Charles D. Nilson, Jr.
Tim Rhodes

SAP
Implementation

UNLEASHED

A Business and Technical Roadmap to Deploying SAP

SAMS | 800 East 96th Street, Indianapolis, Indiana 46240 USA

SAP Implementation Unleashed: A Business and Technical Roadmap to Deploying SAP

ISBN-13: 978-0-672-33004-9
ISBN-10: 0-672-33004-0

Library of Congress Cataloging-in-Publication Data:

Anderson, George W.

  SAP implementation unleashed : a business and technical roadmap to deploying SAP / George W. Anderson, Charles D. Nilson, Jr., Tim Rhodes.

      p. cm.

  Includes index.

  ISBN 978-0-672-33004-9 (pbk. : alk. paper) 1. SAP ERP. 2. Integrated software 3. Business—Data processing. I. Nilson, Charles D. II. Rhodes, Tim. III. Title.

  QA76.76.I57.A65 2009

  004'.36—dc22

                          2009013560

Printed in the United States of America

First Printing May 2009

Trademarks

All terms mentioned in this book that are known to be trademarks or service marks have been appropriately capitalized. Sams Publishing cannot attest to the accuracy of this information. Use of a term in this book should not be regarded as affecting the validity of any trademark or service mark.

Warning and Disclaimer

Every effort has been made to make this book as complete and as accurate as possible, but no warranty or fitness is implied. The information provided is on an "as is" basis. The authors and the publisher shall have neither liability nor responsibility to any person or entity with respect to any loss or damages arising from the information contained in this book.

Bulk Sales

Sams Publishing offers excellent discounts on this book when ordered in quantity for bulk purchases or special sales. For more information, please contact

> **U.S. Corporate and Government Sales**
> **1-800-382-3419**
> **corpsales@pearsontechgroup.com**

For sales outside of the U.S., please contact

> **International Sales**
> **international@pearson.com**

Editor-in-Chief
Mark Taub

Acquisitions Editor
Trina MacDonald

Development Editor
Michael Thurston

Managing Editor
Patrick Kanouse

Project Editor
Tonya Simpson

Copy Editor
Bill McManus

Indexer
Ken Johnson

Proofreader
Paula Lowell

Technical Editor
AJ Whalen

Publishing Coordinator
Olivia Basegio

Designer
Gary Adair

Compositor
Jake McFarland

Contents at a Glance

Table of Contents

About the Authors

George W. Anderson is the Chief Strategist for EDS, an HP Company, providing enterprise applications, thought leadership, and strategic direction on behalf of the Office of the CTO. An avid writer, technologist, student, and speaker, George lives near Houston, Texas, with his wife and three children. George is a certified SAP Technical Consultant, PMI PMP, HP Master ASE, and more, and holds one of several technical editor positions for *SAP Professional Journal*. An SAP consultant for 12 years and IT professional for more than two decades, George has had the privilege of working on numerous implementations, upgrades, computing platform migrations, infrastructure refresh and performance optimization projects, and other enterprise consulting engagements. You can reach him at george.anderson@hp.com.

Charles D. Nilson, Jr., is a Senior Program Manager for EDS, an HP Company. Charles lives near Chicago, Illinois, with his family and has held various SAP project management, program management, and consulting roles. Across a 14-year SAP career, Charles has had the pleasure of working on numerous projects and programs, managing multicultural teams and supporting scores of successful SAP implementations across four continents. With industry knowledge spanning electronics, consumer products, pharmaceutical, and discrete manufacturing companies, Charles is a PMI PMP and is SAP Partner Academy certified in MM and PP. He also holds a Certificate in Integrated Supply Chain Management from MIT and a bachelor's of science in business administration from Elmhurst College in Illinois. An avid sportsman (favorites include kayaking, golfing, hunting, and camping), you can contact Charles at charles.nilson@hp.com.

Tim Rhodes is a Senior Technical Consultant for EDS, an HP Company. He resides in Houston, Texas, with his wife and three children and enjoys reading and conquering steep learning curves. Tim is an eight-year Basis and SAP infrastructure veteran focused on implementing, migrating, and upgrading SAP components and has been working in the information technology field for more than 17 years. An SAP-certified Technical Consultant, Oracle Certified Professional, Microsoft MCSE, and HP Master ASE, Tim recently received his MBA and is a coauthor of the popular *Teach Yourself SAP in 24 Hours,* Third Edition. You can reach him at tim.rhodes@hp.com.

Andreas Jenzer is a Principal Consultant with 11 years of SAP experience spanning the entire SAP systems lifecycle. A proud recent father of twins, Andreas consults to executive-level technology leaders on behalf of HP. He currently focuses on Business Technology Optimization solutions for SAP environments. Andreas is a graduate engineer in information technology and holds a master's degree in service management. Andreas and his family reside in Boulder, Colorado; he may be reached at andreas.jenzer@hp.com.

Sachin Kakade is a Senior Solution Architect and Functional Consultant for HP specializing in enterprise applications such as SAP. He has 17 years of total experience with the manufacturing industry and with SAP implementations, specializing in Supply Chain Management, Business Intelligence, and ERP solutions. Sachin is a certified SAP PP and SAP APO Demand and Supply Planning consultant, and he has provided application configuration, business process reengineering, and architectural solutions for more than a dozen customers. He holds a Bachelor's in Mechanical Engineering from the University of Pune and a diploma in Business Management. Sachin is an outdoor enthusiast and engages in a variety of activities, such as painting acrylic landscapes, playing soccer, and hiking with his family. He can be contacted at sachin.kakade@hp.com.

Jeff Davis is an Independent Enterprise IT Architect and SAP Basis Consultant who lives in Houston, Texas, with his wife and son. With 15 years in information technology and more than 10 years specializing in SAP, Jeff has worked as a Senior Basis/NetWeaver Architect on large SAP implementations throughout the United States, including international and public sector projects. While SAP consulting is his career, Jeff will tell you that his real passions are knowing Christ more and enjoying time with his family. You can reach Jeff at jeff.davis2@hp.com.

Dr. Parag Doshi, Heather Hillary, **Veeru Mehta**, and **Bryan King** contributed significantly to *SAP Implementation Unleashed* as well, sharing their unique expertise and experience in SAP-related fields as diverse as SOA, project leadership, functional configuration, sizing/architecture, enterprise applications implementation preparation, achieving operational excellence, and more. As seasoned consultants, practice principals, and project managers, their real-world implementation lessons learned added a valuable "in the trenches" dimension to *SAP Implementation Unleashed*.

Dedication

George: I dedicate this book to my family—to my wife and children, mom and dad, brothers and sister, and church family, thank you for your encouragement and love.

Charles: I dedicate this book to my family and circle of friends… especially to my wife and best friend, Margie.

Tim: To my wife and family, thank you for your patience, love, and support.

Andreas: To my wife, family, and friends, Thomas and Michel.

Sachin: To my mom and dad, for all their contributions to my life, and to my wife and my son for your patience, love, and encouragement.

Jeff: To my wife, Mandi, and my son, Ealon. Thank you both for all the joy you bring to my life.

Acknowledgments

From George: Thank you, my Lord and Savior, for giving me yet another opportunity to do what I love to do with my friends and colleagues—Your continual blessings and answers to prayer never cease to amaze me. And a big thank you to Tim Rhodes, Jeff Davis, Sachin Kakade, Parag Doshi, AJ Whalen, and especially Charles Nilson, Jr. for jumping in and addressing critical last-minute needs during the development of this book. You guys are pretty awesome as well!

From Charles: Thank you Lord, for providing me the opportunity to work with a gifted group of colleagues in this collaboration. George Anderson, thank you for the opportunity to participate in this project, and many thanks to my family, old and new friends, and colleagues who have sustained and encouraged me in this and other endeavors. Finally, to my bride Margie, thank you for traveling the world with me and for the time to pursue this book project.

From Tim: Thank you my friends and colleagues, especially John Dobbins and John Murdock, for supporting and challenging me over the years, and my family for their patience while I took time from them to work on this and other projects. A special thanks to George Anderson for all the support he has offered both while writing this book and throughout my career.

From Andreas: George Anderson, thank you for the great opportunity to coauthor yet another book. And to my family, thank you for the time to make this book a reality.

From Sachin: Thank you to my Lord and Savior for all of the blessings He continues to provide, to my wife for her patience and support, and to George Anderson for providing me with this opportunity to co-author my first book.

From Jeff: I am continually humbled and amazed at the blessings of serving a loving God. He has favored me with family, friends, and opportunities beyond my wildest dreams!

We Want to Hear from You!

As the reader of this book, *you* are our most important critic and commentator. We value your opinion and want to know what we're doing right, what we could do better, what areas you'd like to see us publish in, and any other words of wisdom you're willing to pass our way.

You can email or write me directly to let me know what you did or didn't like about this book—as well as what we can do to make our books stronger.

Please note that I cannot help you with technical problems related to the topic of this book, and that due to the high volume of mail I receive, I might not be able to reply to every message.

When you write, please be sure to include this book's title and primary author as well as your name and phone or email address. I will carefully review your comments and share them with the authors and editors who worked on the book.

Email: consumer@samspublishing.com

Mail: Mark Taub
Editor-in-Chief
Sams Publishing
800 East 96th Street
Indianapolis, IN 46240 USA

Reader Services

Visit our website and register this book at www.informit.com/title/9780672330049 for convenient access to any updates, downloads, or errata that might be available for this book.

Introduction

Implementing SAP has always been about transformation, or letting go of old ways of doing things in favor of something newer and better. Transformation goes beyond the incremental changes an organization might adopt as it seeks to change. Instead, transformational change is synonymous with revolutionary, rather than evolutionary, change. It's about turning the corner, getting over the hump, or making the leap to a better place. Is it painful? Nearly always. Is it worth it? With a number of exceptions, the answer is nearly always yes. Implementing SAP is one of the few broad transformations that can take not only a business unit but an entire company to the next level, to a place where better information is delivered more quickly, better decisions are made, and ultimately an increased return on information (an old SAP adage that continues to be validated by thousands of SAP's customers) is realized. The trick is doing it right.

Doing It Right

The pain associated with an SAP implementation comes from several different places. End users will be changing both their tools and the way they work. Managers and other decision makers will be changing processes with which they've grown comfortable over the years. Better information will drive these new processes faster, too, bringing with them a different set of issues. And behind all of this, IT organizations will find themselves deploying and managing the most critical suite of companywide business applications they've ever seen. All this change is akin to growth; awkward crawling and hesitant walking at first, followed by a bit of stumbling and a certain amount of falling and getting back up again. Like learning to walk, implementing SAP comes with its share of bruises. Persistent organizations will get through this and see themselves grow more resilient, more self-aware, and ultimately less like the old organization. There's almost no way around all of this; transformational change has great upside down the road but is painful nonetheless.

What if you had a guide, though? Someone who had already navigated these waters and walked these paths? Wouldn't such a thing be worthwhile? Wouldn't a book authored by 10 SAP project managers, functional consultants, and technologists with more than a century of combined experience go a long way toward giving you the peace of mind you need on this journey?

That's where we come in. Our goal is to outline the business, technical, and project management roadmaps necessary to successfully plan for and complete an SAP implementation, and then fill in all the important gaps. We want you to be able to draw upon a deep pool of experience and lessons learned, comfortable in the knowledge that you not only are in good hands, but are also obviously not the first to attempt an SAP implementation. Through this book, you will crawl, walk, and run in record time. You'll make fewer missteps and ultimately cross the finish line closer to budget and your timelines than you ever could have solo. There will still be the underlying discomfort of change, but in retrospect you'll find that your journey has been a whole lot less painful than it might have been. And you'll find that you not only did more with less, but did *better* (than your competitors!) with less, as explained next.

Doing It Better

One of the obvious facts about implementing SAP nowadays is that you're not alone. Upward of 95% of Fortune 500 companies have introduced SAP into their enterprises, as have more than 47,000 other businesses. SAP is everywhere, helping companies change the way they do business, essentially changing their world. Additionally, the information technology underpinning SAP has transitioned from a supporting role (1980s) to something that provides competitive advantage (in the 1990s), to something that also extends where and how business is conducted (2000s). Today, our information technologies are taking us to yet another place, a place where IT and the business are so intertwined and interconnected that IT *is* the business, and the business *is* IT.

None of this is a big secret. Truth be told, in such a me-too world, the increased innovation you might have been sold on relative to adopting SAP might turn out to be less of a competitive advantage than you thought. More likely, bringing in SAP and other enterprise applications nowadays will only bring you up to par with the bulk of your competitors. Enterprise Resource Planning (ERP) solutions in particular are less often the innovative game-changers of years past but rather, for many, have become the required investment necessary to merely re-level the playing field.

So, to be most effective, and to *really* raise the bar compared to your competitors who have already introduced SAP into their environments, you will need to do it better than them. You'll need to innovate beyond the business innovation that comes with implementing SAP's business scenarios and well-integrated applications. Through the very way you deploy SAP and prepare your teams to manage, use, and maintain SAP post go-live, you must find ways to innovate. You'll need to innovate on all fronts, from the way you conduct business, to technical and technology matters, process matters, and even project management approaches and methodologies; it's these innovations that together will fuel your ascent a rung or two higher than your competition.

Implementing SAP is a ton of work, to be sure. We'll help you consider and explore potential innovations at every step along the way. We'll teach you how to boldly sidestep incremental change in favor of strategic revolution—where it makes sense. We'll tell you what your competitors have already done and explain how you can do the same thing better, faster, and cheaper. Beyond this, we'll show you how to gain a competitive edge in the process—how to leapfrog your competitors in ways that really make a difference. They might talk of one day achieving operational excellence, but you'll implement processes, models, and toolsets that set the stage for not only achieving it *today* but reducing ongoing costs and risks in the process. They will speak of creating a custom application that somehow differentiates their business from others, but you will transform your business by adopting best and common business practices to deploy an integrated and accessible set of systems that capitalizes on your unique intellectual property.

Furthering our efforts to help you leapfrog your competitors, we will give you actionable advice and real-world insight spanning everything from project management methodologies to leadership styles, the pending impact of "mega trends" such as green IT, service-oriented architectures (SOAs), virtualization strategies, automated systems management approaches, compelling computing platform refresh strategies, social networking leverage, and more.

How will you innovate? The answer depends on the role you play in your SAP implementation. No role is without opportunity for innovation. For example:

▶ IT architects will be called upon to design systems and solutions that meet business and IT agility needs at a reasonable total cost of ownership (TCO).

▶ Business process owners need to rethink how the company does business, leveraging best and common practices, templates, and approaches in the process.

▶ Developers and functional experts must deliver innovative solutions and approaches, creating an agile enterprise based on a balance of both new and time-tested tool sets.

▶ Organization designers need to work with management and delivery teams to design a purposeful post-go-live organization enabled through automation, creating lean, dynamic, and well-communicating organizations capable of rapidly achieving incremental operational excellence.

▶ Infrastructure teams need to deploy SAP's business applications and underlying NetWeaver technologies in such a way as to pull costs out of IT, thus freeing budgets enough to become nearly self-funding.

▶ Desktop support teams need to quickly assess their current state of affairs and innovate through streamlined SAPGUI deployment along with incorporating Citrix-based or SAP's WebGUI-based user interfaces.

▶ Existing IT shops may find it necessary to innovate in terms of the very platforms deployed for mission-critical enterprise applications, leveraging platform migrations and new technologies to transition to more strategic or cost-effective platforms.

▶ Job scheduling teams might find it necessary to innovate how batch processing is conducted, pulling in third-party scheduling tools that represent yet another way to innovate and create a more agile business solution.

▶ IT operations teams must draw upon tools they have and new SAP-aware systems management applications to create an automated just-in-time monitoring system capable of truly delivering on a single-pane-of-glass, management-by-exception vision, stabilizing headcount while simultaneously freeing up employee bandwidth in the process.

▶ Executive leadership and first-line management must actively and broadly encourage behaviors that build a work culture that's effective, rewarding, and "contagious."

To this last point, contagious cultures and organizations share a number of attributes. They're seen as outstanding places to work, and therefore draw in talent from the company's internal employee pool. Because of this, contagious cultures and organizations suffer little from retention problems. They're naturally innovative, spawn new opportunities for growth, lead the larger organization in terms of adopting and successfully embedding new technologies and business solutions, and act as role models for the rest of the firm. We'll show you what it takes to create and maintain such a contagious culture, beginning with your SAP project teams and culminating in your operational post-go-live staffing models and support organizations.

Our Audience and Approach

So, you're ready to plunge into the world of SAP! Or, maybe you're in too deep already, perhaps even past that critical point of go-live, and need to step back and review where you are and how you got there. Perhaps you're soon going to be involved in a new SAP implementation, or are considering a support or management role at an existing SAP site. On the other hand, you might just be curious about what an SAP implementation is all about. In any case, you have come to the right place.

Our target audience is broad and includes those new to SAP (users, managers, executives, consultants, educators) as well as those looking to simply broaden their view of the SAP solution landscape. Our intention is to provide an end-to-end look at the SAP solutions and technology. After all, there's so much going on with SAP's products, naming conventions, and direction that it's hard for seasoned insiders and other experts to keep up, much less those on the outside looking in.

We suspect that many readers will use this text as a baseline of sorts, comparing their own SAP plans and implementations to what we have provided, looking for new ideas, or alternatives for approaching the problems that are common to all system implementations. Given this commonality, we believe our readers fall into a number of general categories including:

▶ Decision makers, including a firm's executives, key stakeholders, project managers, and others in key leadership positions who need to understand what SAP is, how it is deployed, what an implementation entails, and what a basic roadmap with milestones/critical path items looks like (all without getting bogged down in the technical details, if they want to avoid doing so).

▶ Business analysts, SAP configurators, and power users who are involved with converting legacy business transactions into cross-application enterprisewide business processes connecting a myriad of business communities to one another. These are important folks, as they will essentially make SAP useful to a company's end-user communities.

▶ Information technology professionals, the people who need to plan for, design, test, and deploy the technical infrastructure upon which SAP will run. This is a huge community of potential readers both familiar and unfamiliar with SAP. They'll love the detail in this book, and appreciate how we connect the IT side of a deployment back to the business needs for implementing SAP in the first place.

More specifically, if you fall into one of the following roles, you'll benefit from this book:

▶ Executive leaders tasked with implementing, transforming, or maintaining SAP environments

▶ Stakeholders seeking to understanding the breadth and depth of an SAP implementation

▶ SAP project managers and various business and IT leaders tasked with discrete subprojects related to implementing, supporting, testing, tuning, or training

▶ Business and application consultants, business process owners, and others tasked with supporting or transforming business processes on behalf of an organization

▶ SAP technology consultants, including SAP Basis, NetWeaver, and other engineers and specialists asked to architect, size, configure, and implement SAP solutions

▶ Database administrators (DBAs) and storage area network (SAN) consultants with a need to maintain their piece of the SAP enterprise pie, or simply expand their knowledge

▶ Traditional data center operations and infrastructure management specialists asked to step up and assist in developing or maintaining an SAP IT shop

▶ Network administrators, systems administrators, data center power/utility technicians, and others with similar roles supporting the very groundwork upon which the SAP solution depends

▶ Others internal to (or seeking employment with) an organization, interested in learning the process a company should follow in selecting, designing, and deploying SAP

▶ Technical individuals who are new to (or want to be a part of) the world of SAP—individuals who may be supporting similar enterprise applications or mission-critical environments (mainframes/midframes and more) and who want to make a career move into learning and supporting SAP

▶ Nontechnical business managers/supervisors who are soon to be thrust into an SAP project or environment

A key strength of this book is that it contains enough material to satisfy beginners, intermediate readers, and long-time SAP experts without "dumbing down" the content. It's a hard balance to strike but something your authors have kept in mind throughout the writing process. Another strength is the holistic approach we have taken relative to explaining implementation projects, particularly the three-lane roadmap (business/functional, technical, and project management) that should not only broaden the appeal of this book but make it more relevant to a wider audience. To make sense of everything SAP, the book has been crafted along the lines of a project plan—our central roadmap is therefore steeped in project management. Along the way, we have generously peppered in real-world observations and practical examples to give substance to the journey. As we mentioned earlier, in this journey lies the core value that we provide to you—the chance to benefit from the experiences of others. There's no value and no reason to reinvent the wheel. Frankly, most everything you need or want in regard to an SAP implementation has already been done, and done well, by someone else. Your job can be much simpler and certainly less risky because of them.

Whether you are implementing an SAP supply chain system, customer relationship management system, or a portal to front-end your existing business applications, there are certain tasks that must be planned for and executed across the board. If you're interested in minimizing costs and managing your critical path to a successful outcome, all these tasks must occur in a certain logical order or sequence. With all of this in mind, it seemed rather obvious that a roadmap built first and foremost around a "project plan" made the most sense for the book.

For beginners joining a new implementation project team, we suggest that you read the book sequentially from the first to the last chapter. If you find yourself in the middle of a project, though, feel free to jump to the chapters that best fit your project or timeline status. Of course, in doing so you might well "skip" over knowledge that could very well prove useful, too. We suggest quickly reviewing the Table of Contents, therefore, to determine if it makes sense in your particular case to go back and review any passed-over content. If you're more experienced, you'll find it pretty easy to skip around and read chapters as they apply to you. To keep you reading (rather than flipping back and forth between the appendixes and text), we've taken care to define acronyms in each chapter. This approach is much different from that used in most books, in which definitions and acronyms are explained only the first time they're introduced; we hope you find our approach useful.

Addressing the Real Challenges of SAP Implementations

In a world filled with books on SAP (those of us who work with SAP for a living like to hear it pronounced "ess-aye-pea," by the way), this book is unique. In our review of numerous "how to" and other SAP planning guides over the years, we continually noticed how little attention was given to addressing the *real* challenges related to deploying an SAP business solution or enabling technology. For example, little attention was ever given to

▶ How a particular leadership style may be appropriate given a firm's unique competitive landscape, SAP applications, business environment, and IT skills/competencies

- How to structure SAP business teams, the SAP technical support organization, and the overall project team

- How to build "buy in" with the business folks—the owners and end users to whom the system will eventually be turned over for day-to-day productive use

- How and with what to capture and house all of the information necessary to conduct an SAP implementation

- How to encourage apples-to-apples SAP sizing exercises, and then evaluate each vendor's solution approach on a level playing field

- How to determine realistic high-availability and performance requirements

- How to plan for and develop an SAP data center

- What to include in an SAP operations manual

- How to plan for and execute functional, regression, and load/stress tests

- How SOA fits into the big picture of an SAP implementation

- How to prepare the SAP technical infrastructure and "SAP Basis" teams for the tasks that need to be addressed to actually make it to go-live

- What mix of systems management tools and applications might work best for an IT organization tasked with managing and monitoring SAP

- How to prepare the SAP operations team in terms of staffing and post-go-live tasks

We address all these issues, and much more, from an SAP perspective. And by following the methodical approach outlined earlier, we promote a timeline that coincides nicely with SAP's ASAP methodology and newer SAP Solution Manager–inspired roadmap. This allows project management tasks, functional/business process development, and related technology deployment milestones and resource requirements to be mapped out in lockstep, one with the others.

How This Book Is Organized

As you can tell by now, there's much to cover! This book is organized into several high-level sections, or *parts*. Part I, "Setting the Stage," lays the groundwork for the book and comprises the first six chapters. The bulk of this material is focused on identifying and then marrying business vision with SAP's business applications and something we call *solution vision*. Part I concludes with financial considerations and a chapter on capturing all of the project's inputs, assumptions, and decisions in a knowledge repository.

Part II, "Getting Started," focuses initially on the project management office and project staffing, and then turns to matters of leadership. Next, we address the technical matters critical in setting the groundwork for your SAP hardware and other technology infrastructure, though not before addressing what it means to create a highly available and disaster-tolerant solution.

In Part III, "SAP Realization/Functional Development," detailed technical planning and installation steps are followed up by chapters focused on functional development, tools, best practices, change control, SOA, and testing—all written from a functional or business perspective.

Part IV, "Planning for Go-Live," concludes the book and addresses infrastructure, technical change control, load testing, and essential operational considerations that must be addressed well before the SAP system is ready for productive use. The final chapter goes so far as to outline the events and tasks immediately preceding SAP go-live—tasks that should help create a smooth transition from the firm's old way of doing business to its new, SAP-enabled enterprise business solution.

What Is Not Covered

Although the functional programming, configuration, and work required to make SAP actually *useful* after it is installed is paramount to the overall success of any SAP implementation, we do not go into the details of *how* to configure SAP here. Instead, we leave most of the information related to configuration as well as using SAP's programming language, Advanced Business Application Programming (ABAP), and its more recently supported development option, Java, to the many books, articles, and other documents out there aimed squarely at this kind of activity. When appropriate, we discuss functional development, testing, and other related tasks as they impact our discussions from an SAP implementation perspective, however.

In addition, though we give the topics of business vision and solution vision a great amount of attention, we pretty much assume that you have already selected SAP (or it has been selected for you!) as your enterprise solution package of choice. Certainly, there are a number of choices in the enterprise solutions arena—including products from Oracle, Microsoft, The Sage Group, Lawson, Epicor, and other providers. Pure Internet-based plays and new delivery paradigms such as software as a service (SaaS) and cloud computing offerings are changing the landscape as you read this. However, SAP continues to command the lion's share of enterprise implementations, even recently surpassing a number of "best of breed" specialty applications in terms of popularity. Some of these will be discussed later, but if you are looking for a book that will help you determine *which* enterprise application is right for you, you need to keep looking; outside of basic business vision and application considerations outlined in Chapters 3 and 4, this book presupposes that SAP has been chosen for your enterprise business computing needs.

Real-world Case Studies, Lessons Learned, and Techniques

When we initially discussed this book project, we really liked the idea of sharing the lessons we've collectively learned over the past 10 to 15 years. Giving the book a "real world" flavor from several roadmap perspectives—project management, business/functional development, and technology—was our first concern. For this reason, we have included practical examples, actual customer lessons learned, real-life explanations, tips and tricks, common mistakes you need to avoid, and much more. In our view, material such as this will help the book to not only stand out in a crowd but create a worthwhile reference that's pulled out and *used* time and again. We also wanted to provide a mechanism for applying what you've read in a way that really drives it all home. To this end, we are particularly fond of the ongoing case study we have prepared for you. It starts in Chapter 1 and weaves its way through the entire book. An amalgamation of many different projects we've been a part of, it includes typical issues, questions, and problems—all of which naturally highlight each chapter's material. Who better to learn from than those who have gone before you?

In a nutshell, then, to keep you grounded and to present a well-rounded perspective on SAP implementation, each part, if not each chapter, includes material focused on

- ▶ Project management processes, oversight, and decisions

- ▶ Executive and other decision maker tasks

- ▶ Business or functional business process configuration-focused tasks

- ▶ Technology-focused decisions and tasks

- ▶ SAP developer/programmer-specific decisions and tasks

- ▶ Matters of interest to the end-user community

- ▶ Opportunities for innovation

In conclusion, our experiences are real. They reflect the real challenges embraced and conquered by many different SAP enterprise customers spanning many different industries and geographies. Not all of our implementations have been wildly successful, but, with only a handful of exceptions, we have indeed managed to change and essentially help our customers reinvent their companies through implementing SAP. Our best practices, common practices, lessons learned, and laundry list of problem areas and issues are gleaned from literally a thousand implementations, upgrades, and migrations, including the latest NetWeaver-enabled SAP business solutions. So read on, and position yourself and your company to get it right the first time, do it better than your competitors, and reap the benefits that only 10 guides singularly focused on one thing—helping you—can provide. Thank you again for picking up this book and adding it to your collection.

PART I

Setting the Stage

What It Means to Implement SAP

Implementing SAP continues to be one of the most complex undertakings in the world of business applications and information technology (IT). Based on the sheer number of new implementations in the past several years, the rewards apparently continue to outweigh the effort. SAP enables companies to transform themselves and, in doing so, remain both viable and competitive. To understand and appreciate what this means, though, it is necessary to take a couple of steps back and investigate SAP from a company perspective, a historical perspective, and in terms of roadmaps to implementation.

Welcome to SAP Implementation

The core of the material you are about to read stems from more than a hundred man-years of SAP implementation experience across several hundred midsize and global SAP implementations. Our goal in writing this book is to bridge the gap between selecting an SAP business application or solution and actually going "live" on the application (the act of which makes your investment in SAP finally usable by end users who will spend their work days on the new system). It is our hope that you will use this text as both a reference tool and an informed guide, helping you to steer clear of the hazards and pitfalls common to so many SAP implementations. A good roadmap is multilevel, comprising not only a path outlining how to get from here to there but also a set of markings describing the topology of the terrain. We want this book to be your roadmap.

The Changing Business and IT Landscape

SAP AG (AG is the German equivalent of the term "incorporated") is changing the world around us. The rapid advances in IT hardware and software, and in particular SAP AG's ever-growing umbrella of solutions, have had a profound influence on the way companies today access and manage their data. The role SAP has played in this regard, especially in the past few years, has been pivotal from several perspectives. When faced with competitive threats from arguably its best partners, hot best-of-breed new applications, and innovative methods of extending and hosting ERP (through service-oriented architectures [SOAs] and software as a service [SaaS] offerings, for example), SAP sought to embrace the best of all worlds and evolved to meet its customers and stakeholder needs. SAP AG's growing market share combined with its raw penetration of the Forbes Global 2000 made for a great combination. And recent targeting of the small and medium enterprise (SME) market has opened up new significant and growing revenue streams for SAP. All told, SAP is formidable and here to stay.

One-Stop SAP Shopping

In wishing to share our own experiences regarding implementing SAP, we asked ourselves, "What is the number one reason for putting together this book?" The simple answer: one-stop shopping for "SAP implementation." We have put into this book almost everything a company needs to know or address in terms of planning/organizing for an SAP implementation. Without this book, you would have to hunt through a hodge-podge of SAP installation guides and other papers, SAP web content, miscellaneous documents and articles published by others, and a chapter here and there in the few really good texts that exist today. Instead of starting from ground zero, as so many SAP customers do, you will be able to put together custom project plans, implementation schedules, management justification, and more in just a few days. This is the book we have been waiting for someone to finally write.

In addition, given our breadth of experience, this book comes to you both broad and unbiased. The decision has been made to go with an SAP solution, knowing full well that the risk on the business side is so high that there is little room for risk in the technical implementation. We provide a "soup to nuts" approach relative to how an SAP implementation should be performed beginning to end. We review the different SAP components and modules, how to translate business vision into business processes, and, in turn, how to translate business processes finally into useful SAP functionality. In different chapters of the book, then, we are quick to address challenges relevant to the following:

- ▶ Organizational changes that accompany an SAP implementation will drive sweeping changes across much of the company, from how it conducts business to how the various functional and technology departments are structured to work together.

- ▶ Meeting the project's return on investment (ROI) goals in a timely fashion will impact everything from planning the solution to developing it, testing it, implementing it, and more.

▶ The IT group will tend to think of this as an IT project, and initially will be unaware of the integrated business/technology nature of SAP and how it necessitates a tight partnership between "the business" and IT group.

▶ At the end of the day, the IT department will be faced with implementing a technology solution before the scope of the business solution has crystallized for everyone, and despite the fact that the SAP solution itself is unfamiliar.

Thus, the IT group will benefit from all the help they can receive from people like us who have already made the journey, know the issues, and have dealt successfully with an SAP project's uncertainties. This book will go a long way toward providing the processes, insights, and wisdom that will enable a firm implementing SAP to do the job right, and on time, the first time.

An Unbiased View

As SAP technology consultants, developers, and project managers, our team established years ago that a solution-agnostic approach to SAP consulting kept all of us working. We let the marketing, technology, and engineering folks do their thing while we focused our own efforts on implementation and taking care of our customers. This meant configuring our customers' new, redeployed, or best-of-breed hardware and software components into *solutions*, regardless of the different technology vendors and partners involved. Indeed, we considered ourselves actually quite fortunate when we got involved early enough in a project to allow us to have a hand in the project's technical architecture, design, and selection. In light of this, we have worked with all of the major hardware, operating system, and database vendors upon which an SAP solution is installed. And when we were engaged in SAP development projects, the platform and partners meant next to nothing— configuring business processes is done the same way regardless of whether Hewlett-Packard (HP) or Deloitte does the configuration, and regardless of whether the underlying computing platform is based on HP-UX, AIX, Windows, or Linux.

Finally, we understand that the only reason a firm implements SAP in the first place is to achieve business objectives—to increase competitiveness, identify and capitalize on customer purchasing trends, reduce supply chain costs, make information more widely available across the company, enable better service to customers, improve decision-making capabilities, enhance resource planning, and ultimately improve the execution of the firm's various business processes. In summation, then, the technology and development tools required to implement SAP are simply a means to an end, and not the end itself. Because we realize this, you'll find this to be a better balanced book than otherwise possible.

Why Implement SAP: Enabling Innovation

Introducing SAP into an organization is time consuming, expensive, and subject to creating a whole lot of new challenges. After all, not only will the new system's end users need to be retrained in how they do their job, but the IT organization will need to ramp up on supporting new applications and the various technologies that underpin them. Why go to all this trouble?

The answer is *competitive innovation*, or the ability to introduce the kind of change that gives a firm a leg up on its competition. SAP also calls this business innovation, though its term is actually a bit more limiting than what we've seen in the real world. Innovation with regard to SAP comes in two forms—innovation inherent to introducing new SAP business applications, and the innovation that can be brought to bear relative to how SAP is implemented, deployed, and managed.

The first type of innovation relates to how the system will be used to effect companywide change that presumably reduces operating costs, increases company-internal synergies, helps uncover new revenue streams, and so on. With the exception of introducing ERP (which arguably is more about keeping up with the Joneses than introducing a competitive advantage; see the sidebar for our perspective on this), implementing new SAP business applications will help you to increase your top line and decrease your cost of doing business, or enable other systems to do so.

ERP Implementation Innovation

Almost every company in the Forbes Global 2000—and many near misses—has introduced enterprise resource planning (ERP) systems in-house. To be sure, there's a lot more than just SAP ERP being implemented out there. Oracle and Microsoft have robust ERP offerings, as do several midsize and smaller niche players. Thus, most experts speak of implementing ERP as being less about "changing the game" and more about simply leveling the playing field.

ERP as a broad business solution is no longer perceived as innovative. Yes, the opportunity exists for innovative business processes and practices to be introduced, but implementing ERP is generally perceived as a necessary component of doing business and less of a strategic differentiator than 10 or 15 years ago. Fortunately (for SAP and tens of thousands of customers around the globe) the same can't be said of the robust supply chain, product lifecycle, and customer relationship management business applications available today—applications that still hold the promise of changing the game for those firms who introduce and leverage them for competitive advantage.

The second form of innovation—implementation innovation—is a bit less obvious but just as easy to understand. For starters, a firm that implements a new business application and processes less expensively than its competitors enjoys a better relative capital advantage. If the same company can set up its ongoing IT operations and systems management more cost-effectively, it'll remain in better fiscal shape year in and year out. Finally, if that same company can introduce nimbler infrastructure and IT processes than its competitors, the company's business will be able to change direction and go after new markets more quickly than its less-agile competitors. Combined, such a company will enjoy a significant advantage overall—the kind of advantage that keeps a company in the black and people employed.

Our Take on "Best Practices"

In SAP circles, there's much talk of leveraging best practices. Why? For every thousand implementations, there are nearly a thousand ways to implement SAP but perhaps only several *really good* ways or a single *best* way. In the course of consulting, however, we have determined that there tends to be one or two "best" or "preferred" methods of doing a particular task, or addressing a particular problem.

It is these nuggets of insight and knowledge that we hope to pass on to you, our readers, within the larger scope of covering an SAP implementation end to end. Most of the concepts, practices, and approaches outlined in this book are the result of years of experience designing, deploying, and supporting SAP implementations enabled by technology platforms from Compaq, Digital Equipment Corp., HP, IBM, Sun, and Unisys.

Like SAP AG, we too have endured many changes over the past few years, and have grown both stronger and wiser in doing so. Our projects boast some of the largest, fastest-to-production, and complex business-enabling implementations in the world. We are experts in designing and deploying cost-effective SAP business solutions, pushing the envelope when it comes to embracing new computing paradigms, computing platform groundwork, development tools, and project management approaches alike.

Common Practices

Outside of the two or three preferred ways to plan for, complete, or control a task—whether business or technology oriented—there are oftentimes many more common ways of doing the same thing. These *common practices* stand apart from their best-practices kin in at least one important way—they tend to strike a significantly better balance between what might be deemed best in class and what is deemed acceptable. The classic trade-off cited by those executing common rather than best practices is cost. Best practices are nearly always more expensive to implement than common practices. Common practices fall into the buckets of "good enough" or "good for now" because they do a better job of balancing cost and capabilities. When these "good enough" practices become commonplace, they become de facto common practices.

The Four Priorities of an SAP Implementation

Regardless of whether a practice is "best" or "common," it may be grouped into one of four general areas. We refer to these as the four priorities or primary characteristics of implementation:

- ▶ **People**—End users as well as IT professionals

- ▶ **Processes**—Business, technology, and project management

- ▶ **Technology**—Relative to its adoption and how it enables business innovation

▶ **Money**—Budgetary realities, ROI considerations, and total cost of ownership (TCO) targets

Our parallel implementation roadmaps line up well with these four priorities, all of which must be addressed. That is, attention to only one or a few of these priorities will result in a failed implementation—all four need to be addressed and *balanced* to reflect a firm's unique business and technology landscape. We like to think that the last priority—the money component of an implementation—is perhaps the most central priority of all four, though, because it enables or limits the other three, and itself is limited. Don't misunderstand this point, though. Big budgets do not necessarily equate to successful implementations. At the end of the day, success is found in how money is spent (and saved, or recouped afterward) relative to an implementation. We will do our best to ensure that all four of these areas are well covered in each chapter, as appropriate, along with relevant best practices and common practices. It is our intent to help you build an understanding of the problems and pitfalls you might encounter, and how you might best rectify or avoid them altogether as you march down the road to a successful SAP implementation.

As such, we view this book as simply an extension of our own SAP consulting work, an amalgamation of insight and experience bound together for your benefit in one place. You are now our customer, and we are your (quite inexpensive, thank you) SAP consultants. Given that the efficient and proper use of external consultants is one of many keys to a successful SAP implementation, you're already well on your way to success just by leveraging this book. Nice job.

A Primer on SAP AG and SAP

SAP AG refers to the name of one of the largest software companies in the world, often referred to simply as SAP. The company, consisting originally of ex-IBM folks with a vision of creating an integrated enterprise software solution, is based out of Germany and has been in business since 1972. SAP is also the tag given generically to software created and marketed by SAP AG. The company's most popular application package by far was called SAP R/3, which competed in the *collaborative business solutions* category of software. It was designed to facilitate business operations such as order entry, materials and warehouse management, logistics, sales and distribution, financial and asset accounting, human resource management, and more. Today, SAP R/3 continues to live on at thousands of customer sites, though many of SAP's customers have deployed one of several follow-on ERP products.

Other applications created and marketed by SAP have become quite popular as well. We will cover many of these in detail later, but suffice it to say that SAP has offerings in data warehousing (SAP NetWeaver Business Warehouse, which includes Business Information Warehouse, or SAP BW), supply chain management (Advanced Planner and Optimizer, or SAP APO), customer relationship management (SAP CRM), product lifecycle management (SAP PLM), business-to-business procurement (Supplier Relationship Management, or SAP SRM), and much more. Today, it can be safely said that if there is any system or software need in the enterprise, SAP probably offers a product to fill that need. This is a much different scenario from a decade ago, when SAP was a synonym for a single business application, namely SAP R/3.

A History Lesson

A quick history lesson is in order before we go further. SAP, like its biggest competitors (and partners, incidentally), Oracle and Microsoft, is a business application vendor. All three companies develop and sell software geared toward enabling firms to conduct their day-to-day business. Each provides enterprise-class business software, solutions for small and midsize businesses, platforms for web and application development, software for integrating different systems into one another, and more. SAP comes to the software table from the application side of the house, whereas Oracle has its roots in database management systems and Microsoft is best known for its operating systems and office productivity suite.

SAP was founded to bring forth a novel idea: to develop a software package that integrated and combined a company's myriad business functions together in a manner that reflected business or industry best practices. In this way, a company could replace 10 different business systems of record—such as financials, warehousing, production planning, and so on—with a single system of record, and in the process gain the synergies and communication benefits inherent to maintaining a single version of the truth. Their idea grew into what soon became Systems, Applications, and Products in Data Processing (SAP), or in German Systemanalyse und Programmentwicklung.

The original ex-IBM engineers quickly delivered on their vision to create a multilingual and multinational platform capable of being easily reconfigured from a functional perspective (to enable flexible business processes) as well as from an underlying information technology perspective. Within a decade, SAP was gaining market share through a groundswell of activity propelled by the software's capability to establish standardized business processes in large, complex organizations. After another decade, the company realized growth due to its business application's platform independence, particularly its capability to allow organizations to migrate away from proprietary mainframe solutions to less-expensive infrastructure choices. All the while, SAP's capabilities matured and its market share continued to grow. Today, SAP supports more than 40 languages, 50 currencies, nearly 30 industry solutions, and more than 20 different combinations of popular hardware platforms, operating systems, and database releases.

In less than 20 years after its inception, SAP not only was Germany's top software vendor but was giving IBM and others a serious challenge in the enterprise marketplace; new, large entrants to the enterprise software field emerged during this time, including Baan, Oracle Corporation, PeopleSoft, and JD Edwards. Soon afterward, smaller players began gaining ground as well, including Great Plains and Navision. Though still widespread, mainframes had simply grown too cumbersome and expensive for the majority of companies and other large organizations to deploy and operate. Instead, IT organizations found that smaller, UNIX-based hardware platforms represented better value, while databases from vendors such as Oracle and Informix offered nice alternatives to the old mainframe database offerings.

By the mid-1990s, when SAP began supporting Microsoft Windows and SQL Server, and soon afterward Linux, SAP's place in the enterprise software market was firmly planted— the company's founders had truly delivered on their vision of a multinational, multilingual business solution capable of running on diverse platforms operated and maintained by equally diverse IT organizations. SAP changed both the business and IT worlds faster than anyone would have dreamed possible only a few years earlier. Today, SAP solutions serve more than 82,000 customers across more than 120 countries. And with employees numbering close to 52,000, and a partner ecosystem of several hundred thousand, it's safe to say that SAP is one of the world's largest and most successful employers.

SAP Business Suite Components: The Big Picture

Back in the heady days of 1999 or so, when everything was "dot-com this" and "dot-com that," SAP was already years ahead of the game. R/3 had been Internet-enabled since the introduction of version 3.1G, and the timing was right for SAP AG to introduce a new e-enabled vision of its growing product line. Out of this vision came *mySAP.com*, an umbrella term used to refer to the entire breadth and depth of SAP's e-business solutions and products. Today, mySAP.com has evolved to reflect a broad collection of business solutions (or *application families*)—the SAP Business Suite.

The SAP Business Suite can be thought of as an umbrella encompassing a wealth of general business applications or functionality that represents in turn additional umbrellas underneath which lie specific point products. That is, underneath the SAP Business Suite umbrella are the actual software products that will eventually be used by an end-user community. These software products are generically referred to as *components*. The SAP Business Suite currently comprises five general business application families (see Figure 1.1):

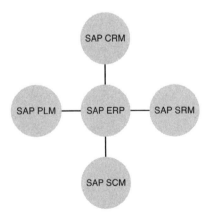

FIGURE 1.1   The SAP Business Suite.

▶ SAP ERP (Enterprise Resource Planning)

▶ SAP CRM (Customer Relationship Management)

- ▶ SAP PLM (Product Lifecycle Management)
- ▶ SAP SCM (Supply Chain Management)
- ▶ SAP SRM (Supplier Relationship Management)

How to Speak SAP: Terms and Terminology

We have already covered quite a few terms and acronyms. However, especially if you are new to or a bit rusty in using SAP's general terminology, you should understand the following list (don't worry about memorizing this right away—to keep the book useful to all levels of readers, we will continue to spell out acronyms and explain key terms throughout the book):

- ▶ **SAP component**—One of SAP's business applications or other products (as opposed to an umbrella term that might instead reflect a group of applications such as SAP Financials).

- ▶ **Instance**—An "installation" of an SAP product that equates to an SAP component with its own set of work processes.

- ▶ **SAP ERP**—An online transaction processing (OLTP) system, the most popular and prevalent SAP component. It includes functionality such as Asset Management, Financial Accounting, Plant Maintenance, Production Planning, Quality Management, Sales and Distribution, Materials Management, Business Work Flow, and more.

- ▶ **Landscape**—The collection of systems supporting a single solution (SAP component) such as CRM, PLM, SCM, and so on. Note that each solution requires its own SAP system landscape.

- ▶ **Three-System Landscape**—Typically, each SAP solution requires a development environment, a quality assurance/test environment, and a production environment.

- ▶ **Central Instance (CI)**—The main "SAP" installation in a system (as opposed to the "database server" installation or dedicated application server instances, and so on). The CI is responsible for managing locks, interserver messaging, and queuing and can be thought of as SAP's executables or binaries.

- ▶ **System**—A collection of SAP instances. For example, an SAP ERP system may consist of a database instance, an SAP CI, two batch server instances (for processing batch or background jobs as opposed to real-time business transactions), and five application server instances (the instances used by end users executing their day-to-day work).

- ▶ **Client**—A legal entity or "business" within an instance—this is what end users actually log in to with their unique user IDs and passwords.

- ▶ **SAPGUI**—SAP's "classic" graphical user interface, which provides a Windows-like look and feel. Other accessibility options exist as well, including a number of web-based user interfaces.

Other terms, such as *SAP NetWeaver* and *SAP* in particular, require a more in-depth definition, even for this introductory chapter, and are covered in the next section. For a truly comprehensive list of SAP acronyms and terms, refer to Appendix B, "SAP Acronyms."

SAP NetWeaver: Enabling Business Solutions

Whereas SAP's business solutions (by way of the SAP Business Suite) represent the applications to be used by a community of end users, there's another set of SAP technologies and products developed to *enable* these solutions. Labeled under another umbrella called SAP NetWeaver, these are SAP's core underlying technology offerings that make it possible to tie together Business Suite components into a unified solution (see Figure 1.2). They include

▶ Portal and collaboration components

▶ Business intelligence, knowledge management, and master data management components

▶ Application platform development tools (J2EE/Java and SAP's proprietary Advanced Business Application Programming, or ABAP)

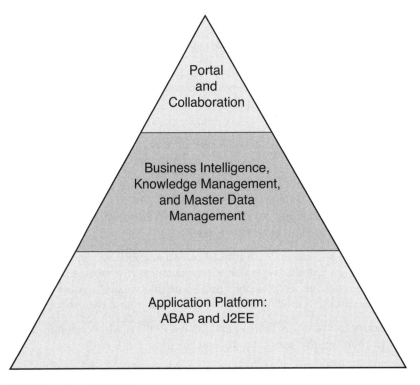

FIGURE 1.2   SAP NetWeaver components.

SAP's NetWeaver Application Server, formerly Web Application Server (WebAS), technical foundation for most of SAP's components. Through the NetWeaver Ap Server platform, SAP not only supports a variety of database and operating syste ......a-tives but also enables communication with external applications created with Microsoft's .NET or IBM's WebSphere development tools. This gives SAP the capability to create extended enterprise solutions crossing diverse product and application classes.

SAP Component Naming Conventions

The underlying software components of any given solution are neatly prefaced with the simple term "SAP" or "SAP NetWeaver," as in *SAP ERP HCM* (SAP's Human Capital Management solution within the ERP component) or *SAP NetWeaver BW* (SAP's business intelligence offering). As you can tell, these products fall under the overall umbrella of either SAP NetWeaver components or SAP Business Suite components. To complicate matters, though, the term SAP is often misused to refer to any business or technical component developed by SAP. For the remainder of this book, we will continue to distinguish between SAP's Business Suite and its NetWeaver offerings. Keep in mind that others will use the term "SAP" to refer generically to any SAP product or component, or to the company itself.

Roadmaps to SAP Implementation

Written from parallel business, technical, and project management perspectives, *SAP Implementation Unleashed* provides you with a high-level roadmap in conjunction with the necessary level of detail across multiple disciplines to set you up for SAP implementation success. We've accomplished this by bringing together matters of business, technology, and project management in one book. We outline these roadmaps in the following sections.

Business Roadmap

Let's face it, the reason an organization introduces SAP has nothing to do with a love for cool technology or global projects. SAP implementations are about satisfying the business's need for business functionality by deploying a business application. For this reason, it's imperative that the business weighs in on the implementation up front as well as throughout the project. Up front, the business must ensure that its needs are being heard and understood by executive management and translated into an appropriate business vision.

After a valid business vision is established and agreed upon, it's time for business software experts to marry the firm's business vision with an application (or suite of applications) capable of actually delivering on the vision. For example, if you have a vision of real-time collaboration and visibility into your product lifecycle (your business vision), application architects and other experts should be able to translate that vision into specific SAP applications and components (or applications and components from Oracle, Microsoft, and a host of midlevel and niche players in the business applications market).

Beyond the initial business vision development and alignment, it remains paramount to an SAP implementation's success that this vision be validated and tweaked as the implementation progresses. Why? Because we don't live in a world where things stand still for the year or two it takes to introduce a complex business application. The marketplace will change, after all, as will the firm's financial, market, and other positions. Strategic vendors and suppliers may change. The firm's appetite for business transformation may change, too; for example, the firm might change its strategic direction or be acquired by another firm with a different view of the future. In all of this, it is therefore important to validate that the implementation's progress lines up with the initial vision plus or minus any changes made down the road. Just as critical, the intersection of the firm's business requirements and strategic technology architecture deserves attention, the latter of which is outlined next.

Technology Roadmap

Just as business requirements need to be not only understood up front but validated and tracked as they change, so too do a firm's strategic technology architecture decisions. Why? Because technology enables firms to conduct business. And just like the business, technology changes over time (as does a firm's appetite for and ability to digest new technologies). Therefore, deploying SAP business applications is impossible without a proper understanding of and commitment to the system's underlying technologies and infrastructure. The combination of these technologies is called by some the *SAP computing platform*, *SAP solution stack*, or simply the *SAP technology stack*. Others refer to this collection of technologies by an old SAP term, *SAP Basis*. Regardless, all of these terms refer to the technology foundation as well as the actual SAP technical installation upon which all development activity and productive operations rely (and for our purposes here, these terms should be treated as interchangeable).

To be sure, many of the challenges related to how an SAP implementation is perceived after go-live fall back to the technologies that have been deployed and how well they've been brought together to provide a well-performing, highly available and agile business system. Integrating all the technologies necessary to pull off a successful implementation is a major achievement. These technologies come together to create an implementation-unique SAP technology stack; the stack is essentially the various "layers" of infrastructure and technology that sit one atop the other in support of an SAP solution, like the different tiers or levels in a three-layer cake. Of course, the SAP "cake" is much higher than simply three layers, and includes the following:

▶ Physical facilities, such as a computer room or other data center hosting site

▶ Power, cooling, and other utility-based core service layers

▶ Physical hardware mounting and racking layer

▶ Server and disk subsystem hardware layer

▶ Firmware layers associated with specific hardware

▶ Operating system (OS) layer

▶ OS drivers, service packs, updates, patches/fixes

▶ Database layer

▶ Database drivers, service packs, updates, patches/fixes

▶ SAP application layer, which in and of itself consists of multiple layers

▶ Internet-enabling layer

▶ SAP accessibility layer, including desktops, laptops, and other devices used to access an SAP solution

Each of these layers can be further broken down into more detailed layers. For example, server hardware covers the individual servers supporting an SAP solution. Drilling down deeper, we find specific memory, CPU, I/O, and other server hardware subsystems or layers, too.

Furthermore, multiple solution stacks typically exist in any given solution. For example, an SAP ERP solution hosted in a data center might consist of IBM Regatta servers running the AIX operating system underneath an Oracle 11g relational database, which in turn hosts an SAP NetWeaver BW business application. In the various front offices, the system's end-user community might rely primarily on a laptop-based technology stack composed of an HP Pavilion running Microsoft Windows Vista, Internet Explorer 7, and the SAPGUI version 7.1. Some of the offices might leverage a Citrix-based solution for SAP access and thus depend on a specific Citrix XenApp technology stack to gain access to the same SAP NetWeaver BW system. Obviously we are interested here in SAP's technology solution stack, but you can apply this same approach to any technology or solution. That is, Microsoft Exchange Server 2007 has its own unique solution stack, as does an Oracle CRM solution or a custom mainframe-based billing application. The enterprise solution differs, and the technology stack will certainly differ, but the approach to building a supported and well-performing solution remains constant.

As you might guess, technology stacks not only are all around you, but are as numerous as they are complex. Perhaps the greatest challenge and greatest achievement is assembling a particular technology stack that both is supported by all the various technology vendors involved in the solution and operates well. Assembling such a supported configuration is by no means trivial! This is one of the reasons why so much time is put into vendor and overall technologies selection—minimizing the number of technology players while bringing together a supportable and well-performing end-to-end solution is the ultimate goal. For these reasons, developing and managing a sensible business-enabling technology roadmap plays a central role throughout this book.

Project Management Roadmap

The project management roadmap serves to wrap up the business and technology roadmaps necessary to implement SAP. It's the glue that cements everything together in a cohesive, manageable manner. Project management enables process discipline, schedule management, and resource management to be effectively applied to an SAP implementation. Together, all three of these roadmaps pave the way to a successful implementation. But it is the project management processes inherent to the roadmap that give the project shape, make it manageable, and therefore make a successful implementation achievable. As such, the project management roadmap is without a doubt the central or most important roadmap—nothing good is possible without it.

Summary

This first chapter answered questions related to what SAP is, its history, key terms, and how SAP may be leveraged to usher in for you a new age of enterprise integration and information sharing.

To this end, we touched upon the difference between the SAP Business Suite and SAP NetWeaver, differentiated between common and best practices, and outlined the three roadmaps to implementation. This should position you, our readers, to not only hit the ground running, but to do so with the confidence that thousands of installations before you have already laid similar groundwork—paving your road to SAP success.

Case Study: Getting on the Same Page

You've been employed by the executive committee of HiTech, Inc., a global provider of technologies and services, to introduce SAP NetWeaver and SAP ERP into the firm's North American operations. The CEO was most impressed with your perspective that SAP requires attention to business, technology, and fundamental project management discipline. Unlike much of his team, he noted that you are focused not just on the technology aspects of deploying SAP but also on how SAP will help HiTech innovate from a business and technology-enablement perspective. To help ground the executive committee, the CEO has requested that you answer several of the committee's basic questions surrounding SAP.

Questions

1. What's the difference between best practices and common practices?
2. The committee understands that SAP is all about introducing change through business innovation. However, what can HiTech do through the implementation itself to introduce SAP in such a way that its very deployment makes a difference to the firm's IT cost model?
3. HiTech tends to look at things from a technology perspective, a by-product of its rich heritage in information and communication technologies. To help HiTech refocus and prioritize, what are the three or four most important things to consider when adopting SAP?

4. Why aren't we using mySAP.com or deploying WebAS, as we did at my last company?

5. The term "SAP" seems to be tossed around pretty carelessly. Is there a good rule of thumb on how to use the term relative to SAP's products and naming conventions?

NOTE

The answers to these questions can be found in Appendix A, "Case Study Answers."

CHAPTER 2

SAP Projects: Characteristics and Themes

In this chapter, we take a closer look at the challenges many firms face prior to deploying an SAP business solution, including the tactical and strategic reasons to deploy SAP, and the project management, architecture, and technical considerations when implementing an SAP solution. We also look at some of the potential reasons for less-than-successful implementations.

What Does an SAP Implementation Look Like?

If you are new to the world of SAP implementations, you're in for quite a ride. If you're a veteran of multiple deployments and are now simply deploying another system, you're still in for a few bumps on the road. There are many reasons for this, including:

▶ No two SAP solutions are exactly identical. Over a period of 30 years, SAP has become a global leader, providing a comprehensive range of enterprise software applications and business solutions for every aspect of business functions irrespective of the size of the business. A comprehensive list of SAP solutions is provided in subsequent sections.

▶ Planning for and deploying an SAP ERP solution for the first time within an organization differs in a number of ways from deploying SAP NetWeaver BW, which in turn differs from deploying SAP SCM or SAP CRM solutions, and so on. Additionally, upgrades, data migrations, and OS/DB migration projects using SAP are also different from a fresh installation of an SAP instance.

▶ SAP solutions solve enterprisewide business problems; hence a project implementation team needs to work with (and include in its own ranks) not only technology folks but also the appointed business liaisons assigned to support the project.

▶ By its very nature, SAP is used to solve exceptionally complicated business problems. So, given its role as an enterprise application and its value in integrating historically disparate data and functions, an SAP solution literally can affect every functional area within the company, including people. Solving these business problems effectively, then, requires a daunting array of hardware and software technology as well, further complicating an SAP implementation.

▶ Some SAP implementations, such as SAP ERP, inherently impact mission-critical business functions. Thus, it is paramount to create additional SAP environments, beyond the production system, that support key development, testing, integration, and other essential activities before deploying an end-to-end network of people and processes using an application that supports, for example, an entire company's financials, supply chain/inventory management functions, human resources management, and data warehousing and reporting needs.

Given all the preceding points, SAP affects how the company will actually do business in the future. Continuously changing economic conditions and efforts to grow the business will propel changes in business processes and procedures, which in turn will need to be embraced by the business community. Therefore, a successful SAP implementation requires a business to continuously develop and enhance the SAP applications to accommodate these changes, explored next.

SAP Implementation: It's All About the Business

If your organization is like most organizations, you have a number of disparate information technology (IT) systems in place that handle the needs of your business. Some of the systems might focus on financial management; others might assist in production scheduling; some might be used for procurement; some might support your sales team in placing and tracking sales orders; and so on. With these disparate IT systems, there is no seamless information flow within the organization, there are broken supply chains, and there are no controls in place to monitor business processes. The costs of maintaining the current systems are out of line, perhaps due to the cost of hardware maintenance, database license fees, application maintenance or upgrade costs, or even the costs of the people supporting these systems. Worse, as costs are incurred to maintain these legacy systems, there is no overall business process or data integration improvement. And, in some cases, if a new business unit is acquired and requires incorporation into the current computing systems, those systems are simply unable to handle the increased user or transaction load, so you end up inheriting the issues and additional disparate systems of the acquired company. The business community (and IT community) has grown tired of a "band-aid" approach to maintaining the current systems.

The business community's needs today include business transformation, collaboration, seamless integration, flexibility, and maximization of profits without sacrificing internal controls. These needs are driven by the continuously changing environment of globalization, better cost and price requirements, shorter order fulfillment cycles, and increased customer expectations. Because of the Internet, not only are large companies doing business on a global level, so are many small and midsize businesses. Almost every business is an end-to-end network of interrelated people and processes. There are businesses that are run totally manually using pen and paper, and that is okay, too, but our focus is the question, what should a business do to keep up with the demands of the global economy? Contemporary firms interested in longevity need to enhance their business, grow, optimize, collaborate, and so forth, using systems and applications. Given this scenario, the more seamless and flexible the network is, the more successful the business will be. As you are going to discover, SAP is the answer to achieving a seamless and flexible network.

The challenge then becomes how to transition from one way of doing things to a new and better way, in essence reinventing the company along the way, while still keeping the company running. This process is analogous to navigating cross country without benefit of a map. Not only is this type of journey extremely difficult, but doing it without benefit of a roadmap, and with little regard to process and best practices, risks putting the entire company in danger.

The changes will be huge, no doubt about it. In the end, not only will a new way of doing things exist, but a new technology stack—the SAP technology stack—will be put into place, a simplified version of which is shown in Figure 2.1.

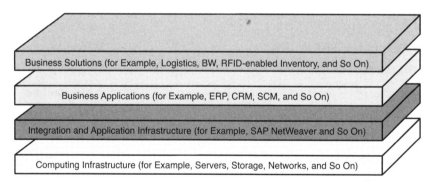

FIGURE 2.1   Another view of the SAP technology stack forming the basis of SAP solutions.

SAP software delivered through an open platform and architecture provides the seamless integration that a business needs. You will be able to optimize the business operations, no matter where they are located or who they involve. You can collaborate with partners, customers, suppliers, contract manufacturers, and even competitors to transform how you conduct business into a competitive advantage. You can develop reporting structures and metrics to monitor and better control business processes in an effort to react quickly and effectively.

Tactical Reasons for Implementing SAP

As you read in the preceding section, there are a number of reasons *not* to remain on a currently implemented business system. However, the people controlling the financial purse strings are usually much more interested in how an SAP solution will address the nagging issues and challenges that crop up in the course of doing business every day. In effect, they tend to say "Don't tell me about problems, show me solutions" before they write the big checks. Our customers have shared the following tactical reasons behind why they chose to implement SAP:

▶ To improve product quality or availability by better managing and reporting on assembly line defects, reducing overall product inventories across warehouses and distribution centers, and enhancing other supply chain functional areas

▶ To improve customer service in terms of increased knowledge of customer trends, status of orders, better turnaround on returns, and so on

▶ To address shifts in customer demand by analyzing buying trends across various geographies, customer demographics, distribution channels, and so on

▶ To provide one system or portal by which to manage activities in a number of other systems "behind the scenes"

▶ To increase competitive advantage by supporting rapid changes to business processes deemed important

▶ To reduce customer billing time

▶ To increase inventory turns/reduce inventories

▶ To decrease lead times for production

▶ To improve the order-to-cash process

▶ To address changing government regulations through integration with standard tax and other systems

▶ To improve resource planning and allocation through better project management

▶ To carry out better supply chain planning

▶ To respond to changing market conditions by rapidly analyzing customer and product trends

▶ To fold all company units into one "system" of record, to have one "version of truth" and a 360-degree view of the organization

Countless other tactical issues that may be solved by an SAP implementation abound in most organizations. We welcome hearing about yours!

Strategic Reasons for Implementing SAP

The strategic reasons for implementing SAP are to achieve general "big picture" goals. As you can see in Figure 2.2, these goals include systems/data and core business application integration, improved operational reporting, improved strategic reporting, and support for creating new or improved business processes. These goals are explained further in the following sections.

FIGURE 2.2   Strategic goals of SAP implementations tend to improve the manner in which the company conducts business.

Application Integration

First, and perhaps most obviously, SAP allows islands of data and processes to be collapsed into a single system. In other cases, a slew of systems may be collapsed into a few better-integrated systems that work seamlessly, such as SAP ERP with SAP SCM, or SCM with SAP NetWeaver BW. In our experience, in fact, it is not uncommon to replace five or more existing systems with one SAP solution—we see this especially in manufacturing realms, where each plant or distribution center tends to hold on to a certain way of doing business (and the corresponding systems) until SAP or one of its enterprise competitors is introduced.

Improved Operational Reporting

When it comes to integrating day-to-day operations across diverse functional or business areas, SAP has been the king of the hill for some time, in the form of online transaction processing (OLTP) systems such as R/3 and ERP. OLTP represents a huge number of business transactions that are executed every day. Out of this daily workload come aggregated reports produced in support of tactical or daily management control. SAP ERP is capable of producing numerous reports that provide real-time operational information. Additionally, summarized data is also available through the Executive Information Systems (EIS) as a method of extracting, combining, and summarizing OLTP data into a true management information system, for use at an operational control level. The unique thing about SAP is that a diverse set of data may be brought together and reported against at other levels as well, and in a real-time manner.

Improved Strategic Reporting

Strategic reporting is also facilitated by a number of SAP components, including SAP NetWeaver BW and Strategic Enterprise Management (SAP SEM). These types of reporting systems, traditionally referred to as decision support systems (DSSs) or online analytical processing (OLAP) systems, focus on supplying information for special reports and analyses typically unavailable from operational data. DSSs also can bring in third-party data (for example, external information on economic and industry conditions) that is simply not available from the day-to-day OLTP systems. SAP became a leader in this kind of strategic reporting with the introduction of SAP NetWeaver BW and the acquisition of Business Objects, and SAP SEM takes these strategic capabilities to the next level by providing dashboard functionality through the enterprise portal. Thus, by using SAP NetWeaver BW, you can provide a 360-degree view of the company through web-enabled (or not) reports and metrics, allowing managers to access and analyze information that ultimately supports better decision making.

Note that without such strategic reporting capabilities, organizations find themselves in a quandary. That is, without the data unification enabled by SAP solutions, strategic reporting is often simply not done. Why? Because, when the data must come from many uncoordinated and disparate systems, the time to collect and analyze the data may exceed the window of opportunity for doing it; the cost may be prohibitive; and quite often strategic reporting may simply entail too much work to do well, only because similar data maintained in different systems is coded differently. For example, we know of a customer that had in its systems multiple vendor numbers for the same vendor. By using the Dun & Bradstreet (D&B) standards and using the D-U-N-S Number to replace all these vendor numbers for a single vendor, the company developed a global spend analysis solution that saved it millions of dollars through better rate negotiations on procurement contracts.

Flexible Business Process Support

Probably the most obvious improvement brought about by SAP involves the opportunity to re-examine business processes and revise them to reflect industry-standard best practices. Often referred to as business process re-engineering (BPR), this long-sought-after goal of an SAP implementation seeks to push analytical questioning throughout each business unit. In other words, BPR dictates that the old ways of doing business should be questioned and, in the case of inefficient or ineffective processes, revised. To this point, we have worked with quite a few companies that, as a result of BPR exercises completed during the SAP planning process, actually injected business process changes into their *current systems* before SAP go-live, simply because the changes were so compelling.

For example, one SAP implementation of ours replaced a number of disparate systems, with accounting, manufacturing, procurement, and inventory systems deployed throughout the organization. Inefficiencies were the rule rather than the exception—the lack of integration between the legacy systems meant that a change in one system necessitated manual changes in each of the other systems as well. Data maintained in one system was not globally available to the other systems, either. Because of the lack of integration, supply chain information trapped in silos hid big holes where dollars were being lost without anyone's knowledge. Ultimately, the task of coordinating and executing all the manual processes necessary to synchronize the systems, and data across all the systems, grew to be too much for the old IT organization.

When SAP was introduced, however, the business folks were forced to get together and agree upon a better solution—re-engineering the business process itself made the difference. Fairly simple changes were made in the current systems, and ultimately the deployment of SAP facilitated an even better implementation of this business process. In the end, it was clear that business opportunities were actually enhanced when re-engineering occurred that focused on supporting better integration and improved processes by *encouraging communication and questioning*, in accordance with the company's strategic objectives and policies.

How SAP Has Benefited Customers in the Real World

From a post-implementation perspective, we thought it would be interesting to identify how a number of our customers truly benefited from implementing SAP. Unlike specific tactical or strategic reasons, these benefits represent the "real world" impact that SAP has had in these organizations or companies. We have left out actual company names, of course, in the interest of preserving anonymity.

- ▶ One company improved its decentralized and uncontrolled procurement processes by implementing SAP Supplier Relationship Management (SAP SRM). By enabling contract negotiations at a global level with regional buying capability, they saved hundreds of thousands of dollars annually through reducing "after the fact" POs, taking advantage of bulk discounts, and reducing rogue buying. The expected savings amounted to approximately $1 billion for every $10 billion spent.

- ▶ One of our customers completely eliminated its legacy system by implementing SAP R/3, getting a return on investment (ROI) of 20% in the first month itself.

- ▶ The same company was also able to reduce a huge inventory of materials because of better planning through SAP planning methods and accurate information availability.

- ▶ Another global company saved more than $1 million annually in employee productivity and on consulting costs by easily acquiring companies and porting their data into its already existing SAP implementation.

- ▶ Compared to its legacy system, another client serviced by one of our teams saved more than $7 million annually by moving its sales, distribution, and order entry system to SAP R/3.

► One of our favorite customers was able to retire its legacy UNIX/enterprise environment running another ERP solution in favor of a Microsoft Windows/SQL Server–based SAP solution, saving $800,000 a year in database licensing costs alone.

► Although the change was not quantified in dollars, one of our customers informed us that its new reporting and DSSs shrank its month-end processes by an incremental two days, thereby providing a jump on the current month's production scheduling, improving cash management, and enhancing its competitive position.

► By implementing global spend analysis through SAP NetWeaver BW, another company had recovered all its implementation costs in the first six months itself.

► One of our team's first SAP CRM customers shared some very interesting data through an ROI study. The results indicated that not only did the project break even in 13 months, but that an increase in average order size of more than 12% (due to rich data-mining capabilities and SAP CRM's campaign-management tools) would serve to maintain better than a 70% internal rate of return over the next two years.

► Attributing its 80% ROI to process cost savings, labor cost savings, and more efficient analysis of its own purchasing activities, another high-visibility SAP SRM customer was able to reduce its number of suppliers from nearly 1,500 to approximately 200.

Over the years we have seen firsthand numerous times that the changes brought about by SAP impacted not only an organization's business processes, but also the very political and power structure of the company. In fact, in hindsight it always seemed pretty clear who stood to lose or gain ground in this regard from the very beginning of the project. Individuals who were known as "squeaky wheels" and "difficult to work with" tended to see their position in the company, or their power base, eroded. Individuals who historically created artificial positions within their company by limiting access to critical information found their jobs eliminated. An SAP implementation breaks down silos and drives collaboration and partnership between different organizations and across different teams of business expertise. People who work well in such environments thrive, while those who focus strictly on localized priorities tend to become obsolete.

Another point often made by our customers post-implementation was that the mix of IT and business personnel working on the SAP implementation surprised them. Although, historically, most IT projects tend to be driven by the IT organizations, time and time again we see a 70/30 or 80/20 implementation team mix—70%–80% business folks, and 20%–30% IT-centric people.

Project Management Considerations

After an organization decides to deploy an SAP solution, it needs to address a number of factors immediately, and preferably in parallel. These factors—tasks, analyses, even marketing of the project internally—are covered in this section.

Promoting Buy-in Throughout the Company

A firm's business executives typically must be convinced that the business units need the kind of help that an SAP implementation is capable of providing. This is done by a *project sponsor* who spends his or her time initially gaining consensus within and between the business areas, functions, and the various IT organizations that will ultimately contribute to supporting the project. As one of a few central figures within the SAP project's steering committee, and generally the person responsible for putting together the membership of the steering committee, the project sponsor's role is key indeed.

We discuss the role of the project sponsor and the makeup and functions of the steering committee in more detail later in this book. For our purposes here, though, the steering committee continues to build upon the momentum put in action by the project sponsor, gaining buy-in and "talking up" the project throughout the company. By working with the various business units to help them understand how important they will be to the project and how much better the project will address their needs, the project sponsor can build excitement and buy-in around the project in these early days.

Finally, until a project-dedicated project manager representing the business organizations is identified, the project sponsor wears this hat, too. Thus, through these important roles, the project sponsor must

- ▶ Project confidence, presenting the SAP implementation with an air of competence in any forum. To this end, the project sponsor must be prepared to give a formal presentation at the drop of a hat, without the presentation appearing too "canned."

- ▶ Be well versed in the SAP project from total cost of ownership (TCO) and ROI perspectives.

- ▶ Tailor language to his or her audience, be it the board room, shop floor, IT group, or a functional department such as accounts payable or manufacturing.

- ▶ Be aware of the politics inherent to the various organizations involved. This includes determining who the informal decision makers are, as well as the ones granted this authority through organization charts.

- ▶ Be truthful and up-front about everything—both personal and professional credibility are on the line at all times. It's impossible to have all the answers all the time, especially in a complex enterprise planning project. Admitting "I'm not sure, but I'll find out" makes a lot more sense than trying to dodge questions or skirt issues.

- ▶ Address questions regarding the potential of changing of roles and responsibilities within the organization as a result of the implementation.

Determining Realistic Service Levels

The term *service level* is by no means new or specific to SAP. As with any IT project, certain minimum requirements need to be communicated by the end-user community to the IT organization tasked with supporting the project. And this needs to take place fairly early in the project, because the technology base of the SAP project itself will be shaped to some extent by these minimum requirements. These minimum requirements become the service levels against which the project will eventually be managed and measured (by way of service-level agreements, or SLAs, which are discussed later in the book). Service levels take a variety of shapes:

▶ **Percentage of uptime, or availability**—For example, a system might need to be in place that will provide 99.9% availability to its end-user community throughout the year.

▶ **Planned versus unplanned downtime**—This is usually expressed in hours per month, or percent achieved per year. A number of our midsize SAP customers plan on four to eight hours of downtime per month, for example, to patch and implement changes to production or test failover and other high-availability processes. Database backups, database reorganizations, and the archiving of SAP business objects represent other common planned downtime events.

▶ **Reactive service levels and related support contracts**—If the system suffers unplanned downtime, the business expects that the problem will be addressed in a certain time period, and resolved within a specific period of time as well. These metrics must be established up front, and then leveraged to draft SLAs with SAP technology stack hardware, software, and systems integration partners.

Work closely with the business groups to nail down what the business perceives as reasonable service levels, and then carefully document these assumptions; later they will need to be clearly understood by the SAP support team, as well as various SAP technology stack hardware and software vendors.

Estimating ROI Early in the Game

Entire volumes of books and complicated expensive software packages have been written with regard to estimating ROI. In fact, Chapter 5, "Financial Impact: ERP Costing and ROI," covers TCO and ROI analysis for SAP in detail. What is important in the earliest stages of the SAP implementation project is "simply" comparing the total one-time expected implementation costs of the project to the in-place systems, and then factoring in recurring costs over something like a three-year time period. An ROI or TCO analysis examines the following areas, in terms of costs and expenses—and does so from an acquisition as well as ongoing cost perspective:

▶ **Processes**—From how SAP infrastructure is deployed to how the system is tested, managed, maintained, technically changed, functionally upgraded, and so on

▶ **People**—Including staffing models, the mix of contractors to employees, the role of outsourcing to augment operations, and more

▶ **Technology**—Comprises the entire technology stack from the data center and its power and cooling facilities to server and storage infrastructure, networks, operating systems, database software, SAP application technology layers, integration technologies, client hardware and software, and so on

Ultimately, a number of sources may be leveraged to gather industry-standard costing data on the "future" solution, from excellent objective resources such as Gartner and IDC, both well-known market research institutes. More challenging, though, can be collecting useful company-specific information when it comes to these areas. Underneath this umbrella of processes, people, and technology are the budgetary/cost categories, including the following:

- Acquisition (technology and people)
- Facilities
- Administration and overhead specific to the solution
- Break/fix labor
- Downtime
- Help desk
- Installation/labor
- Management (asset and systems)
- Operations (computer/systems)
- Planning/evaluation
- Scalability
- Standardization
- Training

Once initial process, people, and technology data are collected on the current systems, a "first-round" and very rough vision of the future solution needs to be assembled. This exercise, though preliminary in many respects, will prove useful time and time again in the next few months. For example, the ROI exercise will be refined via the detailed approaches and processes described later in this book. It will also impact the business and solution visions, covered respectively in Chapter 3, "Business Vision," and Chapter 4, "ERP Solution Vision." Ultimately, the combined ROI analysis/future vision will help drive the sizing process, designing and staffing the SAP functional and support organizations, training approaches and timing, systems management and operations, disaster recovery solution design, and more—all addressed throughout the book as well.

The Importance of a Methodology

Obtaining buy-in from every stakeholder, understanding each and every business requirement, and so on is important, but without the benefit of a methodology such activities can at best only lead to a mediocre, if not very costly, implementation. The methodology that is employed—the structured and repeatable approach to SAP implementation—is what makes all the difference in the world. SAP AG recognized that its customers would benefit from a standard approach to SAP deployment, and developed its ASAP methodology in response. ASAP, or Accelerated SAP, was originally intended for smaller implementations but the approach proved successful in larger SAP rollouts as well, and continues to be used quite successfully even today. Covered in more detail later, ASAP consists of five high-level milestones:

- ▶ **Project Preparation**—This is where the project charter and project plan are developed, the project team is set up, and the project kick-off occurs.

- ▶ **Business Blueprint**—During this phase, interviews are conducted with the business and technical users of the company. Detailed requirements are captured and analyzed and business process mapping occurs on the SAP solution being implemented. Gaps originating between the business requirements and the standard SAP solution functionality are documented and a plan is developed to mitigate these gaps either through business process changes or software enhancements and customization. In short, a detailed design is developed.

- ▶ **Realization**—After the Business Blueprint is signed off by the project sponsor and the steering committee and decisions are made regarding the mitigation of gaps, the actual configuration and customization of the SAP solution takes place. During this phase, test plans and test cases with acceptance criteria are developed in parallel to the development activities. Multiple cycles (usually two or three) of unit testing and integration testing (usually one or two) are carried out in sequence. Further configuration and customization changes are made depending on the outcome of each test cycle.

- ▶ **Final Preparation**—During this phase, the project and the end-user community prepare for the final showdown to migrate their existing/legacy systems and processes to the new SAP systems and processes. Training is carried out, the SAP help desk is established, a cutover plan is developed, and resources are made available when the system cutover actually happens.

- ▶ **Go-Live and Support**—The project team and the leadership agree upon and approve a specific date for go-live. After the cutover activities are completed, the go-live has occurred when users start carrying out business transactions on the new SAP system. The project team members execute the go-live steps to monitor, control, and measure the production activities, and then support the post-go-live production activities for a certain amount of time to ensure a smooth transition of the SAP solution into production.

ASAP evolved into GlobalSAP, and then into ValueSAP, and most recently into SAP Solution Manager, adding methodologies for Evaluation and Continuous Business Improvement (CBI) to its core implementation methodology.

SAP Solution Manager is clearly superior in terms of its capabilities, too. SAP Solution Manager supports you throughout the entire project lifecycle, from Business Blueprint to configuration to production processing. It provides the centralized tools and templates, methods, and preconfigured configuration that not only helps you achieve go-live, but may be used to support ongoing operations and continuous improvement activities after go-live. Robust project monitoring and reporting capabilities exist as well. Issues with the SAP system to be addressed by the SAP developers need to be logged and communicated through SAP Solution Manager for the newer SAP software versions. Plus, SAP Solution

Manager provides a variety of ways to help you manage your project team's educational goals, including *Learning Maps*, which are role-specific Internet-enabled training tools featuring online tutoring and virtual classrooms.

The only downside is the level of software and hardware requirements to run Solution Manager—a separate NetWeaver AS instance is required, for example. Although SAP Solution Manager may arguably represent the best methodology for SAP deployments, other methodologies do exist and can be leveraged for successful project outcomes. All the leading consulting companies and most of the large SAP technology partners offer a methodology for implementing SAP. The key is the degree of experience that the implementation team has with a particular approach, combined with the methodology's capability to support specific SAP components and the challenges inherent to implementing some of these solutions.

Pinning Down the Initial Implementation Budget

Finally, with all the data gleaned during the activities described in the last few sections, you can begin to put together simple preliminary budget figures. Remember, you're just getting the ball rolling at this stage—the actual budget numbers will become more apparent as you move through the first few phases of the project plan and gather all the details surrounding people, processes, and technology. Until that time, though, a rough budget will go a long way toward ensuring that the business requirements and potential technology solutions are in line with each other dollar-wise.

Specifically, you can assemble the following costs for the entire system landscape (whether that's a traditional three-system landscape or larger), as well as some of the basic "people costs":

▶ Data center space capable of housing, powering, and cooling everything listed below

▶ Special power requirements (UPS, power distribution units, redundant power feeds, and so on)

▶ Server hardware (database server, application servers, various integration and Web servers, management appliances, infrastructure servers such as domain controllers, and so on)

▶ Disk subsystem hardware (each system in the landscape requires a database server, and thus a disk subsystem, database, license, and so on)

▶ Network infrastructure (switches, hubs, routers, and all cabling)

▶ License fees and ongoing annual maintenance fees for the operating system for each server

▶ License fees and ongoing annual maintenance fees for the database management system for each database server in every system of the SAP system landscape (a three-system landscape will require three database licenses)

▶ SAP software license fees and ongoing annual maintenance fees

▶ Management system costs (typically an SAP-aware application capable of monitoring the systems holistically)

▶ Incremental computer operations costs

▶ Incremental help desk costs

▶ Break/fix hardware maintenance contracts

▶ System installation (server, disk subsystem, OS, database, and each specific SAP component or product)

▶ Training costs (again, the entire SAP technology stack)

▶ Costs associated with hiring the project manager(s), project coordinator(s), project librarian/documentation specialist, and so on

▶ Costs related to technology-focused team members such as the solution architect, database administrators, SAP Basis and other technical specialists, and so on

▶ Costs related to SAP functional specialists, SAP technical specialists such as ABAP programmers, and other development/business-process experts

▶ Opportunity costs sacrificed by temporarily assigning people to the SAP project, and back-filling their previous line-of-business, technology support, or other roles within the company

Certainly these numbers will change many times during an SAP implementation. But the value of calculating a budget number, even if only 80% accurate, is worth a lot at this stage.

Establishing the General Structure and Roles of the Steering Committee

We have looked at quite a few planning activities thus far. The SAP steering committee (also commonly called the project board) has driven some of these tasks, and the project sponsor specifically has put in his or her share of long hours by now, too. At this time, it makes sense to describe the steering committee's structure as a high-level group tasked with maintaining a focus on creating a high-quality and relevant SAP solution. Depending on the size of the company and the SAP solution being implemented, the composition of the steering committee may change, and some people could be wearing multiple hats. The primary members of the steering committee include the following (see Figure 2.3):

▶ The chair, who is the senior executive tasked with making SAP a reality—that is, the COO (chief operating officer), CFO (chief financial officer), or another very senior appointed delegate.

▶ A representative of each functional area that is to benefit from SAP's re-engineering efforts. For example, this might include representatives from finance, HR, manufacturing, materials, logistics, and worldwide sales.

▶ The project sponsor, if not already identified earlier. In some organizations, this could be the CFO or another executive.

FIGURE 2.3   The makeup of the SAP project steering committee is necessarily broad.

▶ A senior representative of the chief information officer (CIO), or the CIO himself or herself. In some organizations, this could be the internal project manager or the director of enterprise computing systems.

▶ The company-internal project manager, if not already assigned to one of the persons mentioned above (as opposed to other PMs who will be appointed by one or more consulting partners).

▶ The manager or director of enterprise computing systems, if not already assigned to one of the persons above (or equivalent title, usually responsible for the systems currently in place that will be augmented or retired by the addition of SAP).

▶ A senior-level SAP solution architect, or sometimes SAP's appointed project manager (someone who can act as the committee's technical liaison). We refer to this position generically as the SA. The SAP implementation partner may be hired to perform this role.

▶ The implementation partner senior executive, if a consulting organization is hired to help implement the SAP solution at the company.

As we said before, the primary role of the steering committee is to focus the efforts of the company with regard to how SAP will solve problems of a business nature. It is responsible for setting the scope, time, budget, ROI expectations, and general boundaries for the project. It will also develop the critical success factors as a means to monitor and identify the success of the SAP implementation prior to go-live and post go-live. The steering committee could also develop at each phase of the project key performance indicators to measure the success of each phase. Thus, out of necessity, the committee will be heavy with business representatives, who will be required to make decisions that are driven by the nature of SAP and the cost/benefit/capability trade-offs of technology. Making these decisions will require understanding the impact of the information presented. To make good decisions, the committee members will need to familiarize themselves with SAP's disciplined and thorough approach to designing business processes.

Very early in the process, the committee will need to validate decisions made in regard to the very structure of the business hierarchy as represented within SAP, too, including the mapping of business functions against SAP business objects. For example, every company consists of multiple business units, but how will these units be represented in the SAP solution being implemented? As separate clients, or legal entities? As different sales organizations? As different manufacturing plants, divisions, and cost centers or profit centers? Through the implementation of completely different SAP instances? The choices, and the impact of these choices, impact the very fabric of the solution, underscoring the fact that the committee's business representation is vital to the project's success.

To keep the steering committee grounded from a technology perspective, specific IT-related representatives are required as well. In practice, we tend to see a separate, smaller subcommittee or team that coordinates the work "handed off" to the solution architect or SAP project manager, thus giving these critical resources the bandwidth necessary to focus on strategic, committee-relevant issues rather than low-level technical questions. The smaller technology team reports its findings and observations to the SA and/or PM on a regular basis, who then reports back to the steering committee as required.

With the structure and role of the steering committee explained, we next describe some of the committee's and project sponsor's more important activities.

Pushing Business Unit Buy-in

With buy-in achieved at executive and senior management levels, the job of the project sponsor and project board is to push this buy-in "down" the organization. In other words, all of the various business and IT organizations need to understand that their full support will be required to successfully implement SAP, and that their managers back them 100% in this regard. Formal and informal meetings and conversations with key contacts in each functional organization, and anyone who plays a key role in designing and supporting the business processes employed by these organizations, are key. We cannot say enough about this—picking up the phone and discussing the project may be good enough for some folks, but this will be the time to really foster and develop relationships face to face, too. Success is about embracing change, and then putting in the hours to make it happen. If the business units and their key personnel don't fully embrace the changes that SAP will impose, the implementation will struggle along in three key areas:

> ▶ **Configuration**—This is the process of configuring the SAP components or application modules to align SAP business processes with an organization's business processes. Normally this is an adaptive exercise in which the organization actually *changes* its business process to take advantage of the industry-standard built-in SAP functions. But without an organizational subteam in each business area anxious to

assist in deploying SAP, even the best functional consultants and experienced programmers will be at a loss to get this done right, much less quickly.

▶ **Customization**—This is the process of changing or adding business functions through programming to already existing SAP components or application modules to meet the organization's workflow processes in their entirety. A careful cost-benefit analysis needs to be carried out to decide whether this customization is actually needed for the business to function. To be successful, this would require careful designing by both the functional and technical personnel and thorough testing by the business users. There have been far too many instances in which extreme customization has led SAP implementations to crash to the ground. Unless they are critical business requirements, standard SAP business processes must be adapted, and in some cases workarounds need to occur.

▶ **Day-to-day business**—The pure investment in terms of hours will never materialize in organizations that are not completely on board with the SAP project. Not only will the project falter in these business units, but accomplishing day-to-day business will be more difficult as well. Why? Because an organization that is not embracing the changes SAP brings with it will instead be fighting hard to keep these changes at bay, and that fight will consume a great deal of time and energy that would otherwise be expended in achieving the company's operational goals.

Identifying Major Milestones

While you are developing buy-in of the various business units, you may also begin assembling the pieces of what will eventually become your *SAP Implementation (or Infrastructure) Project Plan* (SIPP). At this stage, the plan is focused on big-ticket items and questions, such as

▶ How many sites and business units are involved with the implementation of the SAP solution?

▶ What is the geographical scope?

▶ When will we nail down the SAP component/solution set that will meet the business's needs? In other words, which business functionality and therefore SAP components are we actually implementing?

▶ Do we have any internal experience available within the company, or a working relationship with knowledgeable resources that we can call upon for help?

▶ How complex are the business processes, and do they cross company boundaries into an extended supply chain with suppliers and contract manufacturers?

▶ When is the right time to share what we know with our SAP technology stack vendors and invite them to either participate in our request for proposal (RFP) process or jump into completing vendor-specific SAP sizing questionnaires?

▶ When can we start putting together the SAP support organization?

▶ How will we address training our SAP technical staff? What about our development staff?

▶ How much lead time do we need to design and implement an enterprise-class data center for SAP, and what is on the critical path?

▶ How soon can we get an SAP development environment and a technical sandbox in place? Do we need a business sandbox as well (given that, for large implementations, a business sandbox is necessary for initial prototyping and piloting)? What other requirements or tasks need to be addressed first?

▶ How will we move our existing master data and key transactional data into SAP, to begin the process of configuring and refining business processes?

▶ When can we begin the testing phase? Staging? When do we bring in the final production gear?

▶ How and when do we perform unit and integration testing?

▶ Should we run a stress test or load test? When? Using what tools and processes?

▶ On what date do we think we can actually "go-live" with our new SAP solution?

▶ Do we need to run the old systems concurrently for some period of time? Will we phase in different plants or facilities over time, or will we cut over to the new system all at once (a "big bang" approach)?

A detailed project plan will be developed during the first phase—Project Preparation phase—of the project, and all of these questions (and more) will be addressed in greater detail throughout the book. For now, you want to lay out a high-level project plan and see what kind of timeframe you're looking at. The complexity of the organization and the scope define the actual project timeline. We have been involved in multiple successful implementations in which the project timeline exceeded several years for very large global implementations. We have also been involved in numerous successful implementations of SAP R/3 and ERP for small and medium businesses using a "rapid approach," the goal of which is to implement the solution in six to eight months with 80% of standard SAP functionality but with zero customization.

So, for example, if go-live is anticipated for six months down the line, then you want to do your best to work "backward" from the go-live date, so that you can better identify the milestones and tasks that lie on the critical path to production. In some situations, you might have to work "forward." For example, in the case of an acquisition, you might need to find out how soon after the acquisition has been signed the new plant can be acquired. In either case, follow the project methodology and the phases (Project Preparation, Business Blueprint, Realization, Final Preparation, Go-Live and Support). If the requirements are well defined, the project is easier to scope; if they are not well defined and the project has a lot of ambiguity, then it takes time to define the scope of the project.

To mitigate scope risk, one approach that you could take is to split the project into two parts. The first part focuses on the Project Preparation and Business Blueprint phases. The deliverable at the end of the Business Blueprint phase is the Business Blueprint design document (BBP), which spells out clearly all the business processes, the gaps, and the solutions to mitigate those gaps. Taking this BBP as an input, the second part (Realization, Final Preparation, and Go-Live and Support phases) of the project can be scoped, enabling you to develop and adhere to more realistic timelines.

Architecture Considerations

In the current global environment, speed, agility, and flexibility are essential to success. Organizations that want to respond immediately to changing business requirements must have an IT landscape that supports greater speed, agility, and flexibility. SAP delivers that IT landscape, primarily with the architectures covered in the following sections.

SAP Enterprise Architecture Framework

Organizations looking to incorporate a service-oriented architecture (SOA) and reap its benefits need a master plan that bridges the business processes with the required underpinning technology. We call this master plan the enterprise architecture (EA). You can refer to either The Open Architecture Group Framework (TOGAF) or the SAP Enterprise Architecture Framework (SAP EAF) to develop your own EA that is relevant for your organization. Every EA you develop will have four conceptual layers: Business, Data, Application, and Technical Infrastructure. You must define these layers clearly early on to avoid potential issues at later stages of the implementation. If you fail to do so, the quality of your EA will suffer, especially in terms of incorporating standards within your organization. Figure 2.4 illustrates how the SAP EAF marries with enterprise SOA.

Following are high-level steps to take to implement an EA with reference to the SAP EAF:

1. Obtain an inventory of what you have in-house in terms of tools, methodologies, the existing EA, and so forth.

2. Compare what you have with the SAP EAF.

3. Get inputs from business and technical personnel within your organization and develop the draft EA for your organization.

4. Share your results with the stakeholders, make changes if their feedback is relevant, and validate the final model with experts in the field.

5. Take steps to implement the EA within your organization.

SAP NetWeaver Platform

The SAP NetWeaver platform facilitates a rapid but controlled business process change. It provides an integrated platform of technologies by which business processes can be implemented quickly and solutions can be deployed rapidly. It has an open architecture and enables quick and easy integration with both SAP and non-SAP software components. SAP NetWeaver comprises the following key capabilities:

▶ People, information, and process integration

▶ An application server platform

▶ SAP's Composite Application Framework (CAF), a development platform

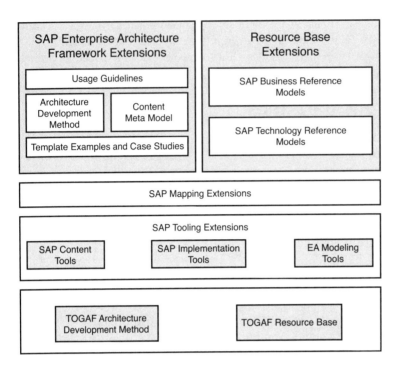

FIGURE 2.4   SAP Enterprise Architecture Framework for an enterprise SOA.

▶ Solution life-cycle management

▶ Key capabilities of security and identity management

We will not dwell on the details of the preceding platforms. Multiple books are available that deal with these topics in greater detail. But here are some of the key IT practices provided by SAP that are supported by the SAP NetWeaver platform:

▶ Helps users improve their productivity through collaboration, knowledge management, and personalized access to critical applications and data

▶ Consolidates, rationalizes, synchronizes, and manages all master data for improved business processes

▶ Increases information visibility of structured and unstructured data

▶ Integrates disparate systems and applications seamlessly

▶ Enables rapid development of custom applications to meet business requirements

▶ Automates application management as much as possible during an application's life-cycle management

▶ Deploys a consolidated technology platform with the capability to allocate computing power according to changing business needs

▶ Supports the design and deployment of an enterprise SOA

Technical Considerations and Constraints

As was covered earlier, the SAP technology stack represents all of the technology layers culminating in a productive SAP installation. But the technology stack applies to each system, and indeed every computer or other piece of gear found in the SAP data center. So, the technology stack applies not only to the production SAP system—the one deployed to actually service the needs of the company—but also to all of the supporting systems that make the production system possible.

Maintaining a bunch of SAP systems to support a single and perhaps small production system may seem like a lot of trouble and expense to go to. After all, each system will require its own hardware, software, and so on—each is a full-blown SAP solution in and of itself.

The SAP System Landscape

Before we get ahead of ourselves, then, let us drill down into the specific purpose or roles that each of these systems will play from a change-management perspective. We have noted in the following list both business process–related changes and technology-driven changes, with the understanding that all of these landscape systems ultimately support and help to maintain a well-performing production system, but not all are required for every different SAP implementation. For example, for an SAP ERP implementation, some companies use a three-system landscape approach and for SAP NetWeaver BW implementations they choose a less flexible, less expensive two-system approach.

> ▶ **Technical sandbox system**—This system is reserved for use by any present or future member of the SAP technical support team to practice and perfect configuring and tuning the SAP technology stack, especially in regard to software component installations, upgrades, integration with other solution components, setup/testing of data replication, backup and restore processes, high-availability hands-on training, and so on. Ideally, then, it should be identical to the production system from a topology perspective (same components), though to save money it does not necessarily have to be configured as robustly (fewer drives, processors, application servers, and so on may be acceptable). Note that because of its technical support role, it is not involved with development activities per se. Development is initiated in the next system discussed.

> ▶ **Business sandbox system**—This system is similar in scope to the technical sandbox, but is used by the functional team (MM, PP, FI-CO, SD, QM under SAP ERP, or DP, SNP, PPDS under SAP SCM, and so on—see Appendix B for more information) and development team (SAP ABAP, HTML, and Java programmers) in support of developing the Business Blueprint document, learning, testing, and practicing their trade. For large implementations, a business sandbox is necessary for initial prototyping and piloting.

> ▶ **Development system**—This system is created and maintained for continued SAP configuration and/or customization, maintenance, and steady-state updates and bug

fixes. This instance also serves as the originator of business process–related configuration and customization changes that will eventually be "promoted" into production.

▶ **Test/QA system**—Also known as the quality assurance system or the integration system, this is one of the most common systems found in even the smallest of implementations. This system is maintained for integration and testing of *business process* configuration changes and so on, prior to eventually promoting these changes into the production SAP system. In other words, all functional changes are promoted from development here and thoroughly tested to ensure that neither this process nor other business processes "break" as a result of a configuration change. It should also be noted that *technical* changes are made here first if, for example, a technical sandbox is not in place and the development system is deemed too critical to initiate changes that may impact availability.

▶ **Training system**—Usually reserved for larger implementations, this system is maintained for ongoing internal training of SAP end-user personnel (that is, "How to Use the SAP GUI," SAP 101 classes, functional business-area training, and so on). In smaller implementations, this role is often served by the test/QA system, on which a separate client can be created specially for carrying out training.

▶ **Staging system**—Usually identical to the production system, this system is used as the last stop for changes in the largest or most mission-critical of implementations. The staging system is often subjected to stress/load tests and other performance tests that reflect what can be expected on the production system, so as to determine the probable impact of a change in the actual production environment *before* this change is promoted to production.

▶ **Production system**—This system supports the business groups and provides for the business needs addressed by the SAP solution implemented. It is the system that the end users work with in their daily activities after go-live, the reason why SAP was implemented in the first place.

▶ **Disaster recovery (DR) system**—This system is implemented when the cost of unplanned downtime exceeds the cost of implementing, maintaining, and supporting a copy of the production system. The DR system (which is usually identical or nearly so to the production system) is located in a different physical location from the production system, and is used "in case" of a disaster—that is, when the production system fails for an extended period of time or is otherwise unavailable. Note how business process changes are applied to the DR system—not from the development system, but typically from the production system itself, in the form of a replicated database or replicated transactions applied to the DR system's database on a regular basis.

A firm's SAP system landscape directly affects how business process changes and technology-derived changes are promoted through the system (see Figure 2.5). Many companies adopt a three- or four-system strategy with regard to SAP, deploying development, test/QA, and production systems, along with a combination DR/staging system or technical sandbox. In fact, one of our customers refers to their technical sandbox as their "best-kept secret" when it comes to maintaining a highly available production operating environment. That is, changes are introduced into the production system only after testing them in their nearly identical sandbox environment, and then further ratified via the development system. And the entire team at this customer site—SAP Basis, DBAs, even computer operations—is very familiar with the technology stack *as they have actually implemented it, because of their technical sandbox.* Further, new hires and others who need to familiarize themselves with how the production system's high-availability cluster operates can do so safely in their hands-on technical sandbox rather than trying to schedule production downtime.

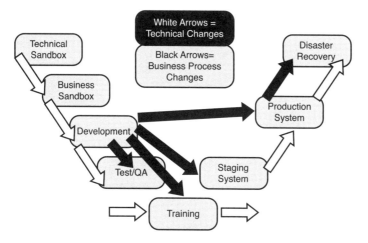

FIGURE 2.5   Changes originate from different systems, and are promulgated differently, based in large part on whether the change is business process driven or technology driven.

Giving Attention to Change Control

The complexity of an SAP implementation can really create problems in the critical area of change control. A company must embrace good technical change control practices. A systemwide approach to managing change must be developed and followed, and it needs to start here and now. There are too many examples of missed SAP go-live dates, and too many botched implementations, to ignore change management.

Ultimately, change control (or change management—the terms are used interchangeably) minimizes system downtime while still allowing the system to benefit from enhanced business functionality or increased future stability due to "bug fixes" and other software/firmware patches. One of our SAP customers describes change control as "staying behind the curve enough to keep the system up." It's a good definition, actually—if a company decides not to jump on the latest and greatest service packs or bug fixes or SAP support packages in its production environment, instead opting to test these changes elsewhere in a methodical manner, that company will enjoy greater system availability. SAP provides the Change Control and Transport System to manage technical changes effectively.

Establishing the SAP Support Organization

With the project plan under development, and progress being made toward a general solutions architecture, you can now turn your attention to considering the organization tasked with bringing the technology together, and ultimately managing it—the *SAP support organization* (sometimes called the SAP technical support organization). A number of forces drive the size and scope of the organization tasked with designing, building, and supporting an SAP implementation. Indeed, the support organization will revise itself shortly before, and again after, the production system goes "live," but for our purposes, we will focus on the following "pre-go-live" requirements that drive how and when the SAP support organization is staffed:

- ► Functional/SAP configuration capability
- ► Technical/programming capability
- ► Accessibility requirements
- ► Availability/high-availability requirements
- ► Performance requirements
- ► Scalability requirements
- ► Security requirements
- ► Administration requirements
- ► Other requirements

We will drill down further into each of these requirements in different chapters throughout this book, too, as the role of this critical organization morphs and changes.

Less Than Successful SAP Implementations

Not all SAP implementations are roaring successes. In this section, we list some of the reasons some SAP projects have failed to meet the expectations of their stakeholders—end users, functional business process–oriented organizations, and the folks controlling the financial purse strings. It should be evident by now that truly a great deal of real risk must be mitigated when tackling an SAP project. Some of the "not best" practices our team has run into are described in the following list. We suggest that you read these carefully and tuck them away for future reference under a big blinking neon banner titled "Lessons Already Learned by Our FAILED Competitors."

- ► **The business is unwilling to change current business processes**—Usually, it is under the guise of keeping things simple so that the implementation goes well and goes quickly. In other cases, we found this to be the result of not having a strong executive order to make decisions and simultaneously having people on the project who are not empowered to make decisions. In reality, though, not wanting to adopt the SAP's best practices with regard to business processes actually represents one of the most common causes of failure for SAP development projects. And when it is coupled with a lack of current-process documentation, the problem is only exacerbated as the configuration and business teams work to figure out how things are really done today.

▸ **No management of general change**—SAP implementation is going to change a lot of tasks that personnel do. Employees might fear that their jobs are going to become redundant or they might simply resist change because of control issues and other factors. Not implementing management of change within the organization can create a negative environment that may lead the project to succumb to politics.

▸ **Not learning from mistakes**—Implementing SAP is an iterative process, in that implementing the various system landscapes and working on the various development and test clients offer opportunities to improve upon even the limited IT processes already in place. A phased approach to implementing SAP (phased in the sense that development is put in first, then testing, then perhaps training, and so on) also lets you learn from your mistakes, so as not to run into the same issues as each new implementation wave begins.

▸ **Ignoring sound technical change control practices**—Putting good change control processes into place is common sense, yet we often see the results of not exercising good change control practices both before and after go-live. More SAP go-live delays seem to result from this "not best" practice than from any other—in fact, usually after something is changed in the system soon to become production, without adequately testing the change first in another environment. Change control needs to be a mindset; without this mindset, it is only seen as an irritating pile of processes and paperwork, until an unplanned downtime event raises change control's visibility again.

▸ **Lack of sound project management**—Although this may be considered a broad "do not do," it's actually common in a number of manifestations. To achieve sound project management, first, be sure to understand and document the desired state solution vision. Second, follow a proven SAP deployment methodology. Third, ensure that the objectives of the implementation are clear and actively managed to completion. And fourth, hire project managers who have leadership, administration, and excellent people-management skills.

▸ **Relying too heavily on third-party consultants**—This is another no-brainer, but a very common dilemma. Having a whole lot of consultants on staff is not the problem (it's the norm, actually). However, providing consultants with all of the opportunities or exposure to SAP at the expense of the company staff (who will be there long after the consultants leave) makes no sense at all. We also see a lot of projects in which the third-party consulting staffs hold too many key roles or positions. Again, the knowledge that these people acquire during the SAP deployment needs to be shared with the home team, not hoarded and carted away. Also recruit good resources to work on the project, and if there are gaps within the organization, fill them with people who you can retain.

▸ **Inadequate training**—Both the business users and the IT department personnel should be adequately trained on the job and as part of the final preparation phase.

All the end users should be provided training pertaining to their new roles and provided proper authorizations.

▶ **Lack of documentation**—Like reinventing the wheel, it's expensive and ludicrous to have to learn over and over again how to do something properly. Documentation regarding the SAP technology stack, and the installation, configuration, support, and operations of each layer of the stack, goes a long way toward improving productivity and increasing uptime. Yet a lack of solid documentation still rates as one of the top areas in which a company fails to measure up, ultimately putting the entire project at risk.

▶ **Lack of buy-in**—We have given the process of developing and securing buy-in quite a bit of attention in this chapter. Buy-in means gaining not only executive-level approval, but also the approval (and a sense of ownership) of the folks who will ultimately use the system. This includes functional organizations and the end users themselves.

▶ **Failing to test adequately**—This problem is more common than most people think. Don't misunderstand; the organizations guilty of this usually *believe* that they have done plenty of testing (and the hours spent in the name of "testing" often bear this out). However, what the numbers fail to reflect is that these failed or delayed projects skimped on either comprehensive integration testing or end-to-end stress testing.

▶ **Scope creep and "bolt-on" madness**—Adding extra features, bells and whistles, and other nice-to-haves has pushed many projects beyond their originally published go-live dates. Not only does the add-on to the project lengthen time to implementation, configuration, and testing, it also impacts day-to-day operations and future support/maintenance needs.

▶ **Insufficient post-go-live support**—A system ill prepared for management and maintenance is doomed to perform poorly over time, suffer from greater-than-necessary unplanned downtime, and generally be viewed as less than successful.

▶ **Inadequate or unclear communication**—Probably the most important consideration for any enterprise-level business/IT project is communication. It can't be too frequent; use the communication mediums at your disposal to ensure that everyone is on the same page.

Summary

We have covered quite a bit of material in this chapter, much of which will be explained in even further detail throughout the remainder of the book. We started off with tactical and strategic reasons for implementing SAP in the first place. Then we looked at the tasks and activities that tend to keep the Steering Committee and Project Sponsor busy in the first few weeks after the decision is made to implement SAP. This included high-level critical tasks such as promoting buy-in, nailing down the real business requirements to be satisfied by SAP, determining realistic SLAs, an exercise in estimating ROI early in the project, translating business requirements into technology drivers, nailing down something of an initial budget, and more. Then we spent some time analyzing the SAP technology stack, discussed the workings of an SAP system landscape, and system architecture, all of which need to be understood at some point to take us to the next level. A discussion on the emerging role of the SAP TSO, and a case study wraps up this chapter.

Case Study: Assessing a Project's Chances for Success

You have been brought on by the CIO of HiTech, Inc. as a project manager. Your first project involves the firm's SAP ERP implementation, for which the CIO is the project sponsor. You have been specifically asked to get involved with the firm's supply chain issues. The project's initial scope involves the company's three primary manufacturing locations and more than 70 stores all across North America. Despite the time and energy being devoted to initiating the project, HiTech's president as well as its CFO do not seem to be very involved with this implementation. In your initial assessment, you've noted that HiTech seems to be facing many other challenges on several different fronts, including the following:

▶ Competition is eating up their market share.

▶ Time to market is slow.

▶ Decision making is based on inaccurate or incomplete information rather than a 360-degree view of the organization; there's no single decision support reporting system.

▶ The company's functional areas have developed silos of information, each having its own systems and IT personnel.

▶ The point-of-sale system is a custom-developed solution that requires constant bug fixes and other attention from both IT and the business groups it serves.

▶ Disparate systems for financials, manufacturing, engineering, procurement, and sales are providing inconsistent information to executive management.

▶ Multiple system vendor maintenance contracts are required because of the multiple systems implemented; these add to cost because of the constant development efforts being carried out to maintain the systems for future acquisitions and growth.

▶ Manufacturing is not streamlined; planners rarely have accurate information related to supply and demand to carry out planning effectively and efficiently.

▶ There are ongoing issues with inventory because of theft and other, unknown reasons.

Questions

1. Which reasons for implementation seem to apply most in HiTech's case?
2. Who seems to be responsible for initiating and cultivating buy-in?
3. Who might make a better project sponsor?

4. With the data center ready for SAP installations, what are the first systems that need to be put in place?

5. Based on your findings for the previous questions, what are some potential reasons why this implementation might fail?

NOTE

The answers to these questions can be found in Appendix A, "Case Study Answers."

CHAPTER 3

Business Vision

An expert in optimizing and simplifying organizational work structures and processes, Bill Jensen tells us that vision is the shortest path between what's in our heads and what people see or hear. From an SAP perspective, the imperative for executive and project leadership is simple—identify what the future state needs to look like from a business perspective, and then socialize, share, and refine it until everyone on the team sings the same tune. With everyone on the same page, the organization will have a realistic shot at effecting authentic change.

Business vision is synonymous with organizational direction. An inconsistent business vision yields unclear direction, making it nearly impossible for an organization to realize a proposed strategy or tangible benefits discussed back in the corporate board room. Once business vision is truly established and then cemented by project leadership and executive communication to the organization's breadth of stakeholders, managers, and individual contributors, an organization can take itself to the next level.

A good business vision starts with a well-articulated mental picture or "mind map" that reflects business needs tempered by an organization's business drivers, "must haves," guiding principles, and more (discussed later in this chapter). But before business vision can be well articulated, sometimes leadership changes must be made. Such changes are often the catalyst for inspiring and casting a new vision and sense of purpose for an organization (see Chapter 12, "Staffing World-Class SAP Project Leadership," for a discussion of leadership styles, roles, and more). Once an executive team appreciates that organizations and people typically resist change in favor of the known, and makes the kind of bold leadership changes often needed to turn the corner from its old way of doing things to embrace a new way, the organization can finally gain what it now needs to take the next step: clarity of purpose. Behind this clarity the organization can gain momentum to innovate and ultimately transform.

Those of us who have been implementing SAP for years typically speak of four strategic dimensions to drive such innovation and growth: a firm's business strategy, its organizational change strategy, its operational strategy, and its technology strategy. Ignoring even one of these is a certain way to spell SAP implementation disaster.

Addressing Strategic Business Needs

In the course of helping thousands of organizations plan for, deploy, and upgrade SAP business applications, we have developed several frameworks, or methodologies, that are useful in giving structure to SAP (and other enterprise application) business projects. Similarly, we developed technical frameworks that are useful for translating business models into application and technology decision trees and ultimately technical solutions underpinning SAP business models (covered in Chapter 4, "ERP Solution Vision"). Helping an organization describe its business model really helps set the stage for the business applications and subsequent technologies needed later. A company might decide its unique business model must reflect the need for the following guiding principles or "big rules," for example:

▶ Overarching business agility and flexibility to address target pricing models, supply chain requirements, changing demand, and so on.

▶ Adherence to the old rule stating that if it can't be measured, it can't be managed.

▶ Auditability and transparency—if it can't be clearly audited, pass on the opportunity.

▶ Focus on particular products and services niches, or several related niches, in an effort to be the best in a few areas (rather than an average player in many industries).

▶ Capability to meet customer deadlines (to create a track record of "we do what we say we do"); a business model focused on meeting customer deadlines and delivery requirements will be optimized differently from a business model focused on delivering flawless or least-costly products, and in turn will require systems and business applications that are highly scalable/similarly able to meet changing business demand.

▶ Disaster resilience and recoverability with regard to the business model itself (and thus the combination of business applications, data, processes, and technologies making up the business model).

▶ Flexible staffing models, or the ability to separate the business and technology staffing models from one another.

▶ Customer data mining and similar business intelligence insight to help the firm decide who to work with, and where to cut their losses (not all customers are created equal—a firm's business model might dictate focusing on the ones that are most profitable or those requiring the least amount of effort).

▶ Negotiation flexibility, which equates to product and services sales model flexibility.

More specifically, an organization might determine that the following are its most critical business characteristics, and then take the time to describe what each of these means to the organization, how the organization benefits, and so on:

▸ **Agility and flexibility**—To achieve an unprecedented level of agility and flexibility, a firm requires an IT platform for SAP that supports virtualization across the lowest layers of the SAP technology stack: server hardware, disk/SAN hardware, and the operating system (OS). Physical assets must be capable of being virtually joined when necessary, and then broken apart again and "shelved" to reduce operating costs. The database layer must similarly be capable of great scalability to meet unknown future demands deemed critical to business success; once business peaks are met, the database layer must support de-provisioning as well, again to reduce cost. Finally, the SAP application layer must be constructed to also support rapid provisioning and de-provisioning, leveraging a pool of resources and a method of proactively scheduling as well as reactively responding.

▸ **Disaster resilience and recoverability**—To ensure the envisioned IT architecture remains viable in the wake of disaster and with regard to Sarbanes-Oxley or other governmental regulations (such as a requirement by defense contractors to meet International Traffic in Arms Regulations or "ITAR" compliance), many firms require significant attention to disaster recoverability (DR). This might be accomplished by splitting production assets across dual data centers along with DR, test, and other assets, for example. In this way, an active-active environment may be built, lowering total cost of ownership (TCO) and enabling scarce resources to be shared and maximized.

▸ **Staffing rationalization and attention to culture/work climate**—We seek ultimately to either in-source SAP infrastructure support or align it with an effective outsourcing partner. Keys to success include staffing rationalization (current employees versus existing outsourcing talent), the ability to retain skills, the need to create a culture in which the to-be SAP architecture platform is respected, and the need to provide an umbrella of companywide systems management, performance management, proactive capacity planning, and cross-application/cross–business unit (BU) business process monitoring. As many clients have shared with us over the years, it's important to design an SAP support model composed of people, processes, and tools that work together to maintain an "ever green" environment. No one can afford to design a model only for it to be put up on a shelf and dusted off now and again; rather, the model needs to be kept alive and thus become capable of sustaining itself.

Note that the specific tools and processes necessary to pull off this vision are not called out. For example, if an organization determines that a focus on process adoption and systems integration represents key business tenets to be followed, a description wouldn't include how the firm would address cross-company data management or process integration (for example, through the deployment of SAP Process Integration)—this decision would be made later. In the same way, the decision by a firm to embrace open and readily flexible integration wouldn't spell out the immediate need for web services or enterprise-ready service-oriented architecture (SOA; via a tool such as the SAP Composite Application

Framework or AmberPoint)—these decisions would also be made later, after the organization agrees that these approaches and tools will enable the company to respond rapidly to new business channels or other new opportunities.

Key Business Drivers

Business vision is tempered or made realistic by way of business drivers such as the following—many of the same kind of characteristics or attributes that help color business vision in the first place:

▶ Ensure that the business's needs drive IT priorities and decisions; business/IT alignment is crucial in that the business must drive IT.

▶ Solicit and define business-originated service-level agreements (SLAs) according to business requirements; alongside system functionality, system availability should be the number one priority across the board.

▶ Address performance requirements; more so than simply addressing system availability, the business requires performance consistent with its SLAs. The organization's vision of the future should dictate the need to maintain good performance even in the wake of rapidly changing business priorities, shifting work loads, potential acquisitions, and so on.

▶ Address yet another top priority: disaster recoverability. The organization's vision should be based on mature provisioning and failover capabilities such that moving business applications between resources located in the same data center is enabled (for high availability, or HA), as is moving business applications between data centers (for disaster recoverability); DR merely becomes an extension of the organization's HA practices and capabilities rather than something completely unrelated and therefore more difficult to achieve.

▶ Enable business flexibility through improved IT agility, so that the business will be able to quickly revisit and adjust its priorities, pursue new opportunities, and so forth. IT agility enables business flexibility at a nonproduction level as well.

▶ Enable business accessibility by providing ubiquitous end-user access—secure, available, and well-performing access around the globe. This includes a robust access strategy, such as a portal or similar user-experience strategy combined with other mechanisms to provide simple and robust access. This dovetails with both a mobile applications and integration strategy and a thin client strategy.

Beyond business drivers, an organization needs to identify what it *really* needs to operate now and in the near future, along with what might prove beneficial or in some other way help the organization take care of business, discussed next.

Must Haves and More

While momentum grows with regard to identifying business drivers, another team reflecting key business organizations should be working through the goals of the SAP project. Their task at this time is to sift through all the drivers and plug them into the basic four-bucket taxonomy covered in Chapter 2, "SAP Projects: Characteristics and Themes."

▶ **Must haves**—These are core capabilities that simply cannot be lived without, such as the need to track and manage inventory and finished products, produce accounting statements, and so on.

▶ **Should haves**—These might include the capability to run reports against an integrated information repository. "Should haves" can be worked around and lived without, but often provide the core foundation of value-adds to a solution.

▶ **Nice to haves**—Also known as extras, these might represent the key differentiators provided in certain business solutions, such as the capability to access a solution using a standard web browser. They do not represent requirements by any means, and often add more cost to a project than value.

▶ **Blue sky stuff**—These include extras that would be really exciting to include, but simply cost too much, or are too complicated to implement, or represent other huge risks. The ability to securely make available your supply chain system to customers, suppliers, and vendors still represents "blue sky stuff" to many organizations, for example (even though it's quite feasible from a technology perspective).

The same list of business benefits put together to get initial approval for pursuing the idea of implementing SAP will suffice as a launching point for moving forward with an SAP project.

Understanding Organizational Change Strategies

As you've no doubt gathered by now, no modern-day organization is as fraught with change as those facing an SAP implementation—disbursed across time zones, geographies, and cultures *and* awaiting a new business system. For this reason, much work has been pursued relative to how SAP should be introduced into an organization. In this section, we explore three different organizational change approaches or models. Use this as background material necessary to understand and develop a conceptual framework for introducing change. Later, in Chapter 11, "Building the SAP Project Team," we will build on the change models or strategies that follow to create an actionable change strategy recommended specifically for SAP implementations.

Lewin's Unfreeze/Refreeze Change Model

A fan of Frederick Taylor's Scientific Management movement, or "Taylorism" as it was called back in the 1920s, Kurt Lewin (the father of modern social psychology) recognized a fundamental flaw of Taylor's rigid time and motion studies: Although steeped in organizational workflow and geared toward maximizing efficiency, Taylorism failed to account for workers' needs. Lewin, a trained physicist with a passion for the social sciences, applied his own scientific background to help explain what he perceived as gaps in organizational and social change theory. And in doing so he created one of the simplest and most effective models for understanding and pursuing organizational change—the unfreeze/refreeze theory of change.

Lewin's work in the physical sciences helped create this model—a three-step analogy based on unfreezing a block of ice so as to make it malleable to change, after which it could then be changed and subsequently "refreezed" into a new shape. The "unfreezing" process is particularly telling. Ice cannot be easily reshaped with a hammer or chisel, as it tends to splinter or shatter. Ice does not respond well to pressure, either; it cannot be forced or squeezed into a new shape. The same tenets hold true for organizations. However, ice *can* be broken down by melting. In this lies the core of Lewin's change process. Those familiar with military boot camp or the police academy understand this change process as well. New civilian recruits are melted—broken down—so that they might become moldable and amenable to change. Once inculcated and indoctrinated or changed, they are then "refreezed" into U.S. Marines, policemen, and so on.

Each of Lewin's three steps in his change process offers unique challenges and opportunities for SAP implementations. In our experience, organizational leaders unfamiliar with managing change often skip steps one and three (unfreezing and refreezing, respectively) and instead jump into the middle of the process, implementing organizational change, without properly readying the organization. Without an organization that is ready and receptive to change, resistance to change logically will result. Lewin underscores this fact, including the need for an organization to be receptive to learning how to do things differently. He points to the need for communicating the "why" behind the impetus for change. With his fondness for scientific survey instruments, it was only natural that Lewin would seek to develop surveys capable of highlighting organizational issues, too—issues with individual and group morale, issues with performance or attitudes, issues reflecting culture, and so on. Organizations unwilling to develop customized employee surveys can take advantage of these standardized instruments.

In step two of Lewin's unfreeze/refreeze change model, the desired change is actually made. This may represent the most difficult step to implement or the simplest one, depending on the approach. The key is to prepare and equip the organization for this change well in advance, such that they are informed about and receptive to the change. This preparation sets the stage for successful change and then the third step in the process—refreezing.

With the change implemented, the final refreezing step may be executed to conclude Lewin's change process. Experience shows that this step is often overlooked, though; the organization is changed in terms of structure or systems, but the newly fashioned or desired culture is never refrozen and therefore the change never becomes a normal part of doing business or conducting operations. According to Lewin, "satisfying needs without changing culture will lead us nowhere." More to the point, just because someone has implemented a new way of looking at or doing things doesn't mean this new way will be preserved. The change needs to be cemented into the organization's very culture as *the* way a particular thing is now done. Making a particular change a permanent part of an updated "business as usual" requires great attention to the final refreezing step in Lewin's model.

Burke-Litwin Organization Change and Performance Model

More current and certainly more complex than Kurt Lewin's unfreeze/refreeze change model, the work of W. Warner Burke and George Litwin and their Organization Change and Performance Model (or more simply, the Burke-Litwin Change Model) more closely aligns with the needs and complexities of the modern workplace seeking to introduce SAP. Burke and Litwin established a 12-factor change model composed of both transformational and transactional elements. The transformational elements—mission and strategy; leadership; the external environment; culture; and individual and organizational performance—balance the more transactional elements of the model including management practices; structure; systems; work-unit climate; motivation, individual needs and values, and task and individual skills.

Burke and Litwin adopted the idea of transformational and transactional factors to help delineate those factors that would typically affect discontinuous change against those more aligned toward evolutionary change. With a bit of thought, it's pretty easy to see how these factors differ. Transformational factors, as the name implies, are responsible for *revolutionary* change. Individually or combined, they affect the *deep structure* or nature of the organization. On the other hand, transactional factors imply continuous improvement or incremental change; hardly transformational, they do not affect the organization's patterns of existence or its deep structure. Instead, incremental changes are often associated with optimizing an existing system or process (compare this to the transformational process of reinventing a system or process).

The granularity of Burke and Litwin's approach gives this "open systems change" model much of its power. Acting as levers of large-scale change, transformational factors may be manipulated to bring about widespread change while their less-impactful transactional counterparts may be used to fine-tune the performance and productivity of an organization. And because the model encompasses both contemporary and germinal dimensions of change, it adapts well to IT-specific needs—even those of geographically distributed and culturally diverse SAP support teams.

Of particular interest, the Burke-Litwin Change Model takes into account culture and its "foreground" counterpart *work climate*. The latter, while less transformational than culture, is the Burke-Litwin Change Model's centerpiece around which all other factors revolve—work climate is critical to organizational performance. It reflects perceptions of how well the team is managed and cared for along with how effectively the team works with one another and other teams to accomplish the mission at hand. Similar to culture, it is nonetheless much more tactical than strategic; culture reflects values and beliefs whereas climate reflects day-to-day operational perceptions. In this, the model holds great value as a predictor as well as an enabler of the change deemed necessary by leadership to catapult organizations forward while increasing performance and securing each organization's longevity.

Orlikowski and Hofman's Improvisational Change Model for ERP

While the preceding models of change generally apply to the modern workplace and have been adapted successfully to SAP implementations, change models exist that have explicit strengths and characteristics mapping specifically to the needs of information technology and end-user organizations deploying or using change-enabling, technology-founded business solutions. Wanda Orlikowski and Debra Hofman, professors at MIT, developed such a model. Orlikowski and Hofman's ERP-relevant Improvisational Change Model comprises people, process, and technology factors within an improvisational structural, cultural, and work practice-derived framework. This model offers excellent contrast to Lewin's unfreezing/refreezing approach to introducing change. Orlikowski and Hofman believe

▶ Change begins with an objective or goal rather than a plan.

▶ Authentic change can't be precisely modeled; rather, the best that change agents can do is to improvise in the wake of change conditions and priorities.

▶ A valid change model must therefore be capable of responding in ad hoc fashion to internally and externally founded change conditions as they naturally occur in an organization's lifecycle.

▶ Contemporary organizations are thus always in a state of flux; the Lewinian concept of refreezing is inapplicable given that change is constant—the organization simply does not sit still long enough to allow for true refreezing.

This latter principle that organizations are always in a state of flux also aligns well with the Burke-Litwin Change Model, as it accounts for external changes—which are unavoidable, occurring in rapid succession today from numerous fronts. Orlikowski and Hofman's model is based primarily on a case study conducted by Orlikowski in 1996. She assessed the use of new technology within an organization, arguing the distinction between deliberate change strategies versus those that evolve. Orlikowski found that organizational change generally neglects emergent change in favor of the well-planned change typically preceding technology-enabled business solutions.

By challenging commonly held precepts that effective organizational change must be planned (and that technology is behind organizational transformation), she challenged the distinction between transformational and transactional change factors such as those described by Burke and Litwin. Orlikowski maintained that organizational transformation was essentially improvisational. Orlikowski viewed ERP implementation, despite Burke and Litwin's perspective that it's simply another business system, as a true change agent. Within this framework of ongoing improvisation and reaction to equally ongoing and inevitable change may be found great value, especially with regard to enabling the virtual teams tasked with constantly deploying, and refining or "reinventing," technology-derived lifecycle change like that brought about by ERP system implementation. Read more about Orlikowski and Hofman's model and more at http://ccs.mit.edu/papers/CCSWP191/CCSWP191.html.

Addressing Operational Strategy: Guiding Principles

The third strategic dimension of SAP implementations, some experts argue that operational strategy might be even more fundamental to organizational success than addressing organizational change. Central to operational strategy is the concept of guiding business principles, which are principles (or mantras or edicts) by which an organization lives. Guiding principles help create the framework an organization seeks when considering different paths or choices; the principles serve a business in the same way that policies guide an organization.

If not overtly identified or already discussed in executive meetings, a number of business-oriented guiding principles tend to manifest themselves during development of a broad business application implementation such as SAP. Similar to filters or a sieve, the guiding principles effectively reduce the options available to a firm in terms of business, solutions/applications, or technologies. Guiding principles may specifically call out a standard or directional preference, call out something to be avoided or circumvented, or take another position somewhere in between. Some examples of such guiding principles are provided in the next few sections. Keep in mind that a firm may elect to spell out many guiding principles or conversely decide that an open approach to business operations precludes creating all but a few of these principles.

Access Strategy

A firm may look at how it provides access to its corporate IT applications and determine that it will live by one or more of the following guiding business principles (for example):

▶ We will enable core business application access via the Web and the company's primary portal.

▶ Where required by power users and developers, we will enable rich access to our business applications via fat-client technology (for example, by way of the classic SAPGUI).

▶ We will avoid access strategies that the business has little or no experience with, including technologies such as the JavaGUI.

▶ On a strict exception basis, we will provide all access by way of our Citrix-based access infrastructure.

Capacity or Applications On Demand Strategy

A firm may take a position relative to how it provisions or "stands up" business applications and decide on one or more of the following guiding business principles:

▶ We will enable the business to do business as needed, where needed, and when needed.

▶ We will quickly provision and host business applications as needed, where needed, and when needed.

▶ Through in-the-box scalability, we will enable the business to scale up and scale down operations to meet demand most cost effectively.

▶ In terms of "de-provisioning," we will enable the business to shrink its investment in IT back to "normal" sizing to reduce overall cost and business asset utilization.

▶ We will better leverage the firm's investment in its business applications by continually refining our comprehensive instance strategy in a way to most effectively meet the business's needs.

Data Services Strategy

A firm may position how it provides data services and identify several guiding business principles, such as the following:

▶ We will deliver on the concept of "data services" rather than provide a discrete one-for-one repository of data for each business group or business application.

▶ We will enable companywide data to be mined via an all-encompassing single data warehouse.

▶ We will avoid the temptation to create an all-encompassing enterprisewide data warehouse and instead satisfy the organization's reporting needs through a federation of corporate and business unit–specific data marts.

Information Technology Location Strategy

From a geographic perspective, a firm may determine that a particular strategy affords an appropriate level of availability or flexibility and describe this position via several guiding business principles:

▶ We will operate on the concept of simplification and consolidation but never deploy or recommend anything less than a dual asset strategy (dual data centers, two node server clusters, and so on).

▶ We will house strategic business assets in two or more locations to minimize business disruption risks from geography-specific disasters; in this way, we will create a foundation for disaster recoverability.

▶ Until we achieve our goal of four data centers (or some other number rationalized by management), we will continually reduce the number of IT data center locations to support our simplification and consolidation strategy.

▶ To maximize our investment and maintain high system availability, we will architect and deploy only business applications that allow for application and data synchronization between locations.

With guiding business principles and operational strategy behind us, let's turn our attention to the final strategic dimension—technology strategy.

Tackling Technology Strategy

The fourth strategic dimension of an SAP implementation—technology strategy—could easily be several books in its own right. Much of this book, in fact, is dedicated to evaluating, planning for, deploying, and operationalizing technology. From a strategic perspective, the earliest of implementation phases requires critically reviewing technology options. We have found that a simple three-tiered approach can help make sense of the technologies used to plan for, build, and operationalize SAP:

▶ **Front Plane**—Front-end technology choices related to the user interface to be deployed to the business communities, primary and backup delivery mechanisms,

> front-end-based printing and faxing solutions, and other accessibility and user productivity matters

▶ **Cross Plane**—Integration technologies and tools used to tie SAP into a firm's larger enterprise, to the Web, or to the firm's customer, supplier, partner, and vendor networks

▶ **Back Plane**—The back-end SAP development technologies, database and application tiers, and all the underlying hardware, OS, and database technologies

Astute readers will notice that this approach is actually not only a very high-level incarnation of our technology stack model but the same approach EDS, an HP Company, takes with regard to agile application architecture. Within each plane exist many choices—alternatives relative to hosting and staffing models, process models, hardware platform choices and configurations, deployment methods and tools, and so on. With so many technology choices, defining even a fairly abstract technology strategy this early in the project helps define the implementation project's timelines, identify key knowledge gaps and other constraints, and highlight resource requirements.

Summary

After exploring the concept of business vision and how strategic business needs, key business drivers, and a host of other factors serve an executive team in creating its business vision, we covered organizational change in terms of how it may be evolutionary and incremental or revolutionary and transformational. We then discussed that in view of today's geographically distributed project-oriented teams and their desired role as organizational change agents, the capability to manipulate and maximize such transformational levers is important not only to organizational agility but longevity as well.

Next we investigated several organizational change models, in the context of operational strategy. To this end, we paid particular attention to four areas (by way of example)—an organization's business application access strategy, capacity/applications on demand strategy, data services strategy, and IT location strategy. A brief discussion about technology strategy concluded the chapter. The real work of combining business drivers, principles, requirements, and solution characteristics into an SAP solution vision is covered in the next chapter.

Case Study: A Business Vision Discussion

HiTech's senior leadership team (LT) has been looking ahead at how the company's business model will fare in the next several years, and is convinced that there are significant opportunities to create shareholder wealth in markets where HiTech has distinct competitive advantages. By the same token, however, the LT is keenly aware of shortcomings across the board—organizational change challenges, supply chain inefficiencies, inability to drill down into client trends and opportunities, unclear business vision, business system integration issues, inconsistent guiding principles, and more. They have asked you, a respected business analyst and long-time business application implementation guru, to come talk with the LT about their business vision and how to translate that into something that not only reflects HiTech's strengths but is actionable and achievable as well.

Questions

1. What are the four strategic dimensions spoken of by long-time SAP implementers that drive innovation and growth?

2. Rather than viewing technology strategy from a detailed technology stack perspective, what three alternative "planes" may be used to more simply illustrate a similar framework?

3. What are the four buckets, or categories, called that reflect the business teams' sifting through all the business drivers and categorizing them?

4. List three organizational change models used previously by SAP implementation leadership teams and note which was developed for large-scale IT projects such as SAP ERP.

5. How might guiding principles include more than just an organization's preferences, standards, or operational principles?

NOTE

The answers to these questions can be found in Appendix A, "Case Study Answers."

CHAPTER 4

ERP Solution Vision

With the understanding we have gained in terms of what an SAP project looks like (Chapter 2, "SAP Projects: Characteristics and Themes") and what constitutes a firm's unique business vision (Chapter 3, "Business Vision"), we are ready to begin refining and communicating a vision of the future state of your SAP solution, or *ERP solution vision*. Think of this as the next step beyond the project's "eyes closed" business vision phase, in which business wants and needs were captured. Now we're ready to take our business-inspired wishful thinking and determine how this vision can be realized by way of SAP's components and technologies. We need to design our SAP solution with an eye toward optimally planning, building, and running it.

What Is an ERP Solution Vision?

One of our customers described the process of creating an ERP solution vision as taking the organization's business vision and giving it legs. Another described it as a way of turning a set of requirements into an SAP-specific application blueprint. Both of these descriptions are good, but there's another aspect to creating an ERP solution vision. As illustrated in Figure 4.1, an ERP solution vision also must be tempered by real-world constraints such as budget, technology, and headcount/staffing realities. In this way, we can sketch an SAP technology- and component-specific design that meets both an organization's business needs and financial goals.

Don't get too hung up on the "ERP" in ERP solution vision—substitute CRM, PLM, SCM, and so on, depending on the particular solution to be implemented. We often use the term ERP rather generically (and incorrectly) to reflect the myriad of enterprise applications that may be deployed. Regardless of the label, in the various roles we have played helping our customers craft such a vision, we have provided advice such as the following to executive leadership teams, senior IT decision-makers, and members of various SAP project steering committees or executive committees:

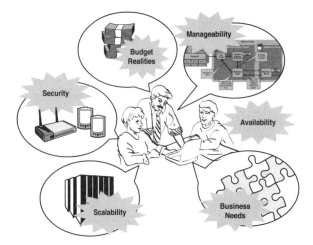

FIGURE 4.1   An ERP solution vision melds company needs and constraints into an achievable SAP-oriented business vision facilitated by technology.

▶ Engage the breadth of people needed for this endeavor quickly; more insight and opinions this early in an implementation project is preferred to too little.

▶ Focus on your core business and how a new potential enterprise solution might better enable that core business to be successful.

▶ Identify the shortcomings of the systems and processes in place today. For example, is customizing the system difficult, expensive, or cumbersome? Are employees forced to duplicate entries in multiple systems, or access different systems for different customers? Is creating a new report for an end user a six-month task? Is the system subject to downtime because of hardware and other technology stack issues?

▶ Clearly define the value that you believe those systems should provide to the business. That is, should the system be available 24×7? Should it be accessible over the Internet or your company intranet? Should it tie together different functional and business areas, or enable real-time decision making?

▶ With the data collected in response to the questions in the previous two bullet points, and with your real business requirements nailed down in Chapter 2, step outside the framework you've collected and again revisit alternatives and "nice to haves." Enlist the assistance of your own long-time end users and the insight of your current IT staff to begin assembling a new solution vision that describes what the system *should* be capable of and therefore the likely SAP components and business scenarios in play.

▶ Don't forget about the data. Answer questions about where the data will reside, how it will be accessed, how it will be integrated, and how much network bandwidth will therefore be required both in *front* of the application (client-side bandwidth) and in between and behind the application (back-end network bandwidth requirements).

▶ Solicit the advice of SAP experts to assist you in identifying real-world product and technology constraints, thereby helping you to refine and document the *characteristics and capabilities* of an SAP solution that can be customized and implemented for *your* company in support of *your* business objectives. This is where SAP-specific advantages, drawbacks, and other realities come into play.

Regarding this last point, SAP experts can be enlisted from many places. We suggest creating a focus team of business, application, and technology specialists from SAP AG itself, from your systems integrator (SI), from your preferred enterprise hardware, software, and services partners, and of course from your own technology teams. There is much to consider regarding solution dimensions, such as availability, accessibility, security, disaster recoverability, and so on (covered later in this chapter). In this way, the entire SAP technology stack may easily be represented (including a certain amount of redundancy, which is very desirable this early in the project).

After your solution vision is initially captured, disseminate it in draft form to initiate a *review process* of sorts—share it with stakeholders, such as senior members of the business groups who will use the solution in their day-to-day dealings and the customer-facing groups who will be positioned to better serve your customers, your information technology (IT) professionals who will be tasked with supporting the solution, and so on. Formally gather and document all of this feedback, so as to begin the process of continuous improvement and ERP solution vision refinement. Update your document or tool being used to track solution dimensions. Ensure that senior and executive-level management concur with the vision as it evolves, and that buy-in is achieved at all levels of your organization. Only after all of this is accomplished can the real work of planning how to actually "get there from here" (sometimes called SAP roadmap planning) commence.

Business Impact

As the business groups begin sharing their thoughts and insights regarding the ERP solution vision, keep in mind the following:

▶ Business processes will almost certainly change with the introduction of your new SAP system, typically reflecting tighter integration and best practices. Therefore, employee roles will change, and jobs will almost certainly be at stake.

▶ Reporting capabilities will dramatically change, which in turn will change what users want from their reports (once they find out that reporting is simpler and more effective, the word will spread quickly—well before go-live is achieved—which in turn could easily affect the direction and velocity of the implementation).

▶ The tools and interfaces used by each employee in the normal course of their job will change, affecting the very nature of how the business conducts business (for example, how quickly the financial books may be closed) and thus the implementation in terms of managing changes and expectations.

During the solution review process, as different end users inevitably demonstrate resistance to the project, consider the points in the preceding list, especially whether their jobs are impacted and to what degree. And just as importantly, consider each individual's personal resistance to change. These two factors represent the key rationale behind exposing only senior members of the different business and functional groups to the new solution vision. With your senior and loyal employees on board and embracing potential changes as their own, you will be positioned as best you can against pockets of resistance lower in the organization.

Technology Perspectives

Before specific SAP software packages, hardware components, and services contracts are procured, a company must come to grips with its *technology perspective*, which is simply how it views its investment in IT resources. Why? Because a firm's technology perspective shapes the architecture, or the very foundation, of a computing solution.

Some companies look at IT spending from a long-term perspective and try to purchase assets with a useful life of perhaps many years. Other companies subscribe to the belief that regular hardware and software refreshes will provide a competitive advantage or a performance advantage over time. Still others seek to stay on one side of the spectrum or the other, investing conservatively in time-proven technology stack components, or on the other hand investing in the latest and greatest high-availability and performance offerings. And finally, others prefer to outsource technology and its requisite support structure.

We like to understand how a company thinks in this regard before attempting to architect an SAP hardware and software solution; it is important for everyone to understand how risk tends to increase as investments in new technology increase, too, promising greater potential reward in exchange. The following list details four very different technology perspectives:

▶ **Conservative**—As the least risky of all approaches, companies that have a conservative technology perspective place availability above all else. They seek mature technology, mature practices, and tried-and-true solutions that *work*, day in and day out. What they potentially sacrifice, then (though in their eyes this is not a sacrifice at all), is anything new—new approaches to accessing their system, new methods of improving availability or manageability, new solution architectures, and so on.

▶ **Mainstream**—Like their conservative brethren, these companies prefer established platforms and products to newer ones. However, the key word here is "company"—they want to have a lot of company when it comes to how they solve their business problems through the use of IT resources. Mainstream companies want to be able to point to a slew of other companies and feel confident that they are not alone, that most of the industry is doing things in a manner similar to theirs.

▶ **Close follower**—Many of our favorite companies to work with tend to be close followers. They seem to leverage their IT investments in proven technology, but with exceptions. That is, although maximizing uptime always remains central, close followers are unafraid to try a few new things to gain a competitive advantage or otherwise position themselves better for the future. Therefore, they take an occasional calculated risk and invest in new products, new technologies, and new approaches.

▶ **Leading edge**—This is the riskiest of all approaches, hence the more popular label "bleeding edge" assigned to this technology perspective. A leading-edge approach places more value on competitive positioning than anything else—it's all about getting a jump on the competition in terms of minimizing cost, reducing downtime (through recent technology advances), increasing response times of customer-driven business transactions, maximizing accessibility (for example, through Internet-based or cloud-enabled vendor/partner access to your order-status system), and so on. Therefore, leading-edge companies must be prepared to spend much more time managing change, as they tend to introduce new products and approaches without the benefit of a "history." In fact, because of this, leading-edge companies are the same ones that tend to find and work through technology problems first.

Note that we did not include outsourcing in the preceding list—the topic of outsourcing as a technology perspective is covered later in this chapter. Key characteristics of an organization's technology perspective and how it relates to the firm's business tenets and overall IT vision also need to be broadly communicated, and might include dimensions like:

▶ Meets business and functional requirements of all business units (BUs)

▶ Enables a firm to leverage its IT staffing model (for example, its shared services model)

▶ Provides a framework to exploit synergies and share resources across BUs

▶ Simplifies and unifies user access to applications and data

▶ Sets direction relative to maintaining common master data across the enterprise

▶ Supports a target architecture and SAP computing platform that is cost-efficient, secure, and resilient

▶ Addresses other solutions and integration points that are vital for a common strategy

▶ Enables the firm to create a common approach while enabling the adoption of a service-based architecture

To accomplish this vision of flexible and high-performance on-demand provisioning, a firm seeking to adopt SAP will integrate its BU-specific stovepipes where possible, essentially breaking out applications and services for BUs only when doing so provides competitive advantage, is necessary in terms of increasing a firm's project execution speed, for legal or regulatory purposes, or achieves some kind of differentiating benefits. Smart firms will consolidate and centralize; for example, on a single companywide *global template* (global production instance) whenever possible, balancing global business process consistency against the potential benefits (and costs!) derived by local customization. It's the age-old argument of centralized versus decentralized applications, only this time it's in regard to SAP rather than your 20-year-old mainframe or 10-year-old client/server applications.

When your technology perspective is clear and you've addressed issues of globalization and local customization, we can start looking at individual solution components and how all this fits together to create a custom system landscape for each particular solution.

SAP Component and Other Considerations

As the different business requirements are hammered out into business scenarios, which in turn are mapped to an ERP solution vision, inevitably a discussion around what *SAP can actually do* emerges. Take care to distinguish between current SAP component capabilities and new features that will be released in upcoming versions of a particular SAP component or technology. Over the last few years, SAP has aggressively released new versions of current SAP components, re-badged existing components and technologies, and added quite a few new components, development tools, and other technologies. So as you begin discussing specific solutions such as SAP's Governance, Risk, and Compliance (GRC) product or how SAP Process Integration (SAP PI) might be useful in tying together a backbone of SAP components with existing applications, it is very important to bring in an expert versed in each solution's current capabilities, shortcomings, and unique technology roadmap.

SAP System Landscape Requirements

As with the SAP components to be implemented, it's also important to determine the SAP system landscape requirements necessary to achieve your solution vision:

▶ Do you need a formal training system for end users?

▶ Will a technical sandbox be required to help your IT staff gain a certain comfort level with new technology?

▶ Will your functional and development/programming team need a business sandbox with which to learn and test?

▶ Will a dedicated load-testing system need to be maintained that is identical to the production system?

All these questions must be answered soon. This is why figuring out details related to your SAP system landscape plays such a big part in this chapter. In essence, though, evaluating the following will help you answer SAP landscape-specific questions as we move forward:

▶ The relative strength or weakness of an organization often determines whether an SAP system landscape component is warranted. For example, a "weak" IT team—a team uneducated about or unfamiliar with a particular technology platform—will benefit greatly from a technical sandbox. Similarly, a development team less than familiar with a unique SAP component/development tool combination will require a business sandbox.

▶ High availability (HA) drives much of the SAP system landscape design, too. The original "SAP 3-System Landscape" discussed in many books and articles over the years evolved out of the need for improved quality and thus availability, for instance. But your particular needs may drive the creation of a more robust architecture on which additional testing is possible.

▶ The ability to recover quickly from a disaster drives the creation of a disaster recovery (DR) system. The term "quickly" is relative, of course, but a backup tape–based restore performed on a newly installed hardware platform usually represents a worst-case baseline.

▶ If performance is critical, adding a staging system to a development/test/production landscape can provide the resources necessary for load-testing or stress-testing changes prior to implementing them in production (or prior to a change management package or "wave" being promoted to production).

▶ If the idea of *simplification* is important to your firm, there are business and technical strategies and approaches designed to do just that—simplify your SAP system landscape. For several ideas put forth by SAP, see "Simplify, Optimize, and Innovate with SAP ERP" at http://www.sap.com/community/webcast/2007_04_SAPPHIRE_US/2007_04_sapphire_us_GE1859.pdf.

Other factors, such as critical security concerns, the ability to manage a particular solution, and so on, will drive the adoption of incremental systems, too. All these factors and characteristics are discussed in detail in the next section.

Business Application Tenets

Just like a business's guiding principles (discussed in Chapter 3), organizations need to establish a set of gates that help decision-makers arrive at business decisions reflecting either current business application standards or the overwhelming need for a new application standard. By way of example, we have worked with a large global firm who laid out the following overarching business application tenets, essentially a framework for investigating and selecting business applications:

▶ All new companywide business applications to be implemented or upgraded will be evaluated from the perspective of "why not SAP?"

▶ Business unit–specific applications, services, master data, and access methods also dictate a "SAP first" strategy.

▶ The firm's unique concept of availability includes five distinct dimensions comprising reliability, performance, disaster recoverability, locatability (with regard to data center strategy), and manageability.

▶ The firm's unique perspective on assurance includes security, integrity, and credibility.

▶ The firm's take on adaptability equates to interoperability, scalability, portability, extensibility, and the firm's unique ability to offer access to services reflecting new operating or computing paradigms.

▶ Several applications are off the table for the near future.

In this way, the firm created a set of boundaries within which the technology and business teams could work to effect change without derailing what the firm considered a couple of key off-limit applications. Similar strategies might also include dovetailing service management (SM) capabilities, solution integration capabilities, and enterprise data management strategies into the firm's business/IT tenets. And to be successful, firms need to proactively address cultural and work climate technology attitudes throughout the IT organization, particularly the concept of change (as discussed last chapter) and why the upcoming envisioned changes are not only good for the company but good for its IT teams.

Another common business tenet relates to pursuing cost savings. Significant savings is not only possible but mandated over the next several years; how SAP is deployed, upgraded, and maintained will lay the foundation for a new cost model. Promises of big savings drive other decisions as well. In some cases, a firm might also state that while its business needs may be addressed by any number of business applications, a particular computing platform is preferred regardless. This can be either very short-sighted or constitute a brilliant move, depending more on hindsight than anything else. That is, in our experience, there are enough cases of SAP customers trying new platforms only to return to them after several painful years to erase many of the success stories.

Marrying Solutions to Computing Platform Standards

When business applications and solutions are understood, basic computing platform standards need to be revisited and nailed down. We have all seen how new business solutions can drive the adoption or requirement for new hardware, software, and middleware standards. The following are typical inflection points for organizations, resulting in new computing platform paradigms:

▶ **Goals and guiding principles**—An organization's stated goal or set of guiding principles may be at odds with fundamental standardization and simplification goals. For example, a position of "strategic hardware diversity" might drive lower costs and avoid problems with locking into a particular hardware or software vendor, but it will also affect the IT organization's innate agility and flexibility (in terms of standing up new business applications, managing and maintaining diverse platforms, and so on) and therefore business agility. Given that business agility is linked directly to application agility, such a principle might actually be counterproductive. It is critical that guiding principles be designed to bolster rather than complicate one another.

▶ **Commodity servers versus proprietary servers**—Pareto's law (the classic 20/80 rule) might be at odds with this; additionally, while a commodity server standard might seem ideal, such platforms might not yet be feasible given the firm's current or desired business model, IT support staff competencies, and so on. In this case, for example, a commodity server footprint representing 80% of all servers might be responsible for only 20% of the overall derived cost savings or other benefits given their inability to scale beyond a certain workload or provide adequate performance beyond a particular threshold.

▶ **Operating system innovation**—More so than innovative attributes held by hardware and middleware, true computing platform innovation is embodied at the OS level. Innovative OS attributes tend to either exist or be absent, and include portability, source code openness, cost, compatibility, integrated innovation attributes (integrating others' innovations), virtualization capabilities, clustering support, manageability, and new-sales marketshare position. The relative degree of innovativeness for SAP's four families of supported OSs can be viewed as lying on a continuum where mainframe/legacy OSs are defined as least innovative followed by UNIX, Windows, and finally the most innovative OS for SAP—Linux. A fifth OS variant, hybrids (typically composed of a mature though less-innovative database server software OS surrounded by application servers running more innovative OSs), sits squarely in the middle of the other four OSs.

▶ **Server virtualization**—This continues to be key to overall IT flexibility and agility; server virtualization is directly tied to OSs, which in turn are supported at varying levels by SAP. For example, not all virtualization overlays are supported for all OSs running production SAP instances (VMware or SAP's Adaptive Computing Controller do not support all of SAP's supported OSs or hardware platforms, for example). And because SAP develops on Linux and Windows OSs first, followed by other OSs, virtualization support typically lags between computing platforms.

▶ **Common network services infrastructure**—Creating a utility model in which network accessibility and bandwidth are ubiquitous (in the same way that power and water utilities are ubiquitous) is generally an excellent idea. Take care to ensure that neither redundancy nor performance is sacrificed for the other.

▶ **Common SAN fabric**—Smart IT organizations seek to create a reliable storage utility in the same way network access and bandwidth may be designed and delivered; ensure your model for obtaining disk space (akin to SAN as a service) balances disk I/O performance (critical to ERP, SAP NetWeaver Business Warehouse [BW], and other component response times) and fundamental disk space allocation. In particular, avoid sacrificing disk spindle counts in favor of fewer "big drives" (fewer physical disk spindles can negatively affect disk performance).

Next, let's visit the SAP system landscape from a design and planning perspective.

SAP System Landscape Dimensions and Characteristics

Remember, a system landscape exists for each SAP solution—if you deploy SAP ERP, SCM, CRM, and PLM, you will in effect be creating four different SAP system landscapes, one for each product. The focus in this and the following few sections, though, is on describing what each one of these SAP system landscapes looks like from a dimensions and characteristics perspective. Dimensions include simplification, performance, high availability, disaster recovery, scalability, the need to support training requirements, security, system accessibility, manageability, and of course cost. In the most general form, an SAP system landscape consists of SAP instances (installations of the SAP database and application software) and SAP servers.

In the Microsoft world of SAP implementations, there is generally a one-to-one correlation between instances and servers (despite the fact that multiple application server instances may coexist pretty easily). That is, the SAP development instance resides on a dedicated development server, the test instance resides on a dedicated test server, and so on. In the world of UNIX implementations, though, multiple instances often can be found on a single "larger" server. For example, both development and test instances can reside on a single server. And multiple application instances can be installed on a single server as well.

Until SAP's Multiple Components in One Database (MCOD) initiative, there was a one-to-one correlation between instances and database systems, too, regardless of the OS platform. An important difference between MCOD and multiple instances on one server exists—MCOD ties the same type of databases within *different* SAP system landscapes together. With MCOD, for example, all development databases used by your SAP ERP, SRM, CRM, and NetWeaver Portal implementations can be one and the same. Similarly, all test databases across SAP ERP, SRM, CRM, and NetWeaver Portal can be bundled together, too. Don't get too hung up on MCOD, however. Although it has its advantages, it has never caught on in the real world, where support packages, kernel updates, database software releases, and so on make it nearly impossible to maintain a highly available MCOD system.

As we move forward with our basic understanding of SAP system landscapes, and seek to understand how your SAP solution vision impacts and is impacted by your landscape decisions, our hope is to achieve the following:

▶ Note the relative importance and relationship of technology perspectives to our solution vision

▶ Understand why each system landscape is important to fulfilling our vision

▶ Note how the presence or absence of a particular system within a landscape impacts the other systems and ultimately the overall solution vision

All these design and planning approaches we cover tend to come into play in one manner or another across all SAP implementations. It's how they are weighted or addressed that makes one system landscape different from the next. Be sure to track and record all the decisions you make with regard to your SAP system landscape configuration. As you work through all the different system landscape characteristics, considerations, and options, document *why* you selected a particular approach or product (SAP or otherwise) and *how* this decision impacts the vision of the project. This documentation must eventually find its way into a knowledge repository, which is simply a documentation vehicle where assumptions, constraints, and so on are all maintained. Read more about the knowledge repository in Chapter 6.

Simplifying Your SAP System Landscape

After spending time with hundreds of customers and SAP implementations, we think it is safe to say that when all things are equal, the desire to *simplify* emerges as an important driver. Simplification takes many forms, too. In the case of the SAP system landscape and how it fulfills our SAP solution vision, the desire to simplify manifests itself in any number of ways:

▶ **Reduce the number of instances**—A particular company might reduce the pure number of instances to the fewest necessary to get the job done right. An organization focused on simplifying administrative, change management, systems management, operations, and other tasks will deploy a three-system or even a two-system landscape, whereas similar organizations without the same simplification goals can deploy more. There are trade-offs, of course. A system landscape without a dedicated test instance will, for example, be forced to perform testing in the same system used for development. Because of these kinds of limitations, simplification achieved through instance reductions is not as common as it has been in the past.

▶ **Reduce the number of physical servers**—A more popular approach to simplification seeks to reduce the number of physical servers in a particular system landscape, by installing multiple instances on a single server. Consolidation of instances in this manner has become quite common in SAP customer environments over the last several years.

▶ **Deploy a shared disk subsystem and tape backup/restore solution**—This also simplifies a very complex piece of the SAP technology stack. It's no surprise that nearly all SAP implementations in the last decade have leveraged shared storage area networks (SANs) or network attached storage (NAS) solutions in addition to data center-wide tape backup solutions.

▶ **Simplify desktop support and maintenance requirements**—As an example, numerous SAP clients have chosen over the years to go with the WebGUI as opposed to the classic SAPGUI approach to system accessibility, eliminating the need to patch and maintain the SAPGUI on all but developer and power user workstations.

▶ **Standardize on a particular technology stack option or approach**—This simplifies support and maintenance and minimizes the need for a variety of onsite or reserved spare parts, the time spent in change management activities, and more.

Although simplification tends to work in one direction by encouraging a "do more with less" philosophy, our next topic goes the other route in that it purposefully introduces complexity and differences between various systems within a system landscape—high availability.

High Availability and the SAP System Landscape

When it comes to high availability, many technology professionals automatically think about what it means to improve the availability of a particular system or hardware component—thoughts of basic HA offerings such as clustering or redundancy come to mind. With regard to the broader topic of how your solution vision impacts your SAP system landscape, though, HA equates to the following:

▶ **Business-driven requirements**—HA offerings and approaches are normally implemented to satisfy specific business-oriented needs, and therefore form an integral part of your overall SAP solution vision.

▶ **Complexity**—HA complicates the SAP system landscape, because HA offerings and approaches tend to only really exist or apply to the production system and, at minimum (hopefully!), another similarly configured system within the landscape.

▶ **Increased support needs**—Because HA offerings are inherently complex, a very real need exists to prepare your SAP support organization in how to install, update, and manage the HA offering and troubleshoot HA issues.

For more details, refer to Chapter 15, "High Availability Considerations and Solutions."

Disaster Recovery Considerations

All companies implement a method of addressing disaster recovery (DR), whether or not they actually realize it. Even companies that do not add a dedicated DR system to their system landscape address DR. That is, their de facto DR plan simply reflects the challenges and timeframes surrounding rebuilding their SAP system from scratch, restoring from their latest tape backup, and imposing upon their end users to manually rekey any new business transactions lost between the last successful tape backup and the point at which the disaster occurred. This doesn't sound like much of a "plan," of course, but it does represent a baseline against which all other DR approaches and solutions can be weighed.

A host of technology-specific DR approaches and considerations are covered later in the book, from those involving disk subsystem data replication solutions, to various clustering solutions, to database- and SAP-specific tactics. But when it comes to sifting the potential layout of your SAP system landscape through your ERP solution vision, two general approaches fall out:

▶ Creating and maintaining a dedicated DR system within your overall system landscape

▶ Outsourcing your DR system to an outsourcing provider

Both approaches are valid, and the first is more traditional. But the time and expense related to setting up, configuring, keeping current, and managing your own DR system explains the recent increase in outsourcing we've seen over the last two years. Companies that outsource the DR component of their SAP system landscape help to preserve their data, and access to this data, in that the outsourcer operates a completely independent data center, typically in a very different geographic location. For smaller and midsize companies with only a single data center, the expense relief is tremendous. On the other hand, if the DR solution is maintained "in-house," so to speak, it will need to be housed in a separate facility. This alone is sure to drive complexity, cost, and even the architecture and makeup of both the SAP system landscape and its individual systems. To read more about DR, see Chapter 16, "Disaster Recovery Considerations and Solutions."

Addressing Training Requirements

The SAP system landscape is directly impacted by the potential need to train SAP end users as well as the system's developers and technical support staff. Three different systems come into play:

▶ **Training**—A dedicated end-user training system is often implemented to assist in teaching users who are new to a particular SAP component *how* to actually use the system. This amounts to business-process training and SAP user interface training (an excellent alternative to creating multiple training clients on the test system, which is busy fulfilling integration responsibilities prior to go-live—the exact time when end users *need* to be trained!). To provide the most value to its students, the training system must be an exact copy of the production system.

▶ **Technical sandbox**—A dedicated technical sandbox system is extremely useful in helping the SAP support organization get up to speed on the entire SAP technology stack, especially with regard to new components and complex HA offerings (rather than attempting to get time on other systems for what could amount to *crash-and-burn* testing).

▶ **Business sandbox**—A dedicated business sandbox (or *development sandbox*) system allows developers who are unfamiliar with a particular SAP component, or faced with integrating multiple components and other legacy systems, the opportunity to pilot new systems in a pure testing environment (rather than on the real development system).

Convincing everyone that such a system is truly required can represent quite a challenge for the "customers" of one of these training systems. In our own experience, we have seen the lack of a technical sandbox really hurt an organization in terms of downtime due to botched infrastructure upgrades and changes to HA technologies and DR processes.

Another colleague of ours has more than once had to strongly push for the adoption of a training system, too. Such a system allows for extensive informal user testing and practice outside formally delivered training. He believes that this extra level of hands-on self-directed training is critical because your end-user community is best positioned of all groups to find business-process operational errors and limitations. And of course it is desirable to correct these issues well before go-live. But a consultant, or even a senior superuser, typically is not positioned to push the adoption and use of a dedicated training system. More often than not, it takes the SAP steering committee, the project's experienced management team, and the prodding of a knowledgeable SAP solution architect to do so. We cannot stress this enough—the risk is huge, in that you do not want to find out too late that not every business scenario works as it did during integration testing (for example, all types of contracts, all types of material movements, all kinds of accounting entries, and so on).

The Performance-Driven System Landscape

When it comes to evaluating your solution vision against the layout of your SAP system landscape, it is important to ensure that the performance of the systems meets the needs of their different end-user communities. Most of the time, of course, the focus is on designing, installing, and configuring a well-performing production system. Performance considerations usually relate back to what an end user will experience while on the system, including

▶ Business transaction *response times*, or how long it takes to refresh your SAPGUI after pressing the Enter key, for example.

▶ How quickly a background or "batch" job will execute, otherwise known as *throughput*.

▶ How quickly a report or other query will make it through the system and actually be printed, sometimes called *latency*.

However, these same performance considerations apply to all the other systems within the SAP system landscape, too. The development system, for example, needs to exhibit excellent performance even while 25, 50, or more developers are banging away at keyboards trying to build your custom SAP solution. Similarly, your test system needs to provide the performance necessary to get through integration testing. Even the training system needs to provide adequate user response times so as to make the actual training experience more than something to be avoided.

High-performance considerations cover the gamut, touching every facet of every system within the landscape. This means that *everything*—from the performance of the network connecting each system, to each server's CPU, RAM, and disk configuration, to each system's OS, database, and SAP component—must be addressed. Starting off on the right foot, with properly sized and configured hardware and software elements, is paramount, of course, but tuning all these technology stack pieces to create a cohesive well-running machine is just as important to achieving excellent performance. Like the weakest link in a chain, a single underperforming solution component will only throttle back the maximum performance otherwise obtainable from your system.

Driving Scalability into Your System Landscape

The need for scalability, such as high availability and excellent performance, is addressed primarily through the sizing process. Scalability does not pay off up front in terms of improved system availability or better user response times, though. Rather, scalability is all about paying for "headroom" in your system, headroom that is not actually needed at present but might be required in the near future. In other words, scalability addresses future planned and unplanned growth in your system.

This growth can manifest itself in a number of ways. In our experience in the real world, we have seen the results of *unplanned* growth hurt companies where scalability was never addressed, as in the following cases:

▶ The number of end users increased at one of our new accounts, not because it did more hiring than it anticipated when its SAP solution was crafted, but because it unexpectedly acquired its competitor and doubled in size. We had six months to project the delta needed in terms of database and application server processing power and RAM requirements, followed by stress-testing the new design and finally implementing it.

▶ More than one of our customers' databases grew so fast that they outstripped the results of their comprehensive three-year database sizing methodology in the first year! In most cases, the system we put in place for these customers was scalable— more disk drives could be added, smaller drives could be swapped with larger ones, and so on. In three cases in particular, though, the database growth was so explosive that a whole new disk subsystem platform needed to be brought in, and the recently acquired current platform was retired (or redeployed) years earlier than expected.

▶ When databases grow quickly, the tape backup/restore solution implemented often grows less effective as well. We have seen this most often in relatively small SAP implementations, where an initial investment in tape backup technology needed to be tossed in favor of tape solutions that backed up more data per tape cartridge, and did so fast enough to not exceed the customer's backup window (time allotted to perform a backup, which usually equates to planned downtime in the case of offline full backups).

▶ It has been a while, but we also had a customer outgrow its network, too. Today, with switched networks and Gigabit Ethernet providing more than adequate bandwidth to every SAP server component, and cheap 10- and 100-Megabit Ethernet prevalent at the desktop, there's no excuse for lacking network scalability (which will prove critical as bolt-ons and other systems are eventually moved to the cloud).

Outstripping the capabilities of your current system such that a new platform is needed probably represents a worst-case scenario. Not only does the current production component need to be replaced, but to support sound change control principles, so does the same component in your test, staging, and/or technical sandbox environments. This is why hardware and software vendors tout things like "highly scalable system architectures," "enterprise versions" of particular OSs and database systems, and so on—though not necessarily needed up front, the headroom that these approaches provide helps an organization feel more comfortable if it winds up growing faster than it expected. And hardware vendors in particular can position their SAP clients for improved scalability by practicing the following:

▶ Specify server platforms that allow additional CPUs and RAM to be added as needed. In other words, avoid "maxing out" the box.

▶ Alternatively, design SAP solutions such that they take advantage of SAP's support for *horizontal scalability*. This is one of our favorite approaches when it comes to SAP application servers, J2EE middleware servers, and web servers—we prefer to max them out with regard to processors, with the understanding that an incremental number of servers can be added at any time should the environment grow to require it (interestingly, although SAP has successfully tested a system running more than 160 application servers, it is rare to find customer implementations with more than 10 or 12, and 4 to 8 is much more common).

▶ Architect a solution for the appropriate level of vertical scalability. In other words, if a two-tier "central system" (where all SAP software components execute on the same physical server) approach to sizing meets today's requirements, perhaps a three-tier solution will provide for unknown scalability requirements. In a three-tiered architecture, one database server and multiple application servers are configured as a single system image.

▶ Architect a highly scalable database platform. As our real-world examples in the preceding list illustrate, this tends to be where a lack of scalability causes the most problems.

Hardware and software vendors alike spend a great deal of time "proving" how scalable their offerings are. As a first step, we suggest that prospective SAP customers review benchmarks, customer references, and feedback, and the results of tests published through whitepapers and other technical documents. We also suggest that you begin considering new approaches to scalability. For example, HP's iCOD (instant capacity on demand) offering touts "capacity on demand"—when and where you need it. When a customer buys a server, for example, it might be fully populated with CPUs. The customer pays for only what is needed in the near term, however. Later, if it is determined that more processing power is required, the customer takes advantage of the in-place processors by merely applying for a license; no intrusive field upgrade or service call is required, and therefore the need for planned downtime is drastically reduced.

The TCO-Driven System Landscape

More than anything else, total cost of ownership (TCO) drives what a solution vision actually looks like at the end of the day, when an SAP solution is implemented and really being used. Discussions on TCO might instead be labeled return on investment (ROI), or might fall under the heading of "investment protection." Regardless, a focus on lowering TCO seeks to find less-expensive solution-stack alternatives that still meet the needs of the business.

When all other things are equal, the following points apply from a hardware perspective when considering TCO:

▶ A hardware vendor's use of common components such as CPUs and memory boards allows flexible sharing of resources between different SAP system landscapes and, in some cases, hardware platforms, too.

▶ Common disk drive form factors reduce TCO by increasing reusability.

▶ Support for hot-pluggable and/or hot-add hardware components eliminates or, in the worst-case scenario, minimizes downtime (can include hard drives, tape drives, power supplies, fans, and even RAM and processors).

▶ Support for redundant components, such as power supplies, disk drives, fans, and so on, also eliminates or minimizes downtime.

▶ The ability to run mixed-speed CPUs or RAM in a particular platform protects that investment—CPUs and RAM do not have to be tossed aside when additional processing power or memory is required.

Outsourcing your entire SAP infrastructure/operations team is another potential method of reducing TCO. In fact, outsourcing can represent the biggest potential TCO factor that a company considers. At this level, though, outsourcing becomes more of a strategic business solution that impacts a lot more than simply TCO. True, outsourcing can cut labor costs by 50%, and enhance flexibility of a technical support organization to easily change as business requirements change, but there are drawbacks and disadvantages as well (discussed later in this chapter).

Another solution vision approach that impacts the SAP system landscape from both a configuration and a TCO perspective is the use of third-party hosting or application service providers. Such providers can drive lower TCO by virtue of their application-specific expertise, above and beyond that provided by in-house staff and traditional outsourcing providers. For example:

▶ A hosting provider can offer a preconfigured technology stack for the particular SAP solution you want to implement. This is one reason why they look so good from a TCO perspective—design, deployment, manageability, operations, and other cost factors are substantially reduced due to a high level of both standardization and core competencies in the services they provide.

▶ Hosting providers enable interesting financing alternatives, in that they partner with various SAP technology partners to make leasing, pay-as-you-go, and other payment methods available.

The hosting market has come on hard times over the last few years. The SAP-focused companies that weathered these hard times seem even better prepared and well positioned to host SAP solutions, however.

Infrastructure Security Considerations

We know of *no* company that does not envision protecting its corporate computing assets. From a technology stack security perspective, not all software vendors are created equal, however. Oracle touts its unbreakable database, UNIX vendors tout the robust security features of their operating environments, and so on.

In our eyes, security features are very important, but good security is more often about creating a secure environment (in terms of firewalls, penetration testing, and so on), locking down, managing, and testing *changes* to a technology stack, and carefully identifying security holes and other weaknesses in new technology stack components before these components ever find themselves in production. Companies that embrace and act upon the idea of protecting their computing assets by maintaining a default configuration in which everything up the technology stack is locked down until a need is validated to exist (in which case a particular aspect of the technology stack is "opened up") will be more secure in the long run.

Manageability Considerations

Few new SAP clients ever look down the road at how they will operationalize SAP from a technology support perspective until the implementation project is well underway. That's not to say that they ignore it, but rather that there's a whole lot of other more pressing needs and decisions to first contend with. By the time go-live looms just over the horizon, though, every single client—without exception—has indicated a growing concern for manageability. Sure, it's there on the project plan, and any number of products can be used to support managing your SAP environment. But the whole field of manageability is more complex *and more work* than you would imagine.

Each layer in the SAP technology stack must be managed; the risk of not keeping an eye on a particular layer or solution component affects the uptime of the entire system. Because each layer is so different from the others, it's nearly impossible to find a single management product that can actually monitor and report on more than a few layers, much less the entire stack. Therefore, the next best thing becomes trying to find a product that can at least interoperate successfully with other products. At the end of the day, three, four, or even more tools and utilities must ultimately be fused together to provide a holistic view of an SAP technology stack. This is challenging, to say the least!

Because of the challenges inherent to managing hardware and software products from a lot of different technology stack vendors, some of our customers have purposely chosen less than "best-of-breed" products for their SAP solutions, if only to minimize the number of software partners involved. Or they have decided to reduce the number of partners and vendors altogether by selecting one of the big enterprise hardware/services vendors. The obvious partners are clear—HP, IBM, CA, BMC, and Sun. For example, if you go with HP and choose to implement an Integrity-based server platform with an HP StorageWorks SAN, running HP-UX 11i, and managed by HP Business Availability Center (BAC), Operations Center, and Data Center Automation Center, the challenges otherwise inherent to managing five or six different vendors' products has just dropped tremendously—not to mention that you would be going with best-of-breed solutions to boot. Similar arguments could be made for going with an IBM- or Sun-based technology stack—IBM even throws a number of SAP-supported databases and middleware into the mix.

The System Landscape and Accessibility

The last area we want to cover with regard to solution vision and the SAP system landscape is accessibility. Many companies over the last three or four years have started with a vision of dumping all application-specific interfaces in favor of browser-enabled solutions, so as to ease the burdens and costs associated with desktop/laptop management while opening up new accessibility approaches such as handhelds and other wireless devices. SAP has supported that vision since 1996, with the introduction of Internet connectivity in R/3 3.1G.

SAP AG offers quite a few accessibility options today when it comes to SAP solutions. The classic SAPGUI represents one end of the spectrum. This approach is safe, very mainstream, and very easy to implement. And the SAPGUI we have today is extremely comprehensive, supporting nearly all SAP components and products through a single interface. But the SAPGUI still represents a typical application-specific approach to accessibility; each end user installs the client on his desktop or laptop, or runs the SAPGUI from a network share, and off he goes.

Other accessibility approaches are available, however. The original WebGUI, for example, is based on HTML and provides connectivity via Microsoft's Internet Explorer and so on. And a more recent addition, the JavaGUI, allows native Java-based access to SAP. Both of these approaches fulfill an Internet-based approach to connectivity, and subsequently simplify the desktop (assuming Internet connectivity is a standard desktop offering at your particular company, of course).

ERP Solution Vision and IT Outsourcing

Outsourcing is what we consider the fifth technology perspective, after the conservative, mainstream, close follower, and leading edge approaches outlined earlier in the chapter in the "Technology Perspectives" section. Most of this book assumes that your company owns and manages the SAP infrastructure necessary to implement your SAP solution. We also assume that the members of your SAP Technical Support Organization (SAP TSO) or overall IT support team are employed or contracted by you, and not by a third-party outsourcing firm. In these final pages of Chapter 4, however, we open the door to considering *outsourcing* these key assets instead.

What drives organizations to outsource? In a recent IDC study, the volatility of our global economy was labeled as the primary consideration. The study put forth several ideas. For example, it was pointed out that making large investments in computing infrastructure is not wise in today's economy. A company should instead let experts in the field of enterprise computing resource management make these investments, leveraging their core competencies in these areas to presumably reduce the organization's cost of IT. All non-core functions should be considered for outsourcing, allowing an organization to instead invest its time and resources in its own core competencies.

This is really no different than in the past, when companies turned to outsourcing firms to cut costs. But today things are a little different, and cost may be less a factor than pure *adaptability*, which is the ability of a company to make changes quickly so as to stay competitive or position itself better with its customers, vendors, suppliers, and so on. In a nutshell, adaptability equates to strategic benefits, rather than the simpler and more tactical cost-cutting benefits realized a decade ago through traditional outsourcing.

Intelligent outsourcing represents one method of becoming more flexible and adaptive, while still cutting costs. Outsourcing can mitigate risks relative to economic uncertainty as well, especially when the outsourcing agreement leverages the core competencies of each party. The really good outsourcing organizations, confident in their ability to execute, are more than willing to assume incremental risk. And with other risk-reward elements coming into play, such as those around meeting service-level agreements (SLAs) and availability targets, the best outsourcers are so convinced that they can do a better job of managing your resources and minimizing your downtime than you can that they're betting their revenue stream—your company's monthly check to them—on it.

With all of this in mind, exactly what should you outsource and what should you keep in-house? The short answer includes anything that is technology-intensive or complex from a process perspective. This easily explains why outsourcing SAP DR responsibilities is growing in popularity—DR meets both criteria in a big way.

Prerequisites of IT Outsourcing

Although companies today can outsource technology or business processes, our focus in the remainder of this chapter is on information technology outsourcing (ITO); business process outsourcing (BPO) is the label given to process-oriented outsourcing. A quick list of ITO prerequisites is in order before we move on, however. To benefit most from an ITO relationship with an outsourcing partner, look for a partner with deep pockets, great quali-fications, and broad geographic coverage. And then consider the following "must haves":

▶ A good outsourcer has both a methodology and a plan for not only helping you transition to its facilities, but transforming your application environment.

▶ The outsourcer must be flexible and able to adapt to your needs, both short-term and long-term. Thus, a clear understanding of the iterative nature of successful outsourc-ing is needed, as both tactical and strategic needs will morph over time. A rigid engagement and change management model will leave you worse off than before.

▶ Effective outsourcers reduce a firm's risk rather than add to it. Managing risk is as important as ever. With the ethical snafus, hand-slapping, and meltdowns of several well-known overseas outsourcing providers, outsourcing decisions made on the basis of cost reductions does not adequately address a firm's need; outsourcing without regard to risk management can prove tremendously more expensive, not to mention disruptive to business, than simply maintaining an existing internally hosted model.

▶ Your firm's goals and objectives must align with the outsourcer's capabilities—if the outsourcer does not specialize specifically in SAP hosting, or is uncomfortable providing references that otherwise prove its capabilities, walk away.

▶ A well-defined and articulated set of expectations must be communicated to the outsourcer. For example, your SLAs, requirements surrounding any systems manage-ment information you want to see on a regular basis, and so on, all must be clearly communicated up front (ensure that SLAs are measured at the application layer rather than at infrastructure layers, for example).

▶ For global outsourcing arrangements, a good cultural fit is very important, too. At minimum, understanding your outsourcer's culture is essential. But it's really helpful to understand specific traits and tendencies. For example, in some cultures people tend to avoid sharing bad news with their clients, or in other cultures, it is not accept-able to answer a question with a simple "no" without providing details as to why.

If both parties meet these prerequisites, and you are comfortable with your potential outsourcer, you are a good fit for at least *considering* outsourcing.

Potential Benefits of Outsourcing SAP Infrastructure

The benefits you should reap from an ITO relationship, compared to retaining control of your SAP assets internally, include the following:

▶ **Less downtime and better availability**—This includes both planned and unplanned downtime, as the outsourcer can presumably leverage its economies of scale, superior maintenance processes, and access to talented SAP personnel.

▶ **The same or greater level of flexibility**—As your business needs change, so too should the system that supports these needs. This should manifest itself in a number of ways, including a full lifecycle offering and "one-stop shopping."

▶ **Better consistency from a personnel perspective**—Although employee and contractor turnover is not what it has been in the past (it's quite reasonable today), a successful outsourcing provider should still be able to retain its scarce technical resources longer than you can.

▶ **Simplified budgeting and financial management of assets**—With a regular payment schedule (plus charges for occasional incremental work), SAP IT budgeting is simplified to writing a single check every month.

▶ **High-quality approach and delivery**—Outsourcers and hosting providers benefit from economies of scale unlike all but the very largest of SAP shops. Because they're in the business of standing up, delivering, and providing access to SAP applications, outsourcers can naturally invest in SAP deployment and upgrade methodologies, testing tools, staff training, and end-to-end systems management suites well beyond the means of most individual firms hosting their own internal SAP systems.

▶ **Reduced IT and supporting costs**—This includes little or no up-front capital expenditures on hardware and infrastructure. This equates to more cash and is especially true when it comes to using offshore outsourcing partners.

To this last point, offshore outsourcing has been described as "counter-recessionary" simply because offshore costing models are so dramatically lower than U.S.-based models—recession or not, you are saving more money than otherwise possible by holding on to SAP assets internally. And with so many other countries beginning to compete successfully with India, which has dominated offshore outsourcing over the last five years (and currently owns 85% of all offshore outsourcing, according to Meta Group), the cost models will only continue to improve over time.

Shortcomings of Outsourcing in the Real World

Historically, it has been difficult to find more than a few success stories where the company was so enthralled with its outsourcing partner that it could not help but tell everyone. Our direct experience with outsourcing is pretty diverse. From the stories our colleagues have shared with us, the following points seem to hold true:

▶ Loss of control seems to be the biggest concern. This relates directly back to the flexibility and adaptability that outsourcers today tout as compelling benefits.

▶ Less than overwhelming cost savings is another concern. Organizations that expect an order-of-magnitude cost reduction may be disappointed. Numbers like this are possible, true, but only if your own organization is so bloated with overhead that you simply couldn't help but reduce your IT bill by half.

▶ There is no perceived difference in the amount of time it takes to resolve system problems. This is especially true if your firm's IT organization does its job quite well, leaving little room for improvement for an outsourcing partner.

▶ Outsource contract timelines vary considerably. One of our large SAP customers was persuaded to sign a seven-year outsourcing agreement a few years back. Seven years! That's an eternity in the world of IT, and the customer is "locked in" until the contract expires, short of turning over a hefty penalty for early termination.

▶ Contractual language related to billing can prove counterproductive. Many customers of ours have signed outsourcing deals structured such that incremental processing power required by the customer during the life of the contract would be billed "per server." In no time, these customers saw their monthly fee rise significantly as the outsourcer increased its revenue stream by meeting new customer SAP requirements with many two-processor servers instead of fewer larger servers.

▶ Fees can add up quickly and thus need to be factored into an organization's initial financial planning. We have been told by customers that they sometimes feel "nickeled and dimed to death" by their outsourcing provider. Every unplanned change to their environment, every new addition to the SAP system landscape, and so on add up to incremental and costly fees that were never envisioned by the original contracting team. Contractual language placing a ceiling on such fees (combined with planning for a 10%–15% uplift in monthly fees during upgrades or platform refreshes) helps mitigate this exposure.

In looking back at the preceding list, it seems that many of the stumbling blocks stem from contractual issues rather than true outsourcing shortcomings. That is, performance problems were hard to find, and it seemed as though service-level agreements and general system availability were not the dramatic issues seen in years past, either. This illustrates just how far the ITO providers have come in the last decade.

Analyzing Outsourcing Versus Doing It Yourself

Just like hosting and managing your infrastructure internally, outsourcing touches every facet of your end users' experience with their SAP solution. However, if an outsourcer can provide the same or better levels of service, responsiveness, and system availability, while successfully retaining the skill sets and expertise needed to keep an SAP solution humming along, and do all of this more cost-effectively than you, by all means consider outsourcing the forerunner in achieving your ERP solution vision.

The next step is to verify not only that the outsourcer is built upon a foundation of sound business fundamentals, but that it can do the following:

▶ Be effectively held accountable to deliver what it promises, through penalties and similar service level–based fees

▶ Show you proof of how it has accepted responsibility for its mistakes and shortcomings in the past

▶ Point to a clear and time-proven methodology for planning, deploying, upgrading, supporting, and otherwise managing the SAP enterprise computing resources of *other* customer organizations

▶ Show you how its own processes and procedures are subject to continuous improvement

Why are these so important? Because they give an organization a way of comparing themselves to the best that outsourcing can provide. And because there is really no cost savings that will ever make it acceptable to circumvent these basic business fundamentals! In other words, flexibility, service, system availability, and authentic customer-service values mean a whole lot more to your end users than price ever will.

Hosting Providers for SAP

Another approach to managing resources outside the boundaries of your internally housed data center is through a hosting provider or application service provider (ASP). What exactly is an ASP? According to IDC, ASPs provide a contractual service offering to deploy, host, manage, and rent access to an application from a centrally managed facility. Such hosting providers are responsible for either directly or indirectly providing all the specific activities and expertise aimed at managing a software application or set of applications. Different providers tend to focus their services in different application areas—hosting traditional file, print, and web services, and enterprise applications such as SAP make up the bulk of these. This is what tends to differentiate ASPs from general ITO and BPO outsourcing providers.

According to Gartner Group, hosting providers deliver application functionality and associated services across a network to multiple customers by way of a pay-as-you-go pricing model. As in traditional outsourcing, the value proposition clearly has to do with providing access to customer applications without the systems, staffing, and manageability challenges. After a couple of cycles of dramatic growth followed by consolidation over the last 10 years, the remaining ASPs are strong and growing again because they provide the following:

▶ Financial advantages (again, the pay-as-you-go model) and flexibility

▶ Consistent accessibility—hosting providers eliminate issues of business application access from an organization's list of to-dos

▶ Inbuilt access to expensive, skilled, and difficult-to-retain IT professionals

▶ Specialized knowledge in hosting SAP and the collection of bolt-on applications common to SAP system deployments

▶ Better reliability than most customer organizations enjoy, in regard to network and other infrastructure resource availability

▶ Ability to host other applications, provide email and web services, and so on

Of course, like ITO providers, an ASP's specific knowledge and experience in supporting SAP solutions, its reputation, its installed base of customer references, and it overall financial stability are critical considerations prior to securing its services.

Summary

In this chapter, we discussed the need and importance of crafting an ERP solution vision prior to designing or implementing SAP. Different technology perspectives were covered, and the importance of refining the solution vision with regard to SAP system landscape dimensions or characteristics was covered as well. After the vision began to take form, we reviewed a few methods of capturing all the data that came together to create the vision—constraints, assumptions, boundary conditions, and so on—including using a knowledge repository. We then wrapped up the chapter with a discussion on IT outsourcing to improve systems manageability, provide excellent resource provisioning, and ultimately create a high-quality customer experience for SAP end users.

Case Study: Developing Your ERP Solution Vision

HiTech's senior leadership team (LT) continues to consider the ramifications of a packaged business application implementation. As one of the LT's respected business analysts and an expert in planning for and deploying business applications, you have been asked to answer several more questions related to the firm's ERP solution vision.

Questions

1. With regard to initially establishing a focus team to help create an ERP solution vision, where might the best participants come from?
2. What are the four primary technology perspectives described in this chapter?
3. Is there a fifth technology perspective? If so, how would you describe it?
4. What are several system landscape dimensions or characteristics that need to be considered and addressed as a part of creating an ERP solution vision?
5. What is the relationship between business vision and solution vision?

NOTE

The answers to these questions can be found in Appendix A, "Case Study Answers."

CHAPTER 5

Financial Impact: Total Cost of Ownership

This chapter takes a closer look at return on investment (ROI) and total cost of ownership analysis, or TCO analysis. The idea at this stage in your SAP project is not to justify the project so much as to determine where and when the costs are incurred within the context of the SAP technology stack and ongoing operations. You also need to be able to compare various technology stack and staffing options and alternatives from a holistic cost perspective. By calculating rough costs before embarking upon major technology purchases, or before fleshing out the SAP Technical Support Organization (TSO) with incremental and expensive human resources, the composition of the solution you eventually go "live" with will not only meet your business needs, but better reflect your budget needs.

TCO analysis is about balancing a firm's SAP technology and staffing requirements against its cost model or budgetary targets. Many years ago, one of our SAP customers put the TCO analysis process in perspective for us—they said that cost (such as the need for system availability, a particular level of performance, and other system characteristics or factors) limited the firm's technology stack choices. The firm's TCO goal was simply another "filter" or decision tree it ran its options through. The goal is simple—ultimately, a trade-off or compromise must be reached where the end-user community, SAP IT organization, and financial bean counters all see eye to eye.

How you achieve that goal is addressed throughout this chapter. The first half of the chapter looks at the decisions made in regard to specific technology stack components: hardware platforms, the operating system (OS) and database selections, high-availability and performance options, and so on. These are one-time implementation costs. The second half of the chapter takes a closer look at recurring costs, such as annual maintenance fees, upgrade/update fees, the cost of downtime to perform such updates, and more. We also look closely at tools and approaches offered by software vendors, hardware partners, and SAP AG alike, designed to reduce TCO and maximize ROI.

Analyzing Total Cost of Ownership

What exactly *is* TCO? Rather than attempting a long-winded all-encompassing definition, consider the following, and refer to Figure 5.1 for a comprehensive visual look at TCO.

TCO analysis is all about determining how to get the best business solution for the least money. But it is much more complex than simply determining the relationship between computing power and budgets. Instead, a key goal of TCO analysis is to understand the cost-benefit trade-offs inherent to different solutions. The three main component costs of TCO are listed next and depicted in Figure 5.1. As Figure 5.1 indicates, these costs span two stages. First, one-time acquisition costs include both product procurement and product installation costs, including training dollars spent in support of installation. Recurring costs include the cost of SAP operations, application management, maintenance costs, the business cost of downtime, and other day-after-day costs.

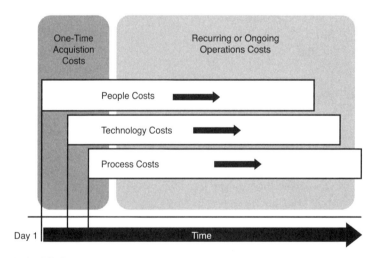

FIGURE 5.1   Both acquisition and recurring costs related to technology, people, and processes play a role in determining a solution's true total cost of ownership.

▶ **Technology costs**—These include costs of the SAP technology stack infrastructure and any hardware and software tools that it comprises or that are used to manage it.

▶ **People costs**—These are the costs of hiring and retaining people who are qualified to deploy and manage the SAP solution, along with the cost of salaries, contractor fees, and so on.

▶ **Process costs**—These include the financial impact that various operational and other processes have on the overall solution costs.

These costs are discussed in depth later in the chapter.

A TCO analysis can help you evaluate different technology stacks, and even help you weigh diverse people and process alternatives such as hosting SAP internally versus outsourcing it. This is possible because TCO addresses both internal (direct salaries) and external (outsourcing contracts) costs, one-time as well as recurring.

And on top of this, a TCO analysis can be either all-encompassing, or quite discrete. That is, TCO can be expressed either in absolute dollars or in percentage differences (deltas) between various choices and alternatives. We use both of these approaches, depending upon the situation, but whenever possible we lean toward delta comparisons. Why? Because a delta comparison is simpler in that only the solution components that differ between two alternatives need to be examined. A delta analysis doesn't cover the absolute costs of one solution over another. Instead, it seeks to identify the *difference* in costs between two different solutions. This usually yields enough information to make a smart decision one way or the other, especially with regard to procurement and people costs. In other cases, though, it becomes a judgment call as to whether one particular approach or solution stack is significantly more expensive than another *in the long run*.

For example, in the past when we were asked to build and analyze TCO models of a Sun/Oracle solution versus a Microsoft Windows/SQL Server solution, each capable of addressing 1,000 concurrent users, we only had to consider a handful of technologies, people, and process issues that differed between the solutions. In the end, the customer deliverable was shorter, more concise, and more applicable than a full-blown TCO analysis, because it was customer-specific and only took the deltas into consideration.

Consider Figure 5.2, which shows two very similar solutions paired in a delta analysis. Because the solutions are similar, only the differences need to be identified, analyzed, and charted here, making this approach simpler and more practical than a complete TCO analysis. You'll note that the solution components with identical costs (regardless of the solution alternative) cancel each other out, making a delta analysis easy to do. Tracking every cost in each technology stack would be a waste of time—only the deltas need to be identified.

Solution alternative 1 looks to be more expensive than alternative 2 for several reasons. For example, alternative 1 requires twice as many DBAs to administer the same size database for each technology stack, and the acquisition cost is four times that of the second alternative. However, from a database operations perspective, each is on par with the other. And the costs associated with the remainder of the technology stack are the same, too, in this case, and therefore not analyzed. Next, let's take a look at how a firm's solution vision comprising technology stacks and their unique process and people costs combine to drive an equally unique cost model.

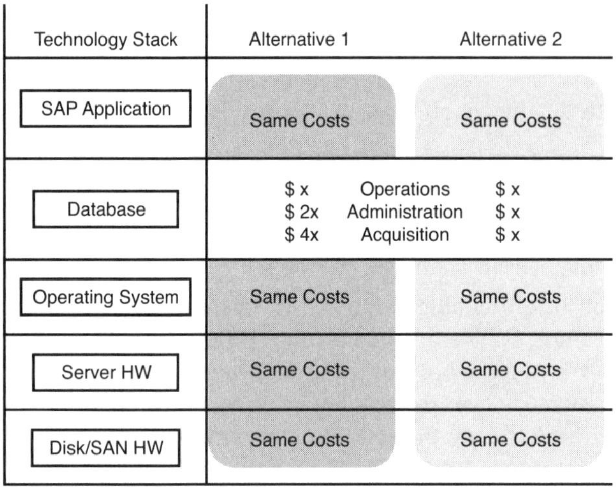

Technology Stack	Alternative 1	Alternative 2
SAP Application	Same Costs	Same Costs
Database	$ x Operations $ x $ 2x Administration $ x $ 4x Acquisition $ x	
Operating System	Same Costs	Same Costs
Server HW	Same Costs	Same Costs
Disk/SAN HW	Same Costs	Same Costs

FIGURE 5.2   A TCO delta analysis represents a quick method of determining, for example, which solution alternative is least expensive from an operations and systems management perspective.

How Solution Vision Drives TCO

Total cost of ownership analysis seeks to measure the lifecycle costs of a particular solution stack—the end-to-end complete costs incurred to own and operate an SAP solution over its useful life. Thus TCO serves to highlight the relationship between cost and performance, illuminating how quickly a particular solution can claim a return on investment.

Returning to Chapter 3 and the various solution characteristics that need to be envisioned and planned for in advance, a number of characteristics were discussed. We have collapsed these into a few key areas or considerations:

▶ High availability (HA)

▶ Disaster recovery (DR)

▶ Performance

▶ Scalability

▶ Security, manageability, and other operations areas

This section focuses on these areas as each pertains to the SAP technology stack from a technology perspective. Later, we will identify people and process considerations inherent to each layer in the stack, such as ongoing operations, infrastructure and applications, systems management, and other processes that are subject to continuous improvement, therefore lending themselves to reducing or increasing TCO.

The Impact of High Availability Requirements

High-availability requirements refer to the need of your SAP solution to suffer from only a limited amount of unplanned downtime. In other words, the higher the level of HA, the more available a solution is to its end users. This availability is often expressed in percentages related to the total number of minutes available in a year. Over time, these percentages have been labeled, giving us the infamous "three nines," "four nines," and "five nines" of availability (which equate to 99.9%, 99.99%, and 99.999% availability, respectively, all of which are covered in more detail in Chapters 15 through 17).

Generally, the higher the level of availability required by the business, the more costly it becomes to procure, implement, and support the system in question; higher availability drives greater TCO. And the relationship between cost and HA is not linear; rather, it grows exponentially as we strive to achieve something closer and closer to 100% availability. Figure 5.3 really puts this into perspective. In our experience, as we move from 99.99% availability to the famous "five nines" of availability, the incremental cost to the business to achieve another 47 minutes of availability could easily exceed $2.9 million, nearly *five times* the cost required to jump from three nines to four nines ($590K). And yet in terms of raw numbers, we only add a fraction of a percentage to our availability targets—a couple more minutes of system availability. For businesses that lose millions of dollars for every minute of unplanned downtime they incur, five nines is the way to go, of course. In our experience, though, the incremental cost is *very often* simply not worth the nearly negligible difference in uptime.

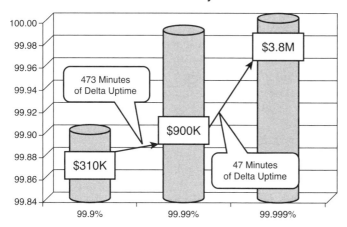

Incremental Availability Versus Cost

FIGURE 5.3   For this fictional enterprise, note the small amount of time or availability gained as we increase our SAP solution's availability from three nines to five nines.

We have always told our customers that we can provide them pretty much any level of availability they'd like—the only issue is money, of course. Many of our customers would commence our initial discussions on HA by telling us that their business demanded "the highest levels of availability" or "little to no downtime." Many of these same companies had failed to do the "five nines of availability" math, however. Their need for this level of availability was little more than a perceived requirement, a desire. After we worked out the budget and ROI numbers together, it was amazing to watch the perceived business requirements nosedive to embrace less expensive technology solutions that are more representative of the business's real needs.

We like to structure the end result of these types of ROI calculations such that they reflect how much the business will pay for that extra few hours or minutes of availability. The real-world numbers have been pretty significant in our experience, in one case running up to another $500,000 over the three-year lifecycle of the project for seven hours less unplanned downtime per year. In other words, giving 21 hours back to the business would cost the business nearly $24K per hour. We then had to pose this question to the customer: "Will you suffer more than $500,000 in lost revenue or productivity if you are down an incremental seven hours a year?" In this one particular case, the cost of downtime escalated pretty quickly with every hour of downtime incurred by our customer, and it indeed required the solution. Most of the time, though, in our experience, the answer is usually one of surprise and our TCO-educated client settles for a lower level of availability that may not be the highest level available, but is *good enough* for IT to deliver to the business what it *needs*.

Good enough—what a great phrase! In these days of redundant and clustered everything, companies often seem to forget that going after that extra tick of availability can really add up, and yet not significantly impact their ability to do business. *Good enough* is all about compromising, settling for 95% of what you desire, but paying only 50% of the cost of a solution that would have satisfied 100% of your desires. Not required, but desired. In so many cases, for so many SAP implementations, *good enough* is the ideal attitude. The decision boils down to identifying business *requirements* versus desires. As we have said before, just do the math. There's nothing like a logical discussion around ROI, TCO, and a technology stack's characteristics to convince the business that *good enough* will serve most companies quite well (not to mention leaving a little money in the project budget for performance awards, recognition, and reasonable go-live bonuses).

Disaster Recovery Requirements That Drive TCO

Similar to HA discussions, determining a company's DR requirements also boils down to how much it costs the organization when the SAP system is unavailable. But whereas HA addresses timelines of minutes and hours, DR discussions focus most often on hours and days.

Figuring out the real cost of downtime after an extended period of time—days—can be quite complicated. Consider the following:

▶ **Seamless failover**—Business processes must usually be capable of failing over to a completely different physical location. Therefore, the technology ramifications are huge, to the point of requiring completely redundant data centers or hosting sites in some cases.

▶ **Roles, responsibilities, and ownership**—Every member of the SAP TSO needs to understand exactly what his or her team is responsible for providing in the event of a disaster, and staff and plan for this accordingly.

▶ **Communications plan**—A communications plan must be developed, tested, and continually retested as the technology stack evolves over time. Similarly, communication vehicles such as escalation plans and even system current-state/as-is and process documentation must be maintained and updated at both the primary and DR sites, and tested regularly.

▶ **Technology issues**—Many technically oriented issues abound, including backup/restore concerns, data synchronization between the primary and DR site, access to the DR site by the system's end users, access to the site by other computing systems (integration touch points), day-to-day operations and management of the DR site in the event of a disaster, and issues with how to fail back over to the primary site (or another site) after the disaster has subsided.

▶ **People issues**—Potential problems such as determining contingency and other backup plans should key people be unavailable to perform their duties in the event of a disaster affect recoverability. Here, the importance of consulting agreements (that is, "consulting on demand" or "reactive services" contracts) is underscored, as is training a backup for each key role, maintaining excellent documentation, and so on.

All of these issues affect cost, and therefore present opportunities to minimize or increase TCO. Most often, our involvement in DR-related TCO exercises has amounted to doing the math between different DR alternatives. In some cases, the math supports building redundant data centers. More often, though, establishing a "mini" data center or putting into place a support agreement with a third party to provide such an environment is more appropriate.

In the best scenarios, a customer is able to distribute its SAP environment across two existing sites, though. For example, it is quite common in our experience to house the production and development systems at one physical location, and a staging or test/QA environment at another physical location. In this way, the site with the staging or test/QA system becomes the de facto DR site. This is generally an excellent approach to addressing disaster recoverability. Consider the following, however:

▶ The system that takes on the role of the DR system must be sized appropriately, based on what the business considers "appropriate" performance after a failover. It is not uncommon to size a DR system for half or perhaps three-quarters of the concurrent SAP end users typically hosted by the production system. In some cases, though, a DR system capable of hosting all production users, batch processes, and so on is mandated by the business. And in worst-case situations, both the production system and a fully functioning staging or test/QA system need to be available concurrently, even in the event of a failover.

▶ The HA built into the DR system must be considered. That is, the DR system may need to be clustered or configured with redundant components to achieve a certain level of availability should it become the production system for an extended period of time.

▶ Along with maintaining the system for its primary purpose of testing or quality assurance, this system must also be kept up-to-date from a DR perspective, consistent with the service-level agreements (SLAs) and other requirements of the business. Therefore, this could entail anything from weekly SAP client refreshes to 15-minute database snapshots replicated across a WAN or other network link, in addition to the load already placed on the system.

▶ SAP end-user access to the DR site must be addressed, because a DR site is no good to anyone if no one can access it. This often involves redundant network links between the client public networks and the DR site. In the best of cases, separate carriers (for example, AT&T and Southwestern Bell) are employed, to avoid single points of failure specific to the carriers themselves. But most often the real challenge here is more a matter of explaining to the end users how to *get to* the production system should it fail over to the other site—which SAP logon group to use, or special DR-only SAPGUI icon to double-click, or ITS server to access, and so on.

▶ The location of each site is critical. For example, there is more risk of a single disaster taking down both the primary and DR sites if they are within a few miles of each other rather than separated by a hundred miles or so. This location issue is common in campus or single-building environments, where the backup site might be only a mile (or a few floors) away from the primary site. Of course, the economics of such a decision are easy to understand—a DR site that is close by will probably be easier to manage and maintain. Our point is this, though—identify the lack of critical "distance" between the two sites as a risk, and either mitigate or minimize this risk.

When it comes to DR and TCO, it is important to focus on the business areas that will cripple the business if interrupted or unavailable. Therefore, core transactional systems responsible for generating revenue, maintaining minimum levels of customer service, and keeping the production lines rolling are generally most often addressed. Reporting systems, internal procurement systems, and other such functions typically fail to garner enough business support to cover the expense of a dedicated DR system or site.

In addition to focusing on the core business areas, it is also wise to establish exactly what it means to say that a business function is interrupted or unavailable. Does this mean eight hours? Three days? A week? Bottom line, when does unavailability become unacceptable? The answer to this question drives failover timelines, impacts SLAs, and more.

The most effective TCO DR analyses benefit from a sound costing model or baseline—such a baseline should reflect how much revenue or productive time may be lost prior to moving business processes over to the DR site. And it should also cover time as a function of dollars, so that the relationship between the two clearly illustrates how losses grow over time.

With this information, you naturally have a better understanding as to how long the business can actually tolerate disasters, including different levels or thresholds of pain. Such a keen understanding will serve to further refine the DR solution down the road, as cheaper and more capable technology solutions continue to evolve and therefore rate delta TCO analyses in their own right. In our opinion, this whole area is probably one of the best places for something beyond a simple delta analysis; understanding the complete DR picture can conceivably mean the difference between surviving a disaster and going out of business a few months later. And with so many people and process considerations, building a good technical solution is simply not good enough.

Performance Requirements and TCO

Like so many other areas of TCO analysis, the more performance sought, the larger the IT budget typically needs to be. The key lies not so much in understanding this, though, as in understanding how to *measure* performance such that it can be factored into a TCO performance delta analysis of solution stack options. In the past, we have characterized SAP performance in terms of

- ▶ End-user response times as related to average and peak periods (like end-of-month peaks, or peaks observed during a seasonal cycle).

- ▶ Dialog steps processed during the peak hour (as a reminder, dialog steps represent units of work in SAP, where one dialog step equates to a user pressing the Enter key or otherwise completing a transaction against the database).

- ▶ Average number of fully completed transactions processed in an hour (like dialog steps, this is another way of measuring *work* completed by the SAP system).

- ▶ Average number of concurrent processes executing in the system while it is under load (easily gathered point-in-time by SAP Computing Center Management System [CCMS] transaction SM66, or historically via any number of SAP-aware systems management applications).

- ▶ Average disk queue length while under load (captured via PerfMon, similar UNIX-based utilities, or most SAP-aware management applications). This kind of performance measurement is most applicable to changes in the disk subsystem or database layers of the SAP technology stack.

- ▶ Average CPU utilization while under load (again, using PerfMon or a similar UNIX utility). This is most applicable to changes in server infrastructure, but also valuable when new disk subsystems are introduced (to observe how a bottleneck moves from the disk subsystem to the server, for example, due to a faster subsystem).

After a measurement is embraced, it is fairly easy to redefine it in preparation for a TCO exercise, in terms of dollars. Thus, transactions per hour becomes "*x* $ per transaction," "% CPU utilization per dollar," and so on.

Furthermore, it is usually easier to perform a delta analysis rather than a full-blown performance analysis. Some of the most common areas of TCO analysis when it comes to performance involve testing new versions of SAP, new disk subsystems, and configuration changes to existing systems. Another area might include a change in operating system, or the application of a service pack or patch to a particular layer in the stack, or the impact of installing multiple SAP Internet Transaction Server (ITS) instances on a single server. In all of these cases, testing the before and after scenarios simply makes the most sense. And it simplifies both testing and success criteria, as absolute numbers tend to not be as important as the delta between the two.

How Scalability Impacts Total Cost

The need for scalability in an SAP system also influences TCO. Scalability is historically addressed by purchasing more than you need when it comes to hardware resources. In this way, headroom is available should it become necessary—for example, in the event of heavier-than-usual end-of-month processing or after new processor- or disk-intensive functionality is added to the system. These "in-the-box" scalability considerations include

- ▶ Deploying a server already configured with additional CPUs, RAM, or disks, in effect *supersizing* the solution to address unknown what-if needs at a later date. In the meantime, such an approach will naturally provide better-than-expected performance of the current solution as well.

- ▶ Configuring a server *capable of scaling* or growing in terms of the number and speed of CPUs, RAM, disk capacity, I/O slots, and so on—without actually adding these components. In this way, the oversized system is ready to grow with only minimal downtime required. Unfortunately, you might wind up buying a more capable platform than you ever need.

- ▶ Procuring a disk subsystem or supporting infrastructure capable of easily housing more data, or supporting rapid expansion of capabilities, instead of buying the exact capacity required for the time being. Such incremental capacity might include a storage system's switched fabric containing a higher available port density than currently required, or a disk subsystem with a few extra empty disk shelves (and therefore ready to add disk drives).

Scalability can also be addressed by virtue of the architecture of the solution. In a classic example, it is common to see a large number of relatively cheap servers employed as SAP application servers, rather than deploying fewer larger but more expensive boxes. In other cases, clustered resources are introduced into the SAP system landscape, providing for both improved scalability and higher availability.

Scalability goes way beyond hardware, though. Even the OS, database, and SAP application components can benefit from buying more than you need. We have many customers who have implemented Windows-based OSs as the foundation for their SAP systems, for instance. The capabilities of different versions within the same family of OSs differ, though. Of course, the more capable versions of an OS are priced at a premium compared to their less capable brethren. Customers who make the decision to purchase the more capable versions without a current need for the capabilities inherent to that version are actually investing in scalability (or simply throwing away their money if the extra capability is never one day required).

What all the aforementioned cases have in common boils down to a simple delta TCO analysis, and the benefits it can provide. Each scenario includes an opportunity to spend more money on something that you may or may not actually need. Depending upon the raw dollars at stake, a quick comparison between the two cost models can make a lot of sense, though.

As you will see later in the book, these kinds of scalability considerations play a common role in architecting your SAP systems. It may be short-sighted to buy exactly what you think you need, because invariably a need will evolve over time that was never addressed during the SAP vision phase. Early attention to scalability and sizing a system for a period of time (that is, a three- or four-year lifecycle, taking into account growth in terms of users, database, and so on) can mitigate this risk.

Other SAP Solution Vision Drivers

Other SAP solution vision drivers impact the solution's TCO. The most prevalent are security, manageability, and operations. That is, the design and architecture of a particular SAP solution may cost substantially more (or less), depending on how these areas are addressed. The tightest security constraints, for example, will dictate deployment of firewalls, lock-down of services and ports, implementation of virus protection, and so on. Each has a particular cost that must be factored in to the total solution cost. And because a variety of firewalls and virus protection methods exist, delta analyses may be appropriate as well between different competing solutions.

A need for implementing the most manageable system, or system that is inherently "operations-friendly," will also affect TCO. There are a multitude of management/ operations approaches and software packages on the market for SAP, for example. Some are OS- or database-specific, not to mention SAP component-specific. Others are supported only on a particular hardware vendor's product line. Still others vary in how much time is required to learn the products, whereas others are more difficult to work with when it comes to managing changes in the landscape.

Lowering TCO Through the SAP Technology Stack

According to findings by the Harvard Business School[1], companies poured $47 billion into enterprise systems in 2001 (not just SAP—all enterprise applications). This did not even include the expense associated with acquiring hardware, conducting training, and procuring implementation services. Therefore, with more than petty cash at stake, an exercise in TCO should represent a "minimum requirement" prior to purchasing the key components of an SAP technical solution. To this end, a number of general factors contribute heavily to lowering solution stack TCO. These include

- ▶ Procurement or acquisition costs, or the cost of initially purchasing SAP technology infrastructure such as servers, OSs, database software, systems management tools, and so on

- ▶ Installation costs, including configuration of the installed product such that it is usable

- ▶ Management and maintenance costs, such as those related to systems and process management, as well as costs related to scheduled maintenance activities

[1] ERP: Payoffs and Pitfalls, *Harvard Business School Working Knowledge, October 2002*

▶ Training, which includes the cost of time off to pursue training as well as the actual cost of attending the training necessary to install and later support a particular component or layer of the SAP technology stack

Another interesting factor that can heavily impact the overall TCO of a particular SAP system landscape and the solution stack(s) inherent to this landscape is the attention paid to *standardization*, covered in more detail next.

Standardization and Total Cost of Ownership

The goal of standardization is to minimize variety, thus simplifying troubleshooting time and expense and therefore TCO while facilitating rapid component replacement when required. Standardization can be applied to individual systems, particular technology stacks, every component within the solution stack, and characteristics or dimensions of the entire SAP system landscape.

Information systems evolve over time. As the demands of end users and other stakeholders force this evolution, care must be taken to ensure that the same standards imposed to create an effective enterprise environment are still enforced. This is essential to minimizing future support costs, so its importance to TCO cannot be underestimated.

However, in the real world of managing SAP solutions post-implementation, maintaining a static SAP computing environment over any real length of time is highly unlikely. Therefore, expending extra effort maintaining exacting standards may very well cost *more* than evolving via changes to the solution stack. One area in particular comes to mind—hanging on to key aging hardware assets with the false hope of keeping TCO lower. Does your organization plan to grow, through new business processes, through additional functional needs, or simply through acquisitions? These kinds of changes are exactly the change agents that not only improve productivity but impact standardization.

How? Consider this: As more end users are added to the organization, or business processes are updated, or new SAP components are added to the mix, incremental changes to the solution stack are almost inevitable. New high-performance hardware with new features, upgraded or new software with its own set of new features, and so on are introduced. Examples abound. For example, SAP ITS for years was only supported on a Windows/Intel, or *Wintel*, platform. So UNIX shops were historically forced to introduce completely new server platforms, OSs, and so on just to Internet-enable their SAP enterprises—so much for standardization and low TCO. Early adopters of new SAP components typically must go with Wintel or Linux-based platforms, too, until the various UNIX ports of each SAP component are completed. At the other end of the spectrum, beyond pilot projects and the like, until recently SAP Supply Chain Management (SCM) liveCache has historically been nearly *always* implemented on UNIX platforms to take advantage of the greater performance provided by such platforms.

If you are running any enterprise application today, this is not news to you. The very standard, very manageable environment you painstakingly assembled and maintained over the course of the first year or two of your implementation today probably looks nothing like the original implementation. Today, if you're like many companies, you probably run a hodgepodge of different hardware, different OSs, and perhaps different database and other application-specific components. You never intended on a hodgepodge, of course. It's simply where you wound up.

Our point here is simply that *standardization* should be looked upon as a goal, not as a black-and-white ironclad reality. SAP IT shops that strive for standardization, but understand that managing change within a standards-based environment represents the real world, will be the most successful at meeting the needs of their end users and customers (and achieve a reasonable TCO outcome in the process). The good news is that ultimately these SAP-driven companies will emerge at the forefront of their industries, as their SAP-enabled business units increase both productivity and profitability compared to their non-SAP-enabled competitors.

Server Considerations

Comparing and evaluating the total cost of owning different hardware platforms has long been a mainstay in the world of TCO analysis. To this end, the SAP technology stack is filled with areas where different platforms and standards can be pitted against one another in terms of acquisition, installation, management, operations, training, consolidation, and other costs.

In the past, we have assisted our customers with evaluating everything from the latest in network infrastructure hardware, to KVM (keyboard, video, and mouse) solutions, to even various power and cooling approaches. But one area in particular has consumed most of our time when it comes to TCO analysis—evaluating server alternatives.

A quick trip down memory lane is in order. Many companies running large SAP enterprises today invested in high-end enterprise computing gear from companies like HP, Sun, IBM, Digital, Bull, and Unisys a number of years ago, leveraging each vendor's respective UNIX operating system. Although historically this type of hardware/software solution had its place in mission-critical environments, it has never been either cheap to own or cheap to operate. A number of years ago, as Intel pushed the envelope in terms of propelling inexpensive processing power into the data center, the world of supporting enterprise applications like SAP turned a corner. Suddenly customers had a choice when it came to meeting the performance requirements of a large processor and disk-intensive application. Scalability was limited initially, however, and availability did not approach the level achievable in UNIX-based clustering solutions.

Enter into the picture Microsoft and its Microsoft Cluster Server (MSCS) technology. Around since the end of 1996, and pioneered in support of enterprise solutions by companies such as Dell and Compaq, MSCS brought a higher level of availability to Intel-based solutions. In 2000, with the advent of Windows 2000 Advanced Server and Data Center Server, Microsoft gave us the most stable and easily managed clusters ever produced out of Redmond, and a large number of Fortune 2000 enterprises began seriously migrating their enterprise applications away from expensive UNIX platforms onto these less expensive yet highly available platforms that performed nearly as well. There were and continue to be trade-offs in terms of managing server consolidation, security, and manageability, but by and large the TCO story has only improved over time.

Today, Intel and other processor-based server platforms vary in every way imaginable—obvious variations include raw processing power, support for various OSs, built-in HA features, internal architecture considerations, form factor (size), support for various memory footprints, general upgradability, ability to add server components and peripherals "on the fly," and of course price. Collect and analyze these data in a spreadsheet-based apples-to-apples fashion that in turn will allow you to compare different platform features, functions, and other capabilities in a comprehensive manner.

Your spreadsheet will also assist you in terms of identifying basic benchmarking data to collect. Server manufacturers often submit their platforms to standard testing batteries such as NetBench, WebBench, WebStress, SPECint, SPECweb99, and so on. On top of this, SAP-certified platforms are often benchmarked using SAP's standard ERP, NetWeaver Business Warehouse (BW), and other benchmarking kits. We recommend collecting this data to support a server delta TCO analysis. Why a delta analysis? Because no "standard" benchmark truly represents the genuine measure of a platform's ability in the real world; this is accomplished via custom benchmarking and proof-of-concept exercises, which are covered in Chapter 33. Standard benchmarks provide excellent data points for server-to-server comparisons.

Disk Subsystem Hardware Dimensions

Similar to server considerations, we must be able to evaluate varying disk subsystems in terms of capabilities, performance, scalability, and so on—with an eye toward how these solution dimensions affect TCO.

We have spent nearly as much time working with comparing and testing various disk subsystems as we have with server platforms. Beyond raw performance and HA options, the most compelling, less-obvious TCO considerations that we have uncovered include

▶ **Setup/installation GUI**—The user interface required by the storage can really make a difference in how quickly an installation or change can be completed. We prefer browser- or Windows-based GUIs, as they tend to take a lot of the guesswork out of *how* a storage system is actually configured. The flip side of this is terminal sessions and command-line-based approaches to configuring and managing storage.

▶ **Density**—The pure number of disk drives and controllers that can be housed in a storage system also makes life easier for the SAP infrastructure or DBA team. With more options and flexibility "in the box," and fewer cabinets to manage, density impacts TCO appreciably. That is, a disk subsystem that can be easily expanded by simply adding more disk drives, rather than requiring the addition of new cabinets, controllers, and disk drive shelves, will prove less costly to procure, manage, and upgrade.

▶ **Management appliances or utilities**—This becomes more critical if additional disk cabinets must be added to an SAP system landscape. A management approach that allows a collection of storage to be managed holistically saves time, simplifies change management processes, and affords greater flexibility.

▶ **In-place upgradability**—A disk subsystem that allows in-place "hot add" upgrades impacts TCO significantly. For example, the ability to upgrade to larger or faster disk drives or enhanced disk controllers, or add or replace HA features such as pluggable fans and power supplies—all while the storage system remains up and running— helps an organization leverage its investment in the disk solution by extending its lifecycle and reducing expensive downtime.

We have also witnessed how network attached storage (NAS) can allow for lower TCO. NAS requires a dedicated storage network of its own, however, to help guarantee minimum service levels, because doing otherwise means impacting users or other services running on existing network infrastructures. This costs money. And the fact that they historically required up to twice the CPU processing power to deliver only a third of the throughput of direct-attached storage devices equates to higher costs, too. Finally, because NAS solutions are often "black boxes" with little to no real tuning capabilities, and are not supported by all SAP computing platform combinations, the highest-performing disk subsystems will probably be found elsewhere.

But our own NAS experience for SAP is limited in this regard. What we have seen in the field indicates that there *could* be immense potential in products that marry the benefits of both NAS and storage area networks (SANs) in a common, networked storage pool. This flexible storage pool promises real interoperability, by providing both file-level (NAS) and block-level (SAN) access to SAP implementations. For companies that have successfully deployed enterprisewide storage organizations, where a single organization is responsible for providing for the commodity storage needs of different business and technology groups, this approach may be right on target.

Operating System TCO

The OS layer gives us another opportunity to affect TCO. We have already shared one of the obvious ways to increase or decrease TCO—by purchasing an enterprise version of a particular OS, versus the standard version. More often, though, our clients have been interested in comparing the virtues and capabilities of one vendor's OS to another vendor's OS in terms of the following:

▶ Support for various SAP products and components, particularly with regard to SAP AG's release strategy for new functional versions

▶ Acquisition license costs and fees, particularly when it comes to calculating initial OS acquisition costs with the OS's costs over time (annual maintenance fees)

▶ Ability to support the performance and scalability needs of the solution, including features such as multiprocessing (and the number of processors that can be supported by a particular version of the OS—that is, 4, 8, 32, 64, and so on), massive RAM footprints, and so on

▶ Ease of administration or management, often impacted one way or the other by the skill sets of the organization responsible for deploying and managing the OS, more so than factors inherent to a particular OS

▶ Ease of patching, data migration, and upgrading, especially in regard to how much downtime must be incurred

▶ Innate OS-level support for HA features such as clustering, redundant network cards and disk controllers, robust security, ability to add new (*hot add*) or replace existing *hot replace*) hardware components without rebooting, and so on

▶ OS support for features that further reduce planned downtime requirements, such as portability or the ability to expand disk volumes on the fly

▶ Value-add capabilities, such as the ability to support dynamic partitioning, directory services, network services such as DNS and DHCP, and more

▶ Third-party support for robust backup/restore solutions, DR solutions, enterprise management applications, other hardware components that may be important to your particular solution, and so on

Additional people and process factors affect TCO, too, such as the time it takes to train a new hire, or the ability to recover from configuration mistakes. And finally, the ability to support a particular SAP technology stack's preferred database solution is critical, as we cover next.

Relational Database TCO

Several database choices exist for most SAP components and products. Historically, though, Oracle databases underpinned the bulk of SAP implementations before the turn of the century. That is why even to this day we continue to be astounded by the fact that 51% of all new SAP sizings that left the doors of Compaq's SAP Competency Center back in 1999 were for Microsoft SQL Server. It is during this period that we saw quite a few changes with regard to database selection, most of it TCO-driven. Oracle's share of new sizings fell to 48% of all of our SAP customers and prospects that year, and the remaining 1.5% was split across DB2 and Informix. Compare this data to information published by Gartner soon afterward, and it becomes quickly apparent that what those of us in the SAP Competency Center witnessed was not a fluke; TCO was driving a huge shift in SAP database demand.

Why the huge interest in SQL Server and, more recently, MaxDB over these past several years? Simple—lower acquisition and management-related TCO at nearly the same performance levels of other database products. True, Oracle Database provides superior performance and scalability. But today, in our eyes the line separating Oracle from SQL Server is quite blurry until you reach systems supporting more than 3,000 concurrent users. Even for MaxDB, where the line should probably be drawn at about 1,000 concurrent users, the reality is clear—the vast majority of SAP systems deployed today would do fine with any database for SAP.

Thus, beyond the database release on which an IT shop might have standardized, the real issue becomes one of TCO. More than a handful of studies and our own experience bear these facts out. If we're talking pure dollars, the numbers don't lie. At something like a quarter of the acquisition costs, half the implementation costs, and half to two-thirds of the management costs of its biggest competitor, SQL Server is substantially less expensive and in *most* cases just as capable when it comes to SAP implementations supporting 3,000 concurrent users or fewer. At a tenth the acquisition and maintenance costs (or less!),

MaxDB is an outstanding alternative any SAP implementation supporting 1,000 concurrent users or fewer should put on its short list for evaluation. Check out the latest Transaction Processing Performance Council (TPC) numbers if you're a performance skeptic (http://www.tpc.org).

By way of example, we've spent the better part of the last 10 years supporting some of the largest SAP-on-SQL Server shops in North America. Because of their decision to run SAP on SQL Server, these SAP shops from a TCO perspective have quite a bit in common beyond simply their database choice:

▶ They employ fewer database administrators (DBAs), when compared to other SAP/non–SQL Server shops that we support.

▶ They benefit from simpler disk layouts, configuration options, auto-tuning, and so on, which tends to make upgrades later on less painful, and day-to-day operations less complex.

▶ About a third of the shops take advantage of the fact that SQL Server supports multiple database instances on a single server, thus reducing hardware-related TCO for testing, training, and development environments.

▶ Great attention is paid to change management, especially given the history of Windows operating environments' tendency to succumb to memory leaks (the result of poorly written third-party drivers, usually). As long as the solution stack remains static, and is changed only after adhering to a tightly controlled "Promote to Production" policy, there is simply no issue running Windows/SQL Server in the enterprise.

▶ More time is spent addressing security holes inherent to the solution stack (the OS more so than SQL Server itself, with some exceptions).

▶ They all enjoy better than three nines of availability, and in some cases four. Remember that 99.9% equates to less than nine hours or so of unplanned downtime per year—outstanding metrics in most anybody's book.

We've had tremendous experience with every SAP-supported piece of database software since the old days of R/3 2x. Without a doubt, we highly recommend that all four SAP-supported databases be at least *considered* for every new SAP implementation where TCO and performance are the biggest factors—run through the math and see for yourself.

SAP Application Layer Costs

At an SAP application layer, beyond licensing and most other acquisition-related technology costs, TCO is most often impacted by people and process issues. Three areas in particular that are key in our experience include

▶ Architecture considerations, especially in regard to distributed three-tiered architectures versus central systems and other architectures

▶ Deployment considerations, such as *stacking*, where multiple SAP instances are installed on a single server rather than deployed across multiple servers

▶ Implementation considerations; that is, choosing between heterogeneous and homogeneous implementations

SAP's support for a distributed architecture allows for multiple low-cost and/or industry-standard servers to replace single-server central systems. These latter "big-box" solutions are inherently easy to deploy and manage, but can cost an order of magnitude more than their distributed solution counterparts. Of course, a few trade-offs need to be taken into account when considering a distributed SAP system. First, the management of many server, disk, and tape resources adds up to more people- or process-related costs in a distributed environment. We have one customer in particular who standardized on a relatively low-end two-processor server for all SAP application servers, web servers, and other infrastructure servers. Compared to the acquisition costs of more capable larger servers, the customer's approach paid off. However, managing 40 servers instead of perhaps 15 consumes a bit of their "savings" every day. The same argument would apply to SAP clients deploying the latest "blade" servers rather than larger ones.

However, managing the SAP system landscape in these cases tasks the SAP TSO more than a more consolidated-server approach would. This is true from the SAP operations team up through the database and SAP Basis/infrastructure organizations. And in our actual customer's case, even with its highly automated SAP monitoring and reporting system, it still incurs significant time penalties when ad hoc uptime and other reports need to be generated for its SAP system landscape—not surprisingly, collecting and analyzing the raw data relevant to 40 servers takes longer than doing so for the raw data relevant to 15 servers.

In addition to the extra management overhead, change management and subsequent upgrades to the solution stack take more time, given that each individual server is subject to firmware, hardware, OS, service pack/patch, database client, SAP kernel, and other per-server updates. Licensing is also a bit more complex than it might otherwise be, again given the sheer volume of OS and database client licenses that must be maintained and managed. Finally, tape backup/restore processes tend to morph into more complex "server restore" processes, as it is easier to rebuild an application server through an automated disk imaging or similar process than to actually back it up and restore from tape in the event of an emergency. This then adds another burden to the SAP TSO, though—maintaining and updating server images for each type of server after each change release or change wave.

The potential TCO benefits of a distributed architecture are many, however, including

▶ The overall technology stack is often not only cheaper to acquire, but still cheaper to manage despite the drawbacks.

▶ High availability may be provided through basic redundancy (less impact to the overall solution if a single SAP application server or redundant web server suffers from unplanned downtime).

▶ Scalability is easily addressed at the application layer by simply adding another application server (and calculating/addressing the performance hit passed on to the database and central instance servers, of course).

▶ Specific workloads can be easily addressed by multiple servers. For example, many SAP shops employ two or three dedicated batch servers in their mix of application servers. Other shops break out update work processes onto separate servers, or in some other way dedicate specific functions to a particular set of servers.

The second key area for minimizing SAP application-layer TCO is in regard to stacking. *Stacking* refers to the ability to install and run multiple SAP instances on a single server. Stacking is very common in UNIX environments, less so in Linux, and even less so in the world of Windows for SAP. You might also want to consider virtual partitioning or virtual machine approaches, such as that provided by VMware. This alternative to stacking lessens the number of servers and is just as manageable as any environment where one SAP instance is installed per OS installation. In addition, though, virtual partitioning allows you to chop up a large server in terms of hardware resources. Thus, it provides the flexibility of allowing you to install an SAP instance based on resource need, rather than based on the maximum capacity of the platform.

Either approach can save a bundle in hardware costs when it comes to deploying pilot, sandbox, development, testing, and training systems. Stacking or virtual partitioning is usually *not* the preferred way to go for production environments, however, as immediate or low-level performance tuning, future capacity planning, and general reactive troubleshooting become more complex.

Finally, whether an SAP system landscape consists of the same or different server environments represents the third area affecting TCO. It probably surprises no one that designing, deploying, and managing a diverse landscape costs more time and money than doing the same for a homogeneous system landscape. However, if the SAP Support Organization is skilled in supporting both UNIX platforms and Microsoft-based OSs, for example, implementing a heterogeneous solution for SAP in the past has significantly decreased both acquisition and recurring maintenance costs. This type of solution seems to manifest itself most often in shops where a large investment has been made in high-end UNIX or IBM mainframes and minicomputers—or where the customer may simply be locked in to the technology and wants to put it to use in the form of an SAP database server. Surrounding these large database servers with relatively cheap Wintel servers can be quite effective and a good TCO move. And given the fact that the SAP connection between the database and application servers is only a simple TCP/IP connection, integration and management of the solution poses no real challenge, either.

Today, given the power of Wintel and low-cost UNIX-based solutions, we see more and more customers actually moving *away* from heterogeneous solutions, however. We believe that this approach served a need quite well for a number of years, but now that need is served equally well by homogeneous systems. One interesting twist to this trend includes the growing role of Linux; it is showing up in more than a few SAP data centers nowadays. Highly capable though very inexpensive SAP-on-Linux application and web servers are especially popular, though we are also seeing entire SAP system landscapes transitioned to Linux. The benefits in terms of OS standardization and access to massive processing power will further reduce TCO while simultaneously elevating Linux higher in the enterprise data center. It is this kind of activity that will certainly drive SAP infrastructure and overall solution stack upgrades, too, covered next.

Upgrading the Technology Stack

While on the subject of SAP technology stack TCO, consider the following. Upgrades are inevitable, and well-timed and well-executed upgrades can be a wonderful method for extending the lifecycle of a stack layer or component. But upgrades get expensive quickly. Every technology upgrade results in significant incremental expense associated with "touching" the production resource rather than outright replacing it. Add to this the costs associated with the following:

▶ Determining *which* upgrade hardware or software part numbers to order adds to the upgrade cost.

▶ Placing and tracking the upgrade order takes time. Because upgrade orders tend to be one-offs, they typically cost more than placing and tracking a new order.

▶ Paying for the update or upgrade component(s), compared to a new component nearly always favors the upgrade in terms of cost.

▶ Coordinating the overall upgrade effort, compared to coordinating a simpler "replacement" effort, costs more.

▶ Managing the change control process associated with upgrading or updating a technology stack component, including increased costs associated with mitigating the risk of dealing with unforeseen compatibility issues not uncovered during testing, is both complex and expensive.

▶ Safeguarding valuable data during the actual process of upgrading, and making that data available again as soon as possible (as upgrades are typically more time-consuming than employing a replacement strategy), affects TCO.

▶ Installing a piece of hardware, such as an additional processor, usually costs more than buying the server already fully populated with CPUs. Why? The cost of service upgrades (that is, buying a processor for a two-year-old server) can be expensive, added to the cost and complexity of scheduling and taking downtime.

It becomes quickly apparent that the costs of a seemingly simple upgrade can well exceed the cost of a straightforward replacement strategy, even when the procurement costs of the upgrade are substantially lower than the procurement costs of a replacement. Our recommendation is to be wary of upgrades and "do the math"—identify and recognize the costs of an upgrade versus a direct replacement, evaluate the deltas, and in the end make an informed decision.

Other SAP Technology Stack TCO Considerations

Finally, before leaving behind the world of technology-based SAP solution stack TCO, a quick look at some final technology considerations is in order:

▶ Backup and restore capabilities continue to top our list of "things that are too complex." We are amazed at how many of both our new and long-time SAP customers are unsatisfied with their backup and restore products and strategies. TCO is certainly important, but given the critical role that a good backup plays in regard to DR, we are inclined to say count yourself lucky if your backup strategy works well at all. Beyond that, disk storage systems that support centralized tape backup (like SANs), and the efficiencies that can be derived by investing in one or a few large tape libraries rather than discrete one-off tape drive solutions, decrease TCO and simplify life with SAP in general.

▶ A variety of SAP-aware management applications and tools exist. We cover many of these in more detail later in the book. As far as TCO is concerned, however, the goal is clear—to replace the mundane tasks of operational reporting and tracking with a package that doesn't require vacation time, fail to show up on Mondays until noon, or forget to collect data one day. In addition, the best enterprise packages will collect and filter against *events* up and down the entire SAP technology stack, both reactively and proactively looking for problems and failures. Finally, the infrastructure required to perform these management tasks should be reasonable, and in our opinion the management application itself should refrain from making internal changes to the SAP component being managed.

▶ Tools that provide connectivity to other systems will eventually become de facto "production" interfaces. In our experience, this means that attention needs to be paid up front to bringing in tools from reputable vendors with support organizations that have an understanding of how their tool or utility works with SAP. Free or "shareware" tools might be nice for a few months, but inevitably some kind of support issue will crop up. Again, do the math—a single support issue, including the time and potential revenue/productivity lost—can drastically impact TCO, especially after changes have been made elsewhere in the solution stack.

▶ The deployment of SAP's user interface, the SAPGUI, can impact TCO substantially as well. One of the most compelling solutions lies in leveraging SAP's WebGUI rather than installing a copy of the traditional SAPGUI on each user desktop. In this way, the desktop is never changed and therefore many fewer user support calls are initiated. Another compelling solution could include Citrix-based solutions and other similar services designed to host the SAPGUI remotely back at the data center, rather than at each user's desktop.

With the technology factor of TCO wrapped up, we can now move to the next two major TCO analysis components—people and processes.

Lowering TCO Through People and Processes

Although the procurement and deployment of technology plays an obvious role in TCO analysis, you must remember that people and processes play equally key roles. No one area is greater than the other two, as is clearly illustrated in Figure 5.4—they are all equally important. Instead, a balance must be achieved.

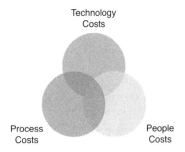

Technology
Costs

Process
Costs

People
Costs

FIGURE 5.4   Technology, people, and processes all play key interdependent roles in evaluating
the TCO of a particular solution.

It is not uncommon, unfortunately, to be inclined to carefully estimate people and technology costs, only to downplay the process costs of a particular solution. Why? Because it
is *easy* to pull together the one-time implementation costs associated with technology, but
usually a bit more difficult to quantify people expenses, and seemingly impossible to
quantify process costs/savings.

Attracting and Retaining Support Staff

A key TCO concern when it comes to people is the cost related to employee hiring and
retention. In a company whose SAP TSO lags dramatically behind IT in general, especially
in terms of technology, the ability to attract and retain high-quality IT people can be
severely hindered. What highly motivated PC technician or systems engineer wants to
continue to support the SAPGUI on a Windows 3.x desktop? What database administrator
wants to work in an Oracle8i environment any longer than necessary? True, there are
plenty of qualified individuals, but as in any other IT organization, the most motivated
and talented individuals typically propel themselves forward as they have always done,
embracing and learning new technology along the way. Meanwhile, those individuals
happy playing with the legacy solution stack components we just mentioned are probably
the same people you had problems training and moving out of your IBM MVS/XA data
center a decade ago.

Not only is finding these older skill sets sometimes difficult, but the annual recurring costs
to retain these skills can actually be higher than the costs of more mainstream solution
components. For example, if you are adamant about maintaining a truly vintage solution
environment (such as SQL Server 7 or perhaps an aging server platform), or insist on
bleeding-edge technology (such as the latest release candidate of a new 64-bit enterprise
version of SQL Server, or the latest HP server released last week), the people-related support
costs will be higher than the costs associated with supporting the mainstream product
(such as SQL Server 2008, or a server platform that has been available for 6–12 months).

So take heed—keeping the incumbent DBA (or SAP Basis guru, client deployment specialist, and so on) is nearly always cheaper than hiring and training a replacement. Our
recommendation is nothing short of common sense. Keep your talented IT people as long
as you can, and have a backup plan. The backup plan should include developing a good

relationship with local contract staffing and consulting firms, and leveraging the assistance of hardware and software manufacturers as needed.

Maintenance Costs

Maintenance costs exist throughout the SAP system landscape, and up and down the entire SAP technology stack. Server and disk subsystem hardware, OSs, databases, and SAP components all usually incur annual maintenance costs (one interesting exception, of course, may be SAP's SAPDB database).

Also, consider the costs of hardware spare inventories, especially after five years, the period when many hardware manufacturers quit manufacturing or remanufacturing spare parts. And then consider the fact that, as your ability to stock these spares decreases, the probability of a component-level hardware failure increases. This explains in a nutshell why so many enterprise and other solutions tend to undergo technology refreshes every three years or so—in addition to the fact that most manufacturers' warranties expire after three years as well.

When it comes to hardware spares, any component or part that is deemed critical to production needs to be carefully considered for "sparing." Usually this means onsite stocking of any part that represents a single point of failure or is otherwise deemed critical.

Instead of stocking a part that sits in a cabinet, however, other methods of stocking are often employed. A key benefit of standardization is the use of identical components throughout test, training, and sandbox environments, for example. Some of our customers even go so far as to house onsite and offsite spare servers and disk subsystems, sometimes "cold" (thus requiring manual intervention to introduce these assets into production should a failure occur within the production environment), but more often "warm" (ready to be pulled into production automatically upon failure of a critical component).

Stocking is also often handled as part of the SLA process, too. In these cases, fee-based arrangements are made with hardware or third-party hardware sourcing partners to provide a part onsite within perhaps four hours after being contacted. Such an approach makes a lot of sense in metropolitan areas where the overhead costs borne by the sourcing partner related to maintaining such a facility or service can be spread out over hundreds of enterprise customers.

Financing Options

Financing alternatives, including leasing, offer an attractive method to retain cash in-house for profit-generating activities that would otherwise be tied up in fixed assets. Leasing in particular allows a company to not only stay near the technology edge, but also treat the expenditure as a tax-deductible operating expense (usually).

For companies with little capital, leasing ensures that they have access to the newest technologies today. Even today, leasing remains an attractive method of financing SAP infrastructure implementations throughout businesses of all shapes and sizes. Seek out leasing entities that allow you to roll up hardware, software, and even consulting expenses into a package deal (and compare the tax implication to a capital asset strategy).

It should come as no surprise that when it comes to TCO, leasing versus purchasing costs demand consideration. Although the exercise to do so can be time-consuming, the potential impact to a firm's books is worth the investment.

Operations and Systems Management Costs

Although it is admittedly difficult to quantify the operations and systems management costs of a solution that is only being planned at this stage, you still need to take a stab at it. Fortunately, questions such as the following can help you put together a delta analysis specific to management costs, as discussed previously:

▶ Does each layer in the SAP technology stack support "manageability" of some degree or other? That is, are there tools, utilities, or management applications available to monitor and manage the various hardware, OS, database, and SAP solution choices you are leaning toward for this particular solution stack?

▶ How much does each tool, utility, or management application cost to acquire?

▶ What annual maintenance fees can be expected of each tool, utility, or management application?

▶ Do the various management tools and approaches work well *together*? For instance, is there a common management framework that can be leveraged, allowing each tool to "snap in" to the framework? Or do any of the tools require specific agents or other components that conflict with other tools' agents?

▶ Does each tool require a dedicated hardware platform upon which to run, or can a common management platform or console be used?

▶ How long will it take for the SAP operations and other SAP Support Organization team members to learn each tool, utility, or management application?

▶ How easy is it to find subject matter experts with experience in the particular management product or approach being considered? And what are the costs of these subject matter experts?

As for other costs, support for the following needs to be understood:

▶ Backup/restore-related tasks and responsibilities, such as the time required to learn and actually use a particular backup solution, monitoring the backup/restore processes, swapping and managing tapes, and so on

▶ Testing DR and HA processes

▶ Change management processes, as necessary

▶ Connectivity to other systems

▶ Client access approaches via the SAPGUI, WebGUI, and other user interfaces

▶ Incremental facilities costs (if, for example, a particular server or disk subsystem platform requires power, cooling, or other facilities infrastructure different from the data center's norm)

For additional management and operations tasks that may need to be evaluated, refer to Chapter 35.

TCO Risk Factors

A value is often placed on the risk inherent to a particular solution stack or process. Given that risk is usually difficult to quantify, a delta analysis is appropriate here, too. In this way, you can compare the risk of employing one method or approach or solution to the risk of employing a different one, and quickly determine the cost difference. We like to perform this exercise using something we call *risk factors*. Risk factors are numbers weighted to reflect the relative risk inherent to changing a particular solution stack layer component. We assign a risk of 0 to 10 to each technology stack layer, where lower numbers are less risky than higher numbers. An assignment of 0 indicates no change to a particular solution stack layer or component and therefore "no" risk. Consider the following subjective evaluations:

▶ The risk in changing server platforms equates to something like a risk factor of 1 if the same server line is brought in, 3 if a new server line is introduced from the same hardware vendor, and 5 if a completely new server vendor is called upon to deliver the new platform. If the server platform is changed, risk is increased more if the server vendor changes as well. That is, it is less risky for an organization versed in HP's UNIX-based servers to bring in a new HP UNIX server than an IBM or Sun UNIX-based server.

▶ If a new storage or disk subsystem is introduced, more risk is incurred than in introducing a new server platform. We go into quite a bit of detail in this regard in Chapter 21 when we explore the SAP data center. Suffice it to say here, though, that the disk subsystem represents the key performance and availability challenge within the solution stack. Risk inherent to introducing a completely new disk subsystem rates a 10 in our book, due to potential issues related to complexity, support, performance tuning, and troubleshooting. Marginal differences in storage (such as a new disk drive standard, or incrementally updated disk array controller) rate a 2. A new storage line from the incumbent storage vendor rates a risk factor of 6, however.

▶ If a new OS is introduced, risk ranges from 0 for the same OS with the same patch or service pack levels, to 2 for introducing a new flavor of UNIX similar to the current UNIX standard, to 4 for introducing a very different UNIX flavor from the standard (say, Linux Red Hat), to 6 or 8 or higher for completely different OSs, such as Microsoft Windows Server 2008 compared to HP-UX 11i—in these cases, we like to evaluate the SAP IT team's technical breadth.

▶ The risk inherent to introducing a new database is also critical. Version changes (that is, the difference between Oracle9i and 10g) represent only a 1 (unless you lose support for a particular SAP solution, which is entirely possible—beware!). Completely changing vendors (from Oracle to Microsoft's SQL Server or IBM's DB2, for example) rates an 8. This is because the database selected for SAP impacts so many other areas—the SAP Basis layer changes, backup/restore processes and utilities are changed, DBAs require retooling, the physical layout of disks differs and there-fore needs to be addressed, clustering solutions need to be reinstalled or completely reinvented, and so on.

▶ Establishing a new SAP Basis standard introduces its own risks. Minor release changes can be nearly negligible. Major release levels incur more risk, though, as new approaches to installing, integrating, and managing the Basis layer need to be taken into consideration. The introduction of the SAP NetWeaver 7.1 technology layer represents a fairly significant change, rating a 6 or so (and perhaps an 8 or more if bringing in the Java stack, however!). The jump from SAP Basis 4.6x to a 6.40 Basis layer would be less risky, though, rating a 3 or 4 (again, depending on the SAP IT organization's current skills and competencies).

What about multiple technology stack changes? For example, if a firm that has standard-ized on UNIX/Oracle but is interested in the low acquisition and management costs inher-ent to SQL Server 2005, it will also need to bring in the new database software and a new server (with some exceptions) and a new OS! Such a decision compounds the risk of merely swapping out the database layer. Add to this scenario the decision to go with a new virtualized SAN, and practically the entire technology stack would represent a serious deviation from the firm's standard.

Summary

One of the most common schools of thought in corporate IT today goes something like this: "If we buy and implement the infrastructure for a new SAP component, and retain the assets for three to five years, we will save substantially in terms of overall SAP Support Organization support costs, help-desk costs, training costs, and minimized peer support as compared to outsourcing everything." Many others might disagree with this statement, backing up their vague claims with "It depends." What we hope we have accomplished in this chapter on TCO analysis is to provide you with an approach to answer these kinds of questions as they relate to your own SAP project.

Case Study: TCO and Risk Factors

HiTech, Inc. is in the process of evaluating a number of different solution stack alternatives when it comes to its planned SAP SCM solution. HiTech is running SAP ERP and SAP CRM today, and already has deep technical expertise in several different midrange HP UNIX server platforms, several recent versions of the HP-UX OS, high-end EMC storage (used by SAP ERP) and HP StorageWorks Enterprise Virtual Array (EVA, used by SAP CRM) storage systems, Oracle9i, and SAP Basis 4x and 6x. These represent a capabilities baseline of sorts, and can be used to calculate how future changes to the technology stack affect risk.

What is *out of scope* for this exercise is an analysis or comparison of the procurement or management costs associated with each solution stack layer/component—this should have already been covered during the technology stack implementation analysis. In HiTech's case, your job is to take a look at different technology stack combinations and alternatives, and assign a risk to each solution layer from 0 to 10, where low numbers are less risky than high numbers.

Therefore, the most risk-averse strategy for HiTech is to go with a solution stack for SAP SCM as similar as possible to its current SAP ERP or SAP CRM standards;, such a low-risk decision would rate a 4, which is simply the sum of the various risk factors, as detailed in the following list:

- ▶ HiTech's current exact server platform is no longer available. The updated platform featuring faster processors and more memory is very close, however. This probably rates a 1 in terms of risk.

- ▶ HiTech's current disk subsystem standard is still available. However, the standard disk drive size and form factor is different, and the firmware on both the disk drives and disk controllers has been updated as well. These minimal changes rate a 2.

- ▶ HiTech's standard OS release is also still available, though the new server platform requires an updated OS patch level. This rates a risk factor of a 1 or 2—a bit more risky than the same exact OS/patch level combination, but not considerably more risky.

- ▶ The particular release of SAP SCM to be implemented leverages the same Basis layer as that employed by SAP ERP, so again there is no impact when it comes to risk—a 0.

Questions

1. Explain how risk differs relative to the technology stack chosen by HiTech.

2. If after conducting a delta TCO analysis one technology stack is rated a 20 and another is rated a 40, is the 40 indeed "twice as good" a potential solution for a firm as the one rated a 20?

3. Explain how HiTech's database software standard—Oracle9i—might rate a 0 in terms of incremental risk.

4. In addition to acquisition costs, what other general category of cost must be included in HiTech's costs analysis?

5. Is a risk factor of 4 good or bad? How might a risk factor of 4 be influenced by adopting a new vendor's server and disk subsystem platforms, and introducing Windows with the same release of Oracle9i? How would adopting a new vendor's server and disk subsystem platforms, a new Windows OS, and bringing in SQL Server instead of Oracle affect the TCO risk analysis?

> **NOTE**
>
> The answers to these questions can be found in Appendix A, "Case Study Answers."

5

CHAPTER 6

Managing Knowledge and the Knowledge Repository

Managing the business, functional, technical, and project management–related knowledge that goes into planning for and deploying SAP is not only an important part of achieving a successful go-live, but also a key process in ensuring that the SAP system operates as intended. We call this process establishing the project's knowledge management (KM) footprint, and we cover this process and related background material in this chapter.

Establishing an Initial Knowledge Management Footprint

There are several reasons why an organization implementing SAP needs to manage its knowledge intentionally and proactively:

▶ Knowledge capture leads to knowledge retention, a much better alternative to having a firm's collective knowledge walk out the door when the consultants finally leave, contractors disappear without warning, or your employees take off for greener and less stressful pastures.

▶ With knowledge capture also comes the ability to transfer and share that knowledge across the organization. Once you have a process for retaining the knowledge that is developed on the project or walks through the front door by way of new employees and consultants, it's time to focus on managing the process of knowledge transfer.

▶ Managing knowledge makes it possible to proactively manage organizational change through access to information when it's needed, where it's needed, and by whom it's needed. A growing, remotely distributed workforce requires knowledge to grow.

▶ Good KM makes it easier to train new employees and retool existing ones seeking to move into a new part of the SAP support organization.

▶ A KM foundation provides background data for pending project tasks; regardless of whether an SAP project is issuing a Request for Information (RFI) to its SAP technology stack partners and prospects or simply going through the standard SAP sizing process, all of the information collected during the activities described in this chapter needs to be captured and documented in the knowledge repository (described in the next section).

▶ A solid KM foundation also enables operational excellence from a technical or systems management perspective. With the details surrounding current state configuration and process or "how-to" procedures, a good KM system goes a long way in helping an organization hum along. And in this, KM reduces unplanned downtime.

▶ Knowledge management makes it possible to avoid repeating the same mistakes; by tracking not only *what* is captured in terms of knowledge but also *why* a particular decision was made, the organization has an easier time managing change down the road, navigating obstacles with wisdom gained from previous assessments and decisions, and so on.

Organizations need a method or mechanism for capturing all this knowledge. More importantly, organizations need a tool for managing and accessing the knowledge, for giving it shape and making sense of it. All of this is accomplished through deploying a knowledge repository, explored next.

Capturing Knowledge: The Knowledge Repository

Knowledge repository is a general term for a tool or document management approach that is useful in capturing project vision, assumptions, constraints, configuration, decisions, and so on; all of this documented data needs a home, after all. Whether a firm selects a fancy knowledge management software package for this role or sets up a basic website with a customized taxonomy (table of contents), a knowledge repository allows that firm to safekeep its system requirements (and so on) while maintaining the capability to pull out this information, reassess it, and share it as necessary. Further, as new information comes to light or questions are posed by prospective vendors, the knowledge repository naturally lends itself to collecting and adding this incremental data to an ever-growing list of constraints, assumptions, potential scope changes (be careful!), needs, and more. Some of us like to think of the knowledge repository as the project's "metadata," or data about the data. The repository thus contains collective knowledge reflecting the following:

▶ Planning and project management–related knowledge

▶ Staffing knowledge

▶ Business vision, requirements, and functionality knowledge

- ▶ Solution vision and application layer knowledge

- ▶ SAP system landscape knowledge

- ▶ Installation and configuration knowledge

We discuss each of these in the sections that follow.

Planning/Project Management Knowledge

All decisions related to project guidelines, control, execution, and so on need to be captured and made available for review, analysis, and updates. Truth be told, most organizations with a formal project management office (PMO) already capture this information and manage it well. For organizations not so fortunate to have a dedicated PMO, the project's knowledge repository should act as the single source of project data, including project plans, tasks lists, schedules, communications and escalation plans, and everything else related to planning and managing the project.

Staffing Knowledge

With any large project comes the need to carefully and purposefully select staff. An SAP project comprises not only a project team (which itself is subdivided into business, development, technical, and other teams), but also a team that will provide the handoff between implementing SAP and managing it as a steady-state component of the business. Thus, operations, help desk, and a host of shared information technology (IT) services teams will come into play. The key with regard to the project's knowledge repository is to track contact data, hiring data, skill set requirements, interview outcomes, offer letters, and so on—everything necessary to ensure that staffing decisions are both transparent and thoughtfully managed.

Business Vision, Requirements, and Functionality Knowledge

It might seem like overkill to some, but capturing the very essence behind the SAP implementation is an important part of managing the project over its lifecycle. After all, business requirements change in light of changing environmental, industry, economic, and company-specific factors. Tracking how the business vision and its underlying requirements change over time makes good business sense. Mapping these changes to the functionality required by the business teams is equally important.

In this case, the knowledge repository can be used to track what is deemed critical for the project (the "must haves") versus what is less important or simply a "nice to have" like we discussed back in Chapter 3. Maintaining a record of all the decisions and other outcomes made in the numerous business and functional requirements meetings also shows that the project is indeed (or not!) capturing and addressing the business's needs. Priorities and dependencies can be captured here as well, so that people looking back a year later can determine why a certain business decision or particular piece of functionality was implemented while other decisions or functionality were put on hold.

Solution Vision and Application/Business Scenario Knowledge

Just like the business vision and requirements, maintaining a record of the project's solution vision—how the business requirements map to specific SAP and other applications to meet the needs of the business—makes good sense. Solution vision, and the knowledge surrounding the SAP applications and business scenarios that are subsequently deployed, reflects the project team's understanding of the project's priorities, constraints, and so on. Maintaining a record of the decisions (and background information) reflecting *what* needed to be implemented, *who* ultimately made those go/no-go decisions, and *why those decisions were made* not only helps keep a project on track but helps ensure that the project's success is viewed through a public lens of transparency, consensus, and buy-in.

It's more difficult to argue that a particular SAP component should have been implemented in a particular way or not implemented at all when the record reveals the background behind all of the solution- and application-specific decisions. Further, with the underlying facts well understood, any gaps between business requirements and solution vision can be tackled more objectively and expeditiously.

SAP System Landscape Knowledge

With regard to each deployed SAP component, the knowledge repository is an excellent tool for tracking why investments were made in infrastructure, servers, disk subsystems, and so on. Just as importantly, the repository can track why landscape trade-offs were made. By way of example, perhaps the SAP NetWeaver BW project could not afford a dedicated training system or technical sandbox due to budget constraints, or perhaps the perception surrounding creating a SAP Solution Manager test system revealed that that particular landscape system wasn't deemed necessary. These decisions, along with the configuration or current-state documentation related to each landscape and component, help minimize finger-pointing later down the road when new requirements arise. And this kind of knowledge is valuable simply from an asset management perspective, as well as from installation, recovery, and performance perspectives.

Installation and Configuration Knowledge

Beyond tracking the decisions and configuration related to each SAP system landscape, capturing the specific technology stack considerations and configuration details related to each SAP component and application is essential. Through this kind of current-state and process/how-to documentation, the various IT teams can back up one another in case of disaster or simply allow a colleague to take vacation or attend a training class. New hires can be more easily trained, while transfers into an organization can more quickly get up to speed with regard to a particular technology stack or solution configuration. The help desk and other support organizations can quickly determine whether a specific configuration (or patch level or kernel level) is associated with known bugs or other problems. And changes to each system's respective technology stack can be tracked and maintained, aiding in troubleshooting and problem resolution down the road.

Knowledge Repository and Management Tools

In our experience, we've come across many different tools and approaches that are useful in capturing and managing a project team's collective knowledge. The SAP Knowledge Warehouse (SAP KW) server is popular, as is SAP NetWeaver's Content Management solution, and various third-party software and portal packages are also available. Many firms continue to house and organize their project data on network file shares and web servers, too.

Using SAP KM and the SAP Knowledge Warehouse

SAP Knowledge Management (KM) and the SAP Knowledge Warehouse (SAP KW, made popular a few years ago) allow you to create and manage knowledge, from custom training materials to ad hoc or technology stack–specific documentation. SAP's tools support version management and include the SAP Library, a helpful SAP Glossary, and insight into SAP's terminology.

SAP KW enables people to conduct full-text searches, search based on file attributes, perform process and workflow modeling, collaborate via check-in and check-out of documents, and perform other basic document management tasks. Publishing is handled by Microsoft's ubiquitous Word and PowerPoint tools while access is enabled through the classic SAPGUI and the popular WebGUI. Supported file formats include the following by default, with the option to support other formats simply by associating their file formats to an application:

▶ DOC

▶ PPT

▶ PDF

▶ HTML

▶ XML

▶ AVI

▶ VCM

Keeping development and production KM repositories is made difficult given that there's no native ability to synchronize. Thus, content managers or power users in the role of content editor may need to update and maintain data in several places initially (until the production environment is truly productive). Some customers tie the production and development KM repository systems together, which enables KM documents to be edited in the development environment (just like source code) before being promoted to production. In the meantime, development users will point their Portal iViews under development to this repository. Benefits include the following:

▶ Similar to the development-production relationship seen in programming, the development server does not need to be sized as robustly as production.

6

▶ A single master repository simplifies synchronization and other management tasks.

▶ Delta document management is simplified as well; no error-prone manual process is required.

▶ Once the taxonomy (in the form of various folders) is created in production, workflows and document approval processes may be implemented.

SAP KM is not without its performance-related and similar challenges, though. The development user community can place a pretty robust load on the production portal, while the connectivity between production and development is subject to performance-impacting security and permission-related settings. If the SAP technical support organization has segregated production and nonproduction subnets (both common and recommended), the systems may have difficulty communicating with one another.

All in all, SAP KW is a solid KM tool that is useful to the entire project team, despite its aging platform. SAP addressed this problem by offering in its newer knowledge management product much of the functionality initially introduced in its legacy knowledge products, as we see next.

Using SAP Content Server for Enterprise Knowledge Management

The SAP Content Server product is a fine tool for collaboratively managing information and documents within (and outside, as necessary) the SAP project team. By enabling the project team to manage distributed knowledge across the company, its partners, and so on, this KM solution supports several different content management scenarios and capabilities.

Germane to our discussion of knowledge management is SAP's support for documentation, manuals, and training material management. SAP's documentation management scenario enables the SAP project team to create and translate documentation, edit and present it, distribute it, and manage and maintain it.

Using Third-Party KM Software Applications

SAP isn't the only knowledge management game in town. Open Source tools such as cyn.in complement older offerings by Novell and IBM typically lumped together as "groupware." IBM also offers Intelligent Miner, a data mining tool similar in functionality to SPSS's Clementine Data Mining (or Knowledge Discovery) Software package. Information Discovery touts the Information Discovery System (IDIS), while PC PACK offers a similar yet portable package of integrated tools useful in managing requirements and maintaining knowledge.

Another favorite tool of ours is Persistent's ECSC (Enterprise Content Search-enabling Connectors). It is an SAP-aware KM tool set that provides Google-like search capabilities while integrating with SAP KM. This tool is earmarked for SAP-on-Windows customers (it runs with SAP NetWeaver 7.0 or 6.0, exclusively on Windows Server 2003 SP2). Features of the Persistent ECSC product for SAP include:

▶ Robust content crawling and retrieval; it crawls all content entities in SAP KM, including the repository, collection, resource, and document.

▶ Secure retrieval and search functionality tied back to SAP KM.

▶ Support for keyword-based search and attribute-based advanced search on metadata.

▶ Support for authorized search using HTTP Basic authentication mechanisms.

▶ Capability to index source documents via its Google Search Appliance.

▶ Assignment of a URL to each KM document for easy access.

Using Popular Collaboration Tools

Over the past five years, when it comes to capturing and maintaining project data, we have seen our customers use Microsoft Office SharePoint Server, Oracle Application Server Portal, and many other similar, competing products. Knowledge management has really benefited from the explosion in knowledge management awareness witnessed during this time. SharePoint, for example, not only is the most popular portal and collaboration framework available today but also offers robust integration with the SAP NetWeaver Application Server, NetWeaver Portal, and SAP's Knowledge Management product. SAP and Microsoft standardized on a position of *collaborative interoperability*, thus making it possible to leverage SAP iViews (its name for its portal components) alongside Microsoft Windows SharePoint Services and its more-capable portal Web Parts. The two software providers share capabilities around Java, .NET, and more than 70 multilanguage business packages as well.

Using Other Legacy KM Approaches

Most of us are familiar with file shares and network directories. These constructs, along with equally simple websites, are often used by firms as short-term knowledge repositories. However, they often have a way of becoming the company's primary knowledge repository as post-implementation budgets shrink and people generally lose interest in the mundane work of documentation management and maintenance.

The problem with these types of legacy KM approaches is that there's usually no enterprisewide taxonomy developed to carefully classify and group the data. Sure, people typically build directory structures or multitudes of web pages, and these can be helpful in the beginning. But after a while, these informal legacy KM approaches become difficult to navigate and therefore more and more difficult to use. Eventually, we tend to see people stop using them altogether—an outcome that puts the entire project in a difficult position as knowledge continues to be developed but only falls by the wayside.

Transferring Knowledge Throughout the Project

Knowledge transfer is often seen as synonymous with training (which explains why many of the knowledge repository products are equally adept at housing and managing training materials). Knowledge transfer is also related to the KM process; without the concept of transfer, KM would be pointless. To transfer knowledge is to capture (or create), organize, and disseminate knowledge through a centralized communications process or tool set. The trick is to coax the knowledge hidden in people, processes, and other tools into a single tool set—a knowledge repository—where it can be refined, categorized, cross-referenced, and generally made more available.

In today's world, the favored communications medium for knowledge transfer is the Internet, though of course knowledge is transferred in many other ways. Knowledge transfer isn't without other challenges, though. Having geographically distributed project teams complicates knowledge transfer simply due to distance and a related lack of speed. Language barriers represent another challenge, as do intergenerational differences, cultural differences, leader-follower relationships, and plain old misconceptions. In some cases, the poor use of figures or other visual cues for sharing complex relationships or representations can exacerbate problems with knowledge transfer. A team's shared beliefs, its exposure to other methods of sharing data, and the prevalence of bad information are other causes of poor knowledge transfer. Finally, basic issues of motivation and trust continue to complicate knowledge transfer.

To create a project team environment or culture in which knowledge sharing and transfer are the norm, practice the following:

- ▶ Identify key knowledge holders across the project team, including people, tools, and processes.

- ▶ Provide incentives to knowledge sharing and transfer.

- ▶ Implement a tool or process that's inherently easy to use; cumbersome tools and processes thwart a project team's best efforts to house and share data.

- ▶ Institute a regular process for transferring data, and execute against it regularly. This might involved one-way or multipath knowledge transfer, the latter of which is preferred given its natural win/win state.

- ▶ Ensure the knowledge repository and associated knowledge transfer policies are measurable.

- ▶ Through organizational and role design, force knowledge transfer within the project team as well as external to it. Establish evaluation metrics that reward knowledge transfer.

As you can see, creating a knowledge-sharing culture cannot happen by accident. The participants in such an environment must be motivated and rewarded.

Summary

Throughout this chapter we focused on understanding the importance of establishing a knowledge management footprint early in the project's lifecycle, backed up by tools and processes culminating in a project knowledge repository. After reviewing the variety of information maintained in the repository, we took a closer look at several popular tools and approaches, and then concluded the chapter with discussions as to how knowledge transfer is best approached and encouraged.

Case Study: KM Business Case Fundamentals

Though HiTech, Inc. continues to implement SAP ERP and the complete SAP NetWeaver portfolio of components, the ERP implementation project team has found little time to capture and organize all the data surrounding the implementation. In some cases, project members are keeping their job-specific documents and deliverables on their company desktops. Several of the business leads have also been dumping their business requirements into a website used primarily for maintaining legacy documentation; the IT team is using a system of network file shares to do the same. Another team is beginning to track project-related documents through SAP's Content Server. You have been asked to put together a business case that demonstrates the need for a more rigorous and comprehensive process for capturing and maintaining the project's knowledge.

Questions

1. Why should an organization seek to capture and preserve its knowledge?
2. What kind of knowledge is typically maintained in an SAP project's knowledge repository?
3. What does the concept of "metadata" mean as it relates to a knowledge repository?
4. Why is it important for the knowledge repository to capture "must haves," "nice to haves," and other priorities and dependencies?
5. What might HiTech leverage internally to implement a knowledge repository?

> **NOTE**
>
> The answers to these questions can be found in Appendix A, "Case Study Answers."

PART II

Getting Started

Project Management Checkpoint 1: Groundwork

Sound project management is based on successfully using proven, time-tested concepts and tool sets. The good news is that the project management body of knowledge has matured to a point at which standard tools and processes are available to support all types of projects. This chapter sets the stage for sound SAP project management.

Project Management Considerations

In times past, project management was deemed to be more of an art than a science. These days, the science of project management has matured to a point at which project management practitioners have readily available a wealth of tools, processes, and techniques that, when properly used, can dramatically increase the likelihood of project success.

NOTE

This chapter is intended to raise your awareness of project management processes and activities. You should conduct further research on your own. Excellent sources for further research include *A Guide to the Project Management Body of Knowledge* (PMBOK Guide), published by the Project Management Institute (PMI), and SAP-specific tools and accelerators.

This chapter presents information that you should consider during all phases of your project, which, as noted in general project management literature, consists of five process groups: initiating, planning, executing, monitoring and controlling, and closing. Of course, SAP has chosen to identify a different set of project phase names, which will be mapped to the generally accepted project management phases in the SAP project–specific chapters of this book.

As you move through this chapter, you will be presented with high-level project management topics; each phase name is based on the process group used during that phase. To keep an SAP project aligned with PMI's popular project management methodology, we recommend (and many of our customers use) general project management labels for the project's phases. For example, rather than exclusively using the SAP ASAP methodology's "Realization" label, we also call this phase of a project the Executing Phase.

In subsequent project management chapters, we will present less-generic, SAP project–centric topics, and we focus on SAP-specific terms or constructs. This includes Chapter 8, "Building the SAP Project Management Office," Chapter 9, "SAP Project Management," and Chapter 11, "Building the SAP Project Team." Chapter 22, "Project Management Checkpoint 2: Revisiting Key Artifacts," and Chapter 30, "Project Management Checkpoint 3: Project Team Retention," provide further insights that expand on the concepts mentioned in this and following project management chapters.

Project Management Basics

Managing an SAP implementation project comprises a great number of tasks, people, conflicting timelines, and competing priorities. From understanding and working effectively within a project's unique cultural and social environment to navigating political factors, working through varying levels of interpersonal and business skills, and more, managing an SAP project presents tough challenges for even the most seasoned project management professional. This section covers many of these concerns. To properly set the stage and ensure we have a consistent foundation, let's turn our attention to project management key concepts.

Project Management Key Themes

Project management is sometimes compared to science—a host of activities, labels, and terminology is associated with project management. Like any profession, there is also a unique set of vocabulary and key themes germane to the project management profession. For example:

▶ **Projects are temporary**—Whereas operational processes (sometimes called base load activities) last indefinitely, projects are temporary: They have a distinct start and finish and usually are undertaken to create a unique product or service. Generally, projects create objects (systems, artifacts, deliverables, and processes) that live on after the conclusion of the project. These objects are the *outcomes* or *results* of the project. In contrast, operational activities typically are continuous. An example of a project is the implementation of an SAP system. An example of a continuous, operational activity is a process that has been enabled by successfully implementing an SAP project, such as the repetitive "order-to-cash" process (which records, prices, acknowledges, picks, packs, ships, and invoices customer orders over and over again).

▶ **Projects are subject to the "triple constraint" concept**—Regardless of size, scope, or outcomes, projects are impacted by three constraints: scope, time, and cost. Successful projects need to strike a balance between these three elements; emphasis on one element almost always impacts the remaining elements. For example, an increase in scope usually changes the schedule and likely the cost.

▶ **Projects can be described by three characteristics**—A project consumes *resources* to complete a sequence of *tasks*, thus achieving the results or outcomes mentioned previously.

▶ **A string of projects equates to a program**—The difference between project management and program management essentially amounts to size and scope (though it must be said that an SAP project can easily exceed the size and scope of entire programs; everything is relative). A program consists of repeated projects or a string of projects that are typically related to one another.

▶ **Managing projects equates to managing iterative processes**—Processes within project management are, for the most part, iterative and follow the cycle: plan the work, do the work, check the work, and act on new information and redirect the work (see Figure 7.1).

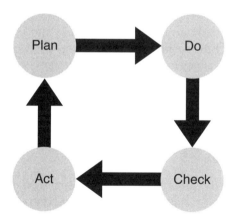

FIGURE 7.1   The plan-do-check-act cycle is paramount to sound project management.

▶ **Projects are subject to failure on many fronts**—Based on the information above and more, projects can fail due to a lack of time or resources, poorly managed resources, unclear requirements, ill-conceived tasks, changes in scope, poor project planning, poor leadership, an inadequate project plan, lack of user or executive leadership buy-in, lack of consensus regarding the project's expected outcomes, lack of communication, technology limitations, an ill-prepared project manager, and more.

▶ **Projects need leaders *and* managers**—While leaders inspire followers to achieve results, a project nonetheless requires managers to manage resources such as budgets, people, processes, and so on. Without both leadership and management, as already mentioned, a project will fail.

▶ **A really good project manager is difficult to find**—In our experience, the most effective project managers balance people and communications skills with personal courage, an ability to successfully juggle competing priorities, and political deftness. This combination of skills and attributes is very difficult to find in a single individual. Where weaknesses are present in an otherwise well-qualified project manager, you might want to initially focus on building a senior project management leadership team that embodies all these attributes and soon after develop the project manager's weaknesses.

▶ **Projects change over time**—Despite the best efforts of the most seasoned project manager or disciplined end-user community, a project as complex and time-consuming as an SAP implementation is bound to have changes. Requirements change, timelines change, technologies change, and people come and go, all of which change the project's scope (or perception of scope). A good change request process (where changes are first requested) and change order process (used to implement the change request after it is approved) is therefore mandatory.

▶ **Rule number one: document everything**—There is no place in project management for oral history. If it is not documented, it did not happen. Rule number two: See rule number one.

We like to remind ourselves that managing an SAP project is akin to balancing science and art—the project management science discussed previously needs to be tempered by the "art" of managing a project in the real world. Beyond the themes and terminology previously mentioned, there's also the concept of project management process groups that merits our attention, next.

Project Management Process Groups

Project management processes are organized into the following five *process groups*, core collections of processes that are related to one another:

▶ **Initiating**—Includes processes that commence the project, including coming to an agreement as to what the project will entail, what is out of scope, and other contractual realities. This includes processes that support defining the project's goal (as previously stated, the iterative plan-do-check-act cycle is followed through project initiating, planning, executing, monitoring and controlling, and closing). The processes in the initiating process group are also used to define and authorize the project, and can further be used to initiate individual project phases.

▶ **Planning**—Includes processes that identify what actually needs to be accomplished, broken down into achievable tasks and milestones. SAP refers to this process as *blueprinting*. The processes in the planning process group are used to define overall project objectives and further refine project objectives stated during the initiating phase, plan the overall course of action and significant steps required to achieve overall project objectives, and define the scope (boundaries) of the project.

▶ **Executing**—Includes processes that support the real work of the project and completing its tasks. SAP calls this realization and final preparation. The processes in the executing process group are used to pull together the resources required to fulfill the project management plan. People, equipment, infrastructure, and physical/geographic project locations are considered in the executing process group.

▶ **Monitoring and controlling**—Includes processes that keep not only project execution but an entire project on track; this helps ensure that overall project scope, cost, and quality remain on plan. The processes in the monitoring and controlling process group are also used to routinely monitor the project's progress by reporting variances to the project management plan (determining which project steps are running ahead of plan, which project steps are running behind plan, and which project steps might require corrective action).

▶ **Closing**—Includes processes that effectively shut down the project (because achieving SAP go-live does not mean everyone is done and can go home!); the closing process group includes processes that describe formal acceptance of the overall project's product, service, or result; is used to document formal acceptance of individual project phases; and brings the project to a successful conclusion. As previously emphasized, formal acceptance equals *written* acceptance.

The aforementioned process groups are recognized across industries and around the world. Each of these process groups is covered in detail throughout this chapter. First, though, a discussion of an SAP project's environment, including cultural, social, international, political, interpersonal skills, and business management expertise, is warranted.

Project Environment

You need to develop a clear picture of the project environment and eventually communicate that picture to all project team members and stakeholders. This section looks at the topics that you need to consider when defining your project environment.

The complexity of a project environment corresponds to how far the business has expanded geographically. Initially, many firms begin with all business activities being conducted at a single location, where all employees, equipment, services, order fulfillment, data centers, and support functions exist within four walls. Subsequently, the firm or business may expand to multiple locations within the same state (or province) or country, requiring that it consider such things as cross-location communications and business transactions and communication across multiple time zones. Additional complexity is added when the firm begins to operate in multiple countries, at which time, in addition to the previous elements, it must consider cross-cultural differences. Let's look at some considerations.

Cultural and Social Environment

As a business expands, consider not only how the project affects people and groups but also how people and groups affect the project. Consider the following possible cultural and social differences:

▶ **Local work rule differences**—Daily work schedule, mandatory or voluntary over-time, and shift differential compensation must be considered.

▶ **Religious differences**—Be aware of the religious customs and traditions, such as holy day observances, that are celebrated by project team members and stakeholders. For example, do not schedule a project cutover or phase closure that occurs when the project members or stakeholders will not be available to support the project.

▶ **Economic differences**—Though it's nearly impossible to enforce, create a culture where salary discussions are frowned upon. Given the diversity in SAP implementation teams staffed by individuals hailing from every corner of the globe, you can be sure to have significant economic backgrounds and differences within your project team.

▶ **Political differences**—Like religious and economic differences, geographically disbursed SAP implementation teams will also represent a variety of political perspectives. Respect differences and actively seek to avoid situations where differences might divide teams. Do your homework so you understand political differences held by members of your team.

▶ **Ethnic differences**—Probably the most complex of all potential differences, ethnic differences can destroy a team founded on insensitivity and ignorance. Establish professional standards of conduct and take care to acknowledge that differences in language, clothing, food preferences, backgrounds, perspectives, and so on exist but nonetheless can have no bearing on the project in terms of meeting its goals and objectives.

Although it's difficult to do, create a culture where differences take a back seat to achieving the project's goals and objectives. Be careful not to inadvertently segregate or separate particular teams or departments from one another. Take steps to bring the project team together, to reward work well done, and embrace the attitude that the right person for a particular assignment has nothing to do with differences but rather with capabilities and attitude. And in cases where someone has infringed upon another's rights or created a less-than-appealing work environment, take swift steps to rectify the problem and set a positive example.

International and Political Factors

In a global economy, we need to consider how activities within the project (and within the system itself that the project establishes) impact commerce that crosses international boundaries. Consider the following factors:

▶ Regional holidays

▶ National holidays

▶ Religious holidays

▶ Local tax requirements

▶ Local import/export regulations

▶ Time zone differences

- ▶ Regional working days

- ▶ Travel requirements for face-to-face meetings

- ▶ Collaboration tools

- ▶ Ecological "green" requirements

Interpersonal Skills and Business Management Expertise

Project team members need to be well versed in organizational and interpersonal skills. After all, the majority of SAP projects are business led rather than IT led. The business folks who are funding these activities are taking an active role in sponsorship and management buy-in and are giving the projects a top-down emphasis. This is unlike the past, where large-scale business projects were often driven from IT organizations up to various business groups and management teams. Basic interpersonal skills required of team members are therefore becoming essential to running a good project, and include the following:

- ▶ Problem-solving ability

- ▶ Motivation

- ▶ Leadership

- ▶ Conflict management

- ▶ Effective communication

General management skills are also needed by all team members, as is a basic awareness of organizational and operational expertise (which, unsurprisingly, maps to SAP functional or technical areas) like the following:

- ▶ Financial management

- ▶ Accounting

- ▶ Sales and marketing

- ▶ Purchasing

- ▶ Distribution

- ▶ Personnel administration

- ▶ Legal and contract administration

- ▶ Logistics and supply chain

- ▶ Information systems/information technology management

- ▶ Problem-solving (yes, it made the list again, this time from an organizational business perspective)

Initiating Phase: Program Preparation

The initiating process group or phase acts to define or authorize a project by formally authorizing a project or the next phase of an existing project. The project initiation phase is very important because all the key activities that occur during this period are needed to establish a project charter (which you will read about later in the chapter). During this process, you take from the project initiator or project sponsor inputs that define the project boundaries. These inputs may then document the organization's business drivers for the project, highlight any alternative solutions that were considered, and, of course, support the recommended solution. In our experience, there are four key initiating activities, each of which are addressed in subsequent sections of this chapter:

▶ Choosing the project initiator or sponsor

▶ Developing the project charter

▶ Developing a preliminary scope statement

▶ Developing a preliminary project budget

Choosing the Project Initiator or Sponsor

The project initiator may or may not be the project sponsor. In a smaller environment, one person may serve both roles. For most enterprises, we have observed that the project initiator and sponsor are different roles performed by two individuals who share a joint vision of the project's goals and objectives. The project sponsor performs the following activities:

▶ Meets periodically with the project management office (PMO) to review progress

▶ Ensures sponsorship through the entire organization

▶ Provides high-level direction and leadership

▶ Articulates the project vision

▶ Drives project communication to the user community

▶ Provides funding and resources

▶ Approves project changes

Developing a Project Charter

Developing a project charter is one of the initiating processes. Project charters are formal statements that describe the business need for the project, formally authorize the project, and link the project to business sponsorship and the business. The following elements may be contained in the project charter:

▶ Project definition and approach

▶ Project description

▶ Project methodology

- ▶ Technical strategy

- ▶ Project impact on the organization

- ▶ Project dependencies

- ▶ Functional scope/system scope

- ▶ Key assumptions

- ▶ Key dependencies

- ▶ Project organization

- ▶ Management organization

- ▶ Roles and responsibilities

- ▶ Project deliverables

- ▶ Project standards and procedures

- ▶ Project control mechanism

- ▶ Scope management

- ▶ Issue management

- ▶ Resource management

- ▶ Change management

- ▶ Project communication

- ▶ Meeting schedule

- ▶ Status report schedule

- ▶ Major milestones

- ▶ High-level schedule

- ▶ Budget summary and estimates

Developing a Preliminary Scope Statement

The preliminary scope statement is a high-level definition of the project that includes input from the project charter, the project statement of work, enterprise/organizational information, the preliminary scope statement documents of the project, project requirements, and high-level deliverables. In addition it establishes project boundaries, such as key assumptions and key dependencies, and describes change management processes. Note that some of the elements in the preliminary scope statement are also reflected in the project charter. Be certain to address these elements in the project charter or project scope statement.

Developing a Preliminary Project Budget

Investments in the future SAP projects are typically identified in a company's long-, medium-, and short-range financial plan. How much you spend on your enterprise system is a function of the number of competing initiatives, the urgency of your implementation, and the size of your overall IT spending. Unfortunately, there is no "ballpark" price for most SAP implementations. The following factors should be considered:

▶ Do you want to do all the work in house?

▶ Are you willing to have some of the work done out of house or remotely?

▶ Are you willing to have most of the work done out of house or remotely?

▶ Are you planning on managing the work, acting as your own "general contractor," or are you hiring a systems integrator to oversee the job?

▶ Is the project so complex that you might require multiple systems integrators?

We believe that, to be prudent, you must consider all of your firm's internal IT and business transformation capabilities, your SAP project's "business case" for implementation, how the SAP project will be funded, your particular budgeting and other financial practices, and your need for outside assistance. Only then can you establish a reasonable project budget.

Planning Phase: Business Blueprint

The planning or business blueprint phase defines and refines project objectives and establishes a formal scope that describes the boundaries of the project. Project boundaries contain desired functionality (end results, objectives, or outcomes), geographic boundaries, the rationale for the project, key constraints and dates, and a host of company-specific, industry-specific, and other special considerations. In short, the planning phase seeks to clearly define what is in scope and, more importantly, what is out of scope, such as

▶ Desired functionality

▶ Company work locations

▶ Project rationale (see the following note)

▶ Project team work locations

▶ Specific exclusions

▶ Scope definition and documentation

▶ Project plan

NOTE

With regard to a project's rationale, consider the following questions: Are you replacing a legacy system? Upgrading an existing system that is about to drop out of support? Adding new functionality or capabilities? Responding to new environmental regulations? Spending funding that would otherwise be lost (don't laugh; this happens)? Or is the project the result or necessary consequence of an acquisition or a divestiture?

Throughout the next few pages we take a closer look at key tasks and activities associated with SAP project planning or blueprinting. Keep in mind that you may start many of these tasks—such as developing your project plan and project standards—earlier in the overall project management process. Be careful not to start too early, however; doing so risks creating project documents that need to be significantly modified (if not completely re-created) before they're useful, which in turn can actually slow down the project rather than accelerate it.

Developing the Project Management Plan

The project management plan is composed of subsidiary plans and defines how those plans will be managed during execution monitoring and controlling and closing. The content of the plan is determined by the project management team and is customized to fit the overall scope and complexity of your project. Key inputs to the project management plan are your preliminary scope statement and enterprise environmental factors, such as the number of your company's physical locations, the locations of your customers, the locations from which the project work will be performed, and whether a systems integrator will be involved or you will act as your own "general contractor." Components of the project management plan include

- ▶ Create implementation schedule
- ▶ Create milestone list
- ▶ Create project schedule
- ▶ Create project standards
- ▶ Validate project budget
- ▶ Create communications plan
- ▶ Create quality plan
- ▶ Create resource management plan
- ▶ Create communication management plan
- ▶ Create training plan
- ▶ Create risk management plan

- ▶ Perform cost estimating

- ▶ Perform cost budgeting

- ▶ Perform contracting planning

- ▶ Create technology plan

- ▶ Create data migration plan

The project management plan is your "playbook," so you should periodically revisit and update it during the lifecycle of the project.

> **NOTE**
>
> The proper care and feeding of the tasks included in the planning process and group will establish a solid foundation on which you can base your project. The old carpenters' saying "measure twice and cut once" comes to mind. The investment you make in planning now will avoid confusion and ambiguities later during project execution.

Addressing Scope Definition and Documentation

Scope definition and documentation comprises the "who, what, where, when, and how" of the project and is based on the project charter, project management plan, and preliminary scope statement. Outputs of this scope definition and documentation process include the project scope management plan, project scope statement, and project work breakdown structure. All of these tools provide the foundation for the project.

Creating the Project Schedule

The project schedule can be viewed as two distinct items: a high-level timeline of key activities (sometimes known as the project Gantt chart) and a work breakdown structure (WBS). The WBS contains project phases, key milestones, key deliverables, tasks and subtasks, task successor and predecessor relationships, task duration, task resource requirements, and associated costs. Although the preceding list might seem daunting, at a high level the project schedule comprises four key components:

- ▶ Activity definition

- ▶ Activity resource estimate

- ▶ Activity sequencing

- ▶ Schedule development

Establishing Project Standards

Project standards are established to provide consistent clarity about scope, project documentation, work breakdown structure, financial budgeting, and acceptance criteria standards. The time that you invest in establishing and communicating a solid set of project standards pays off in huge dividends later. How? By reducing project documentation ambiguity.

Validating the Project Budget

Although the overall project budget that you established during the initiating process might not have changed, you might have discovered by this point that the budget may purchase more or fewer services than you originally anticipated. It is highly probable that new information will cause a change in project scope timing and costs. As project planned expenses begin to solidify, you will have the opportunity to begin separating budget funds into several categories: hardware and infrastructure, software, professional services, internal resources, risk, and contingency funding.

Creating a Communications Plan

In this step you create a communications plan that considers all levels of communications required to keep your stakeholder base informed. Be ready to engage communications specialists from within your firm, supplemented by outside expertise where needed. We recommend tapping your own company's resources first, because they are in the best position to identify effective communications mechanisms within your firm.

Creating the Training Plan

All SAP projects require one type of a training plan or another. SAP projects introduce change into environments. The change that SAP introduces into your environment may impact a small group of stakeholders or impact the majority of your firm's employees. Training may consist of several hours of knowledge transfer, e-learning courses, classroom education, self-taught job aids, or any combination of the preceding elements.

Creating the Data Migration Plan

Although it is possible that the master data that is required for your new enterprise system is entirely contained in your legacy enterprise system, in our experience, master data will be pulled from multiple sources and multiple systems. Understanding your data migration requirements is an arduous process, and developing an approach during the planning phase is a firm requirement. By now, you may have received proposals from several vendors offering to develop a data migration plan. Unless you have done something like this before, we recommend that you hire somebody with expertise in this highly complex area. The processes and tools involved in data migration are complex, to say nothing of how critical the data management and legacy migration process is to creating a sound foundation for SAP.

Creating the RICEF Plan

Reports, interfaces, conversions, enhancements, and forms (RICEF) need to be considered within the overall scope of your project. Remember to keep in mind how the RICEF components affect the project's tasks, effort, and cost of realizing your RICEF objects. It might be helpful to classify reports and enhancements into two groups: objects that must be produced to enable business operations, and optional, "nice to have" objects. An example of a required object is a report of export information, the format of which must satisfy statutory or legal regulations.

Executing Phase: Realization and Final Preparation

So here you are, armed with a complete set of project requirements, a realistic project timetable, a single architectural view of your project and environment, a team of 100% dedicated company resources, systems integrator, and subcontractors. And this is just the *local* team! Your project could possibly have teams working in different geographies, with near-shore and far-shore resources included on those teams as well. We are now where "the rubber meets the road." The executing process or phase brings together all resources required to implement the project management plan, and includes the following execution steps:

▶ Manage deliverables

▶ Review requested changes

▶ Implement change requests

▶ Perform corrective and preventative actions

▶ Update risk management plan

▶ Gather work performance information

▶ Perform issue management

Managing Deliverables

Completion all of your project's work products indicates the completion of individual work products or phases. The end results—the work—are often called *deliverables*. Deliverables must be adequately documented to verify that the work actually occurred, meets requirements, conforms to project standards, and adheres to quality standards.

Reviewing Requested Changes

It is perfectly natural that changes to the project will surface during the planning and executing phases. We recommend that you develop processes for managing and templates for documenting proposed changes. Typical contents of the change template include:

▶ Request date

▶ Requestor's name

▶ Description of the existing solution

▶ Description of the change

▶ Business justification for the change

▶ Change implementation approach and timing

▶ Impact on current project schedule

▶ Cost of change

Periodic review of proposed changes should be a standing agenda item, one that is regularly discussed during project management status meetings.

Implementing Change Requests

Collecting proposed changes, obtaining approval, and implementing properly documented change requests should become a routine project activity. Be certain to document change requests according to your project standards. Remember rule number one: There is no place in project management for oral history.

Performing Corrective and Preventative Actions

The capabilities to anticipate a problem, recognize a problem, react to a problem, and resolve a problem before it becomes a catastrophe are facilitated by corrective and preventative action management. It is our expectation that you, the project manager, have a clear understanding of the types of preventive- and corrective-action tools that are in your PM toolbox and know which tool to use in which situation.

Updating the Risk Management Plan

During the initiating phase, you established a risk management plan. It is now one of the many times to take that plan off the shelf, evaluate whether risk events have or have not happened, adjust the plan, and recognize any new risk events that may have presented themselves. Be sure to record both favorable and unfavorable risk events.

Although it is common practice to include unfavorable risk in your risk management plan, many project teams tend to ignore favorable risk. An example of a favorable risk event is a 30% price decrease in the memory that you are about to purchase for your new environment. The occurrence of this event reduces overall project costs and potentially makes additional funding available to cover additional unfavorable risks.

Gathering Work Performance Information

Managing your project requires gathering information on work performance, such as incomplete tasks, incomplete late tasks, tasks completed ahead of schedule, tasks completed behind schedule, tasks completed with more or less effort than planned, tasks completed with higher or lower costs, and slipping tasks that impact the critical path. It is the project manager's responsibility to recognize negative and positive project variations and react accordingly.

Issue Management Systems

Identifying project issues and managing them with various tools may seem fairly basic to you. In fact, issue management is a very basic process when you are dealing with 15 issues, but it becomes much more complex in environments in which you are managing 500 issues. Select a tool that is strong enough to manage the workload. Features of a good issue management tool include the capability to adequately describe the issue and possible solutions, acceptance criteria to acknowledge issue closure, problem root cause analysis (RCA), and a mechanism for reporting open and closed issue statistics.

As you might imagine, issue management systems vary widely and can be as basic as a single punch list or check list or as complex as a formal database-style *issue management* tool or system. The use of issue management tools is becoming more popular for larger projects in which multiple issue owners need to access and update individual issues, whereas simplistic spreadsheet-like tools have been used in the past. Some projects are beginning to use service call management systems, which tend to be robust, feature-rich issue management systems.

Monitoring and Controlling Phase

Now that you have gathered work performance information, it is time to establish the right monitoring and controlling mechanism and tools for your environment. A weekly or biweekly monitoring and controlling cycle is typical. What is important is that you perform the monitoring and controlling function systematically and routinely. The frequency of your monitoring and controlling cycle is directly impacted by the cost and expense associated with gathering statistics, both of which need to be considered while you are standing up your monitoring and controlling system.

Monitoring and controlling during the initiating, planning, and executing phases of a project are key activities to ensure that overall project scope, cost, and quality remain on plan. Although variances from plan are most definitely normal occurrences, one key goal of this process is to manage routine variances and, more importantly, identify critical "showstopper" variances with enough advance warning to deploy corrective actions and contingency plans to meet project objectives.

> **NOTE**
>
> Managing and resolving project deviations are key activities. Most deviations are expected to be resolved by members of the project team and project management. However, significant, nonresolvable issues must be escalated to the correct resources for speedy resolution. In other words, *escalation is a good thing under the right circumstances.* Do not be afraid to escalate problems to executive decision-makers. In our experience, executive decision-makers expect to be called into play to act as tiebreakers and make the difficult decisions to knock down walls and resolve critical issues.

This section take a look at the following monitoring and controlling areas. Although this is not an exhaustive list, it gives you a good start.

- ▶ Scope verification and scope control
- ▶ Schedule and cost control
- ▶ Quality management
- ▶ Performance reporting
- ▶ Stakeholder management

▶ Communication

▶ Change management and control of the preceding items

The failure to achieve project goals is usually the result of one or more of the preceding areas spiraling out of control. Successful projects devote the appropriate level of energy to these areas. The concepts are simple. However, it is interesting to note that, in our experience, most projects usually do not have all of these areas completely under control. Project teams with a strong focus on all of these areas are typically successful.

Scope Verification and Scope Control

The scope that you spent so much time documenting during the initiating phase of your project is constantly being validated and tested and probably redefined during the planning and executing phases. A reasonable amount of scope creep may be allowable within the bounds of your project. The trick is to define "reasonable." It is up to you and your project team to manage scope and, where required, make appropriate scope additions or deletions.

Some changes can be readily absorbed by the project without requiring significant amounts of additional effort or causing changes to the overall project schedule, whereas other changes will drive cost and effort increases or decreases and require schedule adjustments. In all cases, best project management practice dictates that all scope changes be accurately documented in change orders, presented to the stakeholders, and formally accepted by all parties.

Schedule and Cost Control

The work performance information that you have gathered comprises key input to support schedule and cost control activities. It is likely that your project team will conduct schedule control activities more frequently than cost control activities, primarily because most project management systems provide timely and frequent scheduling control data points, whereas cost information typically takes more time to accumulate. Of course, it is possible to provide timely cost control information as well. Work breakdown structures that reflect best practices will include both activity and cost information, yielding timely cost control information as well. In such systems, variations in schedule will also yield cost variances.

Quality Management

Project quality management is undertaken to ensure that the project's product or results completely satisfy requirements and conform to established project standards. Best practice is to have an independent person or group ("independent" meaning that they are not directly involved with the project) conduct an audit of all project activities and deliverables.

Performance Reporting

Performance reporting consists of comparing actual project performance to planned activities, assessing performance to determine whether preventative or remedial action is needed, and providing timely information in support of status reporting and progress measurement. Gathered information can include the following:

▶ Schedule progress/status information

▶ Deliverable status: complete/not complete/percentage complete

▶ Activity status: complete/not complete/percentage complete

▶ In-progress activities: estimate to complete time

▶ Planned costs/incurred costs

▶ Overall resource utilization

The information provided by performance reporting might indicate that remedial actions are required. Best-of-breed performance reporting stresses timely implementation while offering remedial actions.

Stakeholder Management

Effective stakeholder management is based on a broad understanding of business organizational and management skills. On the business organizational skills side, you need to empathize with the wants and desires of different groups within the organization and work toward satisfying those wants and desires. Solid management skills are necessary to protect overall project goals and objectives. Many teams routinely poll their stakeholders in order to better tune messages to different audiences.

Communication

Best-of-breed projects maintain a regular cadence of communication to all project stakeholders during the monitoring and controlling phase. Let's discuss all the attributes of effective communication that are necessary at this point:

▶ **Communication planning**—Most communication planning occurs during the project initiating and planning phases. We recommend that you conduct a communication requirements analysis to understand the communication and information needs of various stakeholder groups; you need to consider who needs to know what, what needs to be communicated, how will it be communicated, and who will be communicating. Your project contains information that must be communicated to stakeholders. The vehicles used for communication vary from environment to environment.

▶ **Communications vehicles**—A combination of the three communications styles (visual, written, and auditory/spoken) is probably required to get the message across to your audience. Town hall meetings, lunch and learn sessions, and project dashboards are all effective communication vehicles.

- ▶ **Communication cadence**—We recommend that the frequency of communication should, at the very least, match the communication cadence of the organization. Many project teams choose to pick up the pace of routine communication and provide a more aggressive communication schedule containing both off-cycle and on-cycle communication.

- ▶ **Communication language/translation requirements**—During planning, you determined the project's language requirements and, more importantly, stakeholder language requirements. It is not common for a business to formally state that English is its primary language and that all official communication will be in the primary language. However, all stakeholder language requirements need to be understood and accommodated in project communication.

Change Management and Control

The final component of the Monitoring and Controlling phase addresses change management and control. This component reflects the need to manage the previous components—a critical end indeed—and is focused on comparing the current state of your project to what was scheduled (that is, actual project status versus planned status). Pay particular attention to the "control" tasks and other activities that might be necessary to get back on track and *stay* on track.

Closing Phase: Project Closure

The closing process group includes processes that are used to formally wind down and ultimately terminate or "close" all the activities included in your project or project phase. Said another way, processes that are used to formally close any activities that remain open bring about formal closure of the project or project phase. The most important thing to keep in mind is that a successful go-live does not close a project. A project is officially closed only when its stakeholders agree that you have accomplished what was set out to be accomplished in the initiating phase (including all the changes collected throughout the planning, executing, and controlling phases). Several key close-related tasks germane to the closing phase include conducting or performing the following:

- ▶ **Administrative project close**—Used to accurately record the final state of the project's executing phase. This process may contain the following items: final acceptance of the project's work products and deliverables; final tally of project expenses and reconciliation to budget; passing of any remaining project issues to responsible parties; stakeholder/customer satisfaction survey and reporting; reporting of project lessons learned; and formal release of project team members.

- ▶ **Formal client signoff**—Before the project or project phase can truly be considered complete, the SAP customer must "sign off" or agree that the project or project phase has indeed been concluded. Remember rule number one, too, and ensure that you obtain formal acceptance by the client that the project or project phase is complete in *writing*.

▶ **Contract closure**—After formal client signoff has been obtained, the project can be put to rest from a contractual perspective. This typically includes formally releasing all system integrators, closing the "subcontractor door" (the mechanism or process for procuring subcontractor project resources), similarly closing the technology acquisition door, finalizing billing and expense processes, and closing or cancelling unnecessary purchase orders, outstanding sales orders related to the project (if any), and so on.

Summary

This chapter introduced you to important project management concepts and generic project management principles. We covered a lot of ground and exposed you to concepts and processes that you might not have previously considered. In subsequent project management chapters, we will build on these and additional concepts and tune them to the SAP project environment.

Case Study: Project Management Initial Checkpoint

Your employer, HiTech, has decided to replace its legacy ERP solution at 7 of 12 worldwide locations, which are distributed across four different continents. HiTech has leveraged a global ERP solution/template. Worldwide company headquarters are located in Houston, Texas.

Questions

1. Your firm has established English as its official business language for SAP. What are several factors that need to be considered?

2. Through which process group is the project charter established?

3. With regard to the closing phase, what are three closely related tasks that need to be addressed prior to wrapping up a project or project phase?

4. Which three activities comprise the "initiating" process group?

NOTE

The answers to these questions can be found in Appendix A, "Case Study Answers."

CHAPTER 8

Building the SAP Project Management Office

This chapter discusses the project management office (PMO), a centralized business entity that coordinates the overall management of projects contained within its span of control. Sometimes referred to as a project office, program office, or program management office, the PMO is typically responsible for project and program oversight of large-scale or high-profile megaprojects. Like most commonsense ideas, establishing a PMO makes a lot of sense in theory but is more difficult to pull off in reality. After grounding you in PMO concepts at the start of this chapter, we will move on to explore effective PMOs. And because we are examining SAP implementations, we will focus on PMOs that are responsible for managing projects and programs in the SAP domain.

Project Management Office Considerations

The PMO seeks to bring together subprojects and tasks that together represent all the effort necessary to achieve a critical business goal—a megaproject such as an SAP implementation. It's this connectedness and dependencies, combined with constraints such as limited access to people, budget, and other resources, that makes a PMO indispensable.

It is not unusual for the PMO to maintain oversight of project portfolios that contain projects that are not directly related to one another, too. Said another way, a PMO will comprise diverse projects and equally diverse project managers. Project managers will differ in their business backgrounds and experience but will all possess a common project management foundation.

NOTE

Many PMOs provide centralized support functions, such as forms processes, project or program quality assurance, standardized tools, policies and procedures, project, program, or portfolio metrics reporting, cross-project integration, and cross-project resource management. On the other hand, another subset of PMOs is directly responsible for individual project execution. In addition to this variety of roles, a PMO's overall area of responsibility may vary widely from organization to organization. Before building your PMO, take some time to plan its charter, organizational structure, and success criteria. You should be able to define your organization's PMO, including its responsibilities and span of control. For example, in some organizations, the PMO has an executive project stakeholder or decision-maker role complete with full authority to initiate, plan, execute, and terminate projects.

As you will discover, a PMO can perform many functions and play several different project and program management roles. While reading this chapter, remember to differentiate between the PMO's responsibilities and an individual project manager's responsibilities. PMOs manage the overall program, whereas project managers manage and control their individual projects. Both PMOs and project managers are concerned with elements such as scope management, change orders, earned value, risk management, organizational alignment, and stakeholder satisfaction. This chapter gives you information to consider when establishing a PMO; use this information to establish an SAP PMO.

Project Management Office Fundamentals

In this section we will examine program management elements and take a high-level look at creating the PMO. We'll also revisit the number one rule in project management: There is no place in project management for oral history. If it is not documented, it did not happen.

Creating the PMO

A good understanding of the organization's business structure and general business management concepts is required when creating a PMO. Walk carefully here, because when you create a PMO, you create an entity that centralizes some or all of the organization's portfolio and project management oversight functions. Overcoming resistance to change in many organizations can take a considerable amount of time. Best practice is to enlist the support of a program management champion at the executive level. In other words, go out and find the "800-pound gorilla" within the organization who shares the program management vision of, and has the authority to drive change within, the organization.

1. Articulate the type of PMO you intend to build. Consider the functions that the PMO will perform, the PMO's span of control, and how those functions will report within the organization.

2. Sell the PMO concept within your organization and obtain approval and funding to establish the PMO.

3. Staff the PMO to support the functional and organizational requirements. Consider provisions for professional advancement, providing a clear career path that includes concise short- and long-term objectives for PMO members.

4. Periodically examine the role and effectiveness of the PMO. Make the necessary adjustments to reflect the fact that both the PMO and an organization's business units evolve over time.

Program Management Elements

Central administration of the following program management elements provides a consistent framework for guiding projects within the SAP portfolio. You need to consider these program management elements carefully or the portfolio could grow too cumbersome or prove not worth it due to lack of projects.

▶ Shared and pooled resources

▶ Project management methodology

▶ Project standards

▶ Central management of policies, procedures, templates, and accelerators

▶ Centralized change management and configuration management

▶ Datacenter coordination

▶ Central program repository, containing best practices, lessons learned, frequently asked questions (FAQs), SAP landscape and design considerations, and infrastructure design

▶ Project management software; control the operation and management of project tools such as project management software (Microsoft Project, HP Project and Portfolio Management Center, SAP Solution Manager, and Primavera TeamPlay), test management software, dashboards, and other reporting mechanisms

▶ Cross-project communication methodology

▶ On-boarding materials

▶ Project manager mentoring

We discuss some of the most important program management elements in greater detail in the following sections.

Shared and Pooled Resources

Central management of shared or pooled resources makes sense in environments in which individuals with business process–specific knowledge are required to support parallel projects or implementation activities. Consider the following resource types:

▶ Central IT resources with specific SAP skills (unlikely for firms implementing their first SAP component)

▶ System integration partner or subcontractor resources with specific SAP skills

▶ Business process specialists who work either in central IT or in the organization's business units

▶ Local, near-shore, and offshore resource groups affiliated with any number of IT hardware, software, or services firms

Project Management Methodology

The SAP PMO's project management methodology may be based on ASAP, ValueSAP, or SAP Solution Manager (SolMan) tools or methodologies, or other methodologies and tools developed by various SAP systems integrators. Alternatively, the PMO's methodology might be based on an industry-accepted or company-unique non-SAP methodology (such as that espoused by the Project Management Institute). Regardless, at a minimum the following elements need to be included in the project management methodology used by the PMO:

▶ Sample work breakdown structures

▶ Entrance and exit criteria for project phases

▶ Deliverable samples

▶ Business blueprint template

▶ Requirements traceability matrix

▶ Functional specification samples

▶ Technical specification samples

▶ Reports, interfaces, and conversion specifications and templates

On-Boarding Materials

Maintaining a centralized set of on-boarding materials is a best practice that will improve the efficiency of introducing new team members to company processes, templates, reporting standards, and individual project materials. On-boarding is a repeatable process that, once established, will help to increase the productivity of new team members. Key items to include in on-boarding materials are

▶ Company background material

▶ Project/program background material

▶ Work locations

- ▶ Work calendar, by country

- ▶ Labor reporting standards, by country

- ▶ Expense reporting standards, by country

- ▶ Collaboration tools

- ▶ Shared workspaces

- ▶ Access to the SAP system being developed

- ▶ Team contact lists

- ▶ Project templates

For new employees, basic productivity tools such as a laptop, Internet access, and a phone must be appended to this list. Fortunately, contractors and consultants will walk in with these tools (though we've worked with clients who, for security reasons, provided these assets as well).

Project Manager Mentoring

The charter of your PMO may include project manager mentoring. Providing project management thought leadership to your firm's PM community and developing project management as a profession is one way to ensure project delivery consistency. Your PM mentoring program may include:

- ▶ Scope management

- ▶ Time management

- ▶ Cost management

- ▶ Human resources management

- ▶ Procurement management

- ▶ Subcontractor management

- ▶ Quality management

- ▶ Risk management

- ▶ Negotiation

- ▶ Resource optimization

- ▶ Method and tool use

- ▶ Legal/contract standards

- ▶ Project financial management expectations

- ▶ Conflict management skills

To learn more about the various program management elements outlined in the last few sections, refer to the Project Management Institute's website (http://www.pmi.org). It offers a wealth of tried-and-true PMO processes and practices in addition to thought leadership on this topic.

Role of the PMO Within the Organization

Several key inputs affect the structure and behavior of a program management office. For example, business organization considerations, such as where and how the PMO reports up through the organization structure, and the PMO's span of control are important to understand and document. Similarly, the charter of the PMO, which provides the "who, what, where, when, and how" guidelines describing PMO operations, needs to be well communicated. Many PMOs participate in their organization's long-range or strategic planning, maintaining a rolling three- to five-year portfolio plan that supports the organization's long-term goals and objectives and bridges those strategies over to tactical project initiation, planning, and execution activities. Before all else, we suggest that you actively work to define the PMO's structure and its charter, covered in the next two chapters, respectively.

Establishing a PMO Organizational Structure

When establishing a preliminary PMO organizational structure, considerations include managing the project portfolio performance, managing centralized templates and tools, and defining communication/report-out (reporting) mechanisms. The PMO operations block includes processes necessary to ensure healthy projects within the portfolio, issue and risk identification and mitigation, and a status reporting mechanism. The PMO tools block includes all tools and templates used by the PMO, including knowledge capture and reuse, tool expertise, PM mentoring services, and best practice documentation. See Figure 8.1 for a basic PMO structure.

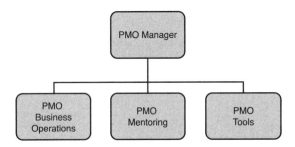

FIGURE 8.1   The project management office structure.

Earlier in this section we talked about the PMO reporting to various units of the organization. The reporting relationship directly impacts how the PMO will operate. In this section we examine the structure through which the SAP PMO reports to the chief information officer (CIO), the chief executive officer (CEO), and individual business units.

Previously in this chapter, we presented PMO organizational report-to relationships. Now, it is time to identify how the SAP PMO fits into the structure. In our experience, the SAP PMO typically reports through the PMO that is attached to the CIO's organization. The SAP projects contained in the SAP PMO portfolio folder will range from technical hardware and infrastructure upgrades, to enhancements to systems interfaced to SAP, to upgrades (for example, from SAP R/3 4.7 to SAP ERP), to SAP functionality enhancement projects.

As you read the following sections, try to identify, based on your project's unique constraints and priorities, the right balance between the benefits and related problems that accompany the various PMO reporting structures that are presented.

PMO Reporting to the CIO

Because we are discussing a large IT/business project, having the PMO report to the CIO (see Figure 8.2) seems like a natural choice. However, an IT-centric PMO presents both pros and cons that need to be considered. Benefits include the fact that infrastructure, data center, configuration, IT change management, and product management and technical requirements gathering all seem to work well when managed from an IT-centric PMO. Challenges include the fact that IT-centric PMOs are great at managing project elements having to do with their home turf but may experience difficulties in communications with the businesses that they serve. A best practice in this regard is to overemphasize business touch points and communications to ensure that the "mouse traps" designed and built (business processes) actually catch the type of mice that the businesses have in mind (that is, serve the business and meet its needs).

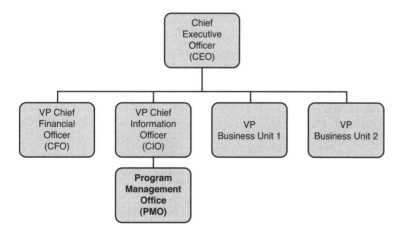

FIGURE 8.2   PMO reporting to the chief information officer.

PMO Reporting to the CEO

A PMO that reports at the executive level (see Figure 8.3) is in a better position than the IT-centric PMO to strike a balance between IT and business concerns. Organizations with PMOs reporting at this level may also tend to classify most temporary activities (that is, activities with a definite start and end) as projects. We usually observe more process rigor in PMOs that are operating at this level, using project management methods to carefully measure projects at the close of the initiating, planning, and executing phases while not being afraid to kill projects that are not delivering desired results. Pharmaceutical companies are good examples of firms that value this type of PMO reporting structure.

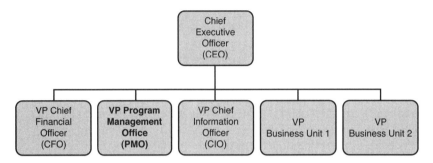

FIGURE 8.3   PMO reporting to the chief executive officer.

PMO Reporting to the Business Units

PMOs typically report to business units (see Figure 8.4) in larger organizations. Projects managed within this type of an organization are more likely to deliver results that are keenly tuned to specific business requirements. However, this type of organization is also more likely to have within multiple business units different applications that all perform the same function, which ultimately drives up the cost of application ownership within the firm.

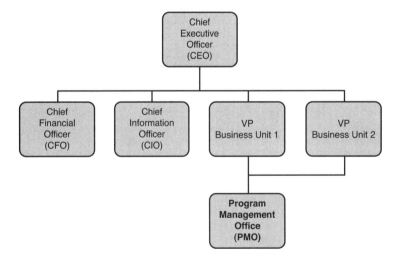

FIGURE 8.4   PMO reporting to the business units.

SAP PMO Project Portfolio Projects

Several types of projects warrant a PMO. Large-scale IT projects with complex resource and timeline requirements are obvious candidates. Any project that can consume not only the firm's resources but require expensive resources outside the firm needs the oversight and direction a PMO provides, too. Consider the following such projects:

▶ Hardware upgrade or technology refresh projects

▶ Other large-scale infrastructure upgrade projects

▶ Interface implementation or enhancement projects

▶ SAP release upgrade projects

▶ Computing platform migration projects (SAP calls these OS/DB migrations)

▶ Improved functionality projects, ranging from incremental functionality enhancements to full ERP system implementations

Developing a PMO Charter

Developing a PMO charter follows a path similar to that of developing the project charter, discussed in Chapter 7, "Project Management Checkpoint 1: Groundwork." The PMO charter contains formal statements that describe the business need for the PMO, formally authorize the PMO, and link the PMO to business sponsorship and the organization. The following elements may be contained in the PMO charter:

▶ **PMO definition and approach**—Describes the PMO, its structure, operating principles, and how the PMO fits into the organization

▶ **PMO/project methodology**—Describes the project and programming methodologies (ASAP, solution manager, and so forth) that will be used

▶ **PMO organizational links**—Describes how the PMO contacts its customers and stakeholders within the organization

▶ **Roles and responsibilities**—Describes PMO roles and may include job descriptions

▶ **PMO standards and procedures**—Provides a high-level listing of PMO operating principles and processes

▶ **Issue management/escalation management**—Describes issue management and escalation management processes and escalation paths at a high level

Measuring PMO Effectiveness

Measuring the effectiveness of PMO processes is part of establishing and managing the PMO. The IT Governance Institute (ITGI) established a governance maturity model (shown in Figure 8.5) useful for PMOs, project managers, CIOs, IT directors, and others tasked with bringing IT projects to fruition. A combination of a framework and an approach, ITGI's Control Objectives for Information and related Technology (CobiT) focuses on strategic alignment, value delivery, resource management, risk management, and performance measurement (see http://www.isaca.org to read more about CobiT and its parent organization). Use the model, which was developed specifically for IT process management, to report on the current state of process acceptance and to set goals for future process acceptance. In doing so, this model will enable an organization to identify its level of achievement relative to PMO process excellence.

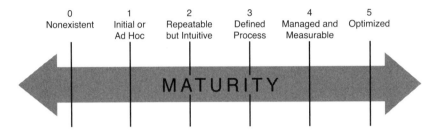

FIGURE 8.5   The IT governance maturity model may be used to measure the extent to which processes are utilized well within the PMO.

Staffing the PMO

Now that we've considered how the PMO fits into the organization, we will focus on PMO staffing considerations. First, we discuss PMO roles generally. Then, we examine how we would assemble a PMO team. We close the discussion by connecting the PMO to the organization.

PMO Roles

Let's begin the PMO role discussion by defining the roles and duties typical of a PMO tasked with managing a significant SAP project:

- **PMO manager**—Responsible for the PMO organization, PMO stakeholder management, providing guidance and thought leadership to the PMO team, staffing, maintaining job descriptions, maintaining budgets, conducting performance reviews, providing career path guidance for PMO members, and managing customer expectations.

- **PMO process/operations manager**—Responsible for establishing and managing the PMO process stack that covers day-to-day PMO operations, and for processes that govern portfolio oversight, cost management and control, schedule management and control, and project support processes.

- **Tools/process manager**—Responsible for maintaining expert-level knowledge of the PMO/project management tool set.

- **Project management mentor**—Responsible for providing mentoring support to the PM community to ensure adherence to a consistent set of project and program management processes. This role is typically responsible for onboarding newly hired project managers into the organization.

▶ **Administrative support**—Responsible for coordinating project manager activities, establishing meeting and conference call schedules, publishing reports or otherwise communicating PMO outcomes, making travel arrangements, acting as the first line of customer relations for the PMO, and performing similar administrative and organization-related tasks.

Remember to staff the PMO to support the functional and organizational requirements, which includes considering provisions for professional advancement by providing a clear career path that includes concise short- and long-term objectives for PMO members.

Assembling the PMO Team

Establishing a PMO within your organization requires a wide range of organizational, operational, program management, and project management skills. Assume for this discussion that you are standing up a new PMO organization. You need to consider the following decisions when evaluating and selecting PMO members:

▶ **Internal promotion**—Spreads a positive message within the organization by providing to employees career advancement or lateral transfer opportunities. Advantage: internal promotion/lateral transfer candidates are already well versed in company culture and practices.

▶ **New hires**—Bring with them experiences gained from working in different company environments and possess skills that augment and expand PMO capabilities. New hires provide a fresh perspective to your PMO organization and practices but need to invest the time required to learn about the organization.

▶ **Project management tool experts**—Important to the PMO and PM community from a tool support perspective. For example, although Microsoft Project might work fairly well out of the box, the PMO must possess master-level competency with this tool and provide guidance to the project manager community regarding how the tool is used today and in the future.

Linking the PMO to the Organization

Let's consider key organizational connections between the PMO and the business organization that is served by the PMO. Identifying PMO customers, links to stakeholders, and links to your management team will help to ensure that the PMO supports your company's goals and objectives.

▶ **Linking to PMO customers**—We cannot overemphasize the importance of maintaining a routine communication cadence with the PMO's customers, including both one- and two-way communication with executive management, IT management, and the business units that use the tools developed by many projects to run their day-to-day business operations. Establishment of newsletters (monthly or quarterly), web pages, and dashboards are all best practices to keep customers informed of PMO activities. It is not unusual to send customer satisfaction surveys periodically to ask your customers to gauge "How are we doing and what can we do to better serve you?"

▸ **Linking to PMO stakeholders**—Stakeholder communication is critical to PMO success; be sure to reach out to all persons, groups, or organizations that are affected by PMO policies, activities or actions. Within the organization, key executives, thought leaders, and informal leaders need to be included in this group. External to the organization, stakeholders may include labor unions, local trade councils, and local government agencies. Consider your own situation to identify stakeholders that might not be mentioned here.

SAP PMO Systems and Tools

Successful SAP implementations number in the tens of thousands and have been supported by many SAP-specific tools and accelerators developed by SAP and a vast number of third parties. It makes good business sense to use proven tools instead of developing your own. At the very least, generic processes, accelerators, and tools need to be tailored for SAP project work. In this section we look at both generic and SAP-specific PMO tools.

Program Management Tools

In the course of planning for and executing an SAP implementation project, good program management tools and people familiar with how to use them are critical to success. Looking through the following listing, you will see some obvious tools, but other items included here might surprise you. The PMO is the keeper not only of the set of project tools, but also of a process stack that clearly describes tool usage and how the PMO's tools fit within the overall program management scheme.

▸ **Project manager on-boarding material**—Introduces new project managers to the organization. Provides company location information, project standards, record keeping guidelines, and access to the PMO tool set.

▸ **Program/project financial management tools**—Enable the PMO to track and describe its project portfolio, project reporting cycle, financial and management tools and accelerators, and supporting processes.

▸ **Time tracking/time management tools**—May include time tracking and time management guidelines, tools, templates, and supporting processes.

▸ **Travel and entertainment expenses tools**—Include applicable company travel and entertainment policy, expense reporting tools/templates, and other tools supporting travel processes.

▸ **Shared team space tools**—Tools that enable the PMO to access and set up a shared team workspace.

▸ **Collaboration tools**—Tools such as Microsoft Communicator and WebEx, telecommunications conference lines, and supporting processes.

▶ **SAP project management methodologies**—Methodologies such as ASAP, Global SAP, ValueSAP, and SAP Solution Manager.

Program Management Templates and Accelerators

The use of centralized templates makes projects more efficient by collapsing repetitive template development tasks, the effect of which standardizes project delivery and removes effort and cost out of your projects. The following list is intended only to get you thinking about this topic. Consider any additional templates and accelerators that make sense for your organization.

▶ **Action, Issue, and Decision Log template**—Describes actions, decisions, status, due dates, follow-up dates, and issue exit criteria

▶ **Risk Log template**—Describes risks, risk events, and risk reserve

▶ **Project organization chart template**—Describes project hierarchy and staff reporting relationships

▶ **Change Request template**—Includes project background information, the specific reason or justification for the change, and a specific description of any cost increase or decrease associated with the change, including dates, resources, locations, and deliverables

▶ **Deliverable acceptance template**—Includes deliverable description, acceptance criteria, and formal project/customer acknowledgment that the deliverable has been completed

▶ **Meeting agenda and minutes template**—Provides a standard form for structuring meeting agendas and minutes

▶ **Project closeout report template**—Includes formal acknowledgment that the project is being closed, that deliverables have been accepted, and that project work papers have been properly archived; also includes project team member and subcontractor evaluations, final financial reports, and release of project team members

▶ **Statement of Work template**—Includes any standard format for providing project background information, scope, scope exclusions, assumptions and dependencies, project schedule (including deliverables and milestones), project organization structure, escalation paths, contract terms and conditions (Ts & Cs) schedule, and project price

SAP Solution Manager

SAP Solution Manager is the successor to the ASAP/ValueSAP methodologies. It contains, for the most part, many of the same tools that will be maintained within the PMO tool set. Solution Manager must be implemented in order for SAP to provide technical support to your company's SAP systems. In addition to solution monitoring, service desk (call center) integration, SAP-specific services and support tools, and change management tools, Solution Manager also contains SAP solution implementation and upgrade project tools.

Of importance to the SAP PMO is the solution implementation and upgrade tool set contained in Solution Manager. Many of the tools that we have been looking at in this section are included, such as project administration, test management, and project repository tools.

SAP's best practice is to utilize to the fullest extent possible the Solution Manager tool set; however, the decision to fully utilize all Solution Manager tools and processes needs to be made by your firm. We recommend that you take a serious look at Solution Manager functionality by contacting your systems integrator or SAP or by reviewing white papers on this topic.

Oh, by the way, Solution Manager is not a plug-and-play application. Implementing or enhancing Solution Manager functionality is not as simple as loading a stack of program CD-ROMs. Solution Manager systems are not installed on your desktop PC and typically reside on a server in your company's data center. You should plan on opening one or more projects to implement a basic Solution Manager system. Solution Manager is genuinely complex.

> **NOTE**
>
> Although the SAP tools contained in Solution Manager are very powerful, many PMOs believe in maintaining a single project tool set for use on all projects and thus do not allow the use of parallel or specialized SAP-specific project tools. We strongly recommend that you use SAP-specific project tools and accelerators for all of your SAP projects. This is a best practice!

Summary

Building on some basic concepts that were presented in Chapter 7, in this chapter we presented PMO basics, discussed the role of the PMO within the organization, and discussed program management systems and tools. We closed the chapter with a closer look at SAP Solution Manager. The subsequent project management chapters look at SAP project management and SAP project staffing in depth.

Case Study: Structuring the PMO

You are working for HiTech, a large, multidivision company operating around the globe. A PMO structure is in place that has the reputation of delivering solutions that are cost effective but usually do not satisfy all of the solution requirements originally articulated by the business. While HiTech's plan is to replace their legacy non-SAP system with SAP ERP, they realize that their PMO issues need to be resolved first.

Questions

1. What type of PMO structure is likely to already be in place?

2. What type of PMO structure might be a better solution to better satisfy business requirements?

3. What are the four steps recommended to create a PMO?

4. Your firm has chosen SAP to replace its ERP system. You are in the middle of the implementation's planning phase and have heard that SAP Solution Manager contains tools and accelerators that you would like to use, so you are considering adding Solution Manager to the scope of your project. What should be considered when making this decision?

NOTE

The answers to these questions may be found in Appendix A, "Case Study Answers."

SAP Project Management

The contents of this chapter begin where Chapter 7 leaves off. Recall that Chapter 7 addressed generic project management topics that are readily applied to all projects and begins to introduce SAP project phase names. Chapter 9 presents SAP project phase names, terms, and concepts. Our discussion of SAP project management needs to begin with an introduction to SAP project phase names and high-level definitions. It is encouraging to note that the SAP project management methodology described in this chapter is a tried and true process that has been used to successfully implement SAP in tens of thousands of firms. Please note that the SAP project phase names differ from the generally accepted project management process and phase definitions previously discussed in this book. We will spend some time at the end of this chapter mapping SAP project phases to the generally accepted project processes.

In previous chapters, we have presented basic project management and program management office (PMO) topics. In this chapter we build upon these concepts and apply them to SAP project management. In addition to reading the material in this chapter, we suggest that you access the Value SAP, ASAP, and Solution Manager materials at the SAP Service Marketplace website (http://www.service.sap.com).

The Five Phases of SAP Project Management

The SAP project management methodology lifecycle has been split up into five phases. Key SAP activities and milestones are described within each phase and are supported by

SAP-specific tools and accelerators that may be used to move the SAP project along. What SAP does *not* provide is a full suite of standard project management tools and processes. We recommend that you combine the SAP-specific methodology's materials and tools with the processes that are described in the initiating, planning, executing, monitoring and controlling, and closing project processes previously discussed in Chapter 7, "Project Management Checkpoint 1." The names and high-level descriptions of the SAP project organizational elements that were introduced in Chapter 2 follow:

- ▶ **Project Preparation phase**—Describes all activities that must occur prior to project kickoff.

- ▶ **Business Blueprint phase**—Develops a specification for required SAP functionality, and reports enhancements and interfaces, SAP organizational structure, and, most importantly, how SAP fits into your company's organizational structure.

- ▶ **Realization phase**—Describes the steps and processes that are followed to enable the functionality described in the Business Blueprint phase. This is also the phase during which your data load and data migration team scrubs legacy and source system data, and develops individual data load tools.

- ▶ **Final Preparation phase**—Describes the steps and processes that are followed to make the business organization and SAP production system ready for go-live. This phase includes delivering end-user training, developing detailed system cutover plans, which include conducting technical make-ready tasks such as backup, restore, and disaster-recovery procedures, cutover dress rehearsals, and final data and open transaction loads.

- ▶ **Go-Live and Support phase**—Describes the steps and processes that turn over the system to steady-state support functions such as data center operations, end-user help desk support team, and application support. This phase also includes formal project closure and sign-off.

Each of these phases is discussed in more depth later in this chapter, in the section "The SAP Project Plan."

In parallel with navigating through the five SAP project phases, it is important that you never lose sight of managing the business implementation. After all, it is the desired new business functionality found in SAP that reflects the real purpose of the SAP project in the first place. We take a closer look at managing the business or functional implementation next.

Managing the Business Implementation

Sometimes referred to as the functional side of an SAP implementation, the business implementation is the portion of your project that connects SAP functionality with the business and describes how SAP will be used to interact with your project's customers. Most of the SAP project activities that have been described in this chapter have revolved around the business and functional side of an SAP implementation.

Some of the key issues that need to be managed on the business implementation side include scope management and stakeholder management and business expectations.

Managing Scope

We witnessed the following hypothetical scope management scenario unfold during most SAP implementation projects.

During the Business Blueprint phase of your project, business process subject matter experts (SMEs) and SAP functionality experts attended workshops whose sole purpose was to determine what functionality/business processes would be supported in your new SAP system. The final delivered system is described in the Business Blueprint document (BBP), which is the key system specification deliverable produced by the Business Blueprint phase. In the following Realization phase, SAP business process experts are configuring the system that you described in the Business Blueprint document. While this is happening, members of the business process and end-user community, like kids in a candy store, are becoming aware of the additional SAP functionality that they would *like* to see turned on. If the new functionality is required to support a process that was inadvertently skipped during the Business Blueprint phase, the change in scope must be documented and agreed upon (sometimes a contract change is required here) before the functionality is turned on.

It is up to the project manager, steering committee, and executive stakeholders to manage changes to project scope.

One way to mitigate scope creep is to record additional "nice to have" functionality as project issues with the intent that the open issues will be considered for implementation following the closure of the current project. Practically speaking, it is highly likely that changes will be made to project scope and that contingency plans and funding needs to be available to accommodate necessary scope change activities during the initiating and planning phases of the project.

Managing Business Expectations

Managing business expectations is really synonymous with managing stakeholder communications. That is, maintaining a constant cadence of project shareholder/stakeholder communications is the primary method of managing business expectations. Your organizational change management plan and activities need to address key questions and concerns that will be raised by the business community, such as

▶ How will the use of this new system change the way that I interact with my external and internal customers?

▶ Has my workforce been trained to be ready for the new system?

▶ If I don't like what I see in the new system, can I change it? In other words, how will the new system impact my day-to-day operations?

Satisfactorily addressing all of these concerns will help the project team gain business acceptance of the new system.

Managing the Technical Implementation

From a project management perspective, the technical implementation enables and supports the SAP business processes that are to be provided to an organization. For purposes of this discussion, let's consider the following elements, located within the domain of the technical team, that might need to be in place beneath the SAP business process layer: system architecture; SAP environments (sandbox, development, quality assurance, training, and production SAP systems, for example); configuration transport management; data conversion; Unicode conversion; SAPGUI; SAP NetWeaver portal; roles and security; output devices; input devices; middleware; infrastructure; servers; change management processes; disaster recovery processes; regression testing; and interfaced systems.

The technical team is responsible for key activities during your SAP project with key dependencies on functional team tasks. To keep your project on track, active communication and collaboration between the technical lead and the project's functional/business process leads is required. Some key activity/dependencies are interface availability, transport management, system landscape, conversion programs, interface testing, the entire Final Preparation phase, and, finally, cutover.

From a project management perspective, the key technical team activities that need to be closely monitored are high-risk activities that occur within finite change windows. A good example of this type of activity would be a requirement to perform all production system data conversions within a 14-hour change window. Risk Mitigation strategy: Prior to attempting this type of activity in the production system, the technical team would perform multiple data conversion simulations in a similar environment to validate that completion of the activity was achievable within the prescribed change window.

The SAP Project Plan

The SAP project plan that we will be examining in this section is one of the components of the project management plan that was discussed in Chapter 7. The SAP project plan is usually stated in a detailed work breakdown structure (WBS), which includes the detailed tasks, activities, and milestones that are required to deliver the system described in your project management plan. Starting with the SAP ECC 5.0 release, the WBS is located in SAP Solution Manager.

Let's begin our discussion of SAP project plans with an examination of the high-level activities included in the five SAP project lifecycle phases: Project Preparation, Business Blueprint, Realization, Final Preparation, and Go-Live and Support.

Project Preparation Phase

The Project Preparation phase describes all activities that must occur prior to project kickoff and includes initial project planning, establishing project procedures, creating a training plan, formal project kickoff, and project quality management planning. A high-level breakdown of the Project Preparation phase follows.

Initial Project Planning

Initial project planning includes obtaining executive sponsorship and funding and defining high-level project requirements and constraints. Additional activities include creating the requests for proposals (RFP) that will be necessary to solicit and evaluate systems integrators and third-party subcontractor firms that will be needed to support your implementation.

As you will see, there is much to do during the initial project planning phase. An initial investment in the following activities will pay off during the project execution phases:

▸ **Create and disseminate the project charter**—See Chapter 7 for an extended list of project charter factors.

▸ **Review and refine the implementation strategy**—This defines the staffing model that will be used (including whether an onshore, near-shore, or offshore model, or a combination of these, will be used), cutover approaches (big bang/turn everything on at once or sequential rollouts of functionality by geographic location), end-user training strategy, and holistic testing plans.

▸ **Determine the project organizational structure**—The project organizational structure clearly states the chain of command and shows the relative relationships of the executive champion, executive sponsor, steering committee, your firm's and third-parties' project managers, your firm's business representatives, the SAP technical team, the SAP functional consultant team, the end-user training team, your firm's business process experts, and interface and bolt-on program SMEs. We recommend that you define escalation paths that will be used to resolve issues and make business decisions when needed by the project.

▸ **Develop the project plan**—The project plan is a formal, approved document used to manage project execution and addresses the following: project start date, design, design freeze, customer sign-off, testing, project end date, project management framework, post-close review, training, risk management, and change management.

▸ **Establish the project schedule**—During the Project Preparation phase, the project schedule includes milestones, respective completion dates, and project phase start and end dates. This schedule is the beginning of your project's detailed WBS and is typically contained in a Microsoft Project plan. The project schedule lists planned dates for performing activities that support meeting the milestones that have been identified in the project plan.

▸ **Address the basics of a data conversion approach**—It is never too early to begin preparing your overall data conversion approach by documenting the data conversion tools that will be used, data locations, and the types of data that need to be converted/included in your new system (customer master, material master, purchasing, production/engineering, assets, and financial records).

▸ **Develop a business acceptance approach**—This includes a high-level description of the approach that will be used to validate the SAP system's readiness for cutover/go-live. Your business acceptance approach will have a direct impact on your testing approach and testing tool selection.

▶ **Define a system landscape strategy**—Determine the number of sandbox, development, quality assurance, training, and production systems that are required to support your implementation. System landscape decisions are also tied to server/infrastructure expenditures, data replication strategies, and training system refresh cycles.

▶ **Set up the development system environment**—Planning and setting up your development system needs to be considered at this stage. In fact, you probably should begin this task early in the planning stage because of the lead times associated with obtaining new hardware and SAP licenses, the goal being to have the development system available early in the Business Blueprint phase of the project.

▶ **Create a basic support approach**—Now is also a good time to begin thinking about how your firm will support the steady-state technical environment and help desk function by defining your approach to online help, help desk system requirements, support staff physical locations, and support staff training requirements.

▶ **Create the project's quality management approach**—Quality management is a topic that is often overlooked. Document the overall approach by discussing the following: How will project quality be measured? What constitutes an adequate quality audit frequency? How will quality reporting be addressed? Will formal auditing be required? Will quality standards be consistent across all businesses that the SAP project is supporting?

▶ **Closure of the Project Preparation phase**—To close this phase, you conduct the documented phase sign-off process as described in your project management plan.

> **NOTE**
>
> When examining an SAP-supplied work breakdown structure (WBS), keep in mind that you are viewing a high-level, detailed task list, not all the detailed tasks that must be successfully executed to stand up your SAP system. You need to add a fair amount of additional content to completely define all of the lower-level tasks and activities.

Establishing Project Procedures

Establishing project procedures consists of the following:

▶ **Define project management standards and procedures**—This includes standards and procedures for such things as time tracking, expense reporting and approval, status reporting, instructions explaining the proper use of forms and templates, and document storage and archiving standards.

▶ **Define implementation standards and procedures**—SAP-specific implementation standards, guidelines, and procedures need to be developed for the following objects: Business Blueprint Document, requirements traceability matrix, configuration documentation, business process design, business scenarios, test scripts, and project deliverable acceptance criteria. Be sure to add detailed activities and deliverables to your project plan for each standards/procedures object that needs to be developed. Also, do not forget to include team training/communication activities in your detailed plan. If you are acting as your own general contractor on this project, you are responsible for pulling this material together. If you are working with a systems integrator partner, the systems integrator will probably have all of this material contained within their project methodology.

▶ **Establish standards and organization**—Conduct a project team standards meeting and communicate the project organization. You need to decide whether standards and project organization are communicated at this time versus during your project kickoff meeting. We recommend that you pass this information to your core team prior to the formal project kickoff meeting.

Creating Training Plans

Creating training plans consists of the following activities:

▶ **Create the project team training plan**—Consider project team background, SAP skills and knowledge, and training gaps that can be satisfied by SAP-sponsored classroom training. It is possible to bring SAP instructors in-house to conduct this training for large groups of individuals.

▶ **Conduct project team (level 1) training**—Training activities of this type need to be scheduled and completed well in advance of the Business Blueprint and Realization phases. The goal of this training is to provide an SAP introduction to members of your in-house project team and is not typically intended to develop the expertise to customize the system. You will be relying on your implementation team's experienced SAP functional and technical consultants to lead system setup, administration, and customization efforts.

▶ **Define end-user training and documentation strategy**—End-user training needs to be considered at this point in time because of the long lead times associated with locating training partners to develop training materials and establishing strategies to deliver training to your end-user community. Some of the tasks in this area include conducting an end-user training needs assessment, selecting end-user training and training document delivery tools, defining SAP training environment requirements, and conducting a course developer's workshop for the individuals who will be writing the training materials. Be sure to include a fair amount of contingency timing in your training plan schedule. It is not uncommon for projects to collapse or reduce training activities to make room for project elements that have fallen behind schedule.

Project Kickoff

Project kickoff consists of the following tasks:

▶ **Organize the project kickoff materials**—Providing high-quality project kickoff materials is very important because, in many cases, they will be your audience's first exposure to project details. This is your first chance to demonstrate executive support for the initiative, set shareholder expectations, provide high-level scope and schedule, and explain the how, where, when, who, and why of your project to a broad audience. It is becoming common practice to prepare executive video or audio messages that can be repeated in subsequent kickoff sessions. The project kickoff materials will also become part of your project on-boarding packet to be presented to team members during the life of your project.

▸ **Organize the project kickoff event**—All the logistical elements that you would normally consider to organize a large business meeting need to be addressed: conference space, presentation materials, telephone dial-in numbers, and real-time collaboration tools (such as WebEx) need to be provided to support the kickoff event. Collaboration tools are becoming more and more important because most project teams are located in multiple locations and time zones. Many project teams conduct multiple kickoff meetings to accommodate teams that are working in different geographic locations and time zones. You may choose to record your project kickoff and make the recording available to anyone who misses the live meetings. Now is a good time to reach out to your company's communication professionals to request that they provide communication and meeting facilitation expertise. Some companies conduct project kickoff meetings at offsite locations, which helps to convey the overall importance of the initiative and helps to focus the entire team on the project without outside interruptions. (No cell phones or laptops allowed!)

▸ **Conduct the project kickoff meeting**—It is important that the project kickoff meeting event be run in a professional manner. Start by presenting a meeting agenda with a time schedule for each segment of the meeting, and then adhere to the schedule. You need to decide where question and answer segments fit into your agenda, record any meeting parking lot items (unresolved issues) that arise during the meeting, and, most importantly, follow up with answers to those parking lot items. Bear in mind that the individuals attending the kickoff meeting will probably be overwhelmed by the sheer volume of material that needs to be presented.

TIP

Deciding where the project document or knowledge repository will be located is important. It is highly likely that your SAP implementation will be resourced with third-party specialists in addition to specialists from within your own organization. Consider the systems that need to be available to the third-party firms who will be participating in your project, and place the knowledge/project repository in a location that can be readily accessed by all data users/team members. Do you plan to locate this repository within your firewall? This makes sense in an environment in which all local and remote team members have firewall access, such as in a firm that provides all team members with company workstations or laptops. In our experience, your project will suffer avoidable data access–related delays if all team members do not have access to the same information and working papers. Bottom line: providing an accessible, firewall-independent knowledge repository is a best practice.

Business Blueprint Phase

The Business Blueprint document describes required SAP functionality, business process definition, customization specification, reports, enhancements and interfaces, organizational structure, and, most importantly, how SAP fits into *your* company's organizational structure and business processes. A common myth is that the Business Blueprint phase is all about preparing the Business Blueprint document. Although preparing the BBP document is a major portion of the work, the following activities are also included in this phase.

- **Address organizational change management**—This needs to be addressed no matter what type of SAP project you are undertaking. In many cases, an SAP implementation will impact the day-to-day jobs of business end users. Unfortunately, many projects fail to conduct effective organizational change management activities, the result of which is that, whereas the IT side of the implementation may go flawlessly, the organizational/business side of the implementation receives poor marks because the business and/or end users were not adequately prepared to operate in the new environment. We recommend a steady cadence of organizational change management activities, beginning with a solid communication plan that is followed up by job reengineering activities and workshops.

- **Conduct technical design planning**—Includes activities that establish the quality assurance, training, and production environments and related infrastructure that were started during the Project Preparation phase of the project.

- **Stand up the development system environment**—The development system planned during the Project Preparation phase needs to be "stood up" (installed) during the Business Blueprint phase and be ready to support the Realization phase when it begins.

- **Design the training plan**—A training plan reflecting the approach that you defined during the Project Preparation phase needs to be devised. Now is also the time to staff and kick off a parallel training project that supports your implementation.

- **Define the SAP organizational structure**—The organizational structure represents a key input for workshops that will be held during the Business Blueprint phase. Expert advice is required during and after the workshops, to ensure that the SAP system that is delivered supports your company's organizational, financial, and cost accounting goals and objectives.

- **Tend to business process definition**—occurs during and after workshops that are conducted during this project phase. The to-be business processes that are defined will become an important element of your Business Blueprint document.

- **Provide RICEF object definition**—With regard to reports, interfaces, conversions, enhancements, and forms, provide the important inputs used to create individual design documents for the SAP system being implemented. Object definition serves as another key output of the workshops that are being held during this period.

- **Initiate the user roles/authorization subproject**—KEY inputs to your user role and authorization scheme will come from your company's internal controls and audit function. This can be a complex set of tasks for new SAP environments and is therefore often viewed as a separate project or subproject of a new implementation.

▶ **Validate initial scope**—Document and verify that the project's scope is agreed upon, and be ready to capture and obtain approval for any changes to the project's scope or schedule (by way of change requests and change orders).

▶ **Share lessons learned**—Capture and disseminate lessons learned, being careful to also share initial assumptions that might have changed and how the implementation team reacted to those changes.

▶ **Create the BBP document**—The BBP describes the SAP organizational structure, RICEF objects, and business processes that will be delivered during the Realization phase. The BBP document is also a key input into any organizational change management activities that will be occurring throughout the life of your project.

▶ **Execute the closure of the Business Blueprint phase**—Conduct the documented phase sign-off process as described in your project management plan.

This is only a partial list; don't lose sight of all the activities that need to be performed and coordinated during the Business Blueprint phase. Although it is possible to slide by with a "meets minimum" approach to completing several of the previously mentioned activities, you do so at your own peril. In our experience, completely addressing all items increases the likelihood of a successful SAP implementation.

Realization Phase

The Realization phase describes the steps and processes that are followed to enable the functionality described in the BBP and includes establishing the system described in the BBP; expanding the technical infrastructure; preparation of the quality, training, and production systems; developing end-user training materials; coordinating activities across a team composed of your firm's business specialists: SAP specialists; and a systems integrator partner (if you chose one). It also possibly will include resources from several third-party firms specializing in various aspects of SAP implementations. It is probable that the Realization phase of an SAP project will contain more moving parts that need to be managed than any other project that has been undertaken by your firm, and it is of utmost importance that solid project management and communication processes are in place to enable proactive management of all project activities.

The following is a list of Realization phase activities. You will discover that many activities build on the approach and materials that were previously developed during the Project Preparation phase.

▶ **Execute organizational change management processes**—These activities should be in full swing during this phase. Be sure to include all levels of management in your communications.

▶ **Create training materials**—It is normal to create training materials as system functionality is validated during the waves of system integration testing. Your goal is to complete all training materials by the end of system integration testing.

▶ **Perform baseline configuration and validation**—This consists of enabling the SAP functionality that supports the processes you have described in your BBP document followed by validation and system integration testing signoff. It also includes delivering configuration control documentation that describes SAP customization settings.

▸ **Develop a unit testing plan**—This is the plan that describes how unit testing will be carried out, including the scope, processes, systems to be tested, tools, tracking and reporting, and supporting documentation.

▸ **Establish quality assurance and production environments**—Server, software, and infrastructure make-ready activities must be performed and completed to support the Realization phase.

▸ **Validate configuration**—Conduct unit testing and system integration testing to validate that system configuration satisfies BBP process requirements.

▸ **Conduct end-user training**—At this point, end-user training should be in full swing. Although most of this work is usually performed by a separate team, you should plan on training material validation tying up some core team resources at a time when you would like to see them 100% focused on the Realization phase.

▸ **Create and update end-user procedures and role descriptions**—These activities are closely linked to organizational change management efforts and probably will involve the efforts of your firm's internal control and audit functions.

▸ **Manage ABAP and custom code development**—Many projects use a combination of onsite, near-shore, and offshore resources to perform this function. The logistics issues involved with coordinating the efforts of teams who could be working on different continents must be considered.

▸ **Develop RICEF objects**—There can be a great deal of work involved with this tasks, depending on your environment. A plan to address the need for SAP "bolt-on" programs, such as sales tax calculation software, is also included in this group.

▸ **Conduct the final integration test**—Many SAP projects choose to perform multiple rounds of integration and validation testing, with the first round of testing led by the SAP consultants/integration partner personnel, followed by a handoff of testing responsibilities to the firm's project team members and, ultimately, key end users. By this time in your project, your key end users will have been trained and be able to perform integration test activities. In some environments, your internal controls/audit function will also be participating in integration testing.

▸ **Conduct business acceptance testing**—Whereas final integration testing validates that the system is performing as described in the BBP, business acceptance testing validates that the system will work using real materials, customers, vendors, and banks. This proves that the realized SAP system will in fact be able to support all business activities immediately following system cutover. In other words, business acceptance testing proves that you are ready to run the business within the new SAP environment. Successful completion and sign-off of business acceptance testing is a prerequisite to the go/no go decision that will occur prior to system cutover.

▶ **Perform knowledge capture**—Before releasing any team members from the project team, be sure that all outstanding requirements for documentation have been met. House this knowledge in the project's knowledge repository.

Final Preparation Phase

The Final Preparation phase describes the steps and processes that are followed to make the organization and production system ready for go-live and include delivering end-user training; conducting technical make-ready tasks such as regression testing; establishing and updating production system change management; backup, restore, and disaster recovery procedures; final data and open transaction loads; establishing connectivity to interfaced systems; and executing detailed system cutover plans within the agreed-upon change window. Typically, at this time we would have already locked down system functionality and would be in the process of completing all activities in support of go-live. It is extremely important that you conduct "enough" cycles of production cutover simulations to minimize the risk during production cutover. Final preparation comprises the following:

▶ **Complete delivery of any remaining end-user training**—Be sure to fill in the gaps and ensure that business users who might have missed training opportunities in the past (due to sick time, shift rotation, and so on) attend training prior to go-live.

▶ **Establish and implement a systems management strategy**—This includes establishing systems operations support, installing and configuring tools to manage and monitor the technology stack, and so on.

▶ **Conduct technical testing**—Verify system administration procedures, backup and restore procedures, printing and fax tests, systems failure scenario testing, and disaster recovery testing.

▶ **Conduct infrastructure and load testing**—This includes volume and stress testing as well as performance testing, covered in greater detail in Chapter 32, "SAP Infrastructure and Platform Testing," and Chapter 33, "SAP Load and Stress Testing."

▶ **Perform mock cutover activities**—Move transports, perform trail data conversions, and perform manual entries. The goal here is to perform enough rounds of mock cutovers to mitigate cutover risks, ensuring that all the bugs have been worked out of the process and that the production cutover will be performed routinely.

▶ **Perform cutover activities**—Move all transports, perform conversions, and perform manual entries. Obtain final approval for go-live by confirming production readiness and verifying that all users are ready to run the business and the SAP environment. It is normal for all hands to be on deck in support of cutover and go-live.

▶ **Execute your production support plan**—Cut over to your help desk, reorganize the SAP TSO to focus on production support, and begin supporting steady-state system operations.

Providing outbound project status communications to all stakeholders is extremely important at this time so that all interested parties have a clear understanding of the schedule and what they, and their organizations, can expect on the first day following successful cutover. Best practice dictates overcommunicating with stakeholders during this period.

Go-Live and Support Phase

The Go-Live and Support phase describes the steps and processes that turn over the system to steady-state support functions such as data center operations, help desk, and first- and second-level steady-state application support. It is normal for most consulting and implementation partner resources to roll off during this period after providing support through one- or two-month end close cycles. This is your last opportunity to conduct knowledge transfer activities before the implementation team is released from the project. This phase also includes final performance evaluations of all employees who participated in the project and formal project closure/sign-off.

Mapping SAP Project Phases to PMI Process Groups

At this point, you might be wondering what the relationship is between SAP project phases and the project management processes that were discussed in Chapter 7. As you might recall, the SAP project phases are used to describe the structure that organizes a complex list of activities into manageable blocks. Within the SAP project phase structure, the project management process groups describe processes that support your project activities (refer to Figure 9.1). Upon examination, you will realize that elements of the initiating, planning, executing, monitoring and controlling, and closing processes mentioned in Chapter 7 are at work within each SAP project phase.

Key takeaway: SAP does a great job of describing project activities, and the Project Management Institute does a great job of describing the project process stack. Successful SAP project execution is realized by performing all activities listed within your project plan, supported by the rigorous execution of the initiating, planning, executing, monitoring and controlling, and closing processes.

Developing Project Management Discipline

Perhaps a better title for this section would be *consistent and rigorous* project management makes all the difference. Given that most project managers are typically A-type personalities who naturally gravitate toward being in complete control of their environments, and considering the fact that most project managers who have been around a while have already developed their own personal set of tools, we encourage your firm to develop a centralized repository of tools, templates, and processes. This repository should be consistently used by all project managers within your firm's PMO or PM community. Bolster this repository with your firm's unique project management processes, materials, and lessons learned. You also might want to include tools and project organization advice from PMI (locate PMI resources at http://www.pmi.org) and SAP as well in your repository.

With your repository in order, we challenge you to next examine current project management behaviors within your organization. Look for opportunities where project management process changes will yield significant improvements to the way in which you manage and execute projects. For example, review the five project process groups that

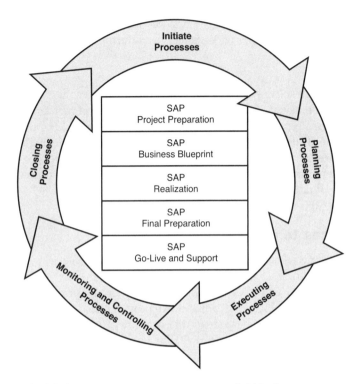

FIGURE 9.1   Project processes map to all SAP phases.

were examined in Chapter 7, compare the processes to the project management process stack that is currently being used within your firm, and ask yourself, "What changes could be implemented that will propel the project management discipline within my firm to the next level?"

In our experience, changes to the process stack yield the biggest bang for your buck. An example of a process change or investment that can pay off is the implementation of several ratio management tools—schedule performance index (SPI) or cost performance index (CPI) project management tools—to use key ratios that are calculated by using cost and schedule information from your project plans to better manage schedule performance and cost performance to plan for all projects within your portfolio.

Additionally, the same microscope that you applied to your project process stack needs to be focused on your SAP-specific project practices to identify key gaps in the way you handle SAP projects. Following gap analysis, you may choose to establish action plans for improvements within your organization. An aggressive program focused on identifying key changes to the established way of doing things can give your company a strategic advantage over your competition. Consider not only areas in which you can collapse cost, but also areas in which an investment in new tools for process improvements is required to move you to the next level. A good example of an additional tool investment that can pay off is to adopt an SAP enterprisewide test management system (such as HP Quality Center) that would establish standard scenarios and templates to be used in current and future SAP implementations and upgrades. In this case, the investment would be in purchasing and learning how to use test management tools and establishing templates and processes that will support your current project and collapse time out of the testing cycle for future projects.

Leveraging Lessons Learned

The goals of recording lessons learned information are to plan for and potentially avoid negative project experiences and, more importantly, to share positive project experiences with those who will follow in our footsteps. The volume of project information that is captured and reused can be correlated to reducing effort and cost in future projects.

Changing the way in which your firm leverages lessons learned is one possible break-through behavior change. Many project teams tend to celebrate completion of significant project milestones and, usually due to time constraints, move on to the next project activity without adequately capturing lessons learned. Although it is likely that the project team collaborated with the firm during the course of project execution, it is probable that the lessons learned information is restricted to the individuals who participated in the project. Consequently, much of this valuable information will be lost to the firm as project team members move on to other roles or leave your company.

How often within your organization do you conduct formal "lessons learned" sessions as projects progress from one phase to another? It is a best practice to conduct lessons learned sessions upon completion of any project phase, and most definitely during the final project close before team members are released for other activities.

If you do conduct lessons learned sessions, how do you make the harvested intellectual property available for reuse? Again, best practice is to make the gathered information available to those who need to know in the future. Many firms establish a central repository that contains lessons learned and frequently asked questions material. Some firms have established an internal SAP Center of Excellence (COE) that is responsible for disseminating this type of information to your internal SAP community. The information is then made available to all the SMEs within the SAP community and to any third parties who are engaged for future project work within your SAP environment.

Your competitors might decide that they cannot afford to organize a formal intellectual property/reuse effort. That is a very compelling reason for you to make a breakthrough investment and reap the rewards that will follow!

Summary

We have taken a trip through SAP project management in this chapter, including a look at managing the business implementation, managing the technical implementation, structuring SAP project plans, describing project management processes, and leveraging lessons learned.

Case Study: Planning for an SAP Upgrade

Your employer, HiTech Inc, has asked you to plan an ERP 6.0 upgrade for one of your SAP systems. The following questions touch upon staffing a technical upgrade, understanding BBP contents, and identifying several approaches to systems integration testing and business acceptance testing.

Questions

1. You have heard this upgrade described by HiTech's SAP Technical Support Organization (TSO) as a technical upgrade. Will SAP functional resources (sales, distribution, logistics, and finance) be required to support your project?

2. What Final Preparation phase activities can be skipped during the production cutover of a technical upgrade project?

3. How many rounds of system integration tests and business acceptance tests are required in a typical SAP project?

NOTE

The answers to these questions can be found in Appendix A, "Case Study Answers."

CHAPTER 10

No Implementation Is an Island: Partners Required

Implementing SAP is nearly impossible without a significant amount of help. The reason should be fairly obvious—complex business, technology, and large-scale project management challenges cannot be addressed by anything but a team characterized as both broad-based and deeply experienced. In this chapter, we take a look at the different types of partners called for in an SAP project, including the RFI and RFP processes, how to select partners, and the pros and cons of employee training versus bringing in consultants and other contractors.

Overview of Prospective SAP Partners

The vast majority of firms who are implementing their first SAP system (or upgrading an existing one) choose to hire an SAP partner to help them with their implementation. Many SAP partners are among the top names in the IT services industry and either offer a comprehensive set of SAP services or specialize in a particular industry or SAP application. Because of the complexity of the overall system to be implemented, and the fact that so many firms simply don't have the requisite exposure to SAP technology, methodologies, and development, choosing an SAP-certified partner is necessary to realize a successful on-time, on-budget SAP project.

Fortunately, the overall business application and IT consulting marketplace has many qualified partners who are certified by SAP to implement its enterprise solutions. These partners fiercely compete for the right to earn a firm's business. They *want* to help your organization implement a business-critical system built on SAP technology if only because of the money. SAP implementations run into millions and millions of dollars in consulting; even the smallest of SAP implementations will quickly consume a $5–$10 million budget, while the largest, multicomponent SAP implementations exceed well over $100 million.

No worries, though. The SAP partner ecosphere is chock-full of capable partners. These partners typically have deep experience implementing SAP projects for firms and have customer references from past projects that you may evaluate as part of the partner selection process. Other partners might have less experience but possess the specific industry expertise (such as healthcare or oil and gas) that tips a consulting partnership decision in their favor. Still other partners may bring unique business application or technology expertise to a project, therefore making them indispensable to new-component implementations (such as the need for Java expertise with the latest SAP NetWeaver Portal deployments). Given all this diversity, it should come as no surprise that SAP partners are divided into three general categories based on their focus areas or areas of expertise:

▶ SAP business and application partners

▶ SAP technical partners

▶ SAP project management partners

Does the list look familiar? It should—the primary SAP partner types parallel our multi-lane implementation roadmap weaving its way through this book. In the remainder of this chapter we'll discuss each of these types of SAP partners and how they can stand alone or come together to pull off a successful SAP project (see Figure 10.1). Along the way, we will take a closer look at how each type of SAP partner participates to ensure a successful implementation of an SAP system.

SAP Business and Application Partners

SAP business partners, often referred to as application consultants or business consultants, focus on specific applications and industry segments. They bring industry and application experience to an engagement to facilitate the mapping of a customer's processes to an SAP system. Often, they will have seen similar business processes or application solutions implemented elsewhere and can provide insight on best practices for applying a functional solution to a business problem (relative to SAP's specific application's capabilities). This may include developing detailed design requirements and implementing customizations to the application through the Java and ABAP programming interfaces. See Figure 10.2 for the numerous industry solutions covered by SAP.

Business consultants have industry domain expertise that they can apply to the implementation of your business processes into business requirements for the customization of SAP modules. Typically these consultants are more business focused than technology focused and may have worked in that particular industry at one point in their careers. Examples of application focus and areas of expertise are

▶ Enterprise resource planning (ERP)

▶ Customer relationship management (CRM)

- Supply chain management (SCM)
- Manufacturing systems
- Financial systems
- Human capital management (HCM)

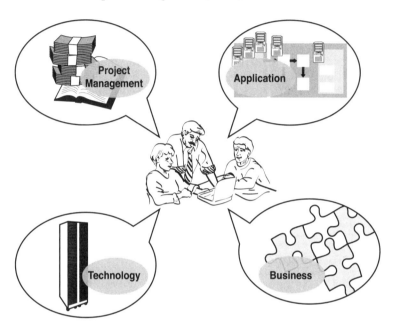

FIGURE 10.1   The SAP partner ecosphere.

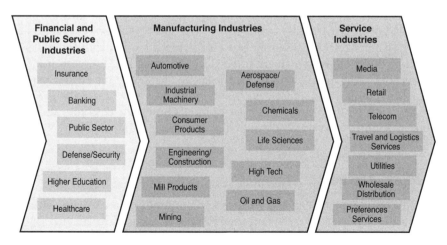

FIGURE 10.2   SAP's industry solutions and areas of focus.

Application consultants have a specific focus area within one of the SAP applications or solution areas. They often have domain expertise on a particular suite of SAP applications such as CRM. Application consultants bring a wealth of knowledge to rapidly prototype or implement design requirements based on the work they have delivered in prior customer engagements of similar size, scope, and complexity.

SAP Technical Partners

SAP technical partners, often referred to as NetWeaver or Basis consultants, focus on systems integration, systems administration, architecture, design, and implementation of an SAP infrastructure. Technical partners typically have expertise in the SAP NetWeaver system architecture components, versus industry or application expertise. Technical partners have broad infrastructure expertise working with the different technology components and platforms that comprise an SAP landscape, including Microsoft Windows, UNIX, and Linux servers, Oracle, DB2, Microsoft SQL Server, and MaxDB database servers, SAP NetWeaver AS Java servers, SAP NetWeaver AS ABAP servers, SAP Central Services, SAP ERP servers, and several other types of servers. Typical areas of expertise for a technology consultant who is SAP Basis Certified are performing system patching, SAP upgrades, migrations to different platforms, performance tuning, and troubleshooting problems with the implementation of SAP on a given platform.

SAP Project Management Partners

SAP project management partners focus on managing the schedule, budget, resources, risk, and deliverables on an SAP implementation. These are project managers who have specific industry and/or application experience with SAP and are able to accurately estimate the scope of deliverables based on prior experience. It is important to have an understanding of the complexity of an SAP system in order to successfully manage it.

As discussed in Chapter 8, "Building the SAP Project Management Office," on larger engagements that span several domains or organizations and last several months, a program management office (PMO) will be established. This is where a project management partner can play a key role, because they possess the breadth and depth to manage the many subprojects that comprise the main project. Larger engagements establish a PMO that is responsible for all deliverables across the entire lifecycle of the engagement and for managing the multiple teams that come on board to deliver their specific pieces of the project. The PMO is oftentimes a shared responsibility between the customer and the partner to ensure that there is accountability and direct visibility into the potential risks that have been identified.

Finding the Right Partner

Your best bet for identifying a qualified SAP partner for your needs on an SAP implementation is to access the SAP website and click on the SAP Ecosystems & Partners link. Figure 10.3 shows the SAP Ecosystem and Partners portal web page (http://www.sap.com/ecosystem/index.epx). Use the Search links in the bottom-right corner of the page to find an SAP service partner for your particular engagement.

FIGURE 10.3   You may search for SAP partners via the SAP Ecosystem and Partners portal web page.

Some excellent SAP services partners to consider are the big IT consulting firms such as Accenture, Capgemini, CSC, Deloitte, EDS/HP, IBM Global Business Services, Infosys, Tata Consultancy Services, and Wipro (along with SAP itself). These SAP partners offer comprehensive consulting services in functional/business, technology, and project management areas.

One thing that you want to look for when evaluating a partner is its track record on prior engagements of similar scope and complexity as yours. Ask potential partners to provide customer references from similar engagements. Also ask them for sample deliverables and sample resumes of their consultants who have done work in a particular area of interest to you for your engagement. When considering which partner to choose, check SAP's website and consider the following selection and evaluation criteria:

▶ **Quality of delivery**—Evaluate the quality of the potential partner's delivery capabilities and ask if its prior SAP engagements have been on time, within budget, and with all requirements completed. These are also questions you can ask of the customer references that the partner provides to you.

▶ **Experience of delivery**—Ask about the caliber and experience of its delivery team within the particular business or functional area for which your project will need some implementation expertise. Make sure that the delivery consultants the partner presents to you are capable of addressing your particular needs. It is not always necessary to have the "A Team" to implement your SAP system. We've heard many organizations in the past express this need to have the partner's best team members assigned to their project. This request usually comes out of a sense of insecurity on the part of the customer, particularly when they don't have a good understanding of the project's scope. Consulting partners are generally very good at weeding out the nonperformers or people who are not competent in a given technology area, but we recommend that you do your homework on vetting the caliber of the team presented to you. By all means, exercise your right to have someone replaced if they don't work out on your implementation team.

▶ **Price range**—Ask what the price range is for the potential partner's consulting services. Ask for a rate sheet on the different tiers of consultants that will potentially be assigned to your SAP project. Also ask whether there are discounts that can be applied.

Other Partners and Vendors

Beyond SAP services partners, there are other partners that you may consider engaging for your SAP system implementation. These include technology and alliance partners, which represent specific platform technologies such as AMD, Cisco, Citrix, EMC, IBM, Intel, HP, Microsoft, Oracle, Red Hat, Sun, and VMware, to name just a few. These vendors represent their different hardware, platform, networking, and storage offerings and can optimize their solution for your particular engagement of SAP technology.

On an SAP engagement, firms often retain the services of their server, storage, and network vendors to implement their technology and ensure that it is configured properly and optimally for their given workload. An example if this would be the setup, configuration, and patching of UNIX servers and SAN storage before the SAP software binaries are installed.

As mentioned earlier in the chapter, you can utilize the SAP Ecosystems and Partners portal to identify specific partners. You may also want to consider working with your account manager representing that particular vendor to engage with their consultants. Bear in mind, many of these consultants representing hardware, storage, and network vendors are pure technologists who are doing this work for firms to ensure that they derive the most value out of the technology the firms have just purchased from the consultant's employer.

Leveling the Playing Field: The RFI

Instead of jumping directly into the SAP business application sizing process by completing several rounds of SAP questionnaires and follow-on sizing documents, many firms choose to author and publish a Request for Information (RFI). We still promote the idea of going through various SAP sizing questionnaires (later, for a number of reasons, including costing), but using an RFI approach can be a lot cleaner method for moving a project along.

Firms often issue an RFI to all potential vendors and consulting partners to gather information about their capabilities. This enables firms to determine how many potential bidders are in the marketplace to deliver services on the implementation of their SAP system. This also serves to level the playing field by identifying other partners beyond an incumbent, making the partner procurement process more competitive and thus less expensive. The RFI itself is an intermediate step in the partner selection process and is not always used. It is often a general description of the system to be implemented and not comprehensive enough to enable potential partners to submit bids. An RFI is most often followed by a Request for Proposal (RFP), discussed in detail in the next section.

Developing a Request for Information

A good RFI takes time to develop on the customer end. It can be as short as 15 to 20 pages or as long as 100 pages (based on the scope of your SAP implementation, the need for legal terms and conditions to be outlined, and more). Your RFI could very well exceed 100 pages if you choose to implement several SAP components or if you employ an ambitious legal department. If you are considering going beyond 20 pages, you should consider issuing an RFP instead (discussed in the next section). An RFI should include or take into account the following:

- ▶ General information, such as your company name and contact information, background data, and why the RFI is being published.

- ▶ Instructions to each potential RFI respondent as to how to complete the RFI, as well as details about the RFI. This includes instructions on how to address questions, details on the proposal process, confidentiality details, any disclaimers, and other administrative details.

- ▶ Terms and conditions, including the scope of the project, payment terms, minimum integration requirements related to existing or legacy systems, and so on.

- ▶ Requirements that must be met by the respondent, including any vendor and account management information you want to capture, the need for other SAP references, details surrounding the pricing model (including leasing versus financing discussions), how to factor in maintenance windows or other planned-downtime windows required of the proposed solution, hardware quotes, requested professional services quotes (for installation, migration of data, training, and so on), and any other information that may help you make a decision (such as each respondent's relationship with SAP, or the various database vendors, or a particular disk subsystem vendor, and so on).

- ▶ Pricing requirements on each proposed product or solution. Inquire whether the vendor is willing to extend a discount level, what the maintenance fees and associated service-level agreements (SLAs) are for each product or solution, and what the warranty period is for any work performed or for specific products provided as part of the solution.

In addition to covering the basics, an RFI normally includes various appendixes that are designed either to share supplemental information about the solution that the customer is seeking to implement, or to enforce a certain type of format for the response. These appendixes might include a template to be used to respond to questions in the RFI. This template may also specify what format (electronic or hardcopy) that the response should be submitted in. For example, organizations often require that we provide an electronic copy along with at least two color hardcopies that need to be submitted by a certain date.

Standardized formatting is often required these days to make it easier and faster for organizations to evaluate the different responses (proposals) that are submitted.

> **NOTE**
>
> The RFI itself is a more abbreviated version of the full-blown RFP that many firms issue for bids on large, complex engagements such as an SAP system implementation. The RFI gives vendors a sample of what's going to be issued later in the RFP.

In our experience, we have found that the kind of information provided in the following seven appendixes is exactly what a potential partner needs to either craft an SAP solution that really meets your needs or to provide you with enough data to make an intelligent decision as to whether that vendor has what it takes to be your partner:

▶ **Existing Equipment Matrix**—Documents what is in place today that must be either replaced by the new system(s) discussed in the RFI, or integrated with these same systems. This may also include a breakdown of existing SAP instances, or other enterprise application installations, that are currently productive. And if a current disk subsystem solution is already in place and expected to be leveraged by the respondent, details must be provided here as well.

▶ **Software to Be Implemented**—In this appendix, the SAP technology stack as you imagine it at this point is shared, including expected versions of each SAP component, database systems, operating system releases, enterprise management packages, and so on.

▶ **Implementation Timetable**—Represents an organization's hard requirements or possibly just a "best guess" as to when the new SAP solution needs to be implemented.

▶ **Reference Form**—Applies to absolutely *all* RFI respondents, though most often is focused on potential hardware, software, and implementation partners.

▶ **Cost Submission Worksheet**—Consists of a standardized worksheet that forces an RFI respondent to price the project *your* way. This allows you to perform true apples-to-apples comparisons after all RFIs have been turned in.

▶ **Staffing Matrix**—Encourages each RFI respondent to consider staffing pre-engagement, during the engagement, and post go-live.

▶ **Sample Agreement with Terms and Conditions**—Allows everyone responding to the RFI to understand up front what kind of legal constraints and financial commitments are expected.

Not all of these appendixes absolutely must be published with your RFI but we highly recommend using them.

An Alternative to the RFI: Iterative Sizing

Some firms either don't have the time or don't have the discipline to go through a formal RFI process. There is no rule that says you must issue an RFI or RFP to select a partner for your SAP system implementation. You may opt instead to work with a preferred partner that you trust and have a prior working relationship with to go through a sizing exercise to define the high-level architecture for your SAP landscape. This is covered in two other chapters in this book.

Whether you elect to publish an RFI or complete a number of SAP sizing questionnaires, all of your hard data and related explanatory reasons for implementing each SAP component in a particular way will be at your fingertips. The ability to share all of this data consistently with all of the prospective hardware and software vendors is important in evaluating potential vendors, because it enables you to perform a more consistent "apples-to-apples" comparison between different vendor's solution approaches later on in the selection process. Further, as new information comes to light, or questions are posed by these prospective vendors, the knowledge repository (outlined in Chapter 6, "Managing Knowledge and the Knowledge Repository") will naturally lend itself to collecting and managing this incremental data of evolving constraints, assumptions, requirements, needs, and so on.

Selecting the Best-Fit Partners: The RFP

The Request for Proposal (RFP) gives a more detailed description than the RFI of the system to be implemented. This is an invitation for partners to submit bids to submit a formal proposal for services to be provided on the architecture, design, implementation, and project management of a comprehensive SAP system. The RFP process levels the playing field among several vendors and brings a sense of structure to the overall procurement process for services. This is often used by firms to compare and contrast one preferred partner against another. Simply put, firms sometimes like to shop around beyond their preferred partner to see if they can get a better level of quality, delivery capabilities, or price.

Drawbacks to leveraging the RFP process are many. First, it places a burden on your organization to produce and publish an RFP that is both comprehensive and useful. If the RFP is "light" on details, a lot of questions will come up during the Q&A period. Worse, a lot of assumptions will be made as the project evolves regarding what is actually in scope versus what is not in scope, which will potentially blur the scope. Spending more time putting together a formal RFP obviously takes time away from employees' "day jobs" and thus costs your organization more money.

From a partner perspective, an RFP is the least-preferred route to working with a customer with whom they've established a great working relationship over several years. It expends a lot of unnecessary energy on both sides of the table. If a partner and customer with an established relationship aren't able to reach an agreement prior to the RFP process, the customer winds up expending time and energy educating someone who is new to their environment and culture, simply for the sake of pursuing a lower price.

A good RFP contains several sections, including

> ▶ **Scope of work**—What's in scope for the implementation, what are the customer's expectations with regard to testing, training, SAP modules to configure and customize, and so on.

10

▶ **Technical abstract**—Details the technical platform, storage, software components, number of concurrent users, number of transactions, database platform, and other characteristics of the system to be implemented.

▶ **Terms and conditions (Ts & Cs)**—The legal stuff that only lawyers and insomniacs will enjoy reading; relates to payment terms, how to handle disagreements or escalate problems, and so on.

▶ **Proposal submission requirements**—Includes requirements such as the RFP's format (typically in a version of Microsoft Word or similar), number of physical copies to deliver, whether these copies should be hard (paper) or soft (electronic) copies or both, and more.

▶ **Bid requirements**—Whether the customer expects a fixed price or to be paid based on time and expense. If fixed price, the payment milestones will often be mentioned in the RFP.

▶ **Customer references**—Includes requests that reflect the responding firm's experience from past engagements that reflect a similar scope and complexity.

▶ **Financial information**—This is required to determine the overall fiscal health of the responding partner or vendor; often includes a balance sheet from the latest 10-Q or a Dunn & Bradstreet credit check report.

▶ **Proposal timeline**—Often includes the Q&A session (referred to as "orals") and the deadline for proposal submission.

In addition to helping solicit bids, an RFP is also used to identify an overall approach to how a system will be implemented. A potential partner may choose to not submit a bid for an RFP if they feel it is not in their best interest to submit one. This choice is often conveyed in writing by the sales manager or partner's customer-specific account manager. After all RFPs have been received, the customer will compare each submitted RFP and select the few that are the best fit for their overall requirements. Firms often invite their short list of potential vendors to deliver an oral presentation of their proposal, their capabilities, and their overall (relevant) experience. This is an opportunity for the customer to size up the potential delivery team and determine if there is a good fit from a technical and cultural perspective. Firms often limit participants to a handful of people from the partner or vendor. It is never a good sign if there are more of the bidder's people at the meeting than people from the firm seeking to implement SAP. The list may include the prospective project manager, lead architect, lead business consultant, and sales/client manager. After a firm has down-selected potential partners on an engagement, they'll often ask for more information to supplement the RFP. Oftentimes this is an opportunity to refine scope and pricing.

Partner Selection Criteria

A common misconception is that firms often choose based solely on price a partner for a complex enterprise system engagement such as SAP. Selection criteria should include the consulting organization's past success and experience with implementing a similarly sized engagement, cultural fit with the firm's team, financial health of the consulting organization, and its ability to manage scope through tight project management discipline. Selection based solely on price is not the best way to select a partner for a complex SAP engagement. The old adage typically holds true that "you get what you pay for."

Having seen this mistake repeated by many clients over the years, common advice we give to clients is to look beyond the price and evaluate the partner's relative quality of oral presentations, evaluate the caliber of its potential delivery team, check references and evaluate resumes provided with the RFP, and track its responsiveness to hitting the timelines in the RFP. When changes occur during the RFP process, the potential partner's ability to incorporate those changes quickly and agilely indicates that the potential partner will be able to address scope changes and unanticipated risks during the engagement without any major disruptions to the overall timeline.

The decision-maker on a proposal often skips to the pricing page and focuses solely on that. Although we understand that their motivation is primarily to stay within budget, they should also consider the quality of delivery and the ability of that partner to make it through the entire project (that is, the caliber of its team and the financial strength of its organization). The last thing you want on a project is to have to throw out one partner in the middle and search for someone else to pick up the pieces and finish the engagement. It is important that an organization considering an SAP implementation keep other selection criteria in mind besides the overall price tag.

Here Come the Consultants!

After the RFP process has been concluded and you have chosen the SAP technology, business/application, and project management partners, it is time to set some ground rules. After all, a great number of consultants will begin showing up at the customer site soon, looking for guidance, tools, operating procedures, and ground rules for delivery. In our experience, these ground rules are best established by the two or three primary project managers—one from the customer or firm (typically aligned with the firm's PMO), one from the primary partner responsible for SAP system configuration, and perhaps another from the computing platform vendor or integrator. Project ground rules should include the following:

- **Project logistics**—Where will the work be delivered? Can it be delivered remotely? Are an office/cubicle and telephone included? Are customer laptops or workstations provided? Is Internet access provided?

- **Working hours**—Are nights and weekends expected? Is this a 24/7 engagement, or strictly Monday through Friday, 8 a.m.–5 p.m.?

- **Project reporting requirements**—Will each team member be required to submit weekly status reports on what they've completed, roadblocks, and upcoming tasks?

- **Expense reporting requirements**—Because partners and vendors often travel from out of town, they often submit weekly travel expenses. Some firms want to see all the receipts, whereas others set a limit on how much they'll pay for hotel, meals, airfare, and ground transportation.

▶ **Project schedule**—What is the critical path, and what are the key milestones between today and the end of the project?

Setting expectations up front is key to maintaining control on a complex engagement, because often there are different resources with specific skills brought in at different times throughout the project, and they will be inclined to do things their way if they do not understand that there are specific standards to meet on a particular project. It is important that everyone coming on board understands what the key success criteria for the SAP engagement are. Common standards of delivery and communication are outlined next.

Quality of Deliverables

Anything delivered to a firm by its consultants and other contracted team members is referred to generically as a "deliverable." With regard to these deliverables, quality is paramount. Be sure that questions relative to your own deliverables—questions such as the following—are addressed proactively and completely:

▶ Is all of the developed and delivered programming code well commented and easy to follow? Is it logical?

▶ Is documentation well written and grammatically correct?

▶ Does the provided documentation address each of your requirements thoroughly enough that a person picked up off the street who knows something about SAP can pick it up and run with it?

▶ Does your test plan address each functional and performance area?

▶ Is the project plan detailed enough to address each deliverable at the work breakdown structure level?

▶ Is there a risk mitigation plan to address each contingency on this project?

▶ Is there a thorough reporting plan of progress?

These are a few things we've identified over the past 20 or so years when looking at the quality of deliverables.

Delivery Timeline

An SAP implementation's timeline should be one of the project manager's top priorities (next to budgeting, scope management, and resource planning). If the PM is late on delivery, you need to ask why and address those concerns quickly to make sure you meet your dates. Legitimate delays should be addressed through a formal change order. Change orders don't always cost money. They are sometimes used to clarify scope and ensure that both sides of the equation are on the same page. We use the term "change order" rather loosely. We recommend that your primary project managers quickly get in sync (and stay in sync) on every detail of the project timeline.

Naming Conventions

Often overlooked in technical delivery, naming conventions are extremely important to maintain consistency when coding, developing new functionality, extending data models, and creating new schemas in the database, servers, switches, LUNS, and node names. The list is extensive. Consistency across the board is important, from the bare metal of a server, network switch, storage area network, or other disk subsystem, to the methods used inside Java's Enterprise JavaBeans (EJB) and more (for details as to how some of these technical naming conventions may be addressed, see Chapter 21, "Developing the SAP Data Center"). We've been in situations in which multicultural teams were brought in and no standards were enforced. Some of the naming conventions conflicted with one another or presented something that made sense in one culture but proved offensive in another culture. It's important to get a handle on this early. Adopt a standard and socialize this with your team leaders to iron out differences and establish a foundation for communication as early as possible.

Documentation Requirements and Standards

Many of us have been in this position: after months of working to create something, creating the documentation reflecting what we've architected, designed, implemented, tested, or delivered somehow falls off our to-do list. Developers are notorious for preferring code development to including inline comments as to how their code is actually intended to work. Technologists are often no better; just look at the documentation for most UNIX or Linux operating system distributions and you'll quickly see how documentation comes second to OS development efforts.

But it's important to lay down the law in advance and set the expectation that *everyone* will be held responsible for documenting what they're doing. The system's longevity is at stake, not to mention the ease with which it may be maintained. Define documentation standards and expectations in advance—and continue holding people accountable for creating usable documentation throughout the project—so you can maintain the system in its entirety long after the consultants have left. Everyone must document their work thoroughly. From coding comments to detailed design specifications, nothing should be left to interpretation or speculation.

The Kickoff Meeting

The first step to getting a project going with a partner is to hold a kickoff meeting in which the key players from the customer and partner teams meet for the first time and review the scope of the engagement, the overall project timeline, logistics, key milestones, deliverables, and critical success criteria. On larger engagements, dozens of consultants might be assigned. The kickoff meeting enables everyone to get aligned and focused on the same objectives and goals.

The kickoff meeting is often followed up by a wonderfully expensive dinner paid for by the partner sales team. Although we don't promote wining and dining as a way to get to know your team members, let's face it: Some of this reflects nothing more than the social

10

bonding necessary to forge relationships across a team that will span multiple organizations and last many months. The bottom line is that the kickoff meeting serves a number of different purposes. It coordinates everyone's expectations as to what the scope of the engagement is for this SAP system implementation while affording people the opportunity to meet each other for the first time and forge working relationships.

Balancing Partners with Internal Resources

Two extremes exist in regard to staffing your SAP project. Achieving a balance comes down to how well you are able to manage the process and set ground rules at the beginning of an SAP engagement. At one extreme, you can hire a partner and let them loose on your project with little oversight, only to find later that the burn rate on consulting and travel fees is going to blow your project budget. If partners or consultants are managed and motivated properly (a really important "if"), then a group of experienced consultants will take you through project preparation, planning, blueprinting, and implementation fairly quickly and complete a successful SAP implementation in several months (versus letting the project drag on for a year or more). There is a coffee mug sold by an online retailer that defines consulting as "If you're not part of the solution, there is plenty of money to be made prolonging the problem." Although funny in a dark humor sort of way, failing to manage your hired guns will result in a project that drags on and piles up consulting fees.

Motivation can be in the form of bonus payments for hitting key milestones, although many firms opt for the stick rather than the carrot (that is, immediate rather than deferred compensation, even with the understanding that deferred compensation typically holds much greater promise of reward). Withholding milestone payments until certain deliverables are met is another option that is often employed. This "big stick" approach will get you results but might impair your working relationship with that vendor or team in the future.

The other extreme is to spend gobs of time and tens of thousands of dollars in training on *each* of your high-potential, intelligent, and investment-worthy internal IT professionals to turn them into inexperienced though SAP Basis–certified and suddenly sought-after SAP professionals. This extreme is even *less* appealing than the other extreme, though. Why? Foremost, because you have practically no chance of actually achieving your ERP solution vision, regardless of how much budget and time you've been granted. Remember that these people have day jobs and often are not 100% dedicated to your project. They may also feel anxious about taking on the full responsibility for delivering an SAP system by themselves without any outside help. And finally, after you've paid to train and certify them, these employees may simply leave for another, higher-paying job and leave your project in a mess. Certainly, a middle ground of sorts must be achieved.

Thus, it became business-as-usual many years ago to employ a staff of perhaps four to nine consultants for every employee or long-term contract IT professional engaged on an SAP implementation. To put it into perspective, a midsize company with 10 resources tasked with implementing and supporting SAP might also bring in another 40 to 90 consultants.

The actual number depends on the SAP solutions or components being implemented, the complexity of the solution (such as the need for the highest levels of availability, or the inclusion of a discrete disaster-recovery system at a remote site), and the number of functional areas (such as materials management, sales/distribution, financials, human resources, and CRM) for which business processes must be defined and deployed. But keep in mind the one-to-four and one-to-nine ratios—they've been proven quite accurate across thousands of SAP implementations.

Finding the right balance between staffing exclusively with consultants and staffing exclusively with newly trained internal resources requires that you determine how much you will benefit from keeping more of your SAP implementation knowledge inside the company versus how quickly you will actually implement SAP. That is, at a particular mix of consultants and internal staff, you will still maintain some level of control (via your own hand-picked staff) and at the same time leverage experienced experts in their fields (consultants). In the next few sections, we examine textbook reasons why using both consultants and trained company employees can make sense for a particular SAP implementation project, and then we delve into educational, real-world examples.

Training Your Own Staff: Intellectual Capital Versus Inexperience

When it comes to training your own staff of SAP professionals, the bottom line is that what you lose in terms of time you gain in terms of employee satisfaction, increased loyalty, and long-term return on investment (ROI). Let's look at the particulars, though, using "pros and cons" approach to evaluation.

Pros: Training your own staff (and doing your best to retain them!) serves to keep key technology and business knowledge inside the company. Sometimes referred to as intellectual capital or tribal knowledge, your own staff must live with the results of what has been implemented and support and maintain the SAP system going forward (whereas the consultants you hire will walk away after the implementation is over and take their knowledge about your SAP implementation with them). Your IT staff can be motivated and otherwise leveraged to provide maintenance and support changes to the SAP solution long after go-live. This practice directly impacts career progression, too, while simultaneously making the organization a better place to work and retaining intellectual capital about how the system was implemented and customized for your organization. And as previously stated, the loyalty gained from investing in your people, and therefore the ROI, becomes compelling indeed.

Cons: Training your own staff will not eliminate the need for consultants. And training does not translate into experience. A seasoned SAP IT professional brings experience to your team and advises and coaches your IT staff on the best practices for implementing an SAP system. Experience comes with time, not by passing a certification exam administered by an IT vendor. In the work we do with clients in the role of information systems architects, technical consultants, and project managers, we have adopted the strategy of knowledge transfer. During the time we're billable to the customer's project, we make sure that the customer's IT staff leverages as much of our knowledge and expertise with implementing their system as they can. This ensures that the IT staff has the opportunity to leverage a seasoned consultant's experience, making the consultant more valuable not only in their role on a project but also in the knowledge that they pass on to the organization that will be supporting the SAP system after go-live.

Also, training simply takes someone to a certain SAP release level, level of functionality, type of hardware platform, or version of a database. Training ensures that your IT staff has exposure to the technology and has passed a certain level of proficiency in understanding the SAP technology environment, but training becomes a very expensive option if, in the middle of an implementation, a newer release or version of a particular SAP technology stack component becomes necessary. Think of it this way: If a consultant's knowledge becomes obsolete, it may be pretty easy to replace him with a different consultant who is knowledgeable or experienced in the newer release. But this isn't true with employees, who must be retooled, only to return to the project with a head full of knowledge but no practical application of that knowledge.

Resources who are trained but not experienced typically take much longer than experienced colleagues to accomplish the same task, often reworking the solution more than a few times until they get it right. If time is abundant, this could possibly be acceptable. But if, like most projects, timelines are pretty tight, the trade-off in time versus cost may simply not make good business sense.

Hiring Consultants: Quality Versus Budget

The training that your internal team members lack (and therefore their inability to meet stringent project deadlines) is more than made up for in general costs. A typical SAP Basis or infrastructure consultant ranges from $40/hr for a junior, self-employed contractor to $150/hr for someone out of a fairly reputable SAP systems integrator, to over $400/hr for a senior enterprise architect from a Big 5 or "Enterprise" hardware or software SAP solutions partner. To be safe, figure that an "average" consultant will cost you $250,000 annually. And this does not begin to include the expenses typical of this kind of arrangement, which normally add another 20%–30%, or $50,000–$75,000 annually, in additional travel costs for consultants traveling to your site each week.

Pros: Using consultants speeds up your time to implementation, no question. But a certain amount of flexibility can also be enjoyed by leveraging consulting resources, too. For example, niche technology areas can be staffed quickly via consultants and short-term contractors, allowing you to continue to meet deadlines even when priorities or business requirements change. Furthermore, if you ever have a problem with a consultant (such as exhibiting a poor attitude, showing up late repeatedly, or failing to actually do the work), then you have great recourse. Let him or her go! Fire him! Get someone else who is qualified, and push hard to not even pay for his "time" that was wasted, or deliverables that were "underdelivered."

Cons: Budget early, and budget accurately. Assume that 65%–80% of your overall implementation costs will go toward funding your consulting staff alone. The costs are high, no doubt about it. But in the long run, as thousands of companies have found, the costs of *not* implementing an integrated enterprise solution such as SAP are even greater when you go it alone without the help of an experienced partner. Can you really afford not to implement such a solution without some experienced hired guns?

Consultants Versus Internal Resources in the Real World

As you have read, there are lots of reasons why it makes sense to use both consultants and internal resources on your SAP project. To reinforce that notion, this section provides real-world examples of situations we have encountered in which a client chose not to strike a reasonable balance between the two extremes.

Forgetting All About the Business

Several years ago we had a client that insisted on leveraging its own resources to implement a CRM solution. The client limited our role to technology support on the platform they had chosen to implement on, which included servers and storage. It cost the customer two times its original budget estimate to implement the CRM system as a result. Although the client had engaged the right resources on the foundational technology layer, it did not consider the value of engaging business/application consultants to help it map its business processes to a cohesive SAP solution.

Money Is No Object!

We had one potential client that started down the path to an SAP implementation two years ago. It brought in experts from one of the big consulting houses to cover almost everything, including project management consultants, project coordination specialists, blueprinting and design consultants, functional consultants, ABAP programmers, SAP Basis and other infrastructure consultants, and so on. The customer named one of its senior managers as the client project manager, but he still had other duties (his day job) to oversee relating to the business, and could therefore be considered a part-time resource at best.

Within a year, this small company was averaging about $50,000 a day in consulting fees and related costs. Annualized, this amounted to more than $18 million, and did not even include budget money spent on hardware for development and test environments, and the SAP and database licenses themselves. For a project that never really got out of the blueprinting phase, the client had literally spent a small fortune.

The project was way over budget and nowhere close to being on time. What happened? Changes in scope gradually crept into the project, unchecked by the customer and client project manager. What started out as an ERP implementation grew into a diverse, multi-component implementation. The business continued to feed requirements to the consulting team throughout the year, and executive sponsorship waffled and eventually succumbed to strong though misguided business leaders. No one was truly in control, especially the client, and only the consulting firm was arguably coming out ahead.

10

In the end, the project was eventually scrapped. Months later, SAP licenses and a pile of hardware in hand, the potential client asked us to propose a new approach to implementing just the core ERP component. Due to weak executive sponsorship, its poor project management practices, and the end user community's general disdain toward the project, we declined. Sadly, economic hard times and probably a deep-seated wariness toward SAP in general served to put this project "on hold" indefinitely; the entire investment was wasted.

Do It Yourself or Die Trying

Another customer of ours actually *did* successfully implement SAP R/3 with "barely" any consulting staff. In fact, the ratio of consultants to client staff was something like 2 to 1. The client took on 90% of the ABAP programming, all of the Basis and infrastructure, and most of the project management itself. It brought in a second-tier (and quite capable) consulting firm to help it for the first few months with general project planning and blue-printing. It also leveraged free consulting resources from three different hardware and software vendors (including us). In all three cases, the vendor provided consulting assistance and introduced new (and therefore not necessarily mature) technology into the SAP technology stack in exchange for the client providing references when the project went live successfully.

The project was not without its share of pain on the client side, however. The normal work week quickly grew to 60 to 80 hours (and then some), as the client painfully learned and relearned how to convert its business processes into ABAP, Java, and HTML code. Case in point, the production database quickly got out of hand, and then SAP tuning consumed all waking hours for nearly a month. New hardware, OS, and database platforms presented their own challenges, too, as the team scrambled to quickly learn and adapt its own operational and support processes to these. All of this could have been avoided with carefully placed consultants tasked with providing good knowledge transfer before they hit the door on their way out.

Nonetheless, the client struggled through all of this, and although it is debatable as to how much time it actually wasted and what the state of the ABAP code is today, the end result was a live system. Go-live came and went without much more pain, and it came on schedule, which we believe amazed most everyone. We hope they don't have to upgrade for a long time!

Summary

In this chapter, we reviewed the different types of SAP partners that can be retained for an SAP engagement: business, technology, and project management partners. We also reviewed the RFI and RFP processes, followed by a closer look at the core selection criteria for selecting a consulting partner to assist a firm with its SAP engagement. We then identified the ground rules to establish at the beginning of an engagement to ensure that the project progresses smoothly. We concluded with a discussion of the pros and cons of training your own staff versus hiring consultants to implement SAP. We underscored the different approaches to staffing an SAP engagement, showing through real-world examples that the ideal solution includes a blended team of a firm's IT staff and an experienced SAP consulting partner.

Case Study: Building the Partner Team

Your employer, HiTech, Inc., has recently purchased the hardware, storage, and SAP licenses to implement an SAP CRM solution to support your sales force and customer contact center. You have been assigned by the project sponsor the task of building a team to architect, design, and technically implement a customized SAP CRM solution for your company. You have been given a budget to work within, and it's your call whether to retain a partner, train internal IT staff on the required SAP technologies, or do both.

Questions

1. What would be your first task in determining which direction to go relative to building a SAP project team of partners?

2. You've decided to identify in the marketplace potential partners with domain expertise implementing SAP CRM. What type of document will you issue to gather information on potential partners and educate them on the scope of your project?

3. You've received bids from interested consulting partners, down-selected to a handful, and asked them to come into your offices to give oral presentations on their proposed solutions. What selection criteria will you apply in selecting the right consulting partner to work with your organization on implementing SAP CRM?

4. After you've selected a consulting partner, what is the first thing your two teams will do?

NOTE

The answers to these questions can be found in Appendix A, "Case Study Answers."

10

CHAPTER **11**

Building the SAP Project Team

Building an effective and well-staffed change-enabling SAP project team is the topic of this chapter. We address questions regarding organizational agility, which change model attributes are most effective, where to find members of the SAP project team, important project team structural matters, and more. How the SAP project team's underlying organizational constructs interact with one another is covered as well. Later in this chapter we also take a look at several sample project structures based on various sizes of SAP projects, and outline real-world examples of approaches and SAP implementation project team models.

Steps for Project Team Success

Building an SAP project team is similar in many ways to building most any team. In our experience, we have successfully used the following four-step process to build the SAP project team:

1. Address organizational size and agility factors, including environmental considerations.

2. Create an effective team structure.

3. Staff key project positions and subteams

4. Empower team members to convert vision into reality.

Once the project team is created, the bulk of the work surrounding team management and controlling and coordinating the work of the project can commence, followed by inevitable redirecting and refining of priorities based on scope changes, environmental factors, and other changes. The steps outlined above are particularly important if only to establish a solid foundation for the project. These and related factors are discussed throughout much of this chapter.

Addressing Organizational Size and Agility

Perhaps the most critical and least understood need of business teams today is agility, or the ability to change easily and responsively as the SAP project and its needs or opportunities dictate. Contemporary change models in the context of virtual, culturally diverse teams are stretched in this regard; agility is rarely noted as a critical transformational factor, if at all. Yet a project team's ability to introduce change by way of an SAP implementation will transform the way a company does business, the role of IT, and more (as we discussed in Chapter 3, "Business Vision"). A lack of project team agility will only set up a team to fail.

Agility is impacted in many ways. A review of successful ERP implementation projects suggests that large physical organizational size or structure is one of the greatest contributors to poor agility. The bulk of organizations implementing ERP are very large companies or institutions (their smaller counterparts simply do not have the financial means to introduce such broad-based business-enabling IT systems as SAP Business Suite). Large companies rarely have all the challenges associated with being large figured out (such as how to change, how to manage resources spread out around the globe, how to access data similarly spread out, how to effectively communicate, and so on). Organizational reach is also one of the fundamental changes with which administrators and managers have had to contend over the last decade. Different from size, an organization's reach complicates agility by slowing down decision making and therefore execution. So, too, do environmental factors, discussed next.

More than ever before, organizational change models must address internal systems complexity as well as external forces and the environment in general, while simultaneously appealing to the needs and requirements of a diverse stakeholder community. To help ensure their survival, organizations spend their entire existence adopting to or warding off these internal and external influences. Especially compelling are external environmental factors, as these factors rarely relate to matters that can be easily controlled or managed yet reflect matters necessary to bring about desired change. From government regulations to new competitors to economic, social, and political conditions, external environmental factors truly test an organization's model and capacity for change. And the rapid, low-cost ability to gather and process data from both inside and outside the enterprise is becoming increasingly critical to organizational longevity.

It is the effective implementation of a change model within a particular set of environmental constraints that sets apart the successful SAP project team from its less-successful counterparts. The rise of geographically distributed project-oriented teams has placed a burden on core organizational change theory today, especially in cases where the team is akin to an island or loosely connected string of islands around the globe—far from local midlevel and executive leadership, isolated in a sense, but critical to organizational success nonetheless.

Advances in information technology have served to propel organizational change, to be sure; with access to data and the ability to synthesize it comes information and therefore power. Across the board, though, certain factors, behaviors, and motivational approaches comprise the essential building blocks for effectively and consistently managing change in the context of virtual teams. Employee empowerment remains essential and universal, for example. A key component of relationship-oriented behavior, employee empowerment must be balanced with employee dependency to link employees with one another such that together they not only appear but operate as "insiders" in the team. This empowerment creates an inspiring work environment (often called work climate) in the midst of changing environmental factors, central to organizational change. Attention to a mix of adaptability, leadership, cultural and work climate factors, organizational design and structure, frequent and consistent communication, and several other dimensions or qualities acts as the basis for change in most of these cases, explored in the next few pages.

Creating an Effective Team Structure

The modern business workplace has become a place of change. Today, both organizations and individuals shift constantly in terms of job and task scope, job breadth, role, physical location, structure, leadership styles, adaptability to change, flexibility with regard to how change is introduced, and much more. That many organizations have reorganized themselves again and again in the last several years is not surprising; successful organizations naturally seek to rebalance and better address challenging business and other external conditions in light of changing global and other environmental factors. Successful at adopting change, the best of these companies enjoy organizational agility hailing from individual as well as organizational adaptability. Tempered through the adoption of behavioral, leadership, and management best practices, companies adept at change are more likely to get through and thrive after an SAP implementation.

The evolution of the modern IT workplace and its ERP subteams tasked with implementing and acting as mission-critical organizational change agents has placed a burden on creating effective teams. In our view, one of the keys lies in adopting an organizationally friendly and well-aligned change model.

Adopting a Change Model

An adaptable change model specifically geared toward addressing the people, process, and technology complexities associated with ERP-initiated change needs to be adopted. Yet how is this adaptability made possible? To be sure, attention to human development factors can lead to organizational behavior and design that not only positions a company for long-term success, but also serves to create, shape, and reinforce a culture willing to reinvent itself for the sake of its customers and other stakeholders, and ultimately its own longevity. Organizational decomposition can help illuminate individual behavioral and other factors, which in turn may be assessed to impact motivation and how the organization must equip itself for change.

We recommend approaches similar to the Virtual Team Change Model (VTCM) discussed later in this chapter, as VTCM highlights the need to actively manage change. A closer look at failed SAP implementations tells us that poorly managed change is a key culprit to failure—especially the kind of non-change seen when SAP is adapted to reflect a firm's existing business model rather than vice versa (see the sidebar "Why Do ERP Projects Fail So Often?"). A good ERP change model can provide a conceptual framework that is useful for describing how project teams should effectively operate to embrace rather than avoid change, in the end providing a "cycle of success" that can be used to implement follow-on SAP components and other enterprise applications.

Why Do ERP Projects Fail So Often?

Most everyone understands that ERP projects are complex, whether predicated on SAP, Oracle, or other software company solutions. At a basic level, an ERP project sets about to adopt a set of best practices for performing various business functions. The difference between a company's current business practices and those that reflect best practices is often a very wide gap. The gap has been described as a chasm, in fact. And leaping across a chasm is no small feat (explaining why a successful ERP project gets so much positive attention). Thus, the real problem becomes one of change—how do you get a firm's people to change the way they do business?

You have to get inside their heads to understand why they do things the way they do, what the benefits and drawbacks are of doing things those ways, and more. And then— another tricky problem—you need to figure out how to convince them that ERP-based best practices will actually make their work life easier once they get over the learning curve. A poor job of convincing leads the business users to constantly push for their old ways of doing business, to the point where they might demand that your new expensive ERP system be modeled after the old software systems to match the way they *used* to work!

Such customization is common, truth be told, but the secret of a really good ERP implementation is to *minimize* this customization. Customizations make the system more difficult to maintain down the road and do nothing to take the business teams to the next level of best practices (which was probably how the new ERP system was sold to the firm's executive leadership team in the first place). Many of the ERP implementation horror stories in the press can be traced back to customization and its antecedents— the inability to change or the overt decision to avoid change. This is why we talk so much about managing change throughout this book! We want your project to be successful and not another negative press release.

Addressing Project Team Design and Structural Evolution

The purpose of organizational design is to create a structure that serves to effectively coordinate organizational tasks and motivate people to achieve an organization's objectives. Organizational structure serves as an adaptive organism shaped in reaction to the characteristics and commitments of participants as well as to influences from the external environment. Such a framework could naturally evolve as an organization's needs or mission changed.

A remotely disbursed team inherently implies time-zone and therefore greater relative cultural differences (whether across town or across countries), both of which demand leadership characterized by excellent communication, relationship, and sensitivity skills. Remote teams require more feedback, acknowledgement, and typically more attention to creating a sense of belonging and connectedness among the team members than their tightly grouped close-proximity counterparts require. To this end, the disbursed team requires project leaders who excel in building cohesiveness while cementing desirable behaviors.

Facing Virtually Managed Project Team Challenges

As companies have grown globally, so have the business organizations tasked with servicing the business. This accounts for their distribution and make-up—increasingly geographically dispersed, loosely connected, and highly decentralized. More and more often they must serve a global user community and therefore need to reflect the same round-the-clock mentality maintained by the business's customers, suppliers, and the organization itself. That such teams are commonplace today is unsurprising. That it all happened in the space of less than two decades presents exceptional organizational challenges, however. Today's dramatically flatter and streamlined organizational structures—the result of downsizing, competitive realities, and economic constraints—have conspired with the changing nature of our global workforce to complicate how organizations work together to effect change and therefore how project teams should be structured and staffed. Challenges include

▶ Enabling planned change while accounting for the need to react to unplanned change

▶ Enabling deep structural change when warranted

▶ Enabling transformational change when warranted, while still promoting the transactional kind of change associated with an organization's gradual evolution

▶ Addressing change when an organization's constituents are physically remote from one another and from local leadership

▶ Addressing change in the wake of multinational, multicultural organizational restructuring and its byproduct, cultural diversity

▶ Realizing the benefits of data visibility and transparency

▶ Accessing the company's data, which is probably as spread out as its people

▶ Communicating effectively given the teams' geographic locations

Recruiting, developing, and retaining project teams are complicated by the aforementioned challenges. Consolidate your project team as best you can (50%–75% is reasonable)

and then recognize that the team will need to be managed virtually regardless of how much work you put into consolidation. Consider the fact that even teams that are completely centralized (a rare situation indeed) still benefit from virtual management techniques, as team members may work from home, be required to travel in response to the project's needs, and so on. Next we take a closer look at some of the key organizational challenges faced by your project team.

Enabling ERP Effectiveness Through Process Orientation

ERP introduces change on several fronts. Access to real-time data enables swift reaction to external environmental changes, for example, while enabling the pursuit of new strategies by way of enlightened internal decision making. ERP enables effectiveness by introducing a process-oriented approach to business and decision making. The widespread organizational changes involved in ERP implementation naturally fall out of the organization's shift in business design from an often fragmented, vertically oriented structure aligned by business areas or functions to a process-based orientation served by an integrated system.

The SAP project team needs to understand that the power of change lies in *managing* the process of change. An effective ERP-enabled organizational change model should therefore align with this process orientation. Years ago, people described such matters in terms of paradigm shifts. Substituting a new process orientation for a legacy functional orientation where the organization rather than individuals serve as the company's change agent is indeed such a shift. Organizational evolution gives way to transformation by way of a Lewinian approach to managing change, balancing stakeholder needs as they ebb and flow from stability to change-oriented and then back to stability.

Maximizing ERP Effectiveness in the Wake of Change

In conjunction with managing the process of change, organizations deploying ERP must be adept at addressing both *planned* and *unplanned* change; both are common, the result of an intended or an unintended result. Despite the origin of a particular change, though, effective change serves to reinvent the organization by encouraging adaptability and increasing the inertia behind the change. It is this inertia that is key—inertia can work to increase both resistance and acceptance to change. As an indicator of direction (whether forward, backward, or sideways), inertia describes an organization's ability to change its behaviors, culture, work practices, and so on. The conceptualization of inertia creates the ability, whether real or based on perception, to view change as continuous.

Furthermore, effective change may be evolutionary or revolutionary; both are equally adept at transforming organizations (though the latter admittedly more aggressively). But while most organizations believe planned change holds the greatest power of transformation, it is actually an organization's response to unplanned change that transforms it most.

Maximizing Effectiveness by Managing Cultural Change

Different from an organization's culture is the concept of cultural differences found among an organization's constituents. ERP teams spread around the globe reflect cultural diversity. Yet this plays a part in establishing a particular company culture as well. The importance of an organization's cultural beliefs and the processes it uses can define the organization; these become inculcated or embodied within an organization's corporate culture. In today's world of geographically distributed, multicultural organizations, developing a consistent corporate culture across distributed sites is challenging but called for—SAP project teams have enough challenges on their plates. Combined with attention to organizational design and flexibility, a set of common beliefs may be cemented to create a uniform corporate culture. Attention to factors that promote sound and consistent communication is called for as well. Through all this, the team is motivated to achieve a higher level of group performance than anything individually attainable; transformational change is given an authentic foothold in the process.

External environments vary in terms of the demands placed on the organization and are often responsible for driving culture change. For example, teams and their constituents anchored in a particular geography will likely be exposed to various external circumstances, values, and situations that differ across cultures and geographies. Methods of vertical and horizontal differentiation may further complicate organizational matters and subsequently the most effective mix of leadership, management practices, and underlying behavioral factors, including the use of functional, product-oriented, customer-specific, and matrix-based organizational divisions. Transformational change factors such as culture are capable of this.

Empowering Team Members to Convert Vision into Reality

The more complex an organization, the more ambiguous the organization's process for enabling teams to change themselves and transform the systems around them. We're big fans of *transformational leadership* (described in Chapter 12, "Staffing World-Class SAP Project Leadership") because it's exactly the tool necessary for empowering a team to convert a project's vision into reality. Different from management practices that are essentially ways of managing tasks, transformational leadership comprises behaviors and practices that *develop people*. Transformational leaders not only bring a vision of the major changes needed in a project team's organizational structure, culture, and way of working, but also empower their subordinates to deliver on this vision in a bigger way—the work represented by the SAP project itself and how the project will change the entire company's structure, culture, and way of working. In this way, such leaders enable organizations to transcend counter-productive structures inhibiting goal achievement, making it possible for organizations and their business communities to agree on the proper path forward. In the next few sections, we take a look at the project team from several perspectives spanning leadership implications, how communication can be augmented in today's socially networked always-on teams, and how decision making can be fast-tracked through fingertip accessible knowledge.

Project Team Leadership Implications

It's been said that it's easier to kill an organization than to change it. Leadership is one of several critical dimensions of planned change (along with strategy, culture, communication methods, and more). With regard to organizational leadership, it is paramount to recognize that old-school autocratic methods of managing people can stifle the very creativity and innovation needed on behalf of the SAP project team. Leadership that is sensitive to culturally diverse, geographically distributed, and therefore virtually managed ERP project teams is called for. No modern-day organization is as subject to failure as those that are disbursed across time zones and cultures while simultaneously tasked with implementing change on behalf of its constituents.

Loosely connected and highly decentralized, SAP project teams need to be constantly finetuned and occasionally reinvented altogether to remain effective long-term. The underlying reasons are many. First, a geographically disbursed team implies a team that, by its nature, must be composed of mature, self-directed, and highly motivated personnel. In the absence of local management, coaching, or similar direction and guidance, only the most competent and self-sufficient teams will actually be successful long-term; others will be less successful and, through a form of natural selection, leave the team. Thus, a successful geographically disbursed team requires consummate professionals of high self-esteem and self-efficacy, which in turn demands a particular leadership style, attention to strategy and mission, adherence to reinforcing a consistent culture for maximum effectiveness, and so on.

To be an effective change agent, certain project leadership styles are preferred; a purely autocratic method is counterproductive, for example, as the latest generations of IT and other professionals often don't respond to this but rather need to feel as though they play a role in shaping their environment and workplace. A leadership style based on rewards might do well in managing the simplest of administrative or organizational tasks, but will do little for building a cohesive team. Even a purely charismatic project leader, while inspiring and interesting to work for, will find it difficult to address the "real" work of SAP project teams—building relationships, managing tasks, taking care of administrative matters, and coordinating completion of tasks.

The Communication Plan: Networking for Success and Survival

Communication is synonymous with pervasive intra-team and team-to-team integration, exactly what is called for in a companywide business project underpinned by a vast technology footprint; there are many ways to fail in the absence of effective and timely communication. Sound and timely communication is essential to well-planned change.

Because of this importance, we recommend creating a project-focused communications plan.

A communications plan connects people and processes with the necessary tools to both maintain the status quo and effect the change called for by the SAP project. Information technologies and tools that enable problems to be rapidly identified, deconstructed, analyzed, and resolved need to be part of your communications plan. These tools are the communication enablers or "glue" that connect business teams with IT teams, project stakeholders with their end-user constituents, and so on. This glue not only enables the Project Management Office (PMO) and overall team to achieve its mission but assists it in building and maintaining a unique, well-connected, trusting, and effective organizational culture positioned to effectively deploy and use its new SAP business application.

As we've mentioned before, SAP project teams today are more often than not virtual teams. Virtual teams present unique communication challenges. In light of global virtual work processes that need to reflect the complexities, uncertainties, and interdependencies within the SAP project, action founded in anything other than sound communication, underpinned by trust while optimized for virtual teams, puts the organization and its constituents at risk of failure. This is especially true for complex multicultural teams—also the norm for SAP implementation projects today—which need communication processes to encompass vertical, horizontal, and diagonal paths to be effective.

Most failures related to introducing new technology-based business systems occur because of a lack of effective communication at the *beginning* of the project. However, implementations can quickly fall off a cliff in the absence of ongoing and effective communications. To keep everyone on the same page, develop a communications plan that encompasses both real-time and offline methods. Real-time methods include using tools such as the telephone along with instant messaging technologies, whereas offline tools such as email, web-based and other status reporting systems, and even social networking systems help connect teams around the clock (refer to the sidebar). To this last point, using homegrown as well as popular collaboration tools we have found that team-based "private" social networks can be especially effective. Combined with wiki- and blog-based communications vehicles, a permanent record of past communications can come in handy throughout the project.

How Advantageous Is Social Networking?

The same executives and other stakeholders who fought for an SAP project are often quick to dismiss social networking as a distracting waste of time. These leaders are missing out on what we believe can become an awesome cultural and work climate equalizer. To be clear, while facebook.com and myspace.com have their place in social networking, we're not talking about these tools. Instead, we'd like to see your project leverage an in-built social framework enabled by SharePoint or a similar collaboration framework and bolstered by wikis, blogs, podcasts, webcasts, and so on. Not only will this approach to social software connect your teams around the globe, but it will increase the team's ability to collaborate, innovate, and solve problems.

In these days of restricted travel and tightened expenses, bringing together the implementation team isn't possible. Social networking tools like blogs and wikis help far-off knowledge workers, business leaders, and technologists become an integral part of a single team focused on solving problems by way of an SAP implementation. Once-disconnected individuals can be given not only a name but a face and a personality—making it a whole lot easier to get work done in the absence of face-to-face communication.

Leadership can use podcasts, webcasts, blogs, email distributions, and other electronically accessible media to share ideas and status updates, inspire the team, and further foster an innovative workplace. These connection points will cement the team in terms of vision and priorities, and go a long way towards introducing change.

Of course, there are dangers inherent to any communication forum. We believe the advantages of social networking far outweigh these potential negatives. Ensure the team understands what's confidential and what's not. Finally, take the time to reinforce what's socially and culturally acceptable and what needs to be avoided. After all, professionalism and high ethical standards need to be maintained in all communications, regardless of medium.

The key is to connect people in as many ways as practical, so that no one is left out and everyone can become a part of the "change process." Said another way, it's all about creating multiple connection points so no one is left in the dark. Whether it's through twitter, IM, email, or the phone, a good communications plan will naturally encourage project buy-in. Down the road, when issues and questions need to be addressed, the broad-based communications network you've developed will help keep the right people engaged and in the know, in turn speeding up decision making and keeping the project on track.

Improving Organizational Decision Making Through Knowledge

ERP systems are well known for their ability to provide better and more useful knowledge to the organizations using them in their day-to-day business. In the same way, successful SAP project teams are known for their ability to access current-state project data, the status and completion percentage of tasks, and so on. The team needs the capability to identify, capture, manage, and use project knowledge as empowering inputs to the decision-making process. We covered this in Chapter 6, "Managing Knowledge and the Knowledge Repository." Access to knowledge grows more and more critical as the project team gets closer to go-live and requires greater agility to rapidly respond to evolving business requests. Facilitated by organizational practices and control systems, knowledge management facilitates decision making and enables communications as well.

Staffing Key Project Positions and Subteams

SAP project responsibilities are typically handed out by the project's leadership team to the business and technical teams making up the overall SAP project team. Additionally, many companies have set up a PMO responsible for maintaining centralized project tools, project portfolio management and support processes, and so on. In this section, we look at staffing key SAP project team positions spanning senior project managers and team leaders, the project executive champion and project board, the customer board, and more. The secret behind successful SAP project teams is building a strong communications framework encompassing executive-level, business-user community, technical team, and other critical stakeholders. A well-structured team maintains business and organizational focus on project activities, issue resolution, and addressing the inevitable issues (and their escalations) as required. Primary components of the SAP project team therefore include the following:

- The PMO (whether internally hosted or aligned with an external organization)

- The program manager

- The project's executive champion or sponsor

- The project board or steering committee

- The customer board

- The business team

- The Technical Support Organization (TSO)

Each of these positions or subteams is explored in the following sections.

The Role of the PMO

As stated in earlier chapters, the PMO provides process and procedural support to all SAP and other projects managed in the PMO project portfolio. The PMO's role is to support the SAP implementation. In addition to this overarching support role, the PMO might also assume the role of a project stakeholder and be a member of the project board.

Understanding the role that your PMO plays within your organization will help to determine where the PMO falls in your overall SAP project or program structure. A PMO that provides forms, process support, and administrator support may not be noted on your organizational structure, whereas a PMO that actively manages projects will probably be included at the steering committee or program board level.

The Program Manager Role

The program manager normally sits on the steering committee and program board and typically understands well the SAP functionality being deployed, the SAP landscape and supporting infrastructure, and the organization, particularly the business organization that is receiving the services that the project is delivering. Good program managers are difficult to find. We suggest looking inside your organization at folks who have led other significant projects or business departments. Alternatively, hire an outsider with a strong industry background and experience with SAP implementations (particularly the SAP component being implemented).

Project Executive Champion

The project executive champion (project exec) role is expected to provide leadership and vision for the project, resolve conflicts and issues that cut across process, business, and geographical boundaries, drive project communication and positioning, and ensure that the delivered system aligns well with the firm's current needs and strategic objectives. Finding a good project exec is therefore critical. In addition to the role expectations that were just mentioned, the project exec that we look for when building a project team demonstrates unwavering support for the project and, acting as a project ambassador at large, works within the organization to give the initiative the appropriate level of visibility within the firm.

Finding the right project exec is especially important in environments in which many project initiatives are in progress. An organization with many active projects demands a lot of time and participation from a limited set of company resources. Be careful to select a champion with enough time to serve the project's needs well.

Building the Project Board

The project board (also commonly referred to as the steering committee) serves a critical leadership component of the overall project team. The project board is a cross-functional team that is responsible for monitoring project progress, advocating project goals and objectives within its organization, and handling project escalations as required. The project board is assembled by locating the executives within your firm who possess a broad understanding of your IT environment, business customer expectations, current initiatives, active projects, data center operations processes, and resource constraints and requirements. In short, your firm's representation on the project board will include executives who are responsible for delivery of the project's functionality to its business unit end customer or have a vested interest in the project's success. Additionally, many project board executives are also responsible for managing the full suite of applications that is provided to the business-user community. In addition to representation from your firm, best practice is to include systems integrator participation and significant third-party subcontractor executive participation.

When you are assembling the project board, be on the lookout for strong, action-oriented leaders who possess a solid understanding of your company and a willingness to "step up" and make business decisions and resolve conflicts when required. Good project board leadership knows when to let the team address issues and when to step in with an edict or guiding principle. These leaders are also comfortable communicating at all levels of the organization to escalate and rapidly resolve issues. When it's time to build the project board, look for people possessing a track record of such action-oriented behaviors coupled with excellent people skills. Combined with industry-specific expertise and knowledge of your unique organization, these folks are highly sought after for good reason—they get things done.

Building the Customer Board

As its name implies, the customer board is staffed with executives who belong to the SAP project's receiving organization—the end-user community who will eventually be served by the SAP project. In a classic enterprise system implementation, the customer board is staffed with the folks who are responsible for delivering your company's goods or services to its customers and includes representatives from sales, distribution, product development, manufacturing, engineering, quality control, cost accounting, and finance.

Ideally, the individuals who are recruited to participate on the customer board possess a broad understanding of how the various business organizations will use the new SAP system. They understand how a centralized and integrated business application like SAP can help the firm do a better job of taking care of its customers while actually reducing the cost of IT. For example, a global firm adopting a single application companywide instead of selecting competing regional applications to support the same process can save money. If customer board members are unable or unwilling to consider such perspectives, the board will have a difficult time pushing authentic change through the organization.

The most important role of the customer board, like the project board, revolves around communication. It's especially important to understand language and local communication norms.

The customer board that is being discussed here may be included as a component of the overall project board or steering committee, depending on the size and origination structure. Regardless of positioning, though, we find that relatively condensed customer boards are most effective. Like any other team, fewer people can agree more quickly on a go-forward strategy. However, the smaller the customer board the more critical each member's background, role, and ability to think strategically.

The Breadth and Depth of the Business Team

Without exception, the business team comes from the business-user community. This team is assembled from members of the organization that is the end customer of the SAP system. These are the folks who are directly responsible for the products and services that your organization delivers to its customers. They are most concerned about finding a reliable solution that satisfies their unique fulfillment requirements, is available for use 100% of the time, is easy to use, and does not require a mountain of resources (and costs) to maintain.

An ideal business team draws from across the organization some of the best talent available who understand the firm, its various business organizations, the firm's products and services, the firm's country-by-country customers, and the financial, environmental, and import/export processes and requirements.

So whom do we select from the business to staff core team project positions? The ideal candidates are the individuals who the organization can do the least without. In retrospect, most successful project teams refer to these people as the rock stars of the organization—without exception, they're talented, well-known, and recognized for getting things done. Assigning your top talent to the business team opens up opportunities for the development of the next wave of key contributors. Project work should be a full-time job for *core team* members. We have seen teams struggling on numerous occasions because project team members were expected to handle all or part of their old jobs in addition to the project work. In addition to moving core team members to a full-time work assignment, it is your choice whether to backfill the project team members' old jobs or save the jobs for their return after project completion. Backfilling may be appropriate if your project is lengthy.

Another important consideration is *team member depth*. Team members need to be experts in their field—real-world experts, too, rather than merely being familiar with a particular discipline or business function. The same staffing philosophy applies to staffing extended business team roles, although full-time assignment to the business team may not be appropriate. Business subject matter experts (SMEs) will be tapped at various phases of the project to support the following activities: requirement definition, system integration testing, business acceptance testing, data cleansing, end-user training, and cut-over preparation.

The SAP Technical Support Organization

Except for its focus on technical rather than business-related skill sets, the SAP TSO is something of a microcosm of the overall project team. It encompasses SAP Basis experts, computing platform (OS, server, and database) specialists, SMEs in front-end client deployment, and various data specialists. The SAP TSO is responsible for designing the SAP system landscape and its respective technology platforms for development, test, training, production, and potentially many other systems. Once designed, the TSO then "stands up" or installs these systems. It then handles the configuration and tuning tasks necessary to align each system's capabilities with the needs of its end-user community. Think of SAP's technical platform as a system with a bunch of knobs. The knobs represent dimensions of the system that can be customized. You might "turn up" the knob responsible for increasing a system's availability or performance, for example, or (to reduce costs, for example) turn down the knob reflecting the system's scalability. And you might even go so far as to completely turn off the knobs representing multiple methods of system accessibility or integration (and by default turn on the knob for exclusive use of the WebGUI or exclusive use of SAP PI, for example).

Once a system is configured to its users' liking, the SAP TSO takes responsibility for the system's care and feeding. This might include handling systems management and maintenance tasks, addressing technology stack changes (either proactively or in light of bugs or security issues), carrying on the critical tasks of quality, regression, and load testing, and more. Because of the SAP TSO's breadth and depth of responsibilities, we provide a complete chapter on staffing this critical organization: Chapter 14, "Staffing the SAP Technical Support Organization." Subsequent chapters detail the TSO's responsibilities with regard to availability (Chapter 15) and disaster recoverability (Chapter 16), the sizing process (Chapter 19), developing the SAP data center (Chapter 21), preparing for and installing SAP Business Suite and NetWeaver components (Chapters 23 through 25), and so on.

An ERP Virtual Team Change Model

SAP implementation practitioners know through experience that many different factors can converge to cripple an otherwise well-positioned SAP project. Size, diversity, geographical distribution, communication challenges, and much more have a direct impact on organizational change and therefore the SAP project team's ability to implement the project successfully.

To position an SAP project team for success, we have developed and used an approach we call the Virtual Team Change Model (VTCM). VTCM allows organizations to introduce a transformational project such as SAP regardless of whether the organization is large or small, well established or new, geographically centralized or dispersed internationally. Similar to a framework or really comprehensive checklist, VTCM encompasses critical change factors such as culture, work climate, leadership, strategy, vision, size, structure, and virtual management composition. VTCM also sustains organizational agility by way of its focus on external factors, the presence of internal systems and ways of doing work, and a systemic approach to reinventing processes rather than people to effect culture change through more easily affected work climate change. For starters, we suggest you employ the following guidelines:

- ▶ **Create the project team from the ground up**—In this way, the team will naturally respect and appreciate the project's purpose and goals.

- ▶ **Build all required skills into the project team**—Leave nothing to chance or outside the reach of the team's influence.

- ▶ **Embrace virtual team management practices**—After centralizing individuals and teams, adopt leadership, management, and communication practices aimed at keeping people motivated, engaged, and connected.

- ▶ **Partner proactively and extensively**—Establish sourcing relationships with large-scale SAP systems integrators and smaller boutique organizations alike to enable just-in-time (JIT) staffing; ensure that any emerging business, technology, and project management needs can be addressed rapidly in case internal resources are unavailable or ill equipped.

- ▶ **Encourage a lean project organization**—Pull resources into the project team who embody the concept of "greater skills in fewer FTEs" (full-time equivalents) which in turn enables lower-cost staffing, simpler communication, faster decision making, fewer points of view to consider, and simpler organizational charts.

- ▶ **Connect everyone**—End-user teams need to have a voice with the project team, which in turn needs to connect and align business and technology teams with one another.

- ▶ **Tie tactical needs to strategic outcomes**—Teams and the tasks they are chartered with fulfilling need to be interconnected to one another and to the project's overall goals by way of prioritization and an effective communications network.

▶ **Address counterproductive inertia**—An organization needs to know itself so that it can nip in the bud any trends drawing it away from meeting its goals; navigating counterproductive inertia can promote cultural and work-climate changes despite the inherent complexity ascribed to implementing SAP and thus changing the organization's culture.

An overarching company culture of transformation, innovation, creativity, trust, communication, and achievement underpinned by basic transformational values is central to effecting positive organizational change. Further, good management practices have long advocated the need for cultivating a shared vision behind which an organization may organize, mobilize, be stimulated, and be inspired. A self-serving transformation-enabling feedback loop may be established in this way. The idea is for the project team's vision to drive its strategy, which in turn drives organizational behaviors. These behaviors need to reinforce the vision but simultaneously encourage work teams to courageously revisit and revise their tactical responses to the project team's strategic vision (in response to changing external and internal factors, for example—factors that are inevitable). By creating a foundation for this level of responsiveness and flexibility, VTCM sets the stage for business and IT transformation in terms of enabled organizational agility.

One way VTCM promotes and sustains agility is by fostering creativity. People need to be encouraged to question the organization's norms. In this respect, the VTCM approach naturally lets an organization look at its culture or the "way things are done around here." By reviewing perspectives from existing and more recently appointed leaders and followers alike, ideas may be solicited so as to approach old situations or ways of doing things in new ways. A culture that invites introspection is more prone to not only accept change, but to drive it internally and do so proactively.

Agility has a direct bearing on how effectively teams can capture and share knowledge—an important structural facet and desired pattern of agile teams. Agility can be reflected in flexible JIT staffing, for example, enabling teams to creatively react to problem situations as well as new opportunities. Either way, JIT staffing enables organizations to innovate as they pursue new revenue, supply chain rationalization, or cost-reduction opportunities. By way of example, organizational agility makes it possible to troubleshoot and resolve issues more quickly, and thus to equip and employ the best person for a particular task rather than employ the person currently available though perhaps inexperienced or ill equipped. Agility then allows process modification to help ensure similar problems are routed to the proper teams and other resources in the future. Finally, agility in this context makes it possible to capture and use knowledge and lessons learned such that the issue at hand is aligned with an accessible, published resolution. By supporting long-term problem resolution, agility conserves scarce organizational resources and reinforces creativity in the process.

Finally, VTCM addresses the negative inertia mentioned earlier in this chapter. Once a project starts rolling forward, it is difficult to change direction despite changes in the environment that might rightly warrant a change in direction (or speed, for that matter). A project team that is knowledgeable in its own deep structure, culture, attitude toward change and complacency, technology biases, work climate, and other change-enabling factors has increased ability to overcome negative inertia—a tenet central to any effective change model or framework. Thus, by understanding itself, a project team can drive toward positive inertia. It gives an organization the ability to create a "culture of change" in light of the fact that organizations and individuals are incapable of directly changing culture. Culture is changed by changing *behaviors*; behaviors are changed by recognizing and rewarding or otherwise encouraging desired behaviors.

Real-World Organizational Examples

You may be asking yourself which organizational approach you should follow to support your SAP project. In many cases, your SAP project organizational structure also informally defines the escalation path that is to be followed for resolving project issues, making the structure that much more important in the overall scheme of things. Instead of providing textbook solutions to answer this question, we have chosen to present some examples of real-world SAP project structure. Some of these project structures contain the organizational elements that have been discussed in this chapter and some do not. The trick to properly defining your SAP organization is to personalize the structure by blending textbook structure examples and your own firm's unique organizational structure requirements. Figure 11.1 illustrates a lean organization that has proven effective in conducting global SAP ERP implementations and upgrades.

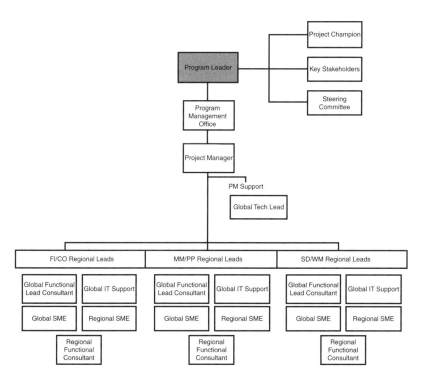

FIGURE 11.1 This SAP project organizational structure has proven itself in the deployment of ERP global templates and upgrades alike.

Figure 11.2 illustrates the potential diversity of subteams found within the SAP project board.

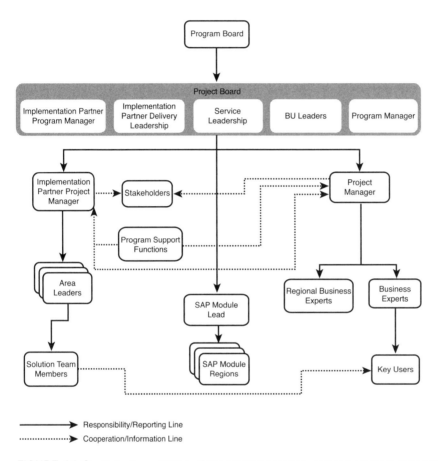

FIGURE 11.2   Note the addition of the implementation partner program manager and delivery leadership to the project board.

Figure 11.3 shows the relationship between a project's systems integrator (SI), customer project manager, and various subteams shown to be especially useful in an SAP upgrade project.

Figure 11.4 illustrates a hierarchy shown to be effective in bringing together geographically distributed project, technical, and ERP support teams.

In Figure 11.5, note that although this organization contains a PMO, the PMO only provides administrative and program support functions. Meanwhile, business teams are represented by various functional row leaders. Such an organizational structure can be easily extended as new business requirements are added to an existing SAP implementation project.

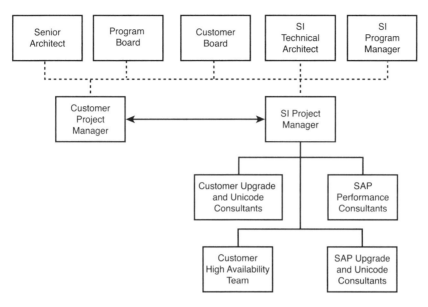

FIGURE 11.3   A time-tested SAP Unicode upgrade project structure example.

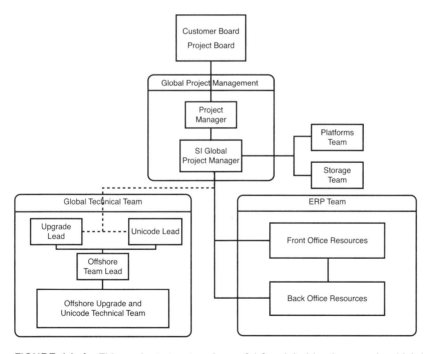

FIGURE 11.4   This project structure is useful for global businesses in which business and IT functions are both large and distributed.

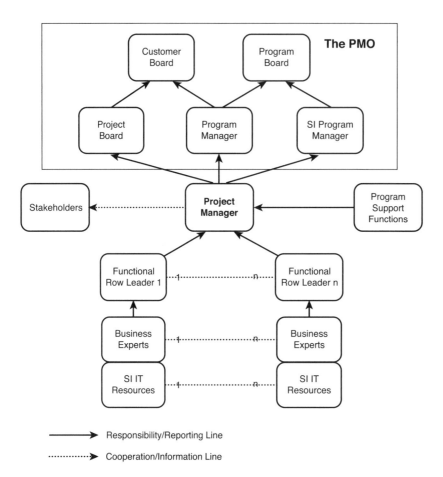

FIGURE 11.5   Consider this organizational structure for medium-sized SAP functional projects that you expect to grow in the future.

Summary

We have discussed building the project team, including which attributes you need to consider when selecting key senior-level project team members. You should be looking for impact executives and other senior leaders who understand the organization and, most importantly, are willing and able to provide senior-level leadership and oversight. Senior project team members must bring to bear their high-level relationships and excellent communications skills to kick off a project on the right foot and keep it on course.

Case Study: Project Team Roles and Structures

You have been tasked by an informal group of business leaders and IT representatives at HiTech, Inc. to provide it counsel regarding building its high-level project team. Your first task is to answer several questions related to key roles and organizational structures.

Questions

1. Given the importance of communication, what similarity is common between the roles performed by the project board and by customer board members?

2. What are some examples of tools that facilitate a good communication plan?

3. Where might the ideal SAP program manager be found?

> **NOTE**
>
> The answers to these questions can be found in Appendix A, "Case Study Answers."

CHAPTER 12

Staffing World-Class SAP Project Leadership

We have already identified how to build an SAP PMO (refer to Chapter 8, "Building the SAP Project Management Office") and how to build an SAP project team (refer to Chapter 11, "Building the SAP Project Team"). With your knowledge of the types of resources and roles required for the PMO and project team, you now need to figure out how to go about staffing the overall project team's leadership. Because the implementation of SAP is a high-priority business-transformation project, it is imperative to find the highest-caliber leadership resources. Having the right people in place can make all the difference in the success of your deployment. To be sure, a number of leadership styles have been adopted over the years by different SAP implementation teams, some wildly successful and others less than so.

But leadership styles are nearly as diverse as the leaders who practice them. Before an organization can select the most effective type of leadership, an understanding of basic leadership styles and principles is necessary, followed by an assessment of the organization's design, constituents, and more. All of this is briefly covered in this chapter as we focus on the critical task of staffing the project's leadership team (LT). Along similar lines, the critical tasks of staffing the business teams are covered in Chapter 13, "Staffing the SAP Business Teams," while staffing the technical support organization is covered in Chapter 14, "Staffing the SAP Technical Support Organization."

Attributes of Effective Leaders

Before we cover the specifics, a quick review of the attributes of effective leaders is in order, particularly as observed through the lens of an SAP implementation. We have noted a number of common leadership traits and personal attributes. First of all, great leaders possess vision. They understand how much progress they and their followers must make to achieve the organization's long-term goals, particularly how the current state of affairs will likely complicate creating a new and better future state. The greatest leaders possess the ability to effectively communicate this vision internally to their organization and externally to outside stakeholders.

Second, great leaders tend to be comfortable with and employ situational leadership, and tend to possess the ability to blend the proper amount of transactional and transformational leadership qualities based on the specifics of the current and desired states. Thus, they prove themselves to be the "right person for the job" time and time again. Great leaders lead by and through ethical example, setting the stage for others to do the same; through their example, they achieve in greater measure than expected.

Finally, great leaders understand how to motivate others to achieve goals beyond their own expectations without the need for contingency theory tactics. Rather than by leadership steeped in fear, coercion, or "management through trade-offs," the greatest leaders know their followers and motivate them to perform for the good of their team rather than expressly for their own good. Such leaders typically exhibit a combination of several different leadership styles, which we'll look at more closely later in this chapter; these leadership styles form a foundation for organizational transformation. Upon such a base, a leader can develop truly transformational leadership behaviors capable of attaining not only greater organizational productivity, but increased follower satisfaction and organizational stability in the long term.

An Introduction to Leadership Theory

A slew of different leadership models have evolved over the years, in response to people seeking within the context of a particular state of affairs to control or incentivize other people to achieve a desired new state of affairs, often through behavior modification and similar means of influencing motivation. Some models, such as Theory X/Theory Y, were developed to be very broad in nature, appealing to humans' desire to distill leadership thought into two readily defined and often mutually exclusive camps (such as people either dislike work or find satisfaction in work). Invariably, though, researchers discovered many exceptions in their attempts to generalize, and these leadership models necessarily morphed, gave birth to new theories, or essentially disappeared. Other leadership models, such as expectancy theory (a basic motivation theory putting forth the idea that hard work yields rewards), were developed to explain humans' likely response within a specific set of conditions when faced with two or more decisions. Still others, such as equity theory (a "justice" theory based on the idea that people seek and value fair treatment and will work to maintain a fair or equitable work environment), sought to explain what dissatisfied humans, rather than what motivated them. These insights proved useful in particular cases and certainly added to the broader body of leadership knowledge. But they failed to reveal the true heart of effective leadership.

Indeed, most leadership theories prior to what we consider contemporary today failed to get their arms around the "big picture" of leadership, instead illuminating only small pieces of a larger puzzle. This is why so many leadership theories have come and gone despite the fact that some seemed to be more effective than others, or proved less useful but nonetheless influential in helping to create or refine new models—they were neither fundamental enough nor wide enough to survive greater scrutiny. Fortunately, in the wake of many of these precursors to modern leadership can be found an easily followed trail congested with lessons learned, best practices for particular circumstances, and even specific leadership methods to avoid.

Authoritarian Leadership

Probably as old as humankind, *authoritarian leadership* was borne of tribes, kingdoms, wars, and the need for control, discipline, and strict attention to commands and orders. In the view of many behavioral theorists, it neither developed nor evolved; rather, authoritarian leadership has existed since the beginning of time, from the point at which one human sought to coerce or influence a fellow human through strength and power, or through headship—leadership granted by virtue of position, class, or appointment. The antithesis of democracy, it represents the culmination of a successful either-or dichotomy. That is not to say that authoritarian leaders cannot exercise a certain amount of democratic behavior—they can and do, reflecting the myriad personalities that make up the human race. Traditionally, though, authoritarian leadership leans heavily toward autocratic tendencies, while its "opposite" leans toward democratic tendencies.

Out of the limitations of valid authority or power came the practice of rewards and punishment. Like the next step of evolution in a well-traveled path, common sense clearly dictated long ago that propping up a leader's lack of formal authority or bequeath of power could be quite effective when done through rewards and punishment. For years, authoritarian leadership was assumed to thrive only in these kinds of highly controlled and disciplined environments, where close supervision prevailed and nonconformance resulted in punitive actions.[1] That is, respect and subsequent productivity was thought to be borne out of the fear of nonconformance, a decidedly unpopular view in most pro-labor contemporary circles today but common up until only half a century ago. This dogmatic use of power and expected compliance, wrapped up in an old-school "rewards or punishment" arrangement, even had some researchers anticipating that authoritarian leadership altogether would become obsolete in our modern world.

You might question whether authoritarian leadership still has any life left in it with regard to the world of large business and IT projects, even when used judiciously relative to rewards and punishments. That is, does it still work today? In our experience, the answer is yes, with the caveat that effective authoritarian leadership is typically at odds with environments requiring two-way communication, negotiation, and even basic fact finding and review. But in the absence of punitive actions, authoritarian leadership has proven itself

---

[1] *Bass, B.M. (1990).* Handbook of leadership: Theory, research, and managerial applications *(3rd ed.).* New York: The Free Press.

over and over again to decrease ambiguity and, in doing so, increase productivity, especially in operationalized and task-based environments. And lest we forget, there is more to authoritarian leadership than autocratic principles working in isolation. More than 2,000 years ago, Sun Tzu shared with us a core nugget of leadership wisdom—that leaders, even autocratic military leaders, must rely on others to be successful, and that leadership was never intended to be a one-man show but rather a knowledge-sharing dialogue between a leader and his followers. Sun Tzu explained in *The Art of War* that this knowledge gleaned from followers enables "the wise sovereign and the good general to strike and conquer, and achieve things beyond the reach of ordinary men," a fundamental tenet of transformational and other modern-day leadership styles: to motivate others to perform beyond what they perceive to be their limits. That transformational leadership could be embodied in a leader exercising authoritarian principles was Sun Tzu's true insight.

It should be noted that Sun Tzu's dialogue between leaders and their followers does not imply democratic discussions, compromises, or negotiations. Again, where communication must necessarily be two-way, other leadership styles prove more effective. Authoritarian "dialogue" is much more one-way than back-and-forth, representing an opportunity for followers to only share (rather than provide insight regarding) their knowledge of a particular situation with their leader, leaving the ultimate decision-making to the wisdom of the leader and his or her newfound knowledge. From a common authoritarian perspective such as that embraced by the armed forces, in time of war any *other* communication vehicle could undoubtedly breed disaster—and cost lives. SAP implementation projects in the most general sense (despite common use of the term "war rooms"!) don't seem to line up with environments conducive to authoritarian leadership.

But despite such perceived limitations, authoritarian leadership continues to prove both enduring and effective. Its effectiveness is broad-based, especially when the threat (rather than need for follow-through) of consequences or opportunity for reward encourages followers to simply follow rather than question. After all, a "Theory X" application of authoritarian leadership will only squash creativity and ultimately productivity and longevity. By its very nature, authoritarian leadership is ideal for addressing very time-sensitive, task-specific, locale-specific, performance-oriented goals, along with goals that are production-centered. Authoritarian leadership works best in cases in which tasks and boundaries are clear, two-way communication is less important, and authority is unquestionable. And best of all, authoritarian leadership works well in conjunction with other leadership styles such as those touched upon later in this chapter.

In cases in which overt or positional authority is lacking or unclear, though, such that an individual fails to possess the true authority to wield control, authoritarian leadership is less than effective. At its extreme, it can be counterproductive, even potentially disastrous. In these cases, effective leadership can be borne from acquiring and growing power granted from followers, rather than authority granted by virtue of position. It is this *delta* between such an individual's authority and the power officially granted to him or her by virtue of position or role that brings us to the next leadership model—servant leadership.

Servant Leadership

Of the different leadership styles discussed herein, *servant leadership* is the only one not borne of authority; power, rather than authority, makes servant leaders effective. Coined by Robert Greanleaf,[2] it is described in this way:

> The servant-leader is servant first... It begins with the natural feeling that one wants to serve, to serve first. Then conscious choice brings one to aspire to lead. He or she is sharply different from the person who is leader first, perhaps because of the need to assuage an unusual power drive or to acquire material possessions. For such it will be a later choice to serve—after leadership is established.

Servant leadership as embodied in the lives and teachings of the Old Testament's Abraham and Moses, followed years later by Jesus, completely changed the face of leadership. This style of leading underscored the fact that effective leaders need not be tied to fear- or rewards-based systems, or a position of headship or authority. Like authoritarian leadership, the greatest testimony to this leadership model's effectiveness lies in its longevity. Servant leadership has probably been taught and handed down throughout the ages more so than any of its contemporaries or successors, simply by benefit of the teachings contained within the Old and New Testaments of the Holy Bible.

Based on the precept that personal gain should be set aside in favor of organizational gain, servant leadership ranges in scope and application like any other leadership model. At one end, the leader of a highly autonomous organization might be perceived as engaging in servant leadership by dealing with organizational barriers and acting as a bridge between the organization and its external environment. At the other end of the continuum, the Book of Romans (15:8–9) proclaims to all people that Jesus came to Earth to serve, teach, and ultimately embody the most selfless act of love and compassion our world will ever know. In both cases, the power to lead *was granted by*, rather than forced upon, those being led. Read that again—servant leadership is effective because those being led willfully place in the hands of others the power to be led.

How did such an effective style of leadership, one completely contrary to anything before it or since, come to be? Many of the answers can be found in Briner and Pritchard's *Leadership Lessons of Jesus*. Servant leaders identify with and actively call their followers, for example, and by virtue of their expertise teach others with authority. Wise servant leaders go so far as to "break bread" with their followers, which not only builds and strengthens personal relationships but facilitates teaching as well. They genuinely care for their followers, and those important to them, to the point of sacrificing personal goals and gain for the betterment of their teams. True servant leaders knows that it is impossible to serve others without giving of themselves, underpinning the tenet that authentic leadership is costly. And above all, servant leaders are both faithful in their commitment and consistent in their embodiment of servanthood—they live out the message put forth in

---

[2] *Greanleaf, R. (2005). "What is servant leadership?" From http://www.greenleaf.org/leadership/ servant-leadership/What-is-Servant-Leadership.html*

the Bible's Book of Matthew (6:24) that says "No one can serve two masters," actively choosing to serve their followers at the exclusion of all others, including themselves.

Servant leadership is certainly the most controversial of the various leadership styles discussed herein. "Breaking bread" with the troops, for example, seems to fly in the face of military practices that actively seek to segregate leaders from those being led. Many would argue that such an outward-focused leadership style, one potentially devoid of organizational overlay, would lack effectiveness in too many situations to be worthwhile in a broader sense. After all, how many organizations are known for rapidly completing orders within the context of such leadership, where formal authority is not actually required and follower motivation stems not from rewards or punishment but from servant leadership in its own right? Having people giving potentially conflicting orders to one another outside the borders of formal authority in a military organization could, in all likelihood, result in communication breakdown within the unit and the bigger command structure as well. Thus, just like authoritarian leadership, there lies limits in where and to what extent servant leadership is indeed effective.

On the other hand, servant leadership in conjunction with or within the umbrella of another style, such as authoritarian or Theory Y leadership, can be phenomenally effective. Case in point, the U.S. Navy SEALs and U.S. Marine Corps Force Reconnaissance both purposely leverage a combination of servant and authoritarian leadership styles to the benefit of their fighting teams and the safety of the United States. At a unit level, relationships are encouraged based on servant leadership; unit leaders and their teams' members go so far as to live, care for, and socialize outside of work together. The resulting bonds of trust and loyalty are unquestionable. This is fostered, however, under the canopy of the larger authoritarian leadership style embodied by the Uniform Code of Military Justice (UCMJ) and further supported by each individual military branch's code of conduct and general orders. Without such "enabling" in this context, servant leadership would not do as well, because the selfish desires of individuals would eventually displace the needs of the team.

Servant leadership can be effective in any number of circumstances and cultures; the presence of underlying principles like those of Judaism and Christianity, for example, need not be a factor, because servant leadership principles hold eternal regardless. The authors know this well—going the extra mile for the team, taking care of one another, and placing the project's needs before individual needs are all important to a successful SAP implementation. Even Sun Tzu tells us that effective leadership embodies treating subordinates as "beloved sons," a label as consistent with Biblical principles as it is relevant today. Doing the right thing for the right reason is timeless.

Transactional Leadership

Although authoritarian and servant leadership are appealing, probably the most common form of leadership—and certainly a style that all of us are familiar with firsthand—is called *transactional leadership*. Transactional leadership is the only one of the leadership styles discussed herein to have its roots in our modern Industrial Age. As the Industrial Age and requisite business world evolved while scientific management developed, managing the efficient completion of discrete tasks became more and more important. Workflows, time and motion studies, and so on helped to create the foundation. But within the context of inherently more efficient organizations came the need for a certain leadership style adept in maximizing the newfound potential for efficiency. Thus was born transactional leadership. Seeking to get things done within the confines of an established system, transactional leadership continues today to be focused on maximizing the standards and processes in place to squeeze the most productivity and profitability out of a particular environment given a unique set of circumstances and constraints. In the laser-sharp single-mindedness of transactional leadership, its adherents can be supremely effective.

Like authoritarian leadership, transactional leadership proponents use contingent reward theory to motivate their followers, seeking to obtain a consistent level of performance in the process. "Do this for me, and I'll do this for you" is commonly heard from transactional leaders. Managing is typically of the "by exception" variety, too, which means the transactional leader tracks deviations from the standard rather than absolute performance. It is in these core factors—contingent reward and management by exception—that the theory of transactional leadership is based. The latter factor may be further split into two components, active and passive, thereby granting an adopter of transactional leadership more insight into their deeper nature as a manager and leader. Naturally, a leader more comfortable with active management-by-exception is not afraid to "change course" and do what is necessary to correct deficiencies. Such leaders may be perceived as micromanagers, and for good reason: They actively seek out performance discrepancies. A passive management-by-exception leader, on the other hand, often refrains from taking any corrective measures until a problem is so serious as to require action.

Thus, understanding the specific type of transactional leader is important to ensuring that they and the team are best suited for one another and the task at hand. In a similar way, it is important to understand where the advocate of contingency leadership sits within his or her own management continuum, discussed next.

Contingency Leadership

As its name suggests, contingency leadership theory states that there is not a single optimal style of leadership but that, instead, effective leadership is based on context or situation. Contingency theory, similar to various other leadership models, pits a task orientation against a relationship orientation. But it does so within a framework of three variables—leader/follower relations, the structure of the task at hand, and the leader's positional power, or power by virtue of his or her position. Research initiated as early as the 1960s has shown how effective this leadership style can be in practice.

In Fiedler's germinal piece[3] on contingency leadership, he proposed two self-esteem-centered leadership styles: one based on the task at hand, and one based on relationships. The idea was that people are inextricably tied to their self-esteem; by understanding one's contingency leanings and preferences, it's possible to ensure a consistent leadership style. And doing so can help a leader assemble tenets of other leadership styles into a cohesive whole, where one style meets one set of needs (for example, personal) while another style meets a different set (for example, the needs of the organization)—leadership based on situation or context. Once leaders understand where they fall on this continuum, they may be more effective leaders, choosing tasks and teams through which they are more naturally inclined, comfortable, and equipped to succeed.

Transformational Leadership

First described by J. M. Burns[4] and later developed by a host of other theorists, this theory defines transformational leaders as those who ask followers to "transcend their own self-interests for the good of the group, organization, or society; to consider their longer-term needs to develop themselves, rather than their needs of the moment; and to become more aware of what is really important."[5] Transformational leaders have also been described in terms of their followers, who often feel admiration, loyalty, respect, and trust toward transformational leaders, the result of which is an increase in the followers' motivation and productivity. Burns[6] described transformational leadership as the ideal relationship between the two, noting that transformational leaders and their followers will "raise one another to higher levels of morality and motivation."

No doubt, you have seen a common theme—despite somewhat differing perspectives, all of these theorists understood that transformational leadership seeks to raise the bar when it comes to individual follower performance. In this, adoptive organizations are poised to achieve operational excellence beyond their expectations. Transformational leadership can be just the game-changer an organization needs to go beyond incremental performance improvements and really make the leap between a current state of affairs and a much more desirable or preferred state.

Wren[7] wrote that transformational leaders tend to be "more willing to share power." Rather than reprimanding or praising their workers to meet organizational objectives, transformational leaders instead develop an expectation of high performance in their employees. With this in mind, Bass outlined the primary role of managers: to become developers of people and builders of teams. Such transformational leadership dictates

---

[3] *Fiedler, F. E. (1967). A theory of leadership effectiveness. New York: McGraw-Hill.*

[4] *Burns, J.M. (1978) Leadership. New York. Harper & Row.*

[5] *Bass, B.M. (1990). Handbook of leadership: Theory, research, and managerial applications (3rd ed.). New York: The Free Press.*

[6] *Burns, J.M. (1978) Leadership. New York. Harper & Row.*

[7] *Wren, D. A. (1994). The evolution of management thought (4th ed.). New York: John Wiley & Sons.*

major changes in an organization's structure, culture, market, and more—changes rooted in enabling, motivating, and empowering individual subordinates. Through this, Bass concludes, followers are themselves converted into leaders as they respond to the requirements of their transformational leader. Through time, such team members and their leaders create a sense of team identity, uplifting the morale, motivation, and even ethics of the team's constituents as they emphasize what can be done for one's organization rather than one's personal self-interests. Transformational leadership therefore bridges some of the old institutional theories with practices and approaches to organizational behavior that inherently help sustain the organization.

Leadership may also be treated as the interactions between team members rather than the traits of isolated individuals. This helps to build a communications grid within the team, thereby facilitating higher levels of productivity and subsequently motivation. However, transformational leadership in conjunction with institutional, cognitive, and social learning theory best exemplifies how an organization can reach its potential within a particular set of circumstances. What's important to remember is that as circumstances change, leadership needs to facilitate the organization's adaptation to these new circumstances, and in doing so continue to assist the revised organization in maximizing its potential as both the environment and the organization evolve.

A good transformational leader exercises charisma and inspirational leadership while stimulating his or her followers intellectually and practicing individualized consideration in the process. This includes learning how to transformationally build, staff, and maintain teams; how to identify and map motivators to individuals; how to take into account cultural factors relative to the manner in which individuals prefer to communicate, follow, and lead; and finally how to find a balance between power and authority such that authority only need be exercised in the direst of circumstances.

Leadership Styles in the Real World of SAP

Although transformational leadership represents the pinnacle of sorts in the world of leadership theory, a combination of many leadership models tends to make up the bulk of most people's leadership style. Understandably, these leadership models ebb and flow as people grow and are exposed to new situations. For example, many of the best leaders embody the essential components of servant leadership as described earlier. In a broader sense, situational or contingency leadership forms the backbone of many contemporary leaders today, while authoritarian leadership is still an important cornerstone for others. And certainly transactional scratch-my-back-and-I'll-scratch-yours can still be effective. Finally, many have witnessed firsthand how transformational leadership can move an organization into new markets, cost models, or broad IT-centric business programs.

If leaders understand where they fall on each dimension's continuum, they may prove to be more effective leaders; the effective contingent leader will select tasks and assemble teams with which they are more comfortable and better equipped to lead. Follower dissatisfaction plays an important role in analyzing leadership effectiveness; when follower motives are met in a haphazard fashion or not at all, organizations rarely achieve maximum efficiency. A better approach is to take the time to identify factors that lead to increased productivity by virtue of various leadership factors to motivate followers.

Finally, it must also not be forgotten that leaders in one realm are potentially followers in another. After all, people with no positional authority will have traditional leadership challenges regularly thrust upon them, while assigned leaders with positional authority may or may not have the power to effect authentic change. In SAP projects, it's important to identify both positional and "de facto" leaders and take the time to develop authentic relationships, understand background data and other context, and be careful to not underestimate exactly how much power followers may hold.

Modeling Ethical Leadership

Leadership is a reflection of personal and corporate character, rooted in personal and cultural values and, above all, an unwavering commitment to integrity. Only with this very personal foundation is business leadership possible in the form of profitability, market share, and so on. The same can be said of leadership within the realm of social groups, institutions, and even families. In the absence of moral and noble character, organizations cannot help but one day implode from within. Role models are an essential component of leadership, as people naturally model their own behavior and actions after those they respect and hold in high regard. Long ago, Sun Tzu[8] shared this single important principle upon which sound management and leadership relies most: the development and application of an all-encompassing standard to which an entire team, including its leader, may be held accountable. Effective leadership is about setting, achieving, and modeling standards. Leadership is about role models.

Modeling ethical leadership is especially important in organizations in the midst of change. Leaders who excel at successfully adapting to change understand the process is neither simple nor speedy. They are better able to motivate and empower others, encouraging creativity and the pursuit of organizational goals in the process. If followers can look to their leaders as a mentor or role model, the organization will be earmarked by a healthier work environment. In this regard, it is paramount that a leader embrace and practice individualized consideration—a quality characterized by personal attention and coaching—lest a key opportunity for transformation be overlooked.

Seasoned leaders have learned firsthand that authority and responsibility should be pushed down to the lowest levels of the organization for maximum effectiveness. Less-senior leaders will find this challenging. The challenge is one of becoming comfortable pushing beyond leadership styles that may no longer prove effective in a multicultural, geographically dispersed project team, and granting followers the authority *they* need to lead effectively. Education is one key, certainly. Sadly, experience borne of repercussions is often another. For these reasons, ethical leadership role models are most desired.

---

[8] *Giles, L. (1910).* The art of war. *(Sun Tzu, Trans.). Barnes and Noble Classics: New York. (Original work published 400 BC)*

Managing Diversity and Cultural Differences

Another critical leadership quality revolves around analyzing and understanding the different skills, experiences, and customs represented by a firm's SAP implementation team. Implementation teams tend to start out diverse and grow even more diverse as partners and vendors supplement the existing team. The opportunity to commit expensive leadership mistakes only increases as the team's diversity increases. Good leaders recognize that this diversity should be sought after, though; research shows that diversity is an asset to be leveraged rather than avoided. It is therefore not enough to simply understand what motivates individuals or teams, or how to best communicate with people of different cultures—in the name of preserving project outcomes and careers, it's also necessary to understand basic cultural factors.

As Bass and Steidlmeier[9] noted, evidence continues to accumulate indicating "that some of the variance in leadership theory and behavior is universal and some is contingent on culture of country and organization." How well a leader leads or exercises control depends less on the leadership traits and values held by the leader and more on the values that the leader's *followers* hold. If these values are consistent between the leader and follower, it is much more likely that the leader will be successful—with no guarantees, of course. The key is to uncover how consistent leaders and followers are in terms of their held values, and to align these values (or makes changes in leadership or the teams) sooner rather than later. Again, IT-centric business project teams today are only becoming more, not less, heterogeneous.

Across the various cultures around our globe, a number of key beliefs, morals, and values appear to be consistent. Among these are the concepts of friendship, love, and honesty. By the same token, other beliefs or values are very culturally dependant. A good leader understands and effectively works within these constraints or challenges, reevaluating behaviors and leader and follower styles as the SAP IT organization and the project's business teams grow more diverse. A leader needs to understand that the term "culture" need not apply exclusively to peoples from different sides of the world—cultural differences apply just as much to parties hailing from different sides of the same town, different parts of New York state, or different parts of North America. An SAP implementation project manager needs to take the initiative to identify the relative weighting of otherwise seemingly consistent values between cultures in an effort to track and maintain the order or sequence of values as they relate to different cultures. This situation makes it clear why leader/follower relationships are especially susceptible to miscommunication and even overt breakdown within a team. Along with traditional communication challenges, it also explains why cross-cultural teams are especially challenged relative to stifling transactionally borne productivity or transformationally inspired innovation.

Some cultures are so decidedly different from others that the "culture gap" between these and other cultures inherently makes for poor leader/follower relations. In these cases, it is

---

[9] *Bass, B. M., & Steidlmeier, P. (1998). "Ethics, character, and authentic transformational leadership." Retrieved from http://cls.binghamton.edu/BassSteid.html*

highly beneficial to provide local leadership at each site, rather than a single instance of centralized yet remote leadership. What does this mean for global SAP implementations? When it comes time to implement country-specific instances or address the gaps between global and local templates, it will be important to provide country-specific local leadership.

Leadership and Achieving Business Goals

At the risk of stating the obvious, all the attention we're putting on leadership is for one reason: to increase our chances of a successful project. Leading a team is a lot of work, after all, and directly impacts team productivity, effectiveness, and longevity, ultimately helping to achieve the project's objectives. That productivity is increased through effective leadership is no surprise. That transformational team leadership may create even greater value through the benefits of employee satisfaction and actualization is an even more pleasant surprise.

For example, the kind of teamwork facilitated through transformational leadership makes it possible for followers to offer up their individual skills, experience, and talents, along with their weaknesses, for the betterment of the team. Like taking one step back and many steps forward, a team aligned toward transformational leadership cannot help but take many steps forward, and perhaps only very few back. In doing so, the team moves inextricably toward rapidly achieving its goals and fulfilling its organization's vision.

Leadership and Motivation

Regarding motivation, basic expectancy theory instructs us that people pursue behaviors they hope lead to pleasurable outcomes. This too is consistent with transformational leadership; as we've seen, transformational leadership compels leaders to identify and understand the factors or "motivators" that actually underpin individual and team actions alike. In doing so, transformational leadership may be brought to bear to assist project teams in better meeting their employees' needs, thereby increasing task and job satisfaction and to some extent employee retention. This underscores the fact that transformational leaders must know not only their followers but themselves as well, and then make adjustments to management and leadership styles such that they mesh well with individual team members. Unaligned motivators weigh heavily on a team's productivity and stifle an otherwise innovative environment, discussed next.

Leadership and Character

Like integrity and other behaviors, leadership is also a reflection of character. With this very personal foundation, business leadership in the form of profitability, market share, and so on is made possible. Thus, even outside of the work world, a leader's character will serve him or her well on many fronts. With regard to family and social goals, a final mention of character lies in the following—once leader/follower relationships are established, the quality of those relationships is subject to change. This results in productivity gains or losses. One of the biggest factors can be found in the personality of the leader. As all of us can attest to, personality differences can drive some leaders into conflicting leader/follower relationships, resulting in a subsequent loss of the leader's—and usually the team's—effectiveness. Leadership borne of character will recognize this situation and proactively work to make changes internally in terms of self, externally in terms of subordinates, or both. All of this is akin to understanding both oneself and the organization, discussed in more detail next.

Understanding the Organization's Leadership Needs

Leaders need to understand their organizations and adapt their leadership style such that they can be the most effective leaders possible. This process of adaptation and reinvention can prove extremely difficult in light of so many complexities inherent to complex organizations—changing priorities, working conditions, and environmental factors; fighting against the status quo; cultural factors; deeply entrenched leaders possessing different viewpoints (or foggy agendas); and so on. What makes the process of change especially cumbersome is a basic lack of organizationally and environmentally specific knowledge. On the other hand, armed with the knowledge of an organization's leadership strengths and weaknesses, competencies and failings, and unfair biases and authentic gifts, a leader focused on truly leading an organization may create a "new normal" in which innovation, intellectual stimulation, self-actualization, and therefore organizational development and preservation are the norm.

In the world of new SAP implementations, transformational leadership—at least initially—is nearly always appropriate; incremental changes, and therefore leaders unequipped to transform their organizations, just won't do. Think about this in terms of revolution versus evolution—introducing a workplace-changing SAP project is all about business (and IT!) transformation or revolution. There's nothing incremental about changing the tools, the systems, and essentially the *way* people get their work done.

Interestingly, once an implementation's go-live date has come and gone, the most effective type of leadership style will almost certainly change. A transformational approach could easily give way to a more transactionally oriented approach centered on helping the organization incrementally refine its processes, for example. A focus on innovation may need to give way to a new focus on achieving operational excellence, including the kind of "continuous improvement" programs necessary to keep an organization lean and focused. Organizations that are used to generous budgets and the ability to spend money may find themselves in the midst of cost-reduction programs. Of course, this could take months or (in the case of successive waves of go-lives) many years. The key for executive-level and other hiring teams is to understand where their organization falls in this cycle, and focus on bringing in the right person for the right time. Once in place, new leaders must then spend some time assessing their organizations and developing the proper leadership plans necessary to transform or sustain—as appropriate—their organizations. Developing project-based and personal leadership plans is covered next.

Developing Project and Personal Leadership Plans

To survive, individuals and organizations alike must be capable of changing. However, the process of change can prove extremely difficult as people and organizations attempt to adapt to new priorities, conditions, environmental factors, competition, and more. To help leaders identify the specifics germane to their unique environment and then navigate their way through, they need a plan—not a project plan per se, but a project leadership plan. Think about it. With a lack of personal leadership prowess and understanding, the potential for a leader to overlook key opportunities to solve business problems, serve others, effectively mentor teams, or live a life less fulfilling than otherwise possible is great. Leadership is an art that must be practiced to be most effective, in a purposeful manner consistent with personal, organizational, and other related goals. For these reasons, development and maintenance of both a project-oriented leadership plan and an individual personal leadership plan is called for. Such plans provide the opportunity to benchmark organizational and individual leadership style as they evolve over time in response to experience, changing priorities, maturity, business goals, and so on.

Although development of a leadership plan provides an opportunity to inventory and introspectively analyze leadership styles, traits, and behaviors, the ability of a leader to make changes on the fly in both the near term and long term is more compelling. That is, noting strengths and weaknesses relative to leadership is valuable (particularly the aftermath of leadership decisions both good and bad). But in the end, the opportunity to learn from the past and introduce "course corrections" justifies creating and maintaining a leadership plan in the first place.

Leadership Plans: Vision and Mission

We like to think that good leaders have a vision, better ones *share* their vision, and the best leaders actively draw in others to embrace and communicate their vision, thus multiplying the leader's organizational impact. Any kind of leadership plan benefits from a well-defined and articulated vision statement backed up by an effective mission statement; an SAP project's leadership plan is no exception. Although vision and mission within the context of leadership and management are tightly related to one another, they are not the same.

Vision is akin to closing your eyes and looking into any number of possible futures, whereas mission speaks to the specific task a person or organization needs to tend to. The lines grow fuzzy as visions morph over time to reflect changing conditions, and missions expand to include multiple lines of business or core competencies. But one thing remains consistent—neither a vision nor a mission statement embodies the "how to" directions required to fulfill the vision or mission. This is left to the discretion of those who focus on operational rather than strategic plans, the execution of which lies firmly in the hands of capable management and leadership teams and their followers.

12

Building an Effective Personal Leadership Plan

With several core leadership models firmly entrenched in our past and current-day culture, a number of leadership style combinations may come together to form a foundation or "leadership pyramid." Interestingly, authoritarian leadership may sit underneath most other leadership models, whereas contemporary models such as transformational leadership can typically be grafted onto most other models. For example, transformational leadership is better enabled when transactional leadership has served to optimize a process or task; with the steps surrounding the successful completion of the process or task not in question, the stage is set for playing "what if" and making fundamental changes. In a similar way, servant leadership can be more effective atop a foundation of authoritarian leadership, as discussed previously, which in turn can enable improved situational leadership. The same holds true for charismatic and transformational leaders.

Other core leadership models, such as servant leadership, can prove effective in initially establishing and growing teams characterized by the need for high levels of teamwork, collaboration, and cooperation. Even better, in some environments, situational or charismatic leadership founded upon a bed of servanthood can usher the team to the next level of productivity and efficiency. The key in this case is authenticity—if the leader is not perceived as a true and consistent servant bound by unwavering morals consistently applied in public and private, he or she will not be granted power in this light; such a leader's effectiveness will crumble. Servant leaders are expected at some level to be quite transformational as well. A good servant leader not only questions the status quo but makes changes deemed necessary to grow the organization. This is contrary to true transactional leaders, who would be satisfied with doing what they could to keep the existing way of doing things alive.

Authoritarian and contingency leadership both help to instill a certain level of discipline and basic productivity within organizations, making for teams that are inherently stable if not overly successful. They work best where authority is clear, and where that authority is not abused in an egalitarian manner. The need for power is much less necessary than, say, in charismatic and transformational leadership styles, though power granted from below naturally advances any person's leadership role. Whereas transformational leadership seeks to instill confidence in an individual's ability to exceed even his or her own expectations, authoritarians get things done by virtue of consequences, whether rewards or repercussions. Similarly, leaders who adopt a contingency style of leadership "get results" through a reward system (where results are typically rewarded with positive reinforcement, though negative reinforcement is common as well when results fail to meet expectations).

As we have seen, contingency, servant, and transactional leadership styles all work well to some extent solo, and all seem to prove even more effective atop a foundation of sound and fair authoritarian leadership. This is probably true of most leadership styles. That is, at work, at school, in the home, and elsewhere, a solid foundation based on hierarchy, rules, and respect for positional authority makes a constructive base from which a good leader can exercise other leadership styles. In this way, the wise SAP executive leader could, for instance, more efficiently achieve goals, more clearly evoke a new vision, be more productive within a particular context or set of circumstances, or promote a more consistent message. And the leader could adopt a more "personal" servant-oriented leadership style, for example, when official influence was lacking and power necessarily had to come from below to make up for an absence of authority from above. Conversely, a fair-minded authoritarian leader with supreme authority could exercise fair and even-handed contingency or transactional leadership behaviors to achieve even higher productivity or greater results.

Implementing a Personal Leadership Plan

All the best intentions are for naught if they are never rightly implemented, for only in practice can a transformational leadership plan, or any plan for that matter, truly act as a change agent. To this end, a good personal leadership plan needs to not only be multifaceted and achievable, but acted upon. First, as discussed previously, a formal vision statement must be drafted, followed by an individual charter that identifies a project's objectives and a team's operational ground rules. In this way, the rules of personal conduct, including standards relative to working with and leading followers in various professional and social circles, are documented and made measurable.

Next, a mission statement must be drafted. Atop this, a description of actionable and measurable transformational leadership steps (such as those focused on coaching, mentoring, team-building, empowering followers, and celebrating team and individual successes) is appropriate. Several of the authors have witnessed the effectiveness of personal leadership implementation plans that reflect the steps to achieving self-actualization as described by Maslow[10] and his disciples, too—another good approach. And we've also seen firsthand how well a personal leadership "pyramid" encompassing the best of different leadership styles and behaviors can work (see sidebar). Our point here is that there are many models. The trick is to choose one that makes sense for the kind of leadership role and team, and then implement it.

Although implementation is critical, only regular follower evaluation and corrective feedback allows for a leadership plan to evolve as the environment in which it is exercised evolves. In this way, it is possible to assist a follower in achieving his or her version of self-actualization, rather than merely hoping one's followers in the end achieve their personal interpretation of what makes them happy. Formal evaluation can serve the purpose of documenting an individual follower's journey along a particular path of leadership, noting not only what is effective but what proves to be counterproductive as well. Ultimately, the evaluation of a leader's leadership plan will prove fairly easy. An effective leader will be known and recognized by the fruit he or she bears, after all.

Building a Personal Leadership Pyramid

In many ways, the stage is set today for transformational, charismatic, or situational leaders to take their otherwise authoritarian, contingency, or transactional organizations to the next level. It is only up to those who occupy leadership positions to recognize their natural tendencies, personal styles, and needs of their organizations and teams

---

[10] Maslow, A. H. (1943). "A Theory of Human Motivation," Psychological Review 50

so as to embrace a more effective *personal leadership pyramid*, a combination of leadership styles and behaviors that "works" for an individual or an organization.

By way of example, Sun Tzu illustrates how effective situational leadership can be when it's poised atop an otherwise authoritarian model. Specifically, Sun Tzu tells us that esteemed leadership is found in the "consistent treatment of men." Such leadership improves productivity because subordinates *want* to put forth extra effort and work harder for their authentic situational and transformational leaders. As described earlier in this chapter, the armed services are another good example. The best military leaders intentionally employ a combination of servant leadership atop an authoritarian foundation to the benefit of their teams and goals alike.

Evaluating Leadership Styles: The Multifactor Leadership Questionnaire

Before an organization selects leadership candidates, it's useful to evaluate them based on their observed leadership behaviors. In this way, an organization has the opportunity to align itself with the appropriate type of leadership from day one. Perhaps an authoritarian style might work best in some cases, whereas a transformational or servant-oriented style might be more appropriate for other organizations. Armed with an understanding of the *kind* of leadership that will probably prove most effective (along with several candidates that seem to fit the bill), the executive board and other senior leaders will have a much better chance of building an effective leadership team.

But how do you evaluate leadership styles? The answer is as broad as the hundreds of tools, evaluation criteria, and leadership questionnaires out there today. We have found Bernard Bass's Multifactor Leadership Questionnaire (MLQ) to be highly effective in identifying leaders and quantifying many of their leadership traits and behaviors. Working with his colleague Bruce Avolio, Bass expanded this tool in 1995 to include nine subscales or dimensions, including

- ▶ Idealized Influence (attributed)

- ▶ Idealized Influence (behavior)

- ▶ Inspirational Motivation

- ▶ Intellectual Stimulation

- ▶ Individualized Consideration

- ▶ Contingent Reward

- ▶ Active Management-by-Exception

- ▶ Passive Management-by-Exception

- ▶ Laissez-Faire

Using the MLQ is straightforward. Leaders can assess themselves (not normally recommended), or followers and others may assess potential leadership candidates. The MLQ version 5X consists of 45 items or questions using a 5-point scale ranging from 0 to 4, where 0 = "not at all," 1 = "once in a while," 2 = "sometimes," 3 = "fairly often," and 4 = "frequently, if not always." In this, the MLQ 5X provides well-balanced insight into a leader's effectiveness despite the weighting and mix of transformational and transactional traits. The tool also measures the absence of leadership, an attitude or trait termed *laissez-faire*. This is an important factor in evaluating leadership styles, as research and our experience have shown that it is the least effective (and from a follower's perspective, the least satisfying) of all measured leadership styles or behaviors. To purchase a (very reasonable) license for using the MLQ, point your browser to http://www.mindgarden.com/products/mlq.htm.

Real-World SAP Implementation Leadership: PM1 Versus PM2

Several of the authors recently assisted a large organization with implementing SAP NetWeaver and the SAP Business Suite, and had an opportunity to use the MLQ as an evaluation tool (at the request of the executive leadership team) of the initial (and much later) the follow-on SAP implementation project managers. The authors sought an objective leadership measurement tool and selected Bass and Avolio's MLQ 5X for several reasons. First, by using a well-known and respected instrument such as the MLQ 5X, biases would be largely removed from the leadership analysis. That is, an instrument shown to be valid and reliable countless times in the past decade would provide an objective platform for analysis. Also, a preliminary review of the organization's leadership trappings and strengths underscored tenets of transformational, contingent, transactional, and laissez-faire leadership; the MLQ 5X emerged as an ideal instrument for measuring leadership given its focus on three of these four styles. In retrospect, using the MLQ in practice was not nearly as daunting as we initially thought. Combined with what amounted to very valid and imminently useful conclusions, we trust you will find the results valuable as well, if not just plain interesting.

Background Data on SapIT

For the purposes of this real-world case study, we refer to the organization each PM worked for as "SapIT." After several false starts and changes in SAP implementation leadership, it was clear that SapIT was challenged by leadership in terms of style, values, and competencies. Historically speaking, some of these leadership styles and those who practiced them were successful; others were less than so. As the company's premier IT support team, the team was always rather large in size and scope, though funded inconsistently and often ill prepared for change. Until just before the SAP project would finally commence, the organization was decidedly laissez-faire at the hands of long-time entrenched leaders.

Strategic IT expenditures were often pushed down into the firm's business units rather than supported at upper IT echelons. In doing so, decisions with regard to the firm's IT infrastructure, applications, and support mechanisms across many different SapIT programs were addressed with little consideration for other programs. With few guiding principles, SapIT benefited from little in the way of technology, business, staffing, or even fundamental IT process standardization and consistency. Different IT-centric business programs shared little in terms of services, expertise, or lessons learned with regard to literally hundreds of technology decisions made over and over again by different project teams and business units. The result was nothing short of problematic; undisciplined spending worked in conjunction with unmanaged hiring, deployment of proprietary IT solutions, and a certain amount of apathy to create a panacea of expensive ill-managed and partially functional business solutions—expensive legacy or "IT stovepipes" incapable of individually supporting complex business initiatives or easily sharing data with other systems of record.

Several years before SAP was actually selected for the firm's enterprise resource planning (ERP) business platform, the SapIT organization was tasked by senior leadership with reviewing the viability of a companywide ERP implementation. The firm had little precedent for understanding ERP. Core financial, accounting, and other business processes had historically been executed within a particular business unit's domain; business units rarely executed processes that spanned different groups. As such, each business unit maintained its own accounting system, materials management system, payroll system, human resources management system, data warehouse, and so on. An ERP system would presumably tie all these systems together.

Given its lack of experience in the matter, SapIT contracted with a well-known management consulting company adept at assessing and planning for large ERP systems. A review of the current state of affairs and other initial findings proved conclusive: The firm was looking at a major undertaking at all levels in the organization, from fundamental leadership challenges, to how to introduce change to many different business units and their respective business user communities comfortable with business-as-usual, to how to incentivize a broad collection of IT resources seeking to maintain their status quo. In all of this, the study uncovered little ERP familiarity and even less ERP expertise.

Shortly afterward, the Office of the CIO (the parent organization responsible for managing IT enablement tasked with facilitating and supporting the firm's business processes) appointed itself companywide "enterprise architect." The organization made the far-reaching decision to establish the firm's technology standards, to broaden its policies and best practices, to develop structures responsible for managing applications, data, and methods of data sharing or interchange, and more. At the same time, a new interim CIO was appointed by the firm's executive leadership team. Change was imminent.

Hiring and Transitioning PM1

Within weeks of being brought in, a new ERP support plan began to take shape in the hands of the new CIO. He hired subject matter experts in project management, total cost of ownership (TCO) assessment, and ERP deployment to give substance to what was slowly evolving into a plan for change. The SapIT leadership team was reorganized and a new program manager was introduced—a personable, charismatic individual with a track record of getting results. This PM (for confidentiality reasons labeled PM1) further reorganized and introduced additional project management and IT business-enablement expertise into SapIT. In addition to several capable colleagues and various business and technology-oriented relationships, he brought with him a passion for both people and process discipline as well.

Although he had no formal leadership training or knowledge of transformational leadership, PM1's adoption of transformational principles (as described earlier in this chapter) helped drive major shifts in SapIT's leadership style throughout 2005 and 2006. PM1 intrinsically changed SapIT's view of leadership and the role it could play in making SapIT successful. More importantly, PM1's leadership by example encouraged individuals throughout the organization to adopt much of the same transformational leadership style. To be sure, PM1's leadership foundation was complex, steeped in situational leadership, transactional leadership, scientific management principles, and a new-found understanding and appreciation of what could only be described as transformational leadership. Placing the needs of his project and project team before himself, PM1 also embodied servant leader characteristics. But for several reasons, which we explore in more detail in the following discussion, PM1 did not remain in his project leadership role beyond two years. One of the reasons reflected an intentional decision by senior leadership; the CIO deemed PM1's initial leadership-focused job as completed. A new leader was deemed necessary to operationalize the ERP project.

Introducing PM2

In year three, a new program manager was brought in to lead SapIT's ERP project through to completion. PM2 not only sat in PM1's recently vacated chair but made broad organizational, partnering, and people changes that at first glance appeared unwarranted. A long-time company employee with far-reaching relationships throughout SapIT and other organizations, PM2 was viewed by senior leadership as the ideal "operational" candidate. With a track record of implementing steady-state operations more so than implementing new projects, in hindsight it was hard to argue with senior leadership's decision—the time for revolution was over, and leadership was now looking for a manager to drive evolutionary or incremental change.

By virtue of previous positional authority and relationships across the organization, PM2 held power unlike anything ever enjoyed by PM1. This proved very helpful as PM2 introduced changes and began to leave his prints on the organization. At first blush, PM1 appeared transformational whereas PM2 seemed to embrace more transactional leadership qualities. PM1 and PM2 were both decidedly distinctive and effective leaders, though; they merely had different strengths and weaknesses. And there were similarities as well. Both exhibited a number of the same characteristics with regard to persuasive abilities, for example. And both had the ability to introduce and manage change. For these reasons, the authors found the entire project intriguing from an SAP project leadership perspective.

How Culture and Diversity Impacted SapIT

Although age and gender diversity were well represented, SapIT was initially a very homogeneous organization in terms of cultural diversity. This created a unique culture within SapIT. As a backdrop for an ERP implementation, SapIT was ill prepared for the diversity inherent to functional configuration specialists, developers, and various technologists hailing from every corner of the globe. The well-known theorist and professor, Henry Mintzberg[11], describes this phenomenon as a collection of social rather than individual processes intervening to create an equally unique mood, atmosphere, operational "style," or culture. For SapIT, finding a leader that could effectively manage the firm's long-time employees as well as the broadly diverse group of consultants was nothing short of critical.

As an outsider initially, PM1 was less successful in some ways than PM2 in understanding and working effectively within SapIT's culture. However, PM1 was instrumental in changing this culture during his tenure, a culture originally slow to embrace change and even slower to adopt it. Through his leadership, PM1 helped guide SapIT along a revolutionary path of change—he managed to get a very large ball rolling, so to speak. To his credit, he also managed to bring most of the in-place organization with him; SapIT suffered from very little attrition even as it added to its ranks monthly.

Leadership Development Failures

PM1 and PM2 were both effective leaders but not without their shortcomings relative to developmental opportunities; although solid leaders in their own right, they both hired lower-level leaders who were ill equipped to work for SapIT. With a lack of personal leadership prowess and understanding, their tendencies to overlook key opportunities to solve the firm's business problems, maximize ROI, serve others, or simply create a workplace less fulfilling than otherwise possible hurt SapIT. These particular new hires did not understand that leadership is an art that must be practiced to be most effective, in a purposeful manner consistent with personal, organizational, corporate, and indeed family and other such related goals. Leadership is about leading people, after all, and people have needs outside of the organization and SAP implementation project they're asked to serve.

Neither PM addressed leadership planning. On behalf of SapIT, developing transformational leadership plans would have been appropriate; such plans would have dovetailed precisely with SapIT's ongoing evolution. It also would have provided the opportunity to baseline or benchmark SapIT's leaders as they too evolved over time in response to further education, inculcation of transformational and other leadership principles, changing priorities and goals, general maturity borne of experience, and so on.

Although development of a leadership plan provides an opportunity to inventory and introspectively analyze a leader's leadership styles, traits, and behaviors, the ability to observe leadership as it develops in the near term and long term is equally compelling.

---

[11] *Mintzberg, H. (1973).* The nature of managerial work. *New York: Harper & Row.*

In this way, it would have been possible to measure leadership strengths and weaknesses relative to leadership outcomes, noting the aftermath of leadership decisions both good and bad. In the end, the opportunity to learn from the past and introduce "course corrections" would have provided the most convincing reason for creating such a leadership plan in the first place.

Transformational Strengths and Weaknesses

In his desire to be effective, PM1 leveraged the concept of shared leadership, discussed earlier—he shared leadership with others, delegating it where he could and mentoring other leaders where it made sense. PM1 understood, applied, measured, and iteratively adjusted its use for maximum effectiveness. This included learning how to transformationally build, staff, and maintain expertise-specific teams within SapIT, how to identify and map motivators to individuals, how to take into account cultural factors relative to the manner in which individuals preferred to follow or lead, and, finally, how to strike a balance between power and authority such that authority needed to be exercised only in the direst of circumstances—again, tenets of transformational leadership explored previously in this chapter.

PM1 embodied what we described earlier as the quintessential transformational leader: one who asks followers to "transcend their own self-interests for the good of the group, organization, or society; to consider their longer-term needs to develop themselves rather than their needs of the moment; and to become more aware of what is really important."[12] Given PM1's strong showing in the five MLQ transformational components—he scored a 3.65 average—it is unsurprising that PM1 was quite successful in the midst of, and indeed driving most of, the changing landscape.

PM1 was also excellent at motivating others and empowering his followers to make decisions. With his high personal expectations both of himself and the team, PM1 sought to develop his team by developing his people. He scored 3.75 on Idealized Influence (attributed) and 3.5 on Idealized Influence (behavior). PM1 was instrumental in establishing the vision and sense of purpose and mission still held by SapIT today. PM1 *breathed life* into his vision—a vision he admittedly gleaned from executive leadership but nonetheless took ownership of and effectively shared. And by gaining the respect and trust of his followers and leadership colleagues alike, PM1 also effectively instilled pride and team spirit in his team—additional tenets of transformational leadership.

PM2 scored much lower in both these two dimensions (2.0 and 1.5, respectively). In the immediate short term, the impact was minimal. But without the ability or desire to continue refining and communicating SapIT's mission, PM2 lost much of the ground covered by his more transformational predecessor. That is, PM2's level of Inspirational

---

[12] *Bass, B.M. (1990).* Handbook of leadership: Theory, research, and managerial applications *(3rd ed.).* New York: The Free Press.

Motivation—including how and to what degree he communicates high expectations, helps focus his teams' efforts, and simplifies complex issues into actionable and simpler terms—was less than desired. Interestingly, PM1 and PM2 scored similarly on this subscale (PM1 scored 3.3 while PM2 scored 2.8). Given his history of effective leadership, it is unsurprising that PM1 was an effective communicator. He infused and inculcated upon his followers the importance of this trait, a key component of inspirational motivation ascribed to transformational leadership that he himself practiced well. PM1 was adept at using metaphors and analogies (an ERP project is "akin to navigating a long river," for example), making conscious use of them to give the project a more tangible handle for grasping otherwise abstract objectives.

With regard to Intellectual Stimulation, the MLQ 5X uncovered a significant delta between the two leaders. At 3.75, PM1 was head and shoulders above his transactional counterpart when it came time to solve problems, promote and reward intelligence, and rationally approach leadership dilemmas. Prior to joining SapIT, PM1 had a history of effectively partnering and co-leading with his colleagues and peers, navigating organizations to success. That PM1 was rarely threatened by others seeking to lead points positively to his ability to find creative solutions outside his own limited knowledge and experience. Meanwhile, PM2 scored only a 1.25 on the Intellectual Stimulation subscale.

The final transformational factor evaluated was Individualized Consideration, or the degree to which leaders provide personal attention, coaching, or sound advice to their followers. By treating followers as individuals and not merely "human resources," this factor spells the difference between long-term employee retention and high turnover. PM1 scored a perfect 4, and PM2 scored a very low 1. This difference in leadership became painfully apparent shortly after PM1 was replaced. SapIT turnover jumped to more than twice what it was under PM1's leadership. Especially worrisome were losses in upper IT and business analyst ranks—it appeared that the personal desires of followers to "stay the course" (referring to the river analogy used so effectively by PM2's predecessor) had diminished over time, and PM1's departure seemed to mark an inflection point for others to make changes as well. Thus, even while the ERP project took an operational turn, the leadership changes made by the executive team seemed to be questioned.

Transactional and Laissez-Faire Strengths and Weaknesses

With a 2.08 overall transactional leadership score, PM1 was much less transactional than transformational. He possessed a good mix of transactional leadership qualities, however. Maximizing transactional efficiency in the name of sound transformational leadership proved a cornerstone of PM1's leadership style; the authors were fortunate to witness first-hand the influence that transformational leadership had in terms of augmenting the effects of his transactional leadership skills.

On the other hand, with an overall transactional leadership score of 3.00 compared to his transformational score of 1.65, PM2 was a transactional leader first and foremost. To be sure, he possessed transformational traits. But the nature of his leadership style hinged much more so on the three MLQ-evaluated transactional factors, particularly

Management-by-Exception (active) and Contingent Reward (3.5 and 3.3, respectively). PM1 scored much lower (2.5 and 2.8, respectively), and particularly lower on the Management-by-Exception (passive) subscale (1.0 versus PM2's 2.75).

Alarmingly, PM2 was also shown to be something of a laissez-faire (think "leaderless") leader; he scored a 3.00 while PM1 scored an admirable 0.50 (for this subscale, the lower the number, the better). Research shows that laissez-faire leadership results in a poorer work ethic and corresponding poorer worker output than that obtained by transactional or transformational leadership. By virtue of its lack of clarity, laissez-faire leadership also culminates in little to no sense of accomplishment, and does little to unite teams (Bass, 1990). Thus, PM2 had a very real opportunity to negate much of the hard work that PM1 invested in terms of team building, mentoring, and essentially transforming the SapIT organization and the firm's way of doing business. Fortunately, PM2's transactional leanings helped offset his tendency to fall back on laissez-faire leadership.

Early researchers insisted that a leader was either transformational or transactional, but never a combination of both. As the authors saw firsthand, though (consistent with more contemporary research), both PM1 and PM2 illustrated how flawed the early researchers' thinking was. Instead, a combination of transformational and transactional leadership behaviors seemed to work pretty well, possibly complementing one another. For example, by following through on transactional agreements, leadership practitioners found that a leader could establish perceptions of consistency, dependability, and trust—all components of transformational leadership. With regard to SapIT, by honoring the conditions of his contingent leadership-inspired transactional style, PM2 also (probably unknowingly) embraced transformational principles even in the midst of his more dominant combination of transactional and laissez-faire leadership styles.

Strengths and Weaknesses Relative to Outcome Factors

With regard to leadership *effectiveness*, the MLQ 5X revealed that PM1 and PM2 differed remarkably. PM1 achieved an average score of 3.67 across all three dimensions. PM2 scored a 2.11. The authors initially believed this dramatic difference to be false. However, upon closer inspection of the three dimensions measured by the MLQ 5X—extra effort, effectiveness, and satisfaction—the authors agreed the numbers reflected reality. Extra effort and satisfaction both varied considerably between the two leaders. For example, while PM1 used methods of leadership that were satisfying (scoring a perfect 4 on this item), PM2 only scored a 1. In the same way, while PM1 heightened the followers' desires to succeed and willingness to try harder (both items were scored at 4), PM2 received a 1 and a 3, respectively. This explains why PM1 scored a 3.5 in satisfaction and a 3.8 in extra effort. Meanwhile, PM2 scored only a 1.5 and a 2. Both leaders measured "closer" in terms of overall effectiveness, however—PM1 scored a 3.67 while PM2 scored a 2.67.

Modeling Transformational Leadership Within SapIT

A major factor that impacted leadership as practiced in SapIT was the team's use of several large systems integrators (SIs) as their integration partners. SapIT was heavily augmented by two SIs in particular. Indeed, the core teams from these third parties represented more than half of the entire SapIT staff. Most of these individuals held long-time intracompany working relationships, and there were a number of lasting friendships within this subset of the SapIT team as well. The SI teams also reflected consistency relative to educational backgrounds, moral beliefs, and other cultural traits. Like a beloved family of sorts, there was little need to muster up false empathy; it existed naturally in light of long-time relationships.

Greater cultural and other venues of diversity came into play with regard to the extended SI deployment teams, though—those individuals and small secondary teams tasked with deploying front-end ERP client access, establishing handheld device connectivity and other mobile access to the backend SAP ERP solutions, supporting the infrastructure deployed in the company's data center, and so on. How SapIT applied transformational principles to effect positive change in the strategies and effectiveness of the overall organization certainly revolved around how well these secondary organizations were melded into the extended SapIT family—how SapIT led remote or virtual teams that simply did not have the benefits enjoyed by onsite local personnel.

To motivate others to achieve goals beyond their own expectations without the need for contingency theory tactics, PM2 should have focused more on selflessly working for the betterment of the team rather than through coercion or what some have called "management through trade-offs"—this would prove challenging given PM2's penchant for contingency leadership. But by self-regulating, remaining flexible, encouraging innovation, and rewarding motivation and achievement, PM2 embodied transformational leadership; in doing so, PM2 set a positive example and modeled both sound leadership and follower behavior, an interesting and even remarkable though essential dichotomy for successful long-term leadership.

As the SAP project grew and waned in response to the project's needs, PM2 was positioned to staff the organization with complementary individuals capable of working well with existing team members. These team members were also more inclined to work well within the constraints and challenges inherent to the project. Social awareness naturally increased across the organization, too, benefiting local and remote teams alike. To this last point, improved social awareness or social competence on PM2's part also set the stage for others to follow his lead. In doing so, the team reinforced its culture of trust, honesty, and awareness of others' feelings—a culture that largely exists today but one that must continue to be reinforced to maximize effectiveness between core and remote teams, and between leaders and followers.

Assisting SapIT in Achieving Its Business Goals and Objectives

PM1 achieved what PM2 could probably never achieve: He turned the course of events within SapIT such that the organization truly evolved into the centralized IT entity it was always envisioned to be but could never quite pull off. PM1 accomplished this purely through his leadership style, for he was without much formal power. On the other hand, once steady-state was achieved, PM2 achieved (in the short term, at least) what PM1 was struggling to do—make progress and streamline processes once the project truly got rolling.

That more transformational principles should be embraced by PM2—especially regarding methods of increasing productivity, minimizing interruptions, maximizing team effectiveness and longevity, and ultimately helping to maintain a happy implementation team—is a bit self-evident. That productivity and morale was increased through his predecessor's effective leadership was also of little surprise. The real surprise was in the level of teamwork achieved followed by the naturally emerging positive business results. PM2 would do well to look at PM1's use of mentoring, too. PM1 established an informal mentoring program that linked directly with the organization's business goals. Within his team, PM1 pulled aside senior technologists and business analysts and assigned each a junior member of the team. This move not only better prepared the team for support, it also aligned the team toward a common objective (successfully implementing the new ERP system) while increasing intrateam communication and commitment.

Conflict Resolution and Other Organizational Considerations

Although PM1 scored better in effectiveness, PM1 was actually less effective than PM2 in resolving internal conflict. Management research underscores the relationship between leadership and employee motivation and morale; no organization reaches its potential without maximizing the loyalty, trust, and confidence of its followers in their leaders. By the same token, as most people can attest to, organizations can be ripped apart by internal feuding. PM2's focus with regard to potential conflicts between the team members, or between those with differing entrepreneurial foci, was to nip them in the bud. By squashing potentially morale-damaging (and therefore productivity-reducing) conflicts, PM2 helped create a culture that simply did not tolerate infighting. PM2 minimized intrateam tensions. PM2 never really focused on actively airing and resolving conflicts, though. This could have been easily accomplished via regular face-to-face communication with the SapIT team, combined with weekly client team meetings and intrateam meetings and conference calls.

PM2 lacked the special brand of charisma held by his predecessor. Authenticity relative to PM2's personal code of ethics made up some of the difference, though—he got things done by virtue of position and ethical example. Better communication skills would have helped, to be sure. But PM2 nevertheless set the stage for organizational longevity, enabling lasting organizational continuity even as technology and customer requirements were expected to continue to evolve rapidly over the next several years. By creating a stable management and leadership foundation within a seemingly chaotic set of evolving circumstances, the authors believe that the SapIT workplace will continue to be a good place to work.

To set the stage for effective conflict resolution, good organizational design was also important. Managing span of control, for example, was important in reducing delays, minimizing time required for coordination, and eliminating most of the confusion surrounding organizations that try to assign too many direct reports to a single manager. The authors are fans of relatively flat organizations, but anything over 10 to 15 people just becomes too cumbersome to manage. PM1 did a great job of establishing a lean organizational framework, and PM2 did a fine job as well in terms of expanding and changing the organization where it made sense.

Additional Strengths and Vulnerabilities

PM1 possessed sound leadership skills and indeed many of the other important management roles and qualities that helped to effectively bring together people from different
backgrounds, cultures, and levels of technical proficiency to build a cohesive team. This
was one of PM1's long-time strengths, and can be attributed to his penchant for servant
leadership as well as his transformational style. In a broader sense, situational leadership,
and in some situations authoritarian leadership, played important roles in PM1's success
as well. His leadership strengths helped create a leadership foundation, true, but it was his
understanding of people and their needs that proved vital to his success as a program
manager and overall project supervisor for the firm's ERP implementation. In studies
conducted by the Gallup Organization and Spherion, supervisor effectiveness was cited as
the primary reason why employees remained employed—not money, not position, and
certainly not pension plans or company cars. To be as effective as PM1, PM2 and his
successors should continue to develop their relationship-building skills. This will go a long
way toward increasing employee and contractor retention rates; organizational climate
will continue to improve as well, making both retention and satisfaction ratings good
predictors of long-term organizational performance.

Beyond leadership, PM2 must understand that vision is also necessary to cement a collection of individuals into an effective team. As we discussed earlier, the concept of vision, or
essentially closing one's eyes so as to look into and see any number of possible futures,
helps a team form a mental picture of where it needs to go, if not how to actually get
there. PM2's predecessor was adept at this; PM2 needs to become more adept at converting
vision into words, and those words into reality. This will also go a long way toward
increasing retention rates and will serve PM2 well in terms of building up the "idealized
influence" dimensions of his own relatively weak transformational leadership style.

SapIT Outcome and Summary

Like taking one step back and many steps forward, a team aligned toward transformationally inspired leadership cannot help but take many steps forward, and perhaps only very
few back (and then, only occasionally, perhaps in light of difficult-to-manage or unanticipated circumstances). A successful assessment of PM1 and PM2 through the lenses of
transformational, transactional, and laissez-faire leadership helped SapIT's executive leadership understand the type of leadership styles shown to be most effective in moving the
organization forward in light of upcoming challenges. By identifying strengths, assessing
gaps and shortcomings, and essentially helping its senior leadership team develop a
project leadership plan, the SapIT organization should thrive over the next several years.

In case you're wondering, PM1 is still transforming organizations today; his special brand
of charisma continues to serve him well. A likeable and engaging leader, PM1 leveraged
his charisma to connect with strangers and colleagues alike to influence decisions and
effect change. And authenticity relative to PM1's code of ethics and morals is seen as a
hallmark of his leadership style in the recent past as well. Together, these traits made it
possible for this transformational leader to make lasting changes well outside of his
immediate circle of influence. A leader with such a fine balance of charisma and moral

authenticity, PM1 proved not only effective in the world of work, but across social, personal, and other dimensions of life.

In the meantime, PM2 also proved to be effective. True, he didn't get the kind of transformational credit his predecessor received, but, then again, that's not why he was hired for the job. After getting through the initial rough spots, PM2 took the organization through several go-lives, internal leadership and organizational changes, a significant change in partnering and resource sharing, and much more. He refined processes and helped the SapIT organization shift its focus from implementation to achieving broad-based operational excellence. In doing so, he pulled off exactly what he was assigned to do—though in a different way than PM1 would have pursued. To both SAP project managers, we say well done!

Summary

In this chapter we explored several leadership models, including authoritarian, servant-led, situational, transactional, and transformational styles. Doing so made it possible to shine a critical light on the broader learning surrounding leadership behaviors and what works in the real world of SAP implementations. Specific tenets of transformational leadership were then introduced, followed by practical methods of implementing both project-based and personal transformational leadership plans. We also noted that truly game-changing organizational transformations, rather than those changes better described as incremental, are made possible through adopting transformational leadership principles. We also presented a detailed case study highlighting two different leadership styles, both of which proved effective.

In many ways, the SAP implementation stage is set today for good transformational, charismatic, or situational leaders to take what are probably best described as transactional organizations to the next level. It is only up to those that occupy leadership positions to recognize their natural tendencies, personal styles, and personality so as to embrace a more effective "personal leadership pyramid" as outlined previously. Wise leaders also need to work to understand their organizations and how existing teams and teams remaining to be formed may be led most effectively. Finally, the best leaders embody the philosophy that leadership without example is empty—perhaps the oldest and yet still most contemporary leadership tenet of all.

Case Study: ERP Program Management Needed

As a member of the HiTech executive leadership team, you have created a subcommittee to identify specific leadership attributes (and eventually bring in candidates to interview) that reflect what the company needs for its pending ERP program manager position. Filling this new position will be challenging. A long-time subsidiary of HiTech called OldBoy needs to be brought onto HiTech's standard SAP-on-Windows/SQL Server computing platform. OldBoy's IT organization reflects a certain amount of bureaucratic military-like authoritarian roots. Further, business as usual is a common theme frequently leveraged to maintain the status quo in the IT team; change is abhorred. OldBoy's IT team is acutely aware that the business is unhappy with its legacy systems and its related inability to collaborate and work more intelligently. Not surprisingly, talk of IT outsourcing has been floating around for more than a year, which has the attention of OldBoy's IT management. Meanwhile, OldBoy's IT teams tend to reflect cubby holes of homogenous skill sets and widely shared biases against anything that doesn't resemble a mainframe.

Questions

1. To bring OldBoy's IT organization into the 21st century, is revolutionary or evolutionary leadership called for? Explain.

2. In terms of a core leadership style or model outlined in this chapter, how might the HiTech executive leadership team best describe the kind of SAP program management leadership style needed to transition OldBoy to HiTech's SAP computing platform?

3. Though its authoritarian roots are evident, from a leadership perspective how else do you envision OldBoy actually getting things done?

4. What role might servant leadership play at OldBoy?

5. Defend the position that the best initial candidate for transforming OldBoy might not be the best person a year or two down the road.

NOTE

The answers to these questions can be found in Appendix A, "Case Study Answers."

Staffing the SAP Business Teams

In the previous several chapters, we discussed building the project management office (PMO), working with SAP partners, and assembling the overall SAP project team. We also briefly touched on the importance of the SAP business team as a component of the overall staffing process and the SAP project's success in particular. In this chapter, we focus specifically on the SAP business teams, including their roles, staffing options, and some real-world challenges inherent to building successful teams.

Best Practices for Building the SAP Business Teams

To begin, it is important to make a distinction between the *business team* and the *technical team*. During an SAP implementation, a technical team is assembled under the leadership of the overall project team. Composed of SAP functional configurators, developers, and a great variety of technologists, this technical team helps introduce standard business processes into a firm (and in many cases also adapts SAP to support the firm's existing business processes). The business team, by contrast, is composed of specialists who help the technical team convert business processes and requirements into an SAP-based technical solution. Given this team's focus, it may be stated that someone works on the "business side" or "business team" as opposed to the "IT side" or "technical team." Also keep in mind that the business team really comprises multiple teams focused on different business functions—so we use the singular and plural notations interchangeably. With all this in mind, let's discuss best and common practices that should be considered when building an SAP business team.

Find Your Visionaries

An SAP implementation often is the largest project that a company has ever encountered in terms of business impact and technology changes. For this reason, the ability of those at both the executive level and on the front lines to carry out the SAP vision throughout the organization is one of the most important success criteria. SAP will impact almost everyone in your company either directly or indirectly and often this change creates anxiety and moves people out of their comfort zone. This makes it imperative that those leading the implementation effort are individuals who embrace change.

People who consider SAP a challenge and an opportunity to better their business rather than an obstacle or distraction are the best candidates. These visionaries will act as the filters of your SAP vision to the rest of the organization, and their attitudes and personalities can make all the difference in your project. These people must be empowered and have the latitude to empower others. The more that individuals feel like they have a stake in the project and are part of the overall vision, the more likely that they will become engaged and buy in to making the project a success.

Find Your Talent

Every department or team has one or more "go-to" personnel, and these are exactly the people who you should tap first to work on the SAP implementation. Their strengths and specific talents may vary, but a few qualities to seek out and focus on generally include

- **Business process experts**—These people understand the detailed inner workings, resource requirements, and connection points describing how a firm does business; they are masters of the end-to-end business processes of a company and therefore play a vital role in redesigning or otherwise changing these processes.

- **Technically savvy**—Individuals who can adopt the new SAP technology changes quickly can become key examples to lead the way for future end users. For instance, savvy web users may be able to intuitively navigate a new portal application and then use their expertise to train the rest of their team.

- **Effective communicators and relationship builders**—No matter how well an individual understands a business process or how technically adept they are, if they do not have the ability to communicate their expertise to others, their benefits are limited. This does not suggest that those who do not communicate well are not still valuable to the project, but those who work most closely with end users, training efforts, and so forth should be your best communicators.

Notice that many of the talents discussed here are intangible qualities. This is notable because the ability to lead, communicate, and teach others will be as important as proficiency in any specific business or technology area as you build your business team. Keep this in mind as we move to the next section on business team roles and tasks.

Business Team Roles

Just as an SAP implementation can touch every facet of business, SAP business team roles can span every level of an organization, from executive leadership to frontline positions. Some of these roles will be permanent jobs and require ongoing coordination with the SAP functional teams over time. Other roles may be only temporary positions for specific phases of the project. Regardless of the level of involvement, all of these roles are important to the success of the implementation.

In this section, we look at three different levels of roles within the SAP business team (executive, management, and subject matter experts) and some of the tasks performed by those who fill those positions. Of course, the exact composition of the SAP business team can vary from company to company based on its size and budget, so consider what might work best for your organization as we move through the section. Also, keep in mind that the SAP business team members had jobs prior to the SAP implementation and often still have those same responsibilities going forward. So, what we are really discussing in this section is how these jobs are impacted or expanded as a result of the project's roles.

Executive Level

In prior chapters, we have discussed project sponsors and project board members that operate at the executive level. Often, these same members also have roles as part of the SAP business team. For instance, the chief financial officer (CFO), while an executive board member of the SAP project team, may still have a supervisory role on the business team and provide direction for the SAP Financials aspects of the project. Likewise, the marketing director may be in charge of handling the communications to the business for all the SAP changes coming to the organization. In this way, executives have responsibilities as members of the SAP business team very similar to their everyday jobs, providing strategic and budgetary direction to management for the business areas for which they are responsible.

For example, a chief operating officer (COO) who is responsible for multiple sales divisions of a corporation may be responsible for the implementation of SAP Customer Relationship Management (CRM) as a strategic shift to improve customer service and provide better tools to the sales force. The duties of the COO have not changed significantly but now SAP CRM is a major component of the COO's budget and strategic decisions going forward. It may also change how the COO collaborates with peers. For example, the COO may be much more concerned now with the activities of the CIO and how technology changes may impact the SAP CRM system on which the COO's division relies.

Management Level

Management jobs on the SAP business teams are often aligned by business process, and this may or may not change during an SAP implementation. Often, it depends on how the business process itself changes as part of process or gap analysis initiatives. Gap analysis is the process of determining delta changes between a current process and a future process or the consolidation of multiple processes into a single process. For instance, if a company with multiple divisions that previously all operated independently implements a single SAP ERP instance, it may perform a gap analysis before it centralizes processes.

The business process managers would work with the SAP TSO (discussed at length in Chapter 14, "Staffing the SAP Technical Support Organization") to perform a gap analysis to consolidate the various processes at each individual division into a single process on SAP. As the business process owners of the organization, managers on the SAP business team work with their functional or technical counterparts in the SAP TSO to plan and implement ongoing business process enhancements to the SAP systems. This can be basic configuration maintenance, such as adding a cost center, or more detailed changes, such as automating the bill-to-pay process. In these scenarios, management works with configuration leads on the SAP TSO to plan the change, agree on timing for implementation, and manage their respective team members who bring the plan to reality.

Subject Matter Experts

SMEs are the human knowledge repositories throughout your organization who perform everyday tasks that keep the business running smoothly. They understand the detailed business processes, know the key vendors and customers, and recognize the integration issues and the exceptions that can arise that require special directives. Accordingly, these SMEs are your most valuable assets on the SAP business team. It is their interaction with the SAP project team and SAP TSO and their input during gap analysis that will ultimately define your blueprint and process standardization for the implementation. In addition, the SMEs function as an extension of the SAP TSO and can take on a variety of helpful roles, including:

▶ **Superusers**—Each department or team usually has one or more people who, due to their proficiency with the business process, the SAP technology, or both, become the teachers and trainers to those who are less experienced. These superusers are often the first from the SAP project team to attend training, and they help relieve the burden on the group by handling day-to-day questions and problems for their particular department or functional area of expertise.

▶ **Trainers**—SMEs can and should be part of the SAP training team. Often, "train the trainer" classes can be performed that allow the SMEs to go back to their teams and facilitate local, ongoing training at their site. Again, this can be a huge service to the SAP implementation because training is often a challenging task, especially in large and geographically dispersed organizations.

▶ **Testers**—As business enhancements and new development are moved through the SAP landscape, SMEs also perform testing in the quality assurance systems to make sure their business transactions are performing properly after changes are made to the system. This will require them to work closely with their functional counterparts to point out problems and recommend process improvements over time.

As you can see, the SAP business team roles, in a lot of ways, mirror the SAP technical and functional roles that operate within the IT departments. Although it is not required, companies often align their organizational structures in this way to create synergies across the business and technical departments (see Figure 13.1). Consider a scenario in which the manager of finance has a counterpart on the SAP team, the SAP configuration owner for the FI module. The manager of finance will have various SMEs on his or her team that will work with SAP FI functional configuration experts on testing and training efforts during the project and for ongoing enhancements. Again, although this structure does not exist for all organizations, you can see how it can streamline processes and communication in the finance area by having alignment across business and technical departments.

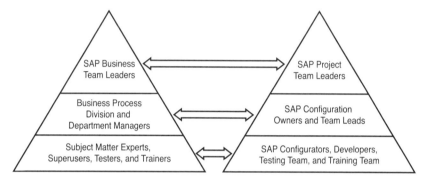

FIGURE 13.1   SAP business teams are "matched" with similar positions found on the SAP project and technical teams.

SAP Business Team Staffing

Because the most likely and most qualified candidates for the SAP business team often are people already working in your business, your approach to staffing the SAP business team may be different from your approach to staffing some of the other teams we have discussed in this book. In fact, you may even question why you need to increase your business staff at all. After all, the team members you need are already part of the organization. Before answering this question, let's consider a common scenario that might help you in your approach toward staffing the SAP business team.

During any SAP implementation, a transition period that can last months or even years occurs during which old processes and new processes are both in place. For instance, until that legacy accounting system is completely retired and converted to SAP, members of the accounting team will still have to maintain and support those as-is processes. Meanwhile, these same people will need to support the SAP team as SMEs, trainers, and testers for the new processes. They may even be asked to join the SAP project team, or at least might be temporarily loaned to the project. In any of these scenarios, it is obvious that new demands will be put on some or all of the business workforce as it adjusts to support existing tasks along with the new project burden. One approach is to leave the status quo and let the same people perform both jobs. However, unless your workers are currently underutilized, they probably already have full-time responsibilities. Likewise, the demands of the SAP project should not be underestimated. For this reason, many companies resolve to staff up utilizing backfill positions. There are two primary approaches used to achieve this goal:

▶ Bring in temporary staffing to learn the legacy process so that current in-house expertise can be used on the SAP implementation. Once the new process goes live on SAP, the temporary positions will no longer be required.

▶ Outsource or hire consulting experts to come in during the transition and train the business team on the new SAP process and functionality. Again, once the process goes live on SAP and the legacy process is retired, the consultants can roll off the project, leaving trained employees to carry on with the new process.

With both approaches, the key is to maintain stability in business operations while simultaneously meeting project goals.

The timing of the staffing approach is also important. At the beginning of any transition, there is an adjustment period. For example, with the earlier first approach, the new hire needs to spend some time working with her internal counterpart before she becomes productive. Similarly, in the second approach, a training period is required while consultants work with onsite experts. In both of these cases, it is best practice to bring in transition positions with plenty of lead time so that, during peak phases of the project, all of the required staff will be up to speed.

Often, a hybrid approach can be used to achieve a balance of backfill roles along with experienced help (see Figure 13.2). Consider an example of a company that is implementing new modules such as finance and logistics within an existing SAP ERP system. In this scenario, the company might use a temporary staffing agency to hire backfill positions for the accounts payable clerks or customer service representatives. This would free up the firm's own SMEs in these finance and logistics areas to focus on project activities. At the same time, the company might bring in functional experts from SAP AG or one of the major SAP systems integrators or consulting firms to work with these SMEs to bring them up to speed on SAP and the new business processes.

Organizing Your SAP Business Teams

Even with the right talent and staffing approaches, the effectiveness of the SAP business team may best be evaluated in terms of how it is organized. In this section, we discuss some of the key factors to consider as you determine the organizational structure of your SAP business team. These include integrating the team for success, organizing it to enable swift decision making, and maintaining balance relative to the classic "workers versus leaders" dilemma.

Integrating for Success

One of the most common organizational pitfalls that can occur early on in an SAP project is to build teams into silos. Depending on project phases and timing, some business areas will build their teams earlier in the project than others will. As a result, planning and business process design can occur in a vacuum without considering integration. For instance,

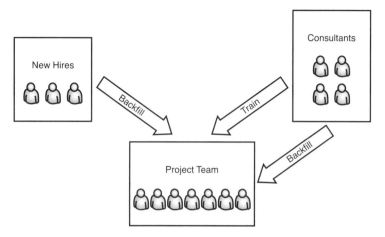

FIGURE 13.2   A hybrid strategy brings in new hires to provide backfill and consultants to work with and train existing employees.

payroll has both SAP Financials (FI) and SAP Human Capital Management (HCM) components that need to work together for the overall payroll process. If either the FI or HCM team begins blueprint and design without including the requirements from the other team, integration points can be missed. This can result in costly mistakes if major configuration has to be redesigned later in a project to accommodate new requirements.

For this reason, the SAP business teams should have cross-functional interaction on a regular basis. An SAP integration team should be formed that includes at least management and senior team members from the various business teams. For instance, team members from the finance, supply chain, and inventory management departments might meet to discuss a bill-to-pay process. It is important here that at least one member of each team have detailed functional experience in the business process represented. Key business process integration points and other potential trouble areas are often exceptions to the rule and may only be recognized by experts with significant specific expertise. It will not always be practical for a representative from each business team to meet as an integrated team on a regular basis, so silo meetings will still occur. The key is to make sure that information across teams is shared at scheduled intervals before final decisions are made.

Organizing for Decision Making

Especially on large projects, SAP business teams can get caught in "analysis paralysis." Earlier in this chapter, we discussed the process of gap analysis. As teams go through this process, there will be varying opinions among the different teams of how multiple business processes should be consolidated into a single business process or what steps should take place in a specific process. Often, there is not a right or wrong answer or one single answer. Avoiding analysis paralysis requires compromise and an organizational structure conducive to decision making. This means someone in the organization, typically at the senior management or executive level, has to evaluate all the information gathered by the teams and make a final decision. This often is difficult and can have political implications in the organization.

Equally important is that teams have accountability to the decision-making process. This responsibility should be assigned at the beginning of the project by the project sponsors. A program manager, or someone who has visibility at a high enough level that represents the project as a whole across business areas, should be involved in these decisions and have the latitude to enforce those decisions. This is necessary to avoid project bottlenecks that can occur when a lack of decision making exists.

Maintaining Balance

As management staffs the SAP business team, it should make sure there is a balance between task-oriented roles and facilitator roles. Said more simply, the team needs the right number of leaders and workers—an unbalanced team will cost more than necessary, slow down decision making, introduce longer project-completion delays, and more.

Facilitator roles are those that manage, plan, or design but do not necessarily carry out specific tasks to implement, develop, or perform. A project manager, for instance, would be considered a facilitator role. Although both task-oriented and facilitator roles are equally important, generally, a team should have more task-oriented roles to ensure that tasks are being performed and goals are being met. If facilitators are creating more work than can be carried out by the rest of the team, an imbalance will occur that can impede progress. While there is no exact science to maintaining balance, it is a topic of which management should be aware so that team organizational structure can be modified over time for optimal efficiency.

Staffing Observations and Lessons Learned

This section outlines several of the common challenges that we have observed regarding staffing and structuring the SAP business team, and how you may avoid them.

Obtaining Top-Down Buy-In

One of the most important factors to ensure the success of an SAP implementation is to obtain buy-in at a firm's executive level. If there is executive-level dissention or apathy relative to the project's purpose or its need, this will certainly trickle down into the ranks of the business. SAP projects are expensive and complex endeavors, and poor sponsorship at the executive level not only sets the stage for confusion but risks wasting a tremendous amount of time and company resources.

Obtaining top-down sponsorship does not mean there has to be full agreement on every aspect of the project. However, there should be a consistent message of support for the overall project. We have seen over the years in the course of our consulting that departmental or agency participation in an SAP project often reflects the attitudes of line management. Proactive teams can be traced to supportive management. Similarly, struggling teams can be quickly linked to managers who are not on board with the implementation. All of this in turn can be traced back to executive-level sponsorship and support. The most successful projects with which we have been involved are those where the most influential members of the organization champion the implementation from the beginning and set an example for others to follow.

Providing Clear Job Definitions

Another major success factor when building the SAP business team is defining clear job roles. Individuals in the organization, especially in the early stages of the project, do not always understand what their place is and how there job is going to change. This can create uncertainty and anxiety, which usually results in a hands-off approach to the project. To avoid this problem, there should be an orientation aspect to training. Whether this comes from SAP AG, partners, or internal personnel that have already received training is immaterial—the key is that expectations are set and managed. The best orientations include both technical and business information. The more that people understand about SAP technology and configuration and how their jobs fit into the bigger plan, the better equipped they will be to provide relevant information to the project. Team members will want answers to questions such as the following:

▶ How will my job change?

▶ What is my role on the project?

▶ Will my job become obsolete?

▶ What new tools will I have to learn to do my job successfully?

Fully answering such questions will ensure that team members feel more comfortable about their roles and thus will perform more competently.

Communicating Regularly with the Business Team

Success of the project requires proper communications with and among the SAP business teams. First, senior management, the PMO, and other umbrella leadership organizations need to communicate effectively with the SAP business teams. Just as important, the business teams need to communicate effectively within each business team. As discussed earlier, the business team is an extension of the SAP project team and, likewise, should be kept abreast of project news, milestones, and challenges so that it stays engaged. Regularly publishing the project status via emails or an informational websites is common, and even full-blown project newsletters have become popular in recent years.

These communications methods help keep continuity among the various teams that need to work together for success. They also provide opportunities to show and share progress with team members who may be struggling in their own areas and slowly losing sight of project objectives. Bogged down in their everyday tasks, such teams and their members might lose sight of the project's larger goal. Regular updates on progress is an easy way to boost morale by keeping team members plugged in, on the same page, and aware of the overall progress being made.

Establishing Work Time Expectations

Inevitably, an SAP project will affect the working hours of those involved. Depending on the culture of the organization and work climate of the individual teams, this may or may not have major impact on morale, productivity, and retention. Regardless, you should establish expectations of working time for the SAP business team. This can be as simple as paying overtime or as complicated as rearranging schedules. For instance, some business process experts may be shift workers who work nights or weekends and now need to be involved in planning meetings that take place during a regular nine-to-five work week. Accommodating them may require a flexible schedule or a new schedule altogether. Similarly, some team members may be required to work on weekends to perform testing activities for project cutover periods. The goal is not only to avoid project delays caused by setting unrealistic schedules but also to keep employees satisfied with their working conditions by establishing expectations up front in the project.

Reviewing Business Team Realities

Business teams will face challenges related to the simple fact that although they know their business, they generally don't know SAP components or how SAP can enable change. Thus, the business teams need to be trained in terms of how the SAP implementation could impact the business, how the business teams should impact the implementation, and more. It's important to address the following business team realities:

▶ **Recognize SAP business team limitations**—Business users are not experts in SAP; they're experts in how business is currently conducted at the firm, and they should have insight into how business may be conducted more efficiently.

▶ **Identify and address knowledge deficiencies**—Business teams need to be trained as early as feasible on the SAP components and products to be implemented. Expectations that this training can be done in any way other than formal SAP-sponsored training courses are typically unrealistic. Additionally, a world-class knowledge repository does wonders to help less-experienced staff navigate and "fill in" important knowledge and experience gaps.

▶ **Balance current workload with the SAP project's demands**—The business team members almost always have a "day job" that needs to get done while the SAP project is in the initial SAP implementation phases. Recognize that the SAP project will likely be the team's "night job" for some period of time, and help team members and their management teams prioritize the project's needs in light of other needs (prioritization is much easier when executive sponsorship is clear and vocal).

▶ **Facilitate excellent business-developer relationships**—The best business teams are well connected to their development and configuration counterparts. Encourage excellent working relationships by carefully associating people of similar temperaments, ways of working, preferred working shifts, and so on.

▶ **Balance experience against inexperience**—Connect less-experienced people with your senior folks to help the project move forward. And for each broad business and technology area, assign and broadly publicize the go-to leaders.

▶ **Focus on staffing quality more so than quantity**—With regard to bringing in the "right" number of business analysts, seek quality (depth and breadth of experience, ability to work well with others, and more) over raw headcount numbers. In our experience, a couple of hardworking and experienced business specialists and seasoned developers can turn around a good solution considerably faster than much larger but less experienced teams.

▶ **Cut your losses early**—Recognize that not all people have the aptitude for adopting change, communicating well, or learning SAP. Further, you may very well run into cases where specific team members simply don't have the time to attend training or invest in the project. Don't be afraid to replace poor performers, less than enthusiastic team members, or overburdened contributors before they significantly impact the project's timing, costs, or general chances of success.

Remember the relationship between resources, scope, and time—each affects the other, in many cases dramatically. The quality of your business teams therefore directly and significantly affects the project's costs and timelines. Seek to fill positions with people who can serve more than one role, as this limits the number of communications connections, helps normalize perceptions, and creates a leaner cost model in the process.

Above all, remember that staffing takes time! Don't settle on creating a "B" team in the absence of an "A" team roster. Build your team by taking advantage of your firm's breadth and depth of capabilities, training to fill in important knowledge gaps, leveraging your knowledge repository, and assigning key functional and other leads. In this way, you can effectively *create* your "A" team despite organizational and other challenges.

Summary

Eventually, the SAP business team will return to conducting business as usual. After one or more SAP go-lives, SAP will be well integrated into your business and part of the everyday process. Until that time, you need to focus on the recommendations in this chapter to build a team for success. As you tackle this challenge, remember that it is important to keep these individuals motivated and focused on the task at hand. This process should start at the top of your organization and filter its way down. Also, consider your organizational structure and look for ways to align the business and technical teams to achieve project efficiencies. The better these teams collaborate and innovate, the better chance you have to achieve business agility and project success.

Case Study: Building the Best SAP Business Team

HiTech, Inc. needs to begin building its SAP business team. HiTech's senior leadership team has several people in mind who seem to be good candidates for leadership positions, but it needs help understanding how to best staff and structure the team. It also is unsure of who the best candidates for several positions might be, and whether to look for help inside or outside the organization. HiTech's senior leadership team has asked you to critically review its people and processes and provide recommendations as to how to optimally approach structuring and staffing the business team. Answer the following questions to assist HiTech with building the best SAP business team possible.

Questions

1. What specific qualities are desirable for SAP business team members?

2. At what levels in the organization may SAP business team members be found?

3. What are some approaches to staffing to consider?

4. In terms of fostering excellent working relationships, how can we encourage the SAP business community (teams reflecting their particular business areas) to plan together rather than planning in silos?

5. With regard to staffing and structuring SAP business teams, what are some key lessons learned from other organizations?

NOTE

The answers to these questions can be found in Appendix A, "Case Study Answers."

CHAPTER 14

Staffing the SAP Technical Support Organization

In Chapter 11, "Building the SAP Project Team," we set the stage for designing and initially creating the SAP Technical Support Organization (SAP TSO, or simply TSO), a key component of the overall SAP support organization. Key positions were staffed and important organizational decisions were made. In this chapter, we take this initial work to the next level. With information gleaned from other chapters in terms of what your particular SAP technology stack will look like and which SAP components you will implement, it is now time to begin the critical task of staffing the bulk of the SAP TSO.

Introduction to Staffing the SAP TSO

From an SAP technology implementation perspective, the SAP Technical Support Organization is the single most valuable resource to an SAP project team. The SAP TSO is a prudently selected group of support personnel that impacts every facet of the system, from architecture decisions to minimizing downtime through intelligent change management, to proactively monitoring system performance and database statistics, to ensuring an excellent user experience, to working calmly through emergencies and crunch times. Carefully staffing the TSO is therefore in order, particularly once the general SAP project team structure and key players have been put in place.

Not all TSO staffing decisions can be made at once, however. In fact, consistent with best practices, our goal at this point is to staff to the 50%–75% level. You must focus on filling positions that directly support your near-term objectives, which are to develop SAP architectures and system platform sizings (covered in Chapters 18, "Introduction to SAP Platform Sizing," and 19, "Conducting the SAP Platform Sizing Process") and to begin installation and implementation of the SAP data center. Later, as you prepare for SAP component installations, execute various testing processes, and address SAP operational matters, you'll staff the remaining TSO roles. In the meantime, skill sets and experience related to the following areas therefore are crucial at this stage in the project:

▶ **Data center infrastructure**—This is the foundation of any IT project. It requires finding people versed in calculating requirements for and implementing power, thermal/cooling, and rack-based server and storage solutions.

▶ **Network infrastructure**—Another foundational area underpinning business applications like SAP, it's imperative to bring in network specialists versed in calculating bandwidth requirements, designing highly available public and private network links, designing high-performance network backbones, and more. Deep knowledge of three-tier client/server architectures, Service Oriented Architecture (SOA), network security, and identity management are also critical.

NOTE

Individuals tasked with supporting data center and network infrastructure, server configuration, and disk subsystems will all probably work under the leadership of the SAP data center lead and hold a "dotted line" reporting relationship to the SAP project. Sometimes their area of responsibility is referred to as the SAP computing platform.

▶ **Server configuration**—This includes capabilities in building out servers (which can include one or more OSs and various server form factors, from server blades to traditional rack-mount servers to large proprietary "boxes"), loading OSs, optimizing rack infrastructure, addressing power and network cable management, and so on.

▶ **Disk subsystem design, installation, and configuration**—Another critical area of responsibility, the disk subsystem specialists play a key role in maintaining overall SAP system availability and performance.

▶ **Infrastructure security, high availability, and disaster recovery**—These specialists may be added to the areas above to bolster the lack of a particular skill set or competency (such as a specific high-availability technical solution or implementation of an SAP computing platform unfamiliar to the team). The SAP TSO needs adequate knowledge at this early point in the project to avoid inadvertently creating bigger problems down the road. In our experience, these specialists often report to the SAP infrastructure/Basis lead or directly to the solution architect.

▶ **Database administration**—One or more DB specialists might be required to work hand in hand under the leadership of the senior database administrator, particularly if the database software being implemented for SAP is unfamiliar to the team.

▶ **Operations**—Basic knowledge of SAP operational activities such as database and file system backup and restore, supporting an SAP help desk, managing enterprise-class print systems, and similar traditional data center "operations" tasks are required early in the project.

▶ **SAP Basis/technology**—To adequately address pending SAP architecture and sizing tasks, the TSO must bring in experienced SAP Basis and technology specialists. With knowledge and experience in the particular SAP components (and common bolt-ons as well as underlying technologies) being implemented, these specialists will be capable of installing and configuring the "empty" SAP shell needed later by the functional experts and development team. For example, if SAP Supplier Relationship Management (SRM) is on the schedule for implementation, you need more than just SAP Basis skills on the team. Depending on the SRM business scenario, you will need SAP Document Builder and SAP NetWeaver Search and Classification (TREX) expertise, experience with Java Virtual Machines, catalog experience, and more.

On the other hand, people skilled primarily in performance tuning and tweaking, interface-level integration, functional development, and load testing are not yet required. If a particular phase of a project is not scheduled to kick off for six months, the people in the job market will be completely different by then, so you're probably wasting everyone's time if you begin the process *too* early.

Jobs and Tasks of the SAP TSO

Taking into consideration the skill sets and experience related to the areas listed in the preceding section, this section takes a closer look at some of the most important SAP TSO jobs and tasks. This includes SAP Basis, OS (and server) support, front-end client deployment, and data specialist roles, each of which are explored next.

Senior SAP Basis Specialist

One of the critical SAP TSO jobs is held by the senior SAP Basis or technology specialist. The objective of the job is to apply knowledge of SAP NetWeaver technology and products, as well as various server databases and operating systems, to support SAP and associated technology infrastructure, landscape environments, and interfacing systems. The senior SAP Basis specialist uses SAP NetWeaver skills to install, migrate, upgrade, and maintain SAP and associated technologies. The SAP TSO staff member performs system refreshes and client copies and applies support packages for SAP ABAP and/or Java stacks, software patches, and fixes.

The senior SAP Basis specialist defines and documents technical system requirements and systems management procedures, creates troubleshooting documents for support and maintenance of each solution, applies database administration knowledge to define an efficient and optimal database layout, implements file structures and disk layouts for SAP installations, and analyzes system performance. The SAP Basis specialist also performs daily and weekly system health checks and is responsible for overall system tuning. Other objectives of the job are problem escalation and resolution, working with SAP AG and other software and hardware vendors to resolve problems, and coordinating all SAP infrastructure change management efforts using the SAP implementation project's change management tools and processes.

Operating System Specialist for SAP

Another critical SAP TSO job is the operating system specialist for SAP, who by the very nature of the role is nearly always a highly regarded server specialist as well. This individual needs to have several years of experience in various operating systems because SAP environments tend to be heterogeneous from an OS perspective. The TSO staff member must be able to generate, tune, configure, and upgrade the OSs in an SAP environment, evaluate system performance, assist in system disaster-recovery situations, define development tools and procedures for daily operational support, and support application activities that require specialized system programming. In addition, the selected individual documents solutions and populates a knowledge database, receives trouble tickets from level-one resources via tracking tools, and provides the necessary support to solve complex and time-critical issues.

Experience supporting various databases and SAP products is a plus. The ability to express complex technical concepts effectively, both verbally and in writing, is critical for this position, as is the skill to work well with people from different disciplines with varying degrees of technical experience.

SAP Front-End Deployment Specialist

The objective of the SAP front-end deployment specialist is to develop, implement, and communicate the strategy required to install, test, deploy, update, and support the SAPGUI and other user interfaces. This individual has to ensure that the SAP front-end deployment strategy is consistent with the back-end SAP component and other business applications from a strategy perspective. The SAP TSO staff member must be able to lead projects and to provide technical expertise to facilitate the deployment of SAP bolt-ons, SAP browser applications, and other front-end-related products. Another task of the SAP front-end deployment specialist is to provide strategic direction and to participate in technical projects across multiple SAP and legacy application teams.

The SAP front-end deployment specialist's ability to develop and implement the technical test environment and methodology required to install, test, and update the SAPGUI and other front-end SAP solutions is critical. This individual must also serve as the liaison with the desktop deployment team to transfer knowledge required to develop automated SAPGUI (or other access methods) installation routines for universal deployment.

> **NOTE**
>
> What if you implement SAP but have failed to consider how end user access to the SAP systems will be provided? We have seen SAP projects almost coming to a halt just because the required SAP front-end release for the back-end SAP system was not supported on a customer's global desktop OS standard. You must verify right at the beginning of the implementation project what the requirements are for the SAP front end, to what extent it complies with your desktop OS standard, and how it can be deployed potentially to thousands of SAP end-user desktops.

SAP Data Specialist

The objective of the SAP data specialist is to develop and execute the detailed design and configuration of the SAP training database system. Afterward, this individual is responsible for developing, loading, and maintaining data that is used to conduct SAP end-user training on various SAP components, particularly the various SAP ERP modules. This SAP TSO staff member interacts regularly with all levels of the project team and business units, assisting team members in the design and testing of solutions, and collaborates with business and other SAP project team partners to deliver solutions that align with the global data strategy for the SAP ERP and other component training systems.

The SAP data specialist is a functional specialist of sorts, translating global business needs into the appropriate data models to deliver required solutions, supporting users on a global basis to understand and resolve training data issues, and more. The data specialist works closely with SAP production support specialists, integration team members, and others to determine global configuration data requirements and to support training exercises. Monitoring global production change requests, and determining the impact and level of work required to support scheduled training exercises consumes much of the data specialist's time as well.

Because the job can be so broad (depending on which SAP components and specific modules are being implemented), good data specialists are difficult to find. The best are skilled at mass-loading transactional data into SAP ERP modules using automated tools like HP's Quick Test Pro (QTP, formerly Mercury QTP) or SAP eCATT. The ability to support instructors tasked with formally training business users, and with helping to develop training materials, is a wonderful plus.

Traditional Approaches to Staffing the SAP TSO

As a result of historically inconsistent staffing practices, several different ways to staff SAP IT organizations have evolved. The method employed most often to staff the bulk of the organization is called the *résumé-to-interview approach*; even today, this is still the most common approach. Companies typically engage their HR organization to seek out résumés of qualified candidates, ideally based on really good input from the SAP hiring manager or team. Because this input is subject to technical interpretation, though, a series of phone screens and quite a few one-on-one interviews are required to even begin to qualify hopeful applicants. Not only does this process take time, but it puts a lot of faith into what appears in the résumé.

A second method of staffing thus naturally evolved out of the necessity to ensure that a candidate's résumé reflected their actual skills. Called the *staff-testing approach*, it forgoes much of the screening-focused interview process in favor of dumping a prequalified SAP candidate into a typical situation (or real-time hands-on "test," hence the name). The candidate then has a certain period of time to solve the problem, or configure the system, or design a solution—whatever is applicable to the job being filled. What a prospective employer discovers using this approach helps them to qualify a candidate in terms of the following:

▶ How the candidate approaches the problem at hand, from a number of different perspectives: organizational skills, problem-solving aptitude, and so on

▶ Whether the candidate has the abilities presented in the résumé

▶ How well the candidate performs under real-world stress

The staff-testing approach has its own limitations, though, in that some folks simply don't test as well as others. And the test itself may not be an accurate representation of what the work environment will be like. Finally, when word of the "test" gets out, it tends to lose its impact or surprise potential, and other tests therefore need to be created on a regular basis. We have even found one of our own tests posted on a publicly accessible website (with incorrect answers, to boot!).

Out of the shortcomings of these first two staffing approaches came a third approach, *try-before-you-buy* (similar to the traditional probationary period approach). This approach shortcuts the interview process and eliminates the need to create and maintain tests by focusing exclusively on putting a candidate to work not only immediately, but for "free." Then, their ability to interact successfully within the framework of the team, and the quality of their actual work, speaks volumes for them. This approach is tempting when two or three equally qualified candidates are vying for the same position. Try-before-you-buy is limited in that it's only really possible when a candidate hails from a consulting organization that can afford to place a person at a prospective customer site for free; the consultant is paid by his consulting organization, but no bill is ever presented to the potential customer during the try-before-you-buy period.

The try-before-you-buy approach is risky, too, in that you are letting a relative "unknown" potentially impact your project. Past working references are therefore critical, as is creating a structured environment for the try-before-you-buy time period. We recommend a trial time of anywhere from a few days to a few weeks. This makes it easier to evaluate and determine whether the candidate is truly a "keeper."

Obviously, all of these approaches have good points and not-so-good points. What you really need, though, is an approach that lets you verify the skills of the candidate, and how well they interact in real-world situations, without spending too much time and money playing around with multiple interviews, test scenarios, and so on. What you need is a comprehensive and quality *rapid deployment* approach to staffing the SAP TSO, covered next.

The Rapid Deployment Approach to Staffing an SAP TSO

The rapid deployment approach to staffing an SAP TSO is based on a hybrid of the résumé-to-hire and staff-testing approaches, with the following modifications:

- ▶ The HR organization is responsible neither for developing technical job descriptions nor for performing technical references; rather, the SAP TSO is.

- ▶ A technical phone screen takes the place of separate general and technical phone screens and interviews.

- ▶ Role-playing via *customer simulation scenarios* during a single "group" technical interview takes the place of testing and multiple technical interviews. This single role-playing technical interview allows for observing both technical and soft skills in action (more detail on soft skills can be found later in this chapter), including how well the candidate performs under real-world stress.

This approach also side-steps the risk inherent to try-before-you-buy, without sacrificing all of the value gained by seeing a candidate in action.

So, with the image of "rapid deployment" in mind, let's take a closer look at a proven process used by more than a few of our own SAP customers (and partner consulting organizations, for that matter). Note, however, that we will be writing mainly from the perspective of the customer (or employer) implementing SAP here, not from the perspective of the technical staff member seeking employment or a contract.

> **TIP**
>
> If you're more interested in the flip side of this perspective, perhaps for your own personal employment education, simply "flip" what is written here. And pay attention—the more you understand what a client is looking for in an SAP job candidate, the better equipped you will be to actually land that position; you will understand your employment opportunities that much better, and how to best sell yourself.

Best Practices for the Rapid Deployment Approach

Before anyone is hired, before even a single interview is scheduled or a single offer letter is sent out, a process needs to be outlined and followed to support rapid deployment, like the one shown in Figure 14.1.

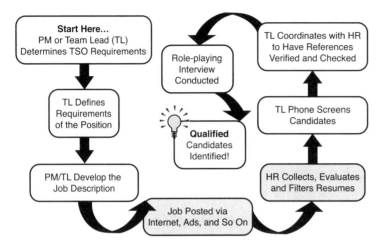

FIGURE 14.1 The Rapid Deployment SAP Staffing Process is not unlike many IT staffing processes, though a few caveats exist.

What we sometimes refer to as the *Rapid Deployment SAP Staffing Process* (RDSSP) is simply a documented set of steps to follow in support of the hiring/contracting process. What underscores the importance of the RDSSP as compared to other IT staffing processes is the fact that the SAP environment is nearly always "mission-critical." This impacts the *quality* of people that need to be considered for positions on the SAP support team. And this in turn affects both the steps and overall timeline in the process, especially with regard to the following exceptions or differences:

▶ **Don't circumvent the hiring process**—It is more important than ever to pay careful attention to following the hiring process. Side-stepping or unduly speeding up the process for staffing SAP project positions will only get you into trouble.

▶ **Check references**—Many hiring processes include a reference check but it fails to mandate the references. Reference checks for SAP project positions are not a "nice to have" but rather a critical piece of data used to validate how well a prospective new hire might fit into an organization. We recommend obtaining three references, preferably from a mix of colleagues and managers or team leaders.

▶ **Obtain detailed references**—The importance of technical and general *detailed references* cannot be stressed enough. Sure, many companies have a policy of not giving references. If you are involved in the hiring process, approach a reference check from a personal perspective (in other words, simply get the reference to talk to you by striking up a personal conversation), and listen and learn. In our experience, even in those companies that frown on giving references, it's easy to find someone willing to talk about one of your prospective new hires. Ask a candidate for the names and contact information of their former colleagues, and then approach your questioning from a "personal reference" perspective.

▶ **Put in the time**—Be prepared to spend time developing job descriptions, checking references, and performing phone screens, interviews, and other follow-up. These need to be handled professionally and thoroughly, in a quality manner. You get what you work for.

▶ **Practice rigor**—Many interview processes used to bring aboard other members of the IT organization encourage, rather than mandate, thoroughness and rigor. You don't have that luxury. Follow up, and follow through, in terms of detailed reference checks, in-depth technical interviews, and well-rounded group interviews using role-playing and customer-simulation environments helps to ensure that job offers are extended to "keepers."

Given the nature of SAP implementations, the right candidates will be flexible, eager to learn, intelligent, and possess excellent people and communication skills. If in doubt, move on to the next candidate.

Each candidate needs to be given the proper expectations as to the scope and timing of the review process. This benefits both parties; nobody needs to waste time on a thorough review and check only to find that the candidate has gone elsewhere in the meantime.

Steps of the Rapid Deployment Approach

The rapid deployment approach to staffing the SAP TSO comprises the following steps:

1. Develop and post job descriptions.
2. Evaluate SAP technical résumés.
3. Perform an SAP technical phone screen.
4. Set up and conduct face-to-face interviews.
5. Rank and evaluate prospective SAP candidates.

Step 1: Develop and Post Job Descriptions

For each SAP implementation, there are literally hundreds of ways that different jobs or occupations can be combined into broad positions of responsibility, or broken down into smaller, cubbyhole positions. Some of our SAP customers have created very interesting and, in the case of some very large implementations, very narrow positions. Creating job descriptions, then, relates directly back to how your SAP TSO is laid out.

Most clients find that advertising for SAP-specific "generalist" positions is the best use of advertising budget and space. For example, an advertisement for an "SAP Server Administrator" or "Network Technician supporting an SAP mission-critical enterprise" or "Oracle Database Administrator for SAP" will tend to yield more qualified candidates than similarly described non-SAP-explicit positions. On the other hand, too much detail might scare away applicants who don't feel they meet 100% of the requirements. For example, advertising for an "Oracle 10.2 database administrator to support a clustered HP-UX 11.31 environment running SAP ERP 6.0" might inadvertently imply to prospects that *only* DBAs with experience on this specific technology stack are desired, and others need not apply. So unless expertise in a complete technology stack is absolutely warranted (perhaps the new hire will be expected to be a "one-man shop" of sorts), word your job descriptions differently. We suggest liberally using words like "preferred" and "desirable" to indicate when a particular skill is not absolutely necessary.

Step 2: Evaluate SAP Technical Résumés

Most hiring firms employ an HR organization to screen and review résumés before they are forwarded to a project team for closer scrutiny. In this way, the HR organization prequalifies prospective new hires, helping to ensure that the project team's staffing or recruiting professionals waste no time on less-than-qualified applicants. When the prequalified résumés start coming in from HR, it's time to take action quickly, for a number of reasons:

▶ The "best of the best" in the SAP job market will find a home somewhere; if you sit on their résumés too long, it won't be *your* home.

▶ The hiring process takes time. The process of posting, technical screening, interviewing, negotiating, sending out an offer letter, and finally setting up start dates can take months.

▶ Even those candidates who are not qualified deserve respect for the time and effort they put into responding to your advertisement. Besides, the SAP job market is sufficiently small that word travels quickly of clients that are unresponsive or difficult to work with. The junior consultant today could very well become the star expert you need next year!

Résumés need to be grouped into job positions and then reviewed against the basic requirements of those positions. A candidate status matrix (CSM) is handy at this point, as it forces an even comparison between all candidates vying for a single position. Further, as shown in Figure 14.2, it gives you a single source document, which you can begin using to track candidates seeking a position within your SAP team. Such a tool is especially useful when shared over the Web or by way of a collaboration tool like a Microsoft SharePoint site, too, as these facilitate sharing candidate information anywhere, anytime, across the SAP TSO, the HR department, and other teams.

Process Steps	Prospects/Candidates				
	Meg Ann	Mike Abe	Phil Lip	Lim Pho	Ash Ley
Date Resume Rec'd	12/19/08	01/04/09	01/05/09	01/10/09	01/10/09
Reviewed by (initials)	MDA	MDA	MDA	KT	KT
Date forwarded to TL	NO	01/08/09	01/10/09	01/12/09	01/12/09
TL Feedback (go/no)	N/A	GO	NO	NO	GO
TL Phone screen	N/A	01/15/09	N/A	N/A	01/15/09
TL Feedback (go/no)	N/A	GO: 📎	N/A	N/A	GO: 📎
Interview Scheduled	N/A	01/17/09	N/A	N/A	01/17/09
Role/Scenario Dev'd	N/A	YES-"A" 📎	N/A	N/A	NO
...	...	...	...	...	...

📎 = data attached

FIGURE 14.2   The candidate status matrix allows for rapid and even comparisons between candidates, and serves as a simple way of initially tracking applicants.

The CSM serves many purposes. First, it is an excellent tool for ensuring that timelines are adhered to throughout the hiring process. For example, when a résumé hits HR's inbox, there should be a time limit set for how long the résumé sits unattended. The CSM helps everyone understand who is responsible for the next step in the RDSSP, and how long it should take to move the candidate from one step to the next. The CSM thus imposes workflow and forces accountability.

The CSM also allows for tracking all vital data on each applicant, from his or her name to contact information to the results of phone screens, interviews, and more. The CSM becomes your tracking system, a single point of reference. And in the beginning of the staffing process, the CSM provides a way to start comparing candidates simply based on their résumés—professional appearance, written communication skills, completeness, all-important spelling/grammar skills, and so on.

Finally, the CSM helps you to manage closure on each candidate. In the end, a candidate is either hired or sent a "Thank you for your interest" note. The CSM enables you to make sure no candidate falls through the cracks (in the sample CSM found in Figure 14.2, the absence of any more scheduled activity triggers a "Thank you for your interest" response from HR).

Don't make the mistake of underestimating the power and value of the CSM. Its use is obvious during the staffing process itself. But the CSM also provides the following compelling benefits:

▶ If you have already interviewed and documented your staffing process, you will not make the mistake of (or waste your time) phone-screening or interviewing the same candidate twice. It happens!

▶ If you are looking to fill a position similar to one that was filled six months ago, and happen to see a familiar résumé in your inbox, the CSM provides a easy way of going back through your notes to determine whether another conversation is worth everyone's time.

▶ The CSM can be used by a company's corporate HR organization to document that the staffing process does not discriminate against any particular race, creed, color, and so on. It's your way of ensuring that you are complying with legal regulations, industry standards, and self-imposed hiring practices.

There are many ways to deploy and use the CSM. Historically, we have seen it deployed in the form of an Excel spreadsheet shared between one or two managers. Problems with this method of sharing data exist, though, especially in terms of version control. As briefly mentioned previously, better methods of sharing and accessing candidate information exist, and include

▶ Creating and maintaining a true candidate database with, for example, SQL Server 2008 (or free options like SQL Server 2008 Express, MySQL PostgreSQL, or Firebird).

▶ Making the database accessible through company-internal file shares, to facilitate access and data sharing.

▶ Providing web access to the database, to allow home-based and remote parties access to a single repository of pre-employment data.

▶ Scanning and attaching all résumés to their individual candidate records.

▶ Tying your Internet or intranet posting process into the database, such that the résumé and other posted information is automatically included for each candidate's record.

The more available the CSM is, the more it will be used. And the simpler it is to update, the more valuable it will become as a tool for truly managing your SAP staffing process. Be careful, though—this is truly confidential data and needs to be treated as such, as issues associated with maintaining this database potentially impact the whole corporation from a legal perspective. Plus, it's important to understand network and other bandwidth requirements when you begin deploying databases over WAN or dial-up links; a poor database choice can bring a network segment to its knees if not implemented correctly.

Step 3: Perform an SAP Technical Phone Screen

Although many companies perform both a general screen and a technical screen, we feel that combining the two is in everyone's best interests. That is, if the only real purpose of a general phone screen is to validate that a candidate is indeed available, that she possesses sound communication skills, and that she seems to fill the basic requirements of a position, this can just as easily be addressed in the first five minutes of a technical phone screen.

Although collecting the responses to phone screen questions is critical, the manner in which the questions are answered is nearly as important. The following list of questions for the technical phone screen emphasizes these "soft" areas. Note that the items placed closer to the front of the list are more weighty; in other words, if you have concerns over the answers you are hearing to the first few items, you might consider cutting the phone screen short and simply moving on to the next candidate.

▶ **Perform the tasks of a general phone screen**—This includes assessing the candidate's availability, communication skills, general experience and background, and perhaps short- and long-term goals. Does the candidate meet the basic requirements of the position and seem to "fit" in to your organization?

▶ **Assess the candidate's preparedness for this phone screen**—Does she have the answers to your questions? Does she ramble on from one question to the next? Is she trying to read from a résumé or set of notes? Does she have a clue about what your company does (has she done her homework) or what the project is all about? The answers to these questions should give you an idea as to the level of importance the candidate places on *preparing in advance*, and even on *customer satisfaction*. You are her customer; how you are treated and spoken to probably reflects how the candidate will treat her customers in the SAP project.

▶ **Record the candidate's attitude toward this phone screen**—Like her level of preparation, this too will likely reflect what you'll see day to day from her should she join your SAP team.

▶ **Note the candidate's tone**—Is the candidate eager to both listen and talk, in a manner consistent with someone anxious to join your team? Does she answer your questions from a negative perspective rather than a positive one? For example, when asked about why they want to leave their current employer, candidates might bad-mouth everyone from their team leader to the SAP project manager to their current company's lack of something or other. This negative perspective needs to be taken into consideration.

▶ **Note whether the candidate raised the topic of salary or other compensation**—At this point, she probably should not have. The information you have shared through advertising the position should provide candidates with a general compensation range. We highly recommend putting off any conversation about compensation until both you and the candidate feel that there is a good fit for employment.

▶ **Note whether the candidate asked any questions after the floor was opened up for questioning**—If so, were they thoughtful? Did these questions reflect that she was actually listening, or were they canned? Importantly, did the candidate *ask for the job*, or in some other way indicate that she is the right person for the position? These kinds of questions give everyone an idea as to how *interested* the candidate is in the position at hand.

We recommend intentional, open-ended questions to encourage a candidate to talk. Specific questions may be key to a particular position, too. Regardless of the types of questions, ensure that these are also included in and tracked by the CSM.

Step 4: Set Up and Conduct Face-to-Face Interviews

Based on a candidate's phone-screen performance and attitude, they may be asked to actually "put on a suit" and show up to be interviewed. The interview is where you get to see the candidate shine. Here, he puts his best foot forward and proves to everyone that he not only has the experience and aptitude to do the job, but that the project simply can't be successful without him.

Interviews take time to plan and conduct. The following list describes a detailed process flow:

1. Start with introductions, and then talk a bit about yourself and the team. Move into discussing the project from a high-level perspective.

2. Move into getting the candidate to talk about his background, including general education. Then move into job-by-job experience, starting with his most recent relevant assignments.

3. Commence the role-playing scenario. Drill down into technical details. Stick with the scenario (get back on track as necessary).

4. Wind down the role-playing scenario. Wrap up with questions and answers and thanks.

Although it might seem like common sense, it's important to note that sometimes attitude, work ethic, and an ability to work with others can be more important than who has the best technical résumé or experience. In fact, as more and more individuals join an SAP team, a new person's ability to work with and on behalf of the team only becomes more and more critical.

Key Interview Techniques and Approaches

The phone screen got rid of the unqualified candidates, and most of the marginal players, too. Now, with a candidate in front of you, you need to determine whether this is indeed the best person for the job. We like the following real-world approaches:

▶ Get business-focused employees engaged in the interviewing process of candidates seeking business-focused positions, such as those requiring liaison-like responsibilities.

▶ Relocate high-level, high-visibility candidates, or candidates interviewing for high-communication positions, from formal corporate settings, to observe these candidates in more real-world settings. A lot of insight can be gained by noting their behavior, language, and opinions at places like the company factory, refinery, or distribution center.

▶ Use a self-assessment form to help determine whether a candidate has the right approach or best mindset for tacking a particular job.

▶ Role-play with three or four interviewers. Especially when it comes to hard-to-fill technical positions surrounding SAP Basis or integration positions, this is one of the best methods of confirming hard-to-prove skill sets.

As we alluded to before, a quality role-playing scenario can bring to light lots of really interesting traits and characteristics in a candidate. What each scenario takes in terms of planning and execution time is more than made up in the quality of the SAP team that is ultimately assembled. The following list suggests several different role-playing customer simulation scenarios:

▶ A troubleshooting scenario of a performance problem in a productive SAP environment, which would include much of the SAP technology stack

▶ A solution vision question appropriate for solution architects and other senior technical resources

▶ An availability issue to help identify how well a candidate balances customer orientation with restoring a system according to procedures (excellent for support, help desk, and similar roles)

▶ A business vision question for senior leadership candidates

▶ A functional configuration scenario (that reflects the SAP components to be implemented) for configuration specialists and developers

▶ A people issue scenario for team leaders and managers, to observe how they might handle a common employment problem, such as the habitually late worker or the worker who often misses deadlines

Interviewing for Basic Qualifications

Aside from role playing, one of the most effective methods of basic technical interviewing revolves around leveraging the technical and business requirements identified in the position description (a job posting or advertisement, for example). This assumes, of course, that the position description or advertisement itself was descriptive and fairly comprehensive. In the sample that follows, an interviewer is looking for a person to fill the role of an SAP infrastructure specialist:

▶ Tell me about your experience supporting other SAP projects.

▶ When it comes to availability, accessibility, scalability, and performance, which do you believe is most important from the SAP end users' point of view, and why?

▶ Explain what you know about a standard three-system landscape for SAP, and how it differs from other system landscape approaches.

▶ How did you gain your experience designing high-availability network solutions for SAP implementations?

▶ What roles did you play in designing, installing, and supporting SAP servers and disk subsystems in past assignments?

▶ How do your current technical certifications and college education fit in with your experience on SAP projects?

▶ What would be your approach if you were asked to install a patch or upgrade into the SAP production environment?

▶ Given your extensive SAP infrastructure experience, what about the position appeals to you most?

▶ How would your colleagues describe you in terms of your work ethic and ability to get things done in a team-oriented environment?

With the preceding list, it should become apparent whether the candidate understands what an SAP business solution looks like from an infrastructure perspective, how changes are implemented, end user orientation, and how well the candidate might be integrated into an existing SAP support team.

Interviewing for Specific Skill Sets

When it comes to determining whether a candidate possesses the deep or advanced skills required of a position, it is usually not enough to ask questions related just to the subject at hand. For example, an applicant looking to hire on as an SAP infrastructure security specialist needs to be asked questions not only specific to SAP security but also related to computer security in general.

We also think there is a lot to be learned about how well a candidate understands a particular technical area by asking them to troubleshoot a specific issue. Consider the following troubleshooting scenarios as we try to fill an SAP DBA position:

▶ A network issue causes problems with an organization's use of log shipping as their disaster recovery solution. This allows you to assess a candidate's breadth of experience and knowledge beyond typical database troubleshooting.

▶ A database simply stops working because its logs become full, for example. This scenario opens up a broad spectrum of possibilities, enabling you to see how a candidate thinks on her feet.

▶ An organization has little experience with capacity planning, performance management, change control, or another important process. Such a scenario helps uncover whether a candidate is not only familiar with such a key process, but what the candidate thinks about process discipline.

It's evident from these troubleshooting scenarios that a lot of real-world value is gained through this type of interview process. Of course, in this particular case, depending on the scenarios you choose, perhaps only a truly skilled SAP DBA might be in a position to intelligently administer these questions (and guide the interview conversation in a manner that best uncovers a candidate's strengths and weaknesses). We suggest that you use these scenarios as templates for creating your own.

Step 5: Rank Prospective SAP Candidates

After the interview is wrapped up, the real fun starts. Again, we recommend leveraging the CSM or some other kind of candidate assessment tool to help compare and evaluate each applicant in the following paper areas—diplomas, certifications, recommendations/references, and so on—as evidenced through the phone screen, interview, reference checks, and other background checks:

▶ General experience

▶ College degree(s)

▶ SAP certification(s)

▶ Other relevant certifications (business, project management, infrastructure, and so on)

▶ SAP-relevant organization(s) and affiliation(s)

▶ Company employee-based recommendation(s)

▶ Other references and recommendations

Next, a closer look at the area of hard technical or business-relevant skills is in order:

▶ Specific experience and skills related to the position

▶ Other skills that may prove complementary to the position

▶ Troubleshooting ability

▶ Verbal communication skills

▶ General intelligence

Whereas having the aforementioned technical and business skills tends to help a candidate *get* a position, having good marks in the following areas tends to indicate the candidate will *keep* his job in your SAP TSO. Use the CSM to compare and evaluate each applicant in the following soft-skill areas:

- ► Level of professionalism (rate from high to low, reflecting the general feel of the interview or any specific events that either transpired or were discussed)

- ► Level of enthusiasm or eagerness (rate from high to low, addressing to what degree a candidate seemed genuinely excited about the prospect of joining your SAP support team)

- ► SAP social personality (rate social skills, from team player to strictly "computer room" personality)

- ► SAP skills personality (rate from "enjoys conquering new learning curves/high stress" to "better suited for maintenance work/low stress")

- ► Level of adaptability (rate from high to low, as evidenced in discussions of how the candidate managed long-term changes in his work or IT environment or career)

- ► Level of flexibility (rate from high to low, addressing how the candidate reacted to short-term problems or issues, such as the need to work over a weekend or stay late to resolve an issue, or the need to travel)

- ► Goal orientation (rate as high goals, some goals, weak goals, unrealistic goals, or no goals, penalizing a candidate only if he or she cannot fashion a response to specific questions such as "What are your short- and long-term goals?")

- ► Overall potential (rate from high to low, stating whether the candidate has potential to succeed in the organization beyond the specific position you are trying to fill)

Given everything in the preceding list, it's apparent that both position-specific skills and soft skills carry a lot of weight in determining the best candidate for a particular SAP position. The ideal candidate tends to be "balanced" across both areas, being not only technically adept or business-process savvy, but also quite strong in many of the soft skills.

And we would be remiss if we failed to mention that any applicant who says he can do anything and everything you want is not someone you want. Why? Because he *lies* (and not very convincingly). Always beware of candidates who seem to answer each of your questions with "yes, I can do that"; if this becomes a pattern, simply start asking for details about where he has done specific tasks before. Drill down into the detail, pull it out of the candidate via role-playing or other means, and pay attention to whether a "yes" turns into a "well...uh...no" after a few minutes.

Bringing New SAP TSO Staff On Board

With the ideal candidates finally identified for your SAP TSO, you now need to actually bring these folks on board. That is, now that you know *who* you want to hire, you need to figure out *how* to make it happen. In the next few sections we explore the hiring process from several different perspectives, followed by a closer look at the new hire's first week.

Internal Transfers

Although it seems contrary at first glance, extending offers to company-internal employees or contractors and transitioning them into the SAP TSO can be especially difficult. This includes folks already associated with the organization's IT function, or contractors supporting another functional part of the business. If the SAP project has been established as a high-priority business-transformation project throughout the company and at all management levels, drafting internal players into the SAP TSO is tricky because you might be taking key contributors from other organizations that are also expected to contribute to the SAP project. Thus, you need to consider the potential for alienating these organizations. An astute project manager will remember this as he exercises his power to draft individuals from other organizations, because both the project's and his own personal post-go-live viability depends nearly as much on the relationships he preserves as anything else. The following points are therefore worth reiterating:

▶ Internal transfers need to be treated with respect. They are members of the corporate "family" who want to make a move to better both themselves and the company. As the hiring entity, this is neither the time nor the place to insist that no transition plan is necessary, or to ignore responsibilities that need to be distributed among the internal transfer's current team. Allow internal transfers to put their affairs in order and transition out of their current positions, out of respect to the organizations losing them.

▶ The organization losing the person deserves some level of flexibility in start dates. A month is not unusual, though sometimes the critical nature and compressed timelines initially seen in an SAP project tend to limit transition time. Regardless, everyone needs to be sensitive to everyone else's predicament and to the needs of what is sure to be a very expensive, very high-profile, and therefore very significant SAP project.

▶ Importantly, the organization losing the person needs to remember that the internal candidate is not leaving the *company*; he is simply changing positions. This is no time for that organization to play power or control games, trying to hang on to their resource until the last possible second—the internal transfer and the company as a whole are the only ones who will be hurt, after all. And a perceived lack of cooperation on the part of the losing organization could very well make its way to the top echelons of the company, tarnishing an organization's image in the eyes of the SAP steering committee and its various stakeholder constituents.

External Consultants and Contractors

Before any external consultants are actually brought in, it is imperative to ensure that you interview the actual person or people who will be onsite. That is, it's still not too uncommon for a third-party consulting firm to allow their best folks to interview, only to follow up by providing their less-senior or less-capable individuals when they win the deal.

Another common mistake is putting the financial arrangements on the back burner during the third-party consulting interview process. Unlike the process for bringing in an employee, both the hiring and consulting organizations must understand financial arrangements up front. In this way, problems surrounding not "getting what you pay for" are mitigated. These financial arrangements are often documented by the consulting party, too—simply request their consulting price list early in the process, with the understanding that all published prices are typically negotiable by 20% or more (especially for long-term contracts, where discounts of 30%–40% are not uncommon). A sample "Consulting Price List" is shown in Figure 14.3; note the detail in terms of classifications of consultants and pricing. It's also not uncommon to obtain sample résumés that reflect the real-world skill sets held and projects worked on by various levels of consultants.

Consultant Job Code	Job Title/Basic Job Description	Part Number	Hourly List Price $	Discounted Price $
TCSUP	Admin & Tech Support	C-ADMIN-EX	65.00	60.00
TCX1K	Junior Consulting Associate	C-CA0A9-EX	110.00	90.00
TCX1L	Consulting Associate 1a	C-CA1A9-EX	150.00	120.00
TCX1N	Consulting Associate 2a	C-CA2A9-EX	175.00	150.00
TCX1O	Consulting Associate 3a	C-CA3A9-EX	195.00	175.00
TCX3P	Project Manager 1a	C-CP1A9-EX	220.00	190.00
TCX3Q	Project Manager 2a	C-CP2A9-EX	250.00	210.00
TCX3R	Project Manager 3a	C-CP3A9-EX	280.00	230.00
TCX3S	Project Manager 4a	C-CP4A9-EX	315.00	250.00
TCX4E	Consulting Manager 1a	C-CCM1A9-EX	220.00	190.00
TCX4F	Consulting Manager 2a	C-CCM2A9-EX	250.00	210.00
TCX4G	Consulting Manager 3a	C-CCM3A9-EX	280.00	230.00
TCX4H	Consulting Manager 4a	C-CCM4A9-EX	315.00	250.00
TCX4A	Consulting Director Id	C-CD0A9-EX	315.00	250.00
TCX4B	Consulting Director IId	C-CD0A9-EX	315.00	250.00
TCX4C	Consulting Director IIId	C-CD0A9-EX	315.00	250.00
DIR6E	Practice Director	C-CD0A9-EX	315.00	250.00
DIR6A	Practice Director Id	C-CD0A9-EX	315.00	250.00
DIR6B	Practice Director IId	C-CD0A9-EX	315.00	250.00
DIR6C	Practice Director IIId	C-CD0A9-EX	315.00	250.00
TCX1Q	Technology Consultant 1a	C-TCAA9-EX	220.00	190.00
TCX1R	Technology Consultant 2a	C-TCBA9-EX	250.00	210.00
TCX1S	Technology Consultant 3a	C-TCCA9-EX	280.00	230.00
TCX1T	Technology Consultant 4a	C-TDAA9-EX	315.00	250.00
TCX2K	Solutions Architect 1a	C-SA1A9-EX	220.00	190.00
TCX2L	Solutions Architect 2a	C-SA0A9-EX	250.00	210.00
TCX2M	Solutions Architect 3a	C-SSAA9-EX	280.00	230.00

FIGURE 14.3   Before bringing on third-party consultants, request a list or document that reflects technical job classifications, descriptions, and pricing.

Finally, to protect everyone and help ensure that business requirements are addressed, every consulting organization should be required to execute a scope-of-work (SOW) or letter agreement (LA). The SOW or LA should include the following:

▶ Scope of the engagement, including what is not included

▶ Specific services to be delivered

▶ Expected length of the consulting engagement

▶ Qualifications of the specific consultants to be engaged

▶ Assumptions made by both parties in terms of who is responsible for providing office, telephone, and PC resources, software and hardware, access to systems, and so on

▶ Price and payment terms and conditions

▶ Who owns the work developed

▶ Confidentiality and rights to ideas, concepts, and techniques developed

▶ Warranty of work to be performed, including recourse if work is performed in an unsatisfactory manner

▶ Contact information, directions, and a process for bringing people into the project, escalating people-related issues, and so on.

▶ Signature page, to be executed by both parties

If a consulting organization is incapable of producing a first-class SOW or LA, its ability to deliver professional consulting is suspect. Pay particular attention to terms and conditions, recourse for work performed in an unsatisfactory manner, and contact information. A quality consulting organization is proud of its processes for ensuring that its work is delivered in a quality manner, and has the references and repeat business to prove it.

External Employee New Hires

Even after all interviews are completed, all references are verified, and everyone agrees that the right person for the job has been found, it's still a lot of work bringing on a new employee. For example, the compensation package itself could take days if not longer to prepare. Details might include nailing down or explaining

▶ Start date

▶ Annual salary requirements

▶ Benefits packages

▶ Sign-on cash bonuses, stock options, or other equity arrangements

▶ Regular bonus schedules (for example, for meeting performance objectives, financial objectives, or other goals)

▶ Workday expectations/typical hours expected

▶ Confidentiality and rights to ideas, concepts, techniques developed on the job, and other intellectual property (IP)

▶ Drug testing and other such programs, including whether these programs are one-time, regular, or random in nature

▶ General companywide information, including how to access employee data, information on employee portals and other similar resources, companywide organizational charts, and more

- Specific organizational information, specifically regarding the SAP TSO and other sister IT organizations, that would prove useful in solving or escalating problems

- Access to and provisioning of company-provided productivity tools and other resources, such as a laptop computer, Blackberry or other personal digital assistants (PDAs), cell phone, email, voicemail, and so on

Then, assuming the candidate accepts the offer, there is much work to be done to simply prepare for the start date. These details are addressed next.

The New Hire's First Week

Regardless of whether a SAP TSO new hire is an employee, contractor (consultant), or internal transfer, many administrative tasks need to be done before they can accomplish any real SAP-related work. These tasks can often consume as much as a week's worth of time, and from the new hire's perspective include

- Attending company- and/or departmentwide orientation

- Obtaining access to specific buildings or sites (project areas, the data center, and any number of various buildings, distribution centers, warehouses, shared meeting space, and so on)

- Obtaining access to the necessary building facilities (parking passes, building or elevator card keys, conference rooms, and project area, business areas, and executive floor access credentials as required)

- Completing new-hire paperwork (W4, benefits forms, and so on)

- Obtaining and setting up physical workspace (office, cubicle, shared area, space in the war room, and so on)

- Working with local management to arrange for the configuration of a desktop/laptop computer, including access to applications or services such as email, the Internet, word processing, presentation packages, spreadsheet applications, and so on

- Setting up printing, faxing, and other business-related day-to-day services

- Ordering business cards (as required, particularly for company-internal resources and senior project leaders)

- Obtaining all contact and organization information germane to the position

- Obtaining data or access to whatever workflow processes make sense for the position

- Attending safety training, legal compliance training, or other typically in-house-sponsored training (often tied to the particular site or building hosting the project resources)

▶ Obtaining all the detailed information required to support the SAP TSO and other sister IT organizations, including identification of and access to specific Internet/intranet websites, collaboration sites, file shares, physical file cabinets, and so on

Summary

You have seen that staffing an SAP TSO is a lot of work. Hopefully, the process offered in this chapter will help streamline things. First and foremost, take care to bring in the right people in the first place. It's infinitely harder and even more time-consuming to develop underperformers or let them go and start over with the recruiting process (not to mention the time that everyone else will waste picking up the underperformer's slack). Stay focused on the types of positions needed immediately, those needed just around the corner, and those that can wait several months. Finally, develop a process that brings new hires into the organization and equips them to get to work. After all, a well-equipped and organizationally knowledgeable new hire will serve your project best.

Case Study: Addressing a Key SAP TSO Gap

To your mixed delight, one of your key SAP TSO team members has been appointed to a management position outside your organization. A highly experienced SAP Basis/technology specialist, this SAP TSO team member will be transitioning to her new role in less than a month—perhaps as early as two weeks from now. It is therefore critical, as the SAP TSO team leader for HiTech, Inc, to find a replacement for this critical position as soon as possible.

Questions

1. Why is it critical for you to find a new team member as soon as possible?
2. Which approaches do you have available to find an SAP Basis specialist?
3. Where might you find a qualified candidate internally within HiTech's ranks?
4. How could one of your SAP implementation project's systems integration partners, GOSAP Consulting (a global provider of SAP consulting, technology products, software, and infrastructure services), help you?

NOTE

The answers to these questions can be found in Appendix A, "Case Study Answers."

CHAPTER 15

High Availability Considerations and Solutions

Before you actually architect (much less technically implement!) an SAP solution, you need to understand the end users' system availability requirements, or the amount of time that the system needs to be available to satisfy the needs of its business user community. In the world of SAP and other enterprise applications, this is referred to as *availability*, and the idea is to provide the appropriate level of *high* availability (HA). It's not enough to be available most of the time—the enterprise solution must be available when the users need it, which commonly means nearly 24 hours a day, seven days a week. The degree of availability thus depends on the requirements of the business. Better availability doesn't come cheap, though—the more available a system, the more money that must be invested up front and throughout the life of the system. And it's generally a steep investment curve.

The trick, then, is for the SAP technical architects to design a system that provides just the right balance of availability without exceeding the project's infrastructure, development, and ongoing operations and staffing budgets. The teams responsible for ongoing operations and staffing need to address process and people considerations that can affect system availability in the same way that the technical architects need to address availability. This chapter seeks to help you not only understand the HA approaches available for SAP but also strike just the right balance between availability and cost of the technology platform underpinning SAP (in case you're curious, people and process considerations related to HA are covered in Chapter 17, "Availability and Recoverability: Organizational Factors"). We also examine the many facets of HA, the concept of failure points, how HA is addressed via the different layers of the

SAP technology stack, when it makes sense to address HA proactively from a planning perspective, and we outline HA best practices and approaches and illustrate typical real-world HA solutions and issues. To keep things simple, we use the general term "availability" when referring generically to either HA or DR.

Introduction to Availability

The successful implementation of a highly available and reliable SAP architecture for an IT organization must balance technical design considerations, process and people considerations, the business or user experience, IT operability, various risks, and overall cost. All these points are key indicators of success for an organization's SAP systems insofar as deploying a highly available business solution is concerned. In our experience, the mission-critical business processes and core business functions of many companies are at significant risk—the kind of risk that's either managed well and thus generally avoided, or simply avoided due to good luck. Consider the following:

▶ Changes to technology, people, and process aimed at achieving a higher level of availability or recoverability do not guarantee a particular level of availability. Architecting a system to achieve four nines (99.99%) of availability can yield a system that only delivers two nines (99%) in reality. The converse is true as well; architecting a system for two nines can yield a system that actually delivers four nines in reality (for a discussion of "nines" see "Determining HA Requirements—The 'Nines of Availability'" later in this chapter).

▶ Steps taken to increase availability *decrease risks* but do not eliminate those risks. Over time, the risk of a failure increases as the technologies, people, and process factors change and the system ages.

▶ The technology supporting an SAP business application acts as the HA foundation. This foundation can be strengthened or weakened based on people and process factors.

The most notable area of concern for many firms today is to maintain a lean IT organization. Throughout the years after the dot-com bubble, economic slowdown, and subsequent roller-coaster of ups and downs, many companies have adopted a policy of handing out more work to fewer and fewer workers. Positions simply haven't been filled after people have vacated them. Instead, in the name of saving money, companies have either inadvertently or purposely chosen to sparingly staff their IT organizations. For many, the result has been to create an organization that's capable of focusing only on day-to-day or core operations; there's little budget or time left to address the broader spectrum of IT operations.

What does this mean to the SAP IT organizations in place today? In short, it means higher risk and less opportunity for differentiation. The strategic long-term needs of the business made possible through IT innovation and process diligence cannot be addressed. More importantly, from a system availability perspective, the ability to manage all the minutiae associated with running an enterprise-class business application characterized by operational excellence, incremental improvement, and best-in-class efficiency (see Figure 15.1) is left unaddressed. Such organizations have only the time, energy, and budget to address the middle of the IT spectrum—core operations. Yet, paradoxically, this increased burden of responsibility winds up being placed in the hands of a very few key technologists. One mistake, one extended leave of absence, or one failed laptop hosting an organization's knowledge can quickly lead to unplanned outages. More importantly, such an issue occurring in the midst of a significant (and eventual) hardware or software failure could easily result in many hours, if not several days, of unplanned downtime.

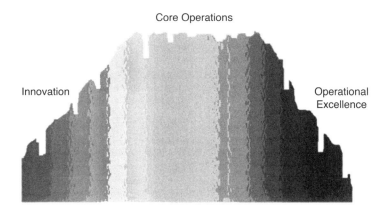

FIGURE 15.1   The energy invested in the spectrum of SAP IT operations spans operational innovation, core operations, and operational excellence.

Clearly, this might represent a risk with which an organization's executive management is comfortable. The risk needs to be identified and managed, however. After all, such an unplanned outage will occur one day, as hardware and software eventually fails, perhaps when the subject matter experts (SMEs) most familiar with it are away. Consider the following shortfalls when organizations focus only on core operations:

▶ When lean IT is combined with knowledge maintained in the heads and on the laptops of only a very few SMEs, not only is availability affected but so are troubleshooting, cross-training, and even new-employee orientation/onboarding—all of which impact recoverability.

▶ When key IT processes (such as restoration from tape to the organization's virtual tape library [VTL] or database or a particular file system, disaster recovery [DR] failback, and the process of IT capacity planning) are not only bereft of documentation, but have not been proven through real-world testing (or are conducted only by way of simulation exercises), the system's exposure to unplanned downtime is significant.

▶ Other important processes may be *missing* key components; an organization's promote-to-production process may be devoid of a load-testing component, for example, which means that any changes to the SAP technology stack will not be proved under load until the company's own production user community stresses the system.

▶ Personnel *workload balancing* can quickly become an issue. Key members of an organization's IT staff may find themselves overworked with baseload activities as well as with new projects, while less-equipped or less-capable colleagues wind up with additional time on their hands simply because they're unable to take on additional load and responsibilities.

Organizations need to "flip" the current state of their IT operations by pulling costs out of infrastructure and thus freeing up investment targeted toward innovation and incrementally improving SAP operational excellence—while increasing system availability and recoverability. This "flip" is illustrated in Figure 15.2.

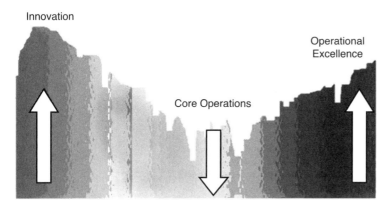

FIGURE 15.2   A focus on operational innovation and excellence naturally drives down the energy required to address core operations.

Organizations need to make some difficult decisions in the short term regarding where and how they spend their budget, how they address staffing, and the rigor with which they pursue and enforce operational process diligence. The issue at hand involves rebalancing or removing costs, particularly people and process costs. HA and its counterpart, downtime, are part of the balancing act that drives cost (among other factors, such as allowable risk, target TCO and budget objectives, acceptable average online user and batch job performance, acceptable peak online user and batch job performance, system scalability requirements, and more).

Availability, Reliability, and Fault Tolerance

Communicated another way, system availability can be discussed as a combination of reliability and fault tolerance. Reliability can be measured in various ways, but a common metric is mean time between failures (MTBF). The vendors of high-end computing platform architectures are often able to demonstrate high MTBF ratings for their systems, commanding significant premiums in exchange. Fault tolerance, on the other hand, involves the capability to provide functionality in the face of catastrophic failure of one or more hardware or software components. Fault tolerance reflects a duplication (or more!) of resources. In our experience, companies tend to focus much more on addressing fault tolerance than on addressing reliability, particularly now that even the least expensive commodity servers tend to provide pretty good reliability. And with mechanisms available for duplicating entire servers and server systems, the observed reliability of a single system or component is growing less and less (albeit still) important.

In the end, HA protects mission-critical business processes, safeguards the data supporting these business processes, and provides flexibility with regard to maintenance windows. Ultimately, the goal of HA is simple—to increase the time that your SAP solution component is up by decreasing both planned and unplanned downtime. However, HA by itself does not address the needs of disaster recoverability or disaster resilience. Tackling *disaster recovery* or *disaster recoverability* (DR) requires taking HA to the next level. It's such a complex topic that it rates its own chapter (see Chapter 16, "Disaster Recovery Considerations and Solutions"). Whereas HA is usually concerned with addressing relatively small downtime outages that range from seconds to perhaps many hours, DR focuses on how to handle downtime that lasts many hours to days, or perhaps even weeks. Thus, whereas HA might simply represent short-term failover solutions or incorporate tactical practices and system characteristics designed to increase general availability, DR speaks directly to how a company continues to do business in the aftermath of a true disaster—anything that disrupts the system enough to warrant doing business using a different set of resources, typically housed in a completely different data center. This is one reason why DR is also often referred to as *business continuity*, and DR solutions themselves as *business continuity solutions* or *approaches*.

Regardless of the label we apply to it, the goal of DR is clear—to protect an organization's production data and business processes from interruptions beyond an acceptable threshold. Our challenge, then, is to determine precisely where this "threshold" lies for a particular business organization—the intersection of long-term uptime and what this costs to maintain versus the organization's budget constraints. Before we get ahead of ourselves, though, let's start by taking a quick look at the common reasons that companies suffer downtime.

Causes of Downtime

According to a Gartner Group study published in 2001, the top reasons for enterprise systems *unplanned* downtime are as follows:

1. Application failure
2. People issues (such as operator errors)
3. Operating system failure
4. Hardware failure
5. Power outages
6. Natural disasters

This list might surprise you. The greatest source of unplanned downtime is not related to hardware failure, nor power-related issues, nor natural disasters (see Figure 15.3). Why? Primarily because these types of issues are commonly planned for and proactively addressed by designing fault-tolerant systems, solutions, and data center facilities. These

Gartner findings are very much in line with what we have seen when we have conducted our own SAP HA troubleshooting and proactive availability assessments.

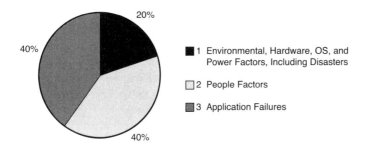

20%

40%

40%

1 Environmental, Hardware, OS, and Power Factors, Including Disasters

2 People Factors

3 Application Failures

FIGURE 15.3   The sources and distribution of unplanned downtime.

The most common reason for *planned* downtime should be no surprise, as it has not changed in years—it's system maintenance, the bulk of which is related to the time required to perform offline database backups. Other system maintenance activities include keeping up to date the hardware, operating system, database, and SAP Basis and application layers of the SAP technology stack. With the common causes of downtime identified, let's identify the ways in which high availability and disaster recovery are similar.

Similarities Between HA and DR

Remember that HA and DR both seek to reduce unplanned downtime to acceptable levels and address planned downtime. To be sure, what is acceptable to one business might not be acceptable to another. Tolerances or expectations with regard to system availability, the cost to maintain that availability, or the cost to mitigate most disaster scenarios naturally varies between different firms (as well as between different business application user communities within the same firm, for that matter). But the up-front requirements to attain a certain amount of HA or DR are similar, as are the general mechanisms for attaining each. Here are some more specific similarities:

▶ Both HA and DR require an evaluation of total cost of ownership (TCO) or return on investment (ROI) to determine the amount of unplanned downtime that is allowable before some kind of alternative action or solution (referred to as *system failover*, or simply *failover*) must be manually or automatically executed.

▶ HA and DR solutions add more complexity to the technology stack, both technology-wise and from a business- and IT-support perspective.

▶ Both HA and DR require in-depth training on the part of the SAP technical support organization, to ensure that each HA and DR solution is understood, deployed, and managed correctly.

▶ Both HA and DR can be addressed or implemented at many different layers of the SAP technology stack.

- HA and DR are in essence *insurance* to the business—incremental budget money spent to protect the SAP solution against a possible disaster.

- Both HA and DR selections tend to drive the architecture of the technology stack. In fact, they very much *restrict* the options of the stack, because only precise combinations of solutions and components work together to create a highly available system.

With regard to this last point, a particular disk subsystem vendor's approach to HA might require a specific operating system or version of the underlying SAP database. Or a certain level of DR might only be available from a hardware vendor's particular line of disk subsystems. In either case, the need for a specific level of availability limits the choices you have regarding the SAP technology stack—you in effect "cross off" many of the lower-level technology stack alternatives in favor of fewer, more highly available options.

Differences Between HA and DR

Ultimately, both HA and DR beg the question "What is my business exposure when my SAP system is down?" Organizations must allocate their limited budgets to properly balance IT costs with business impact and benefits (as outlined earlier). Beyond business exposure, both HA and DR seek to mitigate the risks and costs inherent to this downtime. Key differences exist between HA and DR, however:

- HA tends to be tactical in nature, whereas DR tends to protect the organization from strategic or long term loss. Thus, HA focuses on mitigating component failure within the context of a layer of the technology stack (for example, disk failures, server failures, network component failures, and so on). The focus of DR is on such things as facilities and processes that come into play during the total failure of a data center.

- HA is typically implemented within the SAP system architecture or system landscape, whereas DR is nearly always architected "outside the box"—outside the primary SAP data center facility, and certainly outside specific internal server and disk subsystem HA options.

- HA usually involves SAP technology stack resources in one physical location, whereas DR nearly always entails a second data center site or approach to meeting the business and processing needs of an organization.

- DR tends to require very specific SAP technology stack components. That is, DR approaches tend to be based on a particular technology deployed at one or a few layers of the stack, whereas HA practices exist at every layer of the stack.

- DR recovery tends to be complex and time consuming, often requiring a planned and lengthy failback period; HA recovery is much simpler.

- DR solutions can be quite expensive to procure, implement, and support, significantly more so than HA solutions.

- The DR solution implemented by a firm will be utilized rarely (hopefully), whereas HA and fault-tolerance approaches are exercised quite often. For example, nearly all SAP customers leverage their investments in HA (whatever that might entail) to more rapidly complete planned system maintenance, support change releases/change waves, and support regular activities such as offline database backups and so on. And nearly all SAP systems will suffer from failed disk drives, a failed network card, and the like—failures that can easily be planned for such that no unplanned system downtime is realized.

▶ DR represents a huge insurance policy to the business, whereas HA represents a much smaller one. As with individual medical insurance policies, you hope you never really *need* to exercise your DR site and processes. But they are there if you need them. The trick is to buy the right "plan"—to purchase the proper DR solution required by the business. The last thing you want to find out after a disaster hits your data center is that you signed up for an inferior policy but really needed (based on your business exposure) a class A policy.

Determining HA Requirements—The "Nines of Availability"

Because availability requirements drive the nature of the deployed SAP solution, you must understand these requirements as early as possible in the SAP deployment process. After all, in the same way that business agility is linked directly to application agility, so too is fundamental business availability related to business application availability. Remember, HA and DR requirements limit your choices regarding certain layers in the SAP technology stack. If you make the mistake of purchasing key technology stack components *before* your availability needs are made clear by the business, you risk having to toss out substandard pieces of the stack. So, before you go off and buy servers, database packages, and operating systems, work with the system's intended end users and other project stakeholders to determine exactly the level of availability needed—what we often refer to as the "nines of availability."

A common way of measuring uptime is by *nines of availability*, which refers to the percentage of a year a system is available to end users, such as 99% ("two nines"), 99.9% ("three nines"), or 99.99% ("four nines"). Most often, the actual percentage of time a system is capable of delivering is measured in potential minutes or hours of uptime in a year *not including scheduled downtime* for tasks such as system maintenance (which might include system patching, replacing hardware before it fails, and applying bug fixes via SAP support packages). In other cases, SAP support organizations might include both planned and unplanned downtime when they talk about their nines of availability. Neither is necessarily a better approach than the other (though we tend to prefer to keep planned downtime out of the "downtime" conversations, save for establishing background context). Just be consistent when discussing and measuring system uptime goals.

The greater the number of nines, the less unplanned downtime a system should deliver over the course of a year. To be fair, during a particular year, a system may realize better or worse uptime than what was targeted. Over the course of several years, though, the system's average availability should approximate the nines of availability it was designed to deliver. To keep the nines of availability in perspective, consider the following (and see Figure 15.4):

▶ There are 8,760 hours in most years (365 days times 24 hours in a day)

▶ This equals 525,600 minutes (8,760 hours times 60 minutes in an hour)

▶ This also equals 31,536,000 seconds (525,600 times 60 seconds in a minute)

99% Availability = 88 Hours Downtime

99.9% Availability = 8 Hours 46 Minutes

99.99% Availability = 53 Minutes

99.999% Availability = 5 1/2 Minutes

FIGURE 15.4   The "nines of availability" quickly add up to significantly decreased downtime at the expense of just as significantly increased costs.

Most SAP solutions are architected for somewhere between three and four nines of availability. This correlates to systems that are designed to deliver between 53 minutes and eight hours of unplanned downtime *on average* each year. A solution that's designed for five nines of availability, on the other hand, will be architected to deliver no more than approximately six minutes of unplanned downtime throughout the course of an entire year. Such a system is dramatically more expensive than its three-to-four nines counterparts. Throughout this book, it may be helpful to refer to Figure 15.4 when the topic of nines of availability comes up.

Single Points of Failure

We can now turn our attention to the actual problem areas inherent in our particular SAP technology stack, and ultimately to the SAP solution being deployed. Problem areas are often discussed as *failure points*. An IT-enabled business application naturally falls prey to many different kinds of both business-related and technology-related failure points. Smart business analysts, technology architects, programmers, and others work within cost, timeframe, and other constraints to develop solutions with as few failure points as possible.

Practically speaking, though, it is impossible to develop a complex IT-enabled business application with no failure points. Technology will ultimately fail, regardless of how foolproof it appears. Business process exceptions will occur, no matter how standardized your approach may be. And even the best programming logic will succumb to an unforeseen, and therefore untested, situation—and abort.

The trick is to identify all these potential points of failure and either eliminate or mitigate their capability to cause unplanned downtime. Such points of failure are commonly referred to as *single points of failure* (SPOFs), and they potentially exist throughout the SAP technology stack and the SAP system and application landscape in general. We will walk through each general layer in the stack next, noting advantages and disadvantages of different methods of remediation as we go.

SAP Data Center Infrastructure SPOFs

Potential SPOFs abound in the data center layer more than in any other layer in the technology stack. Fortunately, these potential show-stoppers are some of the easiest to address from a HA perspective. Consider the following:

▶ Data center power must be redundant, from the actual power sources or power grids (which can be safeguarded through the use of a generator), to dual-feed breaker panels, to dual UPSs, to dual power distribution units, to dual power cables feeding dual power supplies in every critical hardware component.

▶ Data center cooling represents an everyday SPOF. We've seen more than a few data centers that cannot withstand the loss of one of their air handlers/air conditioners without the heat rising to the point of forcing equipment power-down.

▶ Network infrastructure, such as power, also benefits from redundancy. This is important from the client network all the way back to the data center. Client network routers, dial-up access devices, VPN connections, and other access points must all be redundant. Similarly, any switches, bridges, hubs, or other network devices also need to be protected through redundancy. Any application that leverages a particular subnet in an attempt to integrate with your SAP solution also becomes a SPOF. Finally, the network cables and individual network cards that facilitate communication to a particular server must be redundant as well.

▶ Data center rack placement can inadvertently become a SPOF, too. For example, one of our customers placed both of its SAP cluster nodes in a single rack, only to have that rack tip over during a maintenance window and completely lose power. In another case, an SAP IT shop (not a customer) had positioned its racks too closely together front to rear, such that serviceability to the production SAP system was impacted when another system (non-SAP in this case) was also undergoing maintenance.

Power Considerations

With regard to power, remember that every critical server, disk subsystem, network component, air handler, and so on should have access to redundant power. For maximum availability, therefore, every component in the chain of power should be redundant, as shown in the example in Figure 15.5.

Additionally, we like to see power cables color-coded. For example, at one of our customer sites, the primary power is supplied through black cables and the redundant power is supplied through gray cables—this reduces human error later on, as it is very clear to everyone which components are protected, and which power source is being drawn upon during maintenance.

There are also some very important tools and utilities available that should play a part in monitoring power. Most UPS vendors offer tools that snap in to popular Simple Network Management Protocol (SNMP)-based enterprise management tools, for example.

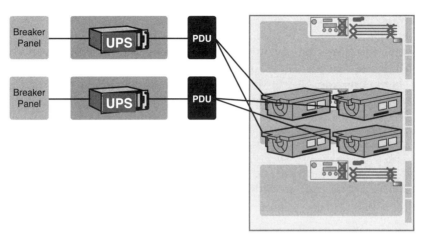

FIGURE 15.5   Power failure fault tolerance starts at each hardware component and works its way back to the data center's central source(s) of power; the key is redundant power supplies and components.

Network Infrastructure

When it comes to network infrastructure, redundancy is key—if an SAP end user cannot gain access to the system because a critical network link is down, the system is in effect "down." Other important areas to consider include the following:

> ▶ Color-coding makes a lot of sense here, too. One client site of ours uses a public network segment for client-to-application server traffic, and another segment for back-end application server-to-DB server traffic. The first segment uses solid-green cable for primary connections and striped green-and-white cable for redundant links. Similarly, the back-end network consists of solid-blue cable for primary connections and striped blue-and-white cable for redundant links. This level of standardization makes troubleshooting simpler, and reduces human errors going forward.

> ▶ Certain software packages or HA solutions require the use of virtual IP addresses, or *relocatable* IP addresses. This may require special software or network drivers that support teaming or pairing network cards into a single virtual network card.

> ▶ Any hardware-based network load-balancing gear must be redundant, too.

> ▶ Some software-based load-balancing solutions do nothing for HA. For example, Microsoft's initial foray into software-based load balancing (NLB; Network Load Balancing) was incapable of detecting higher-layer failures.

> ▶ Similarly, some failover cluster approaches and other HA solutions cannot detect network failures. Thus, these failures need to be detected in another manner—for example, through enterprise management software or hardware-specific monitoring utilities.

▶ Dual-port network interface cards (NICs with two ports on one physical card occupying a single PCI slot, for example) present an opportunity to create a SPOF where none might otherwise exist. Consider the case of one of our SAP customers who implemented a pair of dual-port NICs, but ran both ports from NIC "A" to its client network, and both ports from NIC "B" to its back-end network. In doing this, each NIC became a SPOF. A better approach would have been to take one set of ports from *each* NIC and run it to the public network, and then run the two remaining ports from each NIC to the back-end network.

▶ DR sites probably need to be protected in a similarly redundant manner as previously described in this list. Plus, links to the DR site from the public network also need to be protected. We recommend two links managed by two different service providers—in this way, even provider-specific issues do not become a SPOF.

With redundancy in place as shown in Figure 15.6, even multiple failures throughout an SAP network infrastructure will not take the system out of service.

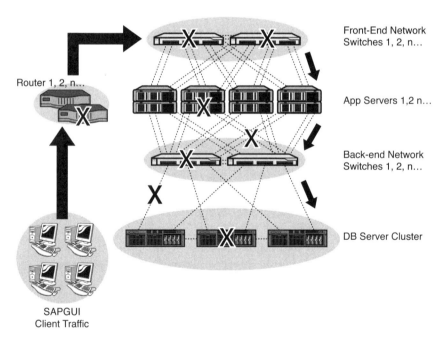

FIGURE 15.6   Network-layer redundancy allows for a variety of discrete and multiple failures while still affording connectivity to SAP (every "X" represents a failed component that still does not impact availability).

Finally, with regard to network components, it's important to proactively monitor these critical SAP solution points as much as any other component whose failure is capable of essentially shutting down your SAP system.

Rack Infrastructure in the Real World

Perhaps surprisingly, the rack infrastructure physically used to house server, network, and disk subsystem hardware represents a very real and very avoidable HA concern. It is important not only to physically install these racks consistent with the vendors' requirements, but also to step back and take a holistic view of what is actually housed in the rack and how this gear is accessed. For example:

▶ SPOFs are created when a specific type of computing resource is installed in only a single rack. Therefore, we always recommend that customers shy away from creating "centralized" racks housing all network components, or all production SAP application servers, or both nodes of a production cluster, or all SAP Internet Transaction Servers, and so on. In this way, loss of power or network services to an individual rack does not automatically (in effect) bring down an entire production system.

▶ Housing heavy components high in a rack may cause the entire rack to come crashing down when the heavy component is pulled out for service. This, and the fact that it's just plain dangerous and contrary to all vendor warnings, should warrant repositioning heavy gear on the bottom of the rack.

▶ Monitors must be placed where they can be seen and therefore used. Before the days of ubiquitous hardware-level and browser-based access, one of our customers installed its rack-mounted retractable video monitors on the top of a row of seven-foot racks. In and of itself, this was not a terrible thing. However, the inconvenience of accessing the monitors eventually impacted production uptime at this small shop—it was so inconvenient and uncomfortable to access their system's monitors that the customer never spent the time needed to proactively monitor its SAP system (and the system crashed due to a very apparent and therefore very avoidable memory leak).

▶ Keyboard, video/monitor, and mouse (KVM) connections need to be considered. Similar to the problems described regarding "centralized" rack configurations, KVM can represent a SPOF if both nodes in a cluster, for example, share the same KVM components. We also like the idea of maintaining two different methods of accessing server resources (to eliminate a single method eventually becoming a single point of failure). Access solutions like Symantec's pcAnywhere, Vector Networks' PC-Duo, Microsoft Terminal Services, HP's Remote Insight capabilities, and any number of KVM over IP solutions can effectively "back up" system access gained through physical KVM connections.

▶ Lack of sound cable management can also compromise HA. That is, cables that are improperly mounted to servers such that pulling out a server wrenches out its power cables will only increase unplanned downtime. Similarly, stuffing all of your power, network, storage area network (SAN), and other cables into an already crowded subfloor not only complicates cable management, but also makes troubleshooting more complex. In fact, in the case of one of our customers, too many piled-up cables actually blocked cool airflow to some of its server racks, resulting in automatic hardware-initiated power-down. Today, ceiling-mounted cable trays for network/SAN

15

cables, combined with subfloor-based power cables, help ensure that they never succumb to this easily avoidable problem again.

▶ Racks stuffed with gear from varying vendors may improperly vent or exhaust hot air. This is especially true in cases where some of the gear draws air from the front and exhausts hot air out the back, while other gear draws cool air from the subfloor and exhausts it out the top, and yet other gear pulls from the top and exhausts into the subfloor.

As one of our SAP clients told us years ago, BTUs are the true enemy of the data center—the high densities and smaller and smaller form factors that we all benefit from only exacerbate the cooling needs of already-crowded data centers. Thus, it is as important as ever to plan well, and plan ahead, not only for data center growth but also for data center cooling requirements.

The Ultimate SPOF—The SAP Data Center

What will happen to your business if your entire data center disappears from the face of the earth? Answering this question consumes many SAP DR specialists' time, and keeps many executives, business process owners, and others awake at night. Certainly, it's expensive to duplicate an entire data center. In our experience, we see more customers duplicate core business processing systems instead, or split business processing and test/development activities across sites. Key concerns relative to duplicating an entire data center include the following points:

▶ Building a DR site is expensive.

▶ Maintaining the site and its equipment is also expensive.

▶ Testing the DR site is both necessary and expensive, too.

▶ Maintaining readiness in terms of people and processes is expensive and time-consuming.

▶ Selling the executive leadership team on the idea of spending a pile of budget money on a resource that will hopefully never be "used" (in effect, an insurance policy) can be difficult.

With regard to testing and maintaining readiness, to reflect the ramifications of a true disaster, not only is time required to conduct the testing, but a tremendous amount of time must be invested in developing and working through disaster scenarios, staffing scenarios, breaks in processes, and so on. We therefore like to identify the hidden benefits of a DR site outside of the most obvious benefit—protection of your core business (which should be enough to satisfy anyone). These include

▶ Leveraging the DR site for end-user reporting requirements.

▶ Using the DR site for testing major infrastructure changes.

▶ Using the DR site for pre-upgrade testing and staging. Staging your preproduction systems at your DR site with the strategy of using them in the event of a primary data center failure can also ease financial pressures associated with building a DR site.

▶ Using the DR site as the definitive testing ground in your change control or change management processes, prior to deploying changes to production.

If you cannot sell the executive leadership team on any of the benefits just discussed, another (perhaps even better) approach is to ask management to consider outsourcing. Instead of spending a fortune on idle computing resources, a company might consider outsourcing its DR needs on a "computing on demand" basis, whereby computing resources are paid for as needed. This can convert large capital expenditures into manageable monthly fees. In the long run, savings can be huge on several fronts. For example, there's less technology for a firm to buy and less time and effort necessary to spend on technology-specific people and process matters. And given the outsourcer's knowledge of HA and DR services, there's generally less risk, fewer unknowns, and fewer headaches. Large SAP outsourcers are doing more and more of this type of DR data center service, including Capgemini, CSC, IBM, HP, SAP in partnership with HP, and others.

Server and Operating System SPOFs

Server-based SPOFs have been recognized and addressed for many years now. Today, what used to be considered "differentiators" between server platforms are no more than commodity traits. Features such as ECC (error code correcting) RAM, redundant/hot-pluggable power supplies, hot-pluggable hard disks, redundant/hot-pluggable fans, hot-pluggable network and host bus adapter cards, redundant battery-backed disk drive controllers, and so on can be found in everything from mainframe-class platforms to entry-level servers. Server manufacturers continue to strive to address HA in their latest computing platforms. Newer features, such as RAID-protected hot-pluggable RAM and hot-pluggable processors, are quickly becoming commodity features as well.

Beyond basic hardware redundancy, a server's operating system (OS) can provide increased availability. HA from an OS perspective is provided by the following:

▶ The ability to software-mirror critical data volumes or partitions—for example, through HP MirrorDisk/UX, Sun Solaris Volume Manager, or Windows Disk Administrator

▶ A highly available file system that supports redundant file allocation tables journaling, and similar features and structures

▶ The ability to apply OS changes or patches "on the fly" or in another manner that eliminates or minimizes the amount of planned downtime such changes require (sometimes called "live upgrade" capabilities)

▶ OS software tools that support the capability to remove, replace, or add redundant hardware components while the system remains up

▶ In the case of UNIX-based solutions, the ability to support Network File System (NFS) redundancy through clustering of the NFS server

As to the last point, clustering support in and of itself is a key feature of an enterprise-class operating system (which is described in detail later in this chapter). Another interesting file system consideration is whether an OS supports *journaling*. A journaling file system is a fault-resilient file system that updates a serial log on disk immediately after a change to the disk, thereby better ensuring metadata and ultimately data integrity. It also allows unsaved data to be recovered, making it an essential feature, in our opinion, of OSs used for SAP applications. Many OSs support journaling. Windows 2008 and its predecessors support it to a great extent, which is why it's unlikely that you will lose an entire disk volume due to corruption, for example, after the system crashes unexpectedly (such as after a power outage). With any OS, though, all of the data yet to be written to disk prior to the crash will still be lost unless it's protected by a disk array controller with battery-backed write cache. On the other hand, the default Linux system (ext2fs) does not journal at all. That means a system crash can more easily corrupt an entire disk volume.

Basic hardware and OS features protect against single-server component failures. The idea is to provide resiliency; in the case of a hardware component failure, the system will still continue to run. But what about catastrophic failures, such as a completely failed system board or the failure of all a server's power supplies (perhaps due to a rogue power spike, itself perhaps due to a failing UPS)? Two possible solutions are readily available, backup/recovery systems and clustering, which are discussed next.

Maximizing HA Through Backup and Recovery Systems

Beyond the HA features built into a file system itself, restoring a file system quickly and without error is left to backup and recovery systems composed of tape (and virtual tape) hardware and tape backup software. Such systems rarely get the attention they deserve, which is surprising, because these systems form the backbone of any enterprise's system recovery capabilities.

Backup and recovery systems have come a long way from the days of reel-to-reel tape and mainframe tape cartridges. Boasting speeds of gigabytes-per-hour throughput, native tape drive solutions today are both robust and fast. And virtual tape drive offerings, which are essentially specialized disk drive subsystems used in conjunction with special software to act like a tape library, can host terabytes of data while giving an organization the capability to back up and restore 100 times faster than its tape counterparts (though a tape-based solution is still recommended for obtaining system images and data backups that can be safeguarded offsite).

Increasing HA Through Clustering

Instead of restoring from tape, wouldn't it be nice to recover from a server crash in such a way as to minimize downtime, through an automated server failover? In cases of complete server failures, hardware and OS vendors have developed server clustering technologies. They come in many different forms and with many different features but have two things in common: OS-based clusters are hardware- and OS-specific, and OS clusters combine a *minimum* of two servers (called cluster nodes) to protect against complete server failure.

It is quite common to cluster SAP systems and the underlying databases using OS-based cluster solutions. In these cases, OS-supported scripts are used to control both failover and resource management. Products such as HP's MC/Serviceguard, IBM's PowerHA for AIX (formerly HACMP for AIX, or IBM High Availability Cluster Multiprocessing), Microsoft's Cluster Services, and various SteelEye products leverage server redundancy and software-based failover mechanisms to monitor clusters and automatically fail applications between nodes. The idea is to detect performance issues or outright server failures, shut down the offending server and its applications, and then automatically restart the clustered applications on an existing cluster server (one of two or more cluster nodes).

Clusters made up of a single node that runs the hosted applications (while one or more other nodes wait around passively for a failover to occur, in which case they become the active node and run the application) are called active/passive clusters. These are common and simple to implement, but they represent a waste of resources in that only one server is ever performing useful work. A smarter approach is to implement an active/active cluster, where all nodes in the cluster actively process work. Naturally, these clusters are more complex and require more careful configuration, particularly clusters comprised of more than two nodes.

Many cluster solutions scale much higher than simply two nodes. IBM's PowerHA for AIX running on IBM AIX servers scales up to 32 nodes, while PowerHA on Linux and Microsoft Windows' cluster services both scale to eight nodes. This allows for many potential nodes to service your SAP CIs as well as your Oracle, DB2, and SQL Server databases, for example, helping keep unplanned downtime to a minimum. For more information on IBM's PowerHA, see http://www-03.ibm.com/systems/power/software/availability/aix/index.html. For HP's Serviceguard, see http://www.docs.hp.com/en/B7885-90013/ch01.html.

Database SPOFs

To many technologists and business users alike, providing HA for SAP often equates to protecting the database "underneath" SAP—the data. Of course, as you have seen already, there is a lot more to HA than simply safeguarding the structure that houses all of your SAP enterprise data. But the database historically represents a key SPOF in SAP installations. Consider the following:

▶ Without the database, neither new nor old transactions can be created or referenced. Thus, all the surrounding SAP infrastructure becomes essentially worthless when the database becomes unavailable.

▶ Until the past several years, the database for an SAP instance could not be split across multiple servers. Of course, Oracle's Real Application Clusters (RAC) solves this age-old SPOF. But the lack of such a solution drove everyone—hardware, OS, and database vendors alike—to create HA approaches and offerings designed to protect either the database itself or the data residing in the database.

Some of these approaches and offerings for protecting the database are discussed next. Keep in mind that these approaches generally protect more than just the database in that they can often be used to duplicate, replicate, or in some other way safeguard an entire server.

Standby Database and Log Replication Solutions

At a hardware level, data is replicated between sites or disk subsystems disk block by disk block. OS-based solutions follow a similar approach, synchronizing the contents of a disk volume block by block. It might be surprising, then, that database-layer solutions replicate the data resident within a database in a different manner. In most cases, a database vendor provides HA in one of two ways:

▶ By replicating data one transaction at a time, applying changes to a standby database via incremental database log updates

▶ By creating a cluster such that the database and all of its associated services may fail over to another server node if the first node fails

Before we cover the various database-layer clustering approaches later in this section, let's investigate log-based replication schemes. An entire database can be replicated to another site, close by or far away, by using a method provided by all enterprise database vendors today—log shipping. This approach is sometimes known as "standby database" or "hot site backup," too, depending on the database vendor involved and the manner in which the data is being replicated. In all the following cases that we describe, the functionality necessary to create these standby or replicated databases is inherent to the database product. In other words, no special SAP server configuration or application-level coding is required to take advantage of these HA solutions.

Oracle Standby Database

Probably the most commonly implemented HA solution for Oracle databases is the standby database. A standby database allows you to keep a nearly synchronized copy of your SAP database at another location. Using a product such as Oracle Data Guard, the general process is quite simple:

1. Set up, install, and configure the standby server on a server at a remote location.

2. Restore a recent full database backup to the standby server.

3. Configure an Oracle standby server (which means put the server in perpetual recovery mode).

4. Systematically copy archived redo logs to the standby server (perhaps every 15 to 30 minutes or so, depending on configuration) as the primary system creates redo logs and archives them.

5. Apply the archived redo logs after a period of time to the standby server, such that the standby server is kept perhaps four to eight hours "behind" the primary server.

By maintaining a delta of four to eight hours between the primary and standby server, it's possible to recover from user errors and other data-manipulation issues that would otherwise be applied to the standby server so quickly that no one would have a chance to realize that an error occurred and still have time to "back out" of it.

With this type of HA solution, if the primary server fails, the secondary server can be put into production rapidly—only the remaining archived redo logs that have not yet been applied to the standby server need to be applied. Worst case, if the standby server never received the last archived redo log, the standby server will only be 15 to 30 minutes behind the primary—this is normally quite acceptable, requiring the end users to log in to the new system and re-enter only 15 to 30 minutes' worth of data and transactions.

Oracle Advanced Replication

Available for many years now, Oracle Advanced Replication allows updates to a primary database to be replicated to many additional databases. This replication occurs automatically, allowing for complete data integrity and transactional consistency. And the really nice thing is that each database, even the replicated copies, can be accessed by end users all day long. One of our favorite implementations of this HA solution allows for the DR site (or any secondary site housing a replica of the primary database) to be used for reporting, thus offloading the primary SAP database from this processor- and disk-intensive daily activity.

With some of the more common transaction and log-shipping approaches behind us, let's look next at how clustering is employed at a database level.

Oracle Real Application Clusters

Oracle Real Application Clusters (Oracle RAC) eliminates the database as a SPOF, and in doing so also provides a certain amount of scalability as additional nodes are added to the cluster. RAC is supported on all the major OSs—Linux, Windows, and various UNIX platforms. Other compelling benefits or features of RAC (as compared to most other cluster solutions) include the following:

- ▶ Transparent client failover capabilities; applications and users are automatically and transparently reconnected to another surviving cluster node, while their queries continue uninterrupted.

- ▶ Ability to add incremental cluster nodes online. In this way, Oracle RAC not only reduces downtime, but also allows SAP to "scale out" through inexpensive commodity servers, rather than "scale up," which eventually drives platform and other expensive technology stack changes.

- ▶ Ability to add incremental disk resources without repartitioning existing drives.

- ▶ Ability to move seamlessly from Oracle's non-RAC database installation to a RAC system, requiring no database unload or reload.

- ▶ Oracle support for all popular operating system and hardware platforms.

Oracle RAC is so effective because of the way in which it uses each database node's data cache. In this method, called *cache fusion*, all local node cache is made available to all nodes in the cluster to satisfy database requests from any node. When an end user's transaction requests a data block, the system first determines whether the request can be satisfied by the cache residing in the locally attached database node. If the data cannot be found there, the request is sent over a high-speed low-latency link—the *interconnect*—to each node's remote caches. If the data still cannot be found, an actual disk read cannot be avoided and therefore a physical disk read is performed—the slowest operation in any

15

enterprise system, and the reason why high-speed disk caches were developed in the first place.

With such tremendous and obvious benefits, why isn't Oracle RAC storming the world of enterprise applications such as SAP? Even after all these years, the solution was only recently deemed generally available (broadly supported) by SAP. Still, the number of RAC installations seems small compared to the potential benefits. We can only guess that price continues to play a pivotal role—the uplift for Oracle RAC is substantial, and this does not include the need for additional hardware and OS licenses.

Oracle Failsafe with Microsoft Windows Cluster Services

In addition to RAC, Oracle also supports clustering on Windows using Microsoft Cluster Services (MSCS) and an Oracle product called Oracle Fail Safe (OFS). Both products are required for Windows environments—from Windows NT to Windows 2008. OFS works by polling the Oracle database resource dynamic link library (an Oracle-specific Windows DLL) to ensure that the database has not failed. If an "Is Alive" message is not returned by the database after three consecutive database polling attempts, a failure status message is forwarded to the cluster resource monitor and the database portion hosted on the presumably failed node is moved over to an existing node.

Oracle Streams

Rather than clustering a database to provide protection, Oracle also offers a technology to replicate data between a source (your production SAP database, for example) and one or more target sources (where a copy of the data is replicated). *Oracle Streams* can be configured to copy data between two or more Oracle databases or between an Oracle database and a mix of Oracle and non-Oracle databases. Oracle Streams also supports copying data internally within a single Oracle database (between different tables, for example), which admittedly only safeguards *some* of the data in your SAP database (and then, only locally rather than to another database hosted at a different geographic site). It is preferable to protect the entire database from disk, server, network access, or entire data center availability issues. After all, if the data is copied locally and the database itself fails, the entire SAP system will be unavailable.

Available on Oracle 9i and greater, Oracle Streams ships only with Oracle Enterprise Edition. Because this solution captures database changes as they are made to the source system, the solution can be configured for near real-time protection (where changes are almost immediately replicated). Oracle Streams does not allow for true synchronous data copies, though; Oracle Streams uses Oracle's Advanced Queuing technology, which employs an asynchronous mechanism for propagating database changes.

Microsoft SQL Server Clustering

When it comes to providing HA for SQL Server, we tend to see both log shipping and MSCS clustering used most often, with the former approach being most popular. Of course, other clustering software packages exist. But unless you want to be a lonely fish in a large sea (that is, the only company around for miles clustering your SAP instance with some unknown or unpopular HA solution), it makes much more sense to go with log shipping or MSCS clustering (enabling you to leverage lessons learned and other experiences from hundreds of other companies and consulting organizations).

Today, clustering SQL Server is simple. SQL Server is cluster-aware and automatically recognizes when it is being installed on a cluster. It requires that its executables be loaded on each node in a cluster, similar to Oracle's approach to clustering on the Windows platform. In this way, SQL Server itself can be easily patched and updated via rolling upgrades. In the past this was not possible—the SQL Server 7.0 executables were maintained out on the shared disk subsystem, for example. Patching or upgrading SQL Server 7.0 therefore meant incurring downtime, because the shared executables only existed in one place.

Microsoft SQL Server Replication

Microsoft's SQL Server replication, which lets you copy database transactions or complete databases from one system to another, addresses HA as well as performance concerns. From an HA perspective, SQL Server replication lets you deploy a failover database capable of picking up as soon as the "primary" database server fails. After a pair of databases are synchronized through a process called snapshot replication, they can then be kept synchronized through transactional replication. Microsoft allows the synchronization to be scheduled or to take place immediately, addressing two different concerns:

▶ Immediate replication ensures that data recovery time is minimized; the primary and secondary databases are kept synchronized transaction by transaction.

▶ Scheduled replication risks loss of data but helps to ensure that user errors may be corrected (assuming they're caught early) before their invalid or inaccurate transactions are committed to the secondary database.

For additional information, see the Microsoft SQL Server 2008 Books Online website, http://msdn.microsoft.com/en-us/library/ms151198.aspx.

SAP Application SPOFs

SAP AG tells us that a disaster is "a situation in which critical components in the SAP environment become unavailable so that service cannot be resumed in a short period," such as a few hours or days or so. Most SAP technology experts agree that the two most critical SAP system components are, first, the database, and second, the SAP instance that runs the enqueue and message services—the central instance (CI).

In previous sections of this chapter, we described a number of methods and approaches for protecting the database. The topic of this section, on the other hand, is how to protect the CI and other SAP-specific SPOFs from both interruptions in service and full-fledged disasters.

Generally speaking, the CI can enjoy a high level of availability by having a standby system available (at a remote site), waiting to be started up in the event of a disaster. When a failover occurs to this standby system, all other application servers that might exist as part of that system have to be restarted, though, or reconfigured to reconnect automatically. The same is true of a cluster node—all application servers must reconnect to the CI after the CI fails (relocates itself) from one cluster node to another. This fact underscores a point made earlier in this chapter that *avoiding* failing services to another system is as important as anything else. We accomplish this goal by piecing together a server with built-in redundancy, hot-pluggable components, support for proactive systems monitoring, and so on, in the hope that most failures will be addressed by this redundancy and therefore not initiate a failover.

Fortunately, the time required to reconnect to the CI is minimal, in the neighborhood of tens of seconds. And through the auto-reconnect SAP profile parameter, this process can be easily automated and therefore appear to the system's end-user community as a nearly seamless reconnect—most users will never even notice a CI failover.

Clustering SAP Components in General

Any number of clustering technologies can be used to "cluster" an enterprise application. Even applications that are not *cluster-aware*, or written in such a manner as to record and track state information needed by a quorum or other cluster-tracking mechanism, can still be clustered. The only drawback is that no state information is maintained. The non-cluster-aware clustered applications can only be automatically stopped and started, as they know nothing about the status of a particular process or package, or the state of end users connected to the system, and so on. But they can still be made part of a package or group, and therefore have other dependencies defined for them (for example, a database service must be started before an application can be started). In this way, great value can still be obtained by clustering non-cluster-aware applications.

SAP has been Microsoft cluster-aware since SAP R/3 3.1i, and "clusterable" through proprietary hardware and UNIX OSs well before then. The manner in which SAP supports clustering differs between different computing platforms. Consider the following:

▶ UNIX-based OSs typically support clustering a DB and a CI as either a single package (where both the DB and CI must run *together* on node A or node B) or individual packages (where each solution component can move independently between nodes).

▶ UNIX-based OSs typically support clustering a production instance running on node A with a nonproduction instance (that is, QA or test) running on another node in a cluster. The idea here is that if the production node fails, the second node will stop the test or QA services, and start up the production services instead.

▶ Application servers are rarely clustered—availability is achieved through redundancy and SAP logon load balancing instead, as these approaches are less expensive and less complicated.

▶ Traditionally, Windows-based clusters have been much more rigid than their UNIX counterparts in terms of what is supported by SAP AG. Only active/active clustering was supported until several years ago, and then only between the DB and CI, where each is defined in a separate group, and each can execute on either node in the cluster. Today, Microsoft supports multiple cluster nodes for SAP.

▸ Windows-based clusters are typically segregated by their role in the landscape. For example, it's common to create a production cluster, a test/QA cluster, and a cluster in a technical sandbox. Unlike UNIX clusters, production cluster nodes are not clustered with test/QA or other nonproduction nodes.

Our point here is simply that the CI can be clustered in an active/passive manner (clustered with a standby server) regardless of OS environment. We have customers doing just that, running heterogeneous systems in which the CI and DB reside on different hardware/OS platforms and therefore cannot participate in a single shared cluster. However, each individual resource—the DB or the CI—can be clustered such that a standby server is sitting idly by, awaiting the failure of its associated DB or CI partner. More often, though, when HA is required for the CI, a product such as SAP's Enqueue Replication Server is brought in, discussed next.

SAP Enqueue Replication Server

SAP's Enqueue Replication Server prevents data loss by copying data to a redundant replication server. When the primary enqueue server fails, the secondary server takes over the role of the enqueue service, maintaining status information on SAP object locks. Key SAP Enqueue Replication Server benefits include:

▸ It is not computing platform or vendor dependent.

▸ It does not change the executables; thus, both HA and non-HA implementations are identical in this regard, simplifying support and change management.

▸ It's fast, both from a failover perspective and in regard to communications between the CI and other SAP elements.

SAP's Enqueue Replication Server takes advantage of a multithreaded architecture to allow parallel I/O to enqueue clients via TCP/IP-driven asynchronous replication. Transactional integrity is maintained because enqueue responses are delayed until the replication is finished. The failover process is as follows:

1. The failure is detected and the original enqueue server is stopped.

2. The virtual enqueue host is switched to the physical host acting as the replicated enqueue server (the "new" enqueue server).

3. The new enqueue server reads its replica copy from shared memory.

4. The enqueue process is actually started on the new enqueue server.

5. The replication server itself is stopped and restarted on any new host available, in an effort to again protect the new enqueue server from failure.

With many of the general SAP-layer SPOFs covered, let's turn our attention to SPOFs relevant to individual SAP components next.

Specific SAP Components' SPOFs

Each SAP component offers unique SPOFs that need to be evaluated and then either eliminated or mitigated in each production system. Remember, all SAP components are subject to the DB, CI, and enqueue (and in the case of UNIX-based systems, NFS) SPOFs already discussed. The following list identifies the SPOFs with which each component is faced, and offers suggestions for improving HA where possible:

▶ **SAP Advanced Planner and Optimizer (SAP APO)**—SAP APO is subject to several unique SPOFs, including the SAP Optimizer and SAP liveCache servers. With SAP APO 3.0A and beyond, APO Optimizers may be active/active clustered at an OS level. For each Optimizer, two RFC (remote function call) destinations are configured, one pointing to cluster node A and the other pointing to cluster node B. Therefore, both nodes can be used during production, and if one Optimizer fails, the transaction is simply rolled back and re-executed on the remaining node. In the same way, liveCache 7.4 and beyond supports more than simple active/passive clustering. Finally, HA can also be augmented through APO-specific monitoring tools such as HP's saplc.mon utility, which is used with MC/Serviceguard to monitor whether APO liveCache is up and available.

▶ **SAP NetWeaver Business Warehouse (BW)**—This component's data extractors represent SPOFs. Extractors are loaded on one or more servers that actually reside in other SAP system landscapes (such as SAP ERP or SAP CRM landscapes). The extractors pull transactional data from their respective systems, and then populate SAP NetWeaver BW with this data. Thus, it's necessary to ensure that the extractor server is not an SPOF by implementing at least two in each landscape.

▶ **SAP Customer Relationship Management (SAP CRM)**—SAP CRM suffers from several SPOFs. First, the Internet Pricing Configurator (IPC) and other special function servers or links to external systems and components are critical failure points. If any of these are not duplicated functionally (for example, through an active/passive cluster), they represent SPOFs. Also, the adapters used by CRM to collect data pose the same challenges as those noted for the SAP NetWeaver BW extractors.

▶ **SAP NetWeaver Master Data Management (SAP MDM)**—If you're implementing SAP NetWeaver MDM (which centralizes a company's master data and therefore naturally creates an SPOF), the MDM server and database must be clustered. Doing so protects the system's data as well as metadata, both of which are necessary for MDM operations. The Global Data Synchronization (GDS) console also must be protected; otherwise, it's impossible to maintain trade items.

▶ **SAP Supplier Relationship Management (SAP SRM)**—Specifically, any catalog server and all connectivity points and software integration products, such as JRun (or other Virtual Java Machines) represent SPOFs. An active/passive cluster is an easy way to resolve this problem. A more compelling approach involves using the staging catalog server or another catalog typically earmarked for testing new products/procurement processes or providing access to vendors to make routine product line changes. Thus, an active/active cluster can be maintained ("active" in the sense that each node is performing useful work, not in the sense that the nodes are both able to share the load between them and thus improve performance).

▶ **SAP NetWeaver Portal**—SAP's portal product suffers from several SPOFs, starting with typical access points "in front" of the portal (such as any hardware-based load-balancing gear front-ending it). Other SPOFs include the LDAP directory server, SAP NetWeaver Search and Classification (TREX), SAP's Portal Content Directory (including IIS files), and the portal catalog, SAP Unification server, and SAP lock server, all of which can be mitigated today by the use of active/passive clusters. Note that for active/active Microsoft Windows clusters, both MSCS and load balancing must be implemented. And, unfortunately, if you are using the Sun ONE (iPlanet) Directory Server, a fully protected active/active implementation is simply not possible. The use of other directory services might enable you to circumvent this shortcoming, however. Finally, if you are implementing Single Sign On (SSO), consider implementing two different mechanisms: SSO with SAP logon tickets and SSO using SAP user IDs and passwords.

▶ **SAP Knowledge Management (KM)**—SAP KM is subject to an important SPOF in the form of the SAP Content Server. Similar approaches discussed for protecting the SAP SRM Catalog Server can be employed here, or an active/passive cluster can be used.

▶ **SAP Process Integration (SAP PI)**—As the message bus or hub linking together SAP and non-SAP business systems, SAP PI (formerly Exchange Infrastructure, or XI) is critical enough to *always* warrant clustering; if you're implementing SAP PI, it must be clustered.

▶ **SAP Product Lifecycle Management (SAP PLM)**—SAP PLM suffers from an SPOF with regard to the Variant Configuration Server, as well as links to all other unprotected SAP components required for SAP PLM functionality.

Certainly, other SAP products and components exist. Do your homework and carefully study any SAP component to be deployed. With the material provided in this chapter underpinning the knowledge you will continue to gather on your own, you should feel pretty competent identifying SPOFs. Don't forget to enlist the aid of your SAP technology stack partners.

Functional and Application-Layer SPOFs

Some of the worst SPOFs we have seen are "self-created." In other words, SPOFs were created where none naturally or previously existed. The following list provides some examples, and hopefully some insight, into how to avoid these:

▶ All SAP user-specific work processes must be distributed, such that a single server does not run all of one type of work process and therefore become a SPOF. This includes Dialog, Background, Update, and Spool work processes. In other words, shy away from creating a single batch server, a dedicated spool server, or a lone update server, unless you clearly understand the ramifications and trade-offs.

▶ Logon load balancing should be configured such that no functional area is designated to a single server (unless, of course, this is determined to be acceptable). Why? Because if this server fails, the functional area is in effect unavailable. Workarounds abound, fortunately—the most common is to allow users to log in to a different logon group when their primary group is unavailable.

▶ Any software loaded on a single server automatically creates an SPOF should that server crash or otherwise become unavailable. Thus, for the highest levels of availability, SAP NetWeaver BW extractors, Vertex accessibility, fax server integration, and similar integration or connectivity points should be configured on more than one server.

Summary

This chapter addressed high availability, comparing it to and contrasting it with disaster recovery. To set the stage, we covered fundamentals such as identifying the cost of downtime and documenting HA drivers. We then explored a method of identifying single points of failure (SPOFs) by examining each layer in the SAP technology stack. As you read, each layer features quite a few opportunities for failure and equally as many solutions and approaches capable of helping maintain a highly available system. In the next two chapters, we build on the material here and take a closer look at DR along with people and process matters that affect HA.

Case Study: Assessing SAP High Availability

As the new CIO at HiTech's manufacturing business unit, you are concerned that the SAP ERP system in place today is not capable of delivering the 4 nines of availability your predecessor promised to the system's business users. In response, you have created an HA assessment team to quickly review and analyze your ERP system's architecture and HA technologies and solutions.

Questions

1. In terms of how you will direct the newly formed HA assessment team to proceed in its analysis, what approach might make the most sense?

2. Why should you include an HA assessment of the data center used to house your SAP system?

3. Are there systems outside of the core SAP ERP system that need to be assessed from a high-availability perspective?

4. Explain to your HA assessment team members the difference between fault tolerance and system reliability. Upon which should they focus their attention?

5. The HA assessment team concluded their analysis and determined that the system as configured could probably deliver only 2 nines of availability. How may more hours (not nines, but hours) of availability need to be achieved to provide a system capable of delivering 4 nines of availability?

NOTE

The answers to these questions can be found in Appendix A, "Case Study Answers."

CHAPTER 16

Disaster Recovery Considerations and Solutions

In the previous chapter we reviewed the concept of system availability and its focus on maintaining the availability of a system day to day. High availability (HA) solutions seek to avoid failures that completely disrupt access to the system, thus minimizing business interruptions. This is done by anticipating common failures or events and then implementing technology solutions, organization staffing models, and processes to either avoid the events in the first place or prevent them from causing unplanned downtime. We like to think that addressing availability is all about eliminating "local" failures as the root cause for otherwise unnecessary downtime.

But what can a company do about events that have not been anticipated or are simply too costly or otherwise overwhelming to address through HA solutions? What about true disasters such as hurricanes and earthquakes that can disrupt access to entire buildings and cities, much less a company's data center? And what about other events, such as widespread network outages, that make it impossible to access a system that's otherwise up and available? In this chapter, we will look at methods and solutions that are useful in mitigating the impact that disasters can have on SAP business applications.

Recovering from Minor DR Issues

Though it may seem counterintuitive, seemingly minor issues can be enough to drive failover of a system from its primary data center to a disaster recovery (DR) site. These kinds of issues vary and include those related to technology, process, and people-derived problems. As we've learned, a good IT organization will address these three areas from an HA perspective first and foremost. If HA measures fail to do the job, then minor issues such as the following (along with the resulting impact or potential impact) may force the applications to be recovered at the DR site:

▶ If the WAN links fail between the data center and the sites hosting end users, highly available redundant links and providers (and potentially Internet access) ensure that users can quickly if not seamlessly get back to work and that the impact to end users is negligible. However, if the redundant links don't work as expected, or a problem occurs that affects all redundant links into the data center (via a natural disaster or widespread power outage that affects resources not backed up by generators or battery, for example), then the applications need to be failed over to the DR site.

▶ If an SAP Basis specialist or DBA inadvertently logs into the "wrong" SAP system (for example, production instead of training, or development instead of the test system) and intentionally brings it down, the system in question may be quickly restarted and be back up again for users to log in to within 30 minutes. This can very easily occur (as all SAP components within the same family "look" the same from an SAP perspective) and yet is quite avoidable (use a color-coding system for the SAPGUI background, such as the default blue for all production systems, yellow for all development systems, and so forth.)

▶ If one of the SAP application servers that hosts the online end users or batch jobs fails, logon load balancing configured for both online users and SAP remote function call (RFC) connections and batch jobs will quickly address the problem. However, a greater load will be placed on the remaining application servers. If several application servers fail (due to a hardware or software failure consistent across the application servers), the remaining servers may not be able to host the workload, especially heavy batch loads with drop-dead completion times. Thus, the entire system would need to be failed over to the DR site.

▶ If an SAP web server or a batch application server that supports batch processing fails, the other server might need to be provisioned to take over the load. The background job needs to be restarted, however, which could impact the job's completion time several minutes to several hours (depending on the job).

▶ If key SAP bolt-on servers or network-provided web services such as those responsible for faxing or calculating sales tax fail or are otherwise unavailable, the system will still run with reduced functionality. If such servers or web services are down for an extended period of time, there could be a significant impact relative to revenue, getting trucks out of the loading docks, or missing material movements subject to enormous penalties. In these cases, the system would need to be failed over.

▶ If an SAP Basis specialist logs in to the wrong system at an OS level and incorrectly updates the SAP kernel or a configuration parameter, or makes a similar mistake, the servers will typically continue to run. Pristine copies of the now corrupted or deleted files may be retrieved from weekly backups and restored, assuming the weekly backup tape is indeed available and readable, and no changes have been made that week (in that case, any changes would need to be reapplied). The impact to end users would be minimal. However, if these servers are rebooted or (in some cases) if the SAP instances are restarted, and the previously corrupted or deleted files have not been restored, the servers will fail to start. This could be rectified easily unless the backup tapes are bad, in which case it might be preferable to fail over to the DR site while tapes are pulled from offsite and tested, data is restored, and updates are made as necessary to get the servers back to a current configuration.

▶ If overall system performance deteriorates enough, basic system availability becomes a factor. After all, a system that provides 10-second response times for online users, or takes 10 hours to process batch jobs that typically take a fraction of that time, is unacceptable. If the problem lies in data or code that has already been replicated to the DR site, there's no remediation available by failing over. However, if the problem is caught in time, or has something to do with the system's underlying computing platform, a DR site failover may be exactly what's needed while the SAP support team diagnoses and remedies the underlying problem.

Other types of minor issues are much less problematic. For example, if changes need to be made to SAP logon load balancing (to introduce another application server or to change an existing server group configuration), all SAP instances in question need to be restarted. This results in several minutes of unplanned downtime. Changes to logon load balancing can result in a system that remains unavailable for users that continue to use their normal load-balanced logon procedures. Contingency should be made for such an event by providing users with the public TCP/IP addresses of several servers they could log in to directly. In this way, unplanned downtime remains very low; the chances of such a misconfiguration issue requiring a failover to the DR site is miniscule. In the same way, if an individual user's batch job fails, it may be restarted or its code remediated (depending on the impact of recently applied support packages and other updates). Often, only a single user is impacted and the code is quickly corrected (or the need to update a profile parameter is identified). Such an issue rarely results in significant job-related downtime, although of course it's conceivable that a widely used job that is incapable of being executed could cause problems for the business. But such a situation wouldn't call for a DR failover. These types of issues are important to identify and weigh, but are generally not problematic for more than a brief period of time and/or for only one or several users. This is a very different situation from more serious issues, however, discussed next.

Recovering from More Severe DR Issues

Unlike the previous issues discussed, if the following issues arise, a firm faces considerably more risk in terms of recoverability and therefore greater exposure to longer unplanned downtime:

▶ If the SAP database server (housing the company's master and transactional data) or SAP central instance server (where the SAP binaries or "executables" reside) fails, cluster software such as HP Serviceguard or Microsoft Cluster Service (MSCS) will orchestrate a local failover in minutes; little unplanned downtime results, though all online users and batch jobs may be minimally affected. However, if both nodes of the cluster fail (they might succumb to the same firmware bug or OS security threat, for example), the application will need to be failed over and restarted, taking anywhere from several minutes to 20 to 30 minutes, depending on the failover mechanism, state of the database, and how long the database roll-backward/roll-forward process takes to complete.

▶ If a database table is inadvertently deleted (accidentally by the IT organization's junior DBA or by an SAP administrator working in the "wrong" system, for example), or a table is corrupted due to a hardware, firmware, or software issue, performing a point-in-time recovery to restore database consistency might cost the firm many hours of lost productivity (more significant downtime is possible, depending on when the last time the database was cloned, snapped and copied, or, worst case, backed up to tape). Such issues should be rare because the users with these rights are typically very few. But the impact of accidents and inadequate training can be dramatic.

▶ If a user or programmer (presumably with the authority to do so) deletes or incorrectly updates a key piece of transactional or master data, the data can be restored in any number of ways, explained previously. However, if the deletion or change is not noticed for some period of time, the data would have been replicated to the DR site and saved on tape. Depending on the tape retention time, the IT organization might be unable to restore the data, or restoring it from an offsite facility might require a lengthy process.

When key personnel take vacation, call in sick, attend training, or leave the firm's employment *and* a hardware or software failure occurs (either randomly or as a result of a mistake made by the key person's backup), the firm's enterprise resource planning (ERP) system could be down for hours if not days. Note that it's the combination of the two events—losing a person and losing the system—that makes for a disaster rather than "just" a minor outage. Key scenarios include

▶ Storage area network (SAN) or server multicomponent failures, or making changes to the SAN or server (for example, carving new LUNs, zoning SAN fabric switches, or updating OS kernels) without the benefit of good current state documentation. In the absence of a senior SAN or server resource, this could spell disaster in the form of lost data, lengthy restores, and impact beyond just a single application (assuming the SAN hosts data for multiple applications).

▶ Changes to the application's underlying cluster configuration without the benefit of good current state and process documentation, particularly when a failover is attempted and fails and the key "cluster" person is out of pocket. Clusters are complicated by the fact that technology, application, and other factors come into play during a failover. Cluster misconfigurations, poorly implemented changes, and a lack of sound troubleshooting practices often conspire to cause more cluster-related downtime than they avoid.

▶ Changes to, or troubleshooting of, the backup and recovery solution can result in major outages. If most of this knowledge is retained in the heads of a very few people rather than in well-maintained documentation, and those people are unavailable or make a mistake, it's quite easy to lose a day of end-user productivity. Backup and recovery solutions are complicated by several factors; many customers back up their databases to disks, which in turn are backed up to virtual or physical tape libraries. Backup software is installed to control when and how backups are performed, and tapes are normally picked up and safeguarded offsite for some period of time. All of these represent possible technology or process failures, and when combined with a people failure spell disaster.

As you can see, good current-state and process documentation goes a long way toward avoiding these kinds of people-initiated disasters. Documentation isn't cheap, though, and poorly maintained documentation can be much worse than none at all. Our advice is simple, if not obvious. Invest in both creating and maintaining documentation. A documentation maintenance process is a must!

Recovering from Major Disasters

If a major natural or manmade disaster occurs, a firm needs to fail over to its DR site. Such a decision is not to be made lightly, of course, but it's better to be decisive and play it safe than to take a wait-and-see attitude and find yourself without the ability to fail over. Companies that wait to fail over face the following challenges:

▶ DR sites that are widely shared with other companies might simply run out of resources—servers, disk space, network capacity, access to onsite personnel who might be needed to help facilitate failover, and so on.

▶ The ability to fail over may be affected, resulting in a greater loss of data than otherwise necessary (and thus requiring additional manual entries to get the system back to current state).

▶ Waiting to declare a disaster might result in the inability to bring up certain applications or run certain business processes because of incremental failures suffered during the "wait." Perhaps a key bolt-on system will be lost, or data needed from a third-party system will become corrupted or unavailable. Such scenarios require an application consultant's investigation to understand the real ramifications on system availability. But to be safe, declare a disaster as soon as it's clear that a disaster is real enough to warrant failover.

▶ The longer a disaster is not declared, the more likely key personnel may become involved in personal matters that take precedence in their eyes over the company's pending disaster scenario. Key personnel may go on vacation, lose their laptops, or in some other way become unavailable. Even if they're available at the primary site, if a disaster requires the system to be failed over to the DR site, access to that site may be constrained (consider the impact if airplanes are grounded, or other transportation out of or into the sites is unavailable, or power and phone lines are down), exacerbating recovery beyond what is promised and delivered by the DR facility, including to what extent tape backups located at the primary site might be needed at the DR site.

Of course, an organization might wait until the last minute to declare a disaster for good reason. It's a lot of work to redirect all business processing and end-user access to another site. Trade-offs made in terms of the DR system's performance, availability, scalability, and so on may give CIOs pause to pull the DR failover trigger. And more importantly, if there's no failback process for reestablishing the primary data center after the initial disaster that caused the failover in the first place has been resolved, or the process has not been well tested, a company could be facing significant work and a ton of unknowns.

It's actually more common than you might think for organizations to rarely (if ever) test their failback strategies. This was a surprise to us as we researched and drew on our own customer-specific experiences. Many of the firms to whom we provide consulting services actually have no formal failback plans at all! Thus, their recovery techniques tend to only serve the company "one way"—to provide a failover mechanism at best. This might indeed be acceptable for many firms, especially those with HA strategies in place that double as DR solutions. For many other firms, though, the lack of a failback plan represents an area that requires additional research and potentially some pretty significant investments, for several reasons:

▶ The DR site may only provide core business application services, and then only support a subset of the enterprise's overall business processes. More simply said, the company may not be able to survive for long at the DR site.

▶ The DR site may be purposely (for cost reasons) staffed and configured to provide less than acceptable levels of availability and performance in its own right, thus impacting the firm's ability to respond to new business needs should it find itself "failed over" for an extended period of time. Such a purposely designed DR strategy begs the question of whether the DR approach is realistic in the first place; if long-term disasters are not really addressed, how likely is it that the DR site will really be needed?

▶ The site might not be instrumented for systems manageability or even basic infrastructure monitoring, thus putting the firm's IT infrastructure and business applications at risk in terms of its inability to proactively predict and address growing performance problems, availability trends, and other issues. With an inability to manage and monitor the DR solution, systems management would be necessarily ad hoc and therefore time consuming, if done at all.

Why a firm intentionally ignores failback varies, but we found that the most prevalent reason is cost. Developing a failback plan takes time and money, and testing the process requires even more time and money. As an insurance policy, this is apparently acceptable. Our recommendation is to do the math—capture all these costs along with the costs of running in your unique DR site for an extended period of time, and the costs of suffering even more unplanned downtime in this environment. With all the numbers in front of you, you'll be positioned to make a more informed decision.

Data Center Strategies for Dealing with Disasters

Many architectural models exist for addressing disaster recoverability from a data center perspective, some of which are outlined here:

▶ **Dual data center strategy**—Such a strategy involves implementing production and nonproduction SAP systems across dual data centers; applications are protected and load balanced across the two data centers (connected via high-speed synchronous communications) such that if one data center fails, all production applications can "fail over" to the remaining data center and continue to run.

▶ **Geographically distributed data centers**—By distributing applications around the globe, presumably an event in one geographic area will have little impact on the others. The trick is to implement application and data tiers capable of being replicated across sites, along with tools that provide the level of synchronous replication necessary to meet the business's service-level agreements (SLAs).

▶ **Multilevel distributed data centers**—The idea is to provide three pairs of highly available data center resources, which may or may not be distributed throughout the world. Hewlett-Packard's own implementation of three pairs of data centers is a good example.

▶ **Hosting sites**—Third-party sites purposely configured and prestaged (or rapidly staged upon declaration of a disaster) for running data center operations in case of a disaster are quite common.

▶ **Pods**—Self-contained data center pods are becoming a popular way of addressing DR requirements, and could play a role in any of the previously mentioned approaches.

The growing use of dual data centers is explored next, followed by a closer look at more traditional strategies.

Dual Data Centers and Virtualization

Having dual data centers enables a firm to combine HA and DR requirements in an approach that's naturally appealing. With dual data centers, applications can be split between sites for availability reasons, failed over to one site to perform infrastructure maintenance at the other site, and more. Firms may also deploy production resources on one site and nonproduction resources (development, test, and so on) at the other site. In all these cases, there's a certain amount of flexibility that enables better system availability, maintenance strategies, resiliency, and more.

Rather than spending a lot of time designing dual data centers that physically address each and every application's DR needs, forward-looking companies today are rapidly adopting virtualization strategies. Tools such as VMware's VMotion, HP Integrity Virtual Machines (Integrity VMs), Microsoft's and Zen's hypervisor solutions, and so on augment a dual data center strategy and provide a number of benefits:

▶ **Flexibility**—Virtualization abstracts the hardware layer from the OS layer and serves to standardize all hardware and software drivers "underneath" the virtual machines. This gives a firm the flexibility to deploy whatever makes sense based on SLAs, budget constraints, IT staffing realities, and so on.

▶ **Hardware independence**—Virtualization enables different hardware platforms (running the same OS) to back up one another. This means that a company's primary data center can leverage high-end and highly available server platforms while the DR site hosts less expensive systems capable of supporting production but without all the bells and whistles. It also eliminates different network cards, disk controllers, systemboard firmware versions, and so on from needing to be maintained between sites. In the same way, OS releases and patch levels need not be identical either; as long as the DR site's servers can host the virtualized production images, the transition is seamless. In the end, hardware independence not only simplifies change management but significantly reduces recovery time.

▶ **Hardware refreshes and cascading**—Because the primary and DR sites need not host identical computing platforms, it becomes much easier for either side to transition to new platforms (hardware refresh). Similarly, this makes it easy for previously used DR resources to be cascaded or repurposed for other existing needs across the enterprise.

▶ **Active/active architecture**—Because the primary and DR sites don't need to be identical and rely on easily started and stopped virtual machines, the gear at the DR site can be used for any number of SAP-related purposes such as testing, training, and development. This makes both the primary and DR sites capable of performing useful work, much like a two-node cluster in which both nodes are active at the same time but back one another up in case the other fails. There's no need for the DR servers to be sitting idly by waiting for a production failure. When DR is needed, the DR VMs can be easily started as the "other" VMs are brought down.

Despite the benefits of virtualization strategies, many firms are still more comfortable with physical DR sites and assets like those described next.

Traditional DR Hosting Facilities and Other Approaches

Rather than rely on a firm's own IT resources or architectural strategies, companies often address disaster recoverability by employing external, third-party, or containerized hosting facilities. Such an approach has several advantages:

▶ Smaller IT organizations lacking secondary data center resources save on the tremendous costs of building and staffing a facility intended to be used very little; capital costs are replaced by easily budgeted expenses.

▶ In the same way, any organization that has neither the time nor the resources to repurpose and "harden" an existing data center site is well served by a DR hosting arrangement.

▶ A hosting center can be selected that's hundreds or thousands of miles away from the firm's primary data center, thus mitigating the risk of a single event affecting access to both the primary and DR sites (though we've seen widespread damage spanning 1000 miles and more—think about the devastating impact that Hurricane Ike had in 2008, from the Caribbean to Texas, Oklahoma, Illinois, and Ohio).

Third-party hosting facilities are quite common. SunGuard, HP/EDS, IBM, and scads of others are happy to rent space, just-in-time equipment, and even access to people. At one end of the spectrum, they'll provide you the space and gear you need and let your team get busy recovering the systems. At the other end of the spectrum, they will set up your servers and disk subsystems, install OSs, rebuild applications, help you resynchronize your data, and get the business up and running. It's just a matter of paying for what you need.

If you plan to do the recovery yourself and have the budget to invest in always-available resources, another method of providing external DR resources is through "containerized data centers" or pods. HP sells such pods in the form of a 40-foot shipping container stuffed with racks of processing power and disk space. These can be customized, of course, to provide just the right capabilities in the best price, power, and space package. Pods represent a great way to quickly drop computing power into remote locations. Sun, Rackable Systems, and several additional big names can also create pods, and others are getting into the market as well.

Disaster Recovery Best Practices

It's no secret that lots and lots of "best practices" exist for high availability and disaster recovery. We have just poured through many of these in detail. But we believe it makes sense to compile a list before we move into more DR-specific considerations:

▶ Actually failing over to a DR site must be a last resort. Therefore, at the lowest levels, or where it makes the most financial sense when everything else is equal, practice availability through redundancy (ATR).

▶ Where possible, cluster resources to maximize availability, or in some other manner provide redundancy of critical solution components. Simple active/passive clustering should be considered as a baseline HA approach, to which other approaches are compared in terms of the degree of availability provided, complexity, cost, and long-term supportability. Stretched clusters spanning the primary data center and DR site, or implemented as part of a dual data center strategy, are ideal DR solutions. And don't forget to create a similar cluster in your testing or sandbox environments, for failover testing and training.

▶ Always perform at least a cursory TCO analysis to determine the point at which downtime exceeds the cost of an HA or DR solution, based on the level of availability requested by the business. This requires knowledge of the number of "nines of availability" (discussed in Chapter 15, "High Availability Considerations and Solutions") that your business truly requires.

▶ Work methodically through the SAP technology stack, identifying single points of failure (SPOFs) at each layer. When you have identified them, refer to the cost of downtime to determine whether it makes financial sense to eliminate or simply mitigate the SPOF.

▶ Step back and look at the SAP solution holistically, to identify less-obvious technology-, process-, or people-related SPOFs that exist outside the SAP technology stack.

▶ Manage user access to data, security rights, profiles, the ability to launch batch jobs, the ability to tie up multiple dialog processes for long periods of time, and so on. In this way, overt denial of service is addressed as well as honest user-originated mistakes and other acts, all of which can easily impact availability.

▶ Keep in mind that DR sites often operate on a first come, first served basis. Thus, access to shared resources can be significantly impacted during large outages (such as

16

a widespread hurricane that causes hundreds of large companies in Florida, Texas, and Louisiana to activate their DR plans at the same time). This could quickly consume all shared resources, leaving several firms with no servers or storage systems to actually fail over to. The solution is expensive, if not obvious: Contractually address this, or provide your own standby resources.

▶ Ensure that the solution finally implemented is documented as is, noting all deviations from a standard installation or implementation. We are big fans of documentation because it serves so many roles—operational processes rely on repeatable processes, DR plans make it necessary to describe how to rebuild each DR-protected SAP solution, and training materials evolve from documentation as well, for example.

▶ Meticulously plan and test all changes to your SAP environment, being careful not to ignore your change control processes even in emergency situations. Improperly tested or executed changes made to a system tend to impact availability as much as anything else, in our experience.

▶ Ensure that all operational procedures are documented and understood—publish HA and DR policies and business continuity plans via a formal communications plan. Furthermore, create and maintain a Disaster Recovery Crash Kit that is accessible both from your DR site and publicly.

▶ Test your HA and DR plans on a regular basis, ensuring that the entire team not only understands and is trained in HA/DR processes but is capable of handling a disaster even when key human resources are missing. One of our favorite ways of testing a DR plan is by removing a senior SAP Basis administrator, backup and restore specialist, or DBA position and then evaluating how the team backfills and otherwise responds to meeting the needs normally addressed by that key position.

Probably the most critical best practice is to develop a DR plan that reflects business and IT realities. In our experience, developing a sound DR plan for SAP encompasses five primary steps:

1. Identify business processes that are truly business critical.

2. Identify the applications (SAP and otherwise), bolt-ons, and other integration points that must remain up and operational to enable the aforementioned business processes to execute.

3. Working with business process owners, develop realistic recovery point objectives (RPOs), which is essentially the amount of data the business is willing to lose. RPOs must be driven by business organizations rather than the IT organization.

4. Working with the IT organization and key business process stakeholders, develop reasonable recovery time objectives (RTOs), which is the maximum amount of time the SAP, non-SAP, and bolt-on systems can be down in the wake of a disaster or other unplanned downtime event.

5. Identify business practices and technology solutions that, together, can meet the organization's RPO and RTO targets in the most cost-effective manner (see Figure 16.1).

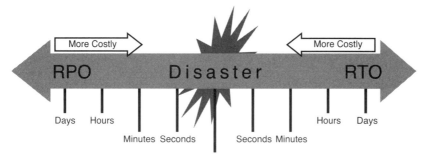

FIGURE 16.1   Both RPO and RTO reflect a time versus cost relationship.

In the end, human error and poor attention to managing change probably cause 60% of what we describe as "avoidable" downtime—that's the unplanned downtime that should never really happen in the first place, which is a lot different from the unavoidable downtime incurred so rarely from actual technology stack failures and honest-to-goodness disasters. In the next few pages, we detail some of these best practices and the challenges inherent to nailing them down.

SPOFs Beyond the SAP Technology Stack

In addition to technology-specific single points of failure, such as those you have already read about that occur at the hardware, OS, database, and SAP layers of the SAP technology stack, SPOFs regarding people and processes exist as well. Consider the following:

▶ All key personnel positions require backups and documented backup plans. This should include earmarking and training internal folks, as well as establishing contractual relationships (for example, executing "consulting on demand" agreements) with third-party resources. This and other "people" SPOFs are discussed in detail in Chapter 17, "Availability and Recoverability: Organizational Factors."

▶ A solution's client strategy could inadvertently create an SPOF, especially if multiple languages are involved. This needs to be addressed in the system landscape.

▶ All processes related to change management, deployment, management, and operations represent potential SPOFs. Two methods of performing each process should be clearly identified and documented in each case.

▶ Tools and approaches used to monitor a system or execute certain processes should also be duplicated. In the best case, manual processes should be documented and tested regularly, ready to be used when automated approaches fail.

▶ Access to documentation must be addressed, especially with regard to disasters. We like the idea of maintaining documentation on a company intranet site or public password-protected Internet site, along with maintaining a printed copy both at the primary data center and at the DR site.

Other SPOFs can, in a sense, be "created" as well. To combat this, our suggestion is to have your entire DR plan reviewed by a new pair of eyes every year. Doing so eliminates oversights caused by people who might be too familiar with the system and therefore prone to assume things are fine that would otherwise warrant further discussion or clarification.

The Disaster Recovery Crash Kit

The DR Crash Kit is your fundamental DR resource, containing everything needed to recover your SAP production environment in the event of a disaster. It is maintained at the DR site itself, and consists of the following:

▶ Software necessary to rebuild the production system, including all OS files, any hardware-specific drivers, the database and SAP installation kit, and all technology stack patches, support packages, service packs, current OS and SAP kernels in use, SAP profiles, and so on. Additionally, this includes any other software packages absolutely required by your production system, such as tax packages or other bolt-ons, that can be added to your SAP environment over its lifetime.

▶ Software necessary to access the production system, including any utilities; SAP licenses; the SAPGUI installation CD; other user interface packages (such as Internet Explorer or legacy UIs); the saplogon.ini, tpparam, and saprouttab files; software used to access the servers and other hardware components (such as Terminal Services, VT100 terminal-emulation software, and so on); the Internet Transaction Server installation kit and a copy of all up-to-date HTML load templates; and so forth.

▶ Administrative and management-related software necessary to ensure operational integrity when your production system is running at the DR site, including backup and restore and related utility programs, UPS control and management programs, hardware monitors and other systems monitors, and so on.

▶ Detailed current state information as to how the system needs to be laid out (such as file system details) or set up (such as hardware specifics related to cabling, physical disk layouts, PCI card slot locations, and so on). We recommend the use of a detailed hardware and software matrix, which is a tool we have used extensively in the past to document just this kind of detailed configuration data.

▶ Step-by-step documentation necessary to install the production system, all access methods, and all operations management utilities and applications. Additional documentation explaining how to restore the database and potentially other critical data (control files, and so on) to a specific point in time is necessary as well. We recommend maintaining both electronic and printed media of all documentation in the DR Crash Kit. And we highly recommend creating and maintaining a Master DR Installation Checklist, which breaks down all installation tasks that must be accomplished, and in what order, along with who is responsible for performing these tasks.

▶ Operational documentation, such as the regularly used daily and weekly checklists, information on how to use your specific enterprise management products, "run books," and so on.

► Administrative items, such as hardware and software service agreements (with contact phone numbers and email addresses for subject matter experts), any special instructions as to how to recall tapes from offsite data storage or acquire replacement gear, escalation procedures, a comprehensive company- and partnerwide phone list, and more.

► An inventory list, so that anyone can quickly tell whether a piece of software or a documented procedure can be found in the DR Crash Kit, or determine that something is missing.

We cannot stress enough how important good documentation becomes during an emergency or disaster. Your goal should be to remove as much as possible of the guesswork related to rapidly reinstalling or failing over a production system under adverse conditions before a disaster ever occurs. This means staying on top of changes as they are made to your production system over time, so that the DR Crash Kit truly reflects what is needed to restore the production system "as is" as it evolves. For example, when changes are made to the SAP technology stack, all installation, support, maintenance, and other operational procedures need to be updated immediately.

Of course, these updated procedures are worthless without the updated requisite software—ensure that the outdated items in the DR Crash Kit are updated immediately with these new versions. And finally, review the entire contents of your DR Crash Kit on a regular basis (such as every quarter). Use the Crash Kit's inventory list as a basis not only to check that every Crash Kit component is present, but to track changes to each component—a good inventory list will reflect the date that any particular item was last updated, by whom, and why.

All this invaluable software, procedures, and so on must not only be maintained at the DR site, but must also be easily available or accessible. As we mentioned before, placing documentation out on an intranet or secured Internet site makes a lot of sense. But we also recommend that the physical components of the DR Crash Kit—such as software CDs, driver disks, restore tapes, and so on—be preserved at a second site, too. This second site might simply be another company site, or even a commercial offsite data storage facility. Or you might make it a policy to keep everything online and dump all data to a file share or website. The point is this: During the middle of a disaster, you want to be able to fall back to another set of media if your primary media fails. We all know that tapes go bad, CDs get scratched, and things sometimes get lost. Protect yourself in this regard, and the extra day or two of effort beforehand may pay big dividends later on.

With regard to the contact information that must be maintained in the DR Crash Kit, we find that keeping information for the following contacts is most useful:

► All members of the SAP TSO, SAP DRO (Disaster Recovery Organization), and especially the SAP recovery team

► Facilities personnel, such as the people responsible for power, network infrastructure, data center and DR site access, and so on

► Any IT infrastructure folks not already covered, such as IT security

▸ Key users from each core functional area or SAP component, to verify after a failover that the DR site is functioning as expected

▸ Key consulting resources, such as those from SAP, your hardware vendor, disk subsystem vendor, OS vendor, systems integrators, and so on

▸ SAP Hotline

▸ Offsite data storage and tape storage personnel

▸ Physical security, should physical access to the UPS room or into the data center (or the building housing the data center or DR site itself) present a challenge

▸ Anyone with whom you have service agreements or contracts, who is tasked with providing or potentially providing support during an emergency

Additionally, access to the Internet (for miscellaneous online SAP technology stack vendor support, or to facilitate Internet-based troubleshooting or access to email) is highly recommended, and often required anyway.

Testing the Disaster Recovery Process

Because recovering from a disaster is so complex and involves many dependencies on technology, people, and processes, your SAP DR process must be integrated with your company's general disaster planning *and then thoroughly and regularly tested*. This process includes identifying how to obtain telephone, network, product deliveries, mail, and other basic services in the event of a disaster, how to ensure your IT staff can access the resources it is responsible for supporting, how to enable end-user access to the specific systems needed to maintain at least minimal business operations, and so on.

Our experience tells us that the DR process is not only inadequately tested, but also increasingly misaligned with the business's needs. Business continuity in the wake of an outage hangs in the balance as IT organizations fail to keep up with changing business requirements, inadequately tracked technology platforms, and changing IT operational processes. Every time a change is made in the data center, or a key how-to recovery process is changed (such as how to recover from tape backups, how to access those tapes from offsite storage, or even how to execute the failover process itself), the DR process is put at risk. Combine these manageable factors with unavoidable events—such as hurricanes, earthquakes, widespread ice storms, power outages of geographic consequence, and so on—and clearly there's much to consider relative to planning for the inevitable disasters looming just over the horizon. To make matters worse, economic, technology, and other factors have conspired to create a world in which instant access is the norm, and even short business disruptions can cause customers to look elsewhere.

With all the technology, people, and process complexities surrounding recovery from a disaster, all of this must occasionally be tested together as well. Why? Because unless you actually test your recovery process, you will never be assured that your particular SAP system can truly be recovered. Make no mistake, IT DR plans are the foundation for business contingency plans. Organizations that scrimp on DR testing to save a few dollars are putting the entire company at risk. DR testing is but another form of an insurance policy. If you do the math (and each organization should, to capture the company-specific, environment-specific factors unique to itself and its industry), DR testing is an inexpensive insurance policy.

A good DR test, then, involves recovering from a simulated disaster to verify not only that you can recover the system, but that you can also use it productively. And a really comprehensive test includes testing people and process SPOFs, not just the failover process to a DR site. That is, a true DR plan forces an organization to actually use every component of its DR Crash Kit and perform every task outlined in the DR plan to determine whether

▶ The DR Crash Kit is appropriately stocked, and a process is in place to keep it up to date (despite the fact that such a process is inherently time consuming and therefore relatively expensive).

▶ The DR procedures actually work.

▶ Any documented steps need further clarification, in the event that a "nonexpert" is called in to perform that particular process or procedure.

▶ Any technology or configuration changes exist that have not been documented. Changes include current-state as well as DR site-specific technology stack details.

▶ All infrastructure services are available and work as expected, such as FTP, DNS, SMTP, LDAP, Microsoft Active Directory, and other (required) necessary network and directory services.

▶ The hardware housed at the DR site, and the supporting network and other connectivity infrastructure, provides acceptable performance; organizations need SLAs not only for their primary data center infrastructure and applications, but also for those applications that are recovered at a DR site.

Actually working through the DR process provides valuable timeline information to everyone, so that, for example, the SAP DRO (and the end-user community) understands how long the recovery process actually takes.

Just how often should a comprehensive DR test be conducted, though? Most experts agree that an annual test is appropriate. Again, though, a rushed-through, ill-planned DR test will do little to assure a company that it can survive a disaster.

Not only is a good DR test comprehensive, it is also unique—no two tests should be identical. DR testing must include members of the actual SAP TSO and other personnel who will be responsible for failing over the SAP environment to the DR site in a real disaster. Don't forget to invite "backups" to recovery tests, too. After all, it's not the abilities of your superstar experts you should be questioning, but rather the abilities of their backups to work through a failover. This will illuminate shortcomings in your training, documentation, and more—exactly the kind of information you need well before a real disaster tests your preparedness. To take this concept of putting people to the test, we're also big fans of seeing how an organization reacts when other key staff members are "killed off" or otherwise made unavailable during the DR test, representing one of the worst implications

16

of a real-world disaster. In this way, the test proves the ability of the rest of the team to pick up the slack and perform a successful recovery.

The DR test also needs to include any third parties that are critical to the recovery. Anyone with whom an SLA or other contractual obligation is in place must be present to prove that they can truly provide the DR services needed in the event of a real disaster. If this level of service is not included in your DR contract and other arrangement, it should be.

Finally, the DR test must cover how an organization communicates status updates to all of its stakeholders—end users, customers, senior management, the SAP TSO, and so on. How will these key stakeholders be kept in the loop? What kind of additional communication responsibilities need to be doled out, and to whom? Answering questions such as these before a disaster makes it easier to focus on recovering from a disaster during the real thing.

Tactical Methods of Increasing Disaster Recoverability

In our experience, even the best-prepared and DR-aware SAP IT organizations have gaps in their technologies and processes. Addressing seemingly small cracks in an organization's recovery armor can add up to precious minutes and hours—time no longer lost in the name of unplanned downtime—and make recovery speedier, too. By way of example, we helped one of our favorite SAP IT organizations recently uncover availability and recoverability gaps that, once filled, will increase its expected level of system availability from an estimated 99.855% to a very respectable 99.959% level of availability. Said another way, this client will move from less than three nines of availability to more than three and a half—through generally very modest changes. Recommended improvements to achieve this level of availability include

> ▶ Create current-state documentation. It is important to note that this documentation must be updated as changes are made to the system. Thus, a documentation maintenance process must be established.

> ▶ Create process documentation, or the how-to documentation necessary to execute processes that affect availability and reliability. This also requires a documentation maintenance process.

> ▶ House all documentation on a publicly accessible secured website so that in the case of a disaster, the documentation will still likely be available.

> ▶ Address gaps in the backup and recovery process, including tape recovery testing (verify tape integrity on a regular basis), publish an offsite storage retrieval and recovery process that includes how to actually restore the production database, and implement a second tape library for redundancy and improved recoverability.

> ▶ Address minor SAP Basis and database technology gaps; automate performance alerts, add redundant work processes to each server, monitor and remediate monthly database growth, and track performance metrics against a baseline.

▶ Address a mixed back-end storage environment and standardize on a single platform and fewer components.

▶ Validate the HA/DR cluster configuration; examine the current cluster and package configuration, startup scripts, monitoring tool setup, alert system, and output, and regularly test the failover process.

▶ Update the promote-to-production process to include a mini load-testing component using software already owned by IT.

The changes described here reflect tactical and therefore limited or minor technology and process updates necessary to create a technology foundation that is available and reliable. As we've mentioned before, process (and people) factors tend to introduce more risk and therefore hold the greatest power of either increasing or reducing a firm's estimated level of availability and recoverability. The technology platform, on the other hand, represents less risk or less of a variable; once an innately available technology platform is deployed, process and people issues tend to drag down the system's availability until they're addressed.

Strategic Methods of Increasing Disaster Recoverability

If a firm addresses not only the tactical gaps outlined previously but also the following people-related availability and recoverability gaps, recoverability in the wake of a disaster can be markedly improved. People issues often constitute a much greater investment and exhaustive level of change than those involving technology (as can process-related issues); because of this broad effect on HA and DR, people matters are usually more strategic in nature. That is, they carry more weight than their tactical counterparts. Process-related matters can fall into this realm as well. Common remediation efforts of a strategic nature include

▶ For lean SAP IT organizations, intentionally augment key IT positions with backup resources who hold the requisite skills and experience related to their particular areas of responsibility; there's no room to train-as-you-go nor is there time to address critical SPOFs in a lean IT organization.

▶ Vigorously pursue cross training both *among* and *between* teams; cross training is difficult and costs time and money but is absolutely necessary for recoverability. Cross training is the most effective way of freeing senior-level people from an oversized workload; it enables a company to normalize its workload.

▶ To avoid inundating already overworked "favorites" with more work, change escalation processes in terms of *who* is assigned to troubleshoot or resolve new issues. Again, the idea is to spread the workload equitably.

▶ If SAP IT team members are incapable or otherwise unable to climb new or steep learning curves regardless of training, make changes to staffing models or areas of responsibility. Skill-set gaps can't be afforded, particularly those that are people related. Sometimes a firm's other admirable promote-from-within policy places people in a role in which they are incapable of mastering the skills necessary to be successful. In this case, the whole team is placed in an unnecessary and potentially very risky quandary.

▶ Rationalize the firm's systems management approach; standardize on fewer but more capable SAP-aware tools, and roll up alerts from other tools to create not only a simpler framework but one capable of addressing a single-pane-of-glass vision. This will help the firm reclaim employee bandwidth, thus making it possible to manage more systems without increasing headcount.

▶ Ensure the firm has segregated its production SAP resources from its nonproduction resources; for example, servers, network infrastructure, and SAN or other disk subsystem infrastructure must be separated between production and nonproduction assets. Creating a single pool of these kinds of assets eliminates the firm's capability to test new services or changes in a truly nonproduction environment, thus creating a situation in which testing winds up being done by real end users in production.

▶ Based on a company-specific study that identifies costs along with capabilities and benefits, implement a virtualization strategy consistent with maintenance, availability, and long-term disaster-recoverability strategies.

Once both tactical and strategic low-hanging fruit have been addressed, a point of diminishing returns is achieved. That is, well-addressed technology, people, and process considerations will ultimately converge in such a way that to improve a firm's estimated level of availability and recoverability, significantly more money will need to be invested. In our experience, this might equate to a five- to tenfold cost to move from four nines of availability to five nines.

Sample Failure Scenarios: Evaluating Your Firm's Recoverability

Smart firms will take the time to identify and assess potential failure scenarios. We like to categorize these scenarios based on technology, people, and process factors, and then drill down into the following:

▶ **Probability**—The probability that the scenario will occur (categorized by low, possible, medium, or high).

▶ **Mitigation strategy**—The steps that the firm has taken to avoid experiencing the failure scenario.

▶ **Business impact**—None, minimal, medium, high, or severe; business impact may also be quantified in terms of the number of minutes or hours of downtime associated with each scenario.

▶ **Recoverability**—The number of recovery minutes or hours associated with each scenario and the ease with which the firm should be able to recover from an outage associated with the failure scenario.

▶ **Tested**—Whether recoverability has been actually production-tested on the production system, simulated on another system, incompletely tested, or untested, or whether recoverability testing has resulted in a status of unknown.

▶ **Peer rating**—How the firm rates compared against its peer group, which should align with others who have deployed a similar technology stack of similar application breadth and depth; evaluation criteria might include below one's peer group, average, or at a level above the peer group.

Sample failure scenarios could include

▶ Loss of basic computing platform facilities, including power, cooling, cable trays, rack infrastructure, and so on

▶ Backup and recovery failure, including loss of the entire tape library, local tape access, or offsite tape access

▶ Failure of the database backup software that houses all backup jobs and job history

▶ A key user's desktop fails, or the SAP Logon Pad or SAPGUI is corrupt

▶ A key user's SAP printing capability fails or is compromised

▶ The LAN suffers a hardware component failure

▶ The WAN connecting the data center and end-user site(s) suffers a link failure

▶ An individual disk drive fails within the SAN (should include data, logs, or executables)

▶ A SAN switch or cable fails

▶ The production database suffers data corruption or deletion (database table)

▶ The database server suffers a hardware failure

▶ The database server suffers an OS failure (other failures in the SAP technology stack should be identified as well)

▶ One or more production application servers suffer from a hardware failure

▶ The entire primary data center is unavailable

▶ The firm suffers a simultaneous loss of both its primary data center and its DR site

▶ A SAN, server, HA, network, or SAP subject matter expert (SME) is unavailable during a disaster or critical failure

▶ An SME logs into the wrong system and brings it down

▶ An SME applies an unintended or untested change to production

▶ After failure to the DR site, user capacity and performance is only half of the actual production system

▶ After failure to the DR site, the firm must continue to do business without access to any number of noncritical bolt-ons (each constitutes its own scenario)

16

▶ After failure to the DR site, the IT organization has little ability to monitor the system while failed over

▶ The IT organization has no tested method of failing back to the primary data center

▶ After failure to the DR site, transportation is affected, with limited access to experts

▶ After failure to the DR site, transportation is affected, with limited access to the offsite tapes necessary to restore the system (should site-to-site replication result in corruption, for example)

▶ Process failure such that technical change management affects stability or performance

▶ Process failure such that the promote-to-production process is compressed

Obviously, more scenarios can be developed. Spend the time to really outline the various issues that could affect you most, and then take the steps to identify how you've mitigated the risk of these failures and what the business impact looks like.

Avoiding High Availability Pitfalls in the Real World

To help you see the importance of high availability and disaster recovery, the following are some real-world scenarios in which SAP enterprise customers failed to give disaster recoverability the attention we have given it in this chapter:

▶ **End-to-end critical points of potential failure**—This UNIX/Oracle customer spent much time working on database and SAP application layer–specific SPOF but missed basic infrastructure SPOFs. A bad network switch and a less than optimally configured NIC (set to autosense rather than hard-coded for 100Mb Ethernet) caused intermittent failures for literally months. Had the customer practiced availability through redundancy and followed NIC configuration best practices, it could easily have eliminated most of its resulting downtime. Had it failed the system over to its DR site and conducted end-to-end load testing on the primary system, it might have quickly found the problem as well.

▶ **Compressing the promote-to-production process**—In an effort to "get a change in fast," this customer did what many of us have done before and compressed the promote-to-production process. Instead of keeping a change in its technical sandbox for a few weeks, and then promoting it to development, test, training, and finally production (which normally would consume another six weeks), the customer pushed the change through in less than a week. We were happy to hear that the customer at least went through the process, instead of ignoring it altogether. In the end, though, a memory leak issue that only manifested itself over a period of time (certainly greater than a week) caused the customer substantial and recurring unplanned downtime.

▶ **Poor documentation**—We provided a customer several viable methods for maintaining its SAP DR processes and procedures. We covered the pros and cons of using websites, file shares, SAP Enterprise Portal, Oracle Portal, Microsoft SharePoint PortalServer, and even a simple Excel Workbook approach to publicly house its documentation. In the end, the customer never actually made a decision one way or the other. And when it suffered an unplanned outage one summer, not only did it have little consistent formal documentation to help it, but the fact that the documentation was spread out all over the place without the benefit of centralization and version control only exacerbated an already tense issue. The customer was fortunate, though; at least it could get to what it had. Imagine what would have happened if access to its various file shares and individual desktops had been compromised.

▶ **Change management shortcomings**—There are so many "keys" to sound change management that we can only recommend reading the change management chapters (Chapter 27, "Functional Configuration Change Control," and Chapter 34, "Technical Change Control") in their entirety. But the real gotchas probably boil down to ignoring change management, poorly documenting and therefore poorly implementing change processes, ignoring the change control process, and overly compressing the promote-to-production process. With regard to this first point, we received a call from a frantic outsourcing partner at 6:30 a.m. one morning. It was in the middle of doing an upgrade but never actually tested the firmware updates associated with updating its disk subsystem to new technology. Four hours later, the partner was back in business, but it far exceeded its SLA for unplanned quarterly downtime that day.

▶ **Employee limitations**—Here's an example of a problem that could easily have been avoided. One of our small SAP-on-Windows/Oracle customers hired a new SAP operator and junior Basis specialist. Familiar with Oracle and SAP, he apparently had no real understanding of hardware, including basic RAID 5 limitations. One day he noticed a disk drive glowing amber instead of the usual green, and he soon determined that he lost a drive on his database. Rather than replacing it, he sat around for weeks looking at the failed drive, comfortable in his ignorant assumption that he could lose plenty more drives before he really needed to worry. He had no idea that the particular RAID group to which the drive belonged was set up for single sparing, and that the single spare had already kicked in as expected and was doing its job of covering for the failed drive. Meanwhile, a couple of hot-pluggable replacement drives were sitting in a data center cabinet a few feet away. Our junior friend learned about his system's limitations the hard way—as bad luck would have it, he lost another drive in the same RAID group (followed by his job later that year).

▶ **Eliminating documentation support**—Another customer laid off two operators, and no specific person was ever held accountable again for maintaining SAP operations and monitoring tasks, including related "how-to" process documentation. As it turned out, no one actually monitored SAP on third shift for months, and a problem eventually cropped up. But with no knowledge of how to identify the issue, much less how to troubleshoot and resolve it, half of the SAP TSO was awakened that night. Imagine what would have happened if the system had needed to be failed over to its DR site; with a lack of knowledge and lack of documentation processes, the failover and system restart could easily have proved catastrophic.

▶ **No training**—In a similar case, a company's HA failover mechanism for SAP ERP worked nicely, but the people who were formally responsible for failing the system back to the original site were reorganized. Many individuals in this reorganized team were new to the team and had been neither trained nor apprised of where to obtain the system documentation. Think about it—no one still on the team had ever actually gone through the procedure for moving the production system back to the original site and pointing end users to it again. The company got lucky and was able to contact one of its former colleagues who had moved into a new role in the company but still remembered the process (and had the documentation, too). Fortunately, their lesson learned paid off before a real disaster occurred.

▶ **No stress testing performed**—This customer opted to incur the risk associated with foregoing stress testing, which had included a provision for testing basic failover capabilities while a load was on the system (at a total cost of $45,000–$60,000). After the customer went live, it found the usual programming issues early on, and discovered some other easily resolved performance problems related to the number of background processes deployed. More importantly, though, SPOFs existed in that the customer deployed only a single server to run all background work processes. The SAP EarlyWatch Service had caught this, and the customer had fixed it weeks before go-live. But an enterprising junior Basis administrator took it upon himself to change it back without understanding the consequences. A stress test would have caught this sooner, both from a performance perspective and in the end-to-end system review that we perform as a prerequisite to testing. And everyone would have understood the consequences.

▶ **People-related SPOF**—Only one person, the DBA, in the entire technical organization at this company knew how to set up and configure the disk subsystem for SAP. When he left the company, though, this fact was not fully understood until the system suffered a failure and many people tried unsuccessfully to access the password-protected system. When that failed to work, the company blew away the system and actually reconfigured the disk subsystem, incorrectly. Lots of people were called that weekend, and it was decided that declaring a disaster would be too expensive and cumbersome versus simply working through the issues one at a time. Bottom line: Availability through redundancy does not apply only to hardware- or process-related SPOFs. It also applies to people.

▶ **Poor communication**—The SAP IT staff went to a lot of trouble to script a really nice failover/failback routine for its production SAP cluster, and it even set up an alternative access method for getting into SAP R/3. But it failed to share how to access the system with the system's end users. This lack of communication rose to the surface as the team ran into a variety of issues during its quarterly mini-DR test, including issues with using the SAP WebGUI versus the classic fat-client SAPGUI. In failover, it could no longer connect to its front-ending SAP system and had to fall back to directly logging in to R/3 using the fat-client SAPGUI.

▶ **Making promises your system can't keep**—A very large customer of ours decided after it had already sized for and purchased its SAP storage solution that it needed an

SAP DR system installed 500 miles away from the primary site. And it needed to meet some really aggressive failover times. Of course, by this time in the project the customer was already live—on a cost-effective SAP-on-Windows solution with which the local IT team was comfortable. The DR solution it actually needed, however, was only supported at that time in a UNIX/Oracle environment and further required a specific model of disk subsystem running a specific version of disk controller firmware. Rather than scrapping the current infrastructure, the IT organization was forced to renegotiate its customer SLAs, able to promise less availability than initially requested. The IT team was lucky that the business was so flexible.

Practically all the downtime illustrated in the preceding scenarios was actually avoidable. Our real-world examples have another thing in common, too—each of these customers would benefit from a regular HA review and more consistent and vigorous DR and business continuity testing.

Summary

After a brief introduction to disasters and the concept of disaster recoverability, we investigated the breadth of disasters spanning minor, more severe, and major disasters. Then we outlined methods of dealing with disasters from a data center strategy perspective, including the role that virtualization might play alongside traditional methods such as hosting. We then covered general availability and DR best practices, SPOFs beyond the SAP technology stack, the role and importance of the DR Crash Kit, and the need for testing the DR process. A look at common tactical and strategic methods of increasing disaster recoverability, followed by real-world recoverability and availability pitfalls, concluded the chapter.

Case Study: Addressing DR Gaps

You've been contracted by HiTech, Inc. to complete a DR assessment for the company's SAP ERP business application. You quickly conclude that HiTech is suffering from significant gaps in its backup and recovery process, outdated DR Crash Kit documentation, clustering shortcomings that could affect failover to the DR site, and basic promote-to-production issues related to compressed change management timeframes.

Questions

1. How might a history of bad tapes and a lack of process documentation, both of which affect HiTech's backup and recovery process, be addressed?

2. What change must be made relative to keeping the DR Crash Kit's documentation up to date?

3. Given that clustering is typically seen as an HA solution, how might the cluster be configured such that it applies to DR?

4. How does HiTech's decision to compress the promote-to-production process from three months to two weeks create a problem?

NOTE

The answers to these questions can be found in Appendix A, "Case Study Answers."

CHAPTER 17

Availability and Recoverability: Organizational Factors

Well beyond technology considerations, it is actually people and organizational considerations that most affect an SAP system's availability. That is, to achieve the greatest level of availability and reliability, a firm needs to have not only the right technology in place but also the right balance of well-trained, knowledgeable, and capable people spread across a well-structured organization. The idea is to create and deploy an SAP organization in which single points of failure (SPOFs) have been identified and mitigated or where well-thought-out SPOFs have been deemed as reflecting acceptable risk.

By way of example, although a system might be architected for three or four nines of availability, the actual downtime observed will nearly always be less. This is due primarily to people factors (and to some extent, process factors that can be tied inextricably to people). People cause problems unlike anything technology is capable of causing. People accidentally drop databases, ignore warnings, forget to validate processes, and make mistakes under stress. Technology, on the other hand, can generally be protected through redundancy and similar mechanisms, as discussed in Chapters 15, "High Availability Considerations and Solutions," and 16, "Disaster Recovery Considerations and Solutions." An organization might deploy a well-architected computing platform boasting automated server clustering in a best-in-class data center. But less-than-complete or otherwise inadequate people issues such as those associated with systems management, documentation and knowledge management, change management, workload balancing, or inadequate subject matter expert (SME) "backup" coverage will reduce the system's as-delivered availability. Systems may also reflect intentional decisions on behalf of IT (or as the result of reduced budgets or headcount) that decrease availability. These decisions or system characteristics might not be inherently negative. Instead, like other system characteristics, they might reflect well-thought-out decisions or risk trade-offs made by an organization over the years—decisions that innately affect availability or system recoverability. In this chapter, we explore how organizational decisions and the people working for those organizations affect SAP system high availability and disaster recoverability.

Organizational Decisions Affecting Availability

With regard to the impact of organizational decisions on availability, the important thing to understand is that while the technology foundation will serve to create an available and reliable system, *organizational (people) matters will increase the risk of unplanned downtime* and ultimately reduce a system's real-world level of availability. We have seen this impact time and again. In our experience, systems that are architected for four nines of availability often might achieve only three-and-a-half nines and sometimes even less. The difference—in this case a loss of more than four hours of planned availability every year—is due to SPOFs related to organizational and people decisions. Consider the following:

▶ A very lean SAP Technical Support Organization (TSO) makes access to particular SMEs absolutely critical in a recovery scenario. It also makes access to the team's shared knowledge that much more critical.

▶ An overly cost-conscious SAP TSO might purposely avoid the cost of training and attending technical conferences in the same way that an individual might opt for less insurance on a car—the cost benefits of low coverage is deemed worth the risk.

▶ In the same way, many organizations might intentionally forgo protecting the SAP database as an SPOF (for example, by not deploying disk-based cloning, DB replication or log shipping software, Oracle Real Application Clusters)—solutions viewed as expensive and unnecessary insurance policies.

▶ An organization also might choose to leave its SAP central instance (CI) unprotected despite the availability of failover technologies such as SAP's Replicated Enqueue. Such a risk normally doesn't have huge exposure in the big picture (in many cases, the SAP CI can be restarted and back in business in minutes), but it's a risk nonetheless.

These are organizational decisions that put people in the position of potentially causing even more downtime than technology failures alone can cause. Think about it—if a database server needs to be restarted, data becomes corrupted, people wearing too many hats hastily do something in error, or the SAP CI fails to start again after a failure, people need to jump in to fix things. At this time, the availability clock continues ticking away but is now subject to ticking even longer in the wake of follow-on mistakes. The following list details several of these mistakes:

▶ A company's decision to forgo database archiving can exacerbate recovery, because database size directly affects recoverability and therefore availability. A 4TB database takes at least twice as long to back up and recover as a 2TB database. In these cases, it's important to take into account the amount of time a database recovery will require. Substantial investments in tape backup and recovery software and hardware, virtual tape investments, and similar solutions might be warranted to get around this people-created situation. And a single mistake in the wake of a previous issue has that much more of an impact when we're talking about recovering 4TB rather than something much smaller.

▶ In the same way, a database growing at 50GB a month demands greater attention to potential people-related issues than databases growing less rapidly demand. In our experience, many typical SAP ERP databases grow between 5MB and 50MB per concurrent user per month (a rule of thumb which also factors in the impact of most batch workloads, incidentally). If a system is growing significantly faster than this rule of thumb, a closer look at the business rules might be in order. Greater-than-average database growth invites longer recovery times and thus subjects an organization to longer downtime in the event of an issue.

▶ An organization may deem that deploying a holistic SAP-aware systems management suite (such as HP Business Availability Center [BAC], BMC PATROL, or CA Unicenter) is simply too expensive. The organization might not understand the value innate to creating a management-by-exception systems management portal capable of providing end-to-end visibility of its SAP systems, or might act in a shortsighted manner and choose to bring in people to do this work manually. In our experience, not only are people more expensive in the long run, but the mundane, tedious work of systems management is rarely done well or managed proactively by people. What starts out as a process-related issue quickly becomes people-related downtime.

▶ An organization's choice of high availability (HA) and disaster recovery (DR) technologies and solutions directly affects availability from a people perspective. Because database storage replication, for example, transmits changed data blocks nearly immediately between two sites, a man-made error initiated at the primary database site is quickly replicated to the secondary. Thus, the lag time to back out of an error condition simply is not available (as it would for HA/DR solutions based on database log shipping configured with a four-hour delay, for example). A corrupted database table is therefore quickly replicated to a clustered server node or stretch cluster/DR site, making it necessary to fall back to a physical tape (or equivalent) to restore the corrupted database table.

▶ When a system's current-state or process/how-to documentation is lacking, a small system glitch can quickly become a major outage, especially in the hands of a novice team member. The same is true of documentation that is not regularly maintained—ill-maintained documentation is often worse than no documentation at all, as outlined in Chapter 16.

▶ When documentation is not accessible, it matters little if the documentation is current or robust; a publicly accessible knowledge repository makes sense for any organization's SAP documentation, software images, patches, and so on. Organizational standards or ignorance may counter this, however, creating an otherwise easily avoidable potential issue.

17

▶ When an organization fails to deploy a nonproduction network, SAN/disk subsystem, or similar set of resources, there's no opportunity to test changes in a nonproduction environment. This puts added pressure on people to introduce fewer changes (to minimize the risk inherent to introducing an untested change). Eventually, though, such changes need to be implemented, thus increasing the risk of unplanned downtime (and the risk of poor performance). What appears to be a budget issue is actually just another poor decision made by people, subsequently putting other people in a place to cause greater downtime.

▶ The decision to deploy a single global SAP instance (rather than several geographically dispersed instances) is yet another decision made by people that can dramatically affect downtime. A global instance implies that there is less time available for planned downtime and therefore less time to conduct regular system maintenance. Shrinking windows of planned downtime not only affect recoverability but wreak havoc on architectural and process decisions—all of which affect how many nines of availability a system can truly deliver.

To be sure, all of the aforementioned decisions reflect technology and process matters. However, they are the result of trade-offs—*decisions*—made by people. Furthermore, the outcomes of these decisions continue to put people in the hot seat insofar as availability is concerned. Organizational design considerations hold similar risks, described next.

Organizational Design and Backup Considerations

Attention to several different organizational factors or methods can increase organizational availability and therefore the availability of the systems they support. Beyond basic people decisions is the matter of how the SAP support teams are structured. To maximize availability and ensure business continuity, organizational dimensions should reflect the following:

▶ **Purpose-built to be as flat as practical**—This enables faster decision making because a broad span of control enables organizations to react quickly to issues. Furthermore, flat organizations naturally minimize management positions and similar overhead positions and therefore costs.

▶ **Intentionally lean**—Create organizations that are intentionally lean (by way of well-planned overlap of roles and responsibilities); avoid creating organizations that grow bloated over time or shrink to anorexic levels in response to poor organizational decisions.

▶ **Few cubbyholes rather than more**—Favor broader team charters over those characterized by narrow disciplines.

▶ **"Intrateam backup"**—Create teams in which multiple skills exist across many different team members; if done properly, this also aligns well with creating a lean team.

▶ **Cross-team backup**—The term we like to use for this is *clustering*. Just as you should have backup within each team, it's advantageous to create a staffing model in which a certain amount of overlapping technical capabilities exist (take care to draw clear boundaries of responsibility, though). We've seen clustering work well when it comes to teams responsible for the database and teams responsible for the SAN—a certain amount of overlap helps during inevitable troubleshooting and creates an environment in which one team can help back up the other during an emergency. Teams with similar synergies include server support and SAN support; server support and network support; and the Basis team and SAP bolt-on team.

▶ **Shared services**—There's no reason to create a staffing model for core infrastructure services when the organization already has such a team—don't reinvent the wheel for SAP's sake (for example, rarely is there a reason to create an SAP-specific network team or data center team).

▶ **Best-in-class physical and virtual organizations**—Virtual teams should overlay the formal IT organizational chart, facilitating change while enforcing accountability, shared services, cross-training, and compactness.

One way to measure organizational effectiveness is to track issues—from where they came and how they were resolved. Overall employee retention is another good measure, because organizations with excessive downtime tend to lose good people (which only makes matters worse, of course). We also look at how frequently such teams are reorganized; "reorgs" can be symptomatic of many issues, all of which do nothing to increase system availability. In an effort to better understand the bearing of people on organizational SPOFs, their breadth of impact, and key methods of mitigating people and organizational risks, we explore potential SPOFs, lessons learned, and more in the following pages.

Support and Project Teams

From an organizational perspective, a careful review of all the various teams that make up the SAP TSO and larger project team is in order. Why? Because potential SPOFs can lie in hiding nearly anywhere. This includes the SAP development team, Basis organization, operations organization, and so on—it is imperative that more than one person be empowered or equipped to make decisions, support technology, work with the business teams, and more, including the following:

▶ Executive leadership team

▶ SAP Project leadership team

▶ Project management office (PMO)

▶ Stakeholder representation (business team representatives)

▶ Data center facilities

▶ Data center operations

▶ Network support team

▶ Server infrastructure support team

▶ SAN and disk subsystem support team

▶ Infrastructure security team

- ▶ SAP user security/authorizations team

- ▶ Database administration team

- ▶ SAP Basis/technology team

- ▶ SAP technical change control team (to manage technology stack changes as opposed to functional or development changes)

- ▶ SAP landscape/environment management team (for scheduling downtime or coordinating training time on a system)

- ▶ Overall SAP Center of Excellence (a common method of bringing together all the functional, business, and development teams under one umbrella)

- ▶ SAP functional change control team (to manage functional and development changes as opposed to technology stack changes)

- ▶ SAP functional/business team(s)

- ▶ SAP ABAP and Java development team(s)

- ▶ SAP globalization and localization team(s)

- ▶ SAP reporting team (especially common in large implementations in which independent business units roll up financial and other data to a holding company)

- ▶ SAP bolt-on or integration point team(s)

- ▶ SAP partner and vendor management organization(s)

Note that teams focused on development and functional support are often subdivided into the SAP components to which they're tied. For example, it's common to host individual SAP ERP, SAP NetWeaver Business Warehouse (BW), SAP Process Integration (PI)/SAP Exchange Infrastructure (XI), and SAP Customer Relationship Management (CRM) development teams in the same way you'll see SAP Financials, Logistics, and Human Capital Management (HCM) teams. Thus, company or project team leadership must be sure to identify backups for not only each team but each discipline or area of responsibility within the team. Getting even more granular, leadership must ensure that backups are identified for each person who is doing anything viewed as specific or unique for the organization. For what should be obvious reasons, don't let a single person be responsible for all companywide financial reporting, everything Java-related within your development team, or everything having to do with SAP NetWeaver Process Integration. One day that person will disappear, after all—even if only to take a day off—and the project could quickly come to a standstill.

Communication Strategy

The old adage "you can't communicate enough" is applicable when it comes to implementing SAP. People need to communicate and be communicated with. Thus, it's important to develop a communication strategy that leverages several different mechanisms. For example, we've seen effective team communications handled well via email, limited instant messenger, and weekly team calls held by management. In other cases, face-to-face communication has been important to kick off a project or key task, followed up by regular conference calls and ad hoc communication.

The most important thing to consider is the method—team leaders, managers, and executives alike need to identify and then use the communication method preferred by their individual contributors, project teams, and formal organizational structures. If you have a team made up of younger people in their 20s, for example, a quick poll will yield a couple of preferred communication mediums—email, texting, and short calls as necessary (the shorter the better). We've worked with other groups who preferred to do nearly all their formal communication over the telephone (and have seen managers uninterested in picking up the phone fail to deliver their projects despite an abundance of outgoing emails). Another communication trend is the use of collaboration portals and similar websites, which can be great for some teams and absolute failures for others. In the same way, team updates delivered through real-time web-based meeting tools can be tremendously effective for the right audience.

Consider how and when your team works, and how it will access team sites and collaboration portals, before you invest a lot of time creating something new. Teams with a need to work asynchronously (around the clock, such as those teams that perform shift-based development activities) may find collaboration portals just the thing for effective communication. Other teams, especially those with poor access methods and tools, might find portals that are tucked away behind firewalls and secured-access VPNs (Virtual Private Networks) more trouble than they're worth. Conducting and then making course changes based on a regular survey of your team's current communications needs and complaints will go a long way toward keeping everyone moving forward and your SAP project on track.

Career Development and Training

Despite all of the competing demands on managers and leaders, career development needs to be a priority. A team's direct manager needs to be motivated and encouraging, looking several years down the road at each of their employees to determine the career path that's best for both them and the company. Though the temptation is huge, good managers can't leave career development exclusively in the hands of their people. Individual contributors don't have the same insight into the organization that leaders (should!) have, nor do they typically have the ability to execute their own training plans. Best case, individual contributors can only help develop their training plans and then trust that the organization will pony up the time and money necessary to put them into action.

Employee retention is an enormous consideration and a key method of avoiding people-related SPOFs. Teamwork needs to be a way of life and an integral part of the organization's culture. Career development and intentionally planned training go a long way toward cementing such teamwork, because this combination creates a foundation for both sharing the workload and moving up the organization. Warning signs of poorly managed, developed, or trained teams may include

▶ Teams that do not take holidays and have little to no opportunity to take time off point to a lack of employee or project team member bandwidth (selling vacation time back to the company can be great for employees short-term, but doing so at every turn inevitably leads to employee burnout).

▶ If employees are rarely promoted from within, there's a gap in existing or potential capabilities, both of which can quickly stall an organization's growth (if not cause its demise).

▶ If employees generally do not feel good about what they're doing or how their job positively impacts the organization, there's a significant chance of en masse exits.

▶ If employees are cubbyholed into a narrow set of duties, they may find their work less rewarding and look elsewhere for intellectual stimulation (on the other hand, some of your best people may be quite happy in a narrow role they love to do; know your people).

▶ Companies and project teams that fail to provide a certain amount of flexibility to work remotely (including from home, from training classes and conferences, and so on) negatively affect a wide range of team attributes including motivation, morale, career development, the ability to stay home with a sick child, the opportunity for networking, and so on. Granted, a work-remotely policy needs to be managed well, obviously.

Longevity is a great barometer of an organization's success; measuring tenure is a common way of measuring satisfaction, though there are many confounding variables in this regard. The very staffing model an organization employs goes a long way toward longevity and creating a great place to work, as we see next.

Staffing and Shared Services

Generally speaking, staffing models for SAP can be characterized as insourced (managed and staffed internally as part of the firm's existing IT organization) or outsourced (managed and staffed by a third party). Neither is necessarily better than the other, though both have their advantages and disadvantages. From an availability perspective, outsourcing can provide an excellent method of obtaining exactly the right resource for a given implementation, software or hardware product, or SAP component. If a company is willing to do its own hunting and recruiting, engaging a contracting or consulting house can provide the same value. Regardless, we've found that SAP IT organizations who use multiple sourcing venues for staffing tend to be successful. Such organizations hire and promote from within as a matter of standard operating practice but also recognize when an outsider with a particular set of skills makes more sense.

Similarly, successful SAP IT organizations have developed a hiring model that leverages their geographic model. If a company's SAP end users will be located around the world, it often makes logical and financial sense to incorporate team members from around the world as well. Sure, there are inevitable communication and cultural factors to consider, including how to delegate work, how to control quality, and how to oversee a global operation. But with all the experience so many people have had with these challenges over the last 10 years, there's a wealth of knowledge and lessons learned available to assist newcomers.

For insourced organizations, another important factor to consider is the SAP IT team's size. An IT organization for SAP can eventually become very bloated with cubbyholes of technical disciplines and domains. These cubbyholes eventually constrain people movement and career development and ultimately beg for IT reorganizations, staff reductions, outright layoffs, and potentially outsourcing. A firm who practices the following will increase its SAP system's availability merely by increasing employee longevity:

▶ Leverage shared services (particularly around network, server, SAN, and infrastructure security tasks and roles).

▶ Leverage co-sourcing with existing or new partners, or any combination (for example, via short-term contractors and consultants).

▶ Embrace breadth and depth in organizational roles, therefore reducing headcount while creating positions that are more interesting and challenging; create an organization with roles requiring more skills held by fewer people or full-time equivalents (FTEs).

▶ Reduce headcount through intelligent IT infrastructure monitoring, process automation, capacity planning, and what-if analysis.

Along these lines, the following section discusses the lessons learned we've captured relative to people-oriented SPOFs.

People SPOFs: Lessons Learned

As we've stated several time already, it's people rather than technology or processes that constitute the greatest cause of SAP system downtime. The people-related considerations and issues that have the most impact reflect two failures back-to-back. On one side, a service, technology, process, or other failure occurs. This in and of itself is often not too problematic. Where things really get messy is when a follow-on issue occurs that exploits a previously introduced failure or weakness. For example:

▶ SPOFs within a particular discipline are a firm's greatest weaknesses. SAN, server and OS competencies, and backup/recovery processes, for example, may each have a single person assigned, and backup skills might be light.

▶ A lack of adequate current-state and process documentation is often the underlying issue behind a basic failure. IT people cause incidents that cause downtime, but a lack of good documentation might be the root cause.

▶ Employee backup must be addressed across the board—each employee needs a backup that has been intentionally trained and each backup requires an easily accessible knowledge repository. Without the knowledge repository, a failure during a primary support employee's absence could spell disaster for the backup employee.

▶ Lean teams also cause downtime, regardless of discipline or knowledge. Eventually someone steps away from the office, goes on vacation, or attends an offsite training class and an issue invariably (and eventually!) occurs. In these cases, excellent process documentation, as well as current-state documentation, are essential; we've seen availability suffer when only one type of documentation is maintained.

17

▶ Backups need to be available 24x7. If Johnny is the only available experienced Basis resource in his group during peak time, he's an SPOF despite the fact that several other trained and experienced Basis resources might be available at other times; this speaks to SPOFs based on the shift or time a backup resource might be available.

▶ Senior-level individual contributors might be too busy with new projects and base-load responsibilities to address proactive monitoring and capacity planning. Junior contributors are then called to fill in the gaps (or the system is simply left unmonitored; in either case, system availability is at risk).

▶ Skill-set gaps between senior and junior contributors may preclude the ability to hand off issues within a team or project; this skill-set gap results in a pool of fewer resources who in turn are required to work on more problems, all of which impacts a firm's capability to pursue SAP tasks that are proactive in nature.

▶ Outside of skill-set gaps, other conditions can cause work to be unevenly allocated; systems and the people managing those systems may be biased toward or against a particular person, role, group, or other construct. Be sure to eye workload from an equitable perspective.

People also need to back up automated processes. That is, a team should be capable of performing manual performance and availability checks of their systems if automated tools or processes fail. How to maintain the system, maintain the ability to perform such manual checks, *and* do the work of the project at the same time is a key issue. Although not absolutely required in every case, our experience is that authentic business transformation is enabled through authentic IT process discipline and management. In other words, a lack of process development and diligence can significantly constrain an SAP IT operation.

Gartner found several years ago that 80% of availability issues related to mission-critical systems were the result of people and process matters, and not technology per se. Giving processes the attention they deserve isn't as appealing as introducing a new business-enabling technology (unless a company is a proponent of the Information Technology Infrastructure Library [ITIL] of processes or a similar process discipline). But this attention is essential to achieving SAP operational excellence. Process discipline is one of the few change levers that holds the key to real innovation—the kind of innovation that can remove costs from an IT operation and thus make room for improved operations and efficiency (through reinvesting in technologies that reduce headcount or return bandwidth to current employees), improved financial performance (through faster return on investment or the ability to return a residual to the business), or both. Process discipline targeted at core operations and operational efficiency can free up capital to reinvest elsewhere, including innovative technologies and approaches that otherwise might find no funding.

The Disaster Recovery Organization

Another organization that exists outside the SAP project team and various technical and business organizations is the SAP Disaster Recovery Organization (DRO). When it comes to people-related SPOFs, few are as important as the roles outlined in the DRO. The number of folks performing these roles may vary from site to site, ranging from a single individual in a small SAP shop to perhaps four or many more people in larger implementations. SAP AG defines, and our experience generally agrees with creating, the following key DRO roles:

- ▶ **SAP recovery manager**—This person is responsible for managing the entire actual DR process from a technical perspective. All DR activities and issues are coordinated through this critical single point of contact.

- ▶ **Communication liaison**—This person is also typically a single point of contact within the DRO, tasked with handling all communication between the SAP technical support teams and upper management, as well as the SAP teams and other technology-focused support organizations inside the firm. By keeping the management team apprised of the recovery status, and handling all phone calls into the DRO, this critical role helps ensure that the technical DR process can continue uninterrupted.

- ▶ **Technical recovery team**—This team comprises from very few to perhaps a half dozen or more SAP technology stack specialists. These folks perform the actual technical DR process, seeking to both manage changes to the recovery plan and coordinate the actual technical recovery as they see fit.

- ▶ **Review/certification manager**—When the system is finally back online (presumably at a DR site, though the recovery process might just as well have been applied at the primary site), this individual coordinates and plans all post-recovery testing and certification with end users, to ensure that no data loss was realized and no other failures were inadvertently initiated.

Organizing the DRO around these four roles is a challenge in and of itself, too. Successful DR is more than simply an exercise in technology; it is an organizational challenge and a great (albeit worthwhile) expense, and thus requires advance planning and commitment from senior leadership. People need to understand their roles, the responsibilities they have during a disaster, and what level of commitment is needed both during real disasters and in support of DR tests.

Decision-makers must be identified early on, too. In other words, who will actually make the call to fail over to a DR site? Who declares the disaster or decides that an event is not worthy of DR actions? In most cases, the recovery manager plays the key role here. But other folks, normally executive level, may play a role too, and certainly systems administrators will be involved by virtue of their support roles—this all needs to be ironed out well in advance.

Finally, basic human resource management must be considered. This might consist of addressing the need to identify and obtain backfill personnel for people unable to fulfill their DR roles during an actual disaster. In turn, internal staffing processes and even external support contracts may need to be revised or put in place.

Where Process and People SPOFs Intersect

Innovative IT organizations tasked with maximizing system availability look beyond technology and people SPOFs and identify how the intersection of people and processes can affect availability. It's this intersection that can prove especially vulnerable. For example, a people failure can act as the last straw in the midst of a poorly executed or managed process. Similarly, a process failure can exacerbate an already bad people situation. We've identified several management-related processes, planning and testing processes, and a host of operational processes you need to pay attention to that intersect with people SPOFs:

- ▶ Knowledge management
- ▶ Change and release management
- ▶ Systems management
- ▶ Capacity planning and resizing
- ▶ Load testing
- ▶ High-availability failover/failback
- ▶ Backup and recovery
- ▶ Server and SAN build/deployment

Clearly, there are more processes that require attention. In our experience, those listed here are key, however. Each of these process/people intersections is outlined in turn in more detail in the following sections.

Knowledge Management Process and People SPOFs

Mismanaging knowledge represents one of the most critical oversights of an organization interested in maximizing system availability. When knowledge is maintained exclusively in the head or on the desktop of one person, an SPOF of great magnitude is created. With regard to knowledge management (KM), we recommend that a firm deploy a process for managing the knowledge it gleans from implementation and follow-on issues and problem resolution. This includes implementing a knowledge repository, as previously discussed. Websites, particularly portals, are effective. Simple file shares with a robust taxonomy can be useful as well, though they tend to become cumbersome over time.

Within the knowledge repository, house issues and problem resolutions, as well as the firm's technology current state and process documentation, various team Shift Turnover logs, and team contact data (telephone/contact data, name/roles data). Operations, development, and Basis teams will likely operate 24 hours a day, 7 days a week, for the last three to six months preceding go-live (if not initially). The knowledge repository also must include organizational charts (to make it easy for other groups, particularly new team members, to locate parties responsible for a specific technology or discipline), service-level agreements (SLAs), and other documents and materials that capture intra- and interteam expectations and responsibilities. Keeping in the knowledge repository documents that explain how to use the tools necessary for implementation and post-go-live makes sense, too, including materials obtained from SAP's training courses. And, of course, all the status reports shared internally and with other teams, including the business status, reports related to uptime/downtime, reports tracking database growth, and so on, need to be preserved.

Combining all of this miscellaneous material in one place serves an implementation team in the same way that training does—it provides a team with yet another knowledge resource. When this kind of knowledge is difficult or impossible to find, a small system outage or condition can lead to greater—and otherwise avoidable—downtime. This is especially true when junior people are given the helm (for example, during an evening shift) and the inevitable system crash or development problem occurs. Avoiding poor KM practices will help your junior person get through such a problem and maintain as much uptime as possible.

Change/Release Management Process and People SPOFs

In many companies, the overall change management process and release management process in particular have matured considerably over the last several years. This is due to the attention that ITIL and similar bodies have given to IT process diligence. A release management agent can be useful to spearhead and provide oversight for the process, lead weekly (at minimum) release management meetings, address scheduling, coordinate inevitable emergency fixes, and act as a single point of escalation. With regard to meetings, every organization that touches or is touched by the SAP implementation requires representation. Most firms have their team leads attend these meetings; be sure that delegates are appointed as well if the team leads are unable to attend the release management meetings themselves. Do the math and you'll see that it is not uncommon to have 15 to 30 people involved in these meetings—anything less shows inadequate attention and prioritization regarding the process. Single points of failure include

▶ **Release management agent**—Such a person naturally becomes an SPOF unless a backup is identified and kept apprised. Assign and cross train a backup who understands how the firm's IT organization is structured, how to get work done, how changing or upgrading the different layers in the technology stack can affect not only the other layers but development cycles, and how the overall release management process impacts raw availability.

▶ **Organizational delegates**—Each technical, development, functional, and business organization requires not only primary representation, but also at least one backup delegate.

▶ **Test plans**—A lack of test plans is another SPOF. Organizational leads or their delegates need to come to the release management meetings with well-vetted test plans that relate to their scheduled changes.

▶ **Backout plans**—In the same way, some kind of documented backout plan is necessary in case the change/release fails. In the real world, these plans might be fairly weak (requiring a reinstallation and refresh of the system is a common catchall). Encourage organizational leaders to think through their backout plans such that the plans require only moderate additional downtime to implement.

Along these same lines, the overall change management process is also fraught with potential SPOFs or other complicating matters:

▶ **Technology stack interdependencies**—Patching the technology stack is complicated by interstack dependencies. For example, you will certainly run into cases in which your UNIX OS can only be patched to a certain level, after which your hardware/firmware might need to be updated, your database software might require patching, and your SAP application layer might even need to be technically upgraded. It's common, therefore, to bundle and execute only two to four patch bundles a year because it can easily take four months or more to get through the process. Engage representatives (and backups) from each technical team to ensure that all dependencies are thought through and planned for.

▶ **Emergency change process**—Despite your best intentions with regard to following a regular change process, you'll need to develop a mechanism and process for applying emergency changes, such as critical security patches, more frequently. Such patches typically need to be pushed through the promote-to-production process in as little as one to two weeks. Be sure to require approval above and beyond the organizational leads who normally attend the release management meetings; it's common for director-level personnel to approve any change requests outside the normal change window, thus ensuring that the change management process has excellent visibility (and potential SPOFs are avoided).

▶ **Unauthorized changes**—The firm needs to track and report all *unauthorized* changes; in many companies, more than a few changes are made without the change control board's knowledge. To be sure, many of these are small changes. But unauthorized changes fail to be reflected in current-state and process documentation, are typically untested, and overall represent a great risk to a firm's SAP system availability. We recommend taking swift action against such team members, including termination for repeat offenders.

▶ **SAP landscape parity**—From a promote-to-production perspective, ensure that the firm has deployed nonproduction assets alongside every production asset. This includes everything from the underlying network infrastructure and storage area network (SAN) infrastructure to testing assets and so on. Never force the organization to introduce *anything* new in the production environment—even something as seemingly innocuous as a minor patch, network reconfiguration, or hardware fix.

Additionally, you'll want to use a tool to audit changes, and ensure that a person is assigned to audit to what extent the tool is used, how the tool is used, and how well the changes are tracked and maintained.

Systems Management Processes and People SPOFs

Overall, poor or incomplete systems management processes will inhibit a company from freeing up employee bandwidth and therefore reducing costs or pursuing the kind of value-add projects that the tools should have enabled. Many companies are in pretty bad shape today with regard to their systems management processes, tools, and investment in people. More often than not, a typical SAP IT organization has a bloated collection of often redundant tools, significant systems management gaps in terms of what the tools actually cover, many different "panes of glass" (each of which requires too much manual intervention), and little automation/poorly designed escalation processes.

For a new implementation, there are many lessons learned to leverage. Start by requiring formal SLAs between the SAP IT organization and the business, along with intra-IT SLAs (for example, between the teams supporting the infrastructure and the SAP Basis/technology support team). The following are systems management rules of thumb for reducing SPOFs:

▶ Approach the systems management process from a bottom-up perspective. Use tools that can "roll up" alerts to higher-level (in terms of the technology stack) tools.

▶ Practice intentional overlapping. Tools must provide a bit of overlap if possible (so that one can corroborate the other tools' findings and thus eliminate monitoring SPOFs).

▶ Do your best to reduce the total number of tools (which will simplify maintenance down the road). Deploying many different tools can quickly complicate systems management; if a tool does not provide a desirable bit of overlap or a critical service, avoid it.

▶ Use your systems management tools to create regular uptime reports that can be discussed during monthly reviews and weekly release management meetings. If the tool can't provide this kind of value, its role in your process should be questioned.

Finally, for issues that may be identified and escalated to specialists to be resolved, take care in managing who these issues are escalated to. In our experience, an organization's top performers tend to get overloaded with such matters (because they're good at resolving problems!), while other people sit idly by. This places a greater load on a few of your best people—who are likely already overworked because they're so capable. Avoid this workload-balancing issue and you'll avoid a common systems management SPOF.

Capacity Planning Process and People SPOFs

Once the SAP IT organization creates a performance baseline, it's important to commence the capacity planning process. This process is used to later resize the SAP production system (in support of technical refreshes, system upgrades, and so on down the road), which explains why many people also call this the resizing process. Capacity planning tracks current workload versus the capabilities of the in-place system. As the workload changes and the technology stack morphs due to regular changes, the system will support the workload differently. The trend will be a narrowing of the system's capabilities and the system's workload, until finally a point is reached at which a technical refresh (new servers, upgraded SAN, and so on) is warranted. From an SPOF perspective, watch out for the following:

▶ Manage capacity planning and performance management separately; they are similar but have a different focus (performance management is end-user focused). Ideally, the same team or person will manage both, and track daily, weekly, and monthly performance alongside capacity planning trends. Be sure you have coverage and backups for both.

▶ Different technical teams tend to track their own layers in the technology stack. Don't use this data exclusively but rather use it as an opportunity to provide overlap; having data collected by individual teams and data collected by a responsible party assigned to capacity planning gives you a chance to correlate performance trends between the network, SAN, servers, database, SAP application, and various bolt-ons and middleware layers in the technology stack.

▶ Beware of warning signs, such as high average server utilization, enormous unchecked SAP disk space growth, and dramatic network bandwidth consumption. It's not the high resource use that's important to note but rather whether the organization is surprised by the growth. A surprised organization is an unprepared organization—highlighting what happens when no time is made for formal capacity planning. The growth might be unavoidable, but managing the growth must be done proactively so that there's time to introduce technology stack changes.

▶ In the same way, if performance management is given little formal attention, there's a good chance that capacity planning isn't getting done properly either. An end-user community that has seen its average response time grow from less than one second to something nearing two seconds is destined to live with poor overall performance while the IT organization scrambles to understand what's happening (to the workload, the technology stack, integration points, business processes, or some combination of all of these).

Capacity planning is one of those processes that doesn't normally get a lot of attention until the process breaks, like the next process we'll take a look at—load testing.

Load Testing Process and People SPOFs

Although best-in-class organizations test their planned changes under load, most organizations fail to understand the benefits of load testing and the downside related to forgoing it. Similarly, although nearly everyone implements some kind of promote-to-production process to test whether planned changes can be installed and configured without error, they don't think about whether the change will hold up under the stress of a user community and batch job workload. Load testing is all about risk mitigation. It affects four areas:

▶ **Performance**—Load testing ensures that business processes and overall functionality execute within SLAs as the SAP technology stack changes, and validates that response times and throughput remain acceptable in the wake of pending changes.

▶ **Scalability**—Load testing enables you to quantify how well a pending technology stack change "scales" before you hit a financial month-end closing cycle.

▶ **Validity**—The ability to validate that several changes can be implemented and shown to work well together under load helps validate a technology stack's evolution.

▶ **Overall system availability**—A system that breaks under the weight of a production load has no business being put into production.

Load testing ensures changes are properly vetted, which in turn mitigates the risk of unplanned downtime. The key question to answer is simply this: Is the availability, scalability, and performance you've signed up to provide (if you're in IT) or required of IT (if you're in the business or in a leadership role) worth the investment in time, money, and processes necessary to load test? Consider the following exposures:

> ▶ Failing to load test puts the SAP IT organization in a situation in which load testing is essentially completed in production; the organization has no idea whether a change will negatively affect the production environment under load. This not only puts SLAs at risk, but creates a situation in which it's unknown whether key business processes can be completed in a particular timeframe.

> ▶ Without load testing, there's no opportunity in the promote-to-production process to corroborate with other teams as a potential change is considered and vetted against potential issues. More simply, the organization loses the ability to trouble-shoot a potential issue before it becomes a *production* issue.

Of course, if the IT organization has failed to create a nonproduction environment to support activities such as load testing, all of this is a moot point; there's no chance of doing load testing outside of the production environment. Do yourself a favor and, as previously mentioned, be sure to deploy nonproduction assets for testing.

High Availability Failover/Failback Processes and People SPOFs

Despite all the attention an organization might give to HA and DR, many firms have no formal failback plans—an important SPOF to quantify in terms of business impact. For these firms, system failover techniques only serve the company one way—they enable failover to a DR site, for example, but don't include failing back to the original site when the site is presumably restored to operations. Such a perceived oversight might indeed be intentional. After all, the failback process will be rarely executed, and failback processes are complicated by company-specific technology, process, and people realities. Forgoing fail-back testing might be acceptable in the same way that foregoing load testing might be deemed acceptable—it's all akin to *not* buying an insurance policy in the hopes that it'll never be required. Like flood insurance, it's easy to believe a failback process is unnecessary.

Many other firms need to make an investment in a DR failback process, though; their business dictates it. More precisely, their combined cost of downtime, less-than-adequate performance, and a likely inability to scale during peak business load dictates it. Without a failback process, a firm is stuck at the DR site indefinitely. Furthermore, even if a failback process is created, if it is never tested then it's also conceivable that the firm will be unable to move away from the DR system after a failover. And that's a bad place to be—DR sites are rarely configured and provisioned for supporting ongoing operations along the lines of the original data center site. The following are typical trade-offs and shortcomings of hosting SAP applications from a DR site:

> ▶ DR sites often are provisioned for core transactional services rather than the breadth of an enterprise; in the case of SAP systems, it's common to fail over SAP ERP, SAP Supply Chain Management (SCM), and SAP PI but leave SAP NetWeaver BW, SAP Supplier Relationship Management (SRM), and perhaps even SAP NetWeaver Portal down (of course, many exceptions and complicating factors need to be considered).

> ▶ Once failed over to the DR site, it's also common that the core DR infrastructure will support only a subset of the enterprise's overall business processes. That is, although SAP ERP may be failed over, it's very likely that not all functionality will continue to

17

work as usual, given that many of the bolt-ons, middleware, and other systems of record may have been left in a down state.

▶ Even with limited SAP functionality and only core transactional services failed over, the DR site is often configured to provide only the least acceptable levels of performance. This naturally impacts the firm's capability to respond to new business needs if it finds itself failed over for an extended period of time, and of course affects day-to-day online transaction and batch job performance and throughput. For example, after a failover to a DR site, a company's SAP ERP system might be running on only a single, less-powerful server rather than a bigger one; this expected performance degradation needs to be communicated with the business community well before a DR failure is ever conducted, if only to be sure that the business agrees that the reduced performance is indeed acceptable for some period of time.

Of course , all of the aforementioned limitations can be solved with money—a solution employed by companies with massive downtime costs or end-user SLA penalties. Such companies will deploy dual data center strategies reflecting production systems mirrored to identical staging, QA, or dedicated DR systems, as discussed in Chapter 16. They understand that one of the primary SPOFs with regard to failover and failback is the DR site itself, and they will give themselves options. These companies will do the downtime versus insurance policy math and therefore know their DR investment threshold. After documenting and vetting out assumptions, constraints, and the impact of extended downtime on the company's business, they might employ a multitiered strategy for DR sites (by designating a backup data center as well as a tertiary data center) followed by contractual specifications calling for access to enough horsepower to run the entire SAP ecosystem indefinitely—bolt-ons and other ERP systems alike. On the other hand, they might intentionally develop a DR strategy comprising significant technology, process, and people gaps—because they understand their business, the risks, and the dollars at stake, their plan will be defendable.

Smart companies seeking to avoid HA and DR SPOFs will be sure to take people factors into account. It's paramount to identify backups for all key roles, figure out how people will get to where they need to be, and figure out what to do in case key people become unavailable in the wake of a disaster. These same companies will also figure out how to obtain access to whatever is required for recovery—whether offsite tapes, tools for deployment and management, access to the company's knowledge repository, access to key DRO decision-makers and other personnel, and so on. By managing the intersection of the HA and DR process and the people assigned to plan for, execute, manage, and control it, smart companies will not only persevere through disasters but come out stronger and be seen as more resilient to such matters by the marketplace.

Backup/Recovery Processes and People SPOFs

SPOFs regarding backup/recovery processes and people are numerous and include the following:

▶ Physical tapes often are created only once a day or once a week. Someone must ensure this occurs successfully. Lack of good tapes represents an SPOF.

▶ How to use, manage, and troubleshoot issues with tape drives, virtual tape libraries (VTLs), and all the other hardware and tape backup software used to back up and recover data needs to be understood by more than one person. This includes the tape backup software used for scheduling jobs and verifying that tapes are indeed good. A single person knowledgeable in these critical technologies is yet another SPOF.

▶ The tape recovery process also needs to be understood by more than one person (and needs to be tested regularly to ensure data is indeed recoverable).

▶ All backup/recovery processes and all involved technologies must be documented in terms of current state (how the system is configured) and operational processes (how-to documentation).

▶ The offsite tape storage process also needs to be understood and documented. There's no use going to the trouble of shipping tapes offsite if you can't get to them when necessary. We've seen firms struggle with obtaining tapes that are safeguarded near their primary data center site but far from the DR site—potential tape logistics issues can occur if air traffic is grounded, ground transportation is shut down, or the company hosting the tapes is unable to be reached (which underscores another area of concern—be sure to have multiple methods of communicating with the SAP project team, all supporting teams, and all vendors and partners).

▶ If you have multiple operating environments for your SAP environment (for example, if you run SAP ERP on HP-UX/Oracle and your SAP NetWeaver BW system on AIX/DB2), don't assume that the backup/recovery processes are similar enough to forgo system-specific documentation and testing. There are enough differences, and perhaps even different software utilities involved, to warrant the investment.

Worst case, the most important SPOF to mitigate revolves around losing a key person in a situation in which processes are poorly documented. Be sure to not only document these processes but update them regularly as required. And just as important, before you ever need to do so in an emergency, be sure to regularly test tape backups and the backup/recovery process to verify they actually work.

Server and SAN Build/Deployment Processes and People SPOFs

Understanding the process used for building out and deploying new server and storage assets can be critical during a disaster. For new HP-UX servers, a firm might employ HP's Ignite server and process to rapidly and consistently deploy new SAP servers. For Windows servers, the same firm might employ multiple methods. Blade servers, for example, might be deployed using Alteris, while other server models might be installed manually or by using an imaging process. Server naming conventions are also important to understand if only to avoid inadvertently bringing down or making changes to the wrong server. And, of course, the process used to patch and maintain servers is critical whether the company is running from its primary data center or from a DR site.

It's also important that the HA software and hardware solutions involved are understood, whether HP-UX Serviceguard clusters, Microsoft's clustering technologies, VMware's clustering approach, and so on. In the same way, how the SAP SAN is configured, how it fails

17

over to the DR site, and how it can be failed back to the primary site are important to understand.

The intersection of all these deployment and configuration processes relative to people during a disaster scenario should be clear—the firm needs to

▶ Invest in creating and maintaining effective current-state and process documentation

▶ Ensure that each SME has an equally effective (or nearly so; the documentation should cover any gaps) backup

With intersecting people/process matters behind us, let's take a look at real-world best practices.

Real-World People-Related Availability Best Practices

It's no secret that lots and lots of best practices exist for HA and DR. We have stepped through many of these in detail throughout the last several chapters. But we believe it makes sense to compile a top-ten list here of people-related considerations:

▶ **Practice availability through redundancy**—At the lowest level, or where it makes the most financial sense when everything else is equal, practice availability through redundancy not only for technology but for people—no job, no task, and no single role should be mastered by a lone guru.

▶ **Employ clustering**—When it comes to organizations, employ clustering in the same way you employ it for servers and applications. Cluster your resources—your teams—to back up one another. This will help maximize availability and provide redundancy of critical resources and organizations tasked with managing key components of the SAP ecosphere.

▶ **Analyze total cost of ownership**—Performing a cursory TCO analysis to roughly determine the point at which downtime exceeds the cost of an HA or DR solution is as important from a people perspective as it is from a technology perspective. Invest in DRO and DR-related services and processes to the point where the math shows your remaining risk of downtime to be equal (and thus palatable) to your DR investment. Do the math!

▶ **Identify SPOFs**—Work methodically through the SAP technology stack, identifying SPOFs from a people perspective at each layer. When you have identified them, refer to the cost of downtime to determine whether it makes financial sense to duplicate, back up, or simply reduce and mitigate each SPOF.

▶ **Review processes**—In the same way, review the processes identified in this chapter to identify less-obvious process/people intersections that can yield significant SPOFs—such SPOFs can have an enormous impact if not properly addressed.

▶ **Be aware that people issues come in many other different forms**—Access to data, infrastructure security rights, profile/authorization rights, the ability to launch resource-intensive batch jobs, the ability to tie up multiple dialog processes or eat up gigabytes of memory for long periods of time, and so on, all reflect availability problems originating with people. By identifying the various ways people in your organization can affect system availability, you address overt denial of service as well as honest user-originated mistakes and other acts.

▶ **Ensure that each SAP business application or solution is documented from a current-state perspective**—Access to this kind of information is one of the key ways of avoiding significant downtime issues, particularly when new hires or junior hires are part of your SAP implementation and post-go-live support team.

▶ **Ensure that all operational procedures and other how-to processes are documented and understood**—Publish HA and DR policies and business continuity plans via a formal communications plan. Furthermore, create and maintain a Disaster Recovery Crash Kit at your DR site, as covered in Chapter 16.

▶ **Meticulously plan and test all changes to your SAP environment**—Be careful not to ignore your release management and change control processes even in emergency situations. Improperly tested changes historically impact availability as much as anything else we've seen. The people side of this is especially important—after all, it's people who decide whether a process will be circumvented.

▶ **Regularly test your HA and DR plans, including failback processes**—Ensure not only that the entire team understands and is trained in HA/DR processes, but that the team is capable of handling a disaster even when key personnel are missing. Put your DR plan to the test by "killing off" a key technology guru or decision-maker, and then sit back and watch how the team backfills and otherwise responds to meeting the needs normally addressed by that key position.

As discussed throughout this chapter, people and process errors hold the potential to really impact a system's availability and recoverability. In our experience, poor attention to managing change probably constitutes half of all otherwise avoidable downtime issues—the kind of outages that should never really happen in the first place. This downtime is much different from the unavoidable and typically very rare downtime hours incurred from actual technology failures and honest-to-goodness disasters. If you keep in mind that people and process failures tend to exaggerate their effects on one another, you'll have the proper mindset when it comes to identifying and mitigating people-related and organizationally related SPOFs.

Summary

This chapter wrapped up our discussions of system availability and recoverability initiated in Chapter 15 and further detailed in Chapter 16. We took a close look at the organizational and people factors affecting a system's availability and recoverability, including organizational design and backup considerations and people-specific SPOFs. The role of the SAP DRO and its members set the stage for examining how management, operational, planning, and testing processes intersect with people SPOFs to exacerbate risky conditions. Real-world availability and recoverability lessons learned and best practices concluded the chapter.

Case Study: The Impact of People and Process on DR

After an initial misstep, HiTech, Inc. is seeking to reorganize its SAP support structure in a way that inherently increases system availability. HiTech's board has been pulled in, given that several competing perspectives relative to how the organization might be best aligned have been presented by a number of business and technology executives. HiTech's CIO—and your boss—has asked you to help her defend a position based on marrying HiTech's focus on process diligence with an organizational structure that eliminates people as SPOFs. Help her construct answers to the board's questions.

Questions

1. Explain how processes and people intersect to cause availability issues.

2. What are several methods an organization can use to increase its own availability and therefore that of the systems it supports?

3. Identify several key processes that intersect people SPOFs and therefore require attention from a system availability perspective.

4. What are the four primary roles discussed with regard to the SAP Disaster Recovery Organization (DRO)?

> **NOTE**
>
> The answers to these questions can be found in Appendix A, "Case Study Answers."

CHAPTER 18

Introduction to SAP Platform Sizing

Enterprise customers who are looking to set up a data center with an SAP infrastructure that supports their business needs have a wide range of choices today. In previous chapters, we have explored various considerations that go into choosing the appropriate configuration for a new SAP deployment. Because SAP is available on many popular operating systems and hardware platforms, the choices are almost endless. Even within a particular hardware and OS family, there is a range of choices. Some standard methodology is needed to be able to make a decision based on multiple parameters such as cost, availability, growth, performance, extensibility, and more. This methodology or process is called the *sizing* or *infrastructure blueprinting* process and is the topic of this chapter.

The SAP Sizing Process

The SAP sizing process seeks to convert what was imagined in the business vision and ERP solution vision phases on the SAP project into a basic infrastructure plan. At the completion of the sizing process, the SAP Technical Support Organization (TSO) responsible for deploying the technical infrastructure underpinning SAP applications will finally have its long-awaited blueprint—including server and storage configurations. With this information, the TSO will be ready to place orders for infrastructure hardware and software and any necessary consulting services. While our focus here is predominantly on new implementation blueprinting, the SAP sizing process is triggered by any of the following:

▸ Designing a new SAP system

▸ Creating a new SAP instance (from simply adding a new application server to an existing system to designing a new landscape component such as a training or business sandbox system)

▸ Adding new business functionality to an existing instance (which typically requires additional infrastructure horsepower, hence the need for sizing)

▸ Upgrading the SAP component (such as adding new business functionality, but with broader consequences leading to even higher demands on the platform)

▸ Consolidating multiple SAP installations on the same database

▸ Consolidating multiple data centers for centralized management

▸ Merging SAP installations across different companies

▸ Conducting a migration from one OS or database release to a different OS or database release

▸ Retiring obsolete hardware and software in favor of new servers running the same OS and database (also called a hardware refresh)

▸ Increasing or reducing seasonal or permanent usage

Sizing is also viewed as the process of converting functional component-specific performance and capacity requirements into hardware and software infrastructure requirements. In this chapter and the next, we will discuss the various steps involved in detail. The sizing process is an iterative one requiring regular communication between the customer and the vendors. This allows for iterative refinement in the sizing configurations, as shown in Figure 18.1.

Sizing an SAP instance and mapping the requirements to specific hardware components is an important requirement both at the start of a project and on an ongoing basis after going live. This is important for capacity management as well as when introducing new functionality. In this chapter we look at the various factors that go into sizing SAP installations. Consider the process of sizing as a workflow similar to the one depicted in Figure 18.2.

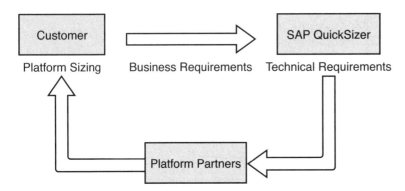

FIGURE 18.1   Platform sizing is an iterative process.

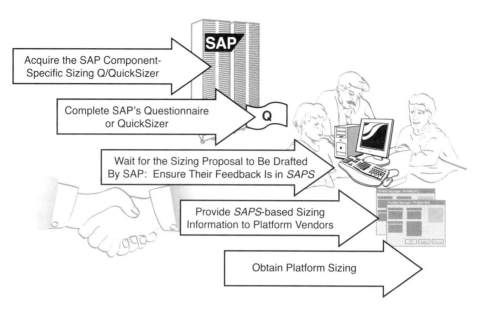

FIGURE 18.2   The sizing workflow.

Typically the sizing process involves the following steps:

1. Collect high-level requirements per functional component.
2. Fill out a QuickSizer questionnaire from SAP.
3. Receive SAPS requirement per functional unit.
4. Pass to different vendors the SAPS and the QuickSizer ID along with other information.
5. Receive vendor-generated sizing proposals to satisfy the functionality.
6. Iterate to ensure that everyone's on the same page, accept a proposal, and start the project to convert the infrastructure.

SAP Sizing Terminology

Before diving into the various ways to perform sizing of SAP installations, let's look at some of the terms commonly used in the process. The following are some of the important terms and concepts that come up in sizing:

▶ **Users**—There are different ways of measuring the number of users that need to be supported by the infrastructure.

▶ **SAPS**—A standard unit of measuring SAP performance; SAP provides this measurement to platform vendors to enable the performance of various platforms for specific SAP release levels to be compared.

- **Tiers**—An SAP installation is divided into multiple tiers, which can be placed on the same system or on multiple systems.

- **Scale-up and scale-out configurations**—Decide whether to have everything on one box or distributed across several boxes.

- **High availability, reliability, and fault tolerance**—Each of these can be costly to implement, so it is important that you know where you need them.

- **Homogeneous and heterogeneous configurations**—Choose between the same processor and OS versus different processor architectures and/or OS.

In the sections that follow, we explore these terms and put them into the overall context of the SAP sizing process.

Users

One of the most important factors in sizing is looking at the number of users that the configuration can support. This is not as easy as you might think because users can be defined in many different ways, including the following:

- **All named users**—These are users who will be provided a unique SAP ID or account (synonymous with the number of licensed users)

- **Logged-on users**—Users who are logged on to the system (regardless of whether they are actively performing work or on a break)

- **Workplaces or front ends**—Can map to multiple users

- **Sessions**—The number of active instances of the SAPGUI or other front ends (the average across a large population is between 1 and 2 sessions per logged-on user)

- **Concurrent users**—The number of logged-on users who are active in the system and thus working simultaneously; in our experience, anywhere from 20% to 50% of the named users are concurrent users

The relevance of these terms to the sizing process can differ depending on the goal of the sizing process. For example, whereas the number of concurrent users can be relatively useful information to feed into the system, the number of named users (the most easily available information) is rather meaningless to provide any accurate sizing guidance. The number of concurrent users can be most helpful to decide appropriate sizing. But even this term is quite subjective because, ideally, we want to understand the number of concurrent transactions at any given second and the modules they touch. So SAP sizing methodologies define three kinds of active users based on "think time"—that is, the time spent between their interaction with the system.

- **Low user**—Processes an average of 10 interaction steps per hour.

- **Medium user**—Processes an average of 120 interaction steps per hour.

- **High user**—Processes on average 360 interaction steps per hour, or every 10 seconds. This is typical of a user working in a call center or performing data entry.

Along with the number of users supported by a configuration, there is another metric used to enable comparison of different hardware equipment—SAPS. We discuss SAPS next.

Introduction to SAPS

SAP AG provides benchmark tools with standard workloads that are specific to the various applications supported. Platform vendors can execute SAP's benchmarks and publicly report their benchmark results, which in turn can be used for comparison purposes by prospective SAP customers. These benchmarks are communicated in terms of the number of SAP Application Performance Standard (SAPS) that each platform configuration can support. Because SAPS are hardware- and platform-independent, they enable SAP platform apples-to-apples comparisons (the greater the number of SAPS, the more capable the platform).

This hardware independence feature also enables SAP platform providers to size and configure a particular workload—measured in SAPS—on various hardware and operating system platforms (often simply called a computing platform). We take a closer look at how SAPS aids the sizing process later in this chapter.

We find the practice of comparing platform-specific SAPS useful for customers who have already decided to implement SAP and are trying to select an infrastructure capable of addressing their project workload. Platform vendor benchmark results are submitted to and are monitored by the SAP Benchmark Council. The council includes industry representation but is primarily shepherded by SAP. Note that a single SAPS unit of measurement "describes the performance of a system configuration in the SAP environment... and is derived from the Sales and Distribution (SD) Benchmark, where 100 SAPS is defined as 2,000 fully business processed order line items per hour. In technical terms, this throughput is achieved by processing 6,000 dialog steps (screen changes), 2,000 postings per hour in the SD benchmark, or 2,400 SAP transactions."[1] With regard to the SD benchmark, fully business processed means the full business process of an order line item: creating the order, creating a delivery note for the order, displaying the order, changing the delivery, posting a goods issue, listing orders, and creating an invoice.

SAP provides more than 20 other benchmarks corresponding to different applications and modules. SAP's Sales and Distribution (SD) benchmark is the most popular SAP benchmark, however, because it is one of the oldest and claims the highest number of platform vendor submissions. Therefore, it is often used as a primary comparison benchmark. The SAP SD module provides functions ranging from creating an order to its delivery, including

- Request for Quotation (RFQ)
- Sales orders
- Pricing
- Billing
- Warehouse processes such as picking

---

[1] *SAP 2008 SAP Benchmark Glossary, http://www.sap.com/solutions/benchmark/glossary.epx*

▶ Packing

▶ Shipping

The SAP SD module provides sales support, such as tools for managing information on sales leads and competitor activity, and the sales information system provides an early warning of market trends. When a customer places an order, the SD module is able to extract information from the database, such as the customer's address, sales activity, and credit limit. The SD module works with modules such as Materials Management (MM) and Production Planning to check on material availability and estimate the earliest possible delivery date for the order.

The SD module provides information to employees about orders that are due for delivery. It works with the MM module to pick the completed goods from the warehouse and supports activities related to packaging and the creation of shipping papers. Once delivery is initiated, the SD module carries out billing automatically. This information is immediately available to the Financial Accounting and Controlling modules.

Scalability can be measured by comparing the results of two different configurations, keeping other factors equal except for the component whose scaling is under review. For example, adding more memory to the same system and retesting gives us information on how the benchmark scales with increasing memory.

SAPS can also be used to determine a rough price/performance measure; for example, a system capable of supporting twice the SAPS of another platform, while costing 1.5 times more, provides better price/performance. In practice, this kind of information is used by sizing partners to illustrate their particular platforms' capabilities. Figure 18.3 depicts a fictional chart comparing various hardware selections from different vendors based on their respective SAPS scores.

Tiers

SAP applications are implemented on multiple tiers, all or some of which can be installed on the same server or "box" (or multiple servers). The primary tiers are

▶ **Client tier**—This is the tier upon which the SAPGUI and other SAP user interface software components are installed to connect to SAP. The client tier is traditionally a desktop, laptop, or other front-end computing device that ultimately connects to an SAP business application by way of an intranet or Internet connection (the latter often accomplished through a VPN tunneling across several security firewalls).

▶ **Presentation tier**—This is the tier presented to the client when it connects to SAP and runs the web server (the SAPGUI, WebGUI, or other interface).

▶ **Middle, or Application, tier**—One or more middleware web components and SAP functional components sit on this tier. This is where all the business logic is implemented.

▶ **Database tier**—This is where the persistent (permanent, in that it's maintained on disk rather than in temporary memory) data is stored.

Performance per Processor

Sample SAP ERP Analysis

Sample Server Platforms	CPU Type	SAPS per CPU	Max Cores	Scaling Factor	SAPS for a system with 1-32 CPUs								
					1	2	4	6	8	12	16	20	24
Server 200	2000	800	4	0.92	1,600	3,072	5,672	0	0	0	0	0	0
Server 1000	1600	900	4	0.95	1,800	3,510	6,678	0	0	0	0	0	0
Server 2000	1600	500	8	0.92	1,000	1,920	3,545	4,921	6,085	0	0	0	0
	2200	750	8	0.92	1,500	2,880	5,318	7,381	9,127	0	0	0	0
	2400	950	8	0.92	2,660	5,107	6,736	9,349	11,561	0	0	0	0
Server 4000	2200	800	16	0.92	1,600	3,072	5,672	7,873	9,736	12,647	14,732	0	0
	2400	900	16	0.92	1,800	3,456	6,381	8,857	10,953	14,228	16,574	0	0
	2600	1000	16	0.92	3,200	6,144	11,344	15,746	12,170	15,808	18,415	0	0
Server 8000	2800	1000	16	0.95	2,000	3,900	7,420	10,596	13,463	18,386	22,395	0	
Server 16000	2500	1200	32	0.91	2,400	4,584	8,380	11,523	14,127	18,067	20,770	22,623	23,894
	3000	1400	32	0.91	5,600	10,696	19,553	26,888	32,962	42,157	48,463	52,787	55,752
Server 32000	3000	1450	32	0.94	8,700	16,878	31,791	44,969	56,613	75,992	91,122	102,935	112,157
	3200	2000	32	0.94	12,000	23,280	43,850	62,026	78,086	104,816	125,685	141,979	154,700

FIGURE 18.3   Charts depicting server models and SAPS make comparisons easier.

The back end (database) and the middle tier (application servers and web servers) can all reside on the same physical server if needed or on different servers. Picking one configuration over the other depends on several factors. The database tends to require higher availability and fault tolerance because it hosts the persistent data. In addition, application servers such as the central instance (CI, which handles messaging, spooling, and queuing of requests to the applications and so forth) require a similar level of failover capabilities to avoid trashing a transaction or having the entire system come down.

On the other hand, sometimes the rest of the application servers can be on commodity hardware, because SAP is fairly robust in shifting the load when a system goes down (whether planned for scheduled maintenance or unplanned). Good horizontal scaling of performance makes it feasible to add multiple hardware servers for application servers.

The database is often clustered for high availability (HA). Oracle has been pushing its Real Application Clusters (RAC) architecture for this purpose for a while now. However, using this configuration is not widely encouraged by SAP and has been unproven beyond a certain size (significant scaling issues are seen beyond four instances). As a result, customers typically go with a scale-up box in which to house the database.

Scale-Up and Scale-Out Configurations

Given that there are multiple tiers, if we add different functional components, we are faced with choices regarding various kinds of configurations. Traditionally we break the choice into one of scale up versus scale out. *Scale up* implies single big server system architectures, whereas *scale out* implies multiple smaller servers. Traditionally, enterprise SAP data center designers have preferred scale-up configurations, which are typified by large

18

RISC-based proprietary architectures from vendors such as HP, IBM, and Sun. The architectures provide support for a very high number of processor cores underpinning a single OS image. Multiple SAP tiers can run together. A big advantage of such systems is that the server consolidation that naturally falls out of such a design innately reduces system administration and management costs. These systems are also known to possess higher reliability features than their "small box" counterparts and so are preferred for the database tier at the very least. A large system such as the HP Superdome, for example, can often handle both the SAP application and database tiers together on the same system (and multiple SAP components, for that matter).

SAP's own architecture gives its customers a choice, however. SAP's business applications scale very well horizontally; the application tier can be installed across scale-out configurations which tend to be created from several smaller "commodity" servers. With the steady improvement in power and performance of x86 servers, this is fast becoming a configuration of choice for all but the largest systems. In fact, with the x86 processors staying ahead in bringing multiple cores per processor, it is easy to find eight-core processors in slim configurations such as the recently popular blade servers.

Blade servers bring further improvements in standardization and manageability that reduce the usual additional cost when dealing with multiple systems. The powerful servers can sometimes also handle the database tier. Having multiple systems can provide separate sandboxes for different functional components and can allow for additional capacity as needed by simply adding another box on the tier.

A third possibility is to combine the benefits of scale-up and scale-out management by hosting hardware and software partitions on a large box to separate the tiers. Most vendors' large servers provide for partitioning at different levels. Some examples are

▶ **Hardware partitioning**—A set of processors can be set up as a separate machine altogether. In some systems, such as HP's nPars using cell-based systems, these can be electrically separate as well.

▶ **Soft partitions**—Allow an independent OS-based sandbox (such as vPars) that provides partitions in multiples of processors.

▶ **Partitioning within a core**—The capability to split a single processor core into many micro-partitions (rather than allowing multiple partitions to span multiple cores). IBM's Power Architecture provides excellent micro-partitioning capabilities.

▶ **Virtual machines**—Allow for sub-CPU or multiple-CPU partitions to be configured across multiple processors at the same time.

These partitioning options enable you to put the different tiers on the same system.

High Availability, Reliability, and Fault Tolerance

Previously covered in depth in Chapter 15, various infrastructure options can be differentiated based on how much fault tolerance, reliability, and high availability (HA) they provide. We will see later in this chapter that vendors can map sizing requirements into different HA configurations. Often, to break the tie between multiple options, we look at the reliability, HA, and fault-tolerance capabilities of the configurations.

Heterogeneous Configurations

Homogenous SAP system architectures represent the bulk of SAP systems in place today. With the multiple choices available for the processor architectures as well as the operating systems supporting SAP, it is possible to create a heterogeneous configuration, however—a special architecture often called a *hybrid*. Hybrids are known for providing a moderate level of innovation at a moderate cost and thus fall smack in the middle of the computing platform innovation continuum. A classic example of a hybrid involves running the application tier on Microsoft Windows (or a SAP-supported Linux OS) on x86 servers while the database tier runs on HP-UX on an Itanium system (or a similar UNIX variant). Such a configuration can bring significant cost savings by keeping the servers that are essential to system availability—the database and the CI—on costlier though more highly available servers while spreading out the more risk-tolerant application servers on commodity hardware platforms. Hybrids are generally perceived as less innovative than their homogenous Windows and Linux counterparts, but more innovative than their mainframe or UNIX counterparts. Hybrids represent an excellent method of achieving a more equitable balance between availability and cost. However, such hybrid or heterogeneous configurations include hidden costs and complexities:

▶ The cost of systems administration with regard to supporting multiple environments (and their underlying technology stacks) adds up quickly.

▶ The hardware cost is provided for in depreciation over time; however, the need for multiple systems administrators with expertise in the different OS environments can be an additional cost, more than making up for the initial savings.

▶ Subtle differences exist in SAP versions and patches across multiple environments, complicating change control and release management.

▶ Although it's available on all the systems, SAP tends to have separate patch levels and even different release dates for primary versus secondary platforms, further complicating a firm's capability to consistently roll out updates and SAP upgrades.

▶ Failover solutions for HA solutions are complicated (if they work at all) when different operating environments are involved.

As discussed earlier, the database and the CI could be set up on a more reliable system. Typically, for HA, we would then set up a second identical system as a failover system. As a failover system, this second system would likely be unused most of the time. It makes economic sense to run other application servers on that system. This would leave these two systems with the database and some application servers, and it would be preferable to use the same architecture for other application servers given the earlier comments. All

18

these considerations should go into the total cost of ownership consideration when comparing solutions from multiple vendors.

Sizing the Installation

To model and predict the capacity needs of an installation, we must start by assessing the needs as accurately as possible. The first step is to measure what we can and estimate what we can't. There are two primary ways to size an installation: through questionnaires and through tools. When there is limited information, such as with new instances or when we don't have access to the systems (for example, if we are a third party), we need to rely on detailed questionnaires. Questionnaires can help establish an approximate baseline in a complex configuration. If we are resizing for upgrades or refreshes and have access to systems, we can use tools to measure the current capacity utilization, which can help with the sizing.

Typically we use a combination of techniques. For example, for initial sizing, we could supplement a questionnaire with actual measurements on a sample configuration using the primary transactions to be used in the instance. For resizing, we could first get an idea of the overall requirement from questionnaires, and then install a tool on the specific systems, such as HP's Discovery tools from the Mercury tools stack, to obtain actual performance information. The fastest and simplest mechanism for collecting a system's basic business requirements is found in SAP's own QuickSizer, explored next.

SAP QuickSizer

SAP provides a service called QuickSizer that, as the name suggests, helps you do some quick sizing to get a rough estimate of hardware requirements. It helps convert requirements spelled out in business terms to requirements spelled out in infrastructure terms.

The QuickSizer website is at http://service.sap.com/quicksizing. An SAP Service Marketplace ID is required to access this site (and indeed many of SAP's sites). You can register for a login ID, also known as an S-user ID because these IDs start with the letter *S*, at the Service Marketplace homepage (http://service.sap.com). Access is based on your SAP customer number and is controlled by an administrator at your company. Like all of SAP's protected sites, the QuickSizer service is free.

After you've logged in to the QuickSizer site, you can complete an online questionnaire by providing information such as number of users, expected response times, planned downtime, required uptime, and so on for the various SAP applications and modules to be used. At the end of the exercise, QuickSizer estimates hardware requirements in terms of CPU, memory, disk space, and network bandwidth. The server requirements are quoted in terms of an SAP-specific unit of measurement called *SAPS*, a platform-independent performance metric described in more detail earlier in the chapter.

Because QuickSizer assumes standard modules configured in standard ways and also 65% server load for optimal performance, additional guidelines are typically used to further refine its output. Often, the output can be compared to standard configurations for quick back-of-the-envelope planning for the SAP landscape. QuickSizer uses two independent models for sizing: user based and throughput based. The outputs of the two approaches in QuickSizer can vary. By using both approaches, we can get a better sense of what the real sizing needs are.

User-Based Sizing

When doing initial planning at a very early stage, one of the easiest values to estimate is that of the number of users. This value also maps well between business terms and technical terms. For example, a business can typically estimate to a high degree of accuracy the number of users who need to connect to an HR system.

The SAP QuickSizer provides sizing estimates based on this information, and this is typically the first step in sizing. However, user-based sizing suffers from the highest inaccuracy and can only be used as an approximation. The users of an SAP system may differ in terms of the type of access they have to the system and the number of operations they execute in a given amount of time. The variation per user is one of the main reasons it is difficult to size accurately. As discussed earlier in the chapter, we rely on definitions of low, medium, and high active users for sizing.

Throughput-Based Sizing

Throughput analysis requires more effort in the beginning to estimate input to QuickSizer but yields much more accurate results. This analysis requires expected data volume and throughput per component and business process, including the number of objects created and their frequency. This type of information tends to be available later in the planning process, so throughput analysis is done in the second phase when more details are available on the planned landscape.

Limitations of the QuickSizer Approach

Although QuickSizer is a very useful tool to do initial estimates in the face of limited data, it is not without its shortcomings. QuickSizer brings limitations and other issues to the sizing process, several of which are outlined here:

▶ QuickSizer makes a lot of assumptions about resource requirements based on transaction volumes and the vendor's estimates on how the transactions will utilize the resources. This contributes to a high degree of inaccuracy (in some cases as high as 40%), which is acknowledged by SAP, who suggests using both user- and throughput-based sizing to get at least two data points.

▶ SAPS and the mapping to various non-SD modules all rely on standard workloads, whereas in real life it is rare to find an application instance that mirrors these workloads closely.

▶ It is difficult to incorporate customization factors (such as the impact of custom programming, specially configured batch jobs, and so on). In general, customization can add an extra 30% worth of load to an SAP system.

18

- ▶ User response times are an important consideration for the customer; however, the SAP QuickSizer doesn't provide this information adequately, except indirectly through its "65% server utilization" assumption.

- ▶ One of the aims of QuickSizer is to provide vendor-independent output. This requires the vendor to provide the appropriate SAPS values, which are not always available for all kinds of servers or specific server configurations. This leads to more estimates.

- ▶ It is difficult to plan a landscape directly through QuickSizer. For example, the utility doesn't help model the best ways to combine various modules on the same hardware. QuickSizer sizes them as if they all use dedicated resources.

- ▶ Similarly, SAP QuickSizer doesn't help determine scale-out versus consolidation differences. Other factors such as system administration cost and spares availability are useful in choosing the appropriate landscape infrastructure.

It is for these reasons that better sizing approaches are used later in the project design to get more accurate results. In particular, QuickSizer is not used much for post-installation resizing exercises, except sometimes for quick back-of-envelope calculations. Other models are used to solve delta- and upgrade-sizing needs. Part of the reason is, with a production system in place already, it is far easier to get actual data based on real resource use with regard to the current set of users and throughput requirements for the customized installation.

The Questionnaire

SAP and its platform partners often use customized questionnaires or surveys to gather data related to sizing. The questionnaire is an interesting study for someone new to SAP infrastructure planning, because it also highlights the way one must approach planning a deployment or SAP platform migration. The online form provides a list of the various applications and modules in the left navigation pane and collects information on each of those applications and modules on the main page as you pick the specific module you plan to implement. If a module cannot be covered by QuickSizer, it provides a link that takes you to an offline document that provides information on how to size for that module. Questions that need to be answered are diverse, and may include providing the following information:

- ▶ Initial project information and customer data, dates, and so forth

- ▶ Choice of one or more of production, consolidation, and development systems

- ▶ The type of database, its version, and size of data

- ▶ The operating system name and version

- ▶ Any system-system communication requirements

- ▶ Definition of a workday as a range of specific hours

- ▶ Planned system uptime per weekday (and conversely unplanned downtime that is acceptable)

- Hard disk mirroring and RAID requirements (though often related to desired high availability, these data might also be requested from a system performance perspective)

- Backup process and frequency

- Hardware high availability, UPS and generator availability, and so forth

- Choice of failover server and configuration

- End-user network connection

- Server network connection

- Front-end elements such as SAPGUI and Web Dynpro for the various modules

As discussed earlier, QuickSizer provides both user- and throughput-based sizing. The user-based sizing tables take the number of low-, medium-, and high-usage concurrent users. The throughput-based sizing tables take actual SAP module objects into account. The results are delivered in terms of SAPS (discussed next), memory and disk (in megabytes), and I/O in terms of the number of inputs and outputs per second. In addition, the components are divided into categories labeled, as with clothing, XS, S, M, L, XL, and XXL. Such "T-shirt sizing" is especially common for newly introduced SAP applications. For example, up to 6,400 SAPS might equate to a CPU classified in the S category, while up to 12,800 might equate to CPUs in the M category.

Obtaining Vendor SAP Sizing Questionnaires

SAP developed the QuickSizer with the help of its primary hardware vendor partners. QuickSizer provides capacity requirements using platform-independent terms such as SAPS, gigabytes of disk space, megabytes of memory, and so forth. The customer then goes to the appropriate hardware vendor, who has other tools that take the SAPS values and helps the customer choose appropriate hardware elements. This is where the actual SAP landscape plan is generated.

The usual process is for the customer to fill out the SAP QuickSizer questionnaire, obtain an SAP-supplied project ID, and then pass the project ID to one or more platform vendors. The vendors then can apply further refinements to come up with the appropriate sizing (the sizing is therefore the output of the sizing process initiated by filling out a QuickSizer questionnaire). To assist them in creating a first-rate sizing, many vendors create customized vendor-specific sizing questionnaires, surveys, or sizing request forms; check with each vendor's SAP-specific Competence Centers to obtain detailed questionnaires (which complement QuickSizer by providing more detailed configuration choices). Most vendors' SAP Competency Centers and their sizing tools can be accessed online; in alphabetical order, these include

- **Bull**—http://www.bull.com/sapsizing

- **Dell**—http://www.dell.com/sapsizing

- **Fujitsu Siemens**—http://www.fujitsu-siemens.com/sap/quicksizing.html

18

- ▶ **HP**—http://h71028.www7.hp.com/enterprise/cache/42968-0-0-225-121.html

- ▶ **IBM**—http://www-03.ibm.com/support/techdocs/atsmastr.nsf/ 84279f6ed9ffde6f86256ccf00653ad3/906cb61e9729a72a8625707b0012ed15? OpenDocument

- ▶ **Sun**—https://www2.sun.de/dc/forms/reg_us_2302_906.jsp

- ▶ **Unisys**—http://www.unisys.com/about__unisys/partners/sap__alliance.htm

We generally recommend working with every vendor that has invested in an SAP compe-tence center (and therefore has specific expertise in designing well-performing highly available infrastructures for SAP), reflects your firm's IT hardware and software standards (or desired standards), and actively contributes to SAP's benchmark sites (inferring that the vendor is staying relatively current with regard to testing new computing platforms on the latest releases of SAP's software).

Using SAPS Values

The hardware vendors release SAPS values for specific configurations of their hardware platforms, enabling SAP's prospective customers to design a configuration themselves. A smarter approach is to directly engage each platform provider, give them the SAPS-based workload that needs to be hosted, and then let them use their tools and experience to design a system. The hardware vendors' sizer tools cover most hardware and OS combina-tions provided and supported by the vendors. For example, HP supports various combina-tions of operating systems such as HP-UX, Windows, and Linux on architectures such as Itanium, PA-RISC, and x86. HP's SAP Competency Center has access to SAPS values for the various hardware and OS combinations and uses that information as the basis for creating sizing or hardware template configurations (also called reference architectures). Some of these values are publicly available through SAP SD (Sales and Distribution) benchmark submissions. Other SAPS values are internally measured by the vendor (and not published) or are extrapolated from previous platforms based on new system processor speed and other system differences.

By way of example, let's examine two benchmark submissions—Certification #2006067 published by HP and certification #2006065 published by Sun (incidentally, the certifica-tion numbers themselves are nothing more than a way for SAP to track individual plat-form benchmark results). These two submissions were two months apart, reflected two-tier submissions, and were based on identical dual-core AMD Opteron 2.8GHz processors running SAP ERP 2004 on Windows Server 2003. Although the two systems (HP's DL585 G2 and Sun Fire x4600) fit in identical 4u form factors, the HP system had only half as many cores as the Sun system (8 versus 16) and only half the memory (32GB versus 64GB). Still, the HP system reported a higher SAPS figure (1978 versus 1650). As a result, it can be surmised that the HP system supports more than twice the number of users per core (495 versus 206), a fact attributable to hardware and software optimization factors well beyond mere processor speed. It is for this exact reason that SAP benchmarks can be so useful—it's not enough to compare platform vendors based on processor speed or the number of configured processors.

An SAP SD benchmark takes into account much more than a relatively "small" benchmark such as SPECint takes into account. Each of these factors acts like an extra knob that can be appropriately tuned to obtain optimal performance. We list some of these factors later in this chapter, but this is by no means an exhaustive list. Although analyzing the value or configuration of a platform factor toward the overall performance seems possible when we examine similar configurations, it can only be done qualitatively. For an actual quantitative differentiation, we need to do the experiments on the same system, while tweaking only one knob at a time, to really gain an understanding of how well one platform compares to another.

CPU, Memory, Disk I/O, and Networking Performance

A two-tier SD benchmark presents a relatively uniform CPU-intensive load on the system. During the high phase of the benchmark, average CPU utilization should be close to 99%. Less than 10% of all cycles are in the OS kernel, including interrupt handlers. The database normally accounts for 5% to 10% of all cycles. The remaining CPU cycles—roughly 85%—are consumed by SAP work processes.

Like most SAP R/3 and ERP code, the transactions executed by the benchmark are written in SAP's ABAP programming language and stored in byte-code format on the database. As a result, the work processes spend a large portion of their time in the core ABAP interpreter modules and in the standard C library code, most importantly the memcpy() and memcmp() functions.

SAP tends to scale very well horizontally, so increasing the number of CPUs can provide an excellent jump in performance. Compared with more database-intensive workloads, such as the well-known TPC-C benchmark published by the Transaction Processing Performance Council (see http://www.tpc.org/), the SD benchmark has a relatively small cache footprint. On the full 16-cell (128-core) platform configuration, the data cache miss rate is less than 1.3 misses per 1,000 instructions. The disk I/O rate is relatively low, averaging around 70Mbps, roughly 65% of which is made up of sequential writes to the Oracle log file.

Total network traffic is in the range of 230Mbps, or a little over 1Kbps per user. If Gigabit Ethernet connections are used, this can be handled without making the network a bottleneck. For a two-tier system, the dialog servers communicate with the database on the same box, so networking issues decrease further.

Operating Systems

Because most of the computations happen in user space, the kernel doesn't take up significant cycles for an SD benchmark. However, the OS can provide other features that can affect the benchmark results. For example, for large systems, cell local memory usage or hyperthreading support can increase the performance enough to beat another vendor's product.

The other area in which the OS is significant is in handling the scalability as the number of software threads and processes increases to accommodate rising load. The capability to manage multiple kernel threads and the development of efficient OS schedulers help ensure that an OS's performance can scale up well as the workload increases.

Database Versions

Although most databases (DB2, Oracle, MaxDB, and SQL Server) are supported on all major operating systems, some are not. For example, Microsoft SQL Server is supported only on specific Microsoft Windows platforms. Thus, if the database is selected first, it can limit which OSs may be selected.

All relational database management systems (RDBMSs) exhibit their own performance strengths and weaknesses in specific parts of a transaction. So it should be no surprise that the database release and configuration play a major role in SAP benchmark scores. There are submissions for Oracle, DB2, SQL Server, and MaxDB, on multiple platforms, and the scores differ on the same hardware configuration when the RDBMS is noted as one of the only differences. As an example, we can look at two submissions made by HP on the eight-core Itanium2 rx6600 Server. They differed in terms of the OS and RDBMS that were used; one was based on Windows Server 2003 with SQL Server 2005, while the other used HP-UX 11i v3 with Oracle Database 10g. The Microsoft solution boasted 7,730 SAPS supporting 1,523 users, while the Unix/Oracle combination supported 10,780 SAPS and 2,150 users. A subsequent SQL Server 2005 submission on rx6600 boosted its score up to 8,680 SAPS. It's clear that the Unix/Oracle solution was faster. What's unclear is whether the difference in performance can be attributed to the difference in OS or the difference in database software. Locating a published Windows/Oracle benchmark on the same hardware platform would be more telling.

A submission on the four-core rx2660 Server running HP-UX 11i v3 and IBM DB2 database showed 5,480 SAPS, nearly half of the eight-core Oracle Database 10g result, suggesting that the two databases perform similarly for this benchmark on HP-UX. Differences can also be seen in major version changes for the same database. Oracle Database 10g showed a big jump in performance. Some of the difference can be attributed to the major code changes that went into the release. Others come from better utilization of resources provided by the OS and the hardware. For example, Oracle Database 10g R1 and later support technologies that automatically boost performance on a multicell box such as the rx8640 Server or an HP Superdome.

Fostering Apples-to-Apples Sizings

The actual sizing process can be a bit more involved. Various additional factors are added as needed to obtain more accurate sizing. Some of these are system independent. For example, different releases bring their own multiples to be added to the configuration as the transactions get heavier (need more processing power) with each release. That is, a server capable of hosting 1,000 SAPS running SAP R/3 3.1i can support only 530 SAPS with R/3 Enterprise and fewer than 400 SAPS with SAP ERP. Said another way, each subsequent release of SAP's software requires greater platform horsepower to support the same number of users. Similarly, the impact of Unicode requires more beefy server and storage systems to host the same workload.

For these reasons, it is very important to use platform-independent metrics to make a sensible comparison of the capacity and performance capabilities of two completely different configurations. This is why most vendors' SAP Competency Centers initiate the sizing process via the standard QuickSizer questionnaire already filled out by the customer—calculating the number of SAPS a particular platform can support levels the playing field.

Production System Sizing Rules of Thumb

Production systems are typically sized with great attention to the HA and redundancy options available, depending of course on business requirements and IT budgets. This may therefore include hot spare disk drives, hot-pluggable redundant power supplies, redundant network interface cards (NICs) and other controllers, redundant fans, various clustering options, and so on, as outlined here:

- ▶ A replicated database, log-shipping solution, or cluster is typically recommended for production. Although HA options are nearly endless, the need to address the two greatest single points of failure—the database server and SAP central instance—is undisputable.

- ▶ Systems that support hot-pluggable RAM and PCI slots may be important (to help avoid an in-the-box internal server failure that requires a time-consuming server failover simply to keep the SAP system up and running).

- ▶ For maximum performance, the database volume is often configured for RAID 0+1 or 1+0 (thus providing maximum read and write performance as well as the highest level of disk redundancy compared to RAID 5), though this doubles the number of drives, storage systems, and RAID controllers—and therefore cost.

- ▶ For drives located internally in a server, it's preferable to either protect these via mirroring or to include a hot spare. Note that hot spares can almost always be configured to support multiple logical drives, making it easy to support SAP's best practices with regard to separating the OS partition from other partitions.

- ▶ Multiple RAID controllers and/or host bus adapters (HBAs) are often configured, one for the internal OS and paging or swapping partitions, one for executables and logs, and one or more for the actual database volume(s). At minimum, at least two disk controllers and HBAs must be specified—one for the database volume and one for all others.

- ▶ All disk drives should be standardized on a specific speed (for example, 10,000- or 15,000-RPM drives), form factor (for example, a 1" form factor), and so on.

18

▶ A hardware platform-specific minimum of drives should be configured for RAID solutions. More disk spindles always equates to better performance. If in doubt, always select a greater number of smaller-capacity drives rather than fewer larger drives.

▶ To provide maximum performance and availability to the database volume, split the drives as equally as possible across multiple fiber or small computer system interface (SCSI) channels and server I/O buses.

▶ Don't forget to architect a highly available SAN infrastructure. Redundant HBAs, fiber cables, and switches are required for the highest levels of availability.

▶ The default 50/50 read/write ratio for most disk controllers should not be changed unless testing is performed within the customer's specific online transaction processing (OLTP) or online analytical processing (OLAP) environment. Only one exception exists: If the logs reside on a dedicated controller, they may be configured for maximum write performance.

▶ In the past, SAP typically recommended 4KB blocks (or allocation units—at an OS level, which is the default in Windows-based systems). However, testing performed by Microsoft and a number of technology partners has confirmed that 64KB block sizes can increase performance quite dramatically—this is most true when it comes to data volumes (continue to use 4KB for log volumes and other write-intensive volumes).

▶ In large systems servicing 500+ concurrent users, the redo logs or transaction logs should be striped across multiple drives (RAID 0+1) rather than simply across a single pair of drives. For Oracle systems, the origA and origB logs should reside on their own pair(s) of drives, and their size may be increased. These logs are also prime candidates for dedicated array controllers configured for maximum write performance.

▶ Often in production environments, dedicated batch, update, or CI servers are configured, to allow the database server extra headroom (single-function principle).

▶ In terms of CPUs, the use of larger second-level caches benefits both DB servers and application servers. However, the cost incurred in fitting application servers (where memory is typically more important than raw processing power) with processors featuring a large second-level cache typically precludes doing so. Rather, a greater number of smaller-cache processors will serve as well (or better perhaps).

▶ Extra RAM in the database server allows more data to be cached, and hence fewer physical database reads are required once these DB buffers are filled. As always, more RAM is always better!

Beyond HA and other fault tolerant solutions and approaches, sizing methodologies differ in other ways. A closer look at several sizing methodologies is in order.

Understanding Different Sizing Methodologies

SAP sizing can be divided into two main categories: new instance sizing and existing instance resizing (also called post-go-live resizing). Sometimes a new piece of functionality (such as the addition of warehousing or logistics) is added to an existing instance, and that would constitute a new instance sizing. There are various techniques available to carry out these two types of sizing, covered next.

New Instance Sizing

As we start out with a new project, we need to perform sizing for the new SAP instance. Depending on the stage of the project and available information, the sizing process is typically divided into three categories, shown here in increasing order of available information and accuracy:

- **Initial or budgetary sizing**—Also known as high-level user-based sizing, this is typically done at a very early stage of the project when very little detail is available. The planners have a rough idea of the number of users who will interact with the system and some idea of the load expected. This helps develop a high-level hardware and landscape infrastructure plan, and it helps identify the initial solution budget.

- **Detailed throughput-based sizing**—This happens closer to the actual implementation when a lot more detail is available, including a good idea of the required throughput. This sizing is also used to estimate resources for batch-oriented workloads. To come up with the CPU requirements, we look at the actual transactions and documents involved and analyze the number of transactions and documents that must be processed per hour for each of the modules to be used by the business processes. Typically, this stage uses detailed questionnaires and tools to develop a much more accurate picture of an SAP system's underpinning infrastructure.

- **Custom sizing**—Whereas detailed sizing still uses standard modules and application information and assumptions, custom or expert sizing takes into account specific customizations required for this specific instance. This provides the most accurate data and can involve running tests on a sample configuration for high accuracy. In some cases, such as when multiple instances need to be implemented, expert sizing can involve performing initial and detailed sizing on the individual instances and then estimating the overall CPU needs from that. Such an exercise might not take much more time than doing the initial and detailed sizing. When multiple tests need to be performed, the resource and people requirements depend on the size of the tests involved and the number of cycles.

Post-Go-Live Resizing

When an SAP instance is up and running, we still might need to do a sizing exercise based on changing requirements. The six most common triggers are

- **Usage changes**—As the organization's needs change, the expected load on the system can change. This can lead to the existing system reaching the limits of its capacity, or going the other way, leading to wasted capacity. A resizing exercise here can help change the landscape to a more optimal infrastructure.

- ▶ **Changes in user counts**—The number of users accessing SAP can increase (due to merger or acquisition activity or simply from organic growth) or shrink (due to divestures or large-scale work force reductions) over time.

- ▶ **Platform changes**—Many organizations refresh their hardware platforms every three to five years. If the system's workload and applications remain constant, even the most basic platform change warrants a resizing (if only to avoid spending too much on the new platform).

- ▶ **Functionality changes**—Over time, new modules and applications can be added to the mix, or some of the existing functionality might be retired due to reorganization and its migration elsewhere. This would trigger the need for resizing.

- ▶ **New releases**—SAP AG updates its product versions about every two years. The enterprise might decide to move to the new release to use newer functionality or to get off an extended maintenance contract. This is one of the most common reasons for a resizing exercise. SAP AG publishes the expected changes in infrastructure utilization depending on the upgrade versions.

- ▶ **Special projects**—A company might decide to do a UNICODE migration, OS/DB migration, or other project that impacts a combination of platform technologies and functional characteristics. A resizing is essential to ensuring that the new system provides the performance expected by the end user community.

Of the different sizing techniques just described, the QuickSizer aims at budgetary sizing and throughput sizing. A QuickSizer process is typically executed early so that hardware planning can continue in parallel while the rest of the implementation, upgrade, or migration planning is put in place. There are other strategies or further refinement depending on specific needs. The following are some of these strategies:

- ▶ **Expert sizing**—When there are complex configurations and high-volume instances, several techniques are used for sizing, such as averaging multiple QuickSizer outputs to see how different instances would work together. If standard interfaces are used to connect with other SAP instances or with other applications such as Oracle CRM, we look at the size of typical IDocs to come up with sizing factors as well as proper network sizing.

- ▶ **Customer benchmark**—When there is a lot of custom code (often called *Z-ABAP* or *custom ABAP*), performing sizing using standard techniques is notoriously difficult. A single poorly coded Z-ABAP can slow the entire system significantly for a specific transaction. In such cases, it is better to benchmark the actual code and assess the change in system resource utilization as the load increases, and then revisit the sizing process.

Predictive Modeling for Precision Sizing

Approximate sizing works quite well for a lot of organizations' needs, especially as hardware prices continue to come down and it's preferable to keep extra capacity in case of demand spikes. However, rising power costs and data center consolidation efforts erode some of that extra capacity and more precise sizing may be needed using predictive models.

Companies such as HP, IBM, and Hyperformix have developed extensive modeling tools that make it easier to input various factors that relate to sizing. These models can then be analyzed relative to changes in resource needs as the load and user counts/characteristics change. Such models allow you to add other factors that would not normally be handled by standard techniques. For example, we can add requirements for management tools and use the models to better assess between the choice of scale-up and scale-out configurations. Predictive modeling also helps catch capacity issues before they happen. Though they claim around 90% accuracy in their assessments, they can be quite expensive to use.

Summary

After reviewing the sizing process, we defined relevant terms, discussed scale-up versus scale-out configurations, and outlined several important choices surrounding availability. Then we looked at the SAP sizing questionnaire and SAP's QuickSizer utility in particular. A discussion of SAP's hardware-independent method of evaluating different platforms was followed by discussions of CPU, memory, disk I/O, network, OS, and database factors, followed by general sizing best practices, limitations of the SAP QuickSizer, and production system sizing rules of thumb. Sizing methodologies and predictive modeling discussions concluded the chapter, setting the stage for the next chapter focused on actually sizing SAP solutions.

Case Study: Resizing at a Subsidiary

A subsidiary of HiTech, Inc. is seeking to replatform to reduce its total cost of ownership, and they are considering buying less-expensive commodity hardware for this effort. The subsidiary wishes to transition its SAP ERP environment off an aging and increasingly expensive RISC-based IBM platform. Based on its growing in-house expertise with Linux and Oracle, the subsidiary believes retaining its Oracle Database 10g and transitioning to Red Hat Enterprise Linux would be cost effective. The change in OS and hardware necessitates an SAP resizing. As the IT solution architect responsible for the system's availability and performance, you have decided to engage the SAP customer team at Red Hat directly but you have several other questions and have thus considered asking several hardware partners for help.

Questions

1. Which hardware partners should be consulted?

2. How can you ensure that competing hardware partners create SAP sizings that can be compared with one another?

18

3. What is the relationship between named users and concurrent users?

4. When is user-based sizing most appropriate?

NOTE

The answers to these questions can be found in Appendix A, "Case Study Answers."

CHAPTER 19

Conducting the SAP Platform Sizing Process

The previous chapter introduced the concept of sizing SAP systems and discussed the various intricacies involved in determining the appropriate infrastructure. In this chapter, we extend these discussions to include the actual process of sizing.

Primarily, the sizing process involves the following steps:

1. Analyze the company's current and future system requirements.
2. Prepare a basic requirements document and supplement it with SAP QuickSizer data.
3. Prepare a short list of a set of vendors and send an RFP (Request for Proposal) to them.
4. Review and respond to the questionnaires submitted by the vendors.
5. Receive the proposals and review them to select the appropriate vendor.

This process is outlined in detail throughout the chapter.

Analyzing System Requirements

The first step in SAP sizing is to analyze a system's need for resources, which in turn is related to determining how the system's business requirements will be satisfied with information technologies—servers, disk resources, network resources, and so on.

In almost all cases, you will find that the current set of capacity and performance needs differs from what you will need in the future. SAP systems tend to grow, except when a company is divesting itself of a business unit and needs to spin it off as a separate company and therefore a separate SAP system. With growth comes the need for additional CPU, memory, disk, and other hardware resources across several different servers—the database server, the SAP central instance (CI), and any number of SAP application servers, web servers, interface servers, servers used for other bolt-on systems, and so on.

This growth is normally associated with the production system. Beyond the production system, though, the supporting systems such as test, development, staging, training, and so on need to be sized and configured based on their own end-user requirements. For example, a development system might need to be sized for 15 ABAP developers and 5 Java developers, whereas a training system might be earmarked for teaching 40 SAP Financials users.

Down the road, a system must support growth or already be configured for a particular amount of processing headroom. It's typical to size an SAP business application to support three years of system growth. The term "growth" in this case refers not only to the size of the database and the raw number of users accessing the system, but also to the increased complexity in business processes over time (which requires additional horsepower to run essentially the same transaction year over year).

The Requirements Document and Supplementing with SAP QuickSizer

We recommend the following steps be completed to acquire a general SAPS value for each SAP component. With a reasonable SAPS value, you will be in a position to share your workload with SAP computing platform vendors in such a way as to obtain sizings from each of them that in turn can be compared with one another.

▶ For existing SAP environments, obtain an SAP EarlyWatch report that tracks CPU and memory utilization on each server in the landscape (particularly the database server, CI, and online application servers). This can be used to estimate SAPS.

▶ For existing environments, obtain SAP Computing Center Management System (CCMS) data, which is useful in identifying the average and peak online and batch workloads throughout the year. This can be used to estimate the SAPS value as well.

▶ Identify a particular class of server, obtaining its SAPS rating from the vendor's or SAP's website. If the rating is not available, it is necessary to extrapolate the values based on comparable systems. This information can be used to further improve the estimated SAPS values attained from the previous two steps for existing environments. For new environments, this can be used to match servers to SAPS estimates found through other means.

▶ Complete the QuickSizer form for the component to obtain a SAPS number that can be compared with the information previously gathered. To be conservative, select the largest of the SAPS values determined through the multiple steps outlined earlier.

▶ Estimate the level of customization and add a percentage to the SAPS value. The greater the level of customization, the more SAPS required to host the workload.

For each component, provide this information, including the resulting SAPS values, to each computing platform vendor. Along with this data, provide any high availability (HA) and reliability requirements, space and power considerations, preferences related to scale out versus scale up, OS and database preferences (if any), and so on. You must send the sizing requirements and the QuickSizer Project ID to the vendors so that they can respond with their vendor-specific proposals. As discussed in the previous chapter, the vendors will respond with their own sizing questionnaires as well. Vendor-specific questionnaires typically help support or give more credence to what was already provided via the QuickSizer.

The Requirements and Sizing Review Team

The initial requirements document might be generated by the SAP solution architect and the SAP project manager working with other stakeholders to gather requirements. At an early stage, that might be enough, but as the process moves forward (for example, when the time comes to respond to vendor proposals), you need to have more involvement from the various IT and business organizations. This participation increases on behalf of a sizing review team over time, until the final SAP configuration is agreed upon.

Ideally, the sizing review team needs representation from the following groups:

- ▶ Project and senior management

- ▶ SAP architecture

- ▶ HR, sales, and other departments with functional needs

- ▶ Solution- or business-specific software architects (such as those who support companywide reporting solutions)

- ▶ Database administration

- ▶ Data center facilities, operations, and systems management

- ▶ Vendors representing other key infrastructure (for example, when the disk subsystem vendor differs from the SAP server vendor, or in the case of heterogeneous server configurations)

- ▶ IT and help desk support organizations

Each of the groups plays a role in either defining initial business requirements or supporting the system after it's up and running.

Management, SAP Architecture, and Functional Needs

The SAP project manager oversees the review team and is responsible for the entire process. It is her responsibility to ensure appropriate buy-in from senior management and all important stakeholders. It is important to have an escalation process to resolve issues arising from conflicting requirements from different stakeholders. Many a project has been derailed at a later stage because appropriate stakeholders were not involved early enough to weigh in on key decisions.

Typically, the next in command is the SAP solutions architect who owns the technical aspects of the requirements and implementation of the vendor's solution. The solutions architect may work with other functional owners based on the size of the installation, which can range from a single department instance to the company's worldwide SAP installation.

Requirements come from different departments who expect to see an increase or decrease in capacity needs. For example, the sales department might require increased business intelligence, so SAP NetWeaver BW might require more capacity and increased network bandwidth between it and the SAP ERP system. Also, the various departments are important stakeholders and, at the very least, need to ensure that their current needs will continue to be met after any changes. So you will need representatives from each of these departments.

Third-Party Software

SAP is but one of the enterprise software packages running in a company's data center. Most companies tend to have solutions that work with different applications. Common examples are reporting software that works across SAP, Siebel, companywide calendaring, and a whole host of other applications. To avoid disruption with these solutions, you need to ensure that any specific requirements of such software are handled in the proposed solution from the vendor. Some of these might run only on specific operating systems at specific patch levels, for example, and the solution might need to handle that. You accordingly need appropriate representation from architects owning those solutions. Keeping them out of the loop and not taking their requirements into consideration can be a very costly and time-consuming mistake.

Database and SAP Basis Administration

The DBA and SAP Basis administrators are very important, both in terms of providing requirements and in reviewing the vendors' proposals. The database is clearly a very important part of the SAP technology stack, and the sizing requirement takes into account not only the DB software but also the hardware and disk capacity and performance needs.

It is also important to review the vendor's solution to see if the required database software version will run on it. For example, some of the older SAP versions, such as ERP 4.7, tend to support older Oracle database versions, and some of the newer hardware and OSs provide only limited support to those versions.

Similarly, the DBAs and Basis administrators weigh in on solutions that differ in hardware configurations such as those that include clusters of many small server blades versus those predicated on fewer large (scale-up) systems. If there are other applications that also access the SAP database directly, they need to be taken into consideration as well.

Data Center and Systems Administration

Any vendor's solution needs to fit into an existing data center, and thus it is very important to have someone who is knowledgeable about the various policies as well as the capacity available in the data center. Specifically, you must ensure that your requirements include information about the following:

- ▶ **Data center power**—Modern servers have very high power requirements, and some of the aging data centers cannot handle them.

- ▶ **Cooling requirements**—As a corollary of the preceding point, some data centers cannot handle dense solutions such as blades because they don't have appropriate cooling capabilities. Together these can restrict the density allowed by racks.

- ▶ **Floor space**—You need to know whether you can get floor space for the entire solution together or need to split it into multiple locations within one data center or even into multiple data centers.

- ▶ **Hardware models and architecture**—There might be restrictions on specific models to ensure optimal use of spare parts and so forth; similarly, a data center might support only specific architectures such as Itanium2, PowerPC, Intel x86, and so on.

- ▶ **Software policy**—Some companies have strict policies on what software can run in the data center; you need to ensure that the solution proposed by the vendor only requires software that's on the approved list.

- ▶ **Systems administration capability**—Having multiple hardware architectures and OSs leads to extra cost in managing them. This requirement may even enforce specific platforms, such as the use of one Linux distribution over another.

- ▶ **Networking architecture**—Based on the interconnectivity available within a rack and between racks, you might have restrictions in distributing load across multiple servers versus keeping it all within one.

- ▶ **Systems management software**—Management of the entire data center may be done from one management dashboard, such as that of HP OpenView or IBM Tivoli. This might have requirements to ensure that software is supported by the vendor's solution.

Most if not all of these requirements can be collected ahead of time through various checklists and interviews with the help of the Basis administrator. They can then be fed into initial requirements. You also need participation from the data center administrator to verify that the requirements have been met in the vendor's solution. Some requirements, such as restricted software policy, can be critical, because if a preferred solution has a software product that is not on such a list, you will need to initiate the process to get it on that list as early as possible.

19

Help Desk Factors

When things go wrong, the SAP Help Desk is called upon to resolve the issues. It is accordingly very important to keep this support organization in the loop as you go through the sizing process. Ensure that all steps in your change management process are followed and that you have representatives who can speak on behalf of the service desk. Management must validate that the support staff has adequate training in the various technologies being proposed by the vendors, and identify technology gaps. The cost of filling in those gaps through training might be a factor in the selection of one vendor versus another.

Team Factors and Representation

Several of the roles described as part of the sizing review team may be carried out by the same person or handed over to one person to act in proxy. You could, for example, have one person who understands the data center's power and cooling needs and the network and floor capacity. The same person could also be aware of the common dashboard software in use to manage the entire data center. Similarly, you could have the solution architect act as proxy for the various departments, having met them individually during initial assessment of your requirements. Because sizing is an iterative process, you might already have several partners in mind for both SAP- and non-SAP-based technologies. It is useful to keep a representative of each of these partners on the team so that all requirements are fully covered.

Having a more complete list of people allows for, hopefully, more complete requirements being sent in response to the vendor's questionnaire. You can sometimes save a lot of time through a conference call with everyone available to answer the questions that arise. The flip side of that is total chaos if such meetings are not managed right and if there are conflicting requirements. Also, in the 24x7 world that we live in now, getting all the stakeholders on a conference call at the same time could be quite a challenge, especially if it also includes representatives from other vendors.

In case of a large distributed team, you can, as discussed, have one person act as proxy for others, especially for groups with similar needs. And you can use more asynchronous means of communication, such as passing the questionnaire around in email to get responses from people in different time zones. Although this can add to the workload when analyzing multiple questionnaires, any effort put in at this time is useful in the long run. The other alternative is to use automated tools to gather a lot of the information (when you are looking to expand existing capacity) and use the meetings for more specific information.

RFPs, Vendor Questionnaires, and More

In the next few sections, we take a closer look at gathering sizing requirements through the use of vendor-specific questionnaires, the Request for Proposal (RFP) process, and conducting presizing conferences. We also review an alternative approach to sizing—allowing vendors to drive the sizing process.

Sending Out Requests for Proposal

Based on the specific current and future needs, you need to prepare a basic requirements document reflecting as much information as currently available regarding system and workload requirements. This very basic Request for Proposal process is often initiated with SAP's QuickSizer tool, as outlined in the last chapter. With the QuickSizer, you identify as much detailed information as you can about your expected system configuration. Once finished, you are provided a QuickSizer ID that can be shared with your internal sizing review team, the overall Technical Support Organization (TSO), and prospective vendors.

Next, you need to create a short list of vendors. Several factors go into selecting a vendor, including past relationships and experience, as well as who currently provides computing infrastructure in the data center. Big enterprises tend to favor renewing and extending existing contracts because of other benefits such as strategic relationships, platform standardization, and uniformity of systems management tools. At this stage, you might want to cast a wider net, however, so that you can obtain (and leverage against one another) multiple competing proposals. The more SAP sizing configurations available to review, the broader the selection of potential solutions.

You may start out with a basic requirements document and improve it iteratively as you gather more inputs from different stakeholders. Based on the information you provide to the vendor, you would get its own version of the questionnaire to supplement your information and the QuickSizer information. SAP QuickSizer asks high-level platform-independent questions and generates requirements in terms of SAPS. The vendors' questionnaires take this to the next step by analyzing more details and coming up with an appropriate architecture that maps SAPS needs to the various hardware systems in their repertoire, along with other considerations.

The Vendor Questionnaire

Responding to the vendor questionnaire is a critical step, and it needs to be completed well. You might have opportunities to make up for anything missing in subsequent steps, but you would be coming up with some requirements later anyway, so you should ensure that everything known today is well captured in the response. Because you might have questionnaires from multiple vendors and because responding to each questionnaire gets tedious, you might want to continue to add to your initial requirements document so that questions asked in the other questionnaires can simply be responded to using a new version of that document. This also improves your knowledge repository for all future requirements.

As you figure out the responses to the various questions, you need to communicate them back to the vendor. This step is also critical, because the vendors will be designing a solution based on your responses, so accuracy is essential to avoid future iterations. It is helpful to overcommunicate at this stage, and you might want live, in-person meetings or conference calls to ensure that everyone's on the same page.

Sometimes, it is preferable to have multiple vendors in a conference call simultaneously. If this can be pulled off, given other factors such as secrecy of RFPs, you can save time by providing updated information to all of them together. Your representation would at least

19

include the SAP project manager and the solution architect, though others could participate on the call as silent members.

Presizing Conference Call

It is quite helpful to conduct a presizing conference call with each vendor in which you can outline your priorities, discuss biases, identify the skill sets and experience you already have in-house that will prove relevant to managing and supporting SAP, and address just about everything discussed in this chapter thus far. A conference call can provide a lot of this information in a single snapshot. Here are several items worth considering in such a call:

▶ Provide solution vision, SAP Business Suite components and NetWeaver products to be implemented, business drivers, project timelines, key milestones, and other project-specific data.

▶ Determine whether this new SAP component to be sized is being integrated with an existing SAP landscape, replacing a current system, or simply refreshing a current system. This is critical information for vendors providing their solutions.

▶ Review the requirements document, QuickSizer data, vendor questionnaires, and all other communications to ensure that everyone's on the same page, including their understanding of the system's anticipated workload, their definition of "users," and their assumptions relative to batch jobs, integration points, availability requirements, and so on.

▶ Review priorities in terms of total cost of ownership (TCO), performance, availability, scalability, and manageability. The prioritization differences can lead to very different architectures for large and complex installations.

▶ With the help of data center representatives, discuss the limitations in terms of architectures and OSs as well as preferences in terms of scale-up versus scale-out configurations. Also include software limitations such as database software and specific versions.

▶ Just like the limitations above, also discuss opportunities and advantages to capitalize on available skillsets for specific OSs and specific versions of software. This is also a good time to show bias toward costly software for which you already own licenses.

▶ Discuss your tolerance for risk in terms of whether a conservative approach is preferred over a more risky approach (either from a high-level platform selection or specific platform configuration perspective).

▶ Clarify your sensitivity to accuracy in sizing, and whether you're comfortable with very general sizing practices, sizing for optional (unspecified) systems such as business sandboxes or training systems, and so forth. Pay particular attention to how the development, test, and production systems have been sized.

▶ Ensure that the database is sized appropriately for each landscape system (production, development, training, test, and so on).

▶ Address any expected changes in the next year or two so that the sizing exercise does not have to be repeated soon. Provide the vendors with all known changes coming your way, including increase in capacity need and number of users due to seasonal variations, data center consolidation, company mergers, and so on.

▶ Describe in detail current client access mechanisms that will continue to be relevant under new sizing needs.

▶ Disclose preferential vendor relationships. An SAP instance involves several software and hardware components and services. The vendor's solution might involve relationships and partnerships it has with different vendors. If you have preferential relationships with some such vendors and/or have already selected some, you should provide that information to the vendor early on. This can help it formulate its plans accordingly and even decide not to participate if it works with other partners.

▶ Discuss acceptance, stress, and other testing plans and strategies with the vendors so that it is clear ahead of time what is acceptable. This is also a good time to push for a proof-of-concept, especially for new or radically changing infrastructure solutions.

▶ Provide clarifications, if any, on answers to the questionnaires, based on vendors' feedback on the responses.

▶ Discuss the preliminary roadmap and next steps.

The Vendor-Driven Sizing Approach

The previous section described a general guideline for initial discussions; in reality, there could be more points of clarification. But in the spirit of overcommunication to ensure less delays and surprises later, you should try to get everyone on the same page. From your vendor's or service provider's perspective, the same questions can be asked in a different manner:

▶ Why are you implementing SAP? Business reasons will impact landscape decisions, performance and service-level factors, and other considerations.

▶ Are you interested in a low-cost, maximum-value solution? Price sensitivity will drive platform decisions.

▶ Is overall performance and response time the driving factor behind the configuration? The best-performing disk subsystems, RAID (redundant array of inexpensive disks) configurations, and server configurations might be called for.

▶ Is overall availability of the system critical or simply important? How many nines of availability are you looking for? This directly impacts technology decisions related to HA and DR options, along with a host of people and process considerations.

▶ Does your company anticipate growing or shrinking via acquisitions, mergers, or divestitures in the near term? What about long term? These factors impact the need

19

for solution scalability or the ability to easily redeploy and repurpose assets as they are no longer needed.

▶ Is the IT team biased toward one OS over another? It's not uncommon for Unix-focused IT organizations to find other OSs unpalatable.

▶ Is the IT team biased toward a particular database or RDBMS platform? Similar to OS biases, IT teams with history and experience with a particular database product may find competing products unpalatable.

▶ Is the IT team biased toward a particular hardware vendor? As in the OS and database realms, rivalries and favorites exist in this realm.

▶ Do you want the "latest and greatest" technology? The need or desire for the hottest technologies and solutions must be understood.

▶ What level of expertise do you have in regard to implementing and supporting SAP? This experience may drive specification of a particular technology stack or solution approach.

▶ Do you understand the role of, or need for, a technical sandbox for your SAP system landscape? Or training system? An organization's realization of the value such secondary systems provides helps communicate the organization's maturity.

▶ Will you be implementing another SAP component shortly after this system? If yes, this might drive adoption of platforms with a longer lifecycle, or development of a more well-developed standardized platform.

▶ Who has been selected as your systems integration partner or functional/business process partner? This can also drive platform adoption (based on its expertise or core competencies), though it really should have no bearing one way or the other.

▶ Who is your hardware reseller, or are you buying direct? This can indicate price sensitivity and, to some extent, partners and, indirectly, their competencies.

▶ Do you expect to implement any vertical industry solutions as part of your SAP solution? Which ones? This drives core sizing in terms of CPU, RAM, and disk requirements.

▶ What do you perceive to be the greatest risk in implementing this SAP system? This will identify priorities, weaknesses, and other useful information.

▶ Will you be stress-testing the proposed solution prior to go-live? Why or why not? This is a measure of how risk-averse an organization is, and can also be used to justify "super-sizing" or building additional overall capacity into the solution.

To this last point, super-sizing is called for when the risks of undersizing (not specifying a computing platform with adequate horsepower to get the business through month-end financial closing, for example) are worth the investment. Such investment might include additional CPU and memory resources, or greater network bandwidth. Taking this a step further, super-sizing might encompass specifying additional servers and disk space along with HA, DR, or systems management solutions that probably exceed the business's requirements, but are called for "just in case." Once all the questions are addressed, the vendors can begin developing well-conceived SAP solution proposals.

The Sizing Proposal Review Process

After you have followed the steps outlined in the previous chapter to send your requirements to various vendors, sizing proposals will be received from each vendor. These proposals then need to be compared and contrasted. As you have seen, many factors influence the runtime performance and capacity of the SAP installation. Beyond ensuring that each solution appears to meet the business system's core requirements, we suggest reviewing each proposal against the following criteria:

- ▶ **Details and depth of sizing**—Review sizing details to ensure all requested systems have been sized adequately, either through a requirements-based (bottom up) approach or through a solution-based (top-down) approach.

- ▶ **Core infrastructure**—Verify that all hardware elements such as servers, racks, power, networking, disk subsystems, and so on are addressed, along with software requirements such as operating systems, management tools, and other software.

- ▶ **Workload analysis**—Validate how workload was computed. Any of the following can be relevant: number of concurrent or named users, peak transaction load, reporting and batch loads, estimating the impact of customization, and so on.

- ▶ **Backup/recovery considerations**—Ensure that these are addressed by the sizing, including expected backup/recovery throughput, performance, and capacity analysis.

- ▶ **High availability and disaster recoverability**—Confirm that the vendor addressed your HA and DR needs; review their HA and DR solutions from technology and business availability perspectives to validate completeness, your recovery point objectives (RPO) and recovery time objective (RTO), and so on.

- ▶ **Solution completeness**—Ensure that everything that was requested is indeed covered, including future growth scenarios (and how scalability is addressed), the need for holistic or one-pane-of-glass systems management capabilities, and so on.

- ▶ **Assumptions**—Validate any assumptions made by the vendor (such as technology biases, workload growth assumptions, your potential mix of batch load versus online user load, and more).

If two or more sizing proposals are considered top choices, some other factors can be used as tie-breakers. Vendors that provide an end-to-end solution are preferred over vendors that provide a disparate group of solutions. Also, the relationship of the primary vendor with the subcomponent providers is an important factor. Ideally, you want a sizable vendor with a long history and good working relationship with other partners who are part of the solution.

Conducting a Detailed Sizing Review

Using the requirements and sizing team, you need to perform a detailed review of sizing proposed by a vendor. Because the solution is based on your original requirements, you first need to verify that the vendor is on the same page as you. You should use the opportunity to also verify that your original requirements were complete and that you didn't miss anything. If you did, this is a good time to add the missing pieces and, if they are big enough, request another iteration with the vendor.

This is also a good time to check for any "extras" added by the vendor to the sizing list beyond what was originally requested. Such extras can lead to inflated sizing costs and make it difficult to compare offerings of different vendors. Examples of extras are SAN instead of attached storage, or added features such as enterprise management consoles and domain controllers.

Sometimes the "extra" may actually be essential and so goes into the same bucket as other missing things from original requirements. For both these cases, you need to beef up the requirements and recirculate them to all vendors so that they can update their solutions. Similarly, if it looks like the "extra" was added as an honest interpretation of an ambiguity in the requirements, you need to clarify that ambiguity with all vendors as well. If a vendor identified mistakes or other matters that were overlooked, or included a feature that should have been requested, that speaks volumes about its SAP Competency Center; that kind of knowledge should be used as a factor when selecting the best vendor.

Verifying SAP Support for Architected Solutions

It is very important to verify that the proposed solution would be supported by SAP. Sometimes a solution may be very close to a certified solution but not quite. You don't want any surprises in that area. One of the examples is distributed databases. With the size of installations growing and with the increase in relatively low-footprint, high-density blades, a vendor without enough scale-up servers might prefer to split the database tier into multiple systems. This, for example, can be achieved on Oracle using Real Application Clusters (RAC) technology, which Oracle promises works perfectly with SAP. SAP only recently published "general availability" of RAC, however (and still does not support it as of this writing for Windows Server 2008 implementations).

There's always the chance that a specific solution provided by a vendor will fail to pass SAP certification. This has significant implications in terms of the support provided by SAP. To be safe, avoid such solutions. This factor also highlights the limits that certain hardware vendors may face—vendors without a breadth of server offerings. For example, a vendor with a single line of servers may not be in a position to grow with a client who has a rapidly growing SAP landscape; there might be scale-up requirements that simply cannot be met by such a vendor.

As you go through every aspect of the solution to ensure that it is supported by SAP, it is worth contacting SAP directly to verify whether a particular solution is supported. The information can be verified through Competency Centers of the vendors as well, especially because they'd find themselves in the position of supporting the proposed solution. Such verification can avoid a host of post-go-live support issues.

Verifying the Risk of the Proposed Solution

Even though a particular solution or approach may be supported by SAP and its SAP technology partners, that doesn't mean the solution has been installed in the field previously. You must verify whether the proposed solution has been field tested before. You might proceed even if it hasn't been, but it is better to do so in an informed manner. If your risk tolerance is high, you might be the first to try a new technology. Sometimes you just might not have any choice in the matter, however. For example, to minimize the number of changes to your existing infrastructure, you might want to use on your stack an SAP-supported solution that has not been field tested before.

You must ensure that the solution will work, and you need to find that out before you go live with the production instance. This means that you need to do more rigorous testing than you would have otherwise done. In addition, you need proof of concepts done ahead of time on your transactions to catch any issues with the solution.

Other ways of reducing the risk include more thorough evaluation of the vendor's expertise, including the comfort level that its Competency Center has with the solution. You should ask for white papers, reference solutions, and other related documents that can help assess the experience level of the vendor. You ought to do this for all vendors anyway, to reduce your overall risk, but this is especially needed in cases in which you are the guinea pig for a solution.

Verifying SAP Production References

Unless you have worked with a vendor yourself in the past, it is very important to verify its references to ensure that its other customers have smoothly running production instances implemented by the vendor. Validate the following from these references:

▶ The proposed technology stack has been field tested and is running on some production system.

▶ The implementation and configuration experiences were in line with our own expectations from the vendor as well as what the vendor stated they would be.

▶ The system performs adequately and provides expected capacity.

▶ Planned and unplanned downtime numbers are no surprise, or are explainable.

▶ Ongoing operations and support are consistent with our expectations.

The references are a good way to check on a vendor's general past performance too. You should try to hold a face-to-face meeting with the customer and its technical team, to get more details not easily forthcoming otherwise.

Revising Total Cost of Ownership Numbers

Planning is perfect but plans rarely are. There will be many revisions and changes on the path to proper sizing. These will require you to revise your original TCO figures. Only with new TCO numbers in hand can you take the sizing process to the next level and assemble the SAP partners and products necessary to solve your unique business problems.

Additionally, pending the final round of SAP technology stack vendor reviews, pricing is usually revisited. During this time, vendors typically take a fine-toothed comb to their overall solution pricing. Even a few percentage points can add up to big savings in projects ranging from hundreds of thousands to many millions of dollars. It is also common to structure a holdback or price/performance guarantee at this stage in the sizing process. In this way, the solution partners will continue to be motivated to perform to the best of their ability (and rapidly address inevitable integration, performance, or service issues) all the way until the day of go-live and beyond.

Finally, hardware acquisition costs versus ongoing operational, management, and overall support costs for each potential solution need to be revisited. You might find that a seemingly better alternative ends up being suboptimal in the long run. For example, Windows- or Linux-based SAP solutions might actually provide a better return on investment in many cases, but this depends as much on an IT organization's competencies and biases as on the cost of acquiring and managing the technical platform. That is, a team unfamiliar with and unwilling to learn a new technology will be more successful planning for and deploying an infrastructure with which it is comfortable, and the solution's TCO could subsequently be superior to most if not all other solutions. Remember that initial hardware and software acquisition costs are but only one factor in a long list of SAP lifecycle costs.

When business requirements change overnight, or when an initially straightforward SAP implementation grows to include many components and a hundred servers, several hidden costs can emerge that make scale-up, scale-out, or other "new" solutions look preferable in hindsight. In the end, the capability of an IT organization to move against the status quo and bring about authentic change through new technology will require a different kind of leadership. The need for transformational leadership will be critical—the kind of leadership that can energize and bring together a team to achieve a common goal or create a "new normal." Without such leadership, an organization's attempts to introduce a new computing platform could very well be undermined from within.

Selecting Core SAP Technology Stack Partners

With final pricing, apples-to-apples solution comparisons, and a host of other solution and partner-relevant data collected and analyzed, you can now work toward selecting your core SAP technology stack partners with confidence. This is often achieved by holding onsite vendor presentations, during which any final questions can be answered and each vendor has an opportunity to present its overall value and solution proposition.

However, keep in mind that there is no single best way to assemble your final SAP technology stack. That is, in many cases we have seen an SAP customer select its products first—the various technology stack components necessary to deliver on its SAP vision— and then select vendors. But in other cases, we have seen customers select enterprise-savvy

SAP technology and consulting partners first, and only later fine-tune the actual combination of hardware, operating system, database, and even SAP components necessary to achieve their business vision. Either approach can prove successful, though you place a lot more faith in your technology and consulting partners in the latter approach—as you would expect, if they are truly strategic partners.

Evaluating Specialized Technology Stack Vendors

With the core technology stack products and partners selected, you can start filling in any "holes" left in your solution architecture. These holes may be the result of special HA and DR requirements, the need to support special types of system accessibility, and so on. Thus, specialized or "niche" SAP technology stack vendors—such as disk subsystem manufacturers, makers of Internet-facilitating or load-balancing gear, test-tool vendors, and enterprise management and other specialty software vendors—can be brought in after your core SAP technology stack partners are identified. When you don't buy all hardware from a single vendor, you should make sure to verify how support is handled and how intervendor issues are going to be resolved.

The key to assembling a smoothly working solution from multiple vendors is to first limit the players. If similar solutions are available from two different vendors, lean toward leveraging the vendor you already use in your SAP or other enterprise environment. Next, when different vendors are brought in, you must plan in advance how support issues will be addressed. In other words, before you ever encounter a problem, you need to iron out all the details regarding how support is handled and how intervendor problems will be approached and solved. SAP AG models one of the best support approaches by way of its PartnerPort facility in Waldorf, Germany, where many vendors work side by side with SAP AG and to some extent each other. Outside of PartnerPort, the best SAP technology partners also host Joint Escalation Centers, support relationships, and similar support mechanisms between various hardware, software, and other technology vendors. You need to identify exactly with whom your core SAP technology stack partners have their best relationships, and lean toward taking advantage of these communication and escalation bridges whenever possible.

Holding SAP Infrastructure Planning Workshops

Now that you have selected your primary, and probably most of your specialized, solution partners, you must commence the post-sizing implementation planning and scheduling sessions. All the solution partners should be engaged in the initial kickoff meeting, subsequent sessions of which actually span several days. This includes your hardware partners, OS and database (software) partners, the SAP project manager, and any other project managers already identified. The data center manager and any key technical resources should also be present at the kickoff meeting.

Initiating the SAP infrastructure implementation represents a critical milestone in our SAP implementation project plan. As such, many tasks and related milestones of a smaller magnitude need to be identified, discussed, assigned, and managed. These tasks are covered in the next few sections of this book, divided conveniently into three days' worth of meetings and discussions. The overriding goals of these sessions are simple: to understand timelines for implementation, and to place orders for various hardware and software system landscape components.

Day One: Setting the Big Picture

Day one of the infrastructure planning sessions revolves around introductions of key personnel, review of the scope of work to be accomplished, review of the key hardware and software vendors' products and responsibilities, and reiteration of how the infrastructure planning sessions fit into the SAP implementation big picture. Here is a suggested agenda for the first day:

▶ **Introductions**—Key personnel from each technology stack partner, SAP, and the client's project team are introduced. Contact information is shared, as is a job description for each organization and for each person assigned to the project.

▶ **Vision and definition**—The reason for implementing the SAP solution is quickly reviewed, followed by a high-level review of the scope of work to be accomplished by the assembled team. Like the pieces of a puzzle, each partner is made aware of how its own contributions augment every other partner's contributions, in the end making the project possible.

▶ **Project sponsorship and accountability**—The role of each partner and the importance of each role are discussed. The term "project sponsor" is used loosely here because it refers to the individual person from each partner organization tasked with responsibility for completing its piece of the overall SAP project. Normally, the client has long ago identified what they expect from each partner. At this meeting, though, the partner comes prepared to put forth the name of its project sponsor—a high-level single point of accountability representing the partner's interests in the SAP project.

▶ **Project management**—Each partner must also come prepared to introduce its incarnation of a project manager, another loosely used term that simply refers to the single person charged with completing tasks relevant to the partner's role in the project. In our experience, it's best to clarify these roles as much as possible, especially with regard to expectations. The skill sets and qualifications of each project manager are reviewed, too, as are the number of hours expected to be consumed in project-management-related activities.

▶ **Project structure**—The project reporting hierarchy is identified, discussed, and usually revised. That is, the structure of the project's key players, in terms of who reports to whom and how issues are escalated, is covered. In large projects, it's common to publish a project organizational chart along with a scope statement. Status reporting, the use and timing of meetings, and other control and communications processes are ironed out as well. Finally, a schedule for regularly updating the master SAP project plan should be put in place.

▶ **Key milestones**—As they are currently understood, key milestones are identified and discussed. These are subject to change in the next two days of meetings, but discussing them at a high level now helps to prepare everyone for the project in general, and the next day in particular.

▶ **Quality management**—Processes for continuous improvement need to be developed over the next few days and embraced by the team. These processes need to be designed in, rather than "inspected" in. For instance, the use of workflow diagrams, recipes and checklists, and Pareto charts (a bar chart format useful in identifying tasks that fall into the 20/80 rule, where 80% of a project's issues are related to 20% of the tasks or resources) represent quality tools. They promote feedback and continuous updating of documentation, lending themselves to fine-tuning simply by virtue of their use, rather than something that is performed once and never used again.

▶ **Project administration**—How to address time and expense reporting, billing, invoicing, change control, and other administrative functions concludes day one. This might also include any contract administration that remains to be addressed, including updating contracts to reflect delivery and payment schedules, pricing, discounts, performance bonds, and more.

As you can see, this first session addresses the big picture. In doing so, it sets the stage for the next two days, preparing you to turn your attention next to project timelines with regard to the actual technology solutions and system landscapes being implemented.

Day Two: Building a Timeline

Day two commences with a quick synopsis of the previous day, and then the floor is turned over to the client or SAP project manager, who leads discussions detailing the following points:

▶ **Planned go-live date**—By establishing the desired go-live date, an experienced SAP project management team can "work backward" to identify when critical production milestones must be accomplished and therefore when tasks supporting these milestones must commence. This is a good way of constructing or validating a high-level project plan, too, as it typically contains no slack time (free time between tasks) and therefore clearly identifies the project's critical path (project milestones spaced in time such that they represent the shortest possible number of days in which a project can be completed). This by no means results in a truly usable project plan, however! Rather, it serves as a high-level template or perhaps simply as a tool for developing the actual plan.

▶ **Critical SAP system landscape milestones**—After production's go-live date is nailed down, you can work backward to determine when other SAP system landscape systems need to be in place, too. Thus, the need and timing for implementing production, test/QA, training, development, a technical sandbox, and so on can all be determined based on your production go-live date and how much lead time needs to be given to tasks related to other activities.

19

▶ **Key risks**—Identifying risks to the project plan is an excellent method of promoting and then refining timeline discussions. Any risk to successfully completing a particular milestone related to each partner's set of responsibilities needs to be covered, and addressed or mitigated. For key risks, a contingency plan needs to be developed as well.

▶ **Landscape assistance**—As each component within the system landscape is discussed, it naturally promotes the discussion of how much assistance the client thinks it will need in achieving SAP system landscape–related milestones. For example, our teams often get involved with technical sandbox and development implementations, but less so with other environments (outside of production, or at least a review of the production environment prior to go-live). Why? Because after we train our clients in how to plan for and install an SAP component, and leave them with a detailed recipe or checklist for repeating the installation, they usually want to not only prove that the recipe works, but also train their own team and preserve their budget by doing it themselves.

▶ **Realistic timelines**—With the critical path and key milestones identified, and an idea as to which partners will be engaged to support achieving these milestones, pencil in hard timelines for go-live of each SAP component to be implemented and each landscape system. Add as much slack time as possible, and spread it out among the various tasks (we like to see each technology stack partner allotted some amount of slack time). Working backward with these realistic figures should give you an idea as to when hardware actually needs to hit the ground, and therefore when the data center needs to be prepared. Everything else going forward can then be filled in pretty easily on the third day.

▶ **Knowledge transfer**—Before leaving for the day, work to clearly understand both when and how much knowledge transfer needs to take place between the various technology partners and the client. Assign names of responsible parties, assign and document the actual tasks associated with this knowledge transfer, and document the method by which the knowledge will be transferred—hands-on training, written process and procedure documentation, use of high-level or detailed checklists, creation of web-accessible content, and so on. In the consulting world, we call these *deliverables*, because they represent something tangible delivered to SAP clients prior to concluding a project.

The second day of planning sessions can run pretty long. Each partner and the client should come prepared with their individual project plans or detailed timelines. In this way, the master plan can be more easily updated, and valuable time is not wasted trying to recall how long certain tasks take to complete, or how critical dependencies relate between tasks. As an aside, it should go without saying that if the partner cannot produce at least a template project plan based on previous SAP implementations, you should be very nervous—if you are paying for specific expertise in a particular SAP component or supporting technology, you deserve to benefit from other projects' efforts. A previously and successfully used project plan is proof of this experience, for example, and equates to at least a minimum level of credibility.

Day Three: Assigning Resources

Whereas the second day of planning sessions focused on the timelines and the technology being implemented, this final day concludes the planning sessions by assigning names and responsibilities to project plan tasks. Thus, by the end of the day, everyone leaving the sessions will understand not only their own roles, but the roles of the entire team and how everyone's tasks relate to the project as a whole. And in doing so, you will conclude the sizing process, taking it from inception through planning the deployment of your physical SAP system landscape. Tasks to address on the third day include

▶ **Assign names to technology stack technical roles**—Each partner must be prepared to commit the technical resources necessary to achieve its unique solution-stack–related milestones. This includes SAP Basis specialists and NetWeaver technical leads, server hardware experts, SAN/disk hardware specialists, OS installation/tuning specialists, database administrators (DBAs), disk subsystem specialists, SAP component subject matter experts (SMEs), and front-end SAP access specialists. A discussion of the skill sets required to perform the work associated with each partner's tasks, and how its resources fulfill these requirements in terms of experience and education, is standard.

▶ **Assign names to other technical roles**—Each partner must also be prepared to identify its resources to satisfy other technical roles, such as HA or failover specialists, stress-test and load-test experts, functional testing specialists, SAP solution tuning specialists for their particular contributions to the SAP technology stack, and so on.

▶ **Identify administrative key roles**—More than just technology folks need to be identified. Each partner's project administrator or coordinator, account manager, documentation specialist, and other support and administrative contacts need to be documented and shared with the team. In small engagements, it's common to see these people wearing multiple hats, perhaps even sharing technical responsibilities with administrative ones.

▶ **Identify client contacts**—Although this varies, we tend to see most of the following positions held strictly by our clients. Regardless, it's important to understand who is actually responsible for the following areas that fundamentally support or underpin the SAP project: environmental/data center manager and specialist, network infrastructure specialist, data and application migration specialist, training coordinator, operations manager, and help desk manager.

▶ **Refine timelines**—With the details surrounding the technical implementation understood now, it should be possible to refine the timelines associated with each task such that the hours and days expected to complete each specific task are documented. This is called a work breakdown structure (WBS) in project management

19

circles, because it breaks down a project into smaller elements and then ultimately into work packages, which are simply tasks that can be accomplished in approximately 80 hours or less.

▶ **Refine and validate budgets**—Although all partners can now provide their final costing numbers, not everyone needs to be involved with reviewing the budget numbers. Normally, this kind of activity is reserved instead for project management representatives tasked with managing the project's financials. This exercise also helps validate how close each partner came to estimating their costs, based on the imperfect information provided to them during the sizing process.

Students of project management have probably noticed that the three-day planning sessions cover many core project management fundamentals. The sizing process in and of itself represents a large subproject of an overall SAP implementation. So it only makes sense that managing scope, timelines, cost, quality, risk, procurement, human resources, and communications needs to be given the same level of attention here as at the higher overall SAP implementation project level.

Summary

This chapter walked through the remainder of the SAP sizing process initiated in Chapter 18, starting with an overview of the sizing and blueprinting process, selecting key partners, and kicking off the SAP infrastructure planning workshops. Details related to how these workshops should be conducted, including outcomes, concluded the chapter.

Case Study: Sizing for SAP Upgrade and Consolidation

HiTech, Inc. is conducting a large data center consolidation and SAP upgrade exercise. HiTech has been an SAP customer for several years, and SAP forms the backbone of its enterprise processing environment. Recently, HiTech acquired another company which had its own SAP environment running on a different architecture and with different SAP components and versions. For the first six months, to keep the business running, IT worked with the various business units to integrate the systems as best it could. The longer-term plan was to upgrade and consolidate the infrastructure in one data center. This triggered an SAP sizing exercise. You have been tasked with building a sizing review team and leading this exercise.

Questions

1. You understand that an SAP sizing exercise takes time and requires a great amount of input. Explain this to the sizing evaluation team you are tasked with building.

2. What kind of technology biases might your team hold?

3. If the team is only familiar with IBM AIX running Oracle databases, is it reasonable to assume the team could be successful deploying SAP-on-Windows/SQL Server or SAP-on-Linux/MaxDB? What kind of leadership might be called for?

4. When is "super-sizing" warranted?

NOTE

The answers to these questions can be found in Appendix A, "Case Study Answers."

19

Training SAP Staff

In this chapter, we will explore several topics related to training the folks tasked with developing, deploying, and supporting SAP. This includes a review of the primary roles of the SAP technical support organization (TSO), the "delta" training needs that are so often overlooked for each position, and the different types of, and approaches to, effective time-honored training. We will also explain how the SAP system landscape aids in training everyone from end users to various members of the SAP TSO, incorporating several methods of ensuring that delivered training is indeed worth your company's time and money. This last point is especially important in our knowledge-based economy, where unlocking the door to your organization's potential can really pay off in terms of newfound innovation, greater system availability, and improved productivity. To this end, we conclude this chapter with a rundown of individual technical and end-user roles, noting how customer-based feedback can be used to fine-tune or endorse a particular training curriculum.

Introduction to SAP Training

In a perfect world, you would staff your SAP project with highly successful, experienced personnel, people who keenly understand your particular environment and your unique technology stack. The SAP TSO would have all the answers, and the project would come in way ahead of schedule and way under budget. Sleeping in would be encouraged, as would long lunches and lazy afternoons on the golf course, because the team was solving all the inevitable project deployment problems in record time. By the same token, all of your end users would quickly grasp the new SAP-crafted business processes replacing their old way of doing things, training would be delivered to the entire body of end users a few days before go-live, and this training would be perfectly and forever entrenched in their minds.

In the real world of SAP implementations, though, a company is fortunate to assemble a technical team in which everyone is SAP literate, much less experts. Each member of the team typically has a few "gaps" in his or her experience that need to be filled in with training or on-the-job experience. Some of the team members will exit long before the big SAP production go-live handle is pulled, too, leaving you with gaping support holes to fill quickly. Other team members may simply not be up to the task at hand. And shifting technology or functional decisions (no matter how fiercely they are avoided) will create skill-set gaps where none existed previously. To top it off, there will be more than a few end users who resist or never attend training, and even for those who do attend, much of this training will unfortunately go in one ear and out the other before it's ever retained by putting it into practice.

Sound training of the SAP support organization combined with effective and timely end-user training can save the day, though, as we explore next.

Who Needs Training?

Certainly, everyone benefits from training. Our focus initially in this chapter is not on the end users of the SAP solution being deployed but rather on the folks tasked with designing, implementing, and supporting this solution. To help thoroughly cover the broad topic of training, we use the SAP technology stack model.

This method of analysis tends to ignore the leadership positions, such as project management professionals and solution architects, which for our purposes here is fine. That is, we believe that the folks charged with fulfilling these senior positions require deep, long-term experience to be effective. Training can still be useful in filling in tiny gaps or holes, but the benefit overall is minimal compared to other positions. After all, who wants to hire an SAP implementation manager and train him in core project management practices? By the same token, who wants to bring in an inexperienced solution architect and teach her SAP technology from the ground up? Few organizations have that kind of time to do so effectively; the risk to the project's success is much greater than the potential benefit.

In technology stack order, then, let's walk through the following SAP TSO positions, focusing on *delta training*, or training beyond the minimum requirements necessary for each position:

- ▶ **Data center/infrastructure specialists**—These specialists benefit from training in infrastructure installation (rack best practices, for example) and management and monitoring tools used in support of managing data center power and cooling.

- ▶ **SAP network specialists**—Training in static routing, designing and deploying highly available public links, and three-tiered client/server architectures in general is appropriate. Further, hardware-specific training is beneficial when high-performance or high-availability deployment options are being considered, such as network bonding or teaming.

▶ **SAP OS specialists**—Server deployment strategies and any OS-specific approaches to high availability (HA) or disaster recovery (DR) need to be taught. If a scripted approach to re-creating or deploying servers is deemed appropriate, training in the specific scripting language or tool needs to be provided, too, including access to test resources.

▶ **Storage/SAN specialists**—Although training in SAN and disk subsystem architecture can be very valuable, in our experience it's the foundation provided by storage platform–specific hands-on training that keeps things running smoothly. This is especially true of training that is specific to the OS being deployed on the servers attached to the storage systems, and even more so of the HA/DR alternatives being deployed.

▶ **SAP database administrators**—Specific database-layer performance tuning (training offered by the database vendor) as well as SAP-specific database training (training offered by SAP, for example) are both crucial. Knowledge of the storage system, especially with regard to HA/DR, is essential as well.

▶ **SAP Basis specialists**—These experts should already be comfortable with the SAP platform foundation being deployed. Delta training and custom workshops are often quite useful, though, in terms of identifying real-world challenges posed by the newest SAP NetWeaver ABAP and Java stacks.

▶ **SAP application component specialists**—In addition to SAP NetWeaver training and expertise, it's essential to train each application component specialist in their particular SAP product so that they understand core *capabilities* and *shortcomings*. Beyond that, hands-on training leveraging the SAP system landscape is key.

▶ **SAP functional specialists**—Each specialist needs to understand their functional area completely. It's also beneficial to train your functional people in related functional areas. And for functional specialists tasked with deploying business processes across multiple SAP application components, training in each component is wise.

▶ **SAP ABAP, J2EE, and other developers**—Developers must understand their development tools and platforms, especially how each tool is used and optimized in the context of an SAP solution. SAP's formal training and certification programs are highly effective here, as is leveraging various systems within the SAP system landscape.

▶ **SAP integration experts**—Training on the specific tool set or approach is important here, though access to test resources is absolutely essential.

▶ **High-availability and disaster-recovery specialists**—The best HA/DR folks understand their entire technology stack and are aware of the various availability options that may be deployed at each layer of the stack. Training that orients these specialists to the issues and solutions relevant to creating a DR plan, along with how to successfully engage their IT organization and end users, is crucial as well. These

20

specialists must also be provided with specific formal and hands-on training in the core HA/DR solutions to ultimately be deployed, including access to test resources. Finally, an HA/DR specialist needs to understand and comply with the need to help maintain outstanding current-state and process documentation. After all, the lifeblood of the organization—its business applications and data—is at stake in the event of a disaster.

▶ **SAP trainers**—These trainers benefit from exposure to all SAP and other bolt-on solution components (to gain at least a high-level end-to-end understanding of a "typical" SAP enterprise), as well as introductory technology stack training. Beyond this, developing their presentation skills and attending other "how to be an effective trainer" training are important.

▶ **SAP security specialists**—The best security specialists understand all integration touch points that impact security, and how to defend their SAP solution at each layer in the technology stack. Given the evolving nature of an SAP solution, delta training in new access methods, the purpose and placement of firewalls, and applicable SAP application components represents the best use of company time and money, as does technology stack–specific training to fill in any technology holes.

▶ **Front-end or user interface deployment specialists**—Each specialist must be comfortable with planning and deploying the chosen client access strategy, and therefore must understand the pros and cons of why a particular strategy may be selected over another (such as deploying the classic fat-client SAPGUI versus the WebGUI, SAPGUI via Citrix, custom-developed user interfaces, and other similar approaches). These specialists tend to interact face to face with your end users, too, and therefore need to not only be experts in your company's desktop, laptop, and other access devices, but also be comfortable working with the gamut of people employed by your company.

▶ **Documentation specialists**—Documentation specialists are experts at writing clear technical documentation, and cannot take for granted options and details. This is especially true for those folks tasked with creating custom checklists, installation cookbooks, DR processes, and operations how-to procedures. Although they do not need to be experts, technical "overview" training in the areas for which they are asked to provide documentation is important—it will result in less-ambiguous documentation.

▶ **SAP operations/systems management professionals**—These folks benefit from training that is specific to the tools they use. To become adept at monitoring and managing both the stack and the SAP business applications atop the stack, they need hands-on experience with the various enterprise applications and other similar utilities, too (typically provided via a test or technical sandbox environment).

▶ **SAP help desk analysts**—As another customer-facing organization, help desk analysts benefit from broad solution-level training but benefit even more so from training related to the tools used to troubleshoot and manage customer issues or "cases." They need to be experts in these tools, so that they do *not* need to be experts in the entire SAP technology stack and each SAP application component deployed. Further, soft-skills training in communicating with different levels of end users is appropriate. And *Troubleshooting 101* training will serve front-line help desk analysts well, too, especially if this training is focused on issues that usually manifest themselves in terms of end-user response times or access to the system.

Despite its length, the preceding list is by no means exhaustive. But it is *realistic*, reflecting the best places to spend scarce training time and dollars. So, to really help a company track and manage its people from an education and experience perspective, a method like the simple spreadsheet illustrated in Figure 20.1 is useful, if not necessary.

Sample Skill-Set Matrix

INSTRUCTIONS: Enter a 1 for EXPERT, 2 for COMPETENT, 3 for INSTALL ONLY, 4 for EXPOSURE ONLY, and enter "comments" as necessary or for clarification

Manager	Name	Org	Data Center Infrastructure	Cisco/Networking	Compaq/HP Proliant Servers	HP Superdome Servers	Sun UE1000	CPQ/HP SAN/Disk subsystems	HP SAN/Disk subsystems	HP-UX 10x 11i	Linux (SuSe or RedHat)	MS NT	MS W2K
BROWN	ANBONS, JOSE	SAP TSO	1		1	3		1		2	2	1	1
BROWN	BURDOCK, JOHN	SAP TSO		1	1				1	1	3		
BROWN	SANDERSON, GEORGE	SAP TSO			2	1					1	2	
BROWN	TALVE, JON	SAP TSO									1		1
CLARK	BOOKING, MARTIN	SAP TSO	1					2			3		2
CLARK	CLEXLEY, THOMAS	SAP TSO	2	1			4				3		2
CLARK	GONIN, PAUL	SAP TSO	1			2						2	2
CLARK	HEART, ROBERT	SAP TSO	1	1									
CLARK	MITTEN, DAVID	SAP TSO	2										
CLARK	PAIGE, DEVEN	SAP TSO		1	2								
CLARK	PLORTIER, CAROL	SAP TSO	2				4				4		

FIGURE 20.1   The skill-set matrix helps an organization manage training, certifications, and more by identifying who possesses what knowledge.

We call this a "skill-set matrix." Although the idea is simple—a grid of skill sets, certifications, and products cross-referenced to each person—the value is tremendous. This spreadsheet not only identifies who possesses what knowledge, but also in effect identifies *skill-set backups*, or people who back each other up in terms of skill sets, certifications, and experience.

Timing Is Everything

All of us have attended training in one area or another, only to return home and either never put that training to use or use it sparingly months later. Others have attended last-minute training courses but failed to grasp the truly pertinent materials, or be given time to do so afterward, before needing to actually use the knowledge that was supposed to have been imparted. In both cases, the *timing* of the training, and not the training itself, became an obstacle to success. When possible, we recommend that all students attempt to schedule training—whether formal classes, workshops, hands-on sessions, or whatever— far enough out that there is time between the conclusion of the class and the need for what the class taught. From our perspective, one to three weeks of time works out best. This gives you the time you need to address any holes in the knowledge you just gained, by researching or re-reviewing the training materials or simply discussing your questions with colleagues.

On the other hand, training received too soon can equate to nearly wasted time and money. People forget things pretty quickly even in the best of worlds—training them on something they don't need to know or use for more than a month is like throwing away money. At this point, only the course-provided materials and really good notes hold any hope in helping a student refresh his or her memory. Another common method of battling this is to encourage students to actually use their newfound knowledge in test systems. Even better, holding them accountable for teaching their coworkers really reinforces training. This practice truly cements new knowledge into place, in fact, and can help to create pockets of subject matter experts (SMEs) over time, too.

Training and the Role of the SAP System Landscape

We have mentioned generic *test systems* a few times already in this chapter. However, the term is relative, as you can see in the following detailed SAP system landscape breakdown—different systems serve different testing/hands-on training purposes, for very different customer organizations. Remember, not all systems exist in every SAP implementation, either. It's possible, of course, but budget constraints typically limit most SAP customer projects to three to five systems per SAP application component being deployed.

▶ **Technical sandbox**—This system is specifically earmarked for *technical* training, along with providing a platform for technical testing. Thus, it services the training needs of every single member of the SAP TSO (which gives rise to scheduling challenges as different SAP TSO groups jockey for access to the technical sandbox—it's usually in high demand!). The entire production SAP technology stack should be duplicated in this environment, especially when it comes to the server and disk subsystem platforms, HA and DR options, backup/restore products, and other critical or unique solution components.

▶ **Business sandbox**—This system is specifically deployed for the folks who are attempting to model business processes, test integration points (how two systems "talk" to one another), and so on. It is often used to create an approximation of an SAP business solution well before all the business requirements have been identified, if only to determine whether core functionality expected of the system is indeed capable of being delivered.

▶ **Development system**—When it comes to training, the development system should provide perhaps only one or two "sandbox" clients, to allow some degree of trial-and-error testing and experimentation. For firms needing more, a better solution is to implement the previously described "business sandbox" or a specialized "development sandbox," which for all purposes is like a technical sandbox, except that it services developers and the like—the folks tasked with configuring the business processes.

▶ **Training system**—This is the most misunderstood system, in our experience. A "training" system is normally dedicated to supporting SAP end-user training—how they execute business processes in a particular area, how they use the SAPGUI, and so on. But too many times we have seen training systems pulled in a hundred different directions, supporting technology training, development training, integration testing, disaster-recovery testing, and more. All of this extra hands-on training and testing needs to be done, of course, but by using the training system, end-user training time is compromised.

▶ **Test/QA system, or quality assurance, or consolidation, or integration**—Labeled many things over the years, training in the integration and testing of configuration or functional changes is performed on this system in a "training" client.

▶ **Staging system**—Emulating the most mission-critical tasks and business processes to be performed ultimately in production is the role of this system. Thus, performance testing and hands-on training are commonly executed here, supporting the entire SAP TSO much as the technical sandbox does, but in a more formal, less "crash-and-burn" manner. Stress testing is often performed against this environment as well, as staging typically duplicates production.

▶ **Production system**—No formal training of any type should occur on this system (though informal post-go-live "training" is inevitable and expected among end-user colleagues).

▶ **Disaster-recovery system**—This system supports training specific to the DR solution implemented, or any number of HA options that may be used.

As you can see, three of the systems described in the preceding list are especially intended to support training in one form or another. Different systems are focused on providing training environments for technology staff, development staff, and end users. These three *core* training systems—the technical sandbox, business sandbox, and training system, respectively—are each visited next, followed by a discussion of the training necessary for supporting an SAP IT organization's unique SAP technology stack.

Leveraging the Technical Sandbox

Because the technical sandbox should duplicate or closely emulate production, it serves many wonderful purposes:

▶ It supports basic "familiarity" training in your particular technology stack, including the hardware platform, OS, database, SAP application components, and so on.

▶ It allows in-depth HA/DR training, such as that typically needed to support a HA cluster or log-shipping process. The technical sandbox is perfect for hands-on demonstrations and testing.

▶ It gives the staff the opportunity to learn how to perform backup/restore processes, and then actually put the processes into use.

▶ It sets the stage for creating initial current-state and how-to/process documentation, all of which can be easily modified later to fulfill real production-level documentation requirements.

▶ Because the technical sandbox also represents the system from which technology changes are tested and eventually promoted into production, it makes sense to begin establishing and using these procedures as the starting point for change management processes.

▶ All of the operations/management tool sets and applications will eventually need to be learned, used, and understood; a technical sandbox facilitates this best.

▶ All of the experience gleaned from working on this system should help the SAP TSO begin building the contents of the DR crash kit.

With clear value like this, it's no wonder that more and more companies are implementing technical sandboxes for their SAP enterprises.

Using the Development and Business Sandbox Systems

In the days of "simple" SAP R/3 implementations, the development system normally was configured with a couple of sandbox clients—clients specifically created for developing throw-away code and configuration. The development process was simply managed by managing these clients. Today, though, complex multiple-component SAP solutions require a greater level of integration and therefore deeper skill sets. Not only that, but the timelines can be such that not everything goes "live" at once—phased SAP implementations might introduce SAP ERP and SAP NetWeaver Portal first, followed up later by SAP NetWeaver Business Warehouse, and then by SAP Supply Chain Management, for example.

Such an approach demands discrete, client-driven integration testing and training. But the risk to client-independent data found in a shared development/business sandbox system would place each client's development code in jeopardy. For this reason, the value of a dedicated business sandbox became apparent. In terms of providing a system for training, the business sandbox is perfect for configuration specialists and developers.

With a business sandbox, not only can multiple clients be created for education and experimentation, but additional clients can be introduced later to focus on figuring out integration challenges inherent to supporting different project phases. And, consistent with best practices, the real development Golden Client or Gold Master (the client where operational business configuration and all master data is "saved") would still only reside on a single development system, the one housing the data to be actually transported to test/QA. In this light, it is obvious that the term "development system" is really a misnomer; a better term would be "the preproduction repository housing the production future state," in the same manner that the "production system" is really the production business system. It's all a bit wordy, though, so for expediency we'll stick with the old "development" term.

Wringing All the Value Out of a Training System

The role of the training system, or "training," confuses many people, because the label "training" is simply too vague. As we said before, we view the training system as the answer to your end users' hands-on education needs—not the technical team, not the development team, but end users. If the training system is to be shared between different end-user groups, we recommend creating a schedule to help manage who is training with, borrowing, or testing what resources, and how long they intend to keep those resources. With this in mind, the training system becomes useful in several ways:

▶ You can use it to train different groups of SAP end users. Most companies leverage a "classroom approach" to training end users, where 15 to 25 students show up in a physical classroom and learn the specifics of their functional area, for example. Each functional area is provided with its own client, to make it easy to refresh the system afterward (as compared to restoring the entire database).

▶ The act of refreshing training clients from the Golden Client acts as training for SAP operations or the Basis team, too, who will be tasked with refreshing clients on a regular basis before and after go-live.

▶ You can *also* use the training system to assemble and refine further "how-to" documentation, especially documentation needed in support of transports, change management, and other multisystem activities.

When it comes to making the decision as to which training environment to deploy, we recommend erring on the side of conservatism. Why? Because setting things up first and distributing training-focused systems to their respective user communities is easier than spending time managing schedules and priorities for these same communities when it comes to training.

Training to Support Your Unique SAP Technology Stack

Hypothetically, the SAP system landscape should reflect how much you need or value training. That is, an SAP customer with a technical sandbox in addition to development, test, and production systems obviously values its SAP technology team having access to testing and training resources. Another customer with a business sandbox and development, test/QA, staging, and production systems places a whole lot of value on functionality, coding, and creating the best possible end-user experience.

In the real world, most SAP customers deploy dedicated development, test, and production systems only, and try to take care of technical, development, and end-user training by leveraging both a client strategy and a systemwide resource schedule. In our experience, training systems are growing in popularity, though. If the budget is available, we would consider adding a training system according to the following guidelines:

▶ Add a technical sandbox if your HA/DR solution is complex, or if the SAP Basis/infrastructure team is new to the technology stack being deployed.

▶ Add a business sandbox if the coding environment is complex. For example, a shop implementing SAP by using ABAP/4, Java, and the older HTML ITS-based integration

20

mechanisms would benefit from the trial-by-error opportunities and other testing capabilities inherent to a business sandbox.

▶ Add a dedicated training instance if multiple clients need to be maintained and refreshed often to support new-user and similar functional/business process training, or if a large number of end users need to be trained in a short period of time.

This is by no means money wasted. Many of our customers actually redeploy their dedicated training system after go-live—they repurpose it to serve as another dedicated batch application server in the test/QA or staging environment, and perhaps toss any remaining systems or infrastructure resources into the technical sandbox to be used for technology stack testing and education.

Finally, another general way to determine whether one of these dedicated training systems is right for your particular SAP solution is to review the skill sets of your people and identify weak areas across the technology, development, and end-user communities. Then consider implementing one of these training environments based on your weaknesses. And keep in mind what we discussed previously—once your training "gaps" are filled, don't be afraid to redeploy or reallocate your training resources to a new or current system within your landscape. Such frugal management of scarce resources can be one of the keys to a successful training program.

Approaches to SAP Training

In the earliest days of SAP deployments, SAP and its implementation partners were so busy deploying new systems and developing a methodology for doing this efficiently (eventually labeled the "ASAP methodology") that little time seemed to be left to dedicate to technical training. Sure, formal training courses existed, but these were highly sought after and impossible to attend unless you were a partner of SAP or an SAP employee yourself.

Consequently, those of us in the industry back then saw a lot of interesting things occur. Hardware partners such as HP, IBM, Digital, Sun, Unisys, Compaq, and others developed their own internal SAP project-team training, Basis-layer (that is, SAP technology) workshops, and integration-focused SAP training courses. Software partners such as Microsoft and Oracle got in on the action, too. Third parties and other niche players sprung up out of the void, anxious to grab a piece of the SAP implementation budget earmarked for training. And internal organizations within many of the very customer sites deploying SAP were created or mobilized to prepare and deliver both their own end-user and project-team-focused technical training curriculum.

SAP AG finally caught its collective breath sometime in 1997 and released a number of products that really turned the heads of its partners and customers, including

▶ **Information Database (InfoDB)**—Though outdated today, these small training systems consisted of two to three dedicated servers—one ERP (R/3) server, one Information File Store (or data store server, discussed next), and optionally one IDES (covered later in this list). Most of these systems were sized for 20 to 40 users, based in large part on how many users would ultimately use the R/3 system productively.

The InfoDB concept is still alive today and thus worth knowing about, if only for historical context.

▶ **Information File Store (IFS)**—This housed all training materials from SAP, including PowerPoint presentations, various white papers and best-practices documents, configuration documents, technical notes, working labs, and more. Processing power was not critical for IFS servers. Data storage needs, on the other hand, grew quite rapidly from 1997 to 1999, culminating in the need for 70–90GB (which, back in the day of many 30GB SAP R/3 databases, was actually quite large). Later, the combination of InfoDB and IFS grew into what became SAP's first Knowledge Warehouse product.

▶ **International Demonstration and Education System (IDES)**—Later, as the Internet really took off as a means of accessing and delivering data, SAP renamed this the *Internet* Demonstration and Education System, and updated its reach somewhat. Originally based on a fictional motorcycle company, IDES systems were often architected for 20 to 40 users, and allowed these users to enter orders, move materials, perform production planning, and so on—all very real and very typical business transactions. This was accomplished by virtue of the fact that the IDES was completely customized (essentially a fully configured and highly capable training solution "in a box").

In the next few sections, we will walk you through the many approaches we have seen used at customer sites to get their teams up to speed. We will touch on a couple of newer approaches, too, including some that we believe are the most effective training methods employed today.

Formal Classes and Courseware

SAP AG and its key education partners offer formal classroom-based courses scheduled and delivered across more than 70 different training centers over the globe. Many of the formal courses offered by SAP AG are hands-on to a great extent, and many of the functional courses are quasi-technical as well (such as those in which integration to another system is covered). You should know that the huge majority of formal classroom training administered by SAP today is functional configuration training, rather than pure technology-focused or technical/Basis training.

SAP categorizes its education services into the following areas:

▶ Introductory Training

▶ Platform

▶ SAP Business Suite

▶ Business Objects

▶ E-Learning

▶ Additional Topics

20

Refer to the SAP training catalog at http://www.sap.com/usa/services/education/catalog/
index.epx for more information.

Introductory Training

SAP AG offers Introductory Training designed to provide an overview of the SAP solution
architecture and integration. You can choose from three different categories: Solution
Overviews, SAP ERP Business Process Integration and Solution Architecture, and Role-
Specific SAP Introduction. All in all, there are more than 50 courses to select from,
comprising a mix of onsite training and e-learning. Some of the course strings offer a certification at the end of the training.

We recommend these courses for nearly everyone, from the project manager who is tasked
with implementing SAP's NetWeaver platform but needs to understand the basics of the
SAP application supported by SAP NetWeaver, to the super user who doesn't need to have
in-depth knowledge of a specific area but needs to understand from a high-level perspective how an SAP environment integrates, functions, and operates.

You can view SAP's education courses and various technology and functional paths at the
SAP website. To identify and book your course, access http://www.sap.com and click
Explore SAP Education.

Platform

The Platform category is all about the SAP NetWeaver technology platform. This is the
category dedicated to the SAP NetWeaver experts, or SAP Basis specialists as we used to call
them during the SAP R/3 era. The Platform training category literally offers hundreds of
SAP courses. We recommend that you carefully select your training string; otherwise,
you'll spend time and money for knowledge that is nice to have but doesn't satisfy your
training needs. Platform training includes the following:

▶ **SAP NetWeaver**—These core training courses teach you everything you need to
know about SAP's technology platform and how it supports an open and flexible IT
architecture. You can take advantage of overview courses in which you learn how to
leverage SAP NetWeaver as a strategic integration and application platform. In addition, you can choose curriculum paths covering specific SAP NetWeaver components
and functionality.

▶ **SAP Solution Manager**—These courses target both technical and business aspects for
the solution lifecycle of your SAP environment. You find training dedicated to how
the SAP Solution Manager can support your SAP implementation project, from
project preparation to Business Blueprint, and from customizing to project-related
testing. You find training focusing on the SAP operations and how the SAP Solution
Manager can support your daily operation, from Solution Monitoring to Service
Desk, and from Service Delivery to Service Level Reporting. These courses are
extremely helpful for project managers and SAP operations personnel.

▶ **Enterprise Service-Oriented Architecture (SOA)**—These valuable training courses
are dedicated to explaining how to design and take advantage of an adaptable and
flexible IT architecture, and how to develop service-based business solutions. As
for the other training categories, at the end of a training string you can take the

certification test. These certifications are especially important for SAP consultants. We have seen many companies asking the implementation partner to provide the relevant SAP certification along with the consultant's resume. Certifications represent in many cases the culmination of SAP's formal training efforts. Consultants certified in a particular discipline tend to stand out from their noncertified colleagues when all other factors are about equal. SAP certifications also tend to communicate a certain level of core knowledge and expertise, which makes identifying and selecting the "best of the best" consulting resources easier than otherwise possible.

SAP Business Suite

The SAP Business Suite training category is dedicated to SAP's comprehensive family of adaptive business applications. These training courses teach you how to manage your most critical business processes, how to integrate across various SAP applications, and how to collaborate over the Internet. Again, you can choose from hundreds of training courses from several SAP Business Suite applications mentioned over and over again in this book, including:

- ▶ SAP Customer Relationship Management (CRM)

- ▶ SAP Enterprise Resource Planning (ERP)

- ▶ SAP Product Lifecycle Management (PLM)

- ▶ SAP Supply Chain Management (SCM)

- ▶ SAP Supplier Relationship Management (SRM)

Additional Topics

Even though the perception might be that SAP provides solutions only for huge enterprises, SAP is no stranger to the midmarket. Termed by SAP AG as small and medium enterprise (SME) offerings, SAP has been developing and releasing software solutions for small businesses and midsize companies for more than half a decade. SAP's declared goal is to reach the 100,000 customer mark in 2010 by winning even more of these small and midsize businesses; after all, the largest firms in the world are fairly saturated with either SAP or Oracle business applications. It is therefore no surprise that this final training category offers courses for SAP's small and midsize customers. Choose from the following training offerings:

- ▶ Duet

- ▶ Industry-specific training

- ▶ SAP solutions for enterprise performance management

- ▶ SAP solutions for governance, risk, and compliance

Onsite Training Workshops

Instead of forcing a customer to develop and deliver its own training materials, SAP AG introduced what it still refers to as Customer-Specific Training. These fundamental educational services are focused at teamwide training, geared to teaching the SAP TSO and

20

others what they need to know to make a new SAP solution a productive reality. With hundreds of training courses available today, covering a comprehensive standard curriculum, custom training courses and workshops can be quickly developed to fit an organization's specific education requirements.

These workshops can be fine-tuned to cover all application, functional, and technical areas related to your SAP implementation. And the workshops can be hosted either at an SAP training facility or (with the right hardware and other infrastructure) at a customer's own site. Perhaps best of all, though, SAP understands what a customer is looking for in terms of training—SAP has implemented thousands of solutions, and knows what it takes to make it happen and keep them running. So if you simply provide SAP with the training topic, the location, the date, and the time, it can take care of everything else. And that lets SAP's customers refocus their energies on what they do best—their own unique core competencies, which are probably far from developing and delivering customized training courses.

Creating and Delivering Custom Training Curriculum

Despite what we said earlier, there are times when developing and presenting your own materials can still make a lot of sense. In looking back at some of the custom training we have personally created and either presented or left with our SAP customers, we are a bit surprised at the variety—there seems to be no particular area that is more common than another. Bottom line, though, these 1- to 10-day training engagements saved everyone on the project teams a lot of travel and training time, and were certainly cheaper than any alternatives. Why? Because, as a virtual project team member, we knew exactly what each client really needed—we knew where their support or go-live holes were biggest, so to speak, and we knew with what materials and information to fill these holes. Consider the following real-world training engagements in which we have participated:

▶ **SAP Help Desk training**—This customer needed "SAP Help Desk 101" training, and visibility into the resources it had at its disposal after a trouble ticket was created (whom to call both within the SAP TSO and externally).

▶ **SAP Junior Basis training**—Many of our clients have benefited from this hands-on and presentation-based training, in which we walk through the SAP technology stack, preparing SAP infrastructure, performing SAP installations, executing basic Transaction Codes (T-codes) used in support of performance monitoring, and so on.

▶ **SAP Operations training**—We trained SAP operators in basic technology stack monitoring, from the server and SAN hardware layers, up to the OS, database, and applications.

▶ **SAP Sizing/Architecture training**—At one site, the customer wanted to better understand the SAP sizing process (especially as it related to the user/transactional data that can be captured in existing systems, to aid in sizing a new SAP solution). We taught similar workshops for third-party partners and vendors, too.

▶ **Monitoring Procedures/Approaches training**—The client wanted its enterprise management group to hit the ground running. We covered the stack, the client's specific enterprise tools, and how to monitor the system via the SAP Computer Center Management System (CCMS).

All of these custom training courses had more in common than being cheap and effective. First, they served to teach those who would eventually turn around and teach others, too. That is, the materials we created and delivered included speaker notes and handout materials, such that they became "train-the-trainer" self-documenting courseware. And because each set of materials was always disseminated in Microsoft PowerPoint format, the training courses could be easily modified to reflect new conditions or changes in a particular customer's environment.

Second, in lieu of another person standing up in front of a room and talking for four or eight hours at a time, these course materials also served as basic orientation materials for new hires and other personnel tasked with supporting our particular customer's unique SAP technology stack.

Third, simply by virtue of leaving the materials with their respective teams, the materials served as a foundation for both current-state and how-to documentation. This allowed the writing curve to be shortened significantly for some of our customers, and in all cases helped each team to stay fresh as the project progressed and different team members were pulled back and forth between their SAP-specific and other job-related responsibilities.

In closing, custom training and workshops can prove extremely valuable simply because they tend to be pointed and customer-specific. Unlike formal offerings, they are not locked down to an explicit set of curricula.

SAP Knowledge Warehouse

The SAP Knowledge Warehouse (SAP KW), first introduced a few years ago, allows you to create and manage custom training materials. A "version management" feature supports country-specific, plant-specific, and role-specific training. This, combined with a modular approach to reusing training materials, encourages rapid development of training courses, self-tests, assessments, and even course-specific certifications. And SAP KW helps you get a jump-start on both project-team and end-user-based training in two ways. First, it ships standard with the SAP Library (extended application-specific help), SAP Glossary, and SAP Terminology. Second, hundreds of predeveloped fee-based standard training courses are at your disposal, ready to be customized for your specific needs. And because all of this is shipped in multiple languages and SAP release versions, SAP AG has made it pretty easy to support a mixed SAP "legacy" and SAP enterprise.

SAP KW also allows full-text searches, attribute-based searches, process and workflow modeling, check-in and check-out of documents, and other basic document management features. All authoring is carried out using Microsoft Word and PowerPoint, tools common enough to most training developers today, thereby speeding up development. And SAP KW supports transporting documents in much the same manner as development objects are promoted to test and then production systems.

A number of interfaces including browsers (the WebGUI or SAP GUI for HTML) and the Knowledge Workbench make user access to SAP KW–based training easy. SAP KW supports

20

most of the file formats used in the past few years and today, and also enables you to associate other file types to any editor application that might be used by a particular customer or organization.

All in all, SAP KW is an awesome training tool across the board, useful to the end-user community, to the SAP TSO, and even to the project team supporting an SAP deployment. Things changed after the introduction of SAP NetWeaver Portal and SAP NetWeaver Knowledge Management (KM), though, and the "bar" was raised again. Many of the features and much of the functionality initially introduced in SAP Workplace and SAP KW found a new and improved home in SAP NetWeaver KM, as you'll discover in the following section.

Using SAP NetWeaver for Enterprise Knowledge Management

Easy and fast access to any kind of information is central in the age of *knowledge workers*. Enterprise information and collateral play an important role in the decision-making process of companies. The SAP NetWeaver KM application is core for collaboratively managing information and documents within an organization. It takes us beyond where the standalone SAP KW could ever go—it opens the door to managing distributed knowledge across not only your own enterprise resources, but potentially the resources of your technology and consulting partners, and even the Internet. SAP's *Enterprise Knowledge Management* solution provides various so-called IT scenarios:

▶ Content Integration and Management

▶ Content Creation, Publication, and Access

▶ Documentation, Manuals, and Training Material Management

The IT scenario *Documentation, Manuals, and Training Material Management* is the one we would like to focus on in this chapter because it provides an additional training approach. It allows you to create and translate, to edit and present, and to distribute and manage any kind of documentation, manuals, training material, and so forth. To use this IT scenario, the following installable units are required:

▶ Application Server ABAP

▶ Application Server Java

▶ Content Server

▶ Search and Classification (TREX)

▶ SAPGUI

This is a "wider" and smarter approach to managing information. Case in point, it is not only integrated with the Enterprise Portal but actually is required by the SAP NetWeaver Business Warehouse application.

Other Computer-Based and Online Training

SAP was not always the KM powerhouse it finds itself today. Before Enterprise Portal, and even before SAP KW, back in the days of InfoDB and IDES, other companies were eager to fill a rather large training and KM void. RWD Technologies, for example, brought to bear its extensive knowledge and understanding of SAP end-user training to create customized training courses unique to its customers. It was one of the first companies to offer compelling low-cost delivery options, too, such as CD-ROM and online. RWD Technologies was so successful at this that it eventually became one of a select number of SAP KW partners.

SAP AG offers something it calls e-learning, a training approach that is flexible enough to facilitate employee and project-team training both in the office and on the road. SAP describes this as "the ideal choice for a fast-moving workforce" and positions it as a way of ensuring the success of an SAP implementation by ensuring the success of the underlying training. Courses are introduced to project team members by way of their PCs or laptops, bridging the void between the classroom and the fast-paced workplace. And given that any client with a minimum-version browser can attend these training sessions, online SAP training is both easy to access and flexible, allowing the team to maximize its time and work at its own pace, while avoiding travel costs, lost work time, and scheduling conflicts.

SAP TechEd and Similar Venues

We are big fans of SAP's annual technical conference, SAP TechEd. Of course, SAP hosts a number of other annual conferences and events, but none of them is geared toward how to design, implement, integrate, and support SAP solutions, as TechEd is.

TechEd is by far our favorite software-sponsored technology event primarily because it has not (and hopefully never will) succumb to the "marketing guys." Not that there's anything wrong with that, but unless we are attending a future product–based technical session, we prefer to skip the marketing hype. Just take a look at some of the following highlights from a recent SAP TechEd event alone, and you can begin to understand why the technology people skip SAPPHIRE when travel and training budgets are tight:

▶ Hands-on workshops of between two and four hours each were presented. These alone are worth the trip. Everything is staged, ready to go—hardware, software, client/access devices, you name it. Plus, with supporting PowerPoint files and custom exercises and instructors that actually have used their products and know them inside and out (with a few exceptions), these activities represent the best ROI an SAP consultant can obtain outside of actual experience.

▶ As just mentioned, the instructors have real-world knowledge. And they tend to be technical and functional consultants and other technology support personnel rather than "trainers." Thus, what the overall presentations might lack in "polish" is more than made up for in substance.

20

▶ Customer and partner presentations helped to round out the predominantly SAP-delivered technical sessions. These sessions are usually quite special in that they tend to focus or tie back to actual lessons learned—again, the real world.

▶ Business development always plays a part when attending an SAP TechEd event. Every year, we tend to walk away with a few consulting engagements. Finding and spending no-pressure time with an expert in a certain SAP discipline has to be worth a lot in and of itself.

The training, relationship-building, and technical insights received over the four and a half days at SAP TechEd paid for themselves in a matter of weeks. And the camaraderie alone—seeing old friends and making new ones—is invaluable in our small world of SAP. But what TechEd offers that no other education medium offers is a chance to learn from the experts. This includes product developers, designers and engineers, and the customers and consultants who work with SAP solutions day in and day out. These people know things that can't be found on any website or in any book, even this one. Bottom line, we consider SAP TechEd a smart investment of a company's time and money, and expect you will, too.

Creating "Cookbooks" from Product Documentation and User Manuals

Sometimes we refer tongue-in-cheek to the need to read product documentation as "a last resort." Indeed, there are many consultants out there who shy away from product documentation and user/installation guides altogether until it is forced upon them. The reality, though, is that a really good SAP consultant or administrator will *start* with these resources, not somehow wind up there after wasting hours with an aborted installation. It is these latter consultants who "make it happen" day in and day out, while their cowboy colleagues occasionally get lucky but more often than not barely manage to scrape together an operational system.

It's sad that so many of us ultimately have to rely on the various readme files, installation guides, and online help available for a product to actually get it installed. But it's an enterprise application's complexity that keeps folks like us employed to one extent or another; ignoring a 100-page installation guide ultimately wastes everyone's time. Better said, trying to install a complicated SAP application component without the benefit of a checklist, guide, or "cookbook" is mindless.

Training is nice, and online courses are great, but at the end of the day we all still wind up with a stack of DVDs and countless downloads waiting to be installed on a particular piece of hardware. For our team back at HP, this is certainly business as usual, and we are nothing if not comfortable with this fact. But we have a huge advantage over most of our customers—we have several multimillion dollar enterprise solutions labs and the bulk of the entire North American SAP Competency Center at our disposal. So, although we tend to have a lot of fun doing what we do, for the rest of the world we can see how a lack of knowledgeable engineers and the weight of project-driven timelines takes most of the fun out of new-product trial-and-error training.

Fortunately, SAP's documentation is really quite good. Not perfect, no—we spend a considerable amount of time identifying, circumventing, and documenting "gotchas" for our paying enterprise customers. But all things considered, SAP has come a long way from the days of thinly clad and imperfectly translated installation documents (some of us speak German as well and it has been quite interesting to compare the English and German statements SAP makes, especially in their SAP Notes).

The following list solidifies much of what we go through to teach ourselves a new SAP product or a supporting layer in the SAP technology stack—consider it a roadmap of sorts. We hope it proves useful to you, and shortens your workdays a bit (the sequence is only suggested; feel free to jump around a bit unless otherwise noted):

1. Visit http://www.sap.com and search for the relevant topic, such as NetWeaver Application Server, CRM, or APO, and so on, picking up general knowledge of the application component in which you are interested.

2. Visit the http://service.sap.com/instguides website to locate relevant documentation. While SAP's Instguides (Installation Guides) are SAP application component–specific, we find the most value in looking through their Master Guides, which provide the "big picture" in terms of solution architecture, role of the solution, and pointers to more detailed technical resources.

3. You may also access the SAP Library" at http://help.sap.com, to obtain deeper knowledge in a particular area.

4. Visit http://service.sap.com/swdc, and enter your SAP Service Marketplace ID and password, to download actual SAP application components and supporting software/utilities. You must register with SAP AG, and provide your customer number or partner data to gain access to this and many other SAP websites.

5. Once you've reviewed the Master Guide for your particular SAP solution, we suggest carefully reading through the Installation Guide(s), looking for specific SAP notes and other notes to provide clarification.

6. Visit http://service.sap.com/notes, enter your SAP Service Marketplace ID and password, download each of the SAP Notes mentioned in the Installation Guide(s), and read these carefully.

7. Consistent with the recommendations found in the Installation Guide(s), configure a server and storage system that meets the minimum installation requirements.

8. Follow the Installation Guide(s) and walk through an actual installation, being careful to perform every step. Note the "gotchas" and other problems and issues that occur. The best way to accomplish this is to create a document of your own that references the Installation Guide(s) step-by-step (avoid using page numbers, as these numbers change both over time and based on unique printer setups). We call this our "Delta Guide" to the Installation Guide.

9. Using both the Installation Guide and your own custom delta document, go through the entire process again, ensuring that everything needed to perform the installation is indeed covered between the Installation Guide (perhaps 90%) and your own document (the remaining 10%).

20

10. It's important to document the hardware and OS configuration in this custom delta document, too (we like to keep all of our notes and supporting documents in a single umbrella document). We include everything relevant to the SAP technology stack—system board and hardware component firmware revisions, operating system patches and service packs, and so on up through the stack.

By adhering to such a process, we help ensure that an installation is indeed repeatable, and that others who follow us in performing this installation do not experience the same hold-ups and issues that we encountered and eventually solved. All of the steps described in the preceding list are therefore important. But the steps that save the most time are probably the first few—quickly reviewing a high level Master Guide and then a detailed Installation Guide, followed by obtaining the appropriate software, gives you a huge advantage in terms of minimizing training time.

And the last few steps are important as well, for it is these tasks that allow us to create a "cookbook" for a particular technology stack, such that we can run through subsequent installation processes quickly and efficiently, over and over again. As shown in Figure 20.2, these cookbooks create a custom knowledge base over time, serving a host of needs.

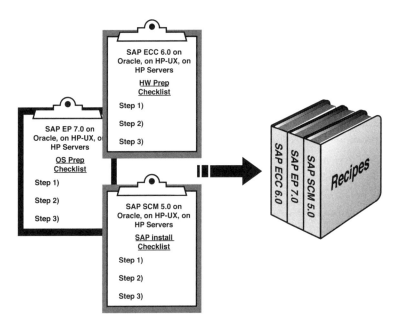

FIGURE 20.2   By creating and maintaining a suite of custom cookbooks for each SAP installation routine, you benefit from a repeatable and rapid system installation process.

So in the end, although formal training courses and custom workshops are great ways to obtain training, many technical professionals learn the basics of doing their jobs by following the same process we outlined in the preceding list.

Feedback Loops: Improving the Value of Training

Feedback loops not only improve the quality of training delivered over time, but can actually help *prove* that the training being delivered is effective, timely, appropriate, complete, and accurate. The best way that we have found to create a really useful feedback loop is to determine who a particular organization's customer is, and then to talk to or otherwise obtain feedback from that customer. For example, to improve the value of end-user training in a particular functional area, it only makes sense that training feedback needs to originate from the people receiving the most benefit from the training—the end users.

It gets more complicated, however, as support organizations grow larger and therefore the "customer" lines grow broader, or get fuzzy. For example, identifying the *real* customers of a particular subgroup within the SAP support organization can be especially challenging. But ensuring that this organization is trained well enough to deliver on all of its commitments is vital to the success of an SAP project, without exception. Thus, it's imperative that each subgroup within the support organization recognize its customers, with the understanding of course that everyone is ultimately working for the benefit of the SAP end-user community.

Functional and Development Consultants

The functional and development teams responsible for configuring an SAP solution have one obvious customer—the end user who eventually will log in to SAP and execute the business processes designed and implemented by this team. However, that day—go-live—lies far out in the future. Meanwhile, the expertise gained as a result of any specific training that the functional/development teams possess *today* needs to be ratified and probably tweaked throughout the life of an SAP implementation.

Who is the functional/development team's customer today, then, before go-live? In the simplest sense, it's the power users and other folks tasked with reviewing and using the code, and ultimately proving that the code being written works. Their regular and impartial feedback is essential to improving the coding and configuration upon which the system relies. This in turn should drive what kind of training the functional and development teams receive, and help to prioritize this training as well.

SAP Technical Consultants

What about the various technical consultants and other team members tasked with designing, installing, integrating, and supporting SAP both before and after go-live? Who is *their* customer? Bear in mind the following:

- ▶ SAP Basis and other SAP-specific implementation specialists are charged with assembling the system to be configured. Thus, we look at the functional and development folks as their customer.

- ▶ SAP administrators are tasked with keeping the system available and well tuned while under development, and later while in production—their customer is first the functional/development team, and later the end-user community.

20

▶ Database administrators are asked to maintain a well-performing and highly reliable database foundation, secure from corruption and resistant to tampering. Because the database serves the SAP instance, so too should the database administrator serve the SAP Basis or SAP infrastructure organization within the SAP TSO.

▶ SAP integration specialists work with other integration specialists, and the SAP Basis group in general, to ensure that an SAP solution operates correctly at a technical level. But they also play a role in ensuring that the integration points provide the required functional integration as well. For these reasons, the functional teams of the core system and other SAP and legacy systems represent customers to these integration specialists, as do the SAP Basis and similar technical teams supporting the technical foundation.

Timely and pointed feedback from each of the customer groups just identified will go a long way in steering training dollars down the right path—where it's needed most. Not all SAP TSO roles fit well into the groups described in the preceding list, though, and have instead been loosely grouped into a general *SAP infrastructure* organization, covered next.

Other SAP Infrastructure Roles

Data center infrastructure teams, staffed with people who oversee the power, rack, and network infrastructure, serve a whole slew of customers. But from a "chain of support" perspective, we believe that their immediate customer is the hardware team. This makes sense in a lot of respects—see Figure 20.3 for an illustrated chain of support.

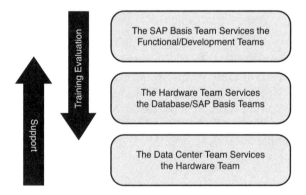

FIGURE 20.3   The chain of support works to promote customer-consumer relationships, all of which ultimately serve the SAP end-user community.

The SAP security team is another subgroup of the SAP TSO that serves many customers while providing an essential and core infrastructure service. Although it could be argued that the SAP security team's primary customer is the SAP Basis team or even the development teams, we are convinced that the end-user community holds the greatest mind share as to how well the security team is performing. If the security team does not do its job well, life is miserable for the end users. If, on the other hand, the security team does its job exceptionally well, the end users will not even remember that there *is* a security team.

SAP Operations/Help Desk

The SAP operations team may be deployed as a subset of the data center operations or infrastructure team, a general hardware support team, or even the SAP Basis organization. But the SAP operations team is accountable to the same primary "customer," nonetheless—the Basis group, charged with providing a highly available technical computing environment for SAP.

On the other hand, the SAP help desk's customer is quite clear. The help desk and its support folks service the end-user community directly. In terms of feedback to guide how training dollars are spent, though, the Basis team will be in an excellent position in this regard. Why? Because many of the issues not resolved by the help desk will naturally be escalated to the Basis team.

Additional SAP Support Specialists

Other support specialists play important implementation roles, too. But by the nature of their positions, it can be very easy to determine their customers. For example, the deliverables created by documentation specialists should be evaluated by whomever the documents are created for. Training specialists should similarly be evaluated by their students. Performance-tuning specialists assisting the database group should be evaluated by the DBAs, and so on. In this way, the combination of training and experience brought to bear in a particular situation is evaluated by the people in the best position to evaluate it, the customers.

In conclusion, then, as we are reminded in Figure 20.4, the real customers serviced by each of the subgroups covered over the past few pages vary considerably. It's our hope that the matrix in Figure 20.4 will help those tasked with managing the quality of training to focus on the proper customer organizations—the groups best positioned to provide really valuable training feedback, and therefore improve the overall SAP implementation across the board both before and after go-live.

Certification Programs

The last method of feedback and evaluation that we cover is certification. SAP's educational services (delivered through SAP Education—see http://www.sap.com/services/education/index.epx) and other SAP technology stack vendors all offer certification programs that not only reflect competence in a particular discipline or product, but also act as excellent feedback. A certification tells others that the holder has achieved a certain level of competency. The certification closes the loop, so to speak, regardless of whether the knowledge being tested was gained through formal training, hands-on experience, self-study, or other methods.

The value of training is nicely captured in process or task-oriented exams, such as those offered by SAP, Microsoft, Oracle, HP, and others. This is why so many companies offer certification programs for their products—they help customers to select people who are qualified or well positioned to be successful in designing, installing, or supporting their products. And certified individuals act as an extension of the company's sales and technical force, too, typically promoting the products with which they are most familiar and certified.

20

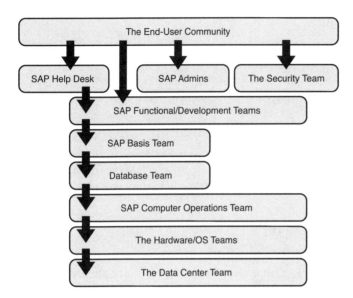

FIGURE 20.4   The quality of training received by one group is easily evaluated by a different group—this constitutes the foundation of a "feedback loop" approach to improving training.

SAP offers a number of certifications on three different levels of expertise: associate, professional, and master. SAP classifies its certifications into several focus areas including application, development, and technology.

Certification exams are scheduled and given in quite a few cities worldwide. The tests are very comprehensive and therefore require quite a bit of preparation to pass. But the results of certification can be impressive in terms of opening doors of opportunity where few existed before.

Summary

In this chapter, we identified, clarified, and described the immeasurable role that training has on an SAP project's success. We then looked closely at the different subgroups within the SAP technical support organization and how these groups benefit from training that's directly supported by a particular system within the SAP system landscape and by various training approaches. Proving that the training received by a particular group indeed met our needs for quality and completeness wrapped up the chapter, positioning us to advance to the next phase in our SAP implementation—developing the SAP data center.

Case Study: Training Technical Staff

You have been working as a consultant for HiTech, Inc. for a couple of years now. You were hired originally to do SAP infrastructure consulting work for HiTech's customers. However, recently there has been an increased demand for SAP NetWeaver consultants.

You have been working more and more in the SAP NetWeaver environment but you have noticed that on-the-job training doesn't answer all the questions nor does it provide you the confidence you are looking for. You are working on a training plan to share with your manager. What are your considerations in this regard?

Questions

1. What is the SAP training you are looking for?

2. When should you attend SAP training?

3. Which three SAP systems within the landscape are specifically targeted toward training, and toward whom are they generally targeted?

4. Would an SAP certification be beneficial? How could you justify the SAP certification?

NOTE

The answers to these questions can be found in Appendix A, "Case Study Answers."

20

CHAPTER 21

Developing the SAP Data Center

In this chapter, we will discuss in detail the processes inherent to building a new data center facility, or transforming your current data center, into a foundation capable of supporting a mission-critical enterprise SAP application and its underlying hardware infrastructure. The goal is clear—to design and build a stable and highly available hosting facility. We will walk through the entire process, from building out the power, network, and rack infrastructure to installing servers and configuring disk subsystems. In essence, by the time you have completed the activities described in this chapter, the SAP system landscape should be ready for the operating system and SAP Basis (that is, the SAP executables or binaries) installations to be performed.

Introducing the SAP Data Center

Data centers come in all different shapes and sizes, from relatively small rooms (or closets!) in the corner of an office building to entire purpose-built buildings. The data center provides many important functions for your SAP infrastructure—everything from providing the power your equipment requires to providing a safe operating environment, including environmental considerations such as temperature and humidity controls, to providing a physical place for all the computer equipment to securely reside. The data center is truly the foundation of a reliable infrastructure because it underpins every other layer in the SAP technology stack.

Although you may have already decided on many of the factors that will contribute to the deployment of this facility, including location, hardware and software vendors, and SAP products and components, availability should typically represent the single most important consideration driving the data center design and build-out. Remember, this application and its resident data will ultimately prove critical to your company's well-being. Should this application and data become unavailable, even for a short period of time, the ramifications to your business operations could be enormous and very costly:

▸ Thousands of users may sit idly by, waiting for the system to come "back."

▸ Trucks may stack up in the loading docks, waiting for bills of lading and shipping orders.

▸ Customers may call in or check online looking for status updates on their orders, only to be told to "try again sometime later, the system is down."

▸ Manual processes may need to be invoked to keep new orders coming in. And to make it worse, eventually these manual orders will need to be keyed into the system when it again becomes available, further impacting the users' time to place new orders.

▸ Manufacturing can come to a halt because the assembly line is dependent on serial numbers or other planning documents generated in SAP.

▸ Reports will be unavailable, impacting decision-making from the boardroom down to the assembly line, and everywhere in between.

Again, the data center in one way or another affects all other layers of the SAP technology stack. For example:

▸ At the lowest layer of the stack are power requirements. We have worked on numer-ous SAP implementations in which as many as 80 new servers, plus related disk subsystem and network infrastructure resources, were deployed over the course of a year, for example. Such a formidable collection of hardware pulls a considerable amount of power. An incorrectly architected power infrastructure will bring down an otherwise highly available clustered SAP solution in a heartbeat—all of the high-availability offerings at other layers in the solution are "powerless" without a well-architected and correctly implemented power distribution system.

▸ Similarly, cooling requirements must be addressed at one of the lowest layers of the stack. All those servers, disks, and network resources just mentioned not only pull a tremendous amount of power but also generate a considerable quantity of BTUs (British thermal units, or units of heat). An inadequate cooling and air-handling system can wreak havoc with availability statistics, again making it impossible to provide a reliable SAP business solution.

▸ Servers, disk subsystems, network infrastructure, and other SAP-related infrastructure all need to be neatly racked and cabled. Poor planning or lack of attention to detail during *physical* deployment quickly contribute to the length of time the system is down. In more than one case, we have seen racks of servers cabled neatly and in an organized manner, only to have all of this work ripped out after someone finally thought to pull out a server for servicing. Why? Because the cabling did not allow enough "slack" for the servers to be actually pulled out more than a few inches (making it impossible to pull off their covers and get inside). In other cases, we have seen high availability (HA) compromised simply because otherwise redundant pairs of cables were routed through the same cable conduits, and the conduit itself failed or was damaged (taking everything out in the process). Finally, poorly positioned data center floor tiles and overweight racks can combine to create a minidisaster when least expected.

▶ SAP's tiered architecture and the potential need for dedicated management, backup, and special-purpose network segments requires forethought in regard to network planning, too. As you will see later in this chapter, neglecting this can impact not only availability and raw system accessibility but also overall performance. In addition, we cannot forget about network firewall security and other network infrastructure considerations that will impact availability—especially for Internet-facing SAP servers such as portals, e-commerce servers, external-facing SAP procurement systems and their bolt-ons, and so on.

▶ Server infrastructure and design directly impact availability, both "in the box" via single points of failure (SPOFs) and "out of the box" when it comes to higher-layer technology stack matters such as failover clustering.

▶ Your disk subsystem, whether a high-performance storage area network (SAN), direct-attached SCSI disk enclosures, or network attached storage (NAS), tends to be the single most important performance factor in our experience (outside of really bad SAP ABAP and Java coding, to be sure). But it is also one of the most easily misunderstood solution components when it comes to HA.

As you have just read, the design and implementation of a company's specific SAP solution stack through a well-planned data center deployment affects availability at all levels of the stack. SPOFs abound everywhere. A lone power source, single power distribution unit (PDU), nonredundant power supply, single network connection to a server, single server hosting a database, and more all represent potential contributors to downtime. And we have not even begun to discuss the database and SAP application layers!

In the remainder of this chapter, we take a closer look at each of the availability factors outlined earlier, as well as operational and other processes that will ultimately impact the net availability of your SAP solution to your end-user population.

First Things First—Standardization

From a high-level perspective, we need to ensure that no detail is overlooked when planning for our SAP data center facility or facilities. Each layer in the SAP technology stack presents SPOF challenges; each layer must therefore be thoughtfully considered with an eye toward eliminating these SPOFs, or at least noting and mitigating risk to the point that it becomes financially acceptable. In the end, identifying and dealing with SPOFs is the essence of achieving HA. This is made possible, in part, through standardization.

Standards impact every layer of the technology stack, and indeed every people-related and process-oriented dimension of an SAP implementation. Fortunately, taking a close look at standards early in the SAP data center planning process forces you to think ahead, and ultimately avoid many pitfalls potentially lurking in the future. Consider the following:

▶ Server naming conventions must be descriptive enough to promote manageability, but short enough to be technically supported by the particular SAP component version (and any other applications that might need to reference this server by name, including systems management applications such as HP OpenView or BMC PATROL).

▶ TCP/IP network naming conventions should help identify what type of server network connection is being made. For example, standards that help to identify public, management, and private network connections required for clusters are quite prevalent in the world of SAP infrastructure.

▶ Disk naming (and drive letter naming for Windows Server 2003) conventions should be published and leveraged for consistency. Such consistency by its very nature impacts availability as well, because the chance of someone "accidentally" bringing a disk resource offline is less likely to occur when the disk name or disk drive letter for the database (for example) tends to be the same throughout the SAP landscape.

▶ Even something as simple as color-coding network cables and power cables can improve system availability. A good color-coding scheme helps avoid unplanned downtime due to someone inadvertently disconnecting or miscabling a vital network or power connection. We have witnessed companies leveraging factors other than simply color, too; the number and thickness of bands in a cable, and even the cable thickness itself can also be used to differentiate otherwise similar cables.

▶ Most SAP shops employ standard HA server configurations. For servers this means "in-the-box" features such as redundant power supplies, fans, processors, network cards, fiber-channel host bus adapters (HBAs), RAID-protected disk drives, RAID- or ECC-protected RAM, and so on. These servers are then deployed in clusters to account for any remaining SPOFs through system redundancy.

▶ As with standard highly available server configurations, most SAP shops also promote an equivalent "high-availability disk subsystem." This usually involves a standard frame or disk chassis, standard drive size (for example, 300GB, 15,000 RPM 1-inch drives), standard redundant disk drive controllers, and redundant disk interconnects back to the server infrastructure, including redundant SAN switches.

▶ A standard operating system (OS) build for HA deployments is typically developed. This would include specific OS release levels, patch or service pack levels, any patches or bug fixes required, other software drivers and their versions, and so on. Nowadays, standard methodologies for deploying customary server images are often employed, leveraging OS-build approaches ranging from traditional disk imaging to custom scripting, deployment of imaging servers, hardware vendor–specific approaches, and so on.

▶ Standardized processes regarding managing all of the aforementioned resources help to minimize downtime across the board.

Other standards exist, of course, but the preceding list should prove useful in identifying the key areas within each layer of the SAP solution stack that must be addressed before a single data center floor tile is ever pulled up, a server is mounted in a rack, or an operating system is installed.

Data Center Physical Requirements

Physical requirements mean different things to different people. In the context of building our data center, we could go into minute details regarding actual construction of the facility, for example. In such case, physical requirements would exist with regard to the following:

- ▶ **Physical construction materials**—Along with related factors such as fire codes, weight-bearing members for roof-mounted AC/environmental units, load-rating factors for the raised floor construction, cable risers or trays, and so on, physical construction materials are fundamental to data center integrity.

- ▶ **Physical security and access**—This includes monitoring systems (card or other systems for doors and window access, and attention to vertical security above the dropped ceiling and below the raised floors).

- ▶ **Location**—Avoid the first floor or top floor of buildings, flood zones, and areas where access may be limited in terms of single stairs, elevators, roads, and so on.

- ▶ **Environmental systems**—These include cooling, heating, and humidity level monitoring, as well as access to published thermal specifications for each component to be housed in the data center, and basic lighting and plumbing.

- ▶ **Environmental controlling systems**—Comprises temperature monitoring and fire suppression capabilities, smoke and water sensors, and so on.

- ▶ **Basic infrastructure accessibility**—Consider the capability of your loading dock or freight elevators from an access perspective, as well as the use of double-protected public access points.

- ▶ **Network operations center (NOC)**—A central operations and monitoring station.

- ▶ **Network considerations**—Access to high-bandwidth multipath data communications circuits or network/Internet connections.

- ▶ **Dual-power infrastructure**—Avoid all SPOFs, even the ones you have no direct control over. Standardize on an approach that marries attention to matters such as 208 volts AC and redundant power grids with more obvious solutions. This includes the availability of generators, generator fuel, battery backup, and so on (this also might include access to two discrete city or state power grids, should HA or DR requirements dictate such a robust power infrastructure).

These details are best left up to the experts who design and build data center facilities. Ensure that at a minimum the preceding points are addressed, however. The next few sections explore power, cooling, and other environmental requirements in more detail.

Power Requirements

From a system availability perspective, power problems can plague an otherwise bullet-proof solution architecture. Power requirements therefore need to be planned for the long term, not merely for the demands of go-live—your SAP environment will only grow, grow, grow. When addressing the power needs of the SAP data center, it is helpful to first analyze each specific server, disk subsystem, network, or other hardware component requiring power, and then work "back" to the ultimate power source. For maximum availability, ensure the following:

▶ Where the highest levels of availability are necessary, each hardware component must support redundant power supplies (otherwise, the remainder of this list is not of any use). Preferably, these power supplies should also be "hot swappable" or "hot pluggable." In this way, in the event of a power failure, not only would the server remain available and powered up on its second power supply, but the failed power supply could be pulled out and replaced without incurring downtime.

▶ Each power supply alone should be capable of keeping the hardware component up and running. That is, if the average load being pulled from one of the power supplies in a dual-power-supply configuration exceeds 50% of its rated capacity, you actually don't have protection from failure of the other power supply! The alternatives are clear—lower the capacity requirements by reducing the number of disk drives, CPUs, and so on, or increase the number of power supplies to three or more, or in rare cases simply replace the current power supplies with higher-rated alternatives.

▶ Each power supply must have its own unique power cable. This is a very common oversight with some of the second-tier server and disk subsystem vendors, where highly available systems might be touted, but reality differs. These HA wannabes often provide only a single power cable receptacle even in their "redundant" power supply configurations. A single *anything* represents a SPOF and should be avoided. Besides, we have actually seen a couple of power cables fail in the real world. What is more likely to occur is that the single power cable becomes unplugged, effectively bringing down the most available server or disk subsystem.

▶ As we indicated previously, color-coding or otherwise differentiating power cables makes it very clear to everyone when things are cabled correctly. The most common implementation of this involves a black cable cabled to the primary power supply, and a gray or white cable cabled to the redundant power supply.

▶ Each power cable must be routed to dedicated, separate power distribution units (PDUs, or power strips, and so on)—whatever is used by the company to centralize many power feeds into fewer, larger-capacity connections. Each PDU needs to be analyzed to ensure that the load placed on this single component, should the other PDU fail, can still be addressed by the remaining PDU. Again, the most common implementation of this is to use black cables to one PDU and gray or white cables to the redundant PDU.

▶ Each PDU must in turn be cabled to redundant uninterruptible power supplies (UPSs). Like the PDUs, these need to be regularly tested and analyzed to ensure that they are indeed "redundant." We have even seen data centers in which the power receptacles from the UPS are color coded, making it easy to verify at a glance that you are indeed using independent power sources. Note that a UPS tends to be equipped to handle only short-term power losses, thus necessitating the next power component listed.

▶ Primary power for each redundant power supply should culminate in redundancy at the breaker boxes as well. That is, each power supply should ultimately receive its power from a dedicated breaker panel, like that illustrated in Figure 21.1.

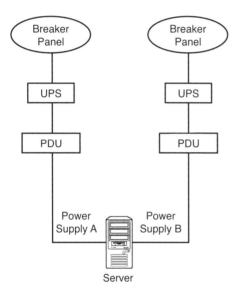

FIGURE 21.1   Note how a completely redundant power infrastructure requires attention not only to hardware components but all the way back to the breaker panels.

▶ The "back-up generator" is a necessity for mission-critical SAP shops. Whereas the UPS provides short-term relief from blackouts and brownouts, a generator can conceivably provide power for days, as long as fuel is available. Select a generator that runs on whatever is most easily accessible or readily available, including diesel fuel, propane, or natural gas.

It is of utmost importance that the generator and the UPS be properly sized to handle the loads placed upon them. Generators must leverage an automatic transfer switch (ATS) to allow them to tie into both the power company (the power utility, or "utility power") and the SAP data center, as shown in Figure 21.2. Critical systems need to be identified and earmarked for generator backup. These systems typically include emergency lighting, emergency environmental and safety controls, the critical SAP data center gear, and in some cases the contents of the entire data center.

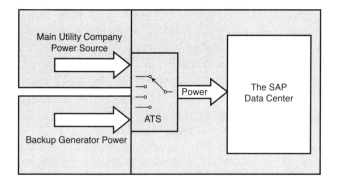

FIGURE 21.2   Without an automatic transfer switch, the actual usefulness of a backup generator is questionable, thereby impacting high availability.

Best practices also dictate that critical computing systems be isolated from the facility's primary power source but capable of accessing this source if required. In this way, the dual sources of power will "back up" one another and facility–related power failures will not impact the enterprise system. Similarly, critical computing system power source failure will not affect the facility.

Using kVAs for Accurate UPS Sizing

UPSs are rated by kilovolt-ampere (kVA). The formula to calculate kVAs is amps × volts / 1,000 = kVA. So if your rack is capable of pulling 69.5 amps, this equates to 16.6 kVAs (69.5 amps × 240 volts = 16,680 / 1,000 = 16.6 kVAs). Never allow your UPS to run above 80% capacity. In our example, 16.8 kVAs is 80% of 21 kVAs. So at a minimum, the rack should have 21 kVAs' worth of UPS.

A Power Plug Oversight
One of our favorite and most popular enterprise SAP server class, the HP ProLiant, serves as the basis for our next example. A wealth of web-based information is available on the ProLiant in the form of something HP calls QuickSpecs. These technical specifications have been published and updated for years, and describe in great detail much of the minutia that is of little interest to anyone but hardcore techies once the SAP system landscape is in place. Prior to that time, though, these QuickSpecs fulfill a number of critical roles. First, quickly perusing this document might reveal, for example, that a particular model and configuration (in terms of CPUs, disks, and so on) of ProLiant draws a maximum of 4.9 amps on a 220-volt line, while producing a moderate 4070 BTUs every hour. These little tidbits of information will help ensure that the data center facilities folks understand how many and what type of power circuits to run. The BTUs, on the other hand, should be fed into a simple model that will determine the minimum rating of the air handlers (cooling/heating system).

The QuickSpecs also specify what type of power plug connectors to use. As with most servers, the power connector from the server to the PDU or UPS is ordered as an option with the PDU or UPS. The real challenge then becomes matching the PDU's power plug with the appropriate power receptacle. Typically, either an L6-20P or L6-30P is called for—in the case of certain PDUs deployed at one of our particular customer's new SAP data center sites, the L6-30P (a 30-amp circuit) was specified by the QuickSpecs.

However, the customer got ahead of itself and, in the interest of meeting deadlines for power, laid enough L6-30P power cables for the new SAN, too, which was to arrive shortly after the servers. When the SAN cabinets showed up, though, the customer couldn't plug them in. The connectors were different—they required the L6-20P receptacles. To this day we are still not quite sure how our motivated customer managed this, but it actually forced its million-dollar SAN power plugs into the wrong receptacles and ran the system this way for perhaps a week before someone noticed that "something just didn't look quite right" under the subfloor. Understand that these two connectors are quite different, and this little engineering feat will begin to sink in—the customer somehow managed to squeeze and twist the male plugs most of the way into the female receptacles. This not only posed a potential safety hazard, but also risked blowing up the customer's 20-amp SAN gear with 30 amps of juice.

The customer got lucky. The SAN had very few drives actually installed and spinning (and therefore drawing power) that first week. However, this simple oversight caused a one-week delay in the project plan while the system was effectively shut down awaiting the proper wiring. In the end, the lost time was made up in the OS and SAP Basis installations, and neither gear nor people were none the worse. But the moral of this story should be clear: Not only should the technical specifications for each piece of equipment be checked and verified, but we should never solve our power problems by brute force. Besides, because all this information is just a click or QuickSpec away, there's really little excuse for misconfiguring or underallocating power and cooling resources.

The Impact of Incorrect Power Cabling

Another common mistake illustrates how the redundancy of power-related components can be rendered useless through lack of attention to cabling and overall power architecture. Our customer in this instance wanted to factor in redundancy at the physical layer of its SAP deployment. Its high-end servers, disk subsystem, and network equipment all supported redundant power supplies, so it took advantage of them. Each power supply on the back *left* side of each server and disk subsystem drive shelf was the recipient of a black power supply cable. This in turn was carefully routed along the left side of the rack enclosures to a PDU dedicated for this purpose. Similarly, each power supply located on the back *right* side was fitted with a gray power cable, and these gray cables were also carefully routed to their own PDU. So far, so good—no SPOFs existed, in that half of the power supplies, cables, and PDUs could fail and the system could still remain up and powered.

However, all the careful preparation and planning that went into this phase of the project was tossed out the window after another few minutes of work. Our customer plugged both PDUs into the same UPS. When the UPS failed, the customer lost 10 servers—servers it assumed were protected through redundancy.

Like power, the next layer in the solution stack also represents a basic necessity for supporting your SAP enterprise—cooling.

Cooling and Other Environmental Controls

One of the biggest causes of hardware component failure is heat. Luckily, planning for cooling requirements has become a lot easier with the popularity of the World Wide Web. That is, nearly every hardware vendor out there today publishes BTU/thermal specifications. Your job is then to simply pull down and "add up" these technical specifications on every piece of equipment you plan to deploy. Don't forget to allow for future growth, either—with server and disk form factors shrinking every year, the heat generated per cubic foot of data center space just continues to grow and grow. Blades in particular have really raised the bar on heat generated per cubic foot and may require special cooling solutions.

To address the next three years in your data center planning efforts conservatively, determine the average BTU output per cubic foot, and then double that number and apply it to any remaining floor space that could conceivably house incremental SAP gear. Don't forget to factor in the fact that air might not move uniformly through your data center and any other cooling dynamics inherent to your facility. In doing so, you will be eminently ready for the day the VP of operations says, "Hey! We're gonna go ahead with that SAP PLM project, so make room for 20 new servers and a couple of fully stocked SAN cabinets in the next few weeks."

As with cooling, air handlers exist that enable you to control and exhaust heat, monitor and fine-tune humidity, and so on. Ensure that new hardware additions to the SAP data center are plugged in to the BTU model as soon as possible, so that you can address any new requirements for cooling. Air handlers, and other large environmental gear like this, require significant lead times when new components or upgrades/replacements loom in the future.

Don't forget to load the proper OS drivers or applets that might be required by your hardware system to shut itself down in the event of overheating or loss of cooling. In the case of the ProLiant, the System Shutdown Service shuts down the server when the heat exceeds a predefined threshold, acting in response to commands from the integrated management features inherent to the ProLiant server platform.

And consider some of the newer trends in air handling and monitoring. For example, HP recently developed a robot that literally rolls around your data center floor looking for hot spots. Upon finding a hot spot, the robot analyzes the conditions and may, for example, signal your cooling system to increase airflow to the area. Or it might instead communicate with your hardware systems to relocate workloads from one system to another. Utilizing a combination of these approaches, HP believes that it can reduce cooling costs for its customers in the neighborhood of 25 percent.

Rack Planning for Data Center Resources

With your highly available power infrastructures laying the foundation for your SAP data center, and attention to environmental requirements already addressed, we are ready to proceed with the next physical data center infrastructure layer—the rack mounting systems for housing all the enterprise computing gear. This section covers

- ▶ Rack layout and design considerations
- ▶ Optimizing rack real estate
- ▶ Rack mounting and related best practices
- ▶ Cabling and cable management

What exactly is a rack? One of my customers describes a *rack* simply as "furniture for computers." In most cases, racks are somewhere between 4 and 7 feet tall, 19 inches wide, and something like 34–39 inches deep, depending on requirements. Racks allow for computer gear—servers, disk subsystems, network components, and more—to be easily mounted, cooled, and serviced in what amounts to a "stacked" configuration. That is, the gear appears to be stacked one on top of the other. In reality, of course, none of it should literally be stacked on top of the other because this makes servicing and cooling the gear quite difficult.

Often, each component is mounted on sliding rails (though less-advantageous fixed rails are still quite popular with some server and rack vendors). These sliding rails facilitate rapid access to the top and sides of each hardware component, where service areas are easily accessed. And something called *cable management arms* make this serviceability possible, allowing hardware systems to be pulled out for service without requiring cables to be disconnected or rerouted. Cabling is detailed later in this chapter.

Rack Layout and Design Considerations

Before you order a truckload of racks, you need to step back and develop a plan for deploying and laying out these racks. A number of best practices should be considered, but nearly as important is achieving some sort of consistency in deployment. This can be accomplished by working with your hardware vendors and demanding detailed deployment guidance as it relates to how servers and disk resources should be mounted, how many racks are required, how they should be optioned, and so forth. You need to get answers to the following questions related to rack placement in terms of metrics and standards:

- ▶ Do the servers and racks match? Determine the airflow design for the equipment to be mounted. Then check to ensure that the racks allow for this design. For example, the HP ProLiant server line has always been designed for front-to-back airflow, thus mandating the use of a rack that supports this. In other cases, servers pull air from the data center subfloor and vent it out the top of the rack. It is therefore necessary to ensure that the servers and racks match each other.

▶ Are your air registers positioned for the best airflow? It is highly recommended that the racks be arranged in a front-to-front or back-to-back manner. Picture standing in between two rows of racks that either face toward each other or face away from each other, and you will understand front-to-front and back-to-back, respectively. For maximum front-to-rear airflow, the *air registers* (the floor tiles with the little holes in them that force out cool air) should be placed in line with the front of the racks. Similarly, air returns located inline with the rear of the racks are a must, too, as shown in Figure 21.3. In this case, the row in front of the servers is referred to as the "cold row" and the row behind the servers as the "hot row." In the case of bottom-to-top airflow, the air registers are instead placed such that the rack sits on top of them.

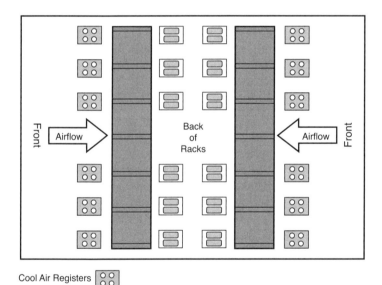

Cool Air Registers

Warm Air Returns

FIGURE 21.3   Placement and layout of racks and floor tile airflow registers/returns are critical to maintaining proper air temperature in the SAP data center.

▶ Is there enough room both in front of and behind each rack to open and close the doors, and to provide the cooling airflow necessary to keep everything running? If not, then reposition the racks, or move the offending gear/walls. Racks need space (25 inches in front and 30 inches in back is suggested, though your specific rack documentation may indicate otherwise).

▶ Would purchasing a top-mounted fan option or split rear door make sense, given the volume of computing gear to be racked? Both enhance cooling to some degree, regardless of airflow direction. We generally recommend top-mounted fans in the densest of racks, regardless of the direction of airflow—these fans help draw component-damaging heat out of the rack as quickly as possible.

▶ Should overhead fire protection sprinkler devices be considered? Check local building codes for acceptable clearances before installing racks underneath such devices.

At this junction, it makes sense to actually diagram rack layouts for your specific data center needs. Again, we recommend working with your data center hosting provider, hardware vendor, or an infrastructure-experienced systems integrator to get this right the first time.

Optimizing Rack Real Estate

When loading equipment into the racks, observe the following best practices and observations:

▶ Put heavier items in the bottom racks; that is, UPSs and large servers.

▶ Address floor-loading weight limitations. For example, never load a rack with all UPSs, because the weight alone will almost certainly exceed the data center's raised floor load-bearing factor. Instead, distribute UPSs evenly across all racks.

▶ Locate monitors and keyboards for maximum ergonomic comfort (based on your particular sitting/standing arrangement). *Do not* locate them on the top of each of your 7-foot racks, as one of our customers did! It's funny reading about this after the fact, but it was no laughing matter at the time.

▶ Attempt to distribute monitors and keyboards such that access to a particular environment is available in two ways. For example, if an SAP staging landscape consists of eight application servers, it would make sense to attach four of them to one monitor and keyboard and the other four to the second monitor and keyboard. In this way, performing maintenance, upgrades, applying patches, and so on is possible from one monitor and keyboard, while the other remains available for business as usual.

▶ Use rack blanking panels to fill in spaces greater than 1U in size (where a "U" is a standard rack unit of measurement equivalent to 1.75 inches). This is important to ensure that good airflow is maintained within the rack enclosure itself.

▶ Install all items of gear housed within the rack—servers, disk subsystems, everything—with their covers and sides on. Running a server without the top cover or side panels, for example, disturbs the flow of air through the computer such that it is not cooled off as effectively as it otherwise would be. In some cases, running a server without the cover and sides will actually invalidate the unit's warranty, too.

Most hardware vendors have software available on their websites to help you plan the optimal rack configuration, and most even provide a list of the necessary components.

Rack Mounting and Related Best Practices

When connecting the power to the racks, heed fault-tolerant considerations. Your servers and disk subsystems should have redundant (or N+1) power supplies. To optimize the power configuration, deploy multiple (at least two) PDUs. We recommend at least one mounted on each side of each rack. All right-side power supplies should be plugged into the right-side PDU, and the left-side power supplies into the left-side PDU. The PDUs should be plugged into separate circuits and breaker panels, as we have discussed previously. These circuits should be adequately sized to meet the potential load demand, which should rarely exceed 80% of their rated capacity if at all possible. In this configuration, if a circuit is lost, only half of the power supplies in each rack will be without power, leaving the other half to continue powering all of the computing equipment—resulting in zero downtime.

Another thing to consider in rack planning is how the servers should be grouped. Ask yourself what makes sense. Some of our clients like to group all development resources together, all test resources together, and so on. The advantage to this is that production resources are easily identified by their location, as shown in Figure 21.4. Others prefer to group all servers together, all disk subsystems together, all network components together, and so on. We suggest that you select either the approach that is used in your data center today or the approach that makes the most sense given the specific SAP system landscape being deployed.

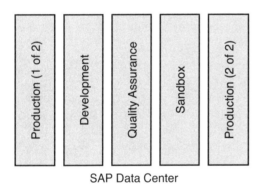

SAP Data Center

FIGURE 21.4   This grouping approach is SAP landscape–centric rather than hardware-centric. Either approach is valid.

Next, let's take a closer look at two very special racking scenarios—racking clustered servers and racking production servers.

Racking Clustered Servers

Regardless of the grouping approach, though, a best practice exists when it comes to clustered servers. Cluster nodes should always be mounted in separate racks, using separate keyboards, mice, and monitors, connected to completely different PDUs and network infrastructure, and so on. In fact, it is a good idea to put the nodes in different areas of the data center if at all possible. Why? Because if the cluster nodes share anything in common, this becomes a SPOF. Because you are clustering to avoid SPOFs in the first place, maintaining separation is critical for these systems.

> **NOTE**
>
> Splitting the servers associated with a particular SAP component (by housing them in physically different areas of the data center) will allow you to maintain availability in the event of a problem in one part of the data center, such as a cooling-, power-, or even rack-related issues. This is especially true of clusters—space them out to avoid issues that take both servers down and therefore eliminate the benefits of clustering in the first place.

Racking Production Servers

When it comes to mounting the production servers in their racks, it is critical to maintain a separation of resources. That is, production should ideally be isolated from all other SAP environments (such as development, test/QA, and particularly sandbox systems) from a power, network, rack, SAN, and server perspective. The production racks therefore require their own power infrastructure, network infrastructure, and so on. The rationale behind this is that you do not want anything that happens in the other environments to affect production, which after all should be your most highly controlled environment. Sharing a single data center resource between production and nonproduction environments will eventually result in unexpected performance or accessibility issues and eventually unplanned downtime.

In the real world, as SANs continue to enable the highest levels of availability and scalability for SAP customers, the line between production and other resources is beginning to blur. Expensive SAN switches, SAN management appliances, SAN-enabled tape backup solutions, and the fiber cabling that ties everything together are often shared between production and development systems, for example. Providing some kind of change management support is important in these cases in which the cost of a sophisticated SAN outweighs the risk of maintaining separate production resources. That is, you still need a test environment—be it a technical sandbox, test/QA system, or whatever—to test the impact of changes to your SAN before implementing them on the production SAN. In our experience, these changes are often firmware- and hardware-related, though topology and design changes also need to be tested as well.

Cabling and Cable Management

If you have ever attempted to squeeze 21 servers into a 7-foot (42U) rack, the concept of cable management should evoke special thoughts of long days and late nights. Cables have shrunk in diameter over the last five years, but not to the extent or in keeping with the trends we have all seen in hardware platform densities. As a result, one of the biggest immediate challenges facing new SAP implementations is how to best route the various keyboard, mouse, monitor, disk subsystem, network, and other cables required for each server. More and more, we see fat cables being replaced by smaller ones, and lots of little cables being replaced by fewer centralized cables. But in the end, there's still a whole lot of cabling to consider!

Alternatives to traditional KVM (keyboard, video, and mouse) cable connections abound today. The following represent two common methods of reducing the number and size of cables (a long-time favorite and a newer alternative):

- Installing a dedicated "computer on a board" into a PCI slot in each server, to facilitate out-of-band and in-band management of the server. Such boards typically require a network connection only, and facilitate communications via a browser-enabled user interface. A fine example is HP's iLo. Depending on the particular server, these boards may come standard with the system, and may even be integrated into the server's motherboard.

- Installing "KVM over IP," which represents another way to shrink various cables into a small single network cable. This method also requires a small server of its own and licensing costs for the particular enabling product.

More often than not, we expect to see the widespread use of cable management arms, tie-wraps, Velcro-wraps, and similar inexpensive approaches. Regardless of the cabling techniques, though, continue to stay focused on *availability*. SPOFs can exist in this realm like any other area—remember that a server might be effectively unavailable when it loses access to its disk or network connections. Effective cable management will enable you to maintain your servers and those around it without having to worry about accidentally unplugging a power cord, SAN, or network cable.

Network Infrastructure for SAP

Given that SAP is architected to support a distributed three-tiered design, a slew of configurations exist that can potentially impact high availability. There are similar performance considerations as well—the database, application, and web tiers are all affected. For example, a public network addresses client requirements while another network interconnects the application servers to the web/Internet layers. If you plan on pulling backups across the network (rather than via a disk subsystem that supports direct-attached SCSI or fiber channel tape drives), a separate back-end network subnet is highly recommended in this case, too. In all cases, Gigabit switched network segments are recommended. The only exception to this rule may be cluster interconnect networks, which can be 100Mbps (or even 10Mbps) switched networks.

We have also had clients who have created a separate management network for security reasons. The idea is that only administrative tools such as Secure Shell (for UNIX or Linux) and Terminal Services Client (Windows) would be allowed access through this network. Furthermore, the network would only be accessible from clients on the internal network, acting as a further defense against anyone outside the client's network hacking into its SAP servers. We have also seen clients go as far as locking down which IP addresses could access Oracle—after changing the default port from 1527. How far you take security really depends on your requirements and the amount of effort (and cost) you are willing to put into it.

> **NOTE**
>
> A few years ago it used to be quite common to establish a network for communication between the SAP application servers and the database. This was called the "back-end segment" or "database segment," and it was necessary for performance reasons. The implementation of Gigabit Ethernet networks has largely eliminated the requirement for this back-end network, however.

Firewalls, Ports, and Other Network Concerns

The application/web tier often consists of a single gigabit subnet. Because the application servers/web servers are usually not considered critical from a backup perspective, dedicated network backup segments are usually not warranted in this case—these servers usually contain fairly static data that lends itself to weekly or other less-frequent backups.

The web tier is typically split, though. In the case of the SAP Internet Transaction Server (ITS), which has been integrated into WebAS and now SAP's NetWeaver Application Server for many years, the client connects to the Web Dispatcher, which is often housed in a secure demilitarized zone (DMZ) for access via the Internet or an intranet, while the SAP application server remains safely behind the firewall, as shown in Figure 21.5. In this way, the network accommodates the performance needs of the enterprise without sacrificing security.

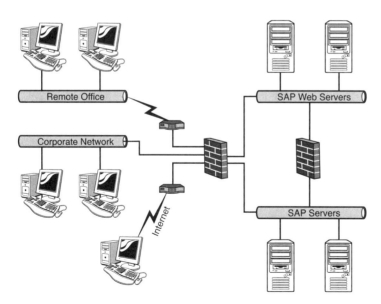

FIGURE 21.5   Firewalls are critical to the security of your SAP systems, especially when accessed from the Internet.

The key to setting up firewalls for SAP networks is to know which ports must be opened. By default, firewalls work by blocking all traffic except that which is explicitly allowed by what are commonly termed firewall rules. Table 21.1 provides examples of a few of the most commonly used TCP/IP ports in an SAP environment.

TABLE 21.1   Commonly Used TCP/IP Ports

Application Service Name	Protocol	Destination Port
sapdpXX	TCP	32XX
sapgwXX	TCP	33XX
sapmsSID	TCP	36XX
SMTP	TCP	25
Microsoft SQL Server	TCP	1433
Oracle	TCP	1527

Network Fault Tolerance

As indicated earlier, there are many ways to architect a network solution for SAP. Simply segregating each layer in the solution stack achieves minimum performance metrics but does not address availability. In fact, it actually increases the chance of a failure, as more and more SPOF components are introduced. Fault tolerance must therefore be *built into* the design, not looked at afterward. To this end, we will next discuss the primary method by which network availability is designed into the SAP data center, using an approach we call *availability through redundancy* (ATR).

Just as a redundant power infrastructure starts with the servers, disk subsystems, and other hardware components, a redundant network infrastructure starts with the servers. Here, redundant network interface cards (NICs) are specified, each cabled to redundant network switches, which in turn are connected to redundant routers. Figure 21.6 illustrates this relationship between the servers and a highly available network infrastructure.

Network fault tolerance starts not only with two (or otherwise redundant) NICs, but also with OS-specific drivers capable of pairing two or more physical NICs into one "virtual" card or NIC. Hardware vendors often refer to this as *teaming* or bonding, but other labels have been used for this important piece of the network puzzle. Regardless of the label, the idea is simple: Pair two or more NICs together and use both concurrently to send and receive the same exact packets of data. Then, use the data on one NIC and its corresponding network segment (referred to as the primary NIC), and discard or ignore the (exact same) data on the other NIC as long as the network is up and things are going well. If a failure occurs with one of the NICs, network segments, or hubs/switches on the redundant path, continue processing packets as always on the primary path—business as usual. However, if a failure occurs with one of the NICs, network segments, or hubs/switches on the primary path, immediately turn to the redundant path and start processing the data moving through this path instead.

Today, most OSs support NIC teaming for high availability. Many OSs also support variations of NIC teaming geared toward improving performance, including network bonding,

The Public Network

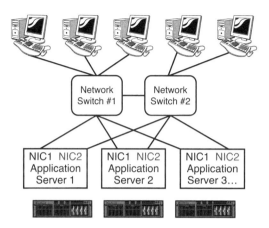

FIGURE 21.6   This example shows what a properly architected highly available network infrastructure may look like for SAP.

adaptive load balancing, Fast EtherChannel, Gigabit EtherChannel, and more. Remember, though, that these latter variations do not necessarily improve availability; teaming must either be inherently supported by or used in conjunction with these different performance-enhancing techniques or approaches.

Not All Server Configurations Support NIC Teaming

Some OSs simply do not support specific network cards when it comes to NIC teaming. Other OSs preclude its use in particular scenarios. For example, Microsoft Windows 2000/2003 Cluster Service specifically prohibits teaming the private interconnect, or heartbeat connection, regardless of the type of NIC—Microsoft simply does not support teaming the heartbeat. Network availability in this case is gained by configuring Cluster Service such that both the private and public networks can send "still alive" messages between the cluster nodes. As an aside, best practices suggest that the private network be preferred for this activity, and that the public network be leveraged only when the private network fails or is otherwise unavailable.

Remember that each NIC in the team should be connected to a different switch, which in turn is connected to a separate router or separate card in a highly available router configuration (as required). Each redundant switch, router, and any other network gear must then be serviced by redundant power to indeed create an *NSPOF*, or no-single-point-of-failure, configuration. Insofar as best practices are concerned, we recommend that you also adhere to the following guidelines:

▶ All network interfaces must be hard-coded or set to a specific speed; for example, 1000Mbps full duplex. Refrain from using the auto-configure function, regardless of how tempting it is to avoid three or four mouse clicks per server to hard-code each NIC setting specifically. This is especially a problem if ignored in clusters or in network environments characterized by switches and hubs servicing different network segments running at different speeds. Using the auto-configure setting can easily mask network problems, including intermittently failing network cards, and ultimately add hours or even days to troubleshooting cluster issues.

▶ Keep in mind that NIC teaming is implemented via a software/driver-level function. Thus, anytime one or more NICs participating in a team are replaced, swapped out, or reconfigured, the team should be dissolved and reconfigured again. Failure to do so could create issues that are difficult to troubleshoot, including intermittent or unusual operation of the NIC team.

▶ Most servers manufactured in the past 10 years take advantage of multiple system busses. Each bus is normally capable of achieving a certain maximum throughput number. For a 64-bit 100MHz PCI-X bus, this number is something approaching 800MBps. To achieve even greater throughput, then, NICs need to reside in different busses. Taken one step further, the idea of multiple buses should also get you thinking about high availability. Remember, an NSPOF solution theoretically relies on redundant components everywhere, even inside the servers. So, multiple PCI buses fit the bill—as an added level of fault tolerance, place the NICs so that they reside on different PCI buses.

▶ If multiple NIC teams are configured (for example, in the case in which redundant connections are preferred to both the public network and the management network), it is important to ensure that the MAC address of the first team represents the primary address of the server. The primary address of the server thus maps back to its name on the public network. This sounds a bit complicated, but Figure 21.7 will help you make sense of it. Here, HP Network Team #1 represents the public team. Furthermore, the MAC address of NIC #1 of this team is the MAC address "seen" by other servers. In this way, both name resolution and failover work as expected.

With our highly available and optimized network infrastructure installed, we can now turn to the next layer in the SAP technology stack—the server.

Server Preparation

In this section, we look at how to best set up and configure servers for their roles in the SAP system landscape. This includes server hardware configuration best practices, details related to deployment and installation, and keys to configuring highly available and well-performing server-based systems.

Optimum SAP Server Configuration Best Practices

When it comes to server configuration best practices, consistency and standardization are the keys. Consistent server configurations and standard server builds or software installations will eliminate a lot of future headaches. Your goals are simple:

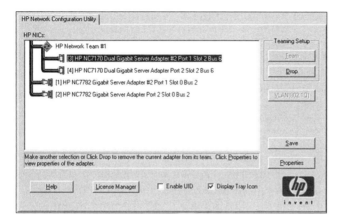

FIGURE 21.7   An unambiguous GUI can help clear up otherwise complicated multi-NIC teaming configurations.

▶ Minimize variety, which really equates to minimizing variables should you ever need to troubleshoot an issue.

▶ Allow for rapid server replacement.

▶ Support your systems management approach.

▶ Support the lowest total-cost-of-ownership model possible.

We cannot say enough about minimizing the number of different server platforms in your SAP landscape. Two or three specific models of servers should be adequate for even the most complex installations or most cost-conscious customers. The benefits are great— fewer platforms for the SAP Technical Support Organization (TSO) to learn to support, less variety in the kind of hardware spare parts that might be stocked onsite, a simpler OS stack (that is, from a software driver perspective), and so on. We recommend the following, considering these best practices regardless of which server platform is deployed:

▶ Use only servers specifically certified by the hardware vendor to support SAP.

▶ Maintain PCI slot consistency—whenever possible, keep all PCI cards in the same slots on all servers across the landscape. For example, if all servers house a public network card in slot 4 and a back-end network card in slot 6, the SAP TSO support staff will be less inclined to make false assumptions or mistakes later should a network issue arise.

▶ Standardize on a particular model of network card, disk controller, HBA, and so on. In this way, not only do you minimize variables from a hardware perspective, you also minimize the variety of software drivers that need to be supported, and the variety of spares that needs to be maintained. In this way, you may even go so far as to swap NICs or HBAs from one server to another, to support troubleshooting without worrying about driver differences, for example. And this approach to standardization simplifies change control as well.

▶ Identify any PCI slot constraints, and ensure that these constraints are documented and followed.

▶ Practice consistency regarding internally housed disk drives; though some exceptions exist, drives housed internal to a server should contain the OS, Pagefile or swap files, and in some cases database or SAP executables. We'll discuss this in more detail later. The point here is that database log and data files should reside on external disk subsystems (certainly normal practice in today's enterprise environments, but worth mentioning again anyway).

▶ Protect all internal disk drives in terms of availability. In some environments, this means attaching these drives to a hardware-based RAID array controller (a high-availability and high-performing controller capable of withstanding the loss of one or more disk drives, depending on the specific configuration), and mirroring the drives. RAID, which stands for *redundant array of inexpensive disks*, may be implemented via hardware or software (though in the latter case only if the OS supports software-based RAID). Note that RAID implemented via software may be configured on standard disk controllers—no special controllers are needed beyond those supported by the OS. For the best availability, the controller and any necessary cables should be redundant as well. We discuss RAID and RAID array controllers in detail later in this chapter.

▶ Attach all external disk drives to a separate RAID array controller (or HBA in the case of SANs or other fiber-based storage systems, also discussed later in this chapter).

▶ Do not use for database or log drives a disk controller that does not support mirrored or otherwise protected cache (which is really just RAM that resides on the controller, to speed up reads and writes) or a disk controller whose cache is not backed up by a battery. Cache allows writes to be posted or acknowledged by the controller, but not actually written to the physical disk drive. In this way, performance is greatly enhanced—the disk controller tells the OS "I have the data" even when it's so busy that it does not have the time to actually write the data to the drive. Meanwhile, the OS is then free to do more work. Later, when the disk subsystem has the time, it commits or writes the data in cache to the physical drives, and the OS and database are none the wiser. However, if the controller loses power, all the writes sitting in the controller's cache never actually make it to the physical disk, and your database becomes inconsistent or corrupted. Resolve this potential issue with battery-backed controllers.

▶ Standardize on specific firmware revisions for all hardware—servers, disk controllers, disk drives, tape drives, and so on. Like software, firmware tells the hardware how to react or what to do, but it resides on a tiny read-only silicon chip on the hardware component itself. Also like software, firmware is subject to changes, bug fixes, and so on. We recommend that a customer maintain a specific revision of firmware on each hardware component consistent with the vendor's SAP Competence Center's advice, testing planned changes in a technical sandbox first. Note that the "latest and greatest" firmware is not necessarily the best, and that a change even at a firmware layer requires the change to be tested and carefully promoted throughout the SAP system landscape (consistent with change control best practices discussed in detail in Chapter 34).

▶ If it ain't broke, don't fix it. After a stable platform is assembled and supported by the vendor's SAP Competence Center, best practices dictate making no changes until forced to. This holds true for hardware components, firmware revisions, software drivers and patches, and so on. Think of it in this way—a lot of work went into assembling a collection of different SAP technology stack layers that actually work well together. Stay away from change *for the sake of change*, and your monthly reports reflecting unplanned downtime numbers will look that much better.

SAP Server Configurations in the Real World

We have seen some pretty amazing SAP server configurations in our day. Think of these examples as more "lessons learned."

More than once we have seen SAP production systems that are clustered in the name of HA but forgo basic availability "in the box." For example, one site chose not to mirror the internal disks located in each SAP cluster node, nor duplicate the requisite controllers and cables. Although this is not absolutely horrifying, it does mean that if a disk drive, controller, or controller cable were to fail, the server would die and the cluster would be forced to fail over to stay up. It has always been our view that it is preferable to never exercise your cluster failover capabilities unless absolutely necessary, primarily because cluster failovers almost always involve some amount of downtime before SAP is available.

One of the biggest problems we used to see with server configurations regarded the use (or misuse) of hosts files. As any network technician knows, the hosts file allows for hostname (server name) resolution back into an IP address. However, if the contents of the hosts file are incorrect, or the hosts file itself is absent (that is, perhaps renamed to *host* rather than *hosts*—another real customer issue), and DNS is not being used, name resolution will simply not work. This problem can manifest itself in a "host" of ways—the SAP Basis installation will fail, the server will seem to be unavailable across the network, and so on. Best practices and experience tell us that the hosts file, if used, should reference all SAP servers in the system landscape, and their IP addresses. Each hostname should be listed twice, once in uppercase and once in lowercase letters. If applicable, cluster alias names should also be defined here. Better yet, avoid the use of the hosts files altogether and leverage your in-house DNS server solution instead.

Blades

Compared to rack-mounted servers, blades are a relatively new advancement in server technology. The idea behind blades is to increase the computing density—in effect, allowing a company to put many more blades in the same space required for conventional servers. With a few exceptions, blades really are just smaller versions of "normal" servers. The exceptions are typically things such as limited internal storage and a smaller number of I/O slots. For servers that are attached to SAN storage or servers that do not have large storage requirements (application servers are a good example of this), blades are a great fit. In practice, we see very few applications where a blade server does not fit the bill. The only disadvantage to blades is that they potentially can expel a great deal of heat in a relatively small space. This is not a deal-breaker, but it does require some consideration with regard to cooling.

An additional benefit of blades may be cable management and SAN and network port consolidation. A blade solution might feature an integrated SAN or network switch—although it might be possible to use a pass-through device when full connectivity is required. The integrated switches simplify cable management by requiring only two connections to the core switch instead of two per server (no SPOFs).

General Storage Considerations

In our experience, perhaps 85% of SAP performance problems end up being storage-related. This is not to say that 85% of *all* SAP problems can be traced back to the storage system—but by the time we are called in, the easy fixes are typically taken care of. So we rarely run into simple SAP profile or database parameter problems, issues with other hardware subsystems, problems with the network, and so forth. Instead, after a quick review of the entire technology stack, we usually find ourselves drilling down into the following:

▶ The model and features of the disk subsystem servicing the systems that exhibit the slow performance

▶ Details as to how the disk subsystem has been configured

▶ Database performance statistics, to quantify how well the database itself performs on the given disk subsystem platform

▶ Specific transaction loads on the system (that is, batch processes or especially heavy online user transactions), especially the top 40 or so transactions identified by transaction ST03 as consuming the most database request time

▶ The ABAP programs (or other code) that is actually being executed by these top 40 transactions (bad ABAP code can make it appear as though there is a disk subsystem issue)

Although a variety of disk subsystems are deployed today in support of SAP solutions, the discussions that follow focus on the predominant disk subsystems being deployed today—SANs—and their storage virtualization capabilities.

Special Considerations for Storage Area Networks

The latest iterations of SANs represent not only some of the fastest disk subsystems ever manufactured, but also everything that customers need in a highly available and scalable disk solution. Not only does a SAN give us the ability to expand quickly, but it also allows us to move data around with ease. Snapshots, disk clones, data replication, and more satisfy HA requirements and help us to address DR, too.

With these new capabilities comes new complexity, of course, and certainly new paradigms. In some cases, we also have a new set of issues that must be addressed when deploying the latest in SAN technology—switched fabric designs, planning for different

21

data access models within the same SAN, providing connectivity to new shared resources such as tape drives and tape libraries, and all the complexity that comes with deploying new software solution sets that interoperate seamlessly (or nearly so!) within the SAN environment. Moving on, let's sneak a quick look at some basic best practices for implementing SAP in a SAN environment.

SAP/SAN Best Practices and Observations

To approach this in an organized manner, we will start with some general SAN observations, and then cover the servers that play a role in the SAN, move to the SAN infrastructure, and finally wrap up with the disk subsystem itself. The following list of observations and best practices has been assembled as a result of hundreds of SAP-on-SAN design or deployment engagements:

▶ Because a SAN is a special network encompassing all components from the HBA to the disk, it is incorrect to call each cabinet of controllers and disks a SAN; instead, the entire connected solution is the SAN. If the development environment is off by itself and is not connected in any way to production, for example, we have in place a development SAN and a production SAN. After these SANs are connected (that is, via a fiber cable connecting one SAN's switch to the other SAN's switch), it then becomes a single SAN.

▶ Each server needs at least a single HBA. Because this represents a glaring SPOF, it is always recommended to install and configure two where HA is important. Both HBAs are cabled to the same SAN, but to redundant switches (discussed later). It is very important to verify that the HBAs are compatible with the server, OS, and storage subsystem before they are ordered. For example, HP certifies different HBAs for Windows and HP-UX, even for the same storage subsystem and server platform.

▶ A server should not connect to two different SANs—connecting to multiple SANs concurrently is not supported. In other words, a single server with two HBAs should not be connected to two different models or implementations of a SAN.

▶ If a server contains two HBAs, it actually has two paths in which to access data on the SAN. To manage this condition, an OS or OS-supported software utility is typically employed on each server connected to the SAN. For example, HP provides a Microsoft Multipath I/O (MPIO) driver for connecting Windows Server 2003 servers to HP storage. EMC PowerPath software is used in EMC storage solutions. In addition to handling multipath management, these software solutions can help to ensure that the HBAs and data access paths are load balanced from a performance perspective.

▶ Each HBA requires what used to be termed a GBIC, or gigabit interface connector, as might each port in your fiber switches. Today, GBICs are more commonly termed *transceivers* and are built directly into the HBAs. Fiber cables then run from each transceiver in each HBA to a transceiver (or otherwise pre-enabled port) in each redundant set of fiber switches.

▶ With regard to fiber switches, different switch vendors can have different rules regarding cascading their switches (to increase the port count available to the SAN, for example). We highly recommend that you reference the specific vendor's documentation for details, with the understanding that many SAN fabrics in use today are limited to very few levels of cascading, or *hop counts*.

▶ SAN switches should be configured with dual power supplies. Two switches are required at minimum to address HA. A fully redundant SAN/server configuration consists of four fiber connections—two to the server, and two to the disk subsystem. These fiber connections should be carefully mapped to the switches so that each controller is connected to two switches, not one.

▶ An access protocol referred to either as "zoning" or "selective storage presentation" is used to ensure that a specific server can access only a specific set of disk drives or virtual drives. The implementation of this varies with the vendor as well as the product set. Regardless, though, be sure to implement one of these access protocols. Failure to do so risks corrupting data.

After connectivity is established from each server to the SAN, disk drives should be allocated or "carved up" on the SAN. Whenever possible, we promote the idea of using a GUI-based tool to address day-to-day SAN management, and a scripted command-line approach for actually configuring a SAN (to allow for rapid cookie-cutter standard SAN installations, for example).

Several sets of disks are needed for SAP, depending on which database vendor has been selected. For performance and availability reasons, all data and log files (including redo logs, archive logs, SQL transaction logs, TempDB, and so on) should reside on the SAN. Furthermore, as long as we are not using a clustering technology that requires local access to database executables, the Oracle, SQL Server, DB2, or other SAP-supported database executables may be located on the SAN as well. When clustering, a RAID-protected quorum drive or similar drive is needed. Responsible for tracking and storing data essential for a cluster server recovery in the event of a network failure, the quorum drive must also be located on the SAN. This presumably allows any cluster node to access the quorum.

There are exceptions, however. For example, clustering SQL Server or Oracle requires that these database executables be installed on each node in the cluster, not out on the SAN. And depending on the clustering solution, a quorum drive construct actually might not be necessary—HP Serviceguard can use a quorum *server*, and Microsoft Cluster Server now supports Majority Node Set with File Share Witness—another method of performing cluster recovery when used with Cluster Continuous Replication (CCR).

Leveraging Storage Virtualization

Storage virtualization is defined by HP as "the transparent abstraction of storage at the block level." The idea of storage virtualization is to minimize the need for parameters that allow fine-tuning, low-level optimization, and tweaking, in favor of allowing the intelligent virtual disk subsystem to take care of everything.

Storage virtualization starts with creating disk groups. The ultimate in high-performance disk performance equates to striping and then mirroring disk partitions across perhaps hundreds of disk drives in a virtual storage disk subsystem within a single disk group.

The ultimate in storage capacity would be achieved by creating a single RAID 5 disk group. It's not an either-or situation—you may decide to create RAID 1 disk groups where performance and availability are paramount and RAID 5 disk groups to maximize available storage (though the difference in performance is nearly negligible in today's world-class SANs).

Once you have created the disk groups, multiple partitions, or drives, may be created and presented to the OS, or a single enormous drive may be created and presented instead. And many storage virtualization technologies automatically create optimally sized and configured RAID drives based on the space available in conjunction with historical data. It's that simple. The various block size parameters, read/write caching algorithms, read-ahead logic, and so on are all under the covers, so to speak. The best storage virtualization disk subsystems allow the few remaining configuration choices to be made via a browser-based GUI, too.

Virtual storage eliminates the physical one-to-one relationship between servers and storage devices, or databases and physical drives. Some important, albeit limited, configuration options still exist, however, and it is these options that concern us next.

Options in the Virtual Array

When it comes to implementing and configuring a virtual array (as opposed to manually selecting and assigning every physical disk in a disk subsystem to higher-level disk constructs as was common prior to the advent of virtual arrays), you have control over the following options:

▶ Follow the manufacturer's recommendations when selecting the number of drives per disk group. For example, HP recommends disk groups with multiples of eight drives.

▶ You can create one or more groups within a physical virtual array storage system. You may decide to create a disk group for logs and a disk group for data drives. The advantage here is that in case of a problem with the data disk group, you still maintain your redo or transaction logs for recoverability.

▶ You can manually create logical unit numbers (LUNs), or disk partitions, and select the group (and therefore disk drives) over which these LUNs will be created. We can create many LUNs or one LUN, whatever is optimal for the need at hand. For example, we might create three 100GB LUNs in a single group consisting of 40 drives, and place our SAPDATA files on these.

▶ Upon creating the LUNs, you can typically specify what RAID level each LUN is to use, and whether caching should be enabled or disabled (although in some virtualization product sets, this is simply not possible). In this way, if required of our solution, we can mix high-density RAID 5 LUNs (for database data files, for example) with high-performance RAID 1 LUNs (for database logs).

Some of the preceding points defy the preaching of many a database administrator or Basis consultant. We can hear them now: "What, one giant virtual disk chopped up into pieces? You can't do that, we're supposed to keep our logs separate from our data! What happened to best practices?" Let them know that best practices can change based on the specific storage solution employed, SAP's recommendations, and particularly each hardware vendors' recommendations. The key to a successful disk implementation is sticking to the hardware manufacturer's best practices—all of them share recommendations based on their storage solutions and the various SAP software components.

On the Road to Implementation

Before we close out our discussions on designing and implementing the SAP data center, it's important to look at how everything up to this point needs to be sustained. SAP deployments progress in phases, or "waves"—each wave brings with it another collection of data center resources that must be planned for, installed, configured, and managed. For example, most new deployments start with bringing in the technical sandbox and development systems. Later, the test, QA, integration, staging, training, and other environments are introduced to the data center. Eventually, the production and DR systems are phased in as well.

Testing the System in the Technical Sandbox

The first time you install SAP in the data center, you will likely do so in a technical sandbox ("sandbox" or "crash and burn system") or similar testing environment. The sandbox will look nothing like the production system is expected to look. In fact, in the haste to get *something* running quickly, many SAP implementations introduce what can only be described as a stripped-down version of what will ultimately grow to be the actual technical sandbox.

The technical sandbox provides valuable hands-on experience to the SAP Basis team, DBA, various infrastructure organizations, and even the computer operations team. It allows each of these technical groups the opportunity to see an SAP installation in action, and begin to realize the fruits of everyone's labor up to this point. Furthermore, it allows the entire SAP TSO the chance to verify what it already should suspect as "holes" in the organization. Specific SAP components such as SAP NetWeaver Search and Classification (TREX) and SAP Enterprise Portal require knowledge and expertise in areas outside simple SAP Basis installations, for example.

As the SAP data center grows and matures, the technical sandbox will grow with it. As a result, the following needs arise:

▶ Every SAP component must be installed and tested in the sandbox prior to installing it elsewhere. Thus, because it's unlikely that anyone wants to maintain a sandbox with multiple SAP instances, robust tape backup/restore capabilities must be introduced in the technical sandbox eventually.

▶ Every layer in the SAP solution stack must be represented within the sandbox. For example, if a web component such as SAP Enterprise Portal or SAP Web Application Server with integrated SAP ITS will play a part in the production system, it also needs to be represented in the technical sandbox.

▶ The SAP operations team should begin to grow comfortable with managing and maintaining SAP, as discussed earlier. This can be accomplished in a number of ways.

For example, the operations team should begin its "career" in SAP monitoring by starting with the technical sandbox. We're talking about more than the SAP Management Console (SAP MC). Other hardware- and software-specific management consoles, such as HP System Insight Manager, HP OpenView, Windows Performance Monitor, UNIX command-line performance utilities, and so on, provide must-have snapshot-in-time and historical trend-analysis value.

With the knowledge gained in performing the preceding tasks in support of the technical sandbox, the SAP TSO will be better positioned to address the needs of the next truly critical system within the SAP landscape—the SAP development environment.

Managing the Development System

When the development system is installed and in place, for all intents and purposes it *becomes* a production system—not for end users in the traditional sense, but for the expensive functional experts and SAP ABAP, Java, and NetWeaver composition environment programmers who will customize this system for many months to come. Therefore, the development system must be treated like a production system with respect to the following:

▶ **Downtime**—Bringing down the development system is unacceptable without plenty of advanced notice. That is, a schedule for planned downtime must be developed, to address various operations and administrative tasks. These might include performing backups, executing client copies and refreshes, and so on. Why? First, because the SAP functional experts and programmers are expensive—without a development environment, these folks will only sit idly by, still billing hourly fees that can easily add up to tens of thousands of dollars for the entire development team. Second, downtime is likely to result in implementation schedule slips, which result in further costs down the road.

▶ **Monitoring**—A proactive approach to monitoring the development system must be put in place immediately, both to minimize unplanned downtime and to quantify that the development system is performing well.

▶ **Backup/restore**—It is absolutely critical that the work being performed by the development team can be safely backed up to tape and preserved offsite in case of a disaster. Why the seriousness? Because the work that goes into the development system to prepare for a production system can easily equate to many millions of dollars in productivity.

By now, you should be well into your SAP implementation. In the next chapter, we will step back and discuss in detail the SAP Basis installations particular to SAP ERP and more.

The Green Data Center

One of today's trends is the movement toward "green" data centers. This trend is probably the result of companies' increasing environmental responsibility and the economic benefits associated with it. The main economic benefit associated with a green data center is the cost savings resulting from power reduction (energy efficiency), and the more expensive energy gets, the bigger this benefit becomes.

The good news is that your company can implement some of the technologies with very little effort—your vendors are building green technologies into the products you buy. One example of this is the Microsoft Windows Server 2008 platform. The default power saving settings out of the box can cut power usage up to 20 percent. Hardware providers are doing their part as well—in a refresh, the new servers are almost certain to be more energy efficient than the ones being replaced.

There are also more advanced technologies being developed. HP has a solution in which sensors are placed throughout the data center, allowing cooling to be directed only where it is needed. IBM has modular rack solutions based on providing cooling within the rack or row of racks. The idea in these solutions is to concentrate cooling where it is needed instead of cooling the entire data center.

Arguably the best solution to conserving power is to eliminate servers. This explains why CIOs tend to focus on both server consolidation and elimination when discussing green initiatives. In most data centers, numerous underutilized servers exist. This might be because the servers were oversized to begin with (or not sized at all) or because it was simply easier to buy another server rather than put an application on an existing server. Server consolidation is all about taking a large number of underutilized servers and making them virtual servers on a relatively few physical servers. The current market leader in the server consolidation space is VMware, although other solutions are available.

There are a number of advantages to server consolidation:

▶ **Capital expenditure**—The company has to buy only the relatively few host machines instead of buying many physical servers (especially in the case of server refreshes or new deployments).

▶ **Power savings**—Servers require power for both operations and the resulting cooling required for the heat they expel. The CPU, network cards, disks, and memory all require power for operation.

▶ **Network and SAN connectivity**—Typically, each host machine has only two network and SAN connections, instead of two per physical server without consolidation. This saves on network and SAN switch ports.

▶ **Cost avoidance**—A significant benefit may be cost avoidance related to space, power, and cooling capacity. For example, expanding a data center that has run out of space for additional racks can be very expensive. Consolidating many underutilized servers into a smaller number of servers can alleviate the need for additional space—saving the company from making a considerable capital investment.

Summary

This chapter covered nearly everything that needs to take place or be addressed when it comes to developing your SAP data center. We worked our way up the SAP solution stack, stopping along our implementation roadmap to discuss data center physical requirements, power and cooling considerations, setting up racks and servers, the need for a robust network infrastructure, configuring disk subsystems, and more.

Case Study: Data Center Facilities

HiTech, Inc. has decided to introduce SAP systems in two data centers supporting 12 worldwide locations. Your task is to assist the CIO with identifying and assessing several critical data center facilities issues.

Questions

1. Name at least four core data center infrastructure services or resources that underpin all SAP applications and therefore are common to all SAP projects.

2. With regard to server racking, is it preferable to house clustered SAP servers in a single rack or in several racks?

3. What are perhaps the two greatest focal areas for going green in the data center?

4. Why is designing and deploying a storage area network or similar high-performance disk subsystem so critical to enterprise applications such as SAP?

NOTE

The answers to these questions can be found in Appendix A, "Case Study Answers."

PART III

SAP Realization/Functional Development

CHAPTER 22

Project Management Checkpoint 2: Revisiting Key Artifacts

Much of this chapter is devoted to revisiting key plans, resource approaches, and other artifacts that have been previously created during the implementation's Project Preparation and Business Blueprint phases. The message we want to convey to you is to avoid investing in or creating "shelfware" documentation. Just as business agility is linked directly to application agility, so too is business livelihood linked to the business project's attention to creating living documents, oversight processes, and so on.

Revising Your TCO Analyses

Considering all of the technology, people, and process factors that can have a positive or negative impact on your total cost of ownership (TCO), it is good practice to perform periodic reviews of your initial TCO analyses. Your TCO model's assumptions are impacted by the cost of various resource elements naturally subject to broad fluctuations. These elements in turn are driven by inevitable changes to the following:

▶ **Project scope**—As the project's scope morphs to presumably better address business requirements (or is cut simply in response to budget and headcount realities), cost is impacted.

▶ **The technology stack's current state**—Validate the status of the currently deployed technology stack versus the stack identified in the initial plan of record; technology standards change over time, vendors fall out of favor, new relationships are struck, release levels and version changes affect the stack, software licensing might be renegotiated, and so on. Even worse, you might find out too late that the particular SAP component you seek to implement is only supported on what your IT organization labels a nonstandard computing platform, adding not only to the project's cost but to its complexity relative to deployment and ongoing operations.

▶ **Data center or hosting venue**—The facilities employed to host your SAP infrastructure, including floor space, power and cooling, hardware components, and more, can quickly grow more costly than budgeted. We have seen the cost of change become a factor too. For example, during a reimplementation of its ERP system, a large customer of ours ran out of cage space it rented from a hosting provider. The provider was unable to extend the cage or provide cages nearby, and for security and logistics reasons could not effectively tie together two physically separate cages. In the end, the client needed to conduct a mini data center move in the midst of its reimplementation, adding significantly to the cost of the project and adversely affecting its timelines and scheduling dependencies.

▶ **Breadth of deployed SAP components and other products**—Revisiting the SAP applications and products being deployed (versus those that were planned for) can quickly uncover otherwise long-forgotten costs. This is particularly true with regard to release or version changes that might have brought with them the need to address unforeseen prerequisites. In the past, for example, we have seen implementations suddenly faced with the need to implement SAP Solution Manager (a project in its own right), introduce new standalone engines into their infrastructure (such as TREX or a Java application server), or the unexpected need to bring in an enterprisewide piece of job scheduling software such as Redwood Cronacle.

▶ **Unexpected tools and support fees**—The need for additional toolsets and other support applications, particularly those associated with deploying infrastructure or conducting any number of testing processes, can add considerably to costs. Consider the impact of quality testing, regression testing, integration testing, load or stress testing, and similar tools purchased last minute, and then add the costs of training, onsite "ramp up" consulting, and other fees.

▶ **Staffing models and headcount**—In response to changing priorities, strategic initiatives, poor scope management, and economic realities, SAP implementation project staffing can change dramatically over time. Changes range from unplanned reductions or increases in headcount to losing key SAP implementation personnel midstream, the need to replace poor performers with new and perhaps more expensive personnel, the loss of a systems integration partner (due to unanticipated mergers or divestitures), and so on. The most prevalent impact is simply underestimating the number of necessary people resources and the time required for those resources to complete their tasks. But we have also seen SAP implementations undergo massive outsourcing initiatives midway through the project in response to executive-level cost-cutting measures (or simply as a way of rescuing a project on a path toward failure).

▶ **Technology process changes**—Seemingly straightforward technical process flows can quickly change in the wake of real-world constraints. High-availability failover and failback processes might need to be revisited in response to the need for increased system availability or to work around issues with disaster recovery requirements. Database backup and restore processes can change midstream after a shared tape-based solution is upgraded or replaced with new technology. And testing requirements might dictate more stringent attention to federal guidelines or regulations governing citizenship, visa status, and so on.

. **Fundamental market forces**—Business-driven economic, geopolitical, and similar external forces, especially those related to a firm's business model, revenue misses, or new business requirements, invite change and therefore affect costs. We also include in this list internal market forces, such as the loss of a key executive sponsor, the need to address key project management or solution architect personnel losses in the wake of competitive recruiting, and more.

As you probably have noticed, TCO impact comes from everywhere. To identify and control risks, costs, and other factors, we generally like to group these areas of impact into technology, people, and process-related domains.

Although our list doesn't reflect it well, not all TCO changes increase cost. There are many opportunities for an SAP implementation project to *cut* costs by cutting scope, reducing headcount, replacing expensive resources with less expensive ones, or automating processes, leveraging standard tools and taxonomies to get a jump on a particular task. The adoption of breakthrough technologies, such as automated testing tools and lights-out server farm management tools, can favorably contribute to your TCO model, yielding dramatic reductions to your overall TCO. Also, be sure to consider the positive impacts of service and process improvements, such as reducing outage incidents or minimizing end-user transactional wait times (and thus increasing the amount of time every end user has to pursue other activities); reevaluating your TCO model need not be a negative exercise.

Beyond reducing costs, a smart project manager or executive board can also help ensure costs don't *exceed* budget. For example, the SAP implementation's IT procurement team might establish fixed-price contracts for personnel, hardware, facilities, and software licenses up front instead of waiting until later in the project, when negotiating clearly favors the vendor rather than the client. Cost-conscious IT teams will also ensure that software components, applications, and enabling tools (such as deployment or systems management software suites) are procured before annual price hikes take effect.

The cadence of the TCO reevaluation process is entirely up to you. We have seen some firms choose to follow their natural audit cycles and basically conduct TCO exercises once a year. Other firms see to it that this type of task is regularly performed by members of their audit team, and other firms revise their TCO model as part of a project or program's risk review cycle. Still other firms rarely think about their TCO model, embarrassed at how poorly they estimated and therefore anxious to bury initial cost predictions.

Revising Your Solution Implementation Plan of Record

Do you recall the implementation plan of record that was developed during the Project Preparation phase of your project? Although the solution implementation plan of record is intended to be a living document, many project teams view this topic as a one-time activity. We consider revising the plan of record to be a best practice. Teams practicing this will

▶ Update the implementation plan of record after each SAP landscape milestone (such as after the development environment is implemented, then again after the test or quality assurance system is in place, and so on).

▶ Periodically update the implementation plan of record as various test cycles and phases are completed.

▶ Present updates and implementation results or outcomes to the steering committee, the project or program board, and other key stakeholders.

In many cases, the changed assumptions and data elements that are noted when this type of plan is revisited will prove quite useful as inputs into your firm's strategic and long-term planning processes. The project's results or outcomes also represent a key set of lessons learned that needs to be communicated and observed (as discussed later in this chapter).

Revisiting Your Staffing Plan

Given that labor will eventually be the element in your project budget that costs the most (overshadowing the incredible expense of software licensing sometime during the Realization phase), it is important to revisit and update your staffing plan, if only to better manage costs. However, there's much to learn with regard to taking a critical look at how your original staffing model has changed over the course of the project:

▶ **Take advantage of repetitive or circular project staffing trends**—Project teams will see the same trends over and over again, both good and bad. For example, we have helped SAP implementation clients note patterns in their need for additional staff based on implementation phases or test cycles. This is especially true of implementations that are phased by business unit or group; the introduction of SAP to a new business unit invariably spells the need to perform several types of testing, address computing platform tuning, and deploy a front-end access strategy, all of which reflect a staffing bell curve.

▶ **Understand employee and contractor retention factors**—By reviewing on a periodic basis who has left the project and why they left, a project team has the opportunity to adjust how it's managing, communicating with, and ultimately retaining its expensive SAP talent. Take the opportunity to review exit interview results, and use this valuable information to tweak leadership appointments, organizational structure, the working relationship between business units, IT organizations, and the SAP project team, and more. Doing so *throughout* the project rather than exclusively at the end of the project will provide much-needed course adjustments.

▶ **Assess staffing changes from a risk perspective**—Perhaps there's a trend in your staffing model or with your staffing partners that merits immediate attention. Staff turnover not only is expensive from a retooling and retraining perspective, but adds risk to a project in terms of how scope is perceived by new hires, how well these new hires integrate with existing teams and processes, and so on. Assessing staffing trends allows a project team to identify and manage its risks more effectively.

▶ **Review staffing changes from a sourcing perspective**—Any dramatic changes that affect the mix of onshore, near-shore, and offshore resources will most definitely impact your project budget. It is surprising how quickly a switch from offshore or near-shore resources to onshore resources can burn through your project's risk reserve (offshore resources are less expensive in terms of real dollars but reflect communication, culture-based, and other potential real-world risks that mandate greater risk reserves).

Taking a critical look at the project's consumption of ongoing people requirements and planned-versus-actual resource costs is simply good business—and project management best practice. It is nearly a certainty that, over time, your staffing assumptions will need to be revisited and updated. Doing so throughout the project, particularly following the completion of major milestones during the Realization phase (and to a lesser extent, the Business Blueprint phase) gives the project team the chance to learn from its mistakes.

Amending Your SAP Implementation Budget

Over the life of your project, as better information presents itself, you need to revise your formal SAP implementation budget. Changes to project scope, schedule, average resource cost, resource mix factors that affect budget, risk reserves brought about by favorable and unfavorable risks that were called out in your risk management plan, and identifying additional risks are all key factors that must be considered when you are revising your budget.

You might be curious as to the value of spending the time to amend the budget. Like the other key artifacts explored in this chapter, a review of the budget holds the promise of identifying trends useful in reducing costs. Waiting to rationalize a budget's planned-versus-actual numbers *at the end* rather than *throughout* the project robs a project team of its ability to leverage budget trends in its favor. For example:

▶ Reviewing SAP training costs versus what was planned might highlight the need for a new method of training, new training tools, a different training partner, or perhaps the implementation of an improved training process.

▶ Noting staffing trends can help justify a change in resource mix or support renegotiating your consulting rates or how expenses are handled. We've seen SAP project leadership teams use monthly variable consulting bills during the Business Blueprint phase as the incentive for creating a less-expensive, fixed-price staffing model for realization, making the project not only easier to budget but less costly.

▶ Tracking the cost of software tools (initial license costs as well as ongoing maintenance and support costs) that assist the implementation from a deployment, management, or testing perspective can prove valuable during contract renegotiations. Best practice dictates marrying outcomes of these tools (that is, how effective they are) against their costs, enabling smart organizations to reduce the price they pay for less-than-effective tools or include "free" training or onsite support as part of follow-on license extensions.

▶ Tracking implementation expenses assists the organization the next time a large enterprisewide business application is implemented. This is especially valuable for organizations implementing multiple SAP components over time, as the knowledge gained during previous SAP projects will help the financial teams plan more effectively and realistically for follow-on projects.

Several of your project's key measures that will likely come out of the monitoring and controlling processes discussed in Chapter 7, "Project Management Checkpoint 1: Groundwork," will also benefit from revisiting the SAP implementation budget. For example, an ongoing comparison of general budgeted or planned costs versus actual project costs often makes its way into weekly staff meetings. Such a basic number serves as a general barometer of the project's status. Similarly, communicating a monthly comparison and analysis of the project's risk reserve helps provide the heads-up that executive committees and project teams alike need to stay on course and close to budget.

Ramping Up and Resourcing the SAP Help Desk

The role that the SAP help desk will play in supporting the overall implementation (and perception of the implementation!) is often downplayed until the big day of go-live looms near. To be successful, though, the help desk needs to be planned for and staffed several months prior to go-live. Waiting until the last minute causes many headaches on several fronts:

▶ In the case of creating a new organization, good help desk personnel are difficult to come by.

▶ Ramping up an existing IT help desk to support SAP is time consuming.

▶ The need for effective escalation and integration processes and smart workflow can't be underestimated.

▶ Implementing knowledge tools (even if this only means providing access to the SAP team's existing knowledge repository) takes time and requires user training.

Simply ramping up an SAP-literate help desk will never make this important end-user support organization successful; you must create a team of professionals knowledgeable in a wealth of diverse areas. Preparing an existing enterprise-focused help desk (for example, one experienced in supporting a large Siebel, Oracle E-Business Suite, or Microsoft Dynamics business application) to take on the world of SAP troubleshooting and problem resolution is no small chore, either. After all, the SAP help desk will tackle issues large and small, with questions originating from end users as well as internal IT and SAP Technical Support Organization (TSO) team members. As such, the staffing and education of this team is vital to the smooth transition from supporting legacy systems to supporting SAP (in conjunction with any remaining legacy systems). In this section, we explore these challenges from several perspectives:

▸ Staffing the SAP help desk

▸ Addressing real-world call volume fluctuations

▸ Training the help desk

▸ Preparing the help desk

▸ Managing end-user perceptions

Given the fact that the help desk represents the first SAP "face" that many new SAP end users will ever "see," their customer-facing role can simply not be underestimated. The help desk is in a position to leave each end user with either a favorable or a poor opinion of the new system, well beyond the issue that prompted their call to the help desk in the first place.

Staffing the SAP Help Desk

Without question, staffing the help desk with enough properly trained, experienced, pleasant, even-tempered, and customer-oriented personnel is critical—all the education, experience, and tools in the world will be worthless in the hands of a lone grumpy support technician a few days after SAP go-live. We tell our SAP clients to view help desk preparation and staffing in terms of a typical bell curve, where the peak of this curve is well *before* go-live. This approach toward preparation will help a client's IT organization when the end-user demand curve faced by the help desk comes into play (normally peaking in the weeks immediately *following* go-live). The need for on-call telephone and online support staff at this time is therefore great, as the largest volumes of help desk calls occur in this timeframe.

In the past, the most common solution for dealing with heavy call volumes was to bring in additional temporary help. As calls tapered off after the first month or two, SAP support teams would scale back the help desk. Downsizing tended to follow the growth of the most frequently asked questions (MFAQs, or simply FAQs) knowledge management (KM) tool—as MFAQs grew and finally stabilized, the number of help desk calls, and therefore technicians, shrank. In other words, when the top 20 or 30 questions became a matter of routine, it was time to replace paid bodies with pleasant on-hold telephone recordings, web-based MFAQs and associated answers, automated online attendants, and so on.

With the rise of good KM toolsets, support center call tracking systems, and service desk applications, greater call volumes can be addressed with fewer people. This benefits SAP support teams in several ways. First, there is less of a need to bring in and train temporary help, only to cut them loose weeks later. This saves time relative to recruiting, interviewing, onboarding, and enabling temporary new hires. Second, much of the collected knowledge held by these individuals would simply walk out the door once the person was no longer needed, providing no benefit to the SAP help desk except in rare cases when this knowledge might have been captured, rationalized, and input into the team's KM tool. Third, typical service desk application support automated call routing, escalation, root cause analysis, issue resolution, and other workflow processes, enabling a smaller team to work smarter than its past predecessors could have.

Addressing Real-World Call Fluctuations

Just like the call volume increase immediately following go-live, the help desk also tends to take additional customer calls after new business processes, functionality, or similar business capabilities are added to the system. This is especially true when this new functionality represents a new SAP component, a new module of an existing component, or a new method of accessing SAP, accessing SAP reports, or doing business. Call volumes reflect these changes, often implemented as quarterly change waves.

In one case, we observed huge call times at one of our accounts where a change to SAP was introduced to facilitate "single sign-on" (where client network IDs were married to their SAP logon IDs to facilitate easy access to network file shares, collaboration sites, printing and faxing resources, and SAP components). However, the necessary communication with regard to exactly *how* to log on to the retooled system had been lacking. The result was a whole lot of extra calls the first two days of the week from people frustrated with their inability to get their day-to-day work done.

In another case, when an account finally added the Sales and Distribution module to its core SAP ERP functionality but failed to adequately resize or reevaluate its in-place computing platform in light of its really poor sales and distribution (SD) implementation, everyone suffered. Response times went through the roof, and the help desk was swamped with calls for days from users across the board—not just the SD users, but others impacted by the system's poor overall database response times.

In the preceding cases, attention to detail and some level of testing prior to major changes in functionality probably would have taken care of both of these issues before they ever came to light. But both cases also serve to underscore the importance of the SAP help desk as a final net, when other nets fail to catch issues or are used improperly.

Training the SAP Help Desk

In the name of pre-go-live training for one of our clients, we assembled a list similar to the one that follows of common SAP help desk questions and scenarios. This list served as a test for help desk technicians, and could also be used as root issues for exercising the team's KM tools. It is by no means a comprehensive list, but represents an excellent smattering of real-world questions and issues. Keep in mind that such a task list can be easily transformed into the foundation for an SAP help desk training plan, though customized for your particular computing and application foundation.

▶ Users cannot print to their previously defined and operational printers. List two reasons.

▶ Users cannot log on to the system. List four reasons.

▶ Explain the process to change a user's SAP password.

▶ How might an SAP user logon and password be impacted by users accessing the SAPGUI via a Citrix session?

▶ Response time seems to be slow, per a user who has called the help desk. Prove that the system is indeed performing to specification by digging out application server statistics and other real-time performance data.

▶ A user can't run a particular business transaction. List three reasons why.

▶ A user calls in and says his job is not completing. How do you confirm this?

▶ Explain the purpose of change management or change control to a user who wants to have a change to production implemented immediately.

▶ Which T-code can you execute to determine whether the previous night's database backup actually completed successfully?

▶ One of the DBAs calls in from a remote vacation spot and needs to know how big the database is today. How do you determine how much of the allocated disk space is actually being used by Oracle (or SQL Server, DB2, or MaxDB)?

▶ The SAP infrastructure or Basis team leader calls in with an urgent request—you need to look at table locks or lock entries. Which T-code do you execute?

▶ A user says that she just ran a transaction and an ABAP dump occurred. How do you look at this dump, or any dump over the past few days?

▶ During troubleshooting, you determine that the system log generated over the last few days should be studied—how do you do this?

▶ Explain how to add the SAP_BC_BASIS_ADMIN_AG activity group to user ZGEANDE.

▶ Management just did another forced early retirement, and you have been requested to lock user ANDEGE. How is this accomplished?

We recommend that you add to this list as required, and use the resulting document to quickly train new hires or refresh folks who might be shared between various IT help desks or support centers. And as stated previously, use such a document to create an MFAQs resource, and to create the foundation for a training plan for your SAP help desk, covered next.

Preparing the SAP Help Desk

When the appropriate staffing plan is in place, both education and access to knowledge tools tend to be the real keys to a first-class support center. Preparing the SAP help desk members for their new support role really amounts to the following:

▶ Mapping tasks and issues (such as those described in the previous section) to those that will actually be faced by the client. This includes paying attention to almost everything at or above the SAP application layer of the solution stack.

▶ Determining the baseline knowledge of the help desk staff. This is often done through IT product and SAP-specific surveys, sample questions, and so on.

▶ Determining the need for formal training versus on-the-job training versus informal employee or consultant-provided knowledge transfer, depending on the baseline knowledge of each help desk technician, your budget, and timing.

▶ Developing and sharing contact information, escalation processes and lists, and so on with everyone on the help desk team—this must also include a description of what each technical and business team is responsible for.

Managing End-User Perceptions

At the end of the day, the SAP help desk, and the SAP support team in general, directly influences how end users *feel* about the new business system. With this in mind, a knowledgeable and courteous support staff can make the difference between a user accepting a one-time short-lived inconvenience and the same user creating and sharing negative long-term system perceptions with colleagues at work.

This issue is huge, and needs to be recognized as such. When a perception is out there—a perception of poor performance or unacceptable up-time, for example—the perception tends to outlive the system itself. We are all familiar with the adage, "you can't squeeze the toothpaste back into the tube." Managing SAP performance and availability perceptions are fine examples of that adage at work.

On the other hand, if the support folks are properly staffed, appropriately trained, and have access to the proper KM tools, they will then be capable of identifying the root cause of a problem, or rapidly escalating the issue to the correct team. The perception surrounding the issue might very well actually turn out positive, in fact. That is, the end user might walk away with a sense of pride in the professional manner in which he and his issue were addressed. This, followed by a timely resolution of the core problem, might even further instill confidence in both the system and support team, on behalf of the end user.

Bottom line, invest in your SAP help desk. These people represent the front line of your SAP support army, and as such signify a great opportunity to help their customer—and your SAP end users—be successful.

Exploiting Cost Management Opportunities

At this stage in an SAP implementation, there are several opportunities to better manage costs, rationalize staffing models, and so on. Two opportunities in particular are most compelling—standard activity assessment and acting on lessons learned, which are addressed next.

Employing Standard Activity Assessment Processes

Many project managers follow a standard script of questions when assessing project activities. Probing in the following areas can help to quickly identify project activities that might need to be closely monitored. The script or process includes

1. Has the scope changed?

2. Will deliverable dates be missed?

3. Have dependencies or assumptions changed?

4. From a risk and schedule perspective, how is the project progressing relative to the following areas or processes:

    a. Budgeting in terms of planned numbers versus actual numbers?

    b. Resource costing, particularly related to people?

    c. Technology deployment and maintenance process?

    d. Deliverable review and approval process?

5. How effective are the project's mitigation plans and strategies proving to be?

Leveraging Lessons Learned

Instead of capturing lessons learned and creating a one-time piece of shelfware documentation, the ideal approach is to periodically revisit key artifacts, plans, and budgets, *and then act on what has been learned.* Making revisions to existing plans and, more importantly, incorporating new lessons learned into existing processes gives a project the opportunity to deliver an improved outcome—a better SAP system—at lower cost and less risk. Utilizing lessons learned and similar intelligence serves as a strategic advantage to organizations that can learn from their mistakes, make course corrections, and more effectively implement SAP. Incorporating lessons learned into documentation and other artifacts creates living documents—another key to making valid course corrections leading to a successful implementation.

Keep in mind that lessons are constantly rising to the surface throughout the project; don't wait to analyze and apply lessons learned months into or at the end of the project, but instead seek to incorporate what you've learned as soon as reasonable. People on the ground—the people actually doing the work of implementing SAP—are perhaps your greatest asset in this regard. These people are full of valuable, pertinent insight into processes that are broken, leaders who are ineffective, relationships in need of repair, and so on. Leveraging lessons learned to improve the delivery of project activities can significantly collapse time and eliminate cost from your project. Our recommendation is to make a point to gather lessons learned at the close of each significant activity or milestone. Furthermore, encourage cross-team meetings to apply these lessons learned to future project activities. And in close, ensure lessons learned are captured in your knowledge repository so that they may be used by follow-on project teams and support organizations.

Summary

Drawing the distinction between shelfware and living, breathing documents, we discussed establishing a regular cycle of revisiting and updating project documentation while emphasizing that information must be regularly harvested throughout the project's lifecycle. Lessons learned represent strategic value to your company, and particularly to your project team. Assess your project's budget, resource costing, technology deployment and maintenance processes, staffing realities, and documentation review processes and be sure to take advantage of lessons learned to reduce ongoing project risk and cost. It is up to project leadership *on the ground* to identify the data points that will yield strategic innovative and competitive advantage.

Case Study: Avoiding Project Shelfware

You have been retained by HiTech, Inc. to assist its SAP project team midstream during its latest SAP ERP implementation. Questions have come up in various team meetings related to maintaining and revisiting several different artifacts created when the project was ramping up. Some of the team members are concerned that they have essentially created shelfware, while other team members feel that project deadlines and priorities mandate not looking back. Answer the team's questions.

Questions

1. When is the best time to capture project lessons learned?
2. How can lessons learned be used to collapse overall project cost?
3. What is an example of a favorable project event and an example of an unfavorable project event that would be captured during lessons learned activities?
4. What project activities will benefit the most from incorporation of the project's lessons learned?
5. How can changes to your project's resource mix impact your project budget?

> **NOTE**
>
> The answers to these questions can be found in Appendix A, "Case Study Answers."

CHAPTER 23

Preparing for SAP Component Installations

The real work in an SAP installation takes place before SAPinst, the System Landscape Implementation Manager, is ever run. There are essentially two ways to complete an SAP installation—the easy way and the hard way. The easy way is to download and read the guides and SAP Notes related to your installation and be fully prepared when you kick off SAPinst. The hard way is to try and figure it out as you go— believe us when we say that the answers to almost all your questions are somewhere in the SAP documentation. We can also attest that if you are well prepared, the SAP installation itself normally goes smoothly—the difficulties normally lie in getting to this point.

SAP installations can be more easily understood when a technology stack approach is taken. First, the operating system must be installed—which requires that the underlying server, network, and storage infrastructure be in place. We discussed these topics in Chapter 21, "Developing the SAP Data Center." Next, all SAP systems (with the exception of some standalone engines) require a database instance. Worth mentioning again, a typical three-system landscape (production, quality assurance, and development) equates to three separate database instances for each SAP component (such as ERP, CRM, and perhaps NetWeaver Portal). Finally, the SAP applications may be installed. If only installing SAP were this simple—SAP applications are inherently complex and the SAP Master Guide is necessary to guide you through the process. After you have developed a master plan based on the Master Guide for each SAP component being installed, you are ready to download the component installation guides and related SAP Notes to ready for the actual install. After a quick run-through of a prerequisite checklist, you are officially ready to run SAPinst and rapidly complete your installation.

For the purposes of this chapter, let us assume we are preparing for the installation of an SAP ERP 6.0 central system for a sandbox environment. We will cover the preparation and planning for a system running Microsoft SQL Server on Windows Server 2003. This is important because the component installations are always based on the OS and database platform combination. To provide a little variety, we also will highlight some of the planning needed for a Solution Manager 4.0 system running Oracle 10.2 on SUSE Linux.

Planning for SAP Infrastructure

This chapter is all about getting ready to do the actual SAP installation. Planning and preparation are the keys to successful installs—both from the perspective of the installation process itself and from the perspective of delivering highly available systems that meet your performance requirements.

In reality, from a technical perspective the installation planning began with the sizing process in Chapter 18, "Introduction to SAP Platform Sizing." During the system architecture and sizing processes you determine whether you are going to install Central Systems, Distributed Systems, are implementing specific High Availability solutions (such as clusters), and so on. Figure 23.1 illustrates a basic sizing—the production system is clustered for high availability, quality assurance is designed as a distributed system, and the development system is designed as a central system.

Production ERP Unicode requires 14,000 SAPS @ 100%							
Function	Load %	Server Model	CPU cores	Speed/ Cache	Ram GB	SAPS@ 100%	OS
DB	33%	rx8640	6	1.6 18M	36	6480	HP-UX 11.31
PTS FO	0	rx8640	6	1.6 18M	36	0	HP-UX 11.31
AS1	33%	rx8640	6	1.6 18M	36	6480	HP-UX 11.31
AS2	33%	rx8640	6	1.6 18M	36	6480	HP-UX 11.31
AS3	33%	rx8640	6	1.6 18M	36	6480	HP-UX 11.31
			30		180	25920	

QA ERP 6.0 Unicode requires 2,310 SAPS @100%							
Function	Load %	Server Model	CPU cores	Speed Cache	Ram GB	SAPS@ 100%	OS
QA DB	33%	rx8640	6	1.6 18M	36	6480	HP-UX 11.31
QA App1	33%	rx8640	4	1.6 18M	24	4340	HP-UX 11.31
QA App2	33%	rx8640	4	1.6 18M	24	4340	HP-UX 11.31
			14		84	15160	

Dev ERP 6.0 Unicode requires 1,155 SAPS @100%							
Function	Load %	Server Model	CPU cores	Speed Cache	Ram GB	SAPS@ 100%	OS
Dev DB	100%	rx8640	4	1.6 18M	24	4340	HP-UX 11.31
			4		24	4340	

FIGURE 23.1   The sizing shows the function or role of the server and the hardware specifications.

Throughout the next few sections, we will explore SAP infrastructure planning in terms of using the Master Guides, installing components, addressing system variants and landscape approaches, and determining the need for standalone engines, whether Unicode is appropriate, and more.

Developing a Master Plan with SAP's Master Guides

Installing SAP used to be pretty simple—you walked through a relatively straightforward SAP R/3 or Business Warehouse installation process and handed over the ready-to-be-configured system to the functional team. Each component had its own system landscape based on ABAP, and there was relatively little complexity. Today, SAP has evolved and things are quite different. Now you have to determine the usage type and associated software units based on your business requirements. Then you must determine how to distribute these components to SAP systems, including determining whether there are any constraints related to the individual component installations. This is where the SAP Master Guides come into play.

The Master Guide is the starting point for the installation of an SAP software component such as SAP ERP 6.0 or SAP CRM 2007. The Master Guides are available for download from SAP Service Marketplace (http://service.sap.com/instguides). You will need a username and password to access the SAP Service Marketplace site; access is based on your SAP customer number and is controlled by an administrator at your company as previously outlined in Chapter 18. The Master Guides deal with the complex issue of architecting and implementing a technical solution based on your business requirements. For example, the ERP 6.0 Master Guide contains the following information:

- **Getting Started**—Includes an overview of the Master Guide, quick links to related information, relevant SAP Notes, and so forth.

- **Cross-Application Overview**—Covers SAP NetWeaver IT scenarios and industry solutions. ERP 6.0 is based on NetWeaver 7.0, so all the NetWeaver capabilities of the NetWeaver platform related to ERP 6.0 are described.

- **SAP ERP 6.0: Technical Overview**—Describes the basic system landscapes used throughout the Master Guide, selection criteria for the optimum system landscape, and the related installation sequence for each system landscape.

- **Key Functional Areas of SAP ERP 6.0**—Lists the processes of the key functional areas, the product instances, system landscape, and implementation sequence. Possibly most important to the technical install, the system landscape details how to lay out the required components by system instance.

- **Software Components Overview**—Provides an overview of the product and content instances.

- **Media Information**—Lists all the media and describes the content.

You probably will use a lot of the information in the Master Guide well in advance of the technical install. It will help you to better understand the product, providing an overview of the various usage types or key functional areas, including product and content instances (CIs). The Master Guide provides the basis for the architecting of the SAP solution based on the business processes, which is then used as an input in the sizing. It provides an overview of the various usage types or key functional areas, including product and content instances, all of which can prove quite complex. For example, the software components in ERP 6.0 include

▶ SAP ECC (ERP Central Component) Server

▶ SAP XSS (Self Services)

▶ SAP SEM (Strategic Enterprise Management)

▶ SAP XECO (Extended E-Selling Components)

▶ Financial Supply Chain Management (FSCM)

▶ SAP Learning Solution

▶ SAP SRM (Supplier Relationship Management)

▶ SAP cProject Suite (Collaboration Projects)

▶ SAP E-Recruiting

The architecture includes the components and the distribution to the systems—key information required for the install process. The Master Guide enables you to create a master plan that includes the following:

▶ The details for the distribution of software units to SAP systems, including usage types AS ABAP and AS Java

▶ The installation sequence used for the product instances and software units, including restrictions that prohibit certain software components from running on the same system

▶ The details for the installation of individual components at a high level, including describing which capabilities are part of the product component install and which are installed as add-ons

It is important to remember that the sizing process is a key determinant in the layout of software units and the number of servers involved. The Master Guide covers everything from putting all the software components on a single server to distributing individual software components to their own server, and everything in between. The Master Guide also includes restrictions that prohibit certain software components from running on the same server.

Having reached the point of knowing what components we are going to install, we are ready to start planning for the individual component installations.

Installation Guides and SAP Notes

At this point, you are ready to download the appropriate installation guide for the SAP component you wish to install. The installation guide depends on the SAP component (for example, SAP ERP 6.0), the kernel (Application Server ABAP, ABAP+Java, or Java only), operating system, and database platform. For example, there is an installation guide titled "SAP NetWeaver 7.0 SR3 ABAP+Java on Windows: MS SQL Server."

The component installation guide covers the planning, preparation, and installation process as it relates to the particular SAP component. Post-installation activities are also covered. The best part about the installation guides is that they not only tell you what you need to do, but often explain exactly how to do it for your OS and database combination. A lot of the information in the remainder of this chapter is based on the SAP component installation guides.

SAP Notes have the most up-to-date information regarding the installation of your component. There will almost always be an SAP Note associated with the OS and the OS and database combination. For example, if you were installing an SAP Business Suite component on Windows/SQL Server, you would want to get the following SAP Notes from SAP Service Marketplace (service.sap.com/notes):

▶ 967123 SAP NetWeaver 2004s/Business Suite 2005 SR2: Windows

▶ 966960 SAP NetWeaver 2004s/Business Suite 2005 SR2: SQL Server

Chances are, if you encounter a problem during the installation of your SAP component, the solution is in one these SAP Notes. We also like to check the related notes listed at the bottom of each of the SAP Notes—you might find something that applies to your situation just by perusing the titles.

> **NOTE**
>
> A good example of how SAP Notes come into play is the situation in which the Oracle prerequisite fails for the number of file descriptors. The SAP Note for SUSE/Oracle explains how to resolve the issue by editing /etc/security/limits.conf and adding the following lines:
>
> ```
> *    hard          nofile         32800
> *    soft          nofile         32800
> ```

We are going to use the installation of Solution Manager on Linux/Oracle as an example throughout this chapter. The first step in the Solution Manager installation process would be to download the following Master Guide and installation guides from SAP:

▶ SAP Solution Manager 4.0 Master Guide

▶ SAP Solution Manager 4.0 SR1 on Linux : Oracle—Installation Guide

▶ SAP Web Application Server ABAP 6.40 SR1 on Linux : Oracle—Part I – Planning and Preparation and Part II – Installation and Post-Installation

You would then need to access the necessary SAP Notes:

▶ 171356—SAP Software on Linux: Essential

▶ 958253—SUSE LINUX Enterprise Server 10: Installation Notes

▶ 980426—Oracle 10.2 Software Installation on New Operating Systems

▶ 1090932—IBM Download Site for Special JDK Builds – iFix

▶ 861215—Recommended Settings for the Linux on AMD64/EM64T JVM

With this information on hand, let's explore different SAP system variants.

Planning for System Variants

One of the planning activities involves determining the system variant or "kind" of SAP installation. There are several variants, the individual components and combination of which must be decided well before you attempt an SAP installation:

▶ Application server (kernel)

▶ SAP database

▶ Central Instance (ABAP)

▶ Central Services (Java)

▶ Application server (also known as a dialog instance)

The planning should determine the type of application server or kernel required for your installation. The Application Server is part of the NetWeaver platform. SAP product instances in the same family are always deployed on the NetWeaver platform, which includes the following application server software units:

▶ Application server ABAP (AS ABAP)

▶ Application server Java (AS Java)

▶ Application server ABAP+Java

Based on the SAP component and the related business process, it might be clear whether a server requires the ABAP, Java, or ABAP+Java stack. For example, NetWeaver Enterprise Portal requires AS Java while ERP Central Component (ECC) is based on AS ABAP. It gets tricky when both ABAP and Java are required in the application environment—then you must decide whether to deploy ABAP+Java or keep the ABAP components separate from the Java components. The implementation of SAP Self-Services is a good example—it is possible to go with an ABAP+Java stack and implement Employee and Manager Self-Services with ECC on a single system. It is also possible to keep the ECC functionality on ABAP and the EP functionality on Java through the implementation of two systems. The decision comes down to availability, scalability, and performance. The sizing process may dictate that one server is not enough to handle both components. Some companies find that because the ABAP stack is more mature than Java, they are reluctant to deploy the ABAP+Java stack for fear of impacting availability of the ABAP components. There really is not a right or wrong answer—it all depends on your company's experience and requirements.

There is also an option to install a Java Add-In to an existing ABAP system. It adds the Java central services instance (SCS) and installs the Java schema in the database instance. However, SAP does not support ABAP dialog instances for an ABAP+Java system—you must install new ABAP+Java dialog instances to replace any existing ABAP application servers.

When you run SAPinst, you will choose from the following system variants depending on your requirements:

- **ABAP Central Instance (CI)**—Installs the kernel plus the services (Message Server and Enqueue) that comprise the CI. The differences between the CI and an application server are the presence of the Message Server and Enqueue service. By default, the sapmnt share or file system is loaded on the CI as well. The sapmnt share is where all the instance profiles and kernel files are stored.

- **Java Central Services (SCS)**—Roughly the Java equivalent of an ABAP CI. If Java and ABAP are installed in the same database, Java has its own schema.

- **ABAP Central Services (ASCS)**—Basically the Message Server and Enqueue services and only exists in a high availability (HA) configuration. The idea behind separating the ASCS from the CI in an HA installation is to limit the resources associated with the central services so that failover occurs quickly. In this case, the CI is really just another dialog instance except that it may be associated with the sapmnt file share or NFS mount point.

- **Dialog instance (application server)**—Dialog instances are synonymous with SAP application server instances; the installation process is very quick and straightforward. The application server is always related to a CI (ABAP) or central services instance (Java). Application servers can run dialog, batch, update, update 2, and spool processes. The only requirement from a server perspective is a local drive to hold the SAP executables. Updated kernel files are automatically copied to the application servers using sapcpe every time the instance is started.

Considering Heterogeneous Landscapes

One of the emerging trends we see in the SAP infrastructure space is the implementation of heterogeneous landscapes in which the dialog instances and central system components run on different OSs. Such landscapes reflect what we often call a *hybrid* computing platform for SAP. The most common variations comprise Windows or Linux application servers tied to a Unix database/CI. The most common reason for implementing hybrids is to reduce the system's total cost of ownership, made possible through low-cost hardware platforms and arguably the two most innovative as well as lowest cost operating system environments, Windows and Linux. Hybrids therefore marry lower costs with the greatest levels of availability, scalability, and performance germane to Unix and legacy or mainframe back-end database systems (thus placing hybrids in the middle of both the TCO and innovation continuums). SAP Note 1067221, "Central Note for Heterogeneous Installation," describes the supported OS and database combinations in a heterogeneous environment.

Standalone Engines

The Master Guides also describe the applicable standalone engines, which may be required depending on the business processes being implemented. Standalone engines are different from "normal" installations in that they are not based on AS ABAP or AS Java. As the name implies, they are standalone applications that provide specific functionality to SAP systems. As a reminder, the following standalone engines are available:

- ▶ Content Server
- ▶ liveCache
- ▶ Search and Classification (TREX)
- ▶ Web Dispatcher
- ▶ SAP Central Job Scheduling by Redwood

Unicode or Non-Unicode

You must decide whether you are going to do a Unicode or non-Unicode installation. If you are a new SAP customer, the decision is easy—SAP requires all new SAP installations (not upgrades) from this point forward be Unicode. It is also pretty easy if the underlying platform is AS Java, which is always Unicode.

SAP first introduced support for Unicode in SAP Enterprise (sometimes referred to as R/3 4.7). Unicode is basically an encoding scheme in which each character is stored in the system in two bytes. In contrast, non-Unicode systems typically store characters in a single byte. The advantage of Unicode is that in global SAP installations, every character from every language can be represented in a single Unicode character. This enables SAP to support multiple languages without adding any codepages (which are required in non-Unicode systems). The downside to Unicode is that it does require more system resources such as disk, processor, and memory. If you need to support multiple languages or are installing a new SAP product in your landscape, Unicode is probably the way to go.

For single languages (except new installations), non-Unicode is probably a safe choice as long as you don't expect to have to support additional languages in the future (via SAP instance consolidation or mergers and acquisitions, for example).

Building Your SAP Infrastructure

To install SAP and any required standalone engines, we first need to have the corresponding infrastructure in place. This includes network, storage, and server infrastructure:

- ▶ Storage requirements must be determined and allocated to the OS.

- ▶ The network information must be obtained.

- ▶ The server must be sized, racked, and connected to the network and storage infrastructure (see Chapter 21).

Believe it or not, from a technical perspective, getting the infrastructure in place for the actual installation is most of the battle—the SAP installation itself is the "easy" part. Keeping a spreadsheet with all the pertinent information on different worksheets (network, SAN, OS, database, SAP) makes it easy to complete the installation—having all the information in a central location makes installation a snap. In the next few sections, we explore the network planning and SAN implementation processes and what is involved with regard to OS preparation and establishing naming conventions.

The Network Planning Process

You will need to set up network communications so that end users can communicate with the SAP servers and for inter-server communication. At most customers, the way this network planning process works is that you give the network team the hostname and server location and they assign IP addresses, make sure the server is connected to the right networks, and possibly enter the hostname into DNS (domain name system). In turn, the network team gives you a spreadsheet with IP addresses, similar to the example shown in Figure 23.2. That's it!

SAP Windows Network Overview				
Server/ Host Name	IP Address	Default Gateway	Subnet Mask	Speed/ Duplex
HOUR3P1	10.51.51.8	10.51.51.1	255.255.255.0	1000/Full
(heartbeat)	192.168.12.8		255.255.255.0	100/Half
HOUR3P1	10.51.51.11	10.51.51.1	255.255.255.0	1000/Full
(heartbeat)	192.168.12.11		255.255.255.0	100/Half
HOUR3CL1	10.51.51.13			
HOUSAPCL1	10.51.51.17			
HOUDBCL1	10.51.51.16			

FIGURE 23.2 Hostname and IP addresses plus the remaining network information needed for successful network communications.

Not so fast, though—if your server is accessed via the Internet or is otherwise located behind a firewall due to security requirements, the process can be a little trickier. In addition to the IP address and hostname resolution, you are likely to have to deal with firewall rules. This typically means that you will have to determine which ports need to be opened in order for the SAP server to operate properly. Once you have given the list of ports/protocols to the network or security team (depending on your company), all that is left is to test the application after the installation to make certain that everything works properly through the firewall.

> **NOTE**
>
> The purpose of a firewall is to make it more difficult for hackers or their malicious software to access your server, by closing down the ports over which communication takes place. For example, by default HTTP communicates over port 80. When it comes to firewalls, more restrictive is generally better—that is, try to open the fewest number of ports required for SAP to operate effectively.

> **NOTE**
>
> If you implement Microsoft Cluster Services (MSCS), you need to keep a few considerations in mind when configuring the heartbeat network. The heartbeat, or private, network is used by the cluster to verify that the nodes are still operating. First, the heartbeat network should not be teamed; redundancy is achieved by making the public network a secondary network for heartbeat communications. Next, the only properties for the NIC should be the IP address and subnet mask—no default gateway or other properties. Finally, keep in mind that the heartbeat network is not very bandwidth intensive—in fact, 10Mbps Ethernet is sufficient.

Storage Area Network Planning

For capacity and performance reasons, SAP databases typically require SAN storage. For the installation to proceed, the storage team must allocate the storage from the SAN. For new storage (typical for new SAP implementations), the storage must be designed for performance and availability. Most SAN vendors have specific recommendations and best practices for configuring their storage for SAP environments. Next, you need to work with the storage team to present the logical unit numbers (LUNs) to the OS. If the storage team is using virtual storage such as the HP Enterprise Virtual Array (EVA), the first step is for the storage team to create disk groups, like those shown in Figure 23.3.

The next step is to create the LUNs on the storage subsystem, which can generally be done from a command-line interface (CLI) or by using a graphical user interface (GUI). The SAP component installation guides detail the storage requirements for each SAP instance, from which the SAN storage requirements can be determined. One method we frequently use is to compile a table of the storage requirements from the installation guide for the entire system landscape, such as the table shown in Figure 23.4. You might notice that for a cluster, the same LUNs are presented to both nodes, and for a Windows cluster there is a quorum drive as well.

EVA Disk Groups				
Disk Group	# of Disks	DG#	vRaid 1 (GB)	vRaid 5 (GB)
LOGS	8	1	387	
DATA	32	2		3097

FIGURE 23.3   The disk groups containing the log and data groups, which follow HP's best practices regarding number of disks in the disk groups (multiples of eight) and separation of logs and data.

SAN Vraid Disk Details						
	Volume		Volume		Volume	
Host Name	SAPexe	AU	Redolog	AU	MirrLog	AU
HOUR3P1	10GB	4K	1GB	4K	1GB	4K
HOUR3P2						
HOUR3D1	10GB	4K	1GB	4K	1GB	4K
HOUR3Q1	10GB	4K	1GB	4K	1GB	4K
	ArchLog	AU	SAPData 1-6	AU	Quorum	AU
HOUR3P1	20GB	4K	40GB x 6	64K	4GB	4K
HOUR3P2						
HOUR3D1	20GB	4K	30GB x 6	64K		
HOUR3Q1	20GB	4K	40GB x 6	64K		

FIGURE 23.4   Table detailing the storage requirements for the servers in an ERP system landscape, including the required SAN LUNs and the file allocation unit (AU) size to be used when formatting the drives in the OS.

After the LUNs are created, the storage team will present the storage to the server. This is accomplished by using the Worldwide Identifier (WWID) of the server's host bus adapters (HBAs) to give access to the LUN. The WWID is a unique string of hexadecimal numbers similar to the MAC address of a network interface card (NIC). The storage team may also utilize SAN zoning, whereby the SAN switch ports are configured to communicate only with other ports in the same zone—similar in concept to virtual LANs (VLANs) on network switches.

One SAN consideration we often encounter is the value of maintaining a nonproduction SAN with components identical to those in the production SAN. At times, customers are reluctant to implement a nonproduction (for DEV, QAS, and test systems) SAN that is the same model/configuration as the production SAN—mostly because of cost. However, not having a SAN to test changes means that the first time a change is implemented is in production—raising the potential of an issue that could ultimately affect availability. Due to this consideration, we almost always recommend purchasing and implementing an identical SAN for nonproduction.

Windows File System Preparation

Now that the storage team has allocated the storage and presented it to the OS, we need the OS team to create and format the partitions. Remember to reference the table you created for the storage team for the file allocation unit sizes when you create the partitions. Best practice for Windows-based SAP systems is to format the data drives with 64K allocation units and log drives with 4K allocation units. You also will want to create a table with the standard drive letters and labels for Windows servers, as shown in Figure 23.5.

You might also choose to implement mount points in Windows Server 2003. The basic idea behind mount points is that a single drive letter can have multiple mount points underneath it that point to physical drives, thereby saving drive letters. This is important only if you expect to run out of drive letters—remember, Windows only has 26 drive letters available (A–Z).

Linux with HP Serviceguard Preparation

Now let's take a look at creating the file systems for a SUSE Linux server with HP Serviceguard. HP Serviceguard for Linux is one of many clustering technologies available for SUSE Linux. Figure 23.6 represents a relatively simple implementation that was done for a Solution Manager sandbox system. Similar to the Windows solution detailed earlier, you would need to work with the storage team to create the SAN LUNs based on either the sizes in the component installation guide or your company's standards. The next step is to create the volume groups vgsaptst, vgnfstst, and vgdbtst, the procedure for which is described in detail in the HP Serviceguard for Linux manual. Notice how the naming convention makes it clear whether the disks belong to the SAP instances (vgsapTST) or the database (vgdbtst). The next steps are

1. Create the logical volumes using lvcreate.
2. Create the file systems using mke2fs.
3. Create the mount point directories.
4. Mount the logical volume to the mount point.

You can also use the graphical YaST Expert Partitioner for these tasks. All these tasks are detailed in the HP Serviceguard manuals.

Standard SAP Drives for Windows Servers			
Location:	Letter:	Label:	Contents:
local OS partition	C: 30GB	OS	OS-Pagefile
local OS partition	D:	CDROM	
local OS partition	E: 30GB	EXE	Oracle Home
local OS partition	P: 20GB	Pagefile	Pagefile
SAN	G: 10GB	SAPexe	SAP Executables
SAN	H: Root Disk	SAPDATA	Root Disk for Oracle Mount Points
SAN	I: 10GB	OraLogA	Oracle Transaction Log
SAN	J: 10GB	OraLogB	Oracle Mirror Log
SAN	R: 20GB	Archlog	Oracle Archive Log
SAN	K:	Data1	SAP Database Files
SAN	L:	Data2	SAP Database Files
SAN	M:	Data3	SAP Database Files
SAN	N:	Data4	SAP Database Files
SAN	O:	Data5	SAP Database Files
SAN	P:	Data6	SAP Database Files
SAN	Q: 4GB	Quorum	MS Cluster Quorum (may be mounted elsewhere as well)
SAN	Y: -varies in size	Diskdump	Copy of DB/Catalog files (online backup)

FIGURE 23.5   A table of standard drive letters and disk labels simplifies maintenance and troubleshooting.

NOTE

It is important to note that SAPinst will automatically create the directories in Figure 23.6 if they do not exist—which is probably not what you want. Before running the installation, you must verify that you have set up the file systems properly and have the required space available.

Network File System Preparation

Notice that Figure 23.6 includes Network File System (NFS) mount points. For Linux, you will generally export the following directories on the SAP global host for distributed or HA configurations:

▶ <sapmnt>/<SAPSID>/exe

▶ <sapmnt>/<SAPSID>/profile

▶ <sapmnt>/<SAPSID>/global

File Systems for Linux Servers with HP Serviceguard Extensions for SAP			
APPLICATION SERVERS			
Mount point	Size	Location	Logical volume or NFS mount
/usr/sap/TST/DVEBMGS00	12 GB	SAN	LV /dev/vgsaptst/lvsapCI
/usr/sap/TST/SCS03	2 GB	SAN	LV /dev/vgsaplst/lvsapSCS
/usr/sap/TST/ASCS02	2 GB	SAN	LV /dev/vgsaplst/lvsapASCS
/sapmnt/TST		NFS mount	DB:/export/sapmnt/TST
/usr/sap/transTST		NFS mount	DB:/export/usr/sap/transTST
/oracle (contains /oracle/client)	200 MB	Local	
/usr/sap	2 GB	Local	
DATABASE (DB) SERVER			
/export/sapmnt/TST	5 GB	SAN	LV /dev/vgnfstst/lvnfssapmnt
/sapmnt/TST		NFS mount	DB:/export/sapmnt/TST
/export/usr/sap/transTST	4 GB	SAN	LV /dev/vgnfslst/lvnfstrans
/usr/sap/transTST		NFS mount	DB:/export/usr/sap/transTST
/oracle/TST	12 GB	SAN	LV /dev/vgdbtst/lvorasid
/oracle/TST/origlogA	1 GB	SAN	LV /dev/vgdbtst/lvoriglogA
/oracle/TST/origlogB	1 GB	SAN	LV /dev/vgdbtst/lvoriglogB
/oracle/TST/mirrlogA	1 GB	SAN	LV /dev/vgdbtst/lvmirrlogA
/oracle/TST/mirrlogB	1 GB	SAN	LV /dev/vgdbtst/lvmirrlogB
/oracle/TST/oraarch	4 GB	SAN	LV /dev/vgdbtst/lvoraarch
/oracle/TST/sapreorg	1.5 GB	SAN	LV /dev/vgdbtst/lvsapreorg
/oracle/TST/sapdata1	80 GB	SAN	LV /dev/vgdbtst/lvsapdata1
/oracle (contains /oracle/client)	200 MB	Local	
/oracle/stage	3.5GB	Local	
/usr/sap	2 GB	Local	
File System for SAP DVDs	20 GB	NAS	

FIGURE 23.6   File system layout for SUSE Linux with HP Serviceguard for Linux for the SAP instances and the Oracle database.

When you install a dialog instance in a distributed system, you need to create the same mount points and mount them for the SAP Global host, the procedure for which is covered in the component installation guide. For an HA configuration such as HP Serviceguard, you need to follow the manufacturer's guides. For Serviceguard, you may choose to run NFS in a separate package to maintain availability.

We are starting to see customers use network attached storage (NAS) devices to export these file systems instead of using the traditional Linux or Unix NFS server. From the Linux application server's perspective, the mount commands for a NAS device are identical:

▶ Mount 10.0.1.18:/vol/export/sapmnt/TST/exe /sapmnt/TST/exe

▶ Mount 10.0.1.18:/vol/export/sapmnt/TST/profile /sapmnt/TST/profile

▶ Mount 10.0.1.18:/vol/export/sapmnt/TST/global /sapmnt/TST/global

▶ Mount 10.0.1.18:/vol/export/usr/sap/trans /usr/sap/trans

Choosing a Server Naming Convention

One of the preinstallation decisions that you must make is what server naming convention to use. It is really useful to know where a system resides, which SAP software component(s) it is running (ERP, NetWeaver Portal, and so on), its role in the environment (development, quality assurance, or production), and its function (database, message server, and so on). Figure 23.7 illustrates an example of a host naming convention in a tabular format. Having such a standard aids administrators by making it easy to identify servers for maintenance or troubleshooting purposes.

SAP Hostname Sample Naming Convention				
Location	Application	Landscape	System Type	Host Identifier
HOU	EC - SAP ERP	D - Development	DB - Database	1
LAX	SR - SAP SRM	Q - Quality Assurance	CI - Central Instance	2
ORD	HR - SAP HCM	P - Production	CS - Central System	3
	BW - Business Warehouse	S - Sandbox (Technical)	AP - Application Server	4
	NP - NetWeaver Portal	B - Sandbox (Business)	BN - Bolt-on	5
	SM - Solution Manager			6
	PI - Process Integration			7

FIGURE 23.7   A table of host naming conventions helps administrators identify servers. In this figure, the Development SAP ERP Central System (combined DB/CI) hostname is HOUECDCS1.

Installing and Configuring the Operating System

With your SAP infrastructure in place (see Chapter 21) and the necessary prerequisites and planning behind us, it is time to get started on the OS installation and configuration. We will now cover some of the SAP requirements and best practices related to OS installation and configuration. To keep things simple, we will focus only on SUSE Linux and Microsoft Windows. Keep in mind that SAP supports several OSs, however. SAP's product availability matrix (PAM—available at http://service.sap.com/pam) lists the supported OS and database combinations. SAP currently supports the following OSs (plus a few lesser-known others) for SAP NetWeaver 7.0 components:

- ▶ HP-UX
- ▶ IBM AIX
- ▶ Microsoft Windows Server
- ▶ Sun Solaris
- ▶ Red Hat Enterprise Linux
- ▶ SUSE Linux Enterprise Server

> **NOTE**
>
> A lot of what applies to Linux is also true for Unix—despite their differences, SAP installation guides regard Linux as a variation of Unix.

Just to make things interesting, we will use examples that also incorporate clustering technologies—Microsoft Cluster Service (MSCS) and HP Serviceguard for Linux. There is a major difference in SAP support for clustering solutions, in that SAP provides the installation tools and documentation for setting up a Microsoft Cluster but leaves support for all other clustering technologies up to the vendor. In reality, this is no big deal, because all the clustering technologies we know of provide more than adequate documentation and support.

Many companies have separate teams responsible for Linux and Windows server builds. Based on the preplanning phase we just covered, these teams are now able to

▶ Assign the IP addresses obtained from the network team

▶ Assign the hostname based on the naming convention

▶ Place file systems on the SAN storage presented by the storage team and the local file systems

Windows administrators will also be responsible for assigning drive letters and formatting the storage.

> **NOTE**
>
> Similar to hostnames, having a standard for drive letter assignment also aids in troubleshooting and maintenance—for example, in the case of Windows-based SAP installations, always place the database log files on the same drive letter. This consistency will simplify post-go-live operations, systems management, and maintenance processes.

Operating System: 32-Bit or 64-Bit?

At this point you should only be dealing with 64-bit OSs. The only reason you would run a 32-bit version of Windows is if there is a 32-bit SAP component that will not run on a 64-bit OS. Otherwise, SAP requires that all instances, with the exception of dialog instances, run on 64-bit systems.

The big deal with 64-bit OSs is that they can manage much larger memory address spaces compared to 32-bit OSs. The old 32-bit OSs were limited to 4GB address spaces, of which 2GB was reserved for the system for each process. The user-addressable space could easily be extended to 3GB with the /3GB switch in the boot.ini file and further extended in some cases via physical address extensions (PAE). This complexity all disappears with 64-bit OSs, which can address an almost infinite memory space—16 exabytes to be exact.

System Drive

To install the OS, we need to partition the hard disks upon which the OS will reside. Notice we said hard *disks*—we highly recommend mirroring the OS partitions or complete drives, such that if one physical drive fails, you can still continue to run from the second drive. These days you have at least three storage choices when it comes to installing the OS:

- ▶ **Mirrored pair**—If you are using a RAID array controller, you must run an array configuration utility to partition the drives prior to the OS install. This readies them to be recognized by an OS. We recommend you create a mirrored pair (also called a RAID 1 set or mirror set). If possible, for maximum availability, place the mirrored drives on separate SCSI buses. This is possible in the case of dual-channel controllers, or with servers where dual SCSI buses reside on the system board. In any case, by doing this, an outage can be avoided if a SCSI bus or cable fails. Not only that, but mirroring increases read performance as well, as both SCSI channels and both disk drives may later conduct work simultaneously. After the disk drives are configured for a RAID set, create a logical drive. This is what will be "seen" by the OS.

- ▶ **Separate PCI buses**—If a standard SCSI or other controller is used (recommended when software mirroring is warranted), the logical volume manager or other software mirroring must be configured. The best hardware option is to use two controllers on separate PCI buses, if possible, to ensure maximum redundancy. The only reason we would recommend software mirroring over RAID controllers is if a RAID controller is not available (which might be the case for some Unix platforms).

- ▶ **Dual HBAs**—If you choose to boot from SAN, make sure you have dual HBAs, such that you can tolerate an HBA failure or any other failure in the path to the storage (SAN switch, fiber cable, and so on). You will need to present the disk to the server using either SAN zoning or selective presentation of the LUN.

Windows OS Partitions and Logical Drives

During the OS installation, make sure to format the system drive with NT File System (NTFS). After the OS installation, carve up the remaining local disks via the Windows Disk Administrator utility, creating a partition for the pagefile and another for executables. Make sure to format all disks with NTFS. If you had a mirrored pair of 300GB drives and a server with 64GB of physical RAM, you might set up the partitions as follows:

- ▶ C: drive (OS)—20GB

- ▶ D: drive (pagefile)—200GB

- ▶ E: drive (executables)—50GB

This layout provides an enormous amount of space for pagefile, and quite a bit of extra space for the SAP executables, just in case. Pagefile sizing is discussed in more depth next.

Pagefile Configuration

You will need to read the SAP component installation guide, because it is no longer possible to make a general recommendation regarding the size of the pagefile. Old rules of thumb (such as 5x physical memory) and other guidelines simply don't apply any longer. For example, the SAP NetWeaver 7.0 SR3 installation guide for Windows/SQL Server recommends the following pagefile sizes for a distributed system:

▶ Central instance and dialog instances: $1 \times RAM + 8GB$

▶ Database instance: $1.5 \times RAM$

Windows OS Configuration Guidelines

The following configuration changes need to be made prior to installing the database and SAP component:

▶ Ensure that all drives were indeed formatted for NTFS (right-click My Computer, click Manage, and then select Disk Management), as shown in Figure 23.8.

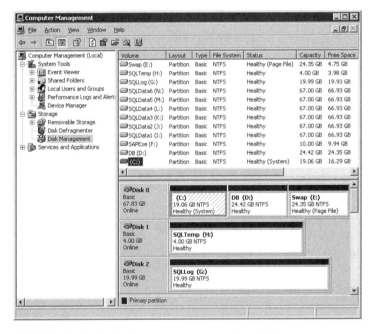

FIGURE 23.8   Verify the volume names, drive letter assignments, and file system types in the Disk Management Microsoft Management Console (MMC) plug-in.

▶ Format data drives with 64KB file allocation units and log and executables drives with 4KB file allocation units.

▶ If not already accomplished, label all remaining disk drive partitions via the Disk Management MMC. For example, label the C: drive *OS*, the D: drive *Pagefile*, the F:

drive *EXES*, the G: drive *LOGS*, the H: drive *DATA1*, the I: drive *DATA2*, and the J: drive *DATA3*. You might also consider changing the CD-ROM to drive letter Z: (or another out-of-the-way drive letter).

▶ Set both the TEMP and TMP environmental variables to point to C:\TEMP. Create the C:\TEMP directory if it does not exist already.

▶ Ensure that the Maximize Throughput for Network Applications option is selected under File and Printer Sharing for Microsoft Networks in Control Panel, Network Connections, Local Area Connections. This impacts how memory/cache is allocated, and can make a significant performance difference.

▶ Load the Simple Network Management Protocol (SNMP) service, in preparation for any systems management agents that will be installed later.

▶ Ensure that the latest Windows 2003 Server Service Pack is applied.

▶ Run Windows Update to apply the latest security updates from Microsoft. After applying the most current updates, turn off Automatic Updates—you do not want to implement any changes without testing them first.

▶ Update the drivers, firmware, and BIOS to the latest supported levels. You will want to check with your hardware vendor beforehand, especially in the case of HBAs, because there might be a recommended/supported firmware and driver level for your storage platform.

▶ Install the systems management agents (that is, HP System Insight Manager, HP OpenView, BMC PATROL, and so on per your standard). Refer to the appropriate management agent installation guide for any other details or prerequisites.

▶ Return to Control Panel, System, Advanced, and click the Performance Settings button. Verify that performance has been optimized for background services on the Advanced tab. This setting ensures that SAP processes are given priority over locally logged-on users.

▶ We highly recommend you install the Windows Server Resource Kit.

▶ Install virus scanning software—your company almost certainly has a standard for Windows servers. Check the vendor's website for recommendations on configuring its product for use with SAP software. In the past, some vendors have recommended excluding database data files because of the risk of data corruption.

▶ Install and configure the backup agent, if applicable. Backup agents that work with `backint` allow you to manage the backup/restore process with SAP tools such as `brbackup` and `brrestore`.

▶ Implement OS hardening, including disabling unnecessary services. Check out the Microsoft whitepaper "SAP Hardening and Patch Management Guide for Windows Server" for some excellent recommendations.

▶ Verify via the Windows Server 2003 Event Viewer that no issues exist from a hardware or OS perspective.

23

▶ Verify via your Systems Management Console (once installed) that no issues exist from a hardware or OS perspective.

▶ After the entire configuration process up to this point has been completed, we highly recommend that you create an automated installation process to easily set up a server that reflects all the activities completed so far in this list. A disk imaging utility such as Ghost is a good way to go. For HP servers, an Altiris RDP server can configure the hardware components, such as the RAID controller, and then install an image. Barring all these automated approaches, a good old-fashioned checklist will serve the same purpose, as long as it is followed precisely.

▶ Verify that you can connect to the server via a remote desktop. Check the Remote tab in Control Panel, System if you encounter any issues.

Creating OS Users and Groups

If you run SAPinst as a member of the domain admin group for Windows or as root for Unix and Linux, the installation will create the users and groups for you. If you cannot get a domain admin or root access, you can complete the installation by manually creating the users. With Windows, you will have to have a member of the domain admins group help you create users and groups in the domain. The two most important users are <sid>adm, the SAP System Administrator account, and ora<sid>, the SAP Database Administrator account. For SQL Server installs, you also have an SAP Service account, as shown in Figure 23.9. By default, these accounts inherit the master password but you can change this during the install.

SAP Products/IDs				
Host Name	SAP Instance	SID	User ID	SAPService ID
hour3p1	ECC PRD	PRD	PRDADM	SAPServicePRD
hour3p1	ECC PRD—FO			
hour3d1	ECC DEV	DEV	DEVADM	SAPServiceDEV
hour3q1	ECC QA	QAS	QASADM	SAPServiceQAS
hour3q1	ECC QA—FO			

FIGURE 23.9   The SAP Service account is used to start the SAP services in a Windows/SQL installation.

NOTE

For Windows, you also have the option of doing an installation with local users and groups, but this is rarely recommended because of the advantages of using domain accounts, such as ease of administration.

Installing the Database Software

The installation of the database depends on the SAP software release and the database software. Currently SAP supports Microsoft SQL Server, Oracle, IBM DB2, and SAP MaxDB database management systems (DBMSs). Again, check the product availability matrix (PAM) on the SAP Service Marketplace (http://service.sap.com/pam) for the list of supported database releases and platforms for your SAP component. For example, ERP 6.0 supports the following database/operating system combinations:

▶ MaxDB for Linux (Red Hat and SUSE), Unix (Sun Solaris, IBM AIX, and HP-UX), and Windows

▶ DB2 for Linux, Unix, and Windows

▶ Oracle for Linux, Unix, and Windows

▶ SQL Server for Windows

We cannot overemphasize the importance of the database to an SAP system. Depending on the component, it will hold all of your company's data as well as the SAP programs—including all the development done by your company. Let's look at some of the key requirements of a database:

▶ **Availability**—The database is a potential single point of failure. The most common way to deal with this is through clustering, although there are alternative solutions, such as the Microsoft database mirroring and Oracle log shipping (see Chapter 15, "High Availability Considerations and Solutions").

▶ **Response time**—The performance of the database is often a key component of response time, although SAP generally recommends it should not exceed 40% of the dialog response time for ERP. You can check the database component of response time in ST03N.

▶ **Scalability**—The database is often the biggest challenge from a scalability point of view as well. You can scale SAP application servers horizontally by adding additional dialog servers (also know as scaling out), but in general databases are limited to a single server, so you must scale vertically (or scale up), which is limited by the hardware platform. This is why until recently the largest databases almost always ran on Unix servers.

Realizing the importance of the database to the overall SAP system, let's examine the installation of two of the more popular database software products, Microsoft SQL Server and Oracle database.

> **NOTE**
>
> You might be wondering at this point how the data gets loaded into the database. The answer is the export DVDs provided by SAP. Essentially, SAP exports the contents of the database of a component after it has been fully developed and tested at SAP. The installation routine takes the export DVDs and imports them into your database. Because SAP software is developed to be database and OS independent, there is only one set of export CDs for each product.

Microsoft SQL Server

SAP requires SQL Server's Enterprise Edition. You can either use the SQL4SAP.VBS script to automatically install SQL Server 2005 and the latest service pack, or follow the manual instructions provided in the component installation guide. You must use the manual process if you are installing SQL Server in a Microsoft Cluster. If you follow the manual procedure, the most important step is setting the collation to SQL_Latin1_General_CP850_BIN2. One thing to note about SQL Server is that you cannot download the database software from the SAP Software Distribution Center on Service Marketplace (http://service.sap.com/swdc).

> **NOTE**
>
> SAP recommends that you always run the latest SQL Server service pack and security updates unless otherwise specified in an SAP Note. Of course, you should carefully test and promote these changes in your other environments before even considering implementing them in production.

The following are some best practices related to the installation and configuration of SQL Server:

▶ The number of data files should equal the number of processor cores in the server (for performance reasons). We typically see four or six data files, although for SQL Server databases spanning multiple terabytes, 12 or more data files is common.

▶ Typically a single transaction log is sufficient. The transaction log is always written to sequentially. For size, 5GB is a good starting point, although you might need to set it larger for a high-volume system.

▶ Set up and monitor frequent backups of the transaction log or it will fill up, thus stopping the database. Many of our customers swear by Quest Software's LiteSpeed for SQL Server backup software.

You can also use SQL4SAP.VBS to install the SQL Server Client Tools. You must install the client tools on every SAP instance unless it is running on the database host. For example, dialog instances almost always require the installation of the SQL Server client.

Oracle Database

In some earlier releases of SAP, the Oracle Database software was installed from an Oracle CD obtained from SAP. In recent releases of SAP, the Oracle Database Server software comes in .SAR files, which are unzipped to a staging area during the SAP install process. Interestingly, the SAP install process still stops and requires the installer to complete the Oracle install before proceeding. The installation of the database software is normally accomplished by running the RUNINSTALLER batch file provided by SAP that contains answers to all the configuration questions normally asked by the Oracle Universal Installer. After the Oracle Database Server installation completes, the current Oracle patch set and any interim patches must be installed. SAP Note 871735 has the information on the latest patch set available for Oracle 10.2, while SAP Note 871096 lists the required interim patches. Oracle Enterprise Edition is required for all applications. In addition, Oracle Fail Safe is required for Microsoft Windows clusters.

> **NOTE**
>
> For some OSs, such as SUSE Linux Enterprise Server 10, you need to update RUNIN-STALLER or it will fail the prerequisite check because it does not recognize the version of the OS.

The following are some best practices related to the installation and configuration of Oracle:

- ▶ For recoverability, keep the archive logs, redo logs, and mirror logs on separate disks.

- ▶ Oracle log files are written to sequentially, whereas data files are a combination of random/sequential reads/writes. In fact, for a typical ERP system most of the disk access is random reads. Because of this, keeping the logs and data separate (as in different disk groups on an HP EVA) may improve performance.

- ▶ It's a great idea to use split mirror backups if backups are affecting performance or your backup window is shrinking.

- ▶ Oracle Real Application Clusters (RAC) is available for some SAP applications but is still not widely used in SAP environments. Companies who require the highest levels of availability and performance should consider RAC, especially if its use in the SAP world becomes more widespread.

The Oracle Instant Client is incorporated in SAP component installations where it is required. For example, a dialog server installation will ask for the location of the Oracle Instant Client software.

Additional Installation Requirements

There are a few other requirements to keep in mind before you start the installation. You will need to generate a Solution Manager key that you will enter during the installation.

You also will need to have a Java runtime environment to run SAPinst. Finally, you will need to have all the SAP media available. You might find the easiest way to accomplish this is to copy the media to a local drive. Let's examine each of these requirements in more detail.

SAP Solution Manager Key

SAP requires that a Solution Manager key be generated for the installation of the latest SAP software components, including ERP 6.0, which necessitates a Solution Manager installation. Solution Manager (SolMan) is an SAP system used to support your other SAP systems. SAP has integrated support into Solution Manager—for example, Solution Manager can be used to open messages with SAP and download SAP Notes. For SAP components based on NetWeaver 7.0 and later, SAP will require the Maintenance Optimizer in Solution Manager to download Support Package Stacks, Support Packages, patches for Java instances, and Legal changes.

Solution Manager provides additional functionality as well, including the capability to generate EarlyWatch reports and provide support to your end users. For now, the important thing for us is that you must have a Solution Manager instance to generate the key required for the install—but if you are in an SAP support role, you must start familiarizing yourself with Solution Manager if you have not done so already.

Java Runtime Environment

The SAP installation utility requires the Java Runtime Environment (JRE). For Windows Server 2003, you also need to set the JAVA_HOME environmental variable and add the Java executables to the path. Keep in mind that you might need to download Java from IBM for 64-bit platforms such as SUSE on AMD64, and that Sun stopped supporting version 1.4.2 (support ended as of October 30, 2008).

> **NOTE**
>
> It is possible to run SAPinst remotely if you are unable to install the JRE on the server—we cover this in the "SAPinst—The SAP System Landscape Installer" section later in this chapter.

For AS Java or AS ABAP+Java, you will need the Java Development Kit (JDK), which includes the JRE. Furthermore, as of NetWeaver 7.0 you will need to download the Java Cryptography Extension (JCE) policy files for strong encryption. You will be prompted for the location of the JCE policy files during the installation.

For a Windows Server running the ABAP stack, the appropriate download is Java 2 Platform, Standard Edition, v 1.4.2 (J2SE). For the Java stack, the appropriate download is Java 2 Software Development Kit (J2SDK) Standard Edition 1.4.2. Both are available from http://java.sun.com/j2se/1.4.2/download.html. Check the JSE Platforms tab on the product availability matrix (PAM) for the supported Java version for your SAP component. Again, the PAM requires a user ID and password and is available at the SAP Service

Marketplace (http://service.sap.com/PAM). For more information on the JDK for your platform, see the following SAP notes:

- 716604—Sun JDK (Windows, Linux, Solaris)
- 716926—HP JDK (HP-UX)
- 716927—IBM JDK (AIX)
- 717376—IBM JDK (iSeries, OS/400)
- 746299—IBM JDK (Linux for z/OS)
- 810008—IBM JDK (Linux on POWER)
- 861215—IBM JDK (Linux on AMD64/EM64T)

Managing CD/DVD SAP Media

You normally receive the installation DVDs as part of the installation package from SAP. However, it is also possible to download the required media from the SAP Software Distribution Center at http://service.sap.com/swdc. You might remember from earlier in this chapter that the final section of the Master Guide covers the required media for the different scenarios. The media also depends on the type of install (variant). For SAP NetWeaver 7.0 AS ABAP, the following media are required by variant:

- Global host preparation:
  - Installation Master DVD
  - Kernel DVD
- Central instance, dialog instance:
  - Installation Master DVD
  - Kernel DVD
  - RDBMS Client DVD
- Database instance:
  - Installation Master DVD
  - Kernel DVD
  - RDBMS DVD
  - RDBMS Patch DVD (if available)
  - SAP NetWeaver Export DVD

In most cases you will want to copy the media to a central location—you will need the same media for the development, quality assurance, and production installations. Plus, for distributed or HA systems, you will end up using the same media on multiple systems.

For example, with Linux we would need the following media based on SAP Solution Manager 4.0 Master Guide and we would copy them to /dvd as follows:

▶ 51032955: SAP SOLUTION MANAGER 4.0 Support Release 3 Installation Master

   Location: /dvd/SAP_Solution_M._4.0_SR3_Inst._Master

▶ 51032956_2: SAP SOLUTION MANAGER 4.0 Support Release 3 Installation Export

   Location: /dvd/SAP_Solution_M._4.0_SR3_Inst._Export

▶ 51031676_1: ORACLE 10.2 64-BIT RDBMS Linux on x86_64 64bit

   Location: /dvd/51031676

▶ 51033032: SAP NETWEAVER 2004S SR2 Kernel 7.00 Linux on x86_64 64bit

   Location: /dvd/NW_2004s_SR2_Kernel_WINDOWS__LNX_X86

▶ 51033272: ORACLE 10.2 Client

   Location: /dvd/ORACLE 10.2 Client

▶ 51031811: ORACLE 10.2 RDBMS Patch 10.2.0.2 LINUX_X86_64

   Location: /dvd/DVD_ORACLE_10.2.0.2_Patches_LINUX

▶ 51032958: SAP SOLUTION MANAGER 4.0 Support Release 3 Java Components

   Location: /dvd/51032958

▶ JCE policy files (http://www6.software.ibm.com/dl/jcesdk/jcesdk-p; you'll need a user ID and password for this site as well)

Prerequisite Checklists

Before we start the installation, we should run through a prerequisites checklist just to make sure everything has been done properly. This is especially important if a lot of different people and subteams within the SAP TSO have been involved in the process up to this point.

Checklist for Windows

The following comprises a list of basic prerequisites prior to installing SAP on the Microsoft Windows platform. Each computing platform has similar requirements.

▶ Check your NIC's network teaming properties.

▶ Verify that the Java Runtime Environment is installed.

▶ Verify that the JAVA_HOME system variable is set and that JAVA_HOME/bin has been added to the path.

▶ Verify that processor scheduling is set to Adjust for Best Performance of: Background Services.

▶ Verify the size and location of the pagefile.

▶ Turn off Automatic Updates.

▶ Verify that Server Optimization is set to Maximize Data Throughput for Network Applications.

▶ Verify the drive letter assignments.

▶ Verify the file allocation unit size for each drive on servers with a database instance, where SQLTemp, SQLLog, and SAPExe (F:, G:, H:) are formatted with 4KB allocation units, and all SAPDATA volumes are formatted with 64KB allocation units.

Checklist for Solution Manager on Linux

We have found that a checklist outlining the basic prerequisites which must be met prior to installing SAP Solution Manager on SUSE Linux is invaluable. The following checklist was developed during the installation of Solution Manager on a sandbox system:

▶ Check network teaming and other network interface properties.

▶ Install the Java Runtime Environment.

▶ Verify whether the following SUSE Red Hat Package Manager resources (RPMs) have been installed: SAP Application Server Base (sapinit) and C/C++ Compiler and Tools.

▶ Verify whether the saplocales RPM attached to SAP Note 171356 is installed. Note: Do not install the Oracle server init package.

▶ Select the MD5 password encryption as the default encryption method used.

▶ Verify swap space—SAP recommendation is 2 × RAM (20GB max).

▶ Verify the file systems.

▶ Verify whether you have downloaded the updated RUNINSTALLER—see SAP Note 980426 for Oracle installation.

SAPinst—The SAP System Landscape Installer

We have finally made it to the point of running SAPinst to install SAP. Before we start, we need to verify the following:

▶ Make sure you have at least 200MB of free space in the temporary directory before starting SAPinst. SAPinst creates the installation directory sapinst_instdir in the temporary directory using the TEMP or TMP environmental variable.

▶ If you are running the SAPinst GUI on the server, set either the JAVA_HOME or SAP-INST_JRE_HOME environmental variable to the JRE. In addition, for Linux or Unix

hosts, set the DISPLAY environmental variable to <host_name>:0.0, where
<host_name> is the host on which you want to display the SAPinst GUI.

Running SAPinst

For central services, dialog, or database instances, you start SAPinst from the Installation
Master DVD as follows:

1. Log in as root (Linux or Unix) or as a Domain Admin (Windows).

2. Copy the Installation Master DVD locally.

3. Navigate to cd <Installation Master_DVD>/IM_<OS>.

4. Execute ./sapinst (Linux or Unix) or sapinst (Windows).

It is possible to run SAPinst from a remote desktop or server. This might be necessary if
you do not have a supported JRE installed, for example. The first step is to make sure you
have a supported JRE on the desktop or server you are planning on connecting from. You
need to set the JAVA_HOME and DISPLAY environmental variables just as you would in a
standard install.

For example, let's say you want to run SAPinst for a SUSE Linux server from a Windows
XP desktop. You would do the following:

1. On the Linux server, run ./sapinst –noguiserver.

2. From the Windows desktop, download the SAP Solution Manager Installation Master
   for Windows and run C:\SAP_Solution_M._4.0_SR3_Inst._Master\
   IM_WINDOWS_I386\startinstgui.bat –host <linux-host>.

3. Run GUI software such as the Virtual Network Computing (VNC) server on the
   Linux server and the VNC client on the Windows desktop to complete the Oracle
   install with runInstaller. The VNC server software is included by default with SUSE
   Linux, and you can download the client from RealVNC's website at http://www.
   realvnc.com.

Navigating SAPinst

The following are key points to remember when running SAPinst:

▶ If you stop SAPinst, you are prompted to either restart the current installation or
  start a new installation after you select the system variant. This is very handy
  because it enables you to restart the installation from where you were instead of re-
  inputting all the parameters.

▶ If you receive an error during the installation, you can view the log, fix the problem,
  and click Retry to continue the installation.

▶ If you are running SAPinst from a remote desktop or server, you can log off and then
  reconnect later when you are ready to proceed.

▶ If you receive an error and need more information than the log viewer provides,
  there are more logs in the sapinst_instdir directory under the system variant you are
  currently installing.

▶ You can navigate to any of the input screens from the Parameter Summary page, even if you select the typical install.

We will examine how SAPinst is put into action in the next two chapters when we look at installing NetWeaver components and the SAP Business Suite.

Summary

This chapter covered all the activities that need to take place before an SAP installation. We started with the planning that takes place using SAP's documentation. Next we prepared for the OS installation by compiling a list of our storage and network requirements. We then covered the OS installation for Windows Server using best practices. Finally, we concluded by identifying the remaining prerequisites for SAPinst.

Case Study: Installation Preparation

You have been tasked with installing the SAP NetWeaver Portal sandbox in preparation for this upcoming Windows-based SAP deployment at HiTech, Inc. Your task is to be fully prepared when the time comes to complete the actual installation.

Questions

1. What guide serves as the starting point for your SAP infrastructure planning activities?
2. If you encounter an error during the database installation, where would you look for a solution?
3. What's a good rule of thumb for Windows pagefile sizing?
4. How would you complete an SAP installation if for some reason you could not directly install the Java Runtime Environment on the host?

NOTE

The answers to these questions can be found in Appendix A, "Case Study Answers."

CHAPTER **24**

Installing SAP NetWeaver Components

In this chapter we introduce you to the SAP NetWeaver installation process, starting with an explanation of the significance of SAP NetWeaver with regard to your SAP implementation. We discussed the importance of the Master Guide in the previous chapter—in this chapter, we walk through the IT business scenarios (an SAP term) with usage types and standalone engines based on the SAP NetWeaver Master Guide. You might remember from last chapter that nearly all NetWeaver-based applications have a similar installation procedure; here, we take a look at each usage type and point out various exceptions and gotchas. We conclude this chapter by walking through several NetWeaver IT scenarios.

NetWeaver Overview

As we've said throughout this book, SAP NetWeaver is one of those terms that means a lot of different things to a lot of different people and is therefore hard to pin down. SAP describes NetWeaver as an open integration and application platform, a development platform, and the technical foundation for SAP's business applications. Because this chapter is about the technical installation of SAP NetWeaver, we will look at it from that viewpoint—a technical one. From this perspective, we can view NetWeaver in a few different ways:

▶ The application platform for SAP Business Suite

▶ A collection of software units (sometimes incorrectly called "applications")

▶ An open integration platform

Let's take a look at each of these in more detail.

Application Platform

NetWeaver is the foundation of the NetWeaver-based SAP Business Suite of applications. SAP ERP, SRM, SCM, CRM, and PLM are all installed on top of SAP NetWeaver Application Server technology. Furthermore, additional applications, such as SAP Solution Manager and the SAP Government, Risk, and Compliance (GRC) applications, are based on the underlying technology of SAP NetWeaver. Different applications require either AS ABAP, AS Java, or both (AS ABAP+Java). For example, SAP Process Integration (PI) requires AS ABAP+Java, SAP NetWeaver Business Warehouse (BW) requires AS ABAP, and SAP NetWeaver Enterprise Portal (EP) requires AS Java. You don't have to remember the requirements for each usage type—SAPinst lists the dependencies for each usage type, as shown in Figure 24.1.

NetWeaver Usage Types

Software units are installation units. Usage types of SAP NetWeaver are software units to be installed and configured. Software units or usage types can be run together with others in one system, they can run separately on different systems. The usage types *Application Server ABAP (AS ABAP)* and *Application Server (AS Java)* are also used as a foundation for other units.

Install	Software Unit	Description	Depends On
☐	AS ABAP	NetWeaver Application Server ABAP	
☑	AS Java	NetWeaver Application Server Java	
☐	BI Java	NetWeaver BI Java	AS Java, EP, EP Core
☐	DI	NetWeaver Development Infrastructure	AS Java
☐	EP Core	NetWeaver Enterprise Portal Core C...	AS Java
☐	EP	NetWeaver Enterprise Portal	EP Core, AS Java
☐	MI	NetWeaver Mobile Infrastructure	AS ABAP, AS Java
☐	PI	NetWeaver Process Integration	AS ABAP, AS Java

FIGURE 24.1   The Depends On column lists the dependencies for each usage type. For example, you can easily determine that BI Java is dependent on AS Java, EP, and EPC.

There are several benefits of running all SAP Business Suite applications on top of a standardized NetWeaver platform. First, the installations are similar because part of the strategy of SAP NetWeaver is to remove the business logic from the application platform. Basically, this means that SAP applications are stored in the database in an operating system– and database-independent format. When you install NetWeaver, the kernel *is* operating system and database dependent—NetWeaver translates the database-independent instructions for your platform. By the way, whenever we say NetWeaver in the context of application platform, we are really talking about either Application Server ABAP, Application Server Java, or Application Server ABAP+Java. You might still see the term Web Application Server (Web AS) used to refer to the Application Server platform— SAP only recently dropped "Web" from the moniker and added ABAP, Java, or ABAP+Java for clarification.

Part of the beauty of NetWeaver Application Server technology is that not only are the installs similar, but the underlying architecture is the same for all applications based on the NetWeaver platform. This means such things as high availability (HA) that are based on the NetWeaver Application Server are similar (if not identical) for all the SAP Business Suite applications.

You might have noticed by now that on the SAPinst menu there are choices for distributed applications and high availability. *Distributed systems* basically are systems in which at least some of the instances run on different servers. A good example of this is if the database and central services run on separate servers—typically for scalability. *High availability* generally equates to clustering, where instances fail over from one server to another in case of failure. In both of these cases, because the computing platform provides these services, the platform is independent of the application. If you understand how to cluster one SAP Business Suite or NetWeaver application, you know how to cluster them all. Figure 24.2 shows the installations required for a Microsoft Cluster Service (MSCS) installation for Microsoft SQL. MSCS is the only HA solution for which SAP provides the cluster installation process—for other platforms, the cluster installation process is documented by the HA vendor.

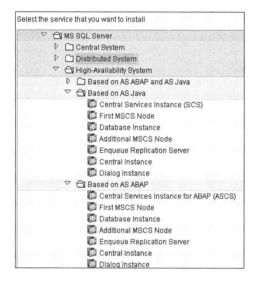

FIGURE 24.2   The installation services for a high-availability AS ABAP or AS Java system. In general, walk through the installation services in sequential order.

The parts of maintaining an SAP instance related to the platform are always the same as well. This means that if you understand how to maintain an ERP server, you have a good bit of the knowledge required to maintain a CRM, BW, or SRM server. This is especially true within each Application Server platform—AS ABAP or AS Java. Remember, the application logic is separate from the platform.

If you have been around SAP, you are probably familiar with the term Basis administrator. A Basis administrator is someone who architects, installs, administers, and monitors the Application Server technology stack. The common application layer (Application Server) makes it possible to maintain systems with different databases or OSs with relative ease. For example, the SAP transactions are always the same in an AS ABAP system. Following are some common examples of transactions that will work on any OS/database combination:

▶ OS06 – Operating System Monitor

▶ DB02 – Database Space (DBA Cockpit)

- ST04 – Performance Overview (DBA Cockpit)

- ST03 – Workload Monitor

- SM50 – Work Process Overview

- SM66 – Global Work Process Overview

- AL08 – List of All Users Logged On

We cover the installation of Application Server technology later in this chapter, including AS ABAP, AS Java, and AS ABAP+Java system installs.

Installable Software Units

Among other things, NetWeaver can be thought of as a collection of installable software units (applications) or usage types. In fact, at one point in time the following usage types were simply standalone SAP components or applications:

- Enterprise Portal (EP)

- Process Integration (formerly Exchange Infrastructure)

- Business Warehouse (BW)

These applications form the basis of the NetWeaver integration platform. Later in the chapter we cover the installation of these installable software units and how to build SAP IT scenarios.

Open Integration Platform

Finally, NetWeaver can be seen as the integration technology tying SAP applications together. SAP Process Integration (PI) is a middleware application that allows applications to exchange information (messages). SAP EP is the common portal interface for SAP applications. SAP BW provides a data warehouse/business intelligence environment for the SAP Business Suite. NetWeaver also integrates with external applications and can be extended to interoperate with Microsoft .NET, Sun's J2EE, and IBM WebSphere. Finally, the Application Server technology includes components such as Integrated ITS that allow SAP applications to be accessed from web browsers.

Installing NetWeaver

You might remember from the previous chapter that we determine the usage types we need for our business or IT scenario from the Master Guide. In case you are wondering, the terms *usage type* and *installable software unit* are used interchangeably by the SAP technical community. The NetWeaver Master Guide refers to IT scenarios that are built using NetWeaver usage types and standalone engines. In contrast, the SAP Business Suite refers to business scenarios—although many of these business scenarios utilize NetWeaver usage types and standalone engines in addition to the Business Suite applications. Keep in mind that they're essentially the same thing.

Look at usage types and standalone engines as the building blocks used to build these scenarios. In this way, a typical IT scenario might be built as follows:

1. The SAP systems are installed based on AS ABAP, AS Java, or AS ABAP+Java.
2. The required usage types are added to the systems (possibly during the initial install).
3. Standalone engines are installed (possibly on different systems).
4. The required clients are installed for the end-user community.

The following is the list of installable software units that are included in NetWeaver 7.0:

▶ Enterprise Portal (EP)

▶ Enterprise Portal Core (EPC)

▶ Process Integration/Exchange Infrastructure (PI/XI)

▶ Business Warehouse (BW, formerly BI)

▶ Business Warehouse Java (BW Java, formerly BI Java)

▶ Application Server ABAP (AS ABAP)

▶ Application Server Java (AS Java)

▶ Development Infrastructure (DI)

▶ Mobile Infrastructure

Keep in mind that EP, BI, and PI were formerly full-blown applications that SAP has now made into installable software units. You could also look at these usage types as modular—many of them are designed to work with multiple Business Suite applications and usage types. For example, EPC is used with BI Java and is also used with ERP to implement the Employee Self-Services (ESS) business scenario. Part of the idea is certainly to lower total cost of ownership (TCO) by making it easy to install these components and build IT scenarios. When we talk about installing these applications, we are really talking about installing the associated usage types. There is no such thing as an Enterprise Portal installation—instead, we need to talk about installing an AS Java system with usage types EP and/or EPC (by the way, the term *SAP NetWeaver Portal* is used frequently today, but the installation guides and processes still speak of *Enterprise Portal*; consider them interchangeable for the purposes of this chapter).

In addition to the usage types, we build IT scenarios with the following standalone engines. Standalone engines are not part of a usage type and they do not run on AS ABAP or AS Java systems. In contrast to NetWeaver usage types, each standalone engine has its own installation routines and architectures. Standalone engines are generally used to extend or improve the NetWeaver usage types. In many cases, the same standalone engines work with multiple NetWeaver usage types.

The SAP systems and standalone engine installation services are shown in Figure 24.3.

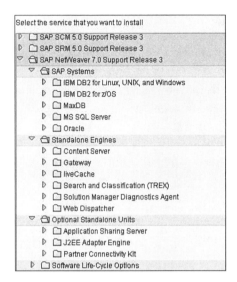

Select the service that you want to install

- ▷ ☐ SAP SCM 5.0 Support Release 3
- ▷ ☐ SAP SRM 5.0 Support Release 3
- ▽ ☐ SAP NetWeaver 7.0 Support Release 3
  - ▽ ☐ SAP Systems
    - ▷ ☐ IBM DB2 for Linux, UNIX, and Windows
    - ▷ ☐ IBM DB2 for z/OS
    - ▷ ☐ MaxDB
    - ▷ ☐ MS SQL Server
    - ▷ ☐ Oracle
  - ▽ ☐ Standalone Engines
    - ▷ ☐ Content Server
    - ▷ ☐ Gateway
    - ▷ ☐ liveCache
    - ▷ ☐ Search and Classification (TREX)
    - ▷ ☐ Solution Manager Diagnostics Agent
    - ▷ ☐ Web Dispatcher
  - ▽ ☐ Optional Standalone Units
    - ▷ ☐ Application Sharing Server
    - ▷ ☐ J2EE Adapter Engine
    - ▷ ☐ Partner Connectivity Kit
- ▷ ☐ Software Life-Cycle Options

FIGURE 24.3   The NetWeaver 7.0 SAP systems and standalone engines are installed using SAPinst from the SAP Business Suite Installation Master for your particular platform; the menu for Windows Server 2003 x86_64 is displayed here.

SAP AG also likes to include the clients that are necessary for a business or IT scenario. The Business Explorer (BEx) is a good example of a client that is required in some BW IT scenarios. Just to be clear, we are talking about a client application that is installed on the end user's desktop in this case.

In the next chapter we will see that SAP Business Suite application business scenarios are built using these same building blocks. First, though, let's take a closer look at a sample IT scenario.

Example IT Scenario—Business Planning and Analytical Services

In this section, we are going to work through an example of how to build an IT scenario with NetWeaver 7.0 usage types and standalone engines. The first step is to determine the SAP systems and usage types. For the Business Planning and Analytical Services scenario, the following SAP systems are required:

- ▶ AS ABAP with BI
- ▶ AS Java with EPC, EP, and BI Java

In addition, the following standalone engines are needed:

- ▶ Search and Classification (TREX)
- ▶ liveCache (optional)

In this case, TREX provides for fast search services for BI metadata. SAP's liveCache can be used as a lock server—this is optional and would only be needed to improve performance in certain circumstances that are detailed in the Master Guide.

Finally, the following clients must be deployed to the end-user community:

- SAPGUI

- Web browser

- Business Explorer (BEx)

- Adobe Reader

You combine systems with usage types, standalone engines, and clients to build NetWeaver IT scenarios.

Installing the ABAP Application Server

We outlined the steps required to prepare for an SAP component installation in Chapter 23, "Preparing for SAP Component Installations," but we consider the following important enough to reiterate at a high level:

1. The SAP NetWeaver Master Guide is the starting point for all NetWeaver installations. You must determine the usage types required for your IT scenario.

2. Download and read the installation guide for your OS and database combination. Both these guides are available (with your login ID and password) from SAP Service Marketplace (http://service.sap.com/instguides).

3. Download and review the SAP notes related to your installation from Service Marketplace (http://service.sap.com/notes).

We simply cannot overstate the importance of reading and following the SAP documentation. We are assuming that, in addition to obtaining the documentation, you have the hardware configured and ready for installation. For more details on the remaining installation considerations, see Chapter 23.

The Application Server ABAP system installation installs the ABAP platform. All NetWeaver installations are started from the SAP Business Suite Installation Master DVD; for example, the BS_2005_SR3_SAP_Installation_Master DVD. Let's walk through a simple installation of an ABAP central system using typical settings for Windows Server 2003 with a Microsoft SQL Server database:

1. Run SAPinst from the SAP Business Suite Installation Master DVD:

    ```
    D:\Install Files\BS_2005_SR3_SAP_Installation_Master\
    IM_WINDOWS_X86_64\sapinst.exe
    ```

2. Select the Central System Installation, as shown in Figure 24.4, and click Next.

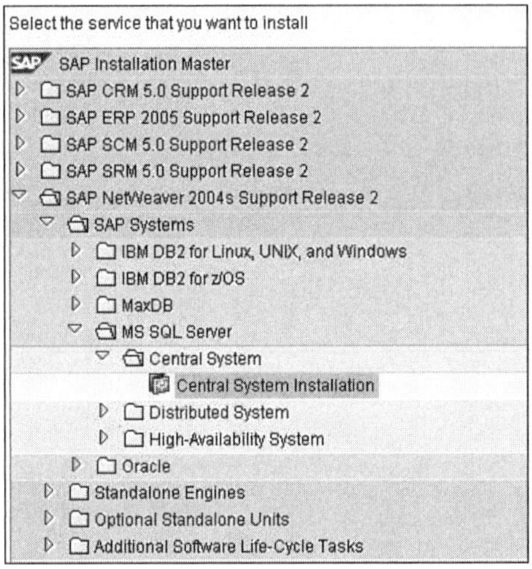

FIGURE 24.4   The Central System Installation installs all the SAP instances on a single host.

We will now step through the actual installation, giving you the SAPinst screen name (for example, Parameter Mode > Default Settings) followed by the input parameter (for example, Typical) and the required action (typically by clicking Next or OK):

3. Parameter Mode > Default Settings

   Typical

   Click Next.

4. SAP System > Software Units

   AS ABAP

   Click Next.

5. SAP System > General Parameters

   SAP System ID: TST

   Unicode (checked – grayed out)

   Click Next.

6. SAP System > Master Password

   Password for all users of this SAP system:

   Confirm:

   Click Next.

7. SAP System > OS User Passwords

   Account: tstadm

   Password of SAP System Administrator:

   Account: SAPServiceTST

   Password of SAP System Service User: xxxxxxxx

   Click Next.

8. Prerequisites checker > Results

We received the following message because the page file was too small: "Your system does not meet some prerequisites or SAPinst could not evaluate them. The checks will be repeated."

Choose Cancel to stop repeating the checks and to continue the installation.

9. Media Browser > Software Package Check

Installation Export NW 7.0 SR3: D:\Install\51033493\EXP1

Click OK.

10. Media Browser > Software Package Check

Installation Export NW 7.0 SR3: D:\Install\51033493\EXP2

Click OK.

11. SAP System > Central Instance

Central Instance Number: 00

Click OK.

12. Media Browser > Software Package Request

UC Kernel NW 7.0 SR3: D:\Install\51032266-kernel\KN_WINDOWS_X86_64

Click OK.

13. SAP System > Unpack Archives

The following archives are checked by default:

DBINDEP\SAPEXE.SAR

MSS\SAPEXEDB.SAR

DBINDEP\IGSEXE.SAR

DBINDEP\IGSHELPER.SAR

Click Next.

14. Parameter Summary

Click Start.

Keep in mind that these are only the parameters requested for a typical installation. If we had chosen to perform a custom installation, we would have had the opportunity to change database configuration settings, database import settings, and more. We could also have selected these additional parameters from the Parameter Summary screen to change the values.

Installing the Java Application Server

AS Java is used to provide the Java (J2EE) platform for SAP NetWeaver systems. The following is an example of a simple installation of a Java central system using typical settings for Windows Server 2003 with a SQL Server database:

1. Run SAPinst from the SAP Business Suite Installation Master DVD:

   ```
   D:\Install Files\BS_2005_SR3_SAP_Installation_Master\
   IM_WINDOWS_X86_64\sapinst.exe
   ```

2. Select the Central System Installation, and click Next.

   Once again we will step through the installation, giving you the SAPinst screen name followed by the input parameter and the required action:

3. Parameter Mode > Default Settings

   Typical

   Click Next.

4. SAP System > Software Units

   AS Java

   Click Next.

5. Media Browser > Software Package Request

   Media Name: Java Component NW 7.0 SR3

   Package Location: D:\Install\51033513\LABEL.ASC

   Click OK.

6. SAP System > JCE Unlimited Strength Jurisdiction Policy Archive

   JCE Unlimited Strength Jurisdiction Policy File Archive: D:\Install\jce_policy-1_4_2.zip

   Click Next.

7. SAP System > General Parameters

   SAP System ID: TST

   Click Next.

8. SAP System > Master Password

   Password for all users of this SAP system: xxxxxxxx

   Confirm: xxxxxxxx

   Click Next.

9. SAP System > OS User Passwords

   SAP System Administrator: xxxxxxxx

   SAP System Service User: xxxxxxxx

   Click Next.

10. Media Browser > Software Package Request

    Java Component NW 7.0 SR3:
    D:\Install\51033513\DATA_UNITS\JAVA_EXPORT_JDMP

    Click OK.

11. SAP System > Central and SCS Instance

    Central Instance Number: 00

    SCS Instance Number: 01

Click Next.

12. Media Browser > Software Package Request

UC Kernel NW 7.0 SR3:

Click OK.

13. SAP System > System Landscape Directory

SLD Destination: Select Register in existing central SLD (default)

Click Next.

14. Parameter Summary

Click Next.

One thing to keep in mind is that, after you have installed AS Java, you cannot install additional Java usage types by rerunning SAPinst. To deploy additional Java usage types to an existing AS Java or AS ABAP+Java system, you must use the Java Support Package Manager (JSPM). Also keep in mind that it is not possible to add the usage type PI via the JSPM—it must be done during the initial installation via SAPinst. This is typically not an issue, because PI should generally be run on a dedicated system.

Installing Application Server ABAP+Java

There are essentially two ways of getting to Application Server ABAP+Java:

▶ Install AS ABAP+Java from the beginning

▶ Add AS Java to an existing AS ABAP installation

Installing AS ABAP+Java from the beginning is as simple as selecting the AS ABAP and AS Java usage types during the installation—that is all there is to it. Of course, depending on your IT or business scenario, you might select other usage types as well. AS ABAP+Java is referred to as a dual stack system.

You can also choose to add Java to an existing AS ABAP system by choosing the SAPinst installation service Java Add-In for ABAP. This has been supported since NetWeaver 7.0 SR1.

It is also possible to add additional usage types based on AS Java while installing the Java Add-In. For example, you could add EPC and AS Java to an AS ABAP system.

There is one caveat to the Java Add-In—you cannot install the Java Add-In to existing dialog instances. In this case, you must uninstall the existing ABAP dialog instance and install a new ABAP+Java dialog instance.

> **NOTE**
>
> Keep in mind that it is not easy to separate or merge usage types. For example, if you choose to install BI Java and EPC on the same server, SAP does not provide tools to later separate these onto separate servers.

One of our key architecture decisions is whether to standardize on the full AS ABAP+Java stack or a subset of it. A growing number of firms are making the decision to install AS ABAP+Java on every server, thereby establishing a consistent image across their entire SAP landscape. This approach requires additional resources and an additional component to maintain (in some cases), but may be easier to maintain and troubleshoot because it is a standard implementation. Other firms have decided to install only the necessary stack components for each SAP installation—AS ABAP, AS Java, or AS ABAP+Java—as required by the business scenario. The advantages of this approach include one less component to maintain (and troubleshoot inevitable issues down the road) and the fact that additional computing resources are made available rather than being tied up by a stack component that doesn't actually need any resources.

This also ties into another decision—whether to install multiple SAP systems (or software usage types) on a single system. Although in many cases it is acceptable to install more than one usage type on a server (check the Master Guide), in practice we often find that customers choose to keep their systems isolated. For example, most customers have an EP landscape, a BW landscape, an ERP landscape, and so forth. There are many factors in deciding how to implement an SAP architecture—performance, scalability, availability, security, and other factors are all affected by the system architecture. The chief advantage of installing multiple usage types on one server is cost savings. We believe that, for most of our customers, SAP is deemed mission critical—they are willing to pay the extra money for the scalability, flexibility, and performance.

Installing SAP NetWeaver Portal

Starting with SAP NetWeaver 7.0 SR2, there are two SAP NetWeaver Portal (again, SAP's documentation still refers to these as "Enterprise Portal") usage types:

▶ Enterprise Portal (EP)

▶ EP Core (EPC)

In case you're wondering, prior to NetWeaver 7.0 SR2 there was only one Enterprise Portal usage type—Enterprise Portal. As the name suggests, EP Core provides the core portal capabilities from the previous EP usage type. The current usage type EP includes the remaining add-in capabilities available in the previous EP and is dependent upon EP Core. Knowledge management and collaboration are two examples of capabilities provided in the EP usage type. The good thing about this arrangement is that it allows you to install just the core portal functionality if that is all you need. This is the case in many situations where the portal provides a consistent web interface to the application. You can determine from the Master Guide whether these usage types are required for your business or NetWeaver IT scenario.

By way of example, the Enterprise Portal usage types are used in the following IT scenarios (among many others):

▶ Running an Enterprise Portal

Usage types: AS Java, EPC, DI (optional—for developing content)

▶ Enterprise Knowledge Management

Usage types: AS Java, EPC, EP (standalone engine TREX)

Installing SAP Business Warehouse

In 2009, SAP changed its nomenclature for its heritage BI offerings back to Business Warehouse (BW); BI is now used by SAP BusinessObjects solutions. For our purposes in this chapter, though, we will use BI and BW interchangeably.

You might have noticed that while there is a BI Java usage type, there is not a BI ABAP or BI usage type. This is because there is not an installation option for usage type BI in SAPinst. To install usage type BI, you first install AS ABAP using SAPinst and then install the SAP NetWeaver 7.0 BI Content via transaction SAINT. Figure 24.5 shows transaction SAINT after the BI Content has been added. Remember to use the latest available version of BI content (in this case it is SAP NW 7.0 BI CONT ADDON 7.04).

```
                Add-On Installation Tool : Installed Add-ons

        Add-ons and Preconfigured Systems installed in the system
  Add-on/PCS   Release     Level  Description
  BI_CONT      703         0007 BI_CONT 703 Upgrade: Meta-Commandfile (D
  PI_BASIS     2005_1_700  0013 PI_BASIS 2005_1_700
  SAP_BW       700         0015 SAP NetWeaver BI 7.0
  ST-A/PI      01J_BCO700  0000 Servicetools for other App./Netweaver 04
  ST-PI        2005_1_700  0005 SAP Solution Tools Plug-In
```

FIGURE 24.5   Transaction SAINT with BI_CONT 703.

You can download the latest version of SAP NetWeaver BW Content from SAP Service Marketplace (http://service.sap.com/swdc) under Installations and Upgrades.

At this point you have the core BI functionality, which runs on AS ABAP. Depending on your business or IT scenario, you may very well require the BI Java usage type as well. BI Java is dependent on AS Java, EPC, and EP—they will be installed automatically if you select the BI Java usage type. BI Java can also be combined with other usage types in addition to the required EP and EPC.

You can run BI and BI Java on the same system or on different systems. The SAP Master Guide recommends running BI and BI Java on separate systems, for higher scalability and flexibility. In fact, as of SAP Enhance Package 1 for SAP NetWeaver 7.0, the default installation option is to install BI and BI Java on separate systems. You can still install BI and BI Java on a single, dual-stack (AS ABAP+Java) system, but some manual actions are required—see SAP Note 1181025 for additional information.

24

Installing SAP Process Integration

Installing the usage type PI is a little different from the other installs in the following ways:

- PI requires AS ABAP and AS Java (dual stack).

- PI requires a dedicated system in the development, quality assurance, and production landscapes.

By default, all the central components (the central Integration Server, Integration Builder, and System Landscape Directory [SLD]) are installed on one host. The service J2EE Adapter Engine (PI/XI) is also part of usage type PI. With regard to PI, remember that the name was changed; PI was previously referred to as Exchange Infrastructure (XI).

Finalizing Other NetWeaver Post-Installation Tasks

After you have finished running SAPinst, you are still not quite done with the installation. To this end, you need to complete the following tasks:

1. Verify logon to AS ABAP, AS Java, and the SAP NetWeaver Portal (if installed).
2. Install the SAP license.
3. Install SAP Online Documentation.
4. Configure a remote connection to SAP support.
5. Apply the latest kernel and support packages.
6. Perform initial ABAP configuration.
7. Perform a client copy.
8. Execute a full database backup.
9. Perform post-installation steps for Adobe Document Services.
10. BI Java and PI: Set the environmental variable CPIC_MAX_CONV.
11. PI: Perform the post-installation steps for usage type PI.
12. EP: Perform the post-installation steps for Application Sharing Server.
13. Verify user security.
14. AS Java, BI, and PI: Run the Configuration Wizard.

These tasks are documented in the installation guide for your OS and database combination. You will find that some of these tasks are OS or database specific. The installation guide details the specific actions required to complete each task for your database or OS. We will guide you through a sample SAP Business Suite installation in the next chapter that includes many of these steps. For now, we will cover a few of the most basic steps and those specific to NetWeaver usage types.

Accessing the Application Server ABAP

Having the SAPGUI installed is a prerequisite for logging in to AS ABAP. Actually, you could log in to the integrated Internet Transaction Server (ITS) with a web browser, also known as SAPGUI for HTML, but most Basis administrators choose to use the SAPGUI.

One reason is that the SAPGUI installation includes the SAP Logon Pad, which makes it easy to log in to multiple SAP systems.

There are two variations of the SAPGUI: SAPGUI for Windows and SAPGUI for Java. SAPGUI for Java is most commonly used on Linux and UNIX platforms, but can certainly be run on Windows as well. The SAPGUI is installed from the NW 7.0 Presentation DVD. If you do not have one, you can download it from Service Marketplace (http://service.sap.com/swdc) under Installation and Upgrades, Frontend Components. You may notice that SAP refers to the client application as a front end—this is because "client" has a different meaning in SAP. In deciding which front end to use, you may want to research the SAP Notes, because there are some limitations to SAPGUI for Java and SAPGUI for HTML. In general, if you have a Windows client, the SAPGUI for Windows is probably your best bet.

You use the SAPGUI to log on to AS ABAP (the application server). You should be able to log on as sap* and ddic to clients 000 and 001. You will probably want to start out by logging in as ddic into client 000.

Accessing the Application Server Java

You access AS Java from a web browser. The URL is http://<hostname>:5<instance_number>00. For example, if my hostname is *testserver* and my instance number is 00, the URL will be http://testserver:50000. You always need to use two numbers for the instance number. And keep in mind that, unless you changed it during the installation, the default user is J2EE_ADMIN.

Accessing NetWeaver Portal (Usage Type EPC and EP)

The portal is also accessed via a web browser. The URL is http://<hostname>:5<instance_number>00/irj. The same rule applies to the instance number, and the default user is J2EE_ADMIN.

Setting Environment Variable CPIC_MAX_CONV

Set the environment variable CPIC_MAX_CONV to the maximum number of simultaneous RFCs to the SAP system, but not less than 200. This procedure is OS dependent (described in the installation guide) and requires a system restart. The installation guide also describes the changes needed to SAP profile parameters gw/max_conn and gw/max_sys on the SAP gateway to support more parallel connections.

Performing Post-Installation Steps for Usage Type PI

You must update the Content Repository (CR) content in the System Landscape Directory (SLD) for usage type PI after SAPinst has finished. You download the latest version of the CR content from SAP Service Marketplace (service.sap.com/swdc) under SAP Support Packages & Patches, SAP Technology Components, SAP CR Content. For additional information, see SAP Note 669669 or download the SLD user manual. You can also learn more about the SLD from the SAP Developer Network (SDN) at http://sdn.sap.com/irj/sdn/nw-sld.

Performing Post-Installation Steps for Usage Type EP

The default installation of usage type EP also installs the Real-Time Collaboration (RTC) Application Sharing Server. You could also install the Application Sharing Server as a standalone engine. In either case, there are a number of post-installation steps you must complete to fully implement application sharing functions in the portal. If you do not intend to use the Application Sharing Server, you should disable it. Otherwise, go to the SAP NetWeaver Library (http://help.sap.com) and search for "Configuring the Application Sharing Server (RTC)" for additional information on configuring the Application Sharing Server.

Running the Configuration Wizard (AS Java, BI Java, and PI)

You must run the Configuration Wizard after installing and patching the system for usage types AS Java, BI Java, and PI. With the exception of BI Java, you should run the Configuration Wizard only one time. You should also patch LMTOOLS—the latest patch is available from Service Marketplace (http://service.sap.com/swdc). You apply the patch using the Software Deployment Manager (SDM). You might notice that, in many cases, before you use an SAP tool for the first time you will need to update the application.

Run the Configuration Wizard as follows:

1. Launch the NetWeaver Administrator from a web browser at http://<hostname>:<http_port>/nwa and log on as the user Administrator.

2. Navigate to the Deploy and Change tab. The system displays the Configuration Wizard and its configuration tasks.

3. Depending on the usage types installed in your system, select a task as described next, and then click Start:

   ▶ **Usage Type Application Server**—You must run configuration tasks NWA_01 through NWA_07 using the Configuration Wizard to configure the SAP NetWeaver Administrator.

   ▶ **Usage Type PI**—You must run configuration task PI_00 using the Configuration Wizard. You will need to reference SAP Note 939592 if you are using a central SLD.

   ▶ **Usage Type BI Java**—You must run the configuration task BIPostInstallProcess using the Configuration Wizard.

4. After the Configuration Wizard has finished, restart your SAP system.

Establishing SAP Printing

Although it is not officially a post-installation step, sooner or later you are going to want to print something in SAP. If you are using the SAPGUI for Windows, you can set up SAP local printing as follows:

1. Go to transaction SPAD.

2. Select Display from the Output Devices menu.

3. Create New Printer LOCL (Output Device, Create) and set up with the parameters for DeviceAttributes, as shown in Figure 24.6.

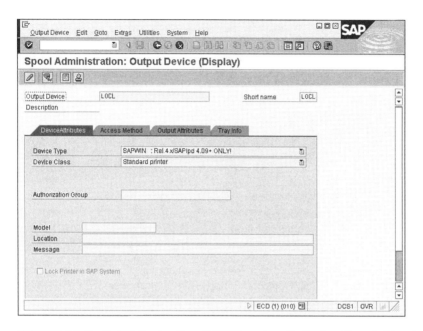

FIGURE 24.6   Select Device Type SAPWIN and verify Device Class is Standard printer on the Device Attributes tab.

4. Enter the parameters for Access Method, as shown in Figure 24.7.

At this point we have completed all the post-installation steps and the SAP system is ready to go. The next steps would be to install any required standalone engines and clients to complete your SAP IT scenario.

Summary

You should now understand how to build a NetWeaver 7.0 IT scenario. The process starts with determining the system type(s) with usage types, standalone engines, and clients using the NetWeaver 7.0 Master Guide. The system type refers to the application platform—AS ABAP, AS Java, or AS ABAP+Java. The next step is to build the systems with usage types and associated standalone engines using the installation guide for your OS and database combination. After performing the post-installation steps, you install and configure the clients (front ends). At this point your IT scenario is ready to use. Keep in mind that these same system and usage types, standalone engines, and clients are also used with SAP Business Suite applications to build business scenarios.

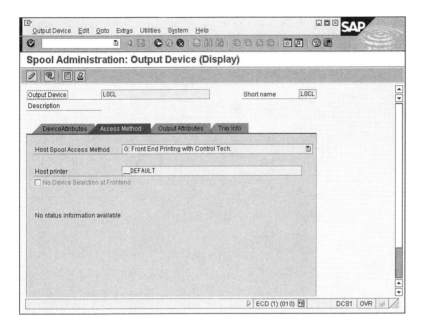

FIGURE 24.7 The access method depends on the printer configuration. For our scenario, the Host Spool Access Method needs to be G: Front End Printing with Control Tech.

Case Study: Implementing a Sandbox

You have been asked by your employer, HiTech, Inc., to implement the NetWeaver IT scenario Running an Enterprise Portal. You will start by installing a sandbox system on Linux with an Oracle database. You will be installing a central system using the default parameters.

Questions

1. How do you determine which software units you need to install for this IT scenario?

2. Will you require the SAPGUI to complete the post-installation steps for this IT scenario?

3. Where would you find a list of the post-installation steps along with the detailed instructions for carrying them out?

NOTE

The answers to these questions can be found in Appendix A, "Case Study Answers."

CHAPTER 25

Installing SAP Business Suite Components

In previous chapters, we walked through all the necessary hardware infrastructure and Operating System (OS) preparation and planning, and are now ready to install SAP Business Suite components. Before we get started, there are a couple of important points to remember regarding these installations:

▶ Each of the components (ERP, SRM, CRM, SCM, and PLM) is based on SAP NetWeaver technology and resides on a NetWeaver application server (ABAP, Java, or ABAP+Java). Because of this standard NetWeaver foundation, the installation routines are very similar with the exception of the standalone engines.

▶ The actual installation of each component will vary based on your business scenario—we'll talk more on this a little later in the chapter.

In this chapter we will walk through the installation of SAP ERP. To be more specific, we will walk through the installation of the ERP Central Component (ECC) on an HP-UX computing platform running an Oracle database.

SAP Business Suite Installation

We have reached the point at which we are ready to install one or more of the following SAP Business Suite applications (depending on our company's specific business requirements and all the required blueprinting and other preparation):

▶ SAP Supplier Relationship Management (SAP SRM)

▶ SAP Customer Relationship Management (SAP CRM)

▶ SAP Enterprise Resource Planning (ERP)

▶ SAP Product Lifecycle Management (SAP PLM)

▶ SAP Supply Chain Management (SAP SCM)

Keep in mind, as covered in Chapter 23, "Preparing for SAP Component Installations," that all the individual applications in a particular version of the SAP Business Suite run on the same version of the NetWeaver platform. For example, SAP Business Suite 2005 runs on SAP NetWeaver 7.0 SR2. A support release (SR) includes the support package stacks in the installation media—NetWeaver 7.0 SR2 includes support package stacks 01 through 09. The advantage here is that after the installation is completed, you do not need to apply these support package stacks. The main point here is that because they are all based on the same version of NetWeaver, the installations are very similar, given the same operating system (OS) and database platform. In fact, the SAP Business Suite applications share a common installation master.

The SAP Business Suite 2005 installation master comprises the following:

▶ SAP NetWeaver 7.0 SR2

▶ SAP ERP 2005 SR2

▶ SAP CRM 5.0 SR2

▶ SAP SCM 5.0 SR2

▶ SAP SRM 5.0 SR2

The real differences in the installations are the business scenarios and the underlying application and technology components, which are described in the Master Guide for each application. In addition to the installable software units, the Master Guide also provides guidance on the installation sequence and the technical system landscape. Obtain Master Guides from the SAP service marketplace by performing the following:

1. Navigate to the "Installation and Upgrade Guides" section of the website.
2. Select the component to be installed (for example, SAP ERP 6.0).
3. Click on the "Planning" link.
4. In the "Planning Information" page you can find links to the Master Guide (along with quite a few other miscellaneous support documents SAP posts to these "planning" sites to assist installers).

Before we walk through an SAP ERP 6.0 installation step-by-step, let's take a closer look at some of the other most popular SAP Business Suite components from a deployment or software component perspective. This will give you an idea of the relative complexity of some of these installations.

SAP SRM Deployment Options and Installation

Within SAP ERP 6.0, SAP Supplier Relationship Management (SRM) can be deployed in the following ways:

▶ By deploying SAP SRM Server as an add-on to SAP ECC Server (so that SRM may run in one client of the ERP system)

▶ By installing SAP SRM Server as a separate component to SAP ECC Server

We tend to see the latter deployment method performed more frequently. Installing SRM can become a very complex process. The SAP SRM Self Service Procurement Implementation sequence, for example, consists of the following high-level installation steps (each of which consists of many more sub-steps):

1. Install SAP NetWeaver Process Integration (PI); optional.
2. Install or integrate SAP R/3, SAP R/3 Enterprise, or SAP ERP.
3. Install SRM Server 5.5.
4. Install SAP Internet Transaction Server (ITS).
5. Install SAP Catalog Content Management 2.0 (CCM) or SRM-MDM (Master Data Management) Catalog 1.0.
6. Install SAP NetWeaver 2004s Search and Classification (TREX).
7. Install SRM Server for SAP Supplier Self-Services (SUS).
8. Install SAP Business Warehouse (formerly SAP NetWeaver BI); optional.
9. Install SAP NetWeaver Portal 7.0; optional.
10. Import the following Business Packages into the portal:

   ▶ Business Package for SRM 5.0

   ▶ Business Package for Supplier Collaboration 2.0

SAP CRM Software Components

Installing SAP Customer Relationship Management (CRM) can also quickly become quite complex. SAP CRM's business scenarios are built upon the following software components:

▶ CRM Core

▶ CRM Mobile Client Component

▶ CRM Handheld Integration

▶ CRM Workforce Management

▶ CRM People-Centric User Interface

▶ Standalone components, which include

   ▶ SAP Content Server

   ▶ Search and Classification (TREX)

> ► SAP Groupware Connector

> ► MapBox

> ► TeaLeaf RealiTea

> ► cProjects for Standalone Installation

► Application Systems—CRM can interface with an ERP 6.0 back end, as well as SAP Business Warehouse (formerly SAP NetWeaver BI), SAP SCM Server, and SAP SRM Server.

► Content Types, which include

> ► Solution Manager Content

> ► Business Packages (Portal Content)

> ► Business Intelligence Content (BI_CONT)

> ► System Landscape Directory (SLD) Content

> ► PI (previously XI) Content

As usual, check the Master Guide for further information.

SAP SCM Software Components

SAP Supply Chain Management (SCM) business processes are built by installing any number of the following software components:

► SAP SCM 5.0—SCM Server, SP07

► SCM Optimizer

► SAP NetWeaver 2004s usage type PI

► SAP ERP 2005—ECC Server

► SAP CRM 5.0—CRM Server

► SAP NetWeaver 2004s usage type BI

► Standalone components

► SAP liveCache

SCM Optimizer is a Windows application and, as such, is only available on Windows platforms (x64 and IA32 as of this writing). After you install SCM Optimizer, you must configure the SCM Server to interface with it.

SAP liveCache is available on a wide variety of platforms. SAP liveCache is a memory-resident database based on SAP's MaxDB. You will learn in the next section how to install it from the SAP Business Suite Installation Master.

Installing Other Components and Products

As alluded to previously, the installation process for many of SAP's components is very similar. To avoid a whole lot of repetition, we chose to avoid detailing every SAP Business Suite component installation. In this section, however, you can read about some of the less common products installed for certain SAP component installations.

SAP Product Lifecycle Management

SAP Product Lifecycle Management (PLM) typically involves one or all of the following applications or business scenario enablers:

- ▶ Collaboration Projects (cProjects)
- ▶ Collaboration Folders (cFolders)
- ▶ SAP xApp Resource and Portfolio Management (SAP xRPM)

Just like every other component we have talked about, the choice of which applications to deploy depends on the business processes you need to support. Following are the applications and their associated business processes:

- ▶ Collaboration Folders (cFolders)
    - ▶ Development Collaboration
    - ▶ Engineering Change Collaboration
- ▶ Collaboration Projects (cProjects)
    - ▶ Project Planning with cProjects
    - ▶ Project Execution with cProjects
    - ▶ Project Accounting with cProjects
    - ▶ Resource and Time Management with cProjects
- ▶ SAP xApp Resource and Portfolio Management (SAP xRPM)
    - ▶ Strategic Portfolio Management
    - ▶ Decision Flow Management

cProject Suite

The cProject Suite is installed as an add-on to SAP NetWeaver 7.0. As usual, you need to read the Master Guide for further information on establishing the system landscape before starting the installation—especially if users will be accessing cFolders from outside your corporate network.

25

In addition to a standalone installation on SAP NetWeaver, the following variants are possible:

▶ cProjects 4.50 can be installed on ERP 6.0 and CRM 5.0.

▶ cFolders 4.50 can be installed on SRM Server 5.5, SCM Server 5.0, and SAP ERP 6.0.

Standalone Engine Options

Additional installable software units or components provided by SAP are the *standalone engines*. Standalone engines do not need to be installed atop NetWeaver; they can be installed and run on their own. The following standalone engines are available from the SAP NetWeaver 2004s Support Release 1 Installation Master:

▶ Content Server (optional database instance MaxDB)

▶ SAP liveCache—based on MaxDB

▶ Search and Classification (TREX)—no database

These engines can be associated with multiple applications. For example, TREX can be used with the following SAP applications:

▶ SAP NetWeaver Enterprise Search

▶ SAP NetWeaver Process Integration (PI)

▶ SAP Business Warehouse (formerly SAP NetWeaver Business Intelligence)

▶ SAP NetWeaver Portal

▶ SAP ERP

▶ SAP Customer Relationship Management (SAP CRM)

▶ SAP Product Lifecycle Management (SAP PLM)

▶ SAP Supplier Relationship Management (SAP SRM)

Other standalone engines you might need to install for a specific business scenario or to better support your SAP system landscape include Redwood's job scheduling software and SAP's Web Dispatcher (used for load balancing).

Installing the SAP ERP Core Component

As previously mentioned, you need to read the Master Guide before you install any of these applications, to determine the software units, NetWeaver usage types, and whether you need to install any standalone engines for your business scenario. In this section, we are going to walk through a relatively straightforward installation involving the ERP Core Component (ECC) 6.0 software unit of SAP ERP 6.0 on HP-UX with an Oracle Database 10g Release 2 (we'll call this Oracle 10.2 for simplicity). We will assume we require ABAP and Java and will be implementing Unicode. Referring back to Chapter 23, we would next want to read through the specific installation guide for ERP 6.0 on HP-UX with Oracle

Database along with the associated SAP Notes (give yourself plenty of time for all the SAP Notes—there's rarely fewer than 20 or 30 that are relevant to a particular computing platform and SAP component combination). Let's assume we have the following in place:

▶ HP-UX has been installed (and the servers, storage, and networks have been configured).

▶ Kernel parameters are set as specified in the SAP component installation guide.

▶ File systems are mounted (available to be used).

▶ Swap space has been configured.

▶ SAP media have been copied to /usr/sap/CD.

▶ The Solution Manager key has been generated.

▶ The Java 2 Software Development Kit (SDK) is installed.

With all these prerequisites met, we can start the actual SAP ERP 6.0 component installation. If you've guessed that the prerequisites could take several weeks to address, you are correct!

1. Log in as root and run `sapinst` as described here:

```
setenv DISPLAY rp34-211:1.0
export JAVA_HOME=/opt/java1.4
export PATH=/opt/java1.4/bin:$PATH
export SHLIB_PATH=/sapmnt/ER5/exe
cd /usr/sap/CD/D51031797/IM_HPUX_PARISC

  ./sapinst
```

2. Select Central System Installation, as shown in Figure 25.1, and click Next.

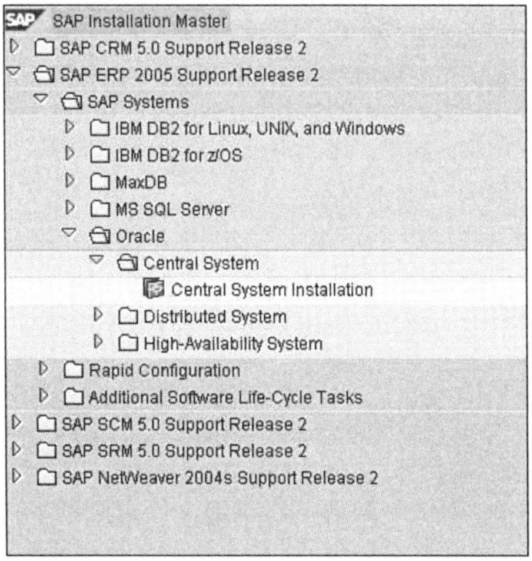

FIGURE 25.1   The SAP Installation Master gives you the opportunity to install the Business Suite applications, NetWeaver components, and standalone engines.

3. Select the appropriate software units and click Next. We are installing ERP Central Component (ECC) with AS ABAP and AS Java, as shown in Figure 25.2.

Install	Software Unit	Description	Depends On
☑	ECC	ERP 2005 Central Component	AS ABAP
☐	BD	ERP 2005 Biller Direct	AS Java
☐	BP ERP	ERP 2005 Business Packages ...	AS Java, EP, EP Core
☐	LSOCP	ERP 2005 Learning Solution ...	AS Java
☐	XECO	ERP 2005 Extended E-Selling ..	AS Java
☐	XSS	ERP 2005 Self Services	AS Java, EP, EP Core, BP ERP

Additional NetWeaver Software Units

Install	Software Unit	Description	Depends On
☑	AS ABAP	NetWeaver Application Serve...	
☑	AS Java	NetWeaver Application Serve...	
☐	BI Java	NetWeaver BI Java	AS Java, EP, EP Core
☐	DI	NetWeaver Development Infra..	AS Java
☐	EP Core	NetWeaver Enterprise Portal..	AS Java
☐	EP	NetWeaver Enterprise Portal	EP Core, AS Java
☐	MI	NetWeaver Mobile Infrastruc...	AS ABAP, AS Java

FIGURE 25.2   This is your opportunity to select the software units required for your specific business scenario.

NOTE

Best practice dictates that you do not install any software components that you do not require. Every installed component requires resources and maintenance and might cause you problems at some point—just say "no" to unnecessary components.

---

4. Enter the location to which you have copied the Java Component DVD and click OK.

5. In the File Chooser, browse to the location of the JCE policy archive you downloaded in advance and click OK, or simply enter the path and then click OK.

6. Enter the SAP System Parameters from your planning worksheet (including the SAP SID, the SAP system mount directory, and whether or not Unicode system will be installed), and click Next. For our purposes, our SID is TST, our mount directory is /sapmnt, and we are indeed implementing a Unicode system.

7. Enter the master password, confirm (retype) it, and click Next.

8. Enter the database parameters (in our case, we will use a Database ID of TST and a database host name of rp34-211) and click Next. Unless you have a specific reason for using a different DBSID, it should be the same as the SAP SID.

9. You might get a message such as the one shown in Figure 25.3 if your system does not pass a check for SAP prerequisites. You can either correct the issues and click OK, or click Cancel to bypass the checks. For example, you may need to click Cancel if you have the latest version of an OS patch that is not recognized by SAPinst (which indeed may or may not be a problem—search SAP Notes to confirm, or use your best judgment).

10. Enter the path to the Export 1 DVD, as follows, and click OK.

Media Name: Installation Export 1 ECC60SR1:

Package Location: /usr/sap/CD/D51031798_1/LABEL.ASC

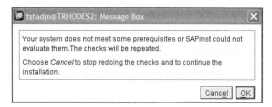

FIGURE 25.3   You can retry the checks by clicking Cancel. If you have evaluated the issues and are comfortable with continuing, simply click Cancel.

11. Enter the path to the Export 2 DVD, as follows, and click OK.

Media Name: Installation Export 2 ECC60SR1:

Package Location: /usr/sap/CD/D51031798_2/LABEL.ASC

12. Enter the path to the Oracle RDBMS DVD, as follows, and click OK.

Media Name: Oracle RDBMS

Package Location: /usr/sap/CD/D51031670/LABEL.ASC

13. Enter the Central Instance Number from the planning worksheet and the SAP Solution Manager Key, as shown in Figure 25.8, and click Next.

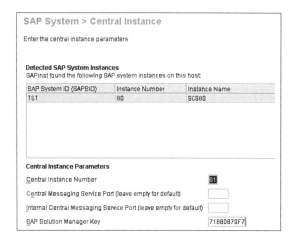

FIGURE 25.4   The Java SCS is detected and you are given the opportunity to enter the central instance parameters.

14. Enter the paths to the Kernel and Oracle Client media, as follows, respectively, and click OK.

Media Name: Kernel NW2004sSR1

Package Location: /usr/sap/CD/D51031791/LABEL.ASC

Media Name: Oracle Client

Package Location: /usr/sap/CD/D51031613/CD_ORACLE_10.2_Client/LABEL.ASC

15. Keep the defaults for the archives to be unpacked and click Next.

16. Enter the path to the Java Component BS2005SR1 DVD, as follows, and click OK.

    Media Name: Java Component BS2005SR1

    Package Location: /usr/sap/CD/D51031807/LABEL.ASC

17. Choose the SLD destination, as shown in Figure 25.5, and click Next.

18. The SLD User Information has the default usernames with the master password—just enter the Object Server Name, and click Next.

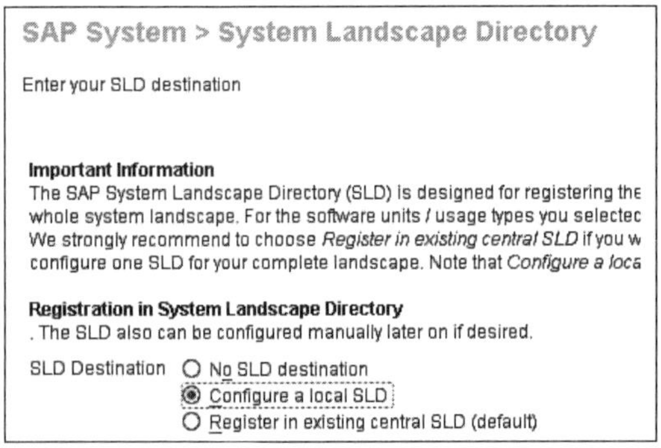

FIGURE 25.5   Select the SLD destination. For a test installation, you might select a local SLD to gain some familiarity with SAP SLD.

19. If you want to revise any of the parameters for the installation, check the appropriate box on the Parameter Summary screen and click Revise. For example, to change the default Oracle Tablespace layout, click the Oracle > Database System check box and click Next.

20. By default, the database administrator password is the master password, but you can change it if you like (so that the DBAs do not possess the master password, for example). You also have the opportunity to change the user ID and group IDs, but this is not normally required. Leave the User ID and Group ID fields blank, and click Next.

21. The Oracle Tablespaces options are part of what SAP describes as advanced DB configuration—check the Advanced DB Configuration box and click Next.

22. In the next screen, check the Sapdata Directory Mapping and Create Tablespaces check boxes to control the database layout.

At this point SAPinst stops the installation for the database installation, as shown in Figure 25.6.

FIGURE 25.6 SAP provides you step-by-step installation instructions for the Oracle database. Make sure you do not click OK until the database installation is complete.

Performing an Oracle-for-SAP Installation

For every major SAP component, database software must be installed as well. The following demonstrates an Oracle database installation:

1. Log in as an Oracle user, set the display, move to the proper directory, and start the installation:

```
su oraer5
setenv DISPLAY hostname:1.0
cd /oracle/stage/102_64/database/Disk1/SAP

   ./RUNINSTALLER
```

The initial screen allows you to enter the inventory directory and operating system group name. Click Next.

2. If you receive a warning message, ignore it.

3. The available Oracle product components are displayed, including those to be installed. Click Next.

4. The prerequisite checks are displayed. Click Next.

5. Another warning may appear. Investigate the reason for each prerequisite check that failed, and click Yes.

6. The Summary screen appears. Note the Oracle Home and path—you will need them for the patch install—and then click Install.

7. The End of Installation screen appears. Click Exit.

8. Install the latest Oracle Patch by performing the following actions:

   ▶ Log on at the OS level with the ora<sid> user. We will use the existing session we already have open.

   ▶ Download the patch set as described in SAP Note 932251.

   ▶ Unzip the Oracle patch using the unzip command:

   ```
   /usr/sap/CD/unzip /usr/sap/CD/D510031810/HPUX_PARISC/
   p4547817_10202_HP64.zip
   cd /usr/sap/CD/D51031810/HPUX_PARISC/Disk1
   ./runInstaller
   ```

   The Oracle Universal Installer (OUI) appears. Obtain version information on the OUI by clicking the About Oracle Universal Installer button. We have seen problems in the past caused by using the wrong (earlier) version of the OUI—ensure you have the latest (or most recently supported for SAP) release.

9. Verify that the Oracle Home name and path are correct, Unless you have multiple Oracle installations, the install normally detects the correct values Click Next, and the Summary screen will be displayed.

10. Run root.sh.

11. The End of Installation screen appears when the patch set installation is complete. Click Exit.

12. After the Oracle database software installation, you need to install the required interim patches, using the Oracle tool OPatch. These interim patches are required in addition to the current patch set. Fortunately, the OPatch tool is quite intuitive.

13. Click OK in the message box shown to complete the installation. The Phase List will be displayed, which helps you track the progress of the installation by showing the phases that have been completed (checked) and the phases that remain. It is important to note that some phases take much longer than others.

Congratulations! You've completed the Oracle database installation for your SAP component. Now you are ready to complete several post-installation tasks outlined in the next section.

Addressing General SAP Post-Installation Tasks

The SAP ERP 6.0 installation guide lists several post-installation activities, including the following:

▶ Verify you can log in to the SAP application server

▶ Install the SAP license

▶ Install SAP Online Documentation

▶ Apply the latest SAP kernel and support packages

- ► Configure a remote connection to SAP Support

- ► Perform the initial ABAP configuration

- ► Run transaction SICK

- ► Install TMS (Transport Management System)

- ► Create SAP Operation Modes via transaction RZ04

- ► Create SAP Logon Groups via transaction SMLG

- ► Set up standard background jobs

- ► Configure printers

- ► Review the system log

- ► Edit the SAP profile parameters

- ► Install languages (I18N)

- ► Maintain address data

- ► Perform a client copy

- ► Perform a full backup

- ► Address user security

In this section, we will highlight some of the more interesting transactions you will use to complete the technical installation of SAP—as always, be sure to follow the installation guide for the specific software component you are installing.

First things first—you need to install the SAPGUI on your desktop in order to log in to complete the remaining tasks in this chapter. After you have installed the SAPGUI, log in to client 000 as user DDIC using the master password. Then proceed with the following steps:

1. Configure the Transport Management System (TMS) with transaction STMS. You may have to enter your company address to proceed. The completed transport domain is shown in Figure 25.7.

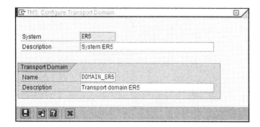

FIGURE 25.7   A simple transport domain is sufficient for test purposes.

2. Check the System Log with transaction SM21. You will receive a Warning message indicating that "This instance was entered in TSLE4."

3. Import profiles with transaction RZ10 (after the profiles are imported, you can easily change SAP profile parameters). From the SAP menu, go to Utilities, Import Profiles, Of Active Servers. The Profile Check Log will provide information reflecting which profiles have been imported, along with any warnings or errors regarding specific profile parameters (see Figure 25.8).

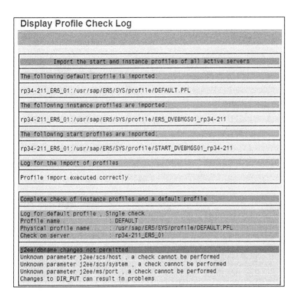

```
Display Profile Check Log


         Import the start and instance profiles of all active servers
The following default profile is imported:
rp34-211_ER5_01:/usr/sap/ER5/SYS/profile/DEFAULT.PFL
The following instance profiles are imported:
rp34-211_ER5_01:/usr/sap/ER5/SYS/profile/ER5_DVEBMGS01_rp34-211
The following start profiles are imported:
rp34-211_ER5_01:/usr/sap/ER5/SYS/profile/START_DVEBMGS01_rp34-211
Log for the import of profiles
Profile import executed correctly

Complete check of instance profiles and a default profile
Log for default profile , Single check
Profile name           : DEFAULT
Physical profile name  : /usr/sap/ER5/SYS/profile/DEFAULT.PFL
Check on server          rp34-211_ER5_01
j2ee/dbname changes not permitted
Unknown parameter j2ee/scs/host , a check cannot be performed
Unknown parameter j2ee/scs/system , a check cannot be performed
Unknown parameter j2ee/ms/port , a check cannot be performed
Changes to DIR_PUT can result in problems
```

FIGURE 25.8   It is not uncommon to receive messages such as these when you import profiles.

4. Create a Basis user with transaction SU01. Copy the DDIC user to BASIS001, for example. Make sure you have given the user any required authorization profiles (such as S_A.System and SAP_ALL).

5. Install the permanent SAP license with transaction SLICENSE; the permanent license is installed with SAP License Administration.

6. Update the SAP kernel; run transaction SE38, execute program RSPARAM, and check Display Also Substituted?. The user-defined value of the DIR_CT_RUN parameter shows the kernel location. Be sure to stop SAP before applying the kernel update. Download the new kernel files from http://service.sap.com/patches and extract them into a temporary directory. We recommend backing up the current kernel directory before overwriting the existing files.

7. Verify that the kernel has been updated by selecting System, Status from the SAP menu.

8. Click the Other Kernel Info button or press Shift+F5. Verify that the kernel has been upgraded in the System Kernel Information screen, as shown in Figure 25.9.

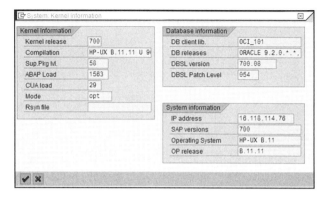

FIGURE 25.9   The System Kernel Information screen lets you verify that the kernel patch installed correctly.

9. Apply the ABAP Support Packages with transaction SPAM.

10. You might need to update Support Package Manager before applying supporting packages. You can download support packages from http://service.sap.com/patches. The Support Package Manager (transaction SPAM) is shown in Figure 25.10.

FIGURE 25.10   You can display and install support packages with the Support Package Manager.

11. Verify that the support packages applied successfully by selecting System, Status from the SAP menu and then clicking the magnifying glass icon under Component

Version. The System Component Information screen displays the release level for each software component, as shown in Figure 25.11.

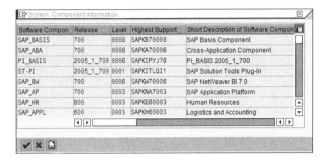

FIGURE 25.11   The System Component Information screen displays the current release and support pack level of each software component.

12. Apply the Java Support Packages with JSPM; start the Java Support Package Manager (JSPM) and then execute the following steps:

   a. Log in as user *root*

   b. Log in as user <sid>adm, for example: **su - er5adm**

   c. Set the DISPLAY variable: **setenv DISPLAY rp34-210:1.0**

   d. Start JSPM by entering the following: **cd /usr/sap/ER5/DVEBMGS01/j2ee/JSPM**

   e. Type the following and then press Enter: **./go**

   f. JSPM may take a few minutes to launch, and then will ask for the password to log on to SDM. Enter the password.

13. Schedule standard jobs with transaction SM36; execute transaction SM36 and click the Standard Jobs button.

14. With regard to scheduling the standard jobs, be sure to click the Default Scheduling button to perform the actual scheduling. Pay particular attention to the Background Job Name and Job Info columns. For example, if you ever notice that the old jobs are not being deleted, look for the SAP_REORG_JOBS job.

15. Generate objects with SGEN; execute transaction SGEN and choose the appropriate option to generate or regenerate objects. SGEN generates (that is, compiles) objects before users access them for the first time, initially improving user response time.

Although the preceding list takes you through only some of the post-installation activities, it should give you a sense of the details that must be addressed after the initial SAP component installation steps are completed. Keep in mind that in some cases the defaults provided by the installation will not be acceptable. For example, you might need to change the database layout for performance reasons. This is where your network of partners and colleagues will prove invaluable. Your system or storage vendor, for example, will be able to provide assistance and best practices. Use your network of people and resources!

Summary

As we have seen, the real differences between SAP component installations lie in the business scenarios and the underlying application and technology components that must be selected and installed. Fortunately, these details are described in the Master Guide for each component or application. In addition to the installable software units, the Master Guide also provides guidance on the installation sequence and the technical system landscape. In the end, although the installation of SAP Business Suite components is similar because they are based on SAP NetWeaver, the software units will differ based on application specifics. And because customers implement different business scenarios (and therefore different software components), installations of the same product will vary between customers. Welcome to the complex world of SAP! Just remember that you need to figure out *what* to install and in what *order*—use your Master Guides, your online resources, and your network of colleagues, and you'll do well.

Case Study: Installing SAP ERP 6.0

You have been asked by your employer, HiTech, Inc., to install SAP ERP 6.0 in a sandbox in preparation for an upcoming SAP implementation. You will be installing SAP ERP 6.0 on HP-UX 11i with an Oracle 10g database. To keep matters simple, you have been asked to install a central system (where the database and application server components are installed on the same physical server) using the default parameters.

Questions

1. How do you determine which software units you need to install for a given business scenario?
2. Should you wait until the SAP ERP 6.0 installation is complete before applying the Oracle patches?
3. What is the transaction used to install ABAP support packages?
4. From where do you download support packages?
5. Before releasing the system to end users, what needs to occur relative to the SAP kernel and support packages?

> **NOTE**
>
> The answers to these questions can be found in Appendix A, "Case Study Answers."

CHAPTER 26

Functional Development

With installation tasks finally behind us, we can begin exploring the process of converting business vision into functional business processes and, ultimately, into SAP functionality. Called *functional development*, this process consumes more time, people, and resources than any other single task outlined in an SAP project. Keep this in mind as you make your way through this chapter—even the most rapidly implemented SAP components require something along the lines of six months of effort, the bulk of which would be consumed by functional development.

An Overview of Functional Development

Implementing SAP solutions to meet business requirements is always a daunting task. It gets even more challenging when the business processes within an organization are complex and the standard functionality provided within the SAP solution is not enough to meet even 80% of the business requirements (a reasonable expectation!). Depending on the type of business an organization is involved in and the depth and breadth of its product and service portfolio, including its geographic reach, it can be categorized as either a simple or a complex organization. Surprisingly, the absolute size of the organization does not really matter in terms of the complexity it reflects. Many small businesses reflect quite a complex business model, while many large organizations have very simple business processes.

Functional development with regard to SAP solutions can be broadly categorized as follows:

▶ **Configuration**—This involves setting up the SAP solution by adding, selecting, and configuring a certain set of available parameters for the business processes to be executed in SAP without making any programming updates.

▶ **Customization**—This involves making programming changes to the standard software solution provided by SAP so that the standard business processes will not behave in a manner different from what is expected, primarily to meet the customer requirements.

The next few sections take a closer look at both the configuration aspects and the customization tools that SAP offers with regard to functionally developing its most common business solutions.

SAP Components and Modules

As we've covered previously, SAP provides business solutions for large enterprises as well as small and medium businesses, including custom industry solutions (IS). Under the covers, the details surrounding the SAP technology stack and SAP service-oriented architecture (SOA) are covered in other chapters. This chapter primarily discusses SAP components and modules associated with SAP ERP Central Component (ECC) and the various tools provided by SAP for application development.

Common SAP ERP Modules

As outlined in Chapters 1, 2, 18, and elsewhere, SAP ERP is SAP's online transaction processing (OLTP) system. It seamlessly integrates financials, cost controls, materials, warehouse management, production planning and shop floor control, quality management, sales and distribution, and much more. The solution caters to a broad range of industry-specific processes in all the areas of business functions within an organization. As a refresher, the following list provides the most common business functions or modules that organizations may choose to implement:

▶ **Finance**—Primarily provides for core accounting payables and receivables, general ledger and special-purpose ledgers, treasury, asset accounting, banking, and credit management.

▶ **Controlling**—Primarily provides for costing processes such as cost center and cost element accounting, internal orders, activity-based costing, product costing, profit center accounting, and profitability analysis.

▶ **Enterprise Controlling and Strategic Enterprise Management**—Primarily provides for business planning and simulation applications and tools for consolidation (legal as well as management).

▶ **Materials Management**—Primarily provides for purchasing, inventory management and physical inventory, logistics invoicing, valuation, material requirements planning and foreign trade and customs business processes within an organization.

▶ **Sales and Distribution**—Primarily provides for sales order processing, which includes inquiries, quotations, scheduling agreements, shipping and transportation, billing, credit management, foreign trade/customs and other sales support functions, such as promotions within the organization.

▶ **Production Planning**—Primarily provides for demand management, sales and operations planning, production planning, material requirements planning, shop-floor control, and capacity planning processes for discrete manufacturing. Additionally provides for business processes for process manufacturing, repetitive manufacturing, and Kanban (which enables just-in-time inventory management).

▶ **Quality Management**—Primarily provides for quality planning, quality inspection, quality certificates, notifications, and quality control processes within an organization.

▶ **Plant Maintenance**—Primarily provides for maintenance of assets and preventive maintenance.

▶ **Human Capital Management**—Primarily provides for personnel management, time management, payroll, training and event management, and overall organizational management.

Each of the preceding modules has its own master data, such as customers for sales, vendors for materials management, bills of materials and work centers for production, general ledger (GL) accounts for finance, cost centers for controlling, and so forth. The master data will have linkages to other relevant functional areas. For example, the work center master data in production is linked to the cost center master data in controlling to calculate the manufacturing cost. Similarly, the vendors share the information between purchasing and finance.

In addition, there is the material master that is used across every business function, and each functional area will have some aspect of its information linked to the material master by way of views. For example, the Sales view of the material master will provide for sales-related information for this material, such as sales taxes, commodity codes, discounts, and so on. Similarly, the Planning view of the material master will provide for procurement or production planning parameters such as lot sizes, material requirements planning (MRP) data describing how the material is planned, procurement and production lead times, safety stock, percentage of scrap that occurs during production, and so on.

Other SAP ERP Modules

In addition to the previously identified modules or business functions, SAP ERP provides for Customer Service, Environmental Health and Safety, Investment Management, Logistics Execution, Project Systems, Real Estate Management, and much more. All these modules are seamlessly integrated with each other within SAP ERP. In turn, SAP ERP is seamlessly integrated within the overall SAP NetWeaver architecture and may be easily tied to SAP's other Business Suite applications such as SAP CRM, SAP PLM, SAP SCM, and SAP SRM.

26

Even with all this available business functionality (to which SAP continually adds through upgrades to new Business Suite components), most SAP implementations reflect a certain amount of customization. In these cases, customer business requirements cannot be configured for an organization using the out-of-the-box standard SAP functionality, and so are provided for through customization or developer tools. Later, if functionality is introduced in an upgrade, a customer can "retire" its custom code and use the built-in functionality of the new release. This customization process will be explored more later in this chapter.

Translating Business Vision into Business Processes

Every CEO has a vision for his or her company, which translates into some business goals that arise from business drivers. *Business drivers* are business conditions, or pressure points, that motivate an organization to seek a solution. Business drivers exist primarily because of the following:

▸ **Pain**—For example, competitors are taking away the customers.

▸ **Directive**—For example, new regulations require compliance by the end of the year.

▸ **Opportunity**—For example, new acquisitions have created silos of information with incompatible systems.

A *business goal*, on the other hand, identifies what a particular business solution should achieve. They are future-oriented targets and provide a decision regarding what to do about one or more business drivers. *Business metrics* are measures of the degree to which the goal is achieved. It is a clear measurable test for a business goal. The vision and the business goals at the CEO level must be propagated to the next level of management—the senior-level executive team, which essentially represents management of each functional area. At this level, each senior-level manager may then develop his or her own business goals and metrics that align with the higher-level direction provided by the CEO while still remaining relevant to the manager's functional area of responsibility. This relationship is depicted in Figure 26.1.

Depending on the number of levels of management and the size of the company, these goals and metrics get propagated to the next levels of management, and each functional manager develops their own goals and metrics relevant for their area and aligned to those developed by the previous level, and so on. These will finally culminate in the business processes in each functional area. For example, as shown in Figure 26.1, the material planning department will carry out materials planning, contract negotiations and better supplier pricing, procurement activities, development of metrics associated with vendor evaluation, and so on. Sales and marketing will set up sales and operations planning in conjunction with manufacturing to carry out demand management and forecasting activities, sales order processing, including customer contracts or scheduling agreements, and so on. Production will establish production planning, capacity planning, and production execution in an effort to reduce inventory carrying cost, improve productivity and efficiency, and so on. Finance and controlling will establish product costing, manage payables

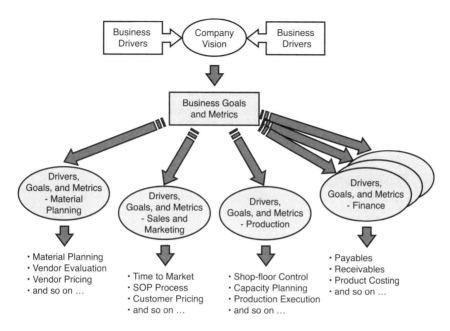

FIGURE 26.1   Translating business vision to business processes takes into account many factors.

and receivables, asset accounting, and legal consolidation, and so on. Each business process will have a metric associated with it wherever possible to measure affectivity.

For example, the CEO of a company might have a vision to grow the company on a global level and increase market share. This may translate to a need for new acquisitions, new products and services, or new offices in other parts of the world. The business drivers in this case might be an opportunity for growth and might arise because of a competitive environment. One of the business goals could be to increase the market share by 20% the following year and 10% each year thereafter. This may result in standardizing the current business processes so that all the regions primarily have one standard business process, the only exception being mandated by the local legal requirements.

Once the CEO provides this vision, including the business drivers and goals, it is propagated to the next level of management, where each functional department will develop its own business drivers and goals. For example, increasing the market share by 20% causes the sales and marketing teams to increase revenue by more than 20%, which may in turn trigger staff augmentation to reach markets that have never been tapped in the past. Materials might have to negotiate to get better discounts from suppliers for better-quality materials. Suppliers will be measured for their on-time delivery and by the quality of the materials. Similarly, manufacturing will have the goal to reduce inventory carrying cost by 15% and to produce against forecasted and firm demand rather than to manufacture products without any real demand, further adding cost. There could be a need to establish a supply chain management (SCM) organization and processes for better forecasting and planning over the extended supply chain. Metrics such as forecast accuracy, sales accuracy, order-to-cash, inventory turns, and so on will be required to monitor the effectiveness of these business processes.

While doing this translation from business vision to business processes, a considerable amount of effort could be spent to carry out this business process reengineering (BPR). Some companies decide not to have this considerable BPR effort spent upfront, but rather to use software solutions, such as SAP ERP and the industry-standard business processes inherent to SAP, to reengineer and establish standard business processes as part of the implementation.

Converting Business Processes into SAP Functionality

During the Business Blueprint phase of the SAP Implementation methodology, business processes are converted into an SAP-specific functional plan—a blueprint. One of the first steps in this process is to understand the current business processes existing within an organization. The first two to five days spent by a functional specialist are intended to obtain an overall high-level understanding of the organization as a whole. Examples include determining such information as how many legal entities exist within each geography and how they are structured financially on a global basis (if a company is of a global nature); how many business divisions exist; how many manufacturing plants and purchasing organizations exist; whether these purchasing organizations are at a regional, country, or global level; the operating principles of each division, plant, profit center, or cost center; and so on. Figure 26.2 provides a pictorial view of a typical manufacturing organization. Information gleaned from such a view is used to model and configure the organizational structure within SAP ERP. The process of doing so is described briefly in the next section of this chapter.

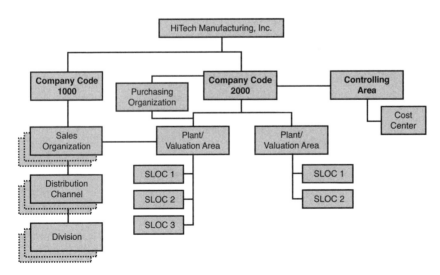

FIGURE 26.2   A typical manufacturing organization.

The functional specialist spends the next few days diving deeply into each functional area, understanding all the current business processes and describing any additional processes identified as part of the visioning exercise described in the previous section. Existing business process documentation is analyzed and discussed with the project team members. Business process flowcharts are developed as a means to capture the information shared by the business process owners and subject matter experts (SMEs). For example, for the typical manufacturing department, the following processes could be identified and documented in the Business Blueprint (BBP) document:

- Demand Management

- Sales and Operations Planning

- Forecasting

- Production Planning

- Goods Issue to Production

- Production Execution for Standard Production Orders

- Production Execution for Rework Orders

- Goods Receipt from Production

- Scrap Process

Figure 26.3 illustrates a business process flowchart for a typical production execution business process. Each process flow diagram contains its subprocesses and decision trees depicted together in a visual format where each row of activity is described as a *swim lane*.

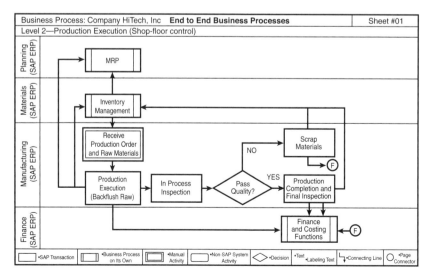

FIGURE 26.3   A typical production execution process in a manufacturing organization.

The flowchart shown in Figure 26.3 depicts not only the business process in detail, but also links to other functional areas, such as Inventory Management, MRP, and Finance. Additionally, it shows the processes that will be executed in SAP ERP, those that are carried out manually, and those being executed in a non-SAP system. In short, Figure 26.3 depicts the business process mapping to the SAP ERP solution and clearly identifies any gaps that might exist within the business process.

The BBP document consists of the following:

▶ Policies and procedures, instructions

▶ Exclusions, if any

▶ Decisions

▶ Change management items

▶ Business process description including business process flow diagrams

▶ Business process mapping to the SAP ERP solution

▶ Local business process requirements (if different from above for legal reasons)

▶ Gap analysis

▶ RICEFS (Reports, Interfaces, Conversions, Enhancements, Forms, and SAPscripts)

▶ Authorization

▶ Data volume per site

▶ Archiving details

▶ BBP acceptance of results—Sign-off by leads

One of the sections within the BBP document is Gap Analysis. Gaps are processes or functionality that does not exist within the standard SAP solution. These gaps are categorized as either critical or "nice to have." A gap can be mitigated with a workaround within the SAP solution or through the process of customization in which the actual SAP programs are changed to accommodate these gaps in business processes or functionality. A cost-benefit analysis is carried out to conclude whether this gap can be mitigated with a workaround or through customization. If the decision is made to add new functionality into the standard SAP solution, then the solution is designed and a detailed design document for this new functionality is developed. This detail design will also include functional specifications of the new functionality to be developed.

The Functional specification will consist of the following:

▶ Policies and procedures, instructions

▶ Business process description including business process flow diagrams

▶ Program changes, including screenshots if available

▶ Test plan details

▶ Functional specification acceptance sign-off

The following section looks at the configuration and customization aspects of functional development.

Functional Development Tools and Approaches

After the BBP document has been developed and the business and IT leads have signed off on the document, the Realization phase commences. Functional experts now initiate the configuration activities and programmers start the customization activities. This phase concludes with the successful acceptance of the results during the unit and integration testing.

SAP Configuration

SAP configuration is a two-step process. The first step is to develop the baseline configuration, which involves configuring SAP ECC based on the information provided during the business blueprint phase. The second step is to fine-tune the configuration further based on the outcome of each unit and integration test scenario. Use the SAP Implementation Guide (IMG), sometimes called the SAP Reference IMG or SAP Customizing Implementation Guide, to actually configure SAP in a step-by-step manner. The SAP IMG is nothing more than a tool for configuration. To begin, from the SAP Easy Access screen, execute transaction code SPRO in the command field. This will start the IMG/Customizing screen, as shown in Figure 26.4.

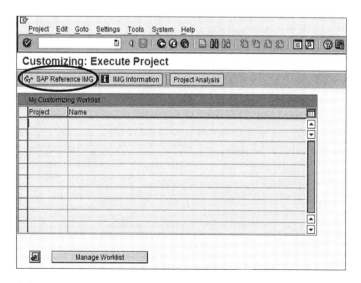

FIGURE 26.4   The Implementation Guide (IMG) screen can vary depending on the SAP components and version you are implementing.

The SAP Reference IMG contains all the SAP business application components supplied by SAP. It serves as a single source for all configuration activities, as shown in Figure 26.5, and can be viewed by clicking the SAP Reference IMG button (circled in Figure 26.4).

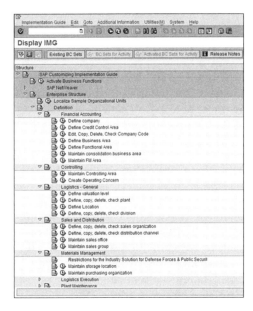

FIGURE 26.5   The Display IMG screen, from which SAP can be customized for your organization.

To configure the organizational structure, define the elements of the organization by configuring the tasks indicated in the figure. Once the organizational structure and the relevant assignments within these elements have been defined, the business processes are configured thereafter. So, the production execution business process can now be configured by drilling down the menu path within the Display IMG screen, as shown in Figure 26.6: SAP Customizing Implementation Guide, Production, Shop Floor Control.

Each transaction under Shop Floor Control will be configured per the business process details documented in the BBP document, the outcome of which will be a fully functional production execution business process. Business processes such as these will be tested as part of the unit and integration testing, and any required changes can be made. When a configuration transaction is executed, the usual practice is to document the details of the task in the IMG itself. Every time any changes are carried out for this task, the details of the change are also documented.

SAP Customization

The term *customization* refers to developing programs not available within the SAP standard functionality to cater to an organization's business requirements. Such customized programs could be used to create the following:

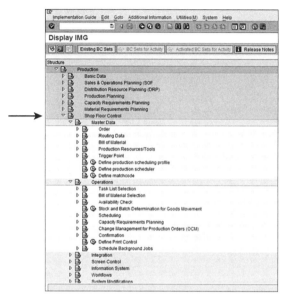

FIGURE 26.6   The configuration tasks for a production execution business process.

26

▶ Reports required to run the business and not available within the SAP solution

▶ Interfaces between SAP and non-SAP systems

▶ Conversion programs to transfer data from the legacy to the SAP solution

▶ Enhancements to the standard SAP programs for additional business requirements

▶ Forms and SAPscripts as documents required for carrying out internal and external business transactions

Also, as discussed earlier during the Business Blueprint phase, gaps might be identified, because the standard SAP functionality might not provide a complete solution for a particular business process existing within an organization. There are situations in which these gaps cannot be mitigated without a workaround. In some cases, even if a workaround exists, it might not be beneficial because it might be time consuming and/or might result in human errors that an organization cannot afford to make. So, an organization may carry out changes to the standard SAP functionality for good reasons. The following tools represent several of the most common and widely used for carrying out customization.

Advanced Business Application Programming

SAP solutions have primarily been developed using ABAP, which dates back to the 1980s. ABAP programs communicate with the database management system of the central relational database and with the presentation layer, which could be an SAP-specific GUI (such as the fat client SAPGUI) or, in the case of web-based SAP applications, a web browser.

The ABAP programming tools can be accessed via the ABAP Development Workbench using transaction SE80 from the SAP Easy Access menu. This is shown in Figure 26.7.

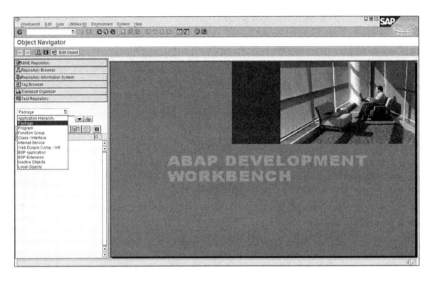

FIGURE 26.7   The ABAP Development Workbench provides a set of tools for developers.

The ABAP Development Workbench provides the following primary functions:

▶ Package Builder

▶ Object Navigator

▶ Web Application Builder for ITS (Internet Transaction Server) Services

▶ Web Application Builder for BSPs (Business Server Pages)

▶ Web Dynpro

▶ Web Services

▶ ABAP Dictionary

▶ ABAP Editor

▶ Class Builder and Function Builder

▶ Screen Painter and Menu Painter

▶ Testing tools such as ABAP Debugger for runtime analysis and performance trace

▶ Transport Organizer

Legacy System Migration Workbench

LSMW is a tool that supports data migration from legacy systems, such as non-SAP systems, to SAP systems. Instead of using individual tables or field contents, this tool migrates user-defined datasets or objects, combined according to business criteria. The following primary features and functions are available:

- ▸ Read data from an input file

- ▸ Display the data (for review purposes)

- ▸ Convert this data to make it compatible to the target system (SAP) requirements

- ▸ Display the converted data (again, for review)

- ▸ Create a batch input session for data transfer

- ▸ Execute the data transfer into SAP

Log files are created for every step executed during the data migration process, and each step can be controlled by authorization so that only the appropriate person having access to a step can execute that step.

To transfer data (master data as well as transactions) between clients in an SAP system or from a non-SAP system into an SAP system, or to set up this data automatically, other tools may be used, such as Application Link Enabling (ALE), Computer Aided Test Tool (CATT), or the application interfaces provided in the Business Object Repository (BOR).

Java and the SAP NetWeaver Development Studio

SAP offers the SAP NetWeaver Developer Studio to create, build, and deploy applications that are compliant with the Java Platform, Enterprise Edition 5 (Java EE 5). Through this toolset, developers have the flexibility to design user interfaces, use Web services, and handle XML-based messages across heterogeneous environments based on the new Java EE 5 standard. The following features and functions are available:

- ▸ Use of the latest Java standards makes development of business applications easier.

- ▸ Service Data Objects (SDO) 2.1 standards make data programming easier.

- ▸ Architecture provides scalability and robustness.

- ▸ Connectivity capabilities makes it possible to interface with all SAP systems adherent to the latest open standards.

NetWeaver Composition Environment

The SAP NetWeaver Composition Environment (SAP NetWeaver CE) provides a service-oriented and standards-based development environment in which developers can easily model and develop composite applications. These applications, commonly known as "composites" (because they combine previously available functions and data sets in a new way), accelerate business process innovation. Composite applications provide data and functions as services. The developer accesses and combines these from the underlying

26

repository to combine them into a new solution for a business process, to add functionality to an already existing application, and so on.

Let's look at a sample composite application. A typical end-to-end process within a manufacturing organization starts with demand creation, wherein a sales order is created for a product ordered by a customer. Based on this demand signal, material requirement planning is executed. Here the bill of materials (BOM) for this product is exploded; the stock at each level of the BOM is checked for its material availability and, if there are shortages, a purchase and a production plan is created. This plan consists of purchase requisitions created for raw materials and planned orders created for manufacturing parts, namely the semifinished and finished parts. Purchase orders are created from these requisitions and sent to the supplier. The suppliers will fulfill the purchase order requirements, and the raw materials will be received into inventory at the manufacturing plant. The manufacturing process will start with the receipt for the raw materials from stock. The raw materials will be processed to subassemblies or semifinished parts and then will be manufactured further to get the final finished product ordered by the customer. The finished product is then picked, packed, and shipped to the customer. The suppliers are paid for their raw materials, and the customer is billed for the product they ordered. The customer then pays the manufacturer of the product.

This end-to-end process consists of sales, planning, procurement, manufacturing, and financial processes. All of these processes are executed in one or more OLTP systems. The product executive wants to monitor the progress of this product through all these processes and needs one view. A developer can develop a composite application using tools and technologies such as the SAP NetWeaver Visual Composer or SAP's Composite Application Framework (CAF) Guided Procedures (CAF GP). A good example is a dashboard-type application residing on the portal. The data extracted from the OLTP systems will be formatted to provide the view, as per the product executive's requirements, where he or she can monitor this end-to-end process from the desktop.

The SAP NetWeaver CE is a must-have in our eyes because it is a key innovation enabler; SAP NetWeaver CE allows an organization to take its SAP business application to the next level and adopt real-world SOA principles. Its model-driven development tools enable developers to create custom services as well as custom user interfaces. And by combining these, a custom workflow or complex business process can be assembled not only quickly but in a manner that enables it to be decomposed and changed again later as business changes dictate. It's this innate flexibility of SAP NetWeaver CE—combined with access to a robust set of existing services and the capability to create new services—that make this tool an indispensable asset for any contemporary SAP developer tasked with quickly standing up new business solutions.

Organizing for Development

The Functional Specification provides the details of the customization requirement that were identified during the Business Blueprint phase for any of the RICEFS (reports, interfaces, conversions, enhancements, and forms, and SAPscripts) objects. Based on the information provided in the functional specifications, the developers will now develop the technical specification for each RICEFS object. The technical specification will provide technical details at the table and field level, including the choice of programming tool that will be used for developing the customizing object.

A *development class* is created for each functional area, such as FI for Finance, MM for Materials Management, PP for Production, SD for Sales and Distribution, and CA for cross-functional.

Whether it is a configuration object or a customization object, a transport number will be created while saving the transaction in SAP ECC. Provide a short description for this transport that outlines the project number, the functional area, and the type of configuration being done—for example, "Project # 1234: Plant Parameters for Plant ABC." The Change and Transport System (CTS) needs to be set up in SAP ECC for this to occur. This is very important to effectively manage technical changes in the SAP environment from their creation to release.

All the transport numbers may be viewed by using the transaction code SE10 from the SAP Easy Access screen, as shown in Figure 26.8.

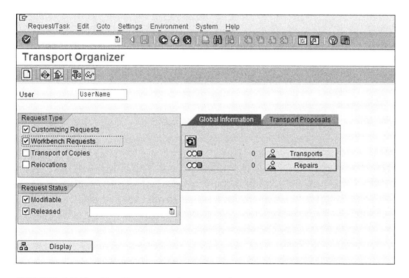

FIGURE 26.8   The Transport Organizer for managing technical changes in SAP ERP.

After the system is configured and the customization objects are developed, the next step is to carry out the unit and integration testing. Test scenarios are developed in which the input data is identified and set up in the system, and the expected outcome is documented. Figure 26.9 illustrates a system test case for the production execution process.

System Test Case ID	1.4	System Test NAME	Production Execution (Shop -floor Control)	Owner	Planners/Production Supervisors
Reference	Level 2 - BP # 1.4			Type	Unit Test
Applications	SAP ECC			Cycle	Cycle # 1
Objective	This is the production execution process where raw materials are issued/back-flushed and then converted to finished goods or sub-assemblies and received into Stock.			Environment	<QAS-client 100>

PREREQUISITES and/or DATA SETUP/Team members

1.	All the master data objects (Materials, Bills of Materials, Customers, Routes, Shipping points, etc.) are created in the SAP ECC system.
2.	All planning parameters are set up in the material master materials (MRP and Work Scheduling views).
3.	Appropriate Planners (MRP Controllers) are assigned and the organizational setup allows for the execution.
4.	The business process 1.5 has been completed.

TRANSACTIONAL STEPS

Step #	Appli-cation	Business Process Step (Description of the Action)	INPUT DATA	EXPECTED RESULTS	ACTUAL RESULTS	PASS/ FAIL (Defect#)	EXECUTED BY
1.0	SAP ECC	Enter confirmation as part of the production execution.	CO11n Production Order# Operations Enter the units being moved	After saving the material movement transactions occur, which signifies back-flushing			
1.1	SAP ECC	Review the material movement transaction	MB03 CO03	Shows back-flushing of raw materials with movement type 261.			
1.2	SAP ECC	Review financial documents for these material movements	FB03 or MB03	Financial transactions exists Db — GL account and Cr – GL Account			
2.0	SAP ECC	If there is scrap, then enter the scrap quantity	C011n Production Order # Operation # Scrap Qty	Scrap qty. enables the net quantity for the next operation to be reflected accordingly			
2.1	SAP ECC	Executive scrap report		These transactions are reflected in the report			

FIGURE 26.9   A sample system test case for the production execution business process.

The business processes are executed as part of the testing, and the actual results are documented. If the actual results do not match the expected results, then configuration and/or customizing changes are carried out until the desired results are achieved. When all the results are accepted by the business lead or the SME, the test case is signed off for acceptance.

Development Best Practices

Organizations have complex business processes that require complex IT requirements. As such, implementing SAP solutions is quite a challenging task. With a large number of successful SAP implementations all over the world, the experiences from these projects can be leveraged as the best practices to improve business operations, decrease the cost of SAP projects, and provide an easier means to identify and mitigate risk, thereby increasing return on investment (ROI). Following are some of the best practices for functional development:

▶ Use a proven implementation methodology.

- Keep customization to a minimum.

- Establish at the start of the project development and documentation standards for configuration and customization tasks.

- Implement "user exits" wherever available. They are trigger points provided in a standard SAP program from which a custom program can be called out.

- If enhancements must be carried out, do not make changes to the SAP standard programs, but rather copy the standard SAP program to a separate program (for example, create a new "Z" program) and make the relevant changes within that program. This avoids customizing an SAP-provided program that's eventually over-written by an inevitable SAP functional upgrade.

- Use the recommended development option from the tool sets for the type of RICEFS object. For example, use LSMW for conversions.

- Instead of using any third-party tools, always leverage the standard SAP tools such as Business Configuration Sets (BC Sets) and extended Computer Aided Test Tool (eCATT).

- Develop clear and concise functional and technical specifications.

- Develop test cases and test scenarios; ensure these reflect end-to-end business processes, including permutations.

- Establish a separate client for customization in the development environment; this supports initial testing that needs to be carried out by each developer prior to executing functional testing.

- Thoroughly test the SAP solution by carrying out multiple cycles of testing, especially for the code or component that has been customized.

- Use automated testing tools wherever possible and where budget permits.

- Establish governance early on for managing technical changes.

- Utilize the SAP Solution Manager tool within the SAP landscape to manage configuration, customization, and to act as a channel for SAP developers to fix bugs, manage upgrades and migrations, and much more.

These best practices are by no means exhaustive, but should set the stage for the kind of process discipline necessary to effectively plan for, deploy, and configure SAP.

Functional Development Lessons Learned

Following are several customer-specific functional development lessons we've learned in recent years:

- **Avoid unnecessary customization**—There are many horror stories of SAP implementations in which an organization decided to extensively customize the standard SAP solution to meet all its whims instead of using the best industry practices. This has created multiyear SAP implementation cycles at the end of which millions of dollars were spent without having gained much in return. The lesson learned here is to use the industry best practices within the SAP solution as much as possible, keep the customization effort to a minimum, and use a workaround wherever possible. An example of a workaround could be to carry out ATP (Available to Promise) based on material availability and forecast (planned independent demand) consumption, rather than customizing the SAP ATP functionality to consider both material and finite capacity.

▶ **Manage change well**—Managing changes well in terms of configuration and customization is not just an important task; it's mandatory. Proper revision controls need to be in place. There are many instances in which, without proper change control procedures, configuration changes were released to the production environment, which then led to the delivery of erroneous information. The result? Poor decision making ultimately cost the company greatly.

▶ **Promote to production carefully**—Like many other businesses, one of our favorite customers sells its products on the Web. To attract customers, this company would run sales of certain electronic products multiple times a week. One of its products usually sold for $1,000. One particular day, however, there was a glitch and the updated price that was uploaded to the Web for this product was missing a zero. The price that its customers saw for this product was suddenly only $100. You can image the ramifications of this error. The company had to honor its commitment and take a substantial loss. The point here is to test and *validate* the updates thoroughly before they are released into the production environment.

The following are more general lessons learned:

▶ **Empower users**—Bureaucracy within an organization can unnecessarily slow down, and even make matters worse for, the successful completion of functional development, despite the leadership support. One way to motivate users to embrace the new technology is to empower them to make decisions.

▶ **Encourage adaptability**—Functional organizations resist change and tend to keep their old ways of doing things, thereby overloading themselves. Instead, they should adapt to the business processes provided within the SAP solution being implemented. Create a culture comfortable with change by rewarding desired behaviors.

▶ **Address standards and templates**—Establish the functional development standards during the Project Preparation phase. Establish templates for all the documentation to be developed as part of the functional development.

▶ **Nail down scope**—Inaccurate scoping of the functional development will cause project delays and project overruns. Also, scope creep is one of the major reasons for project failures.

▶ **Reward positive change behaviors**—Organizational culture in terms of end user attitude toward adopting change will affect the functional development effort. Proper management of change needs to be established during the implementation of the SAP solution so that the development and end user teams work well together.

▶ **Address project communication and training**—Untrained and inadequately informed business users and leadership often slow down the progress of the project because of untimely decision making. Hence, provide enough training during the Business Blueprint phase to key decision-makers.

▶ **Develop appropriate specifications**—functional and technical specifications must be developed to an appropriate level of detail. Be sure to get the end-user teams and overall business community to sign off on the design prior to actual development effort. The business community is notorious for changing its mind, which leads to rework that costs the company a considerable amount of effort.

▶ **Reuse previously developed work**—Leverage existing programs, functions, and configurations already developed and available in the repository. This can have a dramatic impact in terms of rapidly prototyping and developing a functional solution.

▶ **Lock down the system as go-live draws near**—After thorough testing is carried out, freeze the system for any new changes prior to cutover. This applies to functional development as well as technical changes. There are many cases in which last-minute changes affect go-live and not only complicate the new system's introduction but also bring operations to a halt while unforeseen problems are being addressed.

▶ **Prepare for inevitable go-live issues**—Have your developers and configuration specialists available with appropriate authorizations during cutover and go-live to mitigate the risk of a less-than-smooth transition to the new environment. Even minor glitches can impact the perception of the new system's functionality, availability, and performance. Addressing these glitches quickly will minimize fallout.

As shown, functional development issues come from all directions. Therefore, it is critical to reward desired behaviors, leverage previous templates, plan for the worst, and avoid making changes well before go-live. Finally, strive to retain key personnel long after go-live.

Summary

Configuration and customization are the two categories of functional development. These are the foundations of any SAP ERP solution; success of SAP implementations largely depends on these two categories. We also covered several development tools and approaches, how to translate business vision into business processes and finally into SAP functionality, and how to organize for development. Best practices and functional development lessons learned concluded this chapter.

Case Study: Starting the Realization Phase

HiTech, Inc. has just completed the Business Blueprint phase as part of its SAP ERP implementation and is getting ready to start the Realization phase. The functional developers and the programmers are all set to start their configuration and customization activities.

Adequate authorization to the business sandbox and the development environment has been provided.

Questions

1. What is the first transaction code executed to start configuration activities?
2. What will be the first set of configuration tasks carried out?
3. What is the first document required by the programmers to carry out the customization activities?
4. Before starting their activity, what would the programmers develop?
5. What is the transaction code to execute the ABAP Development Workbench?
6. What is the transaction code to view the configuration tasks created via transports?

NOTE

The answers to these questions can be found in Appendix A, "Case Study Answers."

CHAPTER 27

Functional Configuration Change Control

As opposed to managing changes to the technical infrastructure underpinning an SAP implementation (covered in Chapter 34, "Technical Change Control"), functional change control involves managing how the system's functionality evolves through its development, testing, and eventual promotion into the production system. This process, and the various roles and teams involved in managing functional configuration changes, are the topic of this chapter.

Goals of Functional Configuration Change Control

The functional change control process targets several end goals, all of which are described in more detail via the SAP Solution Maps (see http://www.sap.com/solutions/businessmaps/solutionmaps/index.epx):

▶ Improving customer service through product/service quality improvements

▶ Improving regulatory compliance through improved business process transparency and activity auditability

▶ Improving service delivery by way of functional improvements (improved business processes) and technical improvements (such as systems administration)

▶ Maximizing revenue via improved customer retention and loyalty, maximized per-customer profitability, and similar customer-centric management processes

▶ Maximizing security from an overall system security perspective as well as an overall data accessibility perspective

▶ Reducing working capital through greater process efficiency

▶ Optimizing fixed assets and resource management by reducing lifecycle costs, by reducing downtime, and through efficient systems management

▶ Reducing operating costs and therefore increasing efficiency by reducing logistics costs

To achieve these goals, those who are responsible for initiating, performing, and managing SAP functional changes use a host of *change control tools*. Spanning auditing, security, testing, document management, and other disciplines, many of these tools are outlined next.

Change Control Tools

Beyond the change control tools targeted in this section, ultimately many tools are used to manage functional change. Some are used to manage the process of change, others are used to physically manage and promote changes, and others focus on performing the changes themselves. Other tools simply reflect the myriad of templates and accelerators used by functional specialists in the course of their work. See http://www.sap.com/solutions/businessmaps/index.epx for detailed information and pointers.

Change Control Management Tools

Change control management (CCM) tools enable functional developers and change specialists to manage changes in SAP and non-SAP systems in a systematic manner and then to validate that the changes indeed address the initial need. Examples of such tools include the SAP-integrated tools for administering and handling change requests and change documents, and the tools used to authenticate that changes have been made by a particular developer. Attributes of CCM tools include

▶ **Modularity**—Effective CCM tools are intended to be portable between projects and client sites, and therefore need to be flexible enough to prove useful with multiple SAP components, projects, and differing business needs.

▶ **Integrated**—CCM tools must be not only an integral part of the SAP transport system but also tied into each developer's email system (SAPMail at minimum), tied into workflow products, and integrated with any workplace productivity suites.

▶ **Intuitive**—Good tools allow developers and specialists to become productive quickly without much formal training as to how to use the tools.

▶ **Balanced**—Good CCM tools strike a balance between tactical specificity (what you need today) and strategic direction (what you might need very soon). For example, you might standardize on CCM tools capable of tracking functional changes made within service-oriented architecture (SOA), web service–enabled, or virtualized technical environments (to marry functional change management with technical change management discussed in more detail in Chapter 34).

▶ **Generally accepted (or ubiquitous)**—Ideal CCM tools boast user buy-in because they've been previously used by the organization or are already associated with an existing system (a consulting firm might have previously introduced a particular CCM tool that now has become the organization's de facto tool for managing change, for example).

Although far from exhaustive, several types of tools are outlined next.

Electronic Signature Tools

A tool such as SAP's Encapsulated E-Signature Tool enables functional configurations to include electronic or digital signatures within a business process's workflow. A digital signature authenticates that the sender of a message or document, or originator of a business process, is indeed who they say they are. A digital signature also tracks changes (or, in most cases, simply preserves and "locks" the original content to avoid changes).

From a change management perspective, such a tool has obvious advantages. Outside workflow applications electronic signature tools preserve a developer's identity and ensure no other developer touched or modified a piece of code or functionality (or track that such activity occurred, ideal for auditing purposes). We have used SAP's tool for SAP SCM and CRM solutions and have seen it used since the old days of SAP R/3. There are similar tools on the market as well. Regardless, select and standardize on one and reap the benefits.

SAP Enhancement Tools

An *enhancement tool* is nothing more than a tool for customizing what is used to establish audit trails. Draw on it to identify and activate fields for audit trails, to ensure processes are seen through to completion, to manage and activate change documents for data elements, and to activate tables for SAP transaction audit trail creation. Enhancement tools fill in the gap when it comes to SAP transactions that do not do table logging (and therefore forgo an important audit trail mechanism). A basic enhancement tool has been included with SAP's core online transaction processing (OLTP) products since SAP R/3 Enterprise (also called SAP R/3 4.7—the final release of R/3). Called simply the SAP Enhancement Tool, it can address needs at a transaction, table, data element, or change document object level, ensuring log entries for elements activated by the customizing tool are indeed created.

Later versions of the tool are referred to as the Application Enhancement Tool and apply to SAP components such as SAP CRM 7.0 as well. Touted as a tool for structural enhancement, it lets you add a custom field boasting specific and desired business properties. And the tool makes future changes easy in that it lets you view, modify, and re-create (regenerate) your custom fields. You can start the Application Enhancement Tool from your SAP application, from your User Interface Configuration tool, or from a dedicated link. For an informal and very useful blog posting describing the tool and how to actually use it, point your browser to Tzanko Stefanov's article at http://tknight.org/sdn/show/12064. And refer to SAP's site http://help.sap.com (and search on Application Enhancement Tool) for details related to searching for, adding, changing, and deleting custom fields using the Application Enhancement Tool.

27

Document Management Tools

Another useful tool for your functional change management toolbox is a document management tool. These tools should be viewed as synonymous with lifecycle data management and therefore shouldn't be new to an organization that has previously deployed an enterprise business application (whether SAP, another prepackaged application, or something custom). Integrating document management into an SAP business application enables the deploying organization to track how it processes business documents throughout its enterprise.

Document management features are central to SAP Logistics; use Document Management to track functions such as the interfaces between SAP and your bolt-on systems. In this way, you can track documents as they move through your extended enterprise—up to and including where your enterprise stops and your partner, vendor, or supplier systems start. This helps you and your business processes operate with certainty as documents, and therefore data, are exchanged between SAP and other applications.

Issue Management—SAP Notes and the Knowledge Repository

Although we covered the matter of the knowledge repository and the role of SAP Notes earlier in the book, it's worth mentioning the SAP Notes tool here from a knowledge management or issue management perspective. As a management tool, SAP Notes gives you the information you need to fix known errors and other problems with your SAP system. SAP release and support package specific, SAP Notes provides a description of the problem, why the problem is occurring, and how to either fix it or work around it (the latter is often the case when a firm finds itself the first to uncover a problem with SAP; follow-on firms will get to benefit from the solution that SAP will ultimately publish through SAP Notes).

SAP Notes links to component-specific SAP Support Packages (SPs) that solve or work around these issues. This might include steps called *correction instructions* for correcting the issue by way of updating objects in the repository workbench. In fact, if correction instructions are available for your particular fix, you can use SAP Note Assistant to automatically implement the SAP Note(s) necessary to fix your issue. Read more about correction instructions at http://help.sap.com/saphelp_nw04/helpdata/EN/1c/2cee3957f7cd55e10000000a114084/content.htm.

SAP GoingLive Check Tool

The last type of tools useful to the functional change management process are go-live tools, which include many of the tools we have already outlined that are focused on ensuring code quality, maintainability, auditability, and so on. We take a closer look at tools and processes appropriate for ensuring a smooth go-live in Chapter 36, "Preparing for SAP Go-Live." In this section, though, it makes sense to outline SAP's GoingLive Check. The GoingLive Check is a combination of several different functional checks conducted by SAP via a remote connection (as many as five different checks or sessions, focused on activities ranging from planning and analysis to optimization and verification).

This is one of SAP's methods of assessing how well a system will perform for its end-user community prior to actually placing the system in the end users' hands.

The GoingLive Check enables you and SAP both to manage the functional and technical risk inherent to developing and deploying a complex business application like SAP. Through the check, SAP provides recommendations to tune the system in terms of performance, availability, and code or configuration maintainability. Schedule the GoingLive Check two months prior to go-live.

Data Loading Tools

To facilitate the functional change control process, data loading tools are useful if not absolutely necessary. In their absence, a team of data specialists must manually enter and update master and transactional data throughout the course of the implementation. This process becomes especially cumbersome as go-live approaches and test cycles increase in frequency. Testing new or extended functionality, fixing bugs, retesting, and so on occur in a rapidly escalating fashion throughout the last several months of the implementation. Automating or simply speeding up the data uploading and downloading process through tools eliminates much of the repetitiveness, and more importantly eliminates costly and time-consuming errors. This in turn allows a firm to conduct more testing and thus gain greater confidence in their business processes and use cases.

General Scripting and Testing Tools

Any software utility that can drive a Windows GUI can prove useful for loading data. In the past, we have used freeware and shareware utilities such as AutoIT, Microsoft Scriptomatic, Visual Basic scripting, and others to automate a data load process. By automatically walking through a transaction, entering and saving the data, and then repeating the process with a new set of data, automated scripting tools work just fine when data loads are small and time is abundant.

Other tools, such as HP's QuickTest Pro, WinRunner, or LoadRunner, are by no means free but by virtue of their SAP-certified test tool capabilities provide infinitely greater functionality and flexibility. They use SAP's scripting API and are thus SAP-aware and can operate a bit faster and more accurately than their free counterparts. But these tools remain functional or load testing tools simply repurposed for data load functions. And they can still run painfully slowly when, for example, millions of rows of master data need to be loaded into a new system. To get around this dilemma, we often turn to WinShuttle's products, covered next.

WinShuttle

We like WinShuttle's single-purpose approach to data uploading and downloading. Its transactionSHUTTLE tool is made specifically for moving data between SAP enterprise applications and Microsoft Office desktop applications such as Excel and Access. With a special batch option, WinShuttle is fast. Our friends at WinShuttle use a nice wrench analogy to position their product against repurposed testing and scripting tools—if all the customers have available is a wrench, they'll become pretty adept at using it to hammer in nails. But once they get their hands on a real hammer—WinShuttle's products—they'll finally realize just how productive they can be. With regard to a new SAP implementation, WinShuttle tools are most useful in the following scenarios:

▶ **SAP data migration**—Using Microsoft Excel as a staging area for data from legacy systems, WinShuttle's transactionSHUTTLE tool can be used to upload Excel-based legacy data into a new SAP system.

▶ **SAP data maintenance**—During the SAP implementation's realization phase, use WinShuttle tools to make mass changes to SAP master data or transactional data by simply downloading SAP data into Excel, transforming the data in Excel, and then loading the updated data back into SAP. We've seen this process used extensively with regard to material master changes, product pricing changes, customer credit and status changes, and PO delivery date updates.

▶ **SAP data integration**—WinShuttle can also facilitate a certain amount of offline or batch-oriented integration scenarios; use it to load third party-provided data (such as vendor, customer, or partner data) into SAP by way of Excel. Because only a simple mapping exercise is required rather than complex coding or programming, regular updates of P-card statements, UPS or other vendor invoices, or customer purchase orders can be easily completed throughout the testing process (and later, in production).

▶ **SAP data entry**—Post-implementation, use WinShuttle tools as easy-to-use data entry front ends to complex SAP transactions. In this way, WinShuttle can streamline the SAP data entry process (see Figure 27.1).

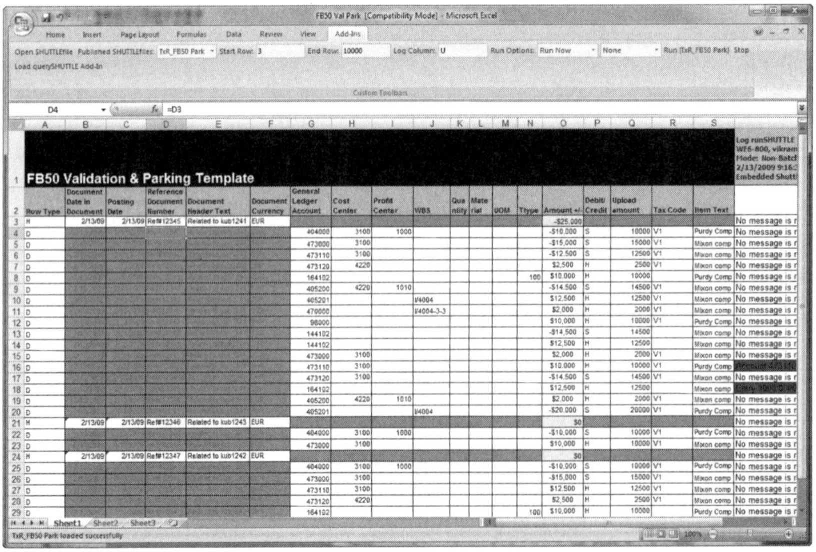

FIGURE 27.1   Use WinShuttle to quickly complete a journal voucher data entry screen for SAP.

WinShuttle's batch input mode makes it much faster than test tools that use GUI scripting mode. And because WinShuttle's security features are more granular than tools like SAP's SE16 transaction, WinShuttle provides superior separation-of-duties capabilities. Not only can the tool be configured to allow a particular user to view only data related to her specific company code or plant, it can also be used to separate the people who *create* scripts from the people who actually execute them.

The Change Control Board

The functional change control process involves several roles typically held by different people who form a formal change control board (CCB). A CCB needs to be established for each unique project. This is not to say that the same board cannot oversee multiple projects. It's unlikely, though, that the same people who understand one part of the business—and how process and functional changes will affect it—will similarly understand other parts of the business to the same degree or depth.

The CCB ultimately decides which changes will be approved and which will be rejected. Board members include the following:

▶ **CCB chair**—Responsible for final decision making in the case of disagreement.

▶ **SAP change control manager (CCM) or project change manager (PCM)**—Responsible for overall planning and tracking of functional development changes within the project.

▶ **Originator**—Responsible for drafting and submitting a new change request and requirements.

▶ **Evaluator**—Responsible to the CCB chair and to some extent the SAP CCM for analyzing the impact of a proposed change.

▶ **Modifier**—Responsible for making the actual changes to code or a piece of functionality in response to an approved change request. Modifiers are developers, configurators, or programmers, and after they make the change, they must promptly report this fact so that it may then be verified.

▶ **Verifier (or functional validation specialist)**—Responsible for testing and determining whether a change was made *well*; changes need to correctly reflect the business requirements spelled out by the originator, and function in the manner in which they were intended.

In our experience, for a large SAP ERP implementation there will be a single CCB with several and perhaps many originators, evaluators, modifiers, and verifiers. The best verifiers are often people who are not intrinsically tied to the project but rather outsiders to some extent. If the same firm takes on another SAP component implementation, such as SAP CRM or SAP PLM, the core of the CCB might be retained (for example, the chair and perhaps the SAP CCM), though new originators, modifiers, and verifiers will likely be brought in. Given the importance of the SAP CCM's role, we take a closer look at it in the next section.

27

The SAP Change Control Manager's Role

The SAP change control manager (SAP CCM or SAP CM, also sometimes referred to as the project change manager, or PCM) is responsible for change control processes, procedures, and tools related to managing an SAP project and the evolution of its specific SAP landscape. The SAP CCM's overarching goal is to establish and maintain a mature change control ecosystem. The SAP CCM helps define and manage the release-management or promote-to-production (P2P) process, cutover process, and transport process. In doing so, the SAP CCM essentially oversees transport processing (across both ABAP and Java stacks—whatever is involved in bringing the system's functionality to bear).

The CCM can't do this alone and thus is called upon to provide daily supervision and overall management of a core team of functional change control specialists (most of whom are tied to the previously discussed CCB in terms of originators, evaluators, modifiers, or verifiers). This also involves establishing and coordinating what might be a global organizational structure tasked with managing change waves across multiple SAP components and system landscapes. Finally, the CCM also needs to document and maintain all these processes, tools, and people, ensuring that the core functional change organization operates seamlessly and autonomously. From a "job description" perspective, the responsibilities of an SAP CCM might be described as follows:

- ▶ Must be an outstanding and prolific communicator.

- ▶ Will work with the project management office (PMO), Technical Support Organization (TSO), and various functional and operational teams to develop P2P (promote to production) release strategies for transports, investigate and resolve transport issues, document root-cause analysis outcomes, and schedule transports.

- ▶ Will be responsible for overseeing all SAP transport processing (ABAP and Java-derived as well as changes that span multiple SAP and non-SAP systems)

- ▶ Will manage and supervise a small group of functional specialists who probably represent a multicultural, geographically distributed team

- ▶ Will help the firm define the global organizational structure required to support change control processes both before and after go-live

- ▶ Must be passionate about documenting processes and ensuring adequate controls and other mechanisms are in place to manage change well

- ▶ Will train and manage a team responsible for transport processes to develop and adhere to change control principals and other operating procedures

- ▶ Will own the tool maintenance processes required for the team to conduct its work

- ▶ With regard to transport and change control procedures and issues, will proactively address audit requirements, maintain team transparency, respond to questions, and publish/address findings uncovered by internal and external audit teams

As such, the qualifications of a good CCM likely comprise

- ▶ High degree of integrity and focus on sound business ethics

▶ Ability to juggle multiple priorities and tasks with excellence

▶ Bachelor's degree or higher required in technical field

▶ Minimum six years of experience developing or supporting distributed enterprise systems

▶ Minimum four years of experience supporting or maintaining similar in scope or size SAP systems (particularly if the overall enterprise solution spans several bolt-ons or non-SAP systems)

▶ Strong understanding of release, change, and software configuration management and the various tools already in use by the firm for change management, digital signatures, and so on

▶ SAP experience highly desired, especially with SAP Solution Manager, the firm's service desk product, and any number of specific BPM (business process management) products

▶ Knowledge of the firm's knowledge management or repository strategy (for example, Microsoft SharePoint), the firm's call center/help desk software (such as BMC Remedy), and the firm's test tool suite, HP Quality Center desired

▶ Experience with audit procedures and a passion for responding swiftly and completely to the outcomes of audit reviews

▶ Process expertise (for example, many CCMs find it desirable to hold Information Technology Infrastructure Library [ITIL] Foundation certification, if only to speak the same language with process experts)

▶ Keen, never-ending attention to detail

This last point cannot be underestimated. Not understanding or avoiding the details will absolutely derail an SAP implementation. It is nearly as critical as communication, arguably *the* most important factor when it comes to change management. Because it is so central to the CCM's success, the topic of communication is further explored next.

Although the SAP CCM has many responsibilities, as just listed, the need to communicate broadly and effectively is most critical. The SAP CCM works with the SAP Project Management Office (SAP PMO), technical teams, support and operational teams, the various business process teams (components of the overall SAP Center of Excellence, or COE), and of course the CCM's own team to ensure all functional changes are initiated, vetted, managed, coordinated, implemented, verified, and shown to be useful. As such, the CCM holds weekly meetings, publishes weekly change board minutes, and communicates extensively through email, workflow tools, and other mechanisms. The CCM's mantra needs to be "no surprises."

SAP Application Layer—Transport Strategies and More

Transport strategies represent a critical piece of the overall change management strategy. For it is by the change management process that business processes are created and changed, support packages are applied, and other changes to the core SAP internals are performed. Historically, SAP provided something called the *Correction* and Transport System (CTS) to perform the work of transports. More recently, SAP renamed it to *Change* and Transport System, and introduced the much-improved Transport Management System to work with Transport Organizer, Workbench Organizer, and Customizing Organizer. Together with the tp and R3trans transport tools, the new system forms a comprehensive, albeit application-focused, change management utility.

The transport strategy or process implemented by an SAP customer should address or facilitate

- ▶ Transport request forms, which should be consistent and complete

- ▶ A process for reviewing the forms before and after the fact, to ensure that the change actually accomplishes its goal

- ▶ A process for approving changes (that is, change management meetings and review boards)

- ▶ A method for ensuring that the transported code indeed passed through the approval process

- ▶ Attention to expedited emergency transports, or those changes that must find their way into production as soon as possible

As we touched upon earlier in this chapter, a process that is automated to the fullest extent possible is highly recommended. Change management tends to be tedious and therefore error-prone—a change control tool or utility is an inexpensive way to mitigate this obvious (and otherwise quite commonplace) risk.

The Process or Workflow of Implementing Change

As in conducting testing, creating and maintaining documentation, and so on, creating a process or workflow is required to manage change in a world-class way. One of our SAP customers tells us that it enjoys an exceptionally smooth change management process by employing the following approach to implementing new changes. For this example, let us assume that the impending major change is with regard to adding SAP ERP Human Capital Management (SAP ERP HCM) functionality to the company's current SAP ERP implementation. An initial budget has been approved, executive/senior management sponsorship is already in place, and the project's CCB has been updated to reflect the addition of SAP HCM expertise.

1. The customer/end-user organization meets with a representative of the CCB or the functional change team directly on a weekly basis. Outside of core leadership, the CCB is composed of a few key technical SAP support resources (based on the nature of the upcoming projects or change waves), business-process and functionally appropriate functional representatives, and the supervisor of computer operations (to cover all bases, this particular team is broader than most and comprises functional as well as technical resources).

2. Based on the change to be implemented, a basic *work breakdown structure* (WBS) or simple "scope of work" is drafted during this meeting (for larger-scope projects, such as adding HCM, people are expected to come to the meetings with their initial WBS prepared instead of consuming valuable time preparing it in the meeting).

3. Success criteria are identified.

4. A priority level for the particular change is established.

5. Test hardware, software, infrastructure resources, end-user liaisons, functional liaisons, and technical liaisons (collectively termed "resources") are identified during this initial meeting.

6. End-user, functional, and technical team leaders are sought, and usually named at this time. For big changes, a change-specific (or initiative-specific) project manager is named as well. Once each weekly meeting ends, each team leader takes with them action items with regard to completing their tasks within the WBS, fleshing out timelines, identifying constraints, and so on.

7. In another meeting attended by all team leaders and the project manager and/or CCM, the tasks and milestones for inclusion into the *Master Project Schedule* (leveraging what this customer calls a *Change Checklist)* are identified. A preliminary timeline is drafted by each team leader, reflecting the needs of the area in which they are responsible.

8. Constraints are reviewed (holiday/vacation schedules, availability of critical resources, and so on), and the meeting ends.

9. The Change Checklists are merged and reviewed at another meeting to ensure that the workflow inherent to each individual area still "works" and "flows."

10. The merged and now revised master Change Checklist is formally reviewed and introduced into the Master Project Schedule some time in the next few days. The CCM owns the Master Project Schedule.

11. The project manager or CCM coordinates with the technical lead, SAP Basis team, and any technology stack partners to ensure that the system's performance, availability, scalability, and other attributes are discussed and addressed as necessary. With regard to this HCM example, it is determined that the existing SAP ERP's database server will eventually be taxed quite a bit more due to the new functionality, the system's application server pool will need to grow, security issues inherent to maintaining employee data will need to be addressed, accessibility to the system via the Web needs to be taken into account, and more.

12. Meanwhile, the technical lead begins to work with the computer operations supervisor to secure technical sandbox or development resources, reserve testing time, and so on, in preparation for the functional team leads to begin testing the proposed changes.

Our customer uses this workflow-like approach to track changes in progress, too. Note that the weekly change management meeting ranges in time from an hour (status update meetings) to perhaps three or four hours (for major functional or infrastructure changes). This HCM scenario would constitute a half-day meeting, for example.

27

Summary

After reviewing the goals of functional configuration change control, we outlined the various change control tools necessary to ensure that an SAP system reflects high code and configuration quality, auditability, and maintainability. This included tools like change control management (CCM) tools, e-signature tools, enhancement tools, audit management tools, document management tools, and more. Then we covered the makeup and role of the change control board (CCB), particularly the various roles of its constituents. Particular attention was given to the role of the SAP change control manager (SAP CCM) and the SAP CCM's great priority—communication. A discussion of transport strategies and workflow priorities concluded this chapter.

Case Study: Meeting with the SAP CCM

As a senior leader at HiTech, Inc., you are curious about how the company will protect its investment in SAP and ensure that the new SAP ERP system functions as expected. In your experience, managing functional change is a key component of delivering a system that indeed meets expectations. You have arranged for a meeting with your SAP CCM to answer a few questions intended to make you more comfortable that HiTech is covering its bases.

Questions

1. What are the various roles or functions within the project's change control board?
2. What is the SAP change control manager's primary responsibility, and why?
3. Why is WinShuttle often better suited for data loading than a functional or regression testing tool or SAP's own SE16 transaction?
4. What are some types of tools that are useful to functional change management organizations?

> **NOTE**
>
> The answers to these questions can be found in Appendix A, "Case Study Answers."

CHAPTER 28

Functional, Integration, and Regression Testing

After the SAP functional configuration and development teams have configured and coded solutions that address the company's discrete business processes, testing beyond simple does-it-work single unit (single user) testing becomes necessary. Said another way, the months of work involved in translating, upgrading, or creating an organization's business processes into SAP best practices must culminate in a comprehensive testing phase well before go-live. No implementation is complete in the absence of functional or "quality" testing; no software project will succeed without it. This chapter focuses on a number of types of business process–specific quality testing that must occur, when each must occur or is appropriate, and how each type helps to ensure a smooth transition from an old way of doing things to an integrated SAP-based approach.

Thus, the focus here is exclusively on *functional business process testing*, which verifies that processes actually execute as expected and create output as expected. Good business process testing can be very resource-intensive, especially when you consider the amount of time consumed in testing, recoding, validating changes, and retesting. Testing consumes a significant chunk of time, requires a great number of people and variety of tools, represents a great amount of potential risk to the project's success, and therefore represents a significant budget item. Testing teams must be assembled and given direction, and everyone must understand that they are engaged in an iterative and very detailed process that will eventually touch every business process, every integration point, and every piece of master data; functional business process testing was never completed in a day.

To complete functional testing as effectively and rapidly as possible, approach it from a lifecycle perspective and adopt automation tools and standardized processes. For starters, we recommend using the ASAP methodology as your testing framework, marrying quality, performance testing, and availability test cycles with ASAP's Realization, Final Preparation, and Go-Live/Support phases. HP has done an admirable job of creating such a testing methodology for SAP; read more about this on SAP's solution extensions web site at http://www.sap.com/solutions/solutionextensions/qualitycenter/index.epx.

To be sure, there are other types of business process testing. Beyond quality testing you'll need to conduct performance testing. An important form of this, called *load testing* or *stress testing*, focuses more on system-level performance by creating a multiuser workload. Its purpose is to ensure that the same business processes validated during functional business process testing will still run well (from a performance perspective) when the SAP business application is under a load similar to what the production environment will eventually endure.

Another permutation of performance testing is called *volume testing*, the purpose of which is to understand the capacity requirements (including elapsed time) of a system. For example, prior to go-live, many companies execute a large volume of transactions similar to what might be observed during month-end closing. The idea is to get an understanding of how quickly the company's books might be closed; in this way, performance limitations can be addressed or simply better understood. Both volume testing and stress testing lead to improved planning and scheduling of resource-intensive system events as well, allowing an organization to set expectations with the system's business user community. Volume and stress testing are covered in detail in Chapter 33.

Introduction to CATT, eCATT, and LSMW

To actually execute business process testing, you need to either bring together a number of very methodical power users willing to work long and tedious hours running and rerunning business process tests, or enlist the aid of an automated test tool. There are some really nice tools out there (which we'll outline later in this chapter), but for starters we look to SAP's very own test organizer called Computer Aided Test Tool (CATT) and its newer kin Extended Computer Aided Test Tool (eCATT). SAP's Business Suite and NetWeaver components include CATT or eCATT *test organizer* capabilities, which let you plan for and manage the various types of testing that take place throughout a deployment. The test organizer lets you organize and manage *test cases*, which are basically documented business processes complete with input, processing, and expected output. CATT and eCATT support automated recording and documenting of test cases, generating input data, and executing these test cases. CATT enables you to capture and create output data as well, in the form of straightforward log reports that facilitate low-level test results examination.

Since SAP R/3 release 3.0, CATT or its successor are not only free, but also have the advantage of being tightly integrated with the system. They're fast, too—by using Batch Input technology, test cases may be executed directly on the SAP application server rather than indirectly via the SAPGUI interface. Furthermore, SAP's tools allow testers to incorporate extensive behind-the scenes checks into their test cases, based on access to data simply not available to the SAPGUI (like verifying the contents of a database table, or performing a field check to verify customizing settings). CATT and eCATT have their limitations though, including

▶ Limited support for external applications that might play a role in an organization's extended enterprise solution. For example, CATT cannot support user interfaces outside of the SAPGUI for Windows or the JavaGUI.

▶ Limited support for distributed SAP system landscapes, resulting in the need to code SAP remote function call (RFC) destinations in your scripts (or to build multiple test cases across your SAP enterprise to simulate an end-to-end business process).

▶ Limited function module support; calendar functions are available, for example, but there is no function module support for tabular parameters.

▶ Controls and other technology (such as tree controls and list viewers) found in more recent releases of SAP and the EnjoySAP SAPGUI are not supported, thereby severely limiting the "testability" of certain business processes.

▶ Limited ability to execute testing remotely; it's possible (again, through RFC calls to SAP systems, or multiple test cases otherwise), but represents a lot of work in terms of script development and management.

Though still useful, CATT was showing its age years before SAP finally developed the more powerful and better-integrated testing tool eCATT (see Figure 28.1); CATT's successor was introduced with Web Application Server 6.20. eCATT supports testing any SAP solution running on SAP Basis layer 4.6C or greater (refer to SAP Note 519858 for current details regarding any support packages that might be required).

Like CATT and eCATT, the Legacy System Migration Workbench (LSMW) is another SAP tool used (since 1998) to support functional testing. As a tool for moving legacy data to SAP by way of recorded transactions, its purpose aligns more with preparing for go-live than executing quality testing. SAP's eCATT and LSMW go hand-in-hand, though, in that it's nearly impossible to test well without the actual data to be used in production. Data can be imported using batch input, direct input, BAPIs (Business Application Programming Interfaces), and IDocs (Intermediate Documents), making it easy (if still not time consuming) to bring data into the QA and other test systems.

Regardless of the tools used, keep in mind that once a business process executes flawlessly over and over again from a functional perspective, basic quality testing takes a back seat to a different type of testing—stress testing. Stress testing takes basic quality testing to the next level, and specific business processes are executed concurrently by many users, in what is also referred to as a stress test or load test (close relatives to capacity planning). In this way, the unit-level activities tested to this point are further refined and proven to ensure that the production system is truly capable of hosting the number and diversity of users and business processes required by the business. Before we examine *how* to approach and actually execute various types of testing, let's step back and take a closer look at the three broad types of business process quality testing first.

28

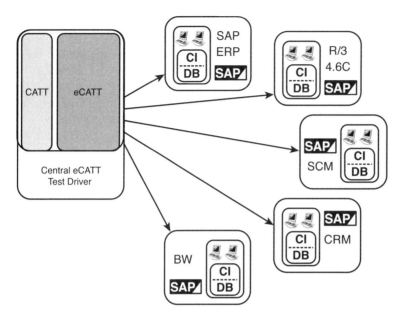

FIGURE 28.1   The value of eCATT as an enterprise testing solution is apparent in the variety of SAP components natively supported.

Three Types of Business Process Testing

Though ensuring high quality applies to all testing, different goals exist in regard to single-user business process testing. In the most generic sense, *functional testing* represents any business process–specific testing executed to ensure that the business process works. In other words, every applicable option, every drop-down menu selection, every radio button, and so on needs to be tested initially, and then retested after every change, and with every valid permutation of master data (again, making LSMW and similar data migration tools key enablers to the testing process).

Integration testing takes functional testing to the next level, ensuring that an organization's business processes work together with other business processes, both within and across multiple functional areas, such that the SAP system as a whole operates as expected. Thus, much of the work prior to go-live falls under the category of integration testing, to the point where it is quite common to maintain a dedicated system within the SAP system landscape for integration testing. Some organizations refer to this system as the QA, consolidation, or test system. Others call it simply integration; we like the term Test/QA. Regardless, the goal of this core landscape component is to allow for end-to-end SAP functional/quality solution testing outside of the primary development system, prior to deploying the business processes to be used productively by end users.

Finally, *regression testing* allows for quickly proving that a specific set of data and processes yields consistent and repeatable results, even when a subset of that data or process changes. Thus, regression testing is all about testing the integrity of a given business process, regardless of the minutiae related to specific changing business logic/coding and programming practices. And regression testing ensures that currently implemented stable business processes continue to work after changes to other business processes are made.

As you see in Figure 28.2, all three types of single-user business process testing combine to create and maintain a functionally useful SAP environment.

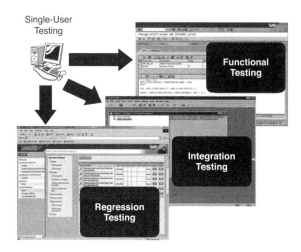

FIGURE 28.2   All three types of business process testing play a part in ensuring that an SAP business application truly delivers what the business requires from a single-user perspective.

In all three types of business process testing, business processes are typically scripted into repeatable business cases, and documented to some extent. Functional tests tend to create the most documentation in terms of volume, as every case must be covered. Integration tests are fewer, and therefore drive less raw documentation. Regression tests tend to be more pointed (very discrete or specific test cases, such as creating a sales order for a specific sales organization), such that the documentation requirements are very detailed but leaner *per test scenario* than in functional testing. Thus, a huge number of specific regression and functional tests are created, perhaps many tens or hundreds of times more than those related to integration testing. Given this relationship, it is nearly always mandated that one set of scripted business scenarios be used for both functional and regression testing, and another set be used for end-to-end complex integration scenarios.

Timing Business Process Testing

There is no general scheduling rule when it comes to testing the functionality of your SAP solution, other than to say simply that testing never truly ends. True, much of it is performed after the initial configuration is drafted in the development environment and subsequently promoted into a QA, consolidation, or integration environment. But if you ask any ABAP or J2EE developer or functional consultant engaged with deploying SAP whether their work ends on the day of go-live, you'll get a quick "not likely." Why?

28

Because it's unlikely that a business solution will not be further refined, or that a process won't be extended, or that a feature won't be added or otherwise modified over time. And preparation for enhancement packages or full-fledged SAP upgrades demands even more functional and integration testing, especially if you're unfortunate enough to have implemented custom routines or user exits. Bottom line, as long as changes are made to the SAP solution, some level of functional, integration, and regression testing will continue to be required as well.

We tend to see functional testing play a significant role in the entire lifecycle of an SAP solution, meaning that it continues until the solution is retired. Because functional testing continues throughout the lifecycle, so too must integration and regression testing. Sure, the quantity of work tends to decrease somewhat after go-live, but it increases just as quickly when a new business group is added to the SAP system, a new plant or distribution center is brought online, or a new product line is released. And it picks up noticeably as legacy and other integration points are brought in or changed, or new functional areas are added to the implementation. And significant changes arise from full-scale SAP upgrades, migrations, or corporate mergers, or when a new business application is added to the SAP system landscape—these and other such activities potentially touch countless business processes, and therefore beg to be thoroughly tested prior to deploying updated processes to production.

In addition to the really "big" changes just noted, other, less-obvious SAP business process changes, such as the following, drive functional, integration, and regression testing:

▶ Adding or modifying custom reports

▶ Adding new output mechanisms, from electronic (via workflow and similar methods) to fax machines and printers

▶ Legal changes, especially those related to tax laws and so on

▶ System or business process enhancements and other similar development activities that essentially refine a specific business process

▶ Various bug fixes and other systemwide updates designed to avoid known or potential issues

▶ Transitioning processes facilitated by older SAP transactions (for example, ME21) to newer equivalent transactions (ME21N) that offer expanded functionality through the use of controls such as drop-down list boxes and tree controls

Again, any change to the system justifies retesting the affected business processes prior to redeploying the updated process to production. Exactly *how* this is accomplished is covered next.

The Critical Nature of Functional Testing

Regardless of the enterprise application or software package being deployed (whether commercial, off-the-shelf [COTS], bespoke, or something in between), the attention given to functional testing directly impacts whether the end product—a productive SAP solution in this case—is successful or worthwhile. In the increasingly complex world of SAP, this has never been more true. SAP continues to add new functionality to mature products such as SAP ERP and SAP NetWeaver BI. Combined with the ever-changing SAP Business Suite and NetWeaver solution offerings, the need to tightly integrate business processes across diverse functional and productivity areas has never been greater. Similarly, the opportunity to really fail has never been as great, either. So it's safe to say that the primary roles of functional and integration testing are more critical than ever. The ASAP/ValueSAP methodologies and their newer counterpart, SAP Solution Manager, go a long way toward generally guiding an SAP test team in its endeavors. But there are a few key roles and areas that remain truly pivotal to successful testing:

▸ The leadership of the team tasked with functional testing

▸ The general aptitude or ability of the configuration, programming, and business processes staff when it comes to testing

▸ The specific experience each tester has in their business area of focus, such as enterprise controlling (EC), asset management (AM) or procurement, fulfillment, and logistics in general

▸ The specific experience each tester brings to the table in terms of other SAP projects and how testing was accomplished

Experience is king, as should be evident in the preceding list. One reason for this is that there is very little formal education offered centered on testing methodologies or building test cases. The training that SAP programming and functional folks receive most often amounts to the experience that each person gains during their paid SAP projects or engagements. Very few functional or SAP Basis courses devote more than a few cursory minutes to functional, integration, or regression testing.

Short of complete failure, what is the risk of inadequately testing an SAP solution? In the best of cases, it is simply that a much less refined system is ultimately offered up as "production." Worst case, though, business processes fail, and key areas of customer satisfaction, manufacturing, human resources management, and so on are put at risk. To address this, employees and consultants alike are often then pulled into "post-production" support roles. In some cases, my programming colleagues seem to never even leave their client site after go-live, transitioning into post-go-live roles while our SAP customers continue to pay for further development and more testing of an end product that in all reality fell short of everyone's expectations. To net it out, then, ignoring or compressing the testing phase in an SAP project can be phenomenally expensive to everyone, affecting not only the project budget but the business's ability to nimbly execute as well.

The Real Value in Integration Testing

When 95% of the coding and configuration ("programming" in the most general sense) has been completed within each SAP component, work can begin in earnest testing how all components integrate to create an enterprise solution. Integration testing must continue to focus *inside* each SAP component, too, to ensure that business processes execute as expected, but *outside* is where most of the work lies. That is, SAP is integrated such that back in the functional testing phase, it was largely validated that the Sales and Distribution

(SD) module of SAP ERP interfaced well and worked as expected with Materials Management (MM), Production Planning (PP), and so on (for example). But in integration testing, what started as a suite of functional test cases was broadened to include an even larger scope of test cases. Thus, we contend that integration testing will not only overlap functional testing, but complicate matters by adding to the need for additional testing.

During this phase in the project, all team members will work together to run through the various scripted and otherwise recorded business processes, noting failures, successes, and unexpected variations or outcomes. Again and again, throughout the testing phase, each team comes together to test its configuration changes. The risks are many:

▶ In a perfect world, it would be ideal to start integration testing after the entire solution has been completely configured at a component level. Normally, though, the teams are fortunate to be 95% of the way there.

▶ After each set of failed integration tests, the teams must go back to their respective drawing boards and address any shortcomings, variations, and errors in their code. The potential exists to introduce new errors into business processes that have performed flawlessly up to this point, however.

▶ The teams must be kept in check against the project scope. It's very easy for an ambitious developer to begin adding "nice-to-haves" or otherwise extra features. This feature creep only adds complexity, though. And it further complicates integration testing as the go-live deadline looms closer and closer.

The next section covers business process testing that most often takes place *after* go-live, although a good bit of it can still occur prior to that big day—regression testing.

The Impact of Regression Testing

Testing how well a business process works after a change is made to the system is the goal of regression testing. This helps to ensure that your changes (or the addition of new functionality, which in itself represents a change, too) do not have a negative effect on business processes already in production or earmarked to be released to production soon. In our experience, we tend to see regression testing activities spike most during migration testing or when a new SAP component is added to and integrated with an organization's enterprise. And regression testing is not uncommon prior to go-live, too, when an organization is going through dreaded scope changes or succumbing to other alterations to the master plan. Overall, though, the bulk of regression testing occurs at the following times after go-live:

▶ When new functionality is added to the currently implemented SAP components or products

▶ Prior to the introduction of new components or products that are necessarily integrated with the SAP enterprise

▶ During the course of normal system maintenance after applying support packages, legal changes, and other patches or fixes

▶ Prior to planned upgrades to new SAP component releases

This type of testing, like functional and integration testing, takes place on the SAP instance implemented for testing—Test/QA, Integration, Consolidation, or whatever you call this special SAP system in your particular environment. Keep in mind, of course, that the actual changes are made in development and then promoted to test/QA and tested again. The changes may be further promoted throughout your landscape. Regardless, after these changes are tested and proven throughout the landscape, they are eventually promoted from the development environment to the production system.

Functional Versus Stress Testing and Recovery Testing

Whereas functional and other such testing is geared toward ensuring that a business process *works*, stress testing or load testing ensures that a business process *works quickly*. That is, functional or quality testing focuses on the correctness of implementation, and stress testing assumes this correctness to focus on how the system behaves during daily and high-load periods. In the real world, after the bulk of the configuration work has been locked down, more attention is paid to functional and integration testing than is ever paid to load testing. A few months before go-live, however, a comprehensive systems and stress test should be executed.

Yet another form of testing may confuse matters. Called *recovery testing*, it is intended to ensure that a business process continues to work as expected in the wake of a disaster. Remember from Chapters 15 and 16 that the ability of a system to continue serving its end-user community in the event of a disaster is the job of the system's disaster recovery (DR) solution. Managed by the DR team, the business may find that the system acts differently after failover to a DR site. Perhaps performance will be impacted. Perhaps several bolt-ons or integration points will be unavailable (either intentionally as a result of a well-thought-out business decision, or unintentionally due to the disaster at hand or a different failure). Either way, quantifying to what extent a system's end users will be able to conduct business after a disaster is the job of recovery testing.

Approaching Business Process Testing

Planning for, executing, and analyzing the results of business process testing is a detail-oriented job, to say the least. And even at its best, it is still phenomenally time-consuming. Historically, much testing has been performed manually. Drawbacks to this approach are fairly obvious though. For example:

- ▶ Each tester representing the business must be able to devote an adequate amount of time to testing. This in turn takes away from the tester's other duties within the organization.

- ▶ Testers brought in from third-party consulting and integration partners are probably not experts in your particular business processes—relevant industry experience is therefore a must. Further, costs can be a huge factor (though in today's world of offshoring, near shoring, and "best shoring," cost is relative).

▶ Testers must be trained in the tools and methodology employed by your team for testing, as well as the method of documenting output and other results such that the data collected is captured and presented in a clear, consistent manner.

▶ Testers need physical resources—office/lab space or a "war room" to easily facilitate coordinated testing, complete with enough physical client devices (desktops, laptops, PDAs, well-equipped phones, and any other access devices that might be used to access the productive system) to actually perform the testing.

▶ Finally, because these expensive human resources operate in "real time" only, the ability to consistently and repeatedly execute business processes is impacted. That is, testers must be present to execute a test, and they must be lucid and otherwise at the top of their game *all day long*. Not only is manual testing time-consuming, but it is prone to errors.

It is because of the drawbacks shown in the preceding list that automated testing tools for SAP have really grown in popularity over the last 10 to 15 years. Tools such as SAP CATT, SAP eCATT, Borland SilkPerformer, Compuware TestPartner, HP QuickTest, and quite a few others negate the issues described in the preceding list in that they

▶ Require fewer expensive human resources

▶ Execute the same tests over and over again without getting bored and making mistakes, or needing a coffee break, and so on

▶ Consistently execute a test much more rapidly than their manual-approach counterparts

▶ Can be easily modified to test a set of variants or other values unique to similar test cases (such as testing the creation of a sales order for many different sales groups or distribution centers)

▶ Act as a single repository for all test cases and related documentation, thus facilitating management of the testing process and key deliverables (many tools are more limited in this respect than eCATT and HP's Quality Center, though, as we will discuss later)

Thus, compared to manual testing methods, the investment in automated testing tools to enable script development consistently pays for itself quickly. Even in the case of third-party tools (for which license fees may range from tens of thousands of dollars to $100,000 and more), the return on investment is still typically rapid—less than a few months.

Third-Party Tools and Other Resources

Whereas the now-defunct AutoTester's products were the first to be certified with SAP, Compuware's TestPartner held the special distinction of being the first product to be certified to run with eCATT. Today, all the popular SAP-approved testing tools support eCATT. In our experience, though, we have seen several different testing tools outside of SAP-approved tools that have been used to drive business process testing. The most basic of these are simple scripting utilities adept at propelling the SAPGUI or WebGUI simply by virtue of being Windows products. More sophisticated products exist, too, as do custom scripting approaches. Basic tools not already mentioned include

- ▶ AutoIT scripts

- ▶ Custom Perl scripts

- ▶ Custom Visual Basic scripts

Most of these represent either older offerings or embody little in the way of SAP-specific capabilities. This is where SAP eCATT represents a quantum leap forward, in that it can handily address integration testing within the SAP framework.

Beyond these basic quality performance tools, vendors like HP, Borland, and IBM have developed SAP-specific quality-focused functional test tool suites. HP's Quality Center is an excellent example of a suite of testing products positioned around an agile development and quality management process to quickly work through the SAP Realization phase. By focusing on the entire testing process for SAP while automating and enforcing quality standards, HP not only eliminates a lot of the risk inherent to the testing process but reduces the time and cost required to implement SAP. HP's "designed for run" lifecycle approach to SAP testing and quality management

- ▶ Facilitates managing SAP's functional requirements

- ▶ Assists in planning testing activities

- ▶ Enables test case scheduling

- ▶ Provides for actually running test cases

- ▶ Tracks functional defects discovered during the testing process

- ▶ Provides reports, graphs, and a handy dashboard reflecting test case quality metrics, findings, and overall status

HP's approach makes it possible to track defects back to their origination in the Business Blueprint phase, giving development and configuration teams the information necessary for SAP project leadership to make better decisions related to how much work might be required to fix issues or even adjust the project's scope.

SAP eCATT Differentiators

The capabilities of SAP eCATT both to drive business process scripts on newer SAP solutions that leverage the SAP Control Framework and to work through the legacy SAPGUI API and interface to external tools make it one of our favorite automated testing tools of choice for pure business process testing.

To access all of this value, Web Application Server (Web AS) version 6.20 is required at minimum, along with SAPGUI version 6.20. The price is right, however, because eCATT is "included" with Web AS (again, as we mentioned in Chapter 24, "Installing SAP NetWeaver Components," you may still see the term Web Application Server or Web AS used to refer to the Application Server platform—SAP only recently dropped "Web" from the moniker and added ABAP, Java, or ABAP+Java for clarification).

Key benefits of eCATT include

▶ It supports remote centralized testing, insofar as being able to drive tests and act as the single test platform for many SAP products, thereby simplifying data and script management.

▶ It supports all SAP components running on SAP Basis Release 4.6C or greater; the core testing tool must reside on Web AS 6.20, but it can test a broader suite of SAP products.

▶ It can be integrated with external testing tools (such as those discussed in more detail in Chapter 33) that may already be used by a particular organization or necessary to support testing business processes that touch non-SAP systems.

▶ It fully integrates with the Test Workbench.

▶ It has tight integration with transaction ST30, SAP's Performance Analysis Tool.

▶ It supports the reuse of test data, by storing this data in separate container objects.

▶ It provides support for various GUIs.

▶ The TCD command allows you to test business processes using the proven batch input technology found in earlier releases of CATT.

▶ The SAPGUI command provides a new flexible test option for transactions that cannot be tested via TCD; precisely, it's the SAPGUI command that supports the SAP Control Framework discussed previously.

▶ Older CATT scripts (called test procedures) may be easily migrated to newer eCATT test scripts. A bit of script tweaking is still required, though, to reflect changes to RFC destinations (created with transaction SM59) and other details that enable eCATT to run tests across multiple SAP instances.

The first point in the preceding list is especially exciting, in that eCATT allows end-to-end SAP solution testing to be executed and managed from a single Web AS 6.20 or newer instance. In the past, test cases usually had to be built and run from each SAP component. That is, every test system within the SAP BW landscape, SAP CRM landscape, SAP SRM landscape, and so on became the de facto testing platform/repository for its component. This complicated business process testing quite a bit, and forced a lot of duplication of effort when it came to maintaining test cases where business processes crossed over to other SAP components or different enterprise applications altogether.

Other test-related areas of importance are impacted too, and are examined next.

Additional People Considerations

With the kind of automated testing discussed thus far, there is a significant potential reduction in human testing resources—people—that may be realized, for the following reasons:

▶ Fewer test execution specialists are needed—as you saw earlier in this chapter, the number of people required is reduced when an automated-tool approach is taken.

▶ Fewer test-case developers and maintainers are needed. However, the people tasked with these responsibilities must understand how their core business processes impact and otherwise touch other SAP components. So, although fewer people may be required, they must be highly qualified across the board—in their business area, in testing, and in general.

▶ The need for testing coordinators is similarly reduced, given the reduction in people needed overall.

However, the number of folks responsible for identifying and fine-tuning the business processes remains pretty consistent regardless of the specific testing approach (manual or automated). Elsewhere in the SAP Technical Support Organization (TSO), headcount remains the same, too.

Process Overview, Constraints, and Issues

When it comes to functional testing, a process is mandatory. We covered a basic lifecycle approach marrying testing with the ASAP methodology earlier in the chapter. Because it's comprehensive and identifies people collaboration considerations, we like the following process outlined by HP with regard to using Quality Center:

1. Subject-matter experts first define SAP functional requirements and testing objectives.
2. Test managers and SAP implementation project leads design test plans.
3. Test managers develop specific test cases.
4. For each test case, test automation engineers or developers tasked with this role create the automated scripts and store them in the test repository.
5. The implementation team's quality assurance (QA) testers run manual and automated tests.
6. The QA team documents each test yields execution results and defects.
7. Developers review and fix the documented defects.
8. The SAP project manager or test lead creates a functional application status report useful for prioritizing test automation engineers, which test cases need to be sent back to the blueprinting team, and which might require a scope change or higher-level management intervention.

Testing includes much more than just testing valid data or combinations of data. Rather, a good testing process also embraces what SAP refers to as *negative testing*, where test cases are created with invalid data. The goal of these particular cases is to determine how well the system recovers or handles incorrect data, and how well the system communicates this fact back to the end user. For example, test cases should be created and tested where invalid customer and material numbers are fed to sales order processes, to ensure that error handling and general feedback is both present and appropriate.

Sound testing also includes experimenting with additional boundary testing as well as all combinations of client and user interfaces—a comprehensive testing process requires true end-to-end execution and analysis. Thus, if the Java-based SAPGUI will exist in your environment, and a particular version of the classic SAPGUI is required to support long-time SAP ERP users, testing must be performed that includes both user interfaces.

Other Areas of Impact

Another area impacted by automated testing regards the number of physical desktops (or other client access devices) needed to perform the testing. Because fewer people are required, fewer SAPGUI, WebGUI, and other access devices used to execute these interfaces are needed as well.

In addition, because scripted test cases are inherently easy to duplicate, fewer test runs are required. This is because every test run executes precisely the same steps, in precisely the same order, as every other test. Omissions, errors, timing inconsistencies, and so on are virtually eliminated with automated testing. By reducing the number of test runs required, we reduce the number of billable hours that consultants will charge a client, and free up valuable hardware resources for other tasks.

Finally, as we outlined previously, a good automated testing approach should not be limited to the tools you currently have on hand. On the contrary, it is always preferable to use a tool that may be "extended" to include third-party testing/scripting tools, to support testing cross-platform, or to allow for testing complex enterprisewide business processes. SAP eCATT is perfectly positioned to address this, too. It allows third-party vendors and software developers to integrate their test tools using the BC-eCATT interface.

Applications that cannot otherwise be tested exclusively with eCATT can leverage this extensibility, thereby opening the doors to testing applications written in HTML, Visual Basic, and so on. With eCATT handling the transport of these additional third-party scripts throughout your SAP test landscape (actually, the SAP Change and Transport System [CTS] performs the actual transports), your centrally managed eCATT scripts can call scripts created by your third-party tools, and then execute them anywhere in the system.

Executing Business Process Testing

At this point in your SAP project implementation, all but the production system is probably deployed. Before testing can commence in the testing environment (or across multiple environments, depending on your situation and the specific business processes being implemented), minimum SAP Release levels need to be in place. Again, ensure that your central test system—the system from which all eCATT testing will be managed and driven—is at Release 6.20 or higher. As of this writing, 4.6C Basis releases are supported.

We further assume that various teams have also been assembled at this point, each geared toward specific functional areas or SAP components. The teams consist of a team lead, and both functional folks and developers working with ABAP, Java, and any other coding or programming languages used in the enterprise. In this way, each team is well positioned to capture the details surrounding a business process, and create the necessary test cases using eCATT. This is accomplished via the Test Workbench, covered next.

Using the Test Workbench

As mentioned before, eCATT is fully integrated with the Test Workbench. This allows the team leader for a specific testing team to

- Assign test configurations to individual testers

- Include test configurations in test catalogs

- Monitor test execution and results

Creating and executing eCATT scripts is straightforward. However, if your particular enterprise needs to test processes outside the scope of eCATT, we suggest that you consider "wrapping" your third-party external scripts in an eCATT script, and then storing them in the SAP eCATT testing platform database. This saves in terms of administrative overhead, complexity, and time spent in managing the third-party scripts.

To "wrap" your third-party scripts, you must first load the third-party tool on the desktop from which you run the SAPGUI that accesses eCATT. This is because when you click the Script button in the SAPGUI, it will actually start the third-party tool and bring up the script you want to edit or maintain. Incidentally, the Script button also allows you to create a new script using your third-party tool.

Prior to executing test cases, create a test matrix that documents all test cases and where the results of test runs may be stored and analyzed. We like to use an Excel workbook for this purpose because it enables us to track multiple test areas—we separate each area by worksheet, labeling the worksheet's tab to make this clear. Plus, this approach allows us to insert input files, output data, screenshots with error messages, a copy of a particularly troublesome script, or other objects that might be useful when sharing or discussing the testing process with others.

Last of all, take advantage of the eCATT system data containers to allow simple administration of the various SAP destinations that come into play when working with a central test system. These data containers eliminate the need to administer essentially the same test scripts in several different systems and the need for "implicit" remote calls.

And remember, leverage the ability of eCATT to maintain and manage all scripts in a single repository. Avoid the temptation to copy scripts and test cases everywhere.

Tracking Data During Test Execution

During each functional, integration, or regression test run, note the date and start times, test run name, run number, version of script executed, version of input data, GUI details, and whether the business process completed successfully, or how far it progressed before it failed. We like to view integration and regression testing in terms of concentric circles to help us document and track failures in terms of where and how often they occur and to what extent they affect other functionality:

- Within the specific SAP component and functional area (for example, SAP ERP SD)

- Within the SAP component (that is, the process completed everything it needed to do within and across the various SAP ERP functional areas)

28

▶ In other SAP components (for example, the process successfully provided data to or pulled data from another SAP component, such as procurement replenishment data shared between SAP ERP and SAP SRM)

▶ In non-SAP applications (to determine, for example, that the process successfully updated an HTML page or a data field on a system outside of SAP)

Maintaining a tiered approach like this helps focus additional development and further testing activity where it is needed most. When a test case has finally completed (whether successfully or not), additional data needs to be collected, and other processes need to be addressed. These post-processing tasks are covered next.

Post-Execution Tasks

After each test run, perform the following post-execution tasks as soon as possible:

▶ Note the output results, such as whether an order number was created and, if so, the actual order number itself. In this way, the order may be reviewed in detail at a later time if necessary.

▶ Note any SAP warnings or errors displayed by the SAPGUI.

▶ In support of "version control," make a backup of any data, scripts, or test cases that have not been backed up yet.

▶ Note basic performance metrics (such as end-to-end "wall clock" execution time, which is simply the end-to-end time it takes to run through a complete business process).

At this stage in testing, achieving excellent performance is not the goal. But really poor performance might drive further business process development down different avenues. And basic performance data serves as a baseline of sorts to share with the folks who will eventually perform any stress testing later in the project.

Compressing the Testing Phase in the Real World

At one of SAP's largest customer sites, this particular client really had a good handle on how to tackle and execute test cases. There was heavy involvement by the various business organizations, resulting in accurate, detailed test cases of all transactions. The customer spent a lot of time getting its input data in order, too, and truly covered in great detail all business processes and its own unique variations. However, for timeline reasons, the customer glossed over what turned out to be two key areas: testing the reporting function—including system-generated, ad hoc, standard or default reporting, and other types of reporting—and training its end users to understand the reports they actually created.

Instead, nearly all the testing was focused on identifying and addressing traditional business processes, specific variants or one-offs, and other highly unique test cases. The rest of the customer's project plan time dedicated to testing was actually consumed by last-minute data loads and similar updates. As this customer told us later, SAP is terrific when it comes to easily drilling down into the details surrounding a specific transaction, and it's great at presenting the big picture. But getting a view of the "middle ground" via custom reporting takes some work, and this work was never thoroughly tested or shared with others.

The customer ultimately obtained all this needed information, but it was sacrificed unknowingly up front just to get the SAP system in place. What does this have to do with business process testing? Simple—a business process is not complete, and therefore not completely tested, until it affords value to the organization that really *depends* upon the business process. For this customer, the fact that the business process worked was nice, but because it could not really leverage the information gleaned from the business process, it was actually of little value until many months after go-live.

Using Testing to Support SLAs in the Real World

Although regression testing is geared toward proving that a business process works or continues to work after a change, we helped one of our customers leverage the data we collected to build a case for establishing minimum service-level agreements (SLAs) and then monitoring adherence to these SLAs. That is, we used the business processes—the workflow surrounding end-to-end business flows—to build timelines that described and supported different business functions in terms of minimum timeframes that could be tolerated between events. These timelines served as the foundation for SLA baselines, because we knew the typical time required to execute a business process under varying system loads.

We later took this same approach and applied it to another customer's Basis/technical infrastructure team, to its benefit. Scripted "Basis business processes" (in this case, scripted CCMS transactions used to monitor the system) were measured against typical response times. Thus, if it took more time than usual to execute a transaction to display all active users, for example, a threshold would be exceeded. This would in turn automatically trigger a message in the customer's problem escalation system, and in doing so notify the senior Basis team, the help desk, and SAP operations. Similar transactions comparing response times, buffer quality, and so on triggered similar messages. All of this became quite useful to the entire SAP TSO after a change control wave took place; monitoring the system in this way provided a "QA" check beyond the scope of basic regression testing, and kept everyone apprised of exactly how well the change control package performed in the real world.

The Weakest Link: Having Too Few Resources

SAP AG touts its products as business products configured by business consultants. True, the functional configuration and development consulting teams who perform much of the functional configuration are often experts in the business first, and configurators, developers, programmers, or test automation engineers second. But this can work against a project team if a balance of both functional experts and development and testing experts is not maintained; inadequate development and testing resources are often the weakest link in a SAP project.

Consider any number of typical business processes in which the base SAP configuration is simply not robust or flexible enough for a particular company. The development team gets around this shortcoming by coding a custom solution in ABAP, Java, or whatever is applicable. A development team consisting of too few real programmers has a decent chance of writing poor enough code that it becomes the solution's weakest link. Poor or inadequate testing only exacerbates this issue. Sloppy ABAP and Java code not only frustrates performance tuners and the end users forced to live with the system day in and day out, but also complicates upgrade attempts later on. And sloppy code certainly plays a role in complicating regression testing throughout the life of the business solution. For these reasons, adopt a sound ASAP-aligned development and testing methodology, engage enough resources to do justice to the project, and leverage automated testing tools wherever possible and financially prudent.

Summary

The focus of this chapter has been on functional, integration, and regression testing. We looked at the value that an automated approach provides, especially in the realm of using SAP eCATT, and at various benefits of using eCATT over other methods or products. We then wrapped up the chapter with an approach to testing, followed by real-world testing experiences. In the next chapter, we take business process testing to the next level and spend time dissecting everything from hardware-level subsystem performance to end-to-end SAP solution stress testing.

Case Study: Building an SAP Test Tool Portfolio

HiTech, Inc. has hired you as an independent consultant to introduce its company-internal SAP configuration and development team to business process testing.

Questions

1. What's the name of the SAP testing tools that are built in to SAP?

2. What other tools should HiTech consider?

3. How might the LSMW tool fit into HiTech's functional testing needs?

4. How does a suite of tools like HP Quality Center assist an implementation test team tasked with functional testing?

5. Why should HiTech use any automated tools at all?

> **NOTE**
>
> The answers to these questions can be found in Appendix A, "Case Study Answers."

CHAPTER 29

Advanced Concepts: Unlocking SAP with SOA and Web Services

Much of this book has dealt with unleashing the power and functions of SAP and achieving implementation success. In this chapter, we present advanced techniques to unlock these great SAP capabilities and serve the rest of the enterprise. Most organization's IT is becoming increasingly heterogeneous and the ease with which SAP can integrate with other technologies becomes an absolute requirement for companies that want to be adaptive. One of the most promising IT transformations occurring in businesses today is to establish a service-oriented architecture (SOA) to achieve much better alignment between business needs and IT capabilities and integrate SAP with the rest of the enterprise architecture. In this chapter, we will visit this topic in terms of opportunities and challenges of SOA, state-of-the-art SOA technologies, a deep dive unlocking SAP functionality via SOA best practice techniques, and specifically with SAP's Process Integration (SAP PI) middleware, and finally establishing a SOA Center of Excellence that governs every aspect of an enterprise SOA initiative.

What Is SOA?

A typical enterprise consists of a heterogeneous landscape that has evolved throughout a company's history. Enterprises today have dozens of technology islands including legacy systems, multiple enterprise resource planning (ERP) systems from different vendors perhaps including SAP, and countless custom-built solutions. It is impractical if not impossible for any single vendor to comprehensively cover an enterprise's needs at the level of detail required. As a result, companies struggle with an ever-increasing problem of heterogeneity, lack of integration, and an inflexible IT environment. Most companies have come to realize that today's inflexible IT systems are limiting their ability to compete or advance their business goals and objectives. Beyond reducing IT costs, an even more strategic objective has come to the forefront—business agility. Companies that have the goal of being a leader of their industries understand that IT is the business, and the current state of inflexible IT is absolutely unacceptable. No longer can systems be built merely to last decades but instead must be designed for inevitable but unknown business changes and connect seamlessly outside its silo. In other words, they must be adaptable practically at the will of the business. For this reason, the journey towards a service-oriented architecture (SOA)—a blueprint for agile architectures—has become one of the most important IT transformations occurring today.

SOA is a distributed computing architectural approach centered on the concept of services that enables an enterprise to execute its business strategy and achieve its business goals. This approach promotes the use of loosely coupled, reusable, standards-based and well-defined services that enable them to be discovered and consumed by independent service consumers. The beauty of SOA is that these services can be assembled much like building blocks to form complex business processes or composite applications. To visualize this composition refer to Figure 29.1, which illustrates a layered view of service-oriented architecture consisting of a set of processes that are made up of several subprocesses and business services. These business services are the basic building blocks for higher-level functionality. In this manner, complex processes do not have to be built from scratch but rather can be formed by an assembly of prebuilt business services, which themselves are made up of business applications and infrastructure. Agility results from the property of "separation of concerns" because each layer of the architecture can be modified without impacting other layers as long as the interfaces are not changed.

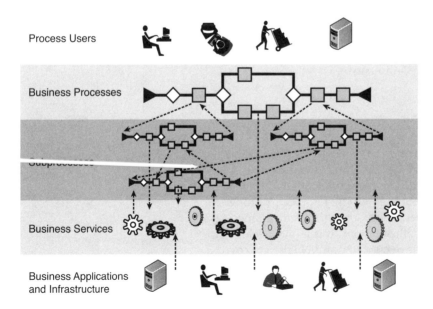

FIGURE 29.1   Layered view of service-oriented architecture.

With SOA, change inherently becomes faster and easier because the architecture is broken up into these layers of processes and services that are designed to be interoperable and used across different business processes and different business contexts. Think of services as essentially building blocks of business functionality that can be assembled and reassembled in multiple ways. This approach not only has the advantage of agility and being "designed for change," it also can reduce costs because services can be reused eliminating the need to reconstruct redundant functionality each time.

The Opportunities and Challenges of SOA

SOA promises to unleash a number of benefits sought by many firms today. According to SAP, SOA is like a blueprint used to create an adaptable, flexible, and open IT architecture that in turn may be leveraged to create services-based business applications. To realize its own vision of such applications, SAP offers in NetWeaver the required technical platform necessary for introducing SOA (among other capabilities, of course). The result is SAP's ability to create real-time enterprise applications that benefit from rapid prototyping and deployment, high reusability, and low development costs. Said another way, the key benefits of SOA center around a drastic increase in business agility coupled with significantly reduced IT costs, all of which are made possible through the concept of reuse. This brings with it both opportunities and challenges, explored next.

Opportunities and Benefits of SOA

Services broken down into their basic tasks naturally lend themselves to fewer integration problems, less code overhead, and so on. Reusability makes it possible for developers to create business-effective as well as cost-effective applications. Based on our own client experiences, some of the specific benefits provided by SOA for SAP (and indeed SOA in general) include:

- ▶ SOA decreases cost by driving reuse and vendor agnosticism

- ▶ SOA increases adaptability by allowing easy modification of IT solutions to meet changing business demands

- ▶ SOA speeds up development by moving the developers' focus from software functions to business functions

- ▶ SOA moves developers' focus to simplicity and modularity, naturally reducing the cost of development

- ▶ SOA helps organizations visualize business processes by creating a tighter link between business needs and IT capabilities

- ▶ SOA enables organizations to develop reusable services ahead of business process definition

- ▶ SOA makes it possible for development organizations to build lean *and* powerful applications

Building SOA-enabled SAP applications from a mix of reusable services allows an organization to deliver the flexibility, agility, and uniformity necessary to change the developer's paradigm from one of spending all their time maintaining code to spending much more time actually *innovating* at a business level. This is the true value of SOA. And building SAP applications from a single suite of enterprise-class reusable services makes an SOA-enabled solution not only achievable but less costly than older development approaches to deploying enterprise applications.

Firms focused on creating a catalog of reusable SOA services will have at their disposal a greater variety of purpose-built and general services. They might construct enterprise-class business applications based on business processes composed of SAP-provided, partner-provided, and partner-based services. And the most innovative firms will add their own internally developed services to their catalog, maintaining them in the name of competitive advantage or selling them at a profit for reusability by other firms. This reflects an interesting dynamic—by spreading development costs out across a much greater breadth than the firm's own developer organization, SOA's usability and adoption for SAP will be increased while associated development costs will be decreased.

Challenges for SOA Realization

Although SOA holds tremendous promise, many organizations will face several challenges in their attempt to ensure success with SOA and actually realize the benefits. For example, business applications predicated on client/server-based enterprise solutions still prevail today despite the presence of SOA and similar architectures. Transitioning from a proven business/IT solution that meets a client's core needs to an architecture that promises greater rewards but requires significant retooling is simply not palatable to everyone—especially organizations already investing millions in an SAP deployment. SAP and its partners can talk of increased business agility and flexibility that comes from SOA, for example, but the obstacles of functional upgrades and technical replatforming costs money, incurs downtime, and is generally disruptive for months. Add to this the need to embrace a new architectural approach and train both IT and an organization's SAP end user community, and it's no wonder that the transition to SOA is anything but slow and deliberate (if attempted at all). Finally, the fact that most organizations tend to upgrade mission-critical applications such as SAP once every five years or so means that SOA-for-SAP hasn't even "come up" in serious discussions at current SAP sites. Other challenges include the following:

▶ **Infrastructure**—SOA requires new infrastructure capabilities for shared services.

▶ **Standards**—Standards continue to mature but change rapidly and make it difficult to maintain competency and consistency.

▶ **Organization and skill sets**—SOA requires a shift in mindset requiring that the organization evolve to embrace SOA. Questions such as "Is SOA and sharing of services part of the culture?" and "How is reuse funded and encouraged?" naturally arise.

▶ **Personnel training**—IT professionals will require retraining in both development and process-related areas.

▶ **Technology**—Questions of which technologies to employ, vendors to partner with, and so on will complicate lifecycle management. As applications support becomes more challenging, specialized SOA management tools will become even more crucial.

▶ **SOA governance and enterprise architecture**—SOA requires a greater focus on governance and overarching enterprise architecture including how to set standards, policy development, strong architectural guidance, and corporate control. Ownership of services must be governed as well as the process for ongoing updating and version control of services.

▶ **SOA testing**—When services are reused in multiple contexts or the same service is used in multiple business processes, the dependencies among these services become difficult to manage. Ensuring that services are reliable and fully tested, adhere to standards and policies, and scale as the needs of the business grows is becoming vastly more complex with the advent of SOA.

The practical benefits of SOA are easy to understand. However, the execution of a practical SOA journey often require a multifaceted approach and recognition of the preceding challenges. Newer technologies have provided amazing new capabilities that greatly mitigate many of these challenges, but it should be clear that these challenges span well beyond technology. The following section presents some of these major SOA technologies available in the market today. Keep in mind, though, that people, organization, and governance issues are clearly recognized to be the toughest challenges facing most organizations attempting a SOA transformation.

SOA Technology

The advent of the latest integration and SOA technologies promise to make SOA implementation a lot easier. However, the number of choices, technologies, and vendors of SOA technology is daunting and can become complex to navigate. In this section, we attempt to introduce some of the major SOA technology and a few of the vendors that exist in this space.

As illustrated previously in Figure 29.1, SOA consists of a set of services and processes that can be assembled together to achieve greater business functionality. As a result of considerable support from tools vendors, technology has been able to make significant strides to enable such an architecture. The "service infrastructure" has evolved to enable the full development, connectivity, runtime management, orchestration, governance, management and monitoring, and testing of services.

Many different technologies enable SOA. It is important to note that all of the technologies described here are not required for SOA and in fact most companies do not employ many of the components. These merely represent options or choices. To further describe SOA technologies, we have introduced some of the major product categories next. Please refer to more detailed texts for a closer review of the categories discussed next; for our purposes here, we determined it was more important to understand the basic components and concepts.

Application Server and .NET CLR

Today, much modern software runs within middleware known as an application server (in the case of SAP and other Java-based software) and as the .NET Common Language Runtime (CLR) for Microsoft-based software. Application servers and their .NET equivalent provide the core application infrastructure to enable distributed programming. As a result, custom software components are independent of the specific hardware node (such as servers) that they run upon. Additionally, application servers provide basic functionality including the ability to scale with or without clustering, persistence, security, fail-over, and other functions typically considered "plumbing." Thus. application servers free developers from having to create custom code specifically addressing all aspects of distributed programming.

Enterprise Service Bus

An enterprise service bus (ESB) is one of the most feature-rich SOA technologies and is often the core component of an enterprise-level SOA. The ESB provides a number of capabilities that enable the connectivity, Simple Object Access Protocol (SOAP) handling, protocol switching, messaging, routing, transformation, and many other functions and features that can make developing and running an SOA much easier. The actual functionality that is contained within an ESB varies from vendor to vendor but typically includes the ability to enable systems integration among heterogeneous technologies. For example, some vendors may include the business process (BP) orchestration engine within the ESB but all vendors make the core underlying communication possible.

Service Registry and Repository

Besides making integration easier, enabling reuse is one of the key reasons for SOA. A basic element of enabling reuse is the existence of a service catalog or some kind of persistence store of the services that are available for reuse. After all, it is difficult to reuse services if there is no single location or store to which one can go to determine what is intended for reuse. This "single location" could be as simple as a spreadsheet; however, to enable enterprise-level sharing of services, many companies use a service registry and repository.

A service registry usually supports the Universal Description and Discovery Interface (UDDI) specification that enables services to be "discovered" and utilized programmatically. UDDI specifies how service consumers or programs can search a directory or catalog of services and then dynamically bind to the service to use it. The service consumer can be bound to the service provider either at compile time (by a developer, for example) or at runtime based on a set of conditions for that particular transaction.

A metadata repository provides substantially more information about the services that are discoverable in the repository. It provides a link to the interface definition described by a Web Services Description Language (WSDL) document if the service is implemented as a web service and can have many custom pieces of useful metadata such as who owns the service, service-level objectives, links to documents and artifacts, describing the detailed behavior of the service, and many other metadata that can be customized by the architects and designers.

Another important functionality that is provided by many registries and repositories is the ability to automate and enforce SOA governance. SOA governance refers to the decision-making process that controls the behavior of who is permitted to use which services, how services are developed and used, and how services may be maintained, version controlled, and so on.

Unlocking SAP Functionality

Unlocking SAP functionality is as much about how well systems integration is addressed as it is about configuring functionality in a particular SAP component. Companies can no longer deliver business value and competitive differentiation when SAP is treated as just another standalone or "siloed" system. Only when data and functionality from SAP is integrated with other data and functionality found throughout the business enterprise can advanced business capabilities become possible, if not evident. Integration is not optional; enterprises must integrate to survive. In this section, we will focus on the various methods to integrate third-party applications with SAP to unlock the potential of a broader and more powerful resulting system.

Systems integration is both an art and a science, marrying people with business applications, processes, and data to create a seamless and useful business system. We have many tools and approaches at our disposal, the most central of which are outlined next.

Application Connectivity Using BAPI and a Web Service

Perhaps the most simple method for connecting a third-party application to SAP is via a Business Application Programming Interface (BAPI) or Remote Function Call (RFC). One way to access data from SAP is a direct read from a SAP table. Specifically, SAP provides a generic function called RFC_READ_TABLE that will pull data from any table. In many cases, an adapter can be used to ease integration to hide the lower level details of SAP. Many companies provide such adapters (such as XI, Tuxedo, and IWAY). If an adapter for the particular scenario does not exist, then the necessary utility objects (for example, SAP Java Connector or SAP .NET Connector) can be downloaded free from SAP Marketplace website (https://websmp108.sap-ag.de/) to develop connectivity mapping objects based on RFC_READ_TABLE function via a Common Programming Interface Communication (CPIC) account in SAP. In both cases, a web service can be built on the connectivity objects (whether provided by an adapter or custom built) and registered in a registry to provide visibility to service consumers. Consumers of the service can download the WSDL document and other instructions to invoke the service. Additionally, the service can be governed, managed, and monitored just like any other service.

Process Integration Using SAP NetWeaver

Many Enterprise Service Bus and BPM products exist to provide integration with SAP. SAP also provides similar technology via SAP NetWeaver. SAP NetWeaver is the core technical infrastructure for enterprise SOA offered by SAP. Agility can be greatly enhanced by decoupling business processes from underlying IT systems. Changes can be made in the business process, such as adding, removing, or changing an existing step of a process flow without interrupting operations or modifying underlying IT systems. A true appreciation of this flexibility is most evident by simply reviewing NetWeaver's architecture. The implementation of a process can be described in three steps:

▶ **Design time**—Design the entire process flow and identify the interfaces that are required.

▶ **Configuration time**—Configure the cross-system processes for an existing system landscape that is specific for each implementation.

▶ **Runtime**—The configuration data is evaluated at runtime and controls communication. You can monitor the message flow by using a central monitoring.

This segregation across the development lifecycle allows a clear separation of duties among different roles (designers and architects, configuration specialists, deployment specialists, operations staff, and so on). Furthermore, the architecture supports the separation of process flow logic, from mapping logic, from data type logic. This is evident with the multiple graphical editors within the Integration Builder that designers and developers use to configure application integrations.

▶ Integration scenarios describe a high-level abstraction of the communication between applications while integration processes are the actual executable processes that will be run within the Integration Server.

▶ Mappings define the structure or value relationships between messages across each interface. Typically a standard is used (or Java archives for more complex transformations).

▶ Context objects mask access to elements or attributes in the payload. For example, deeply nested message structures can be mapped to a shorter designation, eliminating long hierarchy paths.

▶ Data types and message types describe the structure of messages that are to be exchanged using message interfaces. Developers use message interfaces to generate proxies in application systems.

The entire content of the Integration Repository can be shipped and a group of objects can be referred to as *Process Integration Content*, or simply (incorrectly, given SAP's renaming) *XI content*. The XI content can be versioned in the System Landscape Directory (SLD). The System Landscape Directory acts as a central information database, from which the relevant products and systems of the system landscape can be queried for development and configuration purposes, and at runtime.

During configuration time, the cross-system processes are configured for an existing system landscape. The configuration describes how the Integration Server is to process inbound messages during runtime and to which receiver(s) messages must be sent. Unlike the XI content stored in the Integration Repository and developed during design time, the Integration Directory content is not shipped because it varies with each implementation. Routing rules are specified to control the message flow and receiver determinations define the service to which the message is sent. Interface determination determines which sender interface belongs to which receiver interface, and it executes mapping for an interface pair using a map stored in the Integration Repository. Collaboration agreements control inbound and outbound processing. The agreement specifies the options described in the collaboration profile that are to be valid at runtime for a selection of senders and receivers.

At runtime, the Integration Server analyzes the data from the Integration Directory and the System Landscape Directory to process and forward messages from senders. In this way, you can develop applications that integrate SAP applications, internal and external applications, marketplace applications, and middleware components from third-party suppliers.

SAP eSOA, ESR, and the ESC

Built on SAP's own Enterprise Services Architecture (ESA), SAP's version of SOA is called eSOA (Enterprise SOA). SOA may be seen as more generic while eSOA is more specific. Enterprise SOA enables composite applications to be built by assembling enterprise services (a similar concept to web services, though similarly more generic in nature). SAP uses its NetWeaver Enterprise Services Repository (ESR) as the central building block for creating SAP eSOA applications. SAP has engaged not only its internal development team but a broad ecosphere of partners to develop a robust collection of enterprise services. SAP calls this its "inventory of enterprise services," more formally described as SAP's Enterprise Services Inventory. As eSOA's foundation, these enterprise services occupy the ESR and do the job of fulfilling a specific business need. Further, each enterprise service in turn passes data and triggers another enterprise service. SAP describes five principles of Enterprise SOA:

- **Abstraction**—Serves to mask unnecessary or otherwise puzzling details

- **Modularity**—An essential property of enterprise services that enables development of reusable components or building blocks by breaking down services into fundamental units

- **Standardized connectivity**—Necessary to describe and enable data sharing and triggering which in turn can be used to build and combine flexible services into full-fledged enterprise business processes and business solutions or scenarios

- **Loose coupling**—Another necessary property that enable individual services to grow and evolve without requiring a rewrite; loose coupling preserves reusability as well as integration and connectivity between services

- **Incremental design**—Enables changes to be made to a service's composition and configuration without requiring a rebuild

These principles should ultimately provide to SAP's thousands of legacy R/3 customers the last bit of incentive (beyond growing maintenance and licensing costs!) to one day abandon their trusted though increasingly inflexible client/server architectures. Enterprise SOA's flexible and standardized architecture supports business better than did its older architectural counterparts. SAP eSOA simplifies a firm's ability to innovate, integrate with its partners and vendors, and better service its customers. Enterprise SOA unifies business processes and simplifies their deployment and maintenance by structuring complex business applications as merely ad hoc collections of enterprise services.

29

SAP continues to actively engage its development teams and partners to build new services, involving its customers in the process to help identify or initiate and then vet out new potential enterprise services. SAP created the Enterprise Services Community (ESC) to give credence to its concept of enterprise services; the ESC also focuses on defining and refining enterprise services as well.

Another SAP tool, the Enterprise Services Workplace, makes newly published enterprise services available to SAP's customers and partners. SAP also publishes business maps that essentially map services to business processes and solutions. In this way, SAP effectively supports and grows its own vision of SOA and eSOA in particular while simultaneously giving its approach the legs it needs to prove effective in the real world.

Ensuring Success with an SOA Center of Excellence

In this section we describe a prescriptive model for a undergoing a comprehensive SOA transformation and achieving success with SOA. The quest for SOA has become less of a jaunt and more of a journey. Many companies have embraced the potential benefits of SOA but have also recognized that actually realizing these benefits can be a major challenge. What is the best approach for executing this SOA journey, and what are all the pieces that a company should consider in a comprehensive SOA program? Or more simply, "What are all the steps needed to get SOA 'right'?"

A firm needs a proven approach built and preferably tested by numerous *other* customer experiences that outlines all of the steps (both technical and nontechnical) needed to reap the benefits of SOA. Most organizations implementing SOA quickly realize that benefits are not really achieved without a plan for SOA governance. That is, reuse in concept is easy to grasp; however, delivering on the promise of SOA with shared services used across multiple business processes, across multiple business units or organizations, and across multiple cost centers, is much more difficult to pull off. For this reason, we've spent much time helping firms implement an SOA Center of Excellence—the SOA COE.

SOA COE Prescription for Success

In this section, we address these questions via a prescriptive approach that we define here as the SOA Center of Excellence model. An SOA Center of Excellence is a central team that manages all aspects of SOA delivery and establishes a foundational set of processes and artifacts that will accelerate the transformation to an SOA. It is the focal point for SOA activity and SOA governance within an enterprise. The SOA COE is a foundational activity because it guides the rest of the actual design, build, and operate phases of implementing an SOA. It is important to stress that the SOA transformation is a business transformation. Therefore, the COE addresses key requirements and details a roadmap for both business and IT. Key SOA best practices, standards, procedures, and governance processes as well as technologies are set up prior to mass-scale development of services. It is also important to note that for some organizations, an existing architecture team may be empowered to act as an SOA COE and, in some cases, organizations may choose to only go through the roadmap of activities to formalize their strategy without creating a COE organization.

In the latter case, organizations would establish the architecture approach, standards, life-cycle processes, reference architectures, and SOA infrastructure to enable coordinated and efficient SOA development activity downstream but forego the creation of a central team. Either way, the goal of the engagement is to enable organizations to accelerate their journey towards a SOA.

With the rich set of SOA COE artifacts, organizations are able to accelerate their SOA journey because virtually everything they need to do get the SOA transformation started properly is laid out for them including management and governance processes, people/organizational structure, service lifecycle processes, reference architectures, and technology. The COE team is armed with a valuable "toolbag," or comprehensive guide including step-by-step processes, templates, delivery guides, and tools.

Details of the SOA COE Roadmap

The SOA COE provides a detailed step-by-step approach enabling SOA adoption and governance, as well as guiding future implementation. The engagement process consists of two tracks: a management track and a technical track. The management track is tailored for the business, program managers, and lead architects and the technical track is geared towards technical architects and implementers of SOA. For example, key management metrics such as service reuse, refactoring percentages (how much a service has to be modified for reuse), percent reduction in service development effort, and so forth are all laid out in an SOA Metrics Definition guide.

Some of the other management track templates and tools include an SOA COE organization model, engagement model (which implies a consultative model, incidentally), an SOA COE list of roles and responsibilities, and an SOA COE incentive model describing how the organization will encourage teams to develop services that get reused.

Real-World SOA Case Study: HP

In this section, we demonstrate a real-world example of using web services to integrate with SAP. HP has multiple channels in which are products such as desktops and laptops. Unlike the business model of its competitors, HP relies not only on its own direct consumer business through HP's online website but also through retail partner websites such as Costco.com, Staples.com, BestBuy.com, and many others. Prior to the use of interoperable web services, HP had to create and maintain a custom site dedicated to each retailer that would ultimately interface with data and transactions running on HP's SAP ERP back-end system. Additionally, it would take many months for a new retailer to come online and begin revenue-generating transactions.

HP's solution to the retail-partner integration was to deploy a set of web services that could be used by each retailer (see Figure 29.2). In this manner, the core functionality of the SAP ERP system, such as product model definition, configuration rules, order management, and integration with HP suppliers was hidden while retail-centric web services were exposed. The web services that were exposed included the following:

▶ Distribute product catalog

▶ Query product information

▶ Query order status

▶ Validate configuration

▶ Place order

▶ Request price

▶ Request basket transfer

As a result of these web services, HP was able to reduce the integration time for new retailers from 4–8 months down to 2–4 months, greatly speeding up the time to revenue for HP. Additionally, all retailers were able to access these web services from their existing website maintaining their look and feel while still having the flexibility of running their

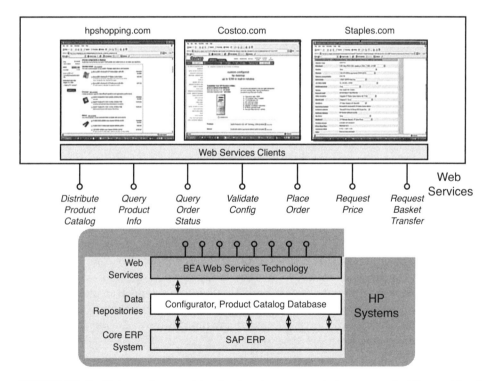

FIGURE 29.2   Web services enables front-end resources to be exposed while masking the back-end ERP system.

own promotions and synchronize a shopping basket between the retailer's items and HP's items. This was the first implementation of a configure-to-order capability between a computer manufacturer and its retailer partners powered by web services and SAP.

Final Thoughts on SOA for SAP

As we have seen, SOA represents a distinct departure from SAP systems that are designed and integrated with other systems from the ground up as well as a departure from deploying prepackaged client/server applications. SOA provides for definitions and methods of building a business-enabling IT infrastructure that makes it possible to not only exchange data between different systems and other data repositories, but to build and extend business processes through reusable and modular developer activity.

For our readers with a background in programming, you have known for years the value of modular programming, where chunks of code can be easily reused. This approach to development takes a bit more time up front, but saves a huge amount of time in the long run, particularly with regard to ongoing maintenance and when widescale business process changes are required. SOA takes the same approach but from an architecture perspective. SOA segregates functionality into modular services, which in turn can be combined and reused to create and more easily change business applications. SAP implementation teams interested in reducing the significant cost of maintaining an SAP system post go-live absolutely must consider and thoughtfully adopt eSOA wherever possible.

Summary

In this chapter, we learned not only what SOA is, but its advantages and challenges. We looked at SOA technologies including the Enterprise Service Bus (ESB) and then investigated how SOA may be leveraged to unlock SAP's functionality. Next, we learned how to marry SOA with SAP through BAPIs, Web Services, and Process Integration, and how SAP integration is enabled through an ESB. We concluded the chapter by presenting a proven approach for introducing and caring for SOA services via the SOA Center of Excellence (COE). The SOA COE provides a prescriptive strategy and approach to help ensure a successful SOA program. It enables organizations to employ a proven technique in addressing SOA challenges. This in turn greatly accelerates SOA implementation and adoption while significantly reducing SOA's inherent risks along the SOA-for-SAP journey.

Case Study: Introducing SOA at HiTech, Inc.

HiTech, Inc.'s senior IT leadership team is considering SOA for SAP. SAP has already been deployed in business units throughout the company, and several new SAP component implementations are currently underway. HiTech's SAP development organization has only limited exposure to service-oriented architecture. You need to answer several questions posed by HiTech's developer organization.

Questions

1. How might SOA be compared to building blocks? What are the advantages of this perspective to the development team?

2. What is the relationship between SAP NetWeaver and the System Landscape Directory (SLD)?

3. What is the primary difference between the Business Process Engine and Workflow Engine?

4. Explain systems integration and how SOA will change the way HiTech will perform systems integration.

NOTE

The answers to these questions can be found in Appendix A, "Case Study Answers."

PART IV

Planning for Go-Live

CHAPTER 30

Project Management Checkpoint 3: Project Team Retention

Because they span one or more years, project retention is critical to completing an SAP project; nothing derails a complex business application implementation like losing key people. In this chapter, we cover six keys to retention spanning motivation, compensation, communications, and more. Prior to addressing these retention matters, we take a critical look at leadership behaviors necessary to properly set the stage (see Chapter 12 for a detailed introduction).

Setting the Foundation: Leadership and Behaviors

At the heart of project and indeed organizational longevity is a concept we're all familiar with: employee retention. Creating an organizational structure, culture, and rewards system that effectively retains its talented workforce is no accident. Organizations seem to constantly reinvent themselves as they bounce between the need to retain their staff, react to marketplace realities, and change with the times. That so many organizations have reorganized themselves again and again in the last several years is therefore not surprising. What *is* surprising is how few of these organizations have reorganized or reinvented themselves well.

Even when we pull SAP completely out of the equation, the modern IT/business workplace has become a place of change. Back in Chapter 12, we talked of leadership approaches that have been shown to be effective in introducing change-enabling systems. Through transformational, servant-led, and contingent leadership behaviors and styles, an SAP project's executive committee, project management office (PMO), and various team leaders can transform their workplace while keeping the organization on track to achieve new heights enabled by change and characterized by adaptability. But how is this adaptability made possible? There are several methods. Attention to human development factors can lead to organizational behavior and design that not only positions a company for long-term success, but also serves to create, shape, and reinforce a culture willing to reinvent itself for the sake of its customers and other stakeholders, and ultimately its own longevity.

Organizational decomposition can also help, by illuminating individual followers and the challenges faced by leadership. And assessing and molding organizational behavior can explain workplace performance in light of the changing workplace landscape. But it's *transforming leadership* that enables change and adaptability within the modern IT workplace—and it's this same transforming leadership that sets the stage for the kind of SAP-centric workforce retention that enables an organization to reinvent itself without running off the tracks. Some of the most important tenets of transformational leadership affecting retention are discussed next.

Intellectual Stimulation

One of the most important attributes a technology or business leader can practice is referred to as *intellectual stimulation*, which is a leadership behavior that promotes and rewards risk taking, intelligence, and innovation, to encourage followers to solve problems in new ways. Leaders need to understand how much they can and should intellectually stimulate their teams.

Too little stimulation jeopardizes the project from the standpoint that the organization—whether technical-, business-, or project management–oriented—will fail to push boundaries that need to be pushed. By way of example, an organization that is unwilling to try new approaches and left on its own will seek to preserve the status quo, and everything from business processes to computing platforms and staffing models will suffer from a lack of innovation.

Pushed too eagerly to innovate, though, and an organization might quickly find itself in territory so unfamiliar and so *risky* that the project's progress will be stalled in the wake of infighting, scrambling to figure out how to support the new system, and so on.

Inspirational Motivation

Good leaders lead, but great leaders inspire and motivate their followers to perform beyond expectations. Transformational leadership motivates and raises a follower's awareness about what's important to achieve, personal values, and other factors intended to support the collective goals and vision of the organization. Transformational leaders uplift the morale, motivation, and morals of their followers to think beyond themselves and serve the greater good. This combination essentially describes one of transformational leadership's greatest attributes: *inspirational motivation.*

How such leadership affects retention is simple: People will not only line up to become part of such an organization, but will stay the course despite project setbacks, less-than-stellar execution, and less-than-excellent working conditions. Inspirational leadership encourages followers to look beyond the immediate and focus on a bright new horizon—exactly what an SAP implementation calls for.

Individualized Consideration

Probably one of the most overlooked leadership behaviors, *individualized consideration*, speaks to the degree to which leaders provide personal attention, coaching, or sound personal advice. By treating followers as individuals and not merely "human resources," this leadership dimension or factor can spell the difference between long-term employee retention and high turnover.

The focus of leaders who practice individualized consideration is to develop some level of relationship with their team members rather than more generically with "the team." The more a leader can build these individual bridges and then grow them through authentic care and feeding, the more apt the organization is to remain intact. Of course, it's more difficult and much more time consuming than might be expected. Personal attention requires knowledge of individuals gained through personal interaction, whether in person, online, or through other settings. And practicing individualized consideration requires an understanding of the type of people and personalities embodied by each individual, which warrants its own discussion next.

Understanding Support Staff Personalities

Companies adept at change can indeed thrive, but as most of us can attest to, poorly managed change is much worse than change itself. In most cases, managers essentially become developers of people and builders of teams. Sure, left alone they might be poor developers and horrible builders, but they're growing their people and teams nonetheless. Thus, it's important to arm the organization's leaders with the tools and insight necessary to keep the team both productive and intact. One way of doing this is by helping leaders understand the personalities of their followers.

What if managers and leaders fail to understand the very people they have been asked to lead? What happens when leadership either purposely ignores or inadvertently overlooks their teams' personalities and individual attributes? In short, nothing positive comes out of such oversight. There's no way for individualized consideration to make a difference, or for intellectual stimulation to be applied when and where it's really needed. Attempts at inspirational motivation may fall on deaf ears, too, as leaders out of tune with their followers will be less likely to strike a chord that truly resonates. For these reasons, a seasoned leader will take the time to understand not only their organizational structure (and how things get done, both formally and informally), but also what makes individuals tick—what motivates them. In our experience leading complex SAP projects around the globe, we've realized that individuals fall into one of two very broad categories or buckets:

- ▶ Project workers, or new project (NP) personality types

- ▶ Steady-state workers, or support/maintenance (SM) personality types

Both of these are described in more detail in the next few pages.

Project Workers: Motivated to Achieve

If your SAP implementation was performed exclusively by NP personality types, you would likely probably finish the design and implementation well ahead of schedule and under budget. These people work hard, love to learn, and thrive under pressure and deadlines. They embrace change, making them perfect candidates for SAP implementations and upgrades. However, you'd quickly run into problems as go-live came and went and the implementation moved into the "maintain" phase. Why? Because project workers are motivated to achieve when the learning curves are steep and the rules can be bent in the name of getting things done. Project workers become less of an asset and more of a liability as implementation goals give way to the need for incremental operational excellence, routine systems maintenance, and stringent change control.

Like anything, employing project workers comes with its share of trade-offs. Some of the trade-offs associated with employing a team of project workers (NP types) are as follows:

▶ They are less interested in formal processes and procedures, and more interested in developing new (or transforming existing) processes.

▶ They tend to be the most challenging people to work with, as they are often accomplished and experienced, with an ego to match.

▶ With their experience and ideas, people naturally turn to project workers as thought leaders within their particular disciplines.

▶ They tend to get bored with repetitive tasks, and therefore tend to be less satisfied and less effective in operations and on-going maintenance and support roles.

▶ They are inclined to put off documentation and other such details, interested instead in "making it work" or "setting it up" and then moving on. If you value timely and precise documentation, you may therefore be disappointed. NP types prefer to churn and burn, leaving documentation to their support/maintenance colleagues.

▶ They find little value in standing still. As such, they need to be kept busy with projects and assignments that challenge them, force them to learn, and generally push them out of their comfort limits. If you can't do this, they'll find a project or an employer who can.

New project types like to make things happen. But as we alluded to, when things transition from project-oriented to more steady-state tasks, you need to begin transitioning a different kind of SAP project person into your organization. As the SAP support organization matures even prior to go-live, a more effective mix of both project workers and steady-state workers needs to be achieved.

Steady-State Workers: Keeping Things Running

The weaknesses of the project workers tend to represent strengths of what are often labeled steady-state workers, or support/maintenance (SM) personality types. These people are motivated by and attracted to different things than what project workers are motivated by and attracted to. Be clear—neither personality type is innately better than the other. You need and want both on your SAP implementation. The trick is to understand the kind of job roles that have been created throughout the organization and then staff them with the best type of worker. For example, steady-state workers prefer roles with regular hours, less travel, more routine or scheduled tasks, and proven documented procedures. They thrive in operational roles or jobs that are less open-ended and more concrete. Steady-state workers prefer to work within a framework defined by roles, responsibilities, lines of authority, and so on. In our experience:

- Steady-state workers often become long-term and loyal employees (or in some cases, long-term contractors).

- Steady and dependable, these people show up every day and often represent the operational "core" of an organization.

- These support personnel are less apt to embrace change as quickly as their project-oriented counterparts.

For new project teams, carefully assess each role and staff accordingly. A team of 20 might equate to an even mix of perhaps 10 of each personality type (or weighted more toward project workers), keeping in mind that several of your project workers will probably transition into new roles or areas as your project nears go-live, while your steady-state workers will take on maintenance roles near and dear to their hearts. An excellent transition from an SAP ERP implementation, for example, might include moving some of the best project workers into roles supporting an upcoming SAP NetWeaver BW or Portal implementation. On the other hand, you might task your best steady-state workers with building post-go-live teams and support processes, stocking the knowledge repository, and so on.

As long as you understand what motivates your team, and take action to meet these needs, you'll be that much more apt to maintain and retain your organization and its most valuable resources. The two types of workers we've described here complement each other in a symbiotic kind of way—it's up to the various SAP business and technical team leads and project managers to ensure the mix of resources reflects what's in the project's best interests.

Keys for Retaining Employees

In the course of assembling and leading SAP implementation teams, we have run across many different leadership styles, management and staffing practices, motivational techniques, and so on. Some of these practices have been shown over time to be quite effective, while others less so. In the next several sections we have brought together arguably the best of these practices. Called "keys to retention," they encompass the following:

- Understanding motivational factors

- Tending to basic compensation

- Providing regular and meaningful communication

- Praising a job well done

- Including performance and other incentive bonuses

30

▶ Addressing training and career path opportunities

Most of the remaining sections in this chapter illuminate what we view as these practical and most important keys to SAP project team retention.

Understanding Team Motivation

It's critical that team leaders, managers, and other leaders actively learn what motivates their team. Motivation is at the heart of leadership. The methods shown most effective in motivating or providing incentive for others to follow vary considerably, though, based on many different leadership and follower attributes. This is where the leadership attributes we outlined previously—intellectual stimulation, inspirational motivation, and individualized consideration—come into play. Understanding what motivates your team underpins everything.

Leadership serves as the foundation for motivation; great leaders can motivate others to achieve goals beyond their own expectations because they *know* their followers. More precisely, these leaders know what makes their people tick. They have taken the time to understand what motivates their team.

Great leaders also know that motivation wanes over time. Motivation is therefore about more than just triggering it up front; motivation must be sustained to be of worth (in terms of not just maximizing productivity but encouraging team retention and follow-on organizational longevity). This comes in many different flavors as we read next, from compensation and communication to providing recognition and more.

Offering Competitive Pay

We would be remiss to not cover the importance of market-leading compensation plans—the kind of compensation plans that take into account current SAP market and technology conditions to reward low supplies of particular skill sets with high dollars, and so on. The last thing your team needs is someone leaving it simply to make a few thousand dollars a year more somewhere else. Here it is, then—pay your people fairly, don't muck with their paychecks, and review salary levels at least annually. Said another way, the matter of pay can easily become an excuse for leaving, but it is often not enough in itself to justify staying.

Salaries and benefits are the groundwork atop which a reward project, if not an entire career, are built. In the real world of SAP consulting and project work, a good salary motivates people to show up at work only for a few weeks. A good raise might even keep someone's interest another week or two. But it's a short-term motivator at best. After that, it's up to the SAP project manager and various technical, business, and functional leads to stay on top of what motivates their team members to continue to excel in their positions. This latter point is critical to understanding the importance of communication, discussed in the following section.

Communicating Regularly and Meaningfully

Good communication is essential right from the beginning and never really takes a back seat in an SAP deployment. From pulling together an organization's solution vision to conducting team meetings, introducing new employees, and so on, regular and meaningful communication sets the stage for a project's success. Regular internal team meetings and broader "stay-in-the-loop" meetings reinforce how important sound verbal communication is—they keep teams moving not only forward, *but in the same direction.*

Weekly and even daily *meeting minutes,* or the details as to who attended a meeting and the subsequent action items discussed and delegated to meeting members, represent a critical written communication forum. Other written forums include regular status updates collected from each team member and assembled into a single SAP project team status update. Collected weekly, these updates often serve as agendas for further discussion, or to ensure that action items are indeed addressed and eventually put to rest.

In all the time we have spent in countless meetings and conference calls with SAP customers and partners, we've noticed that "communication happens" regardless of whether it's driven formally or informally. Our observation is that it's best to be the driver; otherwise, someone else with poor vision will gladly get behind the steering wheel and take you and your whole team off on some pretty crazy tangents. And specifically with regard to holding and attending meetings, we feel the following few points are the most important:

▶ Show up on time, and start on time. It shows respect for others and for the project overall.

▶ Meetings must be short enough for participants to stay focused, and long enough to cover the material to be discussed. We've seen plenty of effective meetings wrap up in 20 minutes, and plenty of ineffective meetings drag on for hours.

▶ Err on the side of shorter rather than longer meetings to at least give everyone a chance to get some real work done today.

▶ Meetings are about communicating direction and vision and helping people stay on track by identifying and figuring out how to remove roadblocks. In this respect, meetings are essentially another way of building the organization's culture and creating a singularly minded community. If your meetings are divisive, you're doing none of this. Figure out what (or who!) needs to change and do it immediately.

▶ If no action items come out of a meeting, the meeting was a waste of time in the first place. Avoid repeating such meetings! Meetings perceived to be a waste of time will be infrequently attended, and thus will serve less and less purpose over time.

▶ If no one documents the action items (that is, via meeting minutes), there is a better chance that they will not get addressed. Action items promote accountability in that they tend to remind the responsible parties that things need to happen before the project can move into the next phase.

30

▶ If no one is assigned to take meeting minutes and publish them to the team within a day or so, less will get done. The person calling the meeting is ultimately responsible for documenting the meeting minutes (though delegating this task is common).

▶ If no one follows up on the status of action items out of meeting minutes, they are less effective, too. In most circumstances, we like the idea of the meeting organizer using the previous meeting's minutes as an initial agenda for the next meeting. For increased efficiency, it may be better to decide on a review schedule for each action item, such that subsequent meetings don't have to address each and every status item, but rather only the ones scheduled for review that day.

▶ Take the time to document all but the most obvious of acronyms in all communications. The number of three-letter acronyms that SAP and its partners not only create but just as quickly assume are universally understood by the rest of us is overwhelming at times.

Regular communication instills confidence in and within a team or organization. And because regular productive meetings and other communications forums allow the team to be involved as a cohesive unit, they tend to promote improved team morale. In essence, you are more apt to feel like part of a successful team charged with a mission, and therefore happier, when regular meetings force action and ultimately progress.

Finally, there is also a link between communication and staff retention in the form of visibility of accomplishments. Most everyone enjoys a meeting in which their own accomplishments are noted and praised. Similarly, checking off action items and other to-dos via posted meeting minutes makes accomplishments visible, and ensures that an individual's effort is noted and acknowledged. People generally like to look good in the eyes of their peers, and they will often work harder to make sure that they are viewed as capable and competent—so be sure to recognize this when you can. The competitive nature in most people will help keep your organization well tuned and productive as long as this kind of peer acceptance goal is pursued and discussed in a healthy manner.

Recognizing and Praising Team Members

Have you ever been told "good job!" by someone who sincerely valued your effort? Words of appreciation like that often do more for morale and team building than any annual raise or Christmas bonus. Sure, we all show up at work to get paid, but what really keeps most of us the happiest is encouraging words of thanks and appreciation. We like to refer to this as the all-important "attaboy" or "attagirl" approach to reducing employee turnover. Sincere and warranted positive feedback means so much to everyone.

Of course, like anything else, if praise is carelessly tossed around, it will lose its significance. A smart SAP project manager or team leader will use positive feedback just enough to keep it both unanticipated and "special." And the best project managers and team leaders will understand that timing is everything, and do their best to deliver timely, well-deserved praise and recognition.

One way to keep one-on-one praise from sounding canned is for a project manager or lead to give it publicly, increasing a member's visibility to her team and with regard to the SAP project in general. In doing this, the PM or lead is putting his people before himself, taking a potential risk by implying that a component of the project's success is less the result of his own personal contribution than it is one of the team member's. In our view, this makes the PM or lead that much better to work for, though the following must be observed:

▶ Public attaboys need to be given to the person or team actually responsible for completing the work or achieving a particular milestone. Doing anything else risks infuriating or disheartening others.

▶ No real good comes out of praise that is distributed for political gain rather than for performance-worthy reasons. The team tends to know the truth anyway, so personal credibility is tarnished if you give politically motivated praise.

▶ Regularly scheduled praise, like that given during monthly meetings or updates, can sound forced. Rather than making praise an agenda item, practice giving it out randomly in the same way that truly outstanding work is typically performed— rarely, rather than on a clock.

▶ If a person is predisposed to giving public recognition, she needs to ensure that it is distributed among different teams and different individuals. This should be easy, as no SAP solution was ever single-handedly implemented. Doing otherwise can easily damage morale.

▶ Too much public praise, like private praise, loses its impact.

While equitable compensation and other incentive plans lay the groundwork for employment, it's the regular use of authentic and well-deserved recognition that keeps many team members grounded during the ups and downs of a complex and stressful SAP project. If you're a leader of a technical, business, or functional SAP support team, think about this the next time you catch your breath between meetings and conference calls: While underperformers take a lot of time and work to elevate their performance or to move them out of your organization, it's a much more difficult and time-consuming proposition to replace even *one* of your SAP superstars, much less several.

Providing Performance and Other Incentive Bonuses

Performance bonuses are great for motivating behavior aimed at meeting goals or deadlines. For example, it's not uncommon to hear about $5,000, $10,000, and larger bonuses being handed out to individual contributors after SAP go-live, and much larger bonuses doled out to those holding key leadership positions. Similarly, cash bonuses and paid time off are also popular ways of rewarding the individuals responsible for meeting key SAP project milestones, such as the completion of the SAP stress test or rapid configuration of a development environment.

Beyond cash, equity is another great tool. Stock options and stock grants that vest over several years have the added advantage of helping retain a team's key contributors well past go-live. In our experience, to make these types of incentive bonuses meaningful, you'll need to use them frequently enough to help everyone understand they're real, and make them impactful enough to encourage everyone to strive for them. A grant of 10 shares (unless they're Berkshire Hathaway shares!) will do little to keep your key contributors around another few years. On the other hand, the potential to earn an equity award equivalent to half one's annual salary will get people's attention.

When doling out cash and other awards, it's also important to stratify the award based on performance. The award for an individual who has clearly outperformed the rest of the team needs to be appropriately sized. In our experience, such an award should be 2 to 10 times the size of an "average" team member's award. The distinction between top performers and solid performers will give everyone something to strive for, and in the end enable those top performers to enjoy an award consistent with their investment into the project's success.

Finally, be sure to establish clear metrics for awards and bonuses well before they're paid out, and do whatever you can to keep these metrics from changing. There's almost nothing worse than expecting a fat payout only to find that the actual check of equity award was calculated in some obscure way that essentially whittled much of it away. Set your targets, establish metrics for measuring those targets, and gladly pay on them when they're achieved.

Many other incentives exist, too, such as providing training. In the name of employee retention, in the next section we cover how to leverage this promise of training to not only bring the right people on board, but to help keep much of the overall team intact.

Supplying Training and Career Path Opportunities

The promise of end-of-project training can be just the encouragement a team needs to drive successful completion of an SAP project, whether the team is composed of employees, long-term contractors, or even consultants. The idea is simple—if you go above and beyond expectations to make the project successful, you'll be rewarded with the opportunity to learn new technologies, SAP components, or functional areas so that you'll be prepared to assist with the next "big thing" at the company or client site. Of course, the real matter at hand is knowing whether such a promise of training is the kind of carrot your team is interested in. Will it motivate them members to achieve beyond your expectations?

It has been our experience, for example, that tasks become mundane over time. Maybe your star SAP technologist has set up ten SAP/Oracle high-availability clusters in the last year alone and is no longer challenged by the prospect of doing another cluster. In this case, the excitement is gone, and the SAP technology honeymoon she might have enjoyed at one time is over. To be sure, your technologist, if she is a support/maintenance type, might be quite pleased with her role. But if she's more of a project worker than a maintenance type of person, the promise of learning a new technology or getting involved in a new project with new training requirements might be just what she needs to stay motivated. This approach could be exactly what's required to keep the individual committed and on schedule with regard to the current cluster project. As an added bonus, ask this team member to identify innovative implementation or configuration alternatives to the standard process (if appropriate)—perhaps there's a less costly, faster, or cleaner method of performing these installations. Reward anything useful that comes out of your request, particularly innovation that's indeed compelling and repeatable.

Compensation Alternatives in the Real World

Although positive feedback, bonuses, training opportunities, and the promise of career advancement certainly motivate most SAP professionals, other compensation alternatives play a key role in maintaining and retaining staff. We think very highly of many of these, and count ourselves lucky to have participated in quite a variety of interesting "compensation alternatives" such as those listed here:

▶ One company we supported for three months would surprise the SAP war room folks at least once a week with a catered lunch. Both the company and the individual consultants benefited greatly. We ate for free without messing around with lunch-time traffic and lines, and the company got an extra 30 minutes of productive time, not to mention the benefit of informal meetings over lunch and the improved morale and loyalty that only really good New York–style pizza and subs can provide.

▶ Still one of our favorites after all these years is the $100-bill story. On a weekly basis during the regular daily status meeting, one of our SAP client PMs would start the meeting by handing out a new $100 bill to the member of the team who solved the nastiest customer problem that week (or achieved some other notable goal). Regardless of the reason for the award, if you're looking for a way to get everybody to your meeting on time, this method works! Even a high-dollar SAP consultant likes a new $100 bill.

▶ Several SAP Basis and other SAP technology or business managers we know would take the whole team out for incredible no-expenses-spared steak dinners on a regular basis. It was always an event to look forward to. And in the case of one of our favorite customers who absolutely loved a good meal, there was never any pressure to skip appetizers or dessert, or eat in a hurry. Or even go back to work or the hotel.

▶ Another client of ours in a very rural part of the Midwest insisted that we, as consultants, get the "good rooms" at the local hotel for our short SAP infrastructure upgrade project. As it turned out, the town was something of a resort in the summer, but nearly emptied out after snow started falling (in September!). And the "good rooms" wound up being enormous suites with huge televisions, fabulous views, and yes, gigantic Jacuzzi-style tubs—not a bad way to spend part of the winter.

▶ An SAP PM we worked for enjoyed treating different members of the team to an afternoon of noncompetitive golf at any number of expensive or select club courses.

30

He did a really good job of taking nearly everyone on the team at least once through the life of the project. Not only was it a great way to put off work for half a day (because the work never actually goes away in the world of SAP consulting or support), it also provided each team member the PM's ear for five or six hours. There's no better way to practice real-world individualized consideration than in your team member's backswing.

▶ An SAP customer support center with which we worked used the "SAP Engineer of the Month" award as a means of rewarding the team member who demonstrated unique troubleshooting or problem-solving skills. Although the honor was nice, the best part of the deal was a paid parking spot next to the client's downtown building. Believe us, it was a coveted award! We've seen several other SAP project leaders effectively use parking as a tool for recognition.

▶ In a twist on the preceding example, one company would give the "SAP Consultant of the Week" two tickets to the city's NBA basketball team when they were playing at home. Even though the team was in pretty sad shape that year, it was still a fun and yet very inexpensive way to break up the week. We've seen many other customers do similar things with professional football, hockey, and of course baseball seats (seeing the Cubs play at Wrigley Field can make a five-day trip away from home seem like a vacation for a night, especially if you go with the peppers and sausage sandwiches and stay away from the large drinks—restrooms are pretty scarce at Wrigley).

▶ Sometimes just having a nice ride makes all the difference. Several of our favorite clients provide (or at least pay the expenses for) convertibles. After a 14-hour day dealing with transports or preparing for the installation of an SAP-on-Windows production cluster, there is nothing quite like throwing the top down in a rental. The California beaches, Texas highways, Sunset Boulevard, the middle of downtown Chicago or Cleveland, near the Bay in San Francisco, or along a lonely stretch of backwoods dirt roads in Canada all become that much more exciting in a ragtop. Trust us, we know.

▶ During the two weeks prior to go-live, one client of ours sprang for a very nice lunch every single day. The only rule was that we could never go to the same place twice. We wound up sampling probably every kind of food available in this small town— what a great couple of weeks!

▶ One of our absolute favorite places to work insisted that every Wednesday be declared "Aloha Wednesday" during the nine months prior to go-live. Why Wednesday, you ask? For maximum turnout—all of your consultants are in town Wednesday, whereas many will opt to leave early if you hold this kind of event on a Friday. Aloha Wednesday equated to half-day work days, volleyball, plenty of liquid refreshments, BBQ chicken or hot dogs or whatever the budget could spare that week, and just plain ol' camaraderie. It is amazing how many technical and business issues can be solved while barbequing chicken, or out on the volleyball court. Good times, good times.

Other kinds of compensation alternatives abound, too, in terms of very simple and inexpensive regular rewards systems. You may prefer, for example, to treat your SAP project team to "consumables," like gift certificates, tickets to the latest movie, and similar one-time-use rewards. Vouchers for $50 meals at really nice or interesting restaurants can be a lot of fun, too. The following are some examples of small gifts and tokens of appreciation that can go a long way in building and maintaining team morale:

▶ One company's project manager gave out weekly awards for the cleanest and messiest work areas. Prizes varied from flowers to gift certificates to company logo shirts and other merchandise. The owner of the messiest work area got a broom or other such token that was rotated from week to week, and they often provided the gift for the following week as well. The whole process was just a fun weekly diversion for the team.

▶ Another company awarded a rotating crystal plaque for the SAP team member of the month, with the name of the latest recipient etched below names of previous recipients. At the end of the year, a ceremony "retired" the plaque, after which it was hung next to other IT and similar group awards near the company's break room. Sure, it just gathered dust at that point, but it was a pretty cool reminder of all the hard work and great camaraderie that went into pulling off the project.

▶ A large SAP hardware vendor's enterprise marketing organization used to treat its SAP Competency Center to regular tickets to basketball and hockey games, with the caveat that they take to the game a customer or other key member in a partner organization. Not a bad way to spend an evening while getting to know your customers (or vendors).

▶ Another favorite SAP customer of ours brought in donuts, bagels, or something similar practically every single morning during the course of a 12-month project. Often, a huge pot of coffee would show up as well. For those of us nonmorning people, this really made getting out of bed a lot easier.

Summary

As you have seen, there are plenty of ways to motivate and ultimately retain your various SAP business, technical, and functional support organizations. Get to know your teams and what motivates them and then use your imagination and budget to give your project a sense of community, camaraderie, and people-focus.

Take the time to understand the two key SAP support staff personalities before you begin filling in organizational charts or planning future projects (or hire into an organization yourself!). If you are a manager or a team leader in an SAP project, pay particular attention to the mix of leadership skills that can prove useful in encouraging employee and team retention—intellectual stimulation, inspirational motivation, and individual consideration. Then take the time to understand the key retention techniques outlined here, from understanding what motivates the team, to addressing salary requirements, practicing regular and meaningful communication, providing performance-oriented and other incentive bonuses, and offering training and career path opportunities.

Pay particular attention to the groundwork created through equitable compensation and other incentive plans. Remember that while underperformers demand a ton of time and work to elevate their performance (or to move them out of the organization), it's a much more difficult and time-consuming proposition to replace your SAP superstars. Finally, never forget the value of well-timed and merited praise. Make it a natural part of your management style, paying special attention to neither miss the right opportunity to praise nor overuse this most important method of keeping your SAP team motivated and onboard for years to come.

Case Study: Retaining Key Team Members

As the technical lead for HiTech, Inc.'s latest SAP implementation (introducing SAP Supplier Relationship Management to the company's internal procurement team), you are in charge of a team of five technologists. Two of your team members are very senior, very experienced, and always ready to take on new challenges, while the other three seem to be reliable but less interested in conquering yet another steep learning curve. Your manager has asked you to put together a retention plan targeted at successfully getting the team through the next nine months.

Questions

1. How would you characterize your team?
2. What are three leadership behaviors that greatly affect employee retention?
3. List at least four of the keys to project team or employee retention we've shared in this book.
4. How might you best reward two of the team's members?
5. How might you best reward the remaining three team members?

NOTE

The answers to these questions can be found in Appendix A, "Case Study Answers."

CHAPTER 31

SAP Infrastructure Operational Considerations

Now that you have your SAP NetWeaver and SAP Business Suite components installed and are preparing for go-live, you are probably wondering what might have been overlooked from an operational perspective. If so, you are right on track, because there are a number of operational considerations that not only deserve your attention but can really get you well positioned for a successful cutover. These areas represent the technology and process "gotchas" that often are overlooked and become the source of problems and challenges in those first weeks and months after go-live. An SAP implementation is a big undertaking on its own, and you do not need unforeseen operational headaches to complicate matters just because you did not know about or plan for them. Some of these topics, such as SAP printing for instance, may be more obvious and may already have your consideration. Other areas, such as the SAP System Copy process, may not yet be on your radar.

In this chapter, we review some of the technologies, processes, and strategies that you want to be thinking about earlier rather than later in your SAP implementation project—these will get you over the hump and help you turn the corner from an implementation to an operational business application. We will also have some tips and helpful SAP transactions, where applicable, to assist you in your journey. Now, let's go turn the corner!

Printing and Faxing Considerations

Although printing and faxing may be simple, day-to-day tasks in any enterprise application, how you print and how you fax and the processes surrounding these tasks can be administratively intensive without proper planning. In this section, we focus not so much on the mechanics of printing and faxing as on the strategies and options available that you should evaluate for your business. As you move through this section, consider the following questions:

▶ Which printing or faxing strategy makes the most sense for my current business model?

▶ In regard to printing and faxing, is it more important for me to offer user functionality to my end-user community or ease of administration for the support personnel?

▶ What common printing and faxing pitfalls is my organization prone to that I can avoid with proper planning?

Printing Strategy

A *printing strategy* for SAP refers to what printing methods or combination of printing methods you will employ for your user community. SAP offers a number of printing methods in its architecture. Before we discuss these options in detail, let us briefly overview the SAP print process and the spool concept.

When a user prints a document, a spool request is first created for that document, as shown in Figure 31.1. A *spool request* is nothing more than a temporary document waiting to be printed at some period in the future, which could be immediate or at a specific date and time. (In fact, "print out immediately" is a specific print option that you can select when printing an SAP document.) This temporary spool request document is waiting on what is known as the output request. In SAP terms, the *output request* is the mechanism that delivers the spool request to a device for output. This could be a physical device such as a printer or another print spool—for instance, a Windows or UNIX operating system spool. Although the print spool concept is a relatively simple process, it is important to understand as we begin to discuss the various SAP methods for printing.

As defined or recognized by SAP, there are seven popular methods for printing:

▶ **Local printing**—Local printing is considered the fastest and most stable of printing methods. It simply involves passing the spool request to the OS spooler on the same host.

▶ **Remote printing**—Remote printing, also called network printing, exists when the SAP spool and the OS spool are not operating on the same host, thus requiring a network to be available to facilitate remote connectivity. For this reason, the performance of remote printing is dependent on a reliable network infrastructure.

▶ **Front-end printing using the SAPGUI for Windows**—Front-end printing, as the name suggests, passes the spool request directly to the OS spooler on the SAP user's workstation. Essentially, the SAPGUI prints to the Windows default printer just like other desktop applications do, such as Microsoft Word.

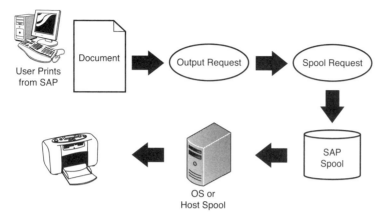

FIGURE 31.1   An SAP document is printed, passed through the SAP spool, and on to the host spool for printing.

▶ **Front-end printing using the SAPGUI for HTML**—Front-end printing using the SAPGUI for HTML, also known as the WebGUI, also works with the front-end workstation; however, the print document is sent as a PDF document to the browser where it can then be printed by the user.

▶ **Front-end printing with control technology**—To understand front-end printing with control technology, you have to first understand the prior generation of front-end printing. Before control technology, SAP required its own Line Printer Daemon (LPD), specifically SAPLPD.exe, to process the handoff from the SAP print spool to the workstation. This executable actually launched in the background every time the user printed to the front end from SAP. Control technology eliminates the need for SAPLPD and calls the Windows printer selection screen directly. Control technology also paved the way for front-end printing with the SAPGUI for Java, which is now available.

▶ **Printing using email**—In addition to traditional spool printing options, SAP also allows for printing via email by sending a PDF document as an attachment. This process uses SAP's built-in SAPConnect-SMTP technology. We discuss SAPConnect further in the section "Faxing Options" later in the chapter.

▶ **Printing Adobe-based forms**—SAP also allows for Adobe-based forms printing as part of its Adobe Document Services technology. This option is discussed further in the next section.

Now that you have a picture of the various printing methods, the next step is to decide which of these options or combination of options might work best in your organization. To assist in this process, we will discuss some common problem areas that you should consider when deciding on a printing strategy.

One of the first items to consider in your printing strategy is whether front-end printing alone will meet your needs. Front-end printing offers the highest ease of administration and maintenance because SAP printers do not have to be mapped to an OS spool server. This means that your Basis administrators and infrastructure teams will not have to maintain a list of dedicated SAP printers, which can be tedious and create challenges as printers are replaced, removed, or upgraded. For this reason, front-end printing is usually the preferred choice, or at least the first choice for most customers.

You might be wondering why you cannot get by with front-end printing alone. Some customers do, but there are several situations in which front-end printing alone might not be sufficient for your business needs. One example is in the area of batch printing. There are two basic options for batch printing: print immediately, or print to the SAP spool without the "print immediately" option. With the second option, this spool request can then be called at a later time and printed via normal front-end printing. If, however, the document needs to be printed overnight so that it is ready the next morning, a local printer or remote printer option is needed so that the document can print without user interaction.

A second situation in which front-ending printing alone might not be sufficient is if a user has a business need to print to a remote printer, such as a printer at another site. Although the user could simply change their default printer on their workstation, this can be cumbersome, especially for less advanced users. If that is the case, a dedicated local or remote printer might have to be configured so that it can be selected by the user in SAP. For example, an HR representative might not want to print a document with sensitive personal information on a public printer. Instead, they would prefer to print the document to a private printer in the HR administrators' office. In this example, a dedicated printer could be set up in SAP that maps directly to the HR Admin printer in a private office.

As a final example, some SAP modules can be configured to print a document during the execution of a business process. For instance, a Material Data Safety Sheet (MSDS) might be printed when a relevant product is ordered or sold. In this case, a dedicated local or remote printer may have to be configured in the module, because front-end printing is not supported in these rare cases.

Now that you have a better understanding of the SAP printing process and printing options, you can make a more informed decision for your organization during your SAP implementation. The next section discusses forms-based printing and SAP's Adobe Document Services.

The Adobe Factor

As of SAP NetWeaver 2004, SAP introduced a new PDF-based form solution as an alternative to the prior SAPScript and Smart Forms technology. These features are now incorporated into both the ABAP Workbench and the SAP NetWeaver Developer Studio. While the purpose of this chapter is not to explore the new suite of Adobe products for SAP, you do need to understand some of the aspects of printing PDF-based forms.

For PDF-based forms delivered by SAP or custom forms created by the development team, Adobe Document Services (ADS) has to be installed on an SAP Java instance to facilitate forms-based printing. Once installed, forms to be printed are sent to ADS in XML format, which returns one or more "parts" for printing. These parts, depicted by the Adobe PDF icon, can then be called from the Output Controller (transaction SP01) and printed either by directly launching the PDF document or by sending the request to a specific printer. Note that printing a PDF-based form to a printer requires a PCL, PostScript, or ZPL printer type. For additional information on configuring ADS and SAP Interactive Forms by Adobe, visit SDN at https://www.sdn.sap.com/irj/sdn/adobe.

Faxing Options

Faxing from SAP is made available via the SAPConnect interface (transaction SCOT), which uses SAP's Business Communication Services (BCS) to send various message types. Although the SMTP and HTTP message types are also supported, SAP faxing is facilitated through the RFC interface for use with third-party software. These companies look to certify their products for use with SAP BCS. Consider the following list of third-party companies certified by SAP for fax messaging technologies:

- Esker DeliveryWare by Esker, Inc.
- Retarus Faxolution for SAP by Retarus GmbH
- AventX Connector for SAP ERP by STR Software
- IXI-UMS Connector by serVonic GmbH
- Crossgate B.I.P. by Crossgate, Inc.
- FACSys Fax Messaging Gateway by emFAST Inc.
- WaveFax Paperless Fax Solution by Wavesource Technologies Co., Ltd.

> **NOTE**
>
> For more information on SAP Certified products, check out the SAP Ecosystem and Partner Catalog at http://sspcatalog.sap.com/catalog/index.jsp.

While these products have various features and levels of functionality, they all work with the SAPConnect interface in similar ways. Let's take a look at some of the common settings in SAPConnect required to fax from SAP.

SAPConnect identifies systems that communicate with SAP as *nodes*, and it supports multiple nodes. For example, you might have a fax node for faxing from SAP, as depicted in Figure 31.2, and an SMTP node for sending email from SAP. In addition, you can have more than one node of each type to handle regional requirements or to load-balance messaging traffic across systems. To create a fax node, the following SAPConnect settings are required:

▶ **Node and Description**—The Node field requires a six-character name to identify the node. Additional text can be provided in the Description field.

▶ **Node Type**—The node type RFC Node should be selected for faxing.

▶ **RFC Destination**—You configure this in transaction SM59, "Configuration of RFC Destinations." Specific information will be available in the documentation for the specific fax solution you have selected.

▶ **Address Type**—Select the Fax radio button from the list of options.

▶ **Address Areas**—This lets you define the criteria for which the node will process. You can use wildcards, and entering * will process all messages. In the case of faxing, a specific country code—for example, US*—can be used to process only U.S.-based fax numbers.

▶ **Output Formats for SAP Documents**—Here you specify the format to which the fax output should be converted. The available document options are HTM, PCL, PS, TXT, and No Conversion.

▶ **Restrict Send Time**—This option allows you to restrict the send time of faxes and prioritize by urgency. This can be used, for example, if you want to send faxes during off-peak hours, when charges are cheaper.

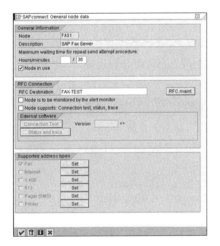 

FIGURE 31.2   By clicking a node, in this case FAX1 in transaction SCOT, you can see the settings. You can further drill down into this information to see the address area and format conversion information.

▶ **Maximum Waiting Time for Repeat Send Attempt Procedure (Hours/Minutes)—** This setting allows you to define the maximum wait time for retrying faxes that might have failed because of a communication failure or busy signal.

▶ **Node in Use—**This check box allows you to quickly enable or disable the node to control messaging traffic.

Before deciding on a fax product, you should prepare a list of business requirements to make sure the product will meet your needs. Although the following points might not cover every decision unique to your organization, they should help you to find the right product and make sure your company is ready for SAP faxing:

▶ Although outbound faxing requirements are the most common, some products and SAP do support Direct Inward Dialing (DID) for inbound fax documents. This requires more complex configurations because internal fax numbers are required for all SAP users that you expect to receive faxes. Consult the documentation of your specific fax vendor for inbound faxing requirements.

▶ Customers who fax should work with their functional teams to determine how customer and vendor master data is maintained. Both SAP and the third-party fax products require that dialing rules be maintained for country codes, area codes, and so forth. For this reason, it is important that master data is input in a consistent manner so that these dialing rules are likewise applied consistently. Otherwise, the result can be a significant number of fax errors due to incorrect dialing, which can be difficult to troubleshoot during production operation.

▶ In regard to troubleshooting, it is very important that you put in place a process for handling fax errors. Depending on how your team is structured, errors can be handled via fax client software by business users, such as customer service representatives, or by technical personnel, such as SAP Basis or fax software administrators. Regardless, it is important that someone monitor faxes for errors and make sure that those in error are re-sent as needed, and re-sent only once in many cases—for example, for invoices or purchase orders, it is important that a duplicate fax not be sent in error. If gone unnoticed, this could result in duplicate orders and create an embarrassing situation with customers or vendors.

SAP Security and Authorizations Management

With SAP implementations comes the addition of new systems and new products, often unfamiliar to your IT department, which presents new challenges. In this section, we discuss SAP security and authorizations management as it relates to infrastructure operations. Specifically, we discuss managing users, roles, and the concept of identity management in an SAP environment and address what topics you should reflect on as you attempt to mesh these technologies and processes into your environment.

31

Managing Users

At one time, managing users in SAP was limited to the ABAP stack of that particular system. Users had to be maintained in the individual R/3, Business Warehouse (BW), or similar systems with no integration. Today, user integration with SAP and non-SAP systems is much more prevalent, made possible by both SAP and third-party technologies. In this section, we introduce the User Management Engine (UME) and Central User Administration (CUA) and explain how they may help you to manage users going forward.

The UME was introduced as a means to centralize users for SAP Java applications. As SAP Java applications continued to grow within SAP landscapes, SAP recognized the challenge in keeping these users (often the same users) in sync. For example, the same users may exist in a company's directory services, multiple SAP ABAP–based systems, multiple SAP Java–based systems, and SAP Enterprise Portal systems. Obviously, this can be difficult to administer from an operational perspective and could create the need for larger security teams in terms of full time equivalents (FTEs). The UME addressed part of this problem by allowing SAP Java–based systems to leverage a user store (also called a persistence store) on a remote system. The UME recognizes the following as valid user stores:

▶ **LDAP directory**—Supported LDAP directories include, among others, Novell eDirectory, Sun ONE Directory Server, Microsoft Active Directory Server, and Siemens DirX.

▶ **SAP ABAP system**—Any SAP system installed with an ABAP stack can act as the UME.

▶ **SAP Java database**—For Java-based systems, the UME can utilize the installed Java database.

Whereas the UME allows a system to leverage a remote user store, CUA can consolidate administration and maintenance of users in one system. CUA defines the controlling system as the *central system* and all other systems as *child systems*, which are updated from the central system via SAP ALE (application link enabling) connections. In this way, the central system acts as the central user repository for all systems in the landscape. Any changes made in the central system are distributed to all child systems automatically. As part of the configuration process, distribution parameters are set so that only common data among the CUA systems is synchronized. This way, any application-specific data that is unique to the child system is not overwritten.

Now that we have reviewed the UME and CUA, let's take a look at an example that utilizes both concepts. Figure 31.3 depicts a combined scenario for a Microsoft environment running multiple SAP products. The SAP Enterprise Portal UME is using Microsoft Active Directory (AD) as its persistence store. As a result, the users assigned in AD will be available in the portal to have appropriate roles assigned. At the same time, the SAP ERP system has been configured as the central system for CUA and for LDAP synchronization with the same Microsoft AD used by SAP Enterprise Portal. Finally, the SAP Business Warehouse (BW) and SAP Supplier Relationship Management (SRM) systems have been set up as child systems in the CUA landscape. As you can see, this provides a great advantage: The user accounts are in sync across all systems, because they rely on the same directory services. Not only does this have obvious administrative advantages but user synchronization offers further benefits in areas such as single sign-on as well as with role management, which leads us to our next topic.

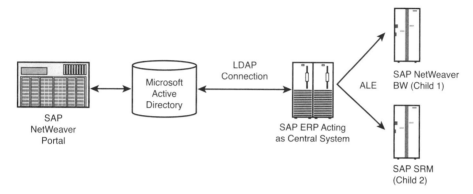

FIGURE 31.3   UME and CUA concepts may be combined to reduce redundant administration tasks.

Managing Roles

The process of managing users is not complete until those users have been assigned roles to control their access in the individual SAP systems. In more complex landscapes that include a mix of ABAP, Java, and Enterprise Portal environments, managing roles, like managing users, can be a challenge. In this section, we discuss managing roles and relate that to the discussion of UME and CUA in the prior section.

SAP security roles, often simply called *roles*, may vary slightly in definition, but in a nutshell, they control user access to objects within an SAP system. These objects may be data, transactions, screens, or a host of other objects common to SAP systems. There are several different types of roles:

▶ **ABAP roles**—ABAP roles are the most common and widely known roles as part of the SAP NetWeaver AS ABAP stack.

▶ **Portal roles**—Portal roles are the standard roles delivered within an SAP Enterprise Portal installation.

▶ **Java roles**—Within the SAP NetWeaver AS Java database, there are two different types of roles, UME roles and J2EE roles.

For the purposes of this section, we focus on the ABAP and Portal roles because they are most commonly used and integrated. ABAP roles control access or authorization to a given SAP back-end system, such as SAP ERP, SAP BW, or SAP CRM. Portal roles control the user interface information. In simplest terms, ABAP roles determine what you can do in a system and the Portal roles govern what you can see. For example, suppose you are a company employee and have access to log in to the company's SAP NetWeaver Portal to maintain your employee information. In the portal, you have to be assigned access to a specific Employee Self-Services (ESS) iView or set of iViews to update your personal information. However, you also have to have authorization to the HR information in the HR module of the back-end SAP ERP system. So, if you have portal access without the back-end authorizations, you'll be able to see the ESS iView when you log in but you won't be able to retrieve any of your personal information from the back end. Vice versa, back-end authorization without the correct Portal roles will result in a runtime error, because you will not be able to view the portal ESS screen.

As you can see, user role management be carefully coordinated to make sure end-to-end access is facilitated. Now let's take a look at managing these roles in the context of our prior discussion on the UME and CUA.

From an administration perspective, roles, like users can be maintained in the UME, in the ABAP system, or in the central system of a CUA landscape. In the case of an SAP Enterprise Portal implementation, the decision on where roles will be maintained has to be architected based on where roles will originate—the portal or the back-end system. Often, this decision is based on which component is in place first and where administrative expertise already exists. For instance, a company that has invested years in developing SAP R/3 or ERP roles and authorizations will likely use the ABAP system or CUA to leverage existing work that has already been performed. Depending on the method used, role administration works as follows:

▶ **Roles administered in ABAP system or CUA**—Existing ABAP roles are uploaded to the portal, and then portal roles are built referencing the ABAP roles from the back-end systems.

▶ **Roles administered in the Portal**—Roles are created in the portal, distributed to the back end or the CUA central systems, and then assigned new or existing ABAP roles at that time. (When you distribute roles from the portal, you can create new authorizations or replace existing authorizations.)

Regardless of the scenario used, the administrator has to work with the technical and business teams to identify and map roles logically between one or more portal systems and the various systems in the landscape as requirements dictate. This planning process is a key success factor as new portals or new ABAP systems are introduced in the environment. It is also important to maintain consistent processes among administrators. Duplicate roles, authorizations, or delta links can clutter the systems if common procedures are not followed. Finally, with integration can come some complexities in regard to troubleshooting for the security and technical teams. For instance, what may appear to be a portal error could be a result of a back-end authorization problem and vice versa. In these cases, it is always a best practice to try and isolate the problem. In this example, if direct access to the back end is available, it may be valuable to log in and validate an authorization error before spending too much time looking into a portal issue that possibly does not exist.

We finish this section with a brief look at SAP's Identity Management product, which will be a major tool in user and role management in the future.

Identity Management

Many of the topics discussed in this section, including user management, role management, CUA, and user and role integration, are now all subtopics of what SAP has labeled Identity Management. In addition, there is also a distinct product available—SAP NetWeaver Identity Management Identity Center. Features include

- Workflow

- Rules and rules-based provisioning

- Meta directory

- Password management

- Audit and monitoring

- Regulatory compliance

Identity Management will build on SAP's existing security expertise by adding workflow capabilities and more business- or task-driven roles. It will also have tight integration with SAP's Government, Risk, and Compliance (GRC) system and offer Identity Services in step with SAP's service-oriented architecture (SOA) offerings. Finally, the product is available today with a migration path for current CUA implementations as well as password management capabilities for both SAP and non-SAP components. For more information, visit the SDN Community at https://www.sdn.sap.com/irj/sdn/nw-identitymanagement.

Archive Considerations in the Real World

Archiving comprises both technology and business strategy considerations, each of which are covered next. In addition, archiving offers a mix of technical and business benefits, including the following:

- **Technical benefits**—From a technical perspective, archiving offers benefits in that it can slow database growth, reduce resource needs, and increase performance.

- **Business benefits**—From a business perspective, archiving can help a customer meet legal requirements, satisfy audits, and support data clean-up efforts.

Archiving Technology

Archiving is standard functionality provided by SAP to relocate data to storage media outside the system. SAP databases can grow large and unwieldy and, over time, cause performance issues and increased maintenance costs in the form of disk requirements. These costs can be further multiplied when systems are required to be redundant and highly available, which results in increased administration and longer restore and recovery times. Archiving involves the process of both removing obsolete data and moving data that needs to be retained but is not required for everyday use.

SAP allows data to be archived via archive objects. Archive objects consist of a compilation of tables containing business-specific data. The purpose of archive objects is to make sure integrity is maintained as data is removed from the system. Figure 31.4 provides a high-level example of the archiving process, which involves three-steps:

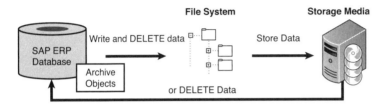

FIGURE 31.4   In this example, database data is written to a file system, deleted from the database, and then moved to offline storage.

1. Create the archive files from database data as defined by the archiving objects.

2. Store archive files to either online (such as file system) or offline (storage tapes, platters, and so on) storage.

3. Delete database data to recover space. Note that deletion of data can be "after write" or "after storage" depending on the exact method used.

The archiving we have discussed to this point is referred to as ADK-based archiving. ADK stands for the *Archive Development Kit*, which is the archive technology framework built into the SAP NetWeaver stack for ABAP. Another form of archiving, called XML-based archiving, is also available for XML interfaces and Java archiving. The XML-based archiving procedure differs from ADK-based archiving in two areas. First, an archive object is written to a single XML file, which is called a resource. In addition, data is written directly to storage instead of being written to an intermediary archive file and then written to storage. More information on XML-based archiving can be found at http://help.sap.com.

Archiving Strategy

While the design and implementation of archiving technology can be relatively simple, the process of archiving and defining functional requirements can be more difficult than it first may seem. The functional data components and archive objects have throughout a company representative stakeholders that have to be engaged for any successful archiving project to take place. For this reason, an archiving strategy should be in place that defines and documents a path forward for deletion and/or retention for each archiving object. Components of a successful archiving strategy should include, but are not limited to, the following:

▶ A current-state analysis of SAP system databases involved in the archive project

▶ Identification of business-relevant archiving objects

▶ Determination of retention periods for each object, including legal requirements

▶ Assessment of reports to be archived (some reports will become obsolete as a result of archived data)

▶ Discussion of report retention strategy (this may require electronic copies of some reports as reference since they cannot be duplicated after archive)

▶ Identification of any archive object integration points where there might be cross-functional impact

▶ Agreement on proper retrieval methods to access archived data

Additional Operational Considerations Prior to Go-Live

As we wrap up this chapter on operational considerations, there are a couple of additional topics that merit review before go-live. Although these items might not be of immediate concern, requirements will often quickly arise, and it is better to be prepared and aware. As an SAP implementation progresses and additional waves of configuration are added over time, keeping current and valid data sets in SAP sandbox, development, testing, and quality assurance environments can be difficult. In this last section of the chapter we take a look at the SAP system copy and client data management, both of which are very relevant to data maintenance across SAP systems.

Using SAP System Copy

Sometime after go-live, there may be a request to have your quality assurance or sandbox system refreshed from production. *Refresh* is a commonly used term to indicate the complete restore of an SAP system back to its functional target state. For example, if system PRD is restored to QAS, there are additional steps required to make changes in the newly restored QAS database to remove references to PRD and/or other production hostnames, RFC destinations, and so forth. This is a critical part of the restore process that is necessary to guarantee the integrity of production data.

At one time, system refreshes were performed as part of a custom process by some companies, but SAP developed a formal process for restoring or refreshing systems to other hosts, the SAP system copy procedure. In SAP terms, a system copy is a duplication of an SAP system using a copy of an existing database. These procedures exist for ABAP, Java, and ABAP+Java systems. System copies take two forms:

▶ **Homogenous system copy**—Involves copying a system to a like OS and database platform

▶ **Heterogeneous system copy**—Used if the goal is to move the system to a different operating system or database

The SAP system copy is a detailed process and can take time to fine-tune for your specific landscapes and environment. For instance, if your organization requests a complete database refresh of your entire QA landscape, multiple restores have to be completed, the system copy process has to be executed for multiple systems, and connectivity among the various systems has to be tested to validate the environment and resume testing activities. This is no small endeavor, so it is recommended that you develop and maintain a comprehensive company-specific system copy procedure. This should be a living document that is reviewed frequently and updated as necessary as new business functionality and enhancements are implemented on your SAP systems. It is important that this become a repeatable process that can be performed in a timely manner as requested during an SAP project lifecycle.

In addition, the security of the target system should also be reviewed as part of the system copy process. For instance, if production data is restored to a sandbox environment and development security is requested, sensitive HR data may be exposed. Processes should be put in place to "scramble" the HR data or to make sure that user security does not allow access (scrambling HR data is usually an ABAP routine developed by the customer to replace sensitive table entries, such as Social Security numbers or salary information, with generic data).

Managing Client Data

Although the SAP system copy procedure is very beneficial when a full database copy is required, production databases and production clients can become very large, requiring increased disk space and long restore periods. In most cases, only a subset of production data is needed to meet development and basic unit testing requirements. Historically, the only way to "build up" data in a client was through load programs using SAP's Legacy System Migration Workbench (LSMW) or eCATT scripts. Today, a number of companies have developed products that assist in the migration of client data from one system to another in a more automated process. A few of the major tools in this area include

▶ SAP Test Data Migration Server (TDMS)

▶ WinShuttle's transactionSHUTTLE tool

▶ EPI-USE Data Sync Manager for ERP

▶ Informatica's Applimation-derived Informia toolset, enabling Data Subset and Data on Demand

These applications, although with varying features and functional expertise, allow client-specific data to be extracted and migrated across systems to create new clients. In addition, they maintain integrity by making sure related data is copied over in a way that ensures transactions are functional on completion. This provides significant value—instead of building a client up via a load program, valid data subsets from existing systems can be copied over in a simple procedure.

31

Summary

While we have covered a wide range of topics in this chapter, the collective goal is to avoid unnecessary operational nuisances in these key trouble areas. All of the technologies discussed are designed to provide a function or feature to benefit your organization, but without proper management and planning, they can become obstacles. The strategy is for your organization to become proactive rather than reactive and spend time innovating rather than troubleshooting. As you move toward go-live, review these operational considerations carefully and make sure you have a process, procedure, or strategy in place to address these topics and continue on your journey toward a successful SAP implementation.

Case Study: Operational Management

HiTech's SAP Technical Support Organization (TSO) members have been asked to work with their counterparts in data center operations to identify key operational concerns that will require planning and support from both teams. As one of the technical leads assigned to this effort, you have been tasked with taking the results from this exercise and providing a brief report to management.

Questions

1. The CIO has dictated that ease of administration is paramount in all technology decisions. As a result, what printing method should be pursued by your organization?

2. The SAP security team is continuing to grow and, consequently, additional systems will be coming into the landscape soon. What can be done to reduce the administration burden and free up time on the security team?

3. Database size continues to increase and may soon begin to impact performance as well as the length of time it takes to back up or recover the database. Management does not want to spend the money to increase disk space because this seems like a short-term solution. What alternatives are there?

4. The HR team has asked for a separate environment with current HR data that it will need to keep in sync with production over time. What options are available to achieve this goal?

NOTE

The answers to these questions can be found in Appendix A, "Case Study Answers."

CHAPTER 32

SAP Infrastructure and Platform Testing

In this chapter we introduce you to infrastructure testing tools. We include a discussion of the various purposes they serve. Further, we show how these tools are used in real-life situations. You will find that all of the tools we cover are freely downloadable from the Web—we have chosen not to cover commercial products here, although several good ones are available. We believe that for the purposes outlined in this chapter, and for the purposes of validating that a production system is well tuned, these free tools will meet all your infrastructure testing needs.

The Goals of Infrastructure Testing

Before a system is turned over to its end-user community for production use, the system needs to be verified in terms of whether its infrastructure is structurally sound and "designed for run." Infrastructure testing provides the following:

▶ **Compare platforms**—By providing a basis for the comparison of two platforms, you will have some idea as to what kind of performance difference to expect. For example, we always compare storage platforms and server platforms in terms of raw performance and throughput. You might also want to compare performance between servers configured with two host bus adapters (HBAs) against those with four HBAs, or to quantify different settings (for example, HBA load balancing algorithms), and so on. In the same way, you might also want to compare the performance of your new servers and storage systems to your existing platforms before you actually deploy them in production.

▶ **Track the performance impact of lifecycle changes**—Infrastructure testing enables you to baseline a system and then retest it throughout its lifecycle (after changes are made to the infrastructure). We believe you should always test disk subsystem throughput after changes are made to the server (for example, after new drivers are installed) or to the storage system (for example, after firmware or configuration updates are made). This is especially true in the case of storage systems (where we find most of the problems that eventually manifest themselves as performance issues). There is real value to having a baseline for comparison when, down the road, you believe you might be experiencing a storage-related performance issue.

▶ **Verify high-availability (HA) solutions**—Infrastructure testing can help you verify not only that a system's availability is maintained, but at which layer in the technology stack a problem might present itself. For instance, infrastructure testing can verify whether a failed HBA or network interface card (NIC) impacts performance. These tools can not only help you to verify that the component is still functioning properly, but also let you know if a component's performance has degraded over time. By way of example, a simple network "ping" test may let you know if a teamed NIC has successfully recovered from a failure, but this test does nothing to tell you anything about the performance of the network team. Running a network testing tool against the server during a staged failure will also give you an indication of the level of performance you can expect with a failed NIC. The same testing could be run in a situation simulating a switch failure or other network core component (and also used to test HBA failures, storage area network switch failures, and more).

▶ **Verify a system is properly installed and tuned**—Test tools provide a means for verifying that both the installation and post-installation tuning have been done to specification. For example, we encountered a situation during a deployment in which running a storage system test tool uncovered a potentially bad situation. The customer's multipath I/O (MPIO) drivers required an additional configuration step be taken when the server was operating as part of a cluster. The extra step was not required in nonclustered environments. Our testing confirmed that the clustered server's throughput was essentially half that of nonclustered servers—the HP MPIO driver was essentially disabling load balancing for cluster nodes. Once the situation was corrected by making the required configuration change (to tell the server's drivers that it was a cluster node), the system's throughput returned to the expected level. This would have been quite problematic had the system gone live prior to understanding this simple change was required.

▶ **Conduct network infrastructure testing**—To a system's end users, well-configured SAP infrastructure equates to a consistent user experience, which in turn often means good response times. This is especially true for users working from remote offices. There are various aspects of the network that can impact remote users from a performance perspective, including bandwidth, network latency, driver efficiency, driver configuration, the effect of dropped network packets requiring retransmission, and so on. Testing in advance using tools such as WAN simulators can prevent you from deploying solutions with unacceptable or merely borderline performance.

The tools we are going to cover later in this chapter operate at the lowest levels of the SAP technology stack, giving you a wonderful low-level performance baseline upon which to build. If the tools show that an updated system performs as well as the baseline system performed, you can be reasonably sure that a newly uncovered performance problem is not operating system, hardware, network, or storage related.

System-Level Stress Testing and Pretuning

Although one of the goals of SAP stress testing is to guide and direct tuning of your soon-to-be-production system, it makes sense to engage in a certain level of *pretuning* as well. This involves testing and tweaking the individual technology stack layers and components to operate well in a standalone manner. When things run smoothly in this respect, you can then more intelligently optimize the entire technology stack to perform as a cohesive solution of integrated components and technologies.

Testing the individual components or layers in your particular SAP technology stack is also often referred to as system-level testing or systems testing, and will save you countless hours and much energy down the road. Key reasons for system-level testing include

▶ To establish a baseline for individual component-level system performance today, to be measured again as your change control processes upgrade these components or introduce new components or technology stack changes.

▶ To simply understand where potential performance bottlenecks might lie in the future. This is also called characterization testing or capacity testing.

▶ To understand where future budget dollars can be best spent—where you get the most bang for the buck when you need your first performance boost.

We cannot overemphasize the importance of validating that your infrastructure is sound before you put it into production. For example, if your network infrastructure is capable of supporting 200% growth in the number of online SAP users, but your disk subsystem can handle only another 30% growth in online users before performance becomes unacceptable, you need to be aware of this. Such information will help drive intelligent upgrades in the future. In a real-world example, one of our customers improperly implemented remote disk mirroring, unknowingly creating a serious database performance issue. Had this customer tested the performance of the disk subsystem *before* implementing disk mirroring, it would have had a baseline. Further testing would have made the customer keenly aware of the consequences of the configuration problem. The customer could have saved itself from a very stressful situation in which its end users were left with a bad first impression of its new SAP systems.

Server Hardware and OS Testing

One of the best attributes of basic tools such as those designed to test server hardware and operating system configurations is that they generally do not require any additional infrastructure—you install and run them directly from the server to be tested. Server and OS test tools focus primarily on CPU benchmarking. Different tools execute different tests, though the results tend to be pretty self-explanatory. A "lower" number is desired for tests that try to crunch their way through a set of problems or calculations (such as calculating the value of pi to several hundred decimal places); in this case, workload is constant while time is the variable. On the other hand, a "higher" number is desired for CPU tests seeking to showcase a CPU's throughput or how much work was processed in a given amount of time. In this case, time is the constant while the workload is variable.

The purpose of executing CPU test utilities is almost always to compare different servers or models with one another or to compare different configurations of a single model. Because these kinds of test tools interact directly with the CPU, there is little point in running these tests again unless something germane to the system changes. We've had customers make system-level changes to cache and pipeline configuration along with the usual BIOS and system-board firmware updates; these types of changes warrant a new battery of CPU tests against which the system's baseline may be compared. In the next few sections, we take a closer look at several CPU benchmarking and testing tools.

MCS CPU Benchmark

MCS CPU Benchmark from MCS Studios is not only powerful but easy to install and run. The results are straightforward and displayed in a text box, as shown in Figure 32.1. Note that higher numbers are desired. You can obtain this tool from http://www.softpedia.com/progDownload/MCS-CPU-Benchmark-Download-30045.html.

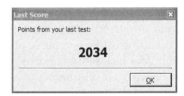

FIGURE 32.1   After a few minutes of execution, the MCS CPU Benchmark score is displayed.

N-Bench

N-Bench is an old but still useful CPU performance measurement utility from AMD, developed by this CPU manufacturer to baseline system performance. N-Bench measures the performance of the CPU by measuring integer and floating-point operations, as shown in

Figure 32.2. It is easy to install and displays entertaining graphics (whose real purpose is to indicate the system is being tested) during its short run.

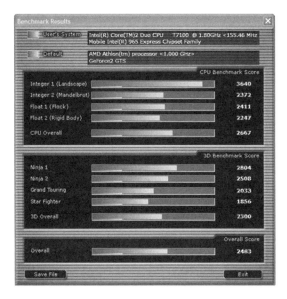

FIGURE 32.2   We are only interested in the CPU benchmarks; for our purposes, the 3D Benchmark scores can be ignored or deselected in Benchmark Settings.

CPUBENCH

CPUBENCH is one of our absolute favorite CPU tools. The program is a single executable from Wandering Idea Software Unlimited. It combines 12 different benchmark tests, providing individual results as well as compiling an overall score for your server's CPU. Many of these individual tests are well known and can be used for great apples-to-apples server performance comparisons. The "options" menu includes a brief description of each benchmark. For example, MFLOPS determines the number of million floating-point operations that the CPU can perform in one second. You can choose which benchmarks to run—you might choose to deselect the KPPS benchmark, for example, as it measures the performance of the graphics card (typically perceived as not worthy of testing when it comes to high-performance application and database servers). For example, a high-end 32 CPU server might display results similar to the following:

- ▶ MFLOPS: 387.35
- ▶ MIPS: 614.8
- ▶ PI: 3421

- Lorenz: 437

- Dhrystone: 3721622

- Whetstone: 1011890

- Nblock: 4766

- Queens: 3015

- Matrix: 2656

- Savage: 1360

- B5: 3719

- Overall score: 10

While the overall score might not prove all that useful, the 11 individual benchmarks are very handy for comparing CPU performance between servers and during a particular server's lifecycle (for example, after the system board's firmware is upgraded or other server maintenance is performed).

Disk Subsystem and Database Testing

The majority of problems we encounter are related to the disk subsystem, so disk I/O tools are especially important. Disk subsystem problems generally show up in the database and "move" to the SAP system in the form of increased response times. Disk I/O tools are used for performance tuning, troubleshooting, validating changes, and comparing disk subsystems.

We use disk I/O tools to validate that the disk subsystem is performing as expected during implementations by running the tools on each database server. You should always test components each step of the way, starting at the most basic level. For example, you should test each node in a cluster before clustering is installed, and again afterward. This also applies to disk subsystem software such as mirroring disk subsystems—the testing should take place before and after implementation to verify that performance is not impacted. Years ago we had a client who suffered through performance issues after go-live only to find they were being caused by synchronous disk mirroring between two sites. If the disk subsystem had been tested at each step of the implementation, as we recommend, the problem could have been discovered before the system went live and users were impacted.

Disk I/O tools can also be used to tune the performance of the disk subsystem—especially performance-critical factors such as HBA disk queue length and load-balancing algorithms. These tools can also help to determine the layout of the disk subsystem, including the number of disk groups and the number of disks in each group.

We have also used these tools to test the performance difference of two HBAs versus four HBAs. You could compare different models of HBAs—even compare a 1Gbps SAN to 2Gbps, 4Gbps, and faster SANs.

Disk I/O tools can also be used to troubleshoot by comparing the current performance to the baseline. If the performance is approximately the same, you can pretty much eliminate as the problem HBAs, drivers, SAN switches, and the disk subsystem itself—everything except the database and SAP.

The same reasoning applies to rerunning the disk I/O tools after changes are made to any component of the disk subsystem. It validates that you have not degraded the performance of your disk subsystem before it is put back in production. In the next few sections, let's take a closer look at several disk subsystem testing tools we have found useful over the years.

SQLIO

SQLIO is a tool from Microsoft that can be used to determine the I/O capacity of a disk storage system. Although Microsoft has several newer tools out, we like the simplicity of SQLIO. We typically use SQLIO to measure the I/O capacity of a database server environment, particularly from the perspective of "what if" scenarios and configuration changes. SQLIO can also be used to verify that the disk subsystem has been properly configured and tuned. Run from a command prompt, SQLIO verifies the lower layers of the SAP technology stack are all working properly, including

- HBA firmware

- OS HBA drivers and other disk components (MPIO drivers, for example), plus the driver settings such as HBA queue depth

- Other OS changes and updates

- Disk subsystem configuration and changes, including disk groups, RAID types, firmware levels, individual disk drive changes, and so forth

- SAN switches, including configuration and firmware changes or other settings

The end result is that you'll know that your disk subsystem is working properly, and you'll have an excellent idea of what kind of throughput the system is capable of hosting—before SAP or database software are installed and brought into the equation.

SQLIO can be downloaded from Microsoft at http://www.microsoft.com/downloads/. Keep in mind that SQLIO is provided as-is—Microsoft does not provide any support for this tool. Microsoft provides an MSI file that installs to a directory such as `C:\Program Files\SQLIO`. From there, you create a batch file to run the SQLIO commands. The syntax is explained in the text files in the install directory. For example, `run.cmd` might include the following commands (where `-b` is the I/O block size you're testing, `-kR` means you're executing a "read" test, `-s60` means the test runs for 60 seconds, and `-Up` includes CPU results in the output):

- `sqlio -Fpfile.txt -b64 -o32 -frandom -kR -s60 -Up`

- `sqlio -Fpfile.txt -b64 -o32 -kR -Up -s60 -fsequential`

- `sqlio -Fpfile.txt -b64 -o32 -frandom -s60 -kW -Up`

▶ `sqlio -Fpfile.txt -b64 -o32 -s60 -kW -Up -fsequential`

▶ `sqlio -Fpfile.txt -b8 -o32 -frandom -s60 -Up`

▶ `sqlio -Fpfile.txt -b8 -o32 -s60 -Up -fsequential`

▶ `sqlio -Fpfile.txt -b8 -o32 -frandom -s60 -kW -Up`

▶ `sqlio -Fpfile.txt -b8 -o32 -s60 -kW -Up –fsequential`

Next, you need to designate the drives where the test data files reside through a parameter file such as `pfile.txt`. In this case, we're running SQLIO using four threads against three data files of 5GB each residing on the K:, L:, and M: drives; SQLIO will create these test data files if they don't already exist:

▶ `K:\SQLIOtest 4 0 5000`

▶ `L:\SQLIOtest 4 0 5000`

▶ `M:\SQLIOtest 4 0 5000`

Finally, to capture the results, redirect the output to a text file (for example, execute the command `run.cmd > results.txt`). You will then want to put the results in a spreadsheet, as shown in Figure 32.3, to create an easy method of tracking performance data over time. For reporting purposes, we like to create a graph of the average throughput in terms of MBps or disk IOs/sec, too, as shown in Figure 32.4.

	hour3p1	dalr3p1	hour3q1	hour3d1
64k Random reads	220.975	258.285	223.68	230.445
64k Sequential reads	230.095	283.89	222.5	228.345
64k Random writes	47.055	49.025	48.54	48.385
64k Sequential writes	46.94	43.16	46.945	47.265
8k Random reads	43.24	51.11	43.52	46.02
8k Sequential reads	54.7	69.22	110.985	102.135
8k Random writes	13.265	15.135	13.775	14.845
8k Sequential writes	16.515	20.47	31.41	27.795
64k Random reads	3535.7	4132.635	3578.9	3687.14
64k Sequential reads	3681.595	4542.345	3560.095	3653.665
64k Random writes	753	784.45	776.685	774.28
64k Sequential writes	751.07	690.655	751.2	756.345
8k Random reads	5535.425	6542.825	5571.29	5891.47
8k Sequential reads	7002.205	8861.005	14207.03	13073.77
8k Random writes	1698.945	1938.09	1763.94	1900.54
8k Sequential writes	2114.31	2620.335	4020.845	3558.34

FIGURE 32.3   Test run output is dropped into an Excel spreadsheet for later trending and on-demand analysis.

Based on our experience, here are some additional testing tips for SQLIO:

▶ Because SQLIO puts a heavy load on the disk subsystem, after the disk subsystem is put into production, run it during off-hours. Even better, run these tests on your nonproduction SAN.

▶ Make sure that the server running SQLIO is the only server placing a load on the disk subsystem; otherwise, the results will be impacted by the other server's disk activity.

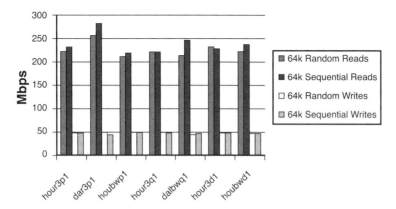

FIGURE 32.4   Presenting the SQLIO results in graphical format makes it easier to compare the results. In this case, the Houston servers were connected to one model of disk subsystem while the Dallas servers were attached to a newer and faster SAN.

▶ Ignore the results of the first test run. During the first test run, SQLIO creates the file(s) on the disk(s) for testing, to be reused in subsequent runs. Because of this, test results are unpredictable; thus, we ignore the results from the first test run.

When you are finished testing, you will probably want to delete the SQLIO files—they do not serve any purpose other than testing, and they can take up considerable disk space.

Iometer

Iometer was originally developed by Intel but is now open source software. Iometer measures I/O performance under a controlled load. It is available for Windows Server, Linux, and Solaris. The major difference between Iometer and the other disk utilities covered in this chapter is that it has a graphical user interface (GUI), as shown in Figure 32.5. If you prefer a nice GUI to a command line, Iometer is the way to go. Another feature we like is the ease with which the results can be saved to a file for later manipulation. A final note is that Iometer can also be configured to perform network testing.

NTIOGEN

NTIOGEN is the Microsoft Windows port of the IOGEN program for UNIX developed by Symbios Logic. It is a relatively straightforward command-line utility—the syntax is explained in the READ.ME file. You could compare a Windows server and a UNIX server by running NTIOGEN and IOGEN, for instance.

IOzone

IOzone is an open-source file system benchmark tool. The really compelling thing about this tool is that builds are available for IBM AIX, HP-UX, Sun Solaris, various Linux flavors, Microsoft Windows, and other operating system environments. This gives an organization considering a new SAP computing platform the opportunity to benchmark and compare server-to-server results—a feature unavailable for most tools given that they're generally OS-specific. You can download it and find out more at http://www.iozone.org.

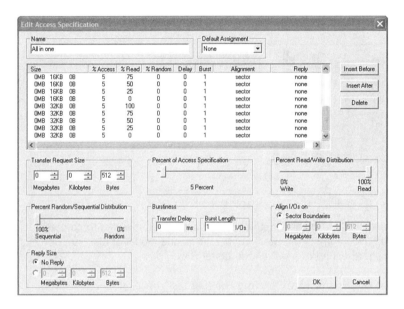

FIGURE 32.5   Iometer's GUI makes it easy to configure the access specifications for the test.

Windows Utilities

Every operating system used for SAP today includes utilities useful for performance benchmarking. By way of example, Microsoft Windows ships with several utilities, such as Microsoft Performance Logs and Alerts that are useful for establishing a baseline and troubleshooting issues. Logging the average disk queue length, as shown in Figure 32.6, is important; it gives you an indication of the normal range for this performance counter. If troubleshooting revealed an increase in this value, you might expect to see increased database times, resulting in increased SAP transaction response times. Understanding what is normal for your system is therefore key. You will want to capture memory and CPU counters for the same reason.

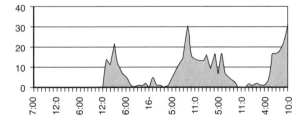

FIGURE 32.6   Viewing the log captured by Performance Logs and Alerts allows you to easily analyze the average disk queue lengths in order to troubleshoot performance issues.

In addition, there are several other Windows utilities we find ourselves frequently using during infrastructure testing:

- ▶ **System Information**—This utility (executed by running the utility `winmsd.exe`) makes it easy to document the current drivers, services, and devices for your server, especially if you export the information to a file.

- ▶ **Windows Task Manager**—This utility provides an easy way to view the current processes and CPU utilization, verify that all CPUs and RAM are "seen" by the system, and check available memory.

- ▶ **chkdsk.exe**—This utility can be used to verify your current disk allocation unit size. It is easy enough to specify the file allocation unit size when you format your drives, but not so easy to verify it afterward. Running `chkdsk` without any options will display the file allocation unit size for the drive.

You will also want to check whether your storage vendor has tools that will allow you to monitor the performance of your storage during these tests.

Network Infrastructure Testing

For the most part, Gigabit Ethernet has eliminated most of the concerns with the back-end SAP networks. The new concerns now involve firewalls and client or front-end networks. This applies to access to SAP systems from the Internet or remote offices via a WAN. These connections pose challenges in terms of bandwidth and latency, which can affect the quality of the end users' experience. It is also important to remember that SAP network traffic varies by system:

- ▶ The traditional SAPGUI is relatively "thin" and requires little bandwidth.

- ▶ Web traffic is more susceptible to latency because of its "chatty" nature.

- ▶ Access to SAP Business Warehouse via the Business Explorer (BEx) can result in large file transfers.

Arguably the best way to test network connectivity is to include a representative remote office or Internet users in the full-blown stress testing, covered in Chapter 33. Many companies also employ WAN simulators to test the user experience with varying bandwidths and latency. However, there are OS tools that will help you establish a baseline or troubleshoot network issues:

- ▶ Simply copy a large file across the network and record the time it takes to complete.

- ▶ The `ping` utility can verify connection to systems and give you a reading on the network latency.

- ▶ The `tracert` utility is used to show the route a packet takes from the source to the destination.

In addition, SAP breaks down network response time for online transactions in ST03. Again, if you establish a baseline of typical network response time, an elevated value will raise flags, allowing you to start looking into the issue before it becomes noticeable to your users.

SAP Failover and Other HA/DR Infrastructure Testing

Testing the high-availability features of your server makes a lot of sense, especially from the perspective of verifying that things have been installed and configured properly. For example, you'll want to

▶ Test HBA availability by disconnecting fiber cables from the HBA. Plug it back in, wait a minute, and repeat for other HBAs.

▶ Test power availability by disconnecting the power cord from one of the power supplies. Plug it back in, wait a minute, and repeat for the other power supply.

▶ Test the local drives by removing a drive from the server and verifying that operations continue. Plug it back in and verify that the pulled drive resumes normal operation.

▶ Test NIC availability by unplugging a NIC cable and verifying the system remains accessible and available. Plug it back in, wait a minute, and repeat for any other NICs.

Further testing can include powering off one of the LAN switches, SAN switches, or power distribution units (PDUs). These tests will prove that you have properly cabled your installation for HA.

Additional Disk Subsystem Testing

You might even want to test how your SAN operates in the event of a disk failure or, as importantly, after a failed disk is replaced. We have seen situations in which degraded performance of the storage subsystem during a disk rebuild impacted user performance. The customer in question subsequently tuned the disk subsystem such that disk rebuilds were given a lower priority. The important thing is to understand what impact, if any, failover situations will have on your SAP system's performance and availability *before* your disk subsystem is put into production.

You should also consider verifying that you are alerted in the event of a disk failure—or even better, that your storage vendor is notified to send a replacement. It is way too common for hardware failures to go unnoticed in remote data centers. Although most storage subsystems are designed to handle a single disk failure without an impact to availability, a failed disk increases the risk of significant downtime in the event of additional failures.

Microsoft Cluster Testing

For Microsoft clustered SAP-on-Windows environments, before you go into production you will want to verify that the cluster is working properly. There is little more frustrating than implementing a cluster only to find that it did not function as expected after a

32

failure. The first thing you will want to verify is that you can fail over resource groups, which are nothing more than packages of resources—disks, IP addresses, and so on. Use Microsoft's Cluster Administrator to fail both SAP and database resource groups between nodes in the cluster. Simply right-click the respective resource group and select Move Group. The resource group should move to the other node and come online. If you have users connected, you should notice that they will be disconnected during the SAP resource group failover, but will remain connected during the database failover—although the users will not be able to complete any activities that require database access until the database is online again.

You will also want to test to make sure that a temporary resource failure does not cause the entire resource group to fail over. You really want to avoid failovers when possible because service to the end users will be interrupted. You can test temporary resource failures as follows:

1. Start Cluster Administrator, right-click a resource in the SAP or database group, and click Initiate Failure. The resource should temporarily go into a failed state and then be brought back online. The resource group should be unaffected.

2. Repeat the Initiate Failure test three more times. The fourth time you click Initiate Failure, the resource group should fail over to the other node. This goes to show that a persistent failure will cause the resource group to fail over. You can, of course, control this behavior for each resource—we would suggest that for noncritical resources you change the settings so that a failure of the resource will not cause the resource group to fail over.

You will also want to complete the following tests to verify that your cluster handles hardware or operating system failures as expected:

▶ Move all the resources to one node and stop the cluster service on that node. The resources should fail over to the other node. Restart the service.

▶ Shut down the node with all the resources (normal shutdown via Start, Shutdown). The resource should fail over to the other node. You could take this test even further by shutting down the power via the power button or removing the power cables— although there is some danger that you might corrupt your database.

▶ Unplug the network cable for the heartbeat network. If you have configured the network priority in the cluster properly, the heartbeat will take place over the public network and no failover will occur.

▶ Unplug a network cable for the public network. If the public network is configured for NIC teaming (best practice), you will not experience any failures. Next, unplug the second network cable for the public network. You should now see the resources fail over the other node, although it may take some time for the failover to occur.

As you can see, cluster testing not only verifies that the cluster is working properly but also familiarizes you with how the cluster functions. You should also record the time it takes for a failover to occur so that you know what to expect if a failure occurs during production.

Testing Tools in Action—Server Comparison

We were tasked on one project with comparing from a performance perspective a new HP ProLiant DL785 32-core server to the customer's existing Itanium2 database server. In addition to the server, a new HP EVA 8100 storage subsystem was also being tested. The customer wanted to verify that the DL785 and new storage could perform better than the existing solution, if only from a pure infrastructure perspective; SAP-specific benchmarking and comparative load testing were out of scope. The test tools we employed were many of the same ones discussed in this chapter:

▶ SQLIO (disk and CPU)

▶ Miscellaneous other disk benchmarks (NTIOGEN, IOzone)

▶ N-Bench (disk, CPU, and RAM)

▶ MCS CPU Benchmark (CPU)

▶ CPUBENCH (multiple CPU tests)

The testing methodology we employed for the storage-related testing involved multiple test runs and a variety of components:

▶ Initial test run to build SQLIO data files

▶ Subsequent tests to validate test run consistency

▶ DL785: Tested different firmware and driver releases

▶ DL785: Tested different load-balancing algorithms

▶ DL785: Tested different PCI-e slots (x4, x8, x16)

▶ DL785: Tested two versus four HBAs

The actual test results revealed the following:

▶ The DL785 was clearly *much faster* from a CPU perspective.

▶ The DL785 and IA64 performed *nearly identically* in terms of sequential write operations (477 versus 469 MBps on the new SAN); the DL785 was much faster in terms of random writes.

▶ The DL785 boasted *much faster read operations* at 1120 MBps throughput—more than 1.1GBps!

▶ Between Shortest Queue Service Time (SQST) and Round Robin (RR), we were able to determine the best HBA load-balancing algorithm; given that SQST and RR were nearly identical, we ultimately recommended going with the default SQST setting.

▶ The best PCI Express slots to house the HBAs was also determined; interestingly, despite the differences in DL785 PCI slots—three different speeds—we found in this particular case that the difference in performance only amounted to a percentage point or two.

▶ We were able to quantify the performance differences between implementing two and four HBAs; in our case, we found a significant difference when it came to reads but only a negligible difference relative to writes.

Even with only two HBAs, the DL785 clearly outperformed this customer's midsized IA64 platform, making it an ideal SAP database server for it. More impressively, with four HBAs the DL785 delivered the kind of scalability and performance necessary for the customer to consolidate multiple SAP production database systems in the long-term. Without this kind of actionable infrastructure testing, such a statement couldn't have been made with confidence.

Summary

You should now have a better understanding of the importance and inherent value of infrastructure testing. We covered several of the tools we use on a regular basis and how they can provide insight otherwise unattainable. Infrastructure testing reduces the risk of implementing technologies that fail to deliver to expectation. The important thing is for you to identify several tools that meet your needs and your budget, establish a baseline, and retest every time you make a change to the environment. This approach will save you from finding out *after* you make hardware or software changes that your overall system's performance has been impacted. You will also have the peace of mind that your individual servers have been properly installed and the individual components have been well tuned for your environment. Once such infrastructure testing is completed, a full-blown stress test or load test is in order to show that everything across the entire SAP technology stack works together and performs as expected—the subject of the next chapter.

Case Study: Infrastructure Testing

HiTech's SAP Technical Support Organization (TSO) has just finished the first SAP installation—the ERP 6.0 environment. You have been tasked with verifying that the installation has been carried out properly and that the individual components are properly tuned. The SAP systems in question are all clustered. You have downloaded the infrastructure testing tools and are putting together the testing plan.

Questions

1. Should you test the disk I/O performance before or after verifying cluster operations?
2. Should your plan include establishing a baseline for CPU performance?
3. Explain how you might want low numbers in some of your CPU benchmark tests and higher numbers in other tests.
4. After you finish the initial testing to verify that the installations are correct and that everything is properly tuned, will you ever need to run the disk I/O tools again?

NOTE

The answers to these questions can be found in Appendix A, "Case Study Answers."

CHAPTER 33

SAP Load and Stress Testing

We are nearing the point where go-live is just around the corner. Although SAP calls this the tail end of the Realization phase, it's also referred to as the Final Preparation phase. We like the latter term, because in our experience, stress testing is an important milestone done in the name of go-live preparation. Stress testing seeks to identify and describe the limits of an IT solution, such as the kind of performance that can be expected day after day and how the system will react when put under the stress of month-end processing, peak batch workload processing, or other weighty business processes.

For SAP solutions, the work of stress testing not only is critical, but is complex and not accomplished quickly. It's hard work, plain and simple. Most anyone can bang together a framework for an SAP stress test based on guesses as to what kind of load the system will be hosting on an average day. But to do a stress test justice, there's much to consider.

Key SAP Stress-Testing Considerations

Before you can conduct an SAP stress test, you must plan and prepare for it. We recommend developing a detailed project plan to ensure nothing falls through the cracks, as articulated next. For starters, your stress test project plan should address the following:

▶ Pretuning your SAP technology stack (covered in Chapter 32, "SAP Infrastructure and Platform Testing")

▶ Selecting a stress-testing approach and tools

▶ Determining the technical skill sets and other resources (including time commitments) required to support stress testing

▶ Setting up and configuring the stress test infrastructure

▶ Analyzing business processes to determine which SAP components, functional areas, and so on will come into play

▶ Setting aside time to work with the business groups associated with these SAP components and functional areas (to record scripts that reflect how the business will actually execute its business processes)

▶ Scripting the business processes identified earlier

▶ Identifying whether there is enough data available to do the scripted business processes justice

▶ Developing a process for "warming up" the database, and then restoring this known state prior to each new test run

▶ Preparing for, executing, and monitoring each stress test run

▶ Collecting performance and other output data

▶ Validating that the stress test runs are valid

▶ Analyzing the data to determine how well the system performed under load

▶ Conducting iterative testing and tuning cycles to increase the system's performance (or meet other objectives, some of which are outlined later in this chapter)

Later, as you prepare for the stress test and begin to better understand the challenges associated with scripting complex business processes, you will make changes to the plan. It's not unusual, for example, to initially underestimate the time needed to find enough valid test data, build the test infrastructure, and even execute the test runs. These challenges and others are covered throughout this chapter. First, though, let's turn our attention to analyzing a system's planned workload, addressing data concerns, and reflecting all this in an updated project plan.

Analyzing Online Users and Batch Processes

You must characterize your system in terms of the business processes that run as a part of the load you want to simulate in your stress test. This is a big part of identifying the mix of business processes, and usually boils down to characterizing online users and background or batch processes—the workload that will be hosted by SAP. Thus, if your goal is to simulate an average day on the system, your mix of online users and batch processes will probably be skewed toward the users. It will therefore be important to characterize which functional areas are represented, and how many users will typically be "active" within each functional area.

If you want to execute a stress test that simulates your peak load on the system (a typical goal), you probably need to run more background processes representing month-end reports, quarterly financial closings, and so on. The nature of the work being performed by the online users will be different, too. For example, warehouse and inventory management users will be closing out inventory reports and displaying and updating material-related information. Financial users will be matching purchase requisitions with purchase orders and clearing out accounts payable and receivable. Manufacturing and supply chain users will be updating and running new demand planning and forecasting jobs while seeking to move as much product out to customers as possible. Business management teams will be updating forecasting models, updating budgets and employee records, and so on.

The less you understand the nature of the business transactions inherent to a particular load, the less likely your stress test will prove useful to anyone. So don't assume you know what kind of load to generate from your stress tests. Ask the business and functional leads! They know the SAP components and SAP functional areas that best represent the load to be borne by the production system. And identify "backup" transactions and processes as well—these may become useful if your first choice in a particular functional area proves too difficult to script or too weak in terms of acquiring useful data necessary to drive the stress testing.

Understanding It's All About the Data!

Though it's probably not obvious at first blush, access to the right data combinations is as important a consideration in selecting a business process for scripting as is anything else. More simply, an easy script is essentially worthless if only a few combinations of data are available for use in a stress test. Why? Because after the data is used by the first "user" during the course of stress testing, all this data is immediately cached at a number of different levels—by the hardware cache in your disk subsystem, by the database software's data cache, and even by the application server's cache. Thus, subsequent executions of the same transaction will be less real-world and much more artificial—the data will be immediately accessible and therefore will drive absolutely no load on your disk subsystem. Recall from previous discussions that truly driving your disk subsystem is a major goal of any type of performance or stress testing. It's the primary "bottleneck" down the road and thus needs to be exercised and tuned.

When it comes to data, you can never really have too much. Valid data is crucial, of course, but quantity is equally important, as just discussed. Exactly how much is enough? The right answer is simple—try to never use the same input data twice during the execution of a test run. If you have a business script that requires a customer number to be input, obtain enough customer numbers so that you don't have to repeat the same one during your test run. If you're moving materials or processing invoices, obtain enough data so that you never have to use the same data during the test run. To be sure, you'll use the same data again and again during *different* test runs. But within a single test run, the goal is to have as much data as is realistic for your business. In our experience, the following approach has proven successful:

1. Think about how long a test run needs to execute. Thirty minutes is pretty typical, with another 15 minutes beforehand needed for ramp-up. Thus, your target should be to supply enough variety in data to support a user running for 45 minutes without having to process the same data twice.

2. Consider how many users need to be tested simultaneously. To complicate matters, you will be running business processes executed by not just a single user (as that level of quality testing was presumably already completed during our functional test cycles outlined in Chapter 28), but by hundreds or even thousands of users during that 45 minutes—each of whom needs their own data so as to place the greatest load on the system.

3. Analyze how long each script within each functional area takes to execute, including "think time" (a reasonable pause between transactions). If you take a relatively fast transaction such as an FD32 credit check followed by a credit line increase, and then factor in a typical think time, it would be safe to say that the entire business process would consume 1 minute of "wall clock" or actual time.

4. Do some math. If your goal (as directed by the business) is to simulate the 20-member financial team's peak load for this particular transaction, you would need to process 900 credit checks or updates throughout the stress test (45 minutes ×1 transaction × 20 users). In the best case, then, you want to have 900 different customer numbers on hand so that you never pull up the same customer data twice (which may or may not be realistic).

5. Consider the future production system's actual needs. If you're simulating an organization with 1,000 users, your data requirements for the earlier scenario would grow to 45,000 unique customers. Is this valid, though? Perhaps 10,000 unique customers is more real-world, therefore yielding less actual—but nonetheless more realistic— load on the system. Then again, if a 20-member financial team will only run a particular transaction a few times a day, perhaps a different transaction (even better, a suite of transactions) would be more realistic for stress testing.

This simple method can work for all transactions, obviously. Work with your business leads to determine what is real and what is actually achievable, and then do your best to simulate the real world with the data available to you. And whenever possible, test business processes with a great amount of data behind them.

Updating Your Project Plan

Now that your basic stress test project plan is beginning to take shape and you have a better understanding of a host of underlying business processes and data, it's time to take a closer look at budgets and goals, and to give some careful thought to which business processes must actually be scripted. And you must determine at what point to invest in procuring a stress-testing utility that supports virtual users, based on which SAP components will play a role in your stress test. Ultimately, all of this will drive intelligent project plan updates as well as underscore the type and amount of scripting required to support the test. Specifically, you must

▶ Evaluate the need for real or virtual users

▶ Analyze which stress-testing tool is most appropriate for your needs and budget

▶ Review and consider which business processes need to be scripted

These three requirements are addressed next.

Real Versus Virtual Users

There will be cases in your stress test plan that will probably not be worth automating or scripting. Examples might include generating a bit of background noise by launching a couple of long-running reports, or easily launching a Material Requirements Planning (MRP) or other lengthy business process. In these instances, it could save time and expense to launch each of these processes through a dedicated "real" SAPGUI session rather than anything that is scripted or handled virtually through a testing tool.

However, if you need to show the impact that more than a few users have on a system, it will be neither practical nor cost effective to do so using "real" physical desktop or laptop clients, each running multiple SAPGUI sessions. Instead, investing in an SAP testing utility that supports *virtual users* is the ticket. Virtual users are exactly like "real" user sessions, with one difference—hundreds of virtual sessions may execute on a single client driver, many more than the six concurrent sessions allowed by recent SAPGUI versions. The virtual SAPGUI sessions are executed behind the scenes via direct SAP Business API (BAPI) calls. In this way, the actual GUI is not required to be displayed, because scripts written to support virtual users don't fill in the contents of a SAPGUI screen by tabbing to it and entering data; they drive business processes through referencing field names, drop-down boxes, radio buttons, and so on through SAP's API. We call such tools "SAP aware."

Tools that support these powerful virtual capabilities must by their very nature support excellent monitoring and reporting capabilities. These features are by no means free, however. An exercise in evaluating price versus capabilities could be warranted in some cases, in fact. But at the end of the day, if you need to drive more than 50 or 60 SAPGUI sessions, you'll save money using virtual testing tools.

SAP-Aware, Freeware, and Inexpensive Testing Tools

The decision of whether to choose SAP stress testing tools that boast an SAP BAPI–certified interface over those that do not comes down to price. Using SAP's BAPI makes a testing tool "SAP aware," in that it can communicate with an SAP system through its standard API. In this way, SAP-aware tools boast the following capabilities that are unavailable in tools that drive a physical SAPGUI (like AutoIT, Scriptomatic, and other popular macro tools that are great for driving activities of a single user in an automated fashion):

▶ They can "screen scrape," meaning they can pull information out of an SAP output screen (such as "transaction completed successfully" or "Order 0006011998 posted for customer 19940425") and use it to populate a variable.

▶ They can read the contents of a field displayed by the SAPGUI even if the field is not actually "visible" on the screen.

▶ They can take this capability one step further and execute transactions without even displaying the SAPGUI; the transaction actually runs, but does so "virtually" or behind the scenes without the need for a user interface. Sometimes this is called Virtual Direct Test (VDT) capability.

▶ They can build on these capabilities and run many users—called virtual users—on the same physical desktops or laptops. By using a high-powered "client driver" such as an eight-CPU server with 4GB of RAM, literally hundreds or even thousands of virtual users can be set in motion.

Tools like this are not cheap, however. The most popular SAP-aware test tool vendors charge between perhaps $100,000 and $250,000 for the privilege of being able to execute 500 virtual users on a single client driver. Some of the best tools include HP (formerly Mercury) QuickTest and LoadRunner products, Borland (formerly Segue) SilkPerformer, Compuware TestPartner, and Rational (owned by IBM) Performance Tester.

Even factoring in the cost of licensing, the savings are still significant in the long run, however, in that 500 networked and managed desktops cost quite a bit more, paying real users to give up a Saturday or sacrifice normal business hours' productivity costs more, and *not* stress testing costs even more. But it is still possible to save some money if you're willing to sacrifice the ability to easily test a lot of users running on a few servers or high-end desktops. You can use other, low-end products that can drive the SAPGUI simply because the SAPGUI is a Windows-based application. Similarly, you can use tools to drive the WebGUI, too. Products hailing from Empirix and SPECweb utilities offer management and monitoring capabilities of a test run at prices ranging from several hundred to a few thousand dollars. For projects truly strapped for cash, the AutoIT scripting utility can be a great way to go, too—not only is it free, but scripts are available over the Internet that have already been customized for various SAP transactions and general functions. So, if you have the client-driver hardware, the infrastructure, and the time but are lacking financial resources for software licensing, this could be the answer for your particular stress test.

Developing Business Process Scripts

With all of the information gleaned thus far, it should be clear which business processes need to be run during the stress test to represent the typical load on the system. Interview the super users and functional specialists to clarify any questions you may have. Further, it should be clear as to what needs to be scripted to represent a month-end close or seasonal peak—whatever represents the system's busiest time.

In identifying these business processes, the specific SAP components upon which these core business processes depend need to be clearly identified. An SAP Financials stress test might exercise SAP Financials exclusively, for example, whereas an SAP-enabled Executive Information System might require to be scripted business processes touching SAP NetWeaver BW, SAP Supply Chain Management (SCM), and even SAP ERP's Production Planning functionality. Use this information to begin planning for how and where you will ultimately develop and test scripts. Will you need a dedicated test environment or technical sandbox? Or will you simply (and more likely) need access to test or development clients within each SAP system landscape? Further, consider how you will ensure that the data in these systems or clients remains static enough to support scripting—there is nothing worse than coding a set of business process scripts one week only to come back the next and find that your data is no longer valid, or the screens in your SAP ERP VA01 sales order transaction have changed!

Differentiating Between Load, Volume, Stress, and Smoke Testing

You're probably curious as to what the difference is between SAP load testing and SAP stress testing. For that matter, you may be familiar with other terms—such as performance testing, volume testing, or smoke testing—and wonder what really differentiates each of these. In general, *performance testing* encompasses all these types of testing—any testing intended to test or validate performance. *Smoke testing* is an exercise designed to completely saturate a system so as to identify at what loads particular system components (such as the amount of server RAM, a system's disk resources, or an application server's profile settings) become bottlenecks. Smoke testing is not about real-world testing but rather about identifying limits and thresholds perhaps useful for capacity planning. For example, we have performed smoke testing on many different customer server platforms and disk subsystems to see where the hardware "breaks." The term originated long ago from a basic form of hardware testing in which a passing mark was awarded if a piece of gear managed to avoid catching on fire during its initial "burn-in."

Load testing refers to exercising a system by placing a typical or average load on it, such as the load associated with an average day of processing invoices, creating sales orders, and so on. This is often called *volume testing* as well. Load or volume testing are the natural stepping stones preceding true stress testing. We prefer the expanded term *average load testing* so as to differentiate it from plain old load testing and true stress testing, but we also tend to use all these terms rather interchangeably.

Stress testing is more about understanding the response-time performance and throughput capabilities of your unique implementation under a particular workload, or better yet under multiple and varying peak workloads. This lets the IT organization validate and quantify performance metrics germane to the proposed system environment, helping everyone understand to what degree the following major subsystems or components function well, and at what point each might represent a blockade to greater performance or throughput:

▸ CPU performance and utilization

▸ Memory utilization

▸ Network design and throughput

▸ Disk subsystem I/O capabilities and overall effectiveness

▸ Database layout and performance

▸ SAP application layer configuration and performance

Conducting real-world stress testing requires access to the production system or a system configured identically (not close—an exact match!). For new SAP implementations, the system earmarked for eventual production use can be made available with a bit of preplanning and coordination with other teams. After go-live, you'll need to schedule downtime to pull off a stress test (for example, in support of a quarterly change wave).

At the end of the day, stress testing is all about giving the project team the peace of mind that comes with fewer surprises at go-live. Stress testing validates that your SAP technology partners did *their* jobs in terms of sizing and recommendations, and that the SAP Technical Support Organization, business teams, developer and configuration specialists, and so on have all done *their* jobs equally well. It's not enough to generate a peak workload and run through a few tests, therefore. Remember that a stress test must be methodical and repeatable; a well-conceived stress test must therefore embrace a sound testing methodology. This in turn consists of various project phases, from planning through configuration, preparation, execution, and finally analysis and documentation. Without well-documented and repeatable processes, your stress test results are suspect at best.

Executive leadership teams that shelve the idea of stress testing to save a few dollars or man-hours are risking being confronted with several surprises on the day of go-live. It has always been our thought that this last big phase in an SAP implementation is too critical and just too risky to forgo stress testing. We want to let you in on a little secret—you can have the peace of mind that comes from stress testing for as little as $35,000 to $100,000. And that's not for a basic "simulation" or generic benchmark test, either; a full-blown end-to-end stress test across multiple SAP components using SAP-aware testing software executing online users and batch jobs running *your* business processes against a copy of *your* actual preproduction database can be yours for the cost of less than an hour or two of downtime. There are also several really good freeware tools, such as OpenSTA, that can be used to script and execute virtualized stress testing. Suffice it to say that with millions of dollars of budget money, tens of thousands of man-hours invested, and your core business processes at stake, an SAP implementation is just not complete without a pre-go-live stress test.

In this chapter, we drill down into the different business and technical reasons why the preproduction system needs to undergo stress testing, and walk you through performing an end-to-end stress test. You will gain insight into some of the tools and approaches that can validate that your solution is ready for the real world, and we'll help you capture the statistics and other data you need to back up those claims of being prepared for go-live.

Testing SAP Components: Basic Methods

SAP stress testing has come a long way from the days of simply testing a firm's SAP R/3 system by bringing in 100 people and sitting them down in front of a slew of desktops loaded with the Windows SAPGUI. Today we have automated tools, great methodologies, plenty of best practices, and a whole lot of lessons learned. This is good, because with the advent of SAP NetWeaver, applications built from SAP's Composite Application Framework, and the latest SAP Business Suite offerings, stress testing across the extended enterprise is necessary like never before.

To execute a stress test, you fortunately do not need to be an expert in these protocols and initiatives, nor necessarily in the systems and products that these protocols bring together. Rather, if you "drive" the business process correctly, and the functional testers have done their work to ensure that the business process executes as expected, you can (theoretically) relax and focus on scripting business processes and then monitoring the stress test. This is great news to anyone faced with otherwise learning a slew of interfaces and products.

However, you're not out of the woods yet. Scripting in different SAP components can be demanding in that each component may need to be addressed differently. And every component includes a database server, which not only needs to be closely monitored but also needs to be warmed and restored prior to each test run. Thus, pure coordination activities rise to the surface as unavoidable and resource-consuming must-haves, lest the stress test results be compromised in terms of integrity and therefore value. This is why SAP's standard benchmarking kits can prove valuable to firms with little time and the desire to compare systems from an apples-to-apples perspective.

Using the SAP Standard Application Benchmark

The "SAP Standard Application Benchmark" is a benchmark kit published by SAP AG and available to SAP's technology partners. Using this tool can be valuable for IT organizations seeking to measure, or "benchmark," a custom SAP IT architecture against configurations that have been tested and published by SAP's hardware technology partners. The downside is that such an approach does not leverage your own customer-specific data and business processes. We therefore find these types of benchmarks most useful when funded (or at least partially funded) by your hardware partner. For example, we have participated in customer-specific benchmark tests, or "bake offs," where we used the benchmark kit to test a custom system built from an HP SAP Competency Center design document. The customers have other hardware partners doing the same work in their respective hardware labs. In the end, by using this benchmark approach, we can compare our configurations and quantify who had the best response time, processed the most dialog steps, and so on.

From the customer's perspective, this works out well—it benefits from seeing a solution in action, and because the same benchmark kit is used by each hardware vendor, the results are very much apples-to-apples; resources and processes used in the execution and monitoring of an SAP benchmark are unswerving and consistent, reflecting dependable benchmark test results. Plus, most of the testing fees are often absorbed by the respective hardware sales organizations looking to close a big sale, making it an inexpensive insurance policy for the customer—it provides oversight to some degree, participates to some degree, and walks away with great data and a sense of the real value proposition that each vendor brings to the table.

Where SAP eCATT Fits In

Another valuable tool provided by SAP is eCATT, or *extended Computer Aided Test Tool*, which was discussed in Chapter 28, "Functional, Integration, and Regression Testing." eCATT is the perfect tool for testing multicomponent SAP solutions, in that it supports the most common releases of SAP products on the market or in data centers today, and can leverage its hooks into SAP to drive complicated back-end processes. But eCATT does not natively support virtual users, relying instead on SAP's testing partners. So although eCATT is a powerful tool for proving functionality and performing regression testing, it really takes a third-party SAP-aware load testing tool such as those found in HP's Performance Center suite of tools to pull off a true stress test.

Using SE38 for Cross-Application Stress Testing

Because of the potential complexities associated with testing business processes that span your enterprise, we find it especially useful to leverage transaction SE38 for testing. SE38 can be scripted to run a variety of reports and other jobs, both online and in the background (running as batch processes). Selecting jobs that not only represent your typical workload but also make calls to other SAP components is one of the most straightforward methods of driving an enterprisewide stress test.

Problems exist with this "easy" approach, of course. First of all, it's doubtful whether all of your key business processes can be neatly executed in this manner. Second, you need to consider how many transactions you actually have that can be started from SE38 *that touch multiple SAP systems* (assuming your goal is a cross-application stress test). Our guess is that there won't be many. Combined, these two challenges tend to make SE38 only a piece of a larger puzzle, then. We like to augment a stress test load with the heavy load that can come from executing simultaneous batch jobs executed in the foreground, for example. The results may guide you as to when and upon which servers you run your batch jobs, where you place your update work processes, and even how to characterize the degree of parallelism in your custom batch processes. The bulk of the puzzle is then completed by scripting business processes that originate in your other SAP systems.

Real-World Preparation and Script Development

In this section we discuss the time and tasks related to developing the business process scripts to be executed during Stress Test Week. Before we begin, understand that the term *Stress Test Week* (Test Week) is used pretty loosely—it's not unusual for this "week" to actually run two or three calendar weeks. We have found that a calendar week, or about five to seven days, tends to represent the average amount of time a company actually stress tests its production environment. This clearly does not include time spent in planning and preparation, but should give you a rough idea of your investment. Unfortunately, we're not talking about 8-hour days and long lunches here, either. For the teams engaged in supporting Test Week, it seems as if no matter what level of preparation is taken up front, Test Week consists of something close to 12-hour days. And the days leading up to Test Week are usually not much better. Consider the following typical workloads we have executed during Test Week:

▶ For a medium-sized R/3 system test long ago, we consumed eight calendar weeks creating over 50 online user transaction scripts across six different R/3 functional areas.

▶ Another stress test engagement required preparation to the tune of four weeks for ERP, and one additional week for SAP's Business Warehouse. We coded 20 discrete online ERP transactions, three batch processes with over 100 variants, and five BW queries and a mix of other transactions in support of this test.

▶ Another pre-go-live ERP stress test required four weeks to script six end-to-end business processes (approximately 30 online transactions representing processes such as order-to-cash and so on), and another week and a half to execute and analyze the test runs.

▶ Another really simple stress test consisting of only five core business transactions consumed two weeks to script and test, and another three days to execute (a short Test Week). Comparing this particular test to the previous tests illustrates the work involved up front; additional scripts become easier to develop after the core work is completed.

Preparing for Test Week takes so long because there's so much to do. We spend a great amount of time with the various business and technical teams identifying functional process flows and workflows, and then gathering enough valid data to support a test. After installing the scripting tool, we spend even more time creating scripts that functionally work; like programming, script development is subject to development iterations, including fixing coding bugs, introducing standard subroutines for error handling and reporting, and so on. During the script development process, we like to hold at least twice-a-week status reviews, too. During each one- to two-hour meeting, we ensure that all testing assumptions still hold true, share status updates related to scripting in the various functional areas, identify issues or problem areas, and share successes. If something is changing (for example, we've often lost our "test clients" due to system refreshes), we discuss what this means to the test project plan.

Fortunately, some of the tasks associated with a stress test can be performed concurrently, such as working through the final test goals and success criteria, determining ways to validate success criteria, making revisions to the test plan and refining a testing methodology, working with the business units or functional teams to understand business processes or verify transaction flows, actually test-executing each transaction, and so on. This gives you an opportunity to *crash* the project schedule, a project management term that implies throwing more bodies at a project to achieve milestones faster. On the other hand, tasks that cannot be crashed imply things that must occur sequentially, one task after the other. A good example of this is testing a script for bugs—each script must be recorded and then set up to run in virtual mode, leveraging variable input before any real bug testing can take place.

When both scripting and the follow-on single-unit testing are completed (including finding more last-minute data, which is not as unlikely as it sounds), the script is ready to be tested by multiple virtual users running concurrently. Single-unit testing ensures that the business process script can be executed by a single user from start to finish without error. Next, understanding how many virtual clients will be needed to emulate the future production environment, including which functional areas and so on, is necessary. Once you have this information in hand, you are ready to progress to the next phase of script development—defining, installing, and configuring your stress test infrastructure.

Stress Test Client Infrastructure

In stress testing, your goal is to run your tests in an environment that, from an infrastructure and configuration perspective, looks like production. In the best of worlds, you run your stress test on your soon-to-be actual production system. This is *always* preferred to any other alternatives, but is sometimes not possible. In that case, an identical staging or disaster recovery system, or something cobbled together that truly represents production, must suffice.

Just as importantly, you need to assemble the "client side" of your production system. It is this client infrastructure that we refer to when we talk about *stress-test client infrastructure*. It is rare for a customer to have enough desktop/laptop clients, network infrastructure, and time to actually assemble a mock client environment—this is precisely why virtual direct testing software products were built in the first place. But you still need some amount of in-place hardware to serve as client drivers. In other words, you need to install one to perhaps four or five servers to provide the client load on the production system. Further, you need one or more computers to control these client drivers. A high-level task list might include the following:

1. Size the client infrastructure. You need to figure out processing power and RAM for the controller, console, and any special monitoring systems required by your stress-testing software.

2. Acquire and install the client infrastructure.

3. Install the SAPGUI where required, being careful in the installation process to include the option to also install SAP development tools. You may need to copy both the `services` and `SAPMSG.ini` files from one of your SAP applications servers to your client drivers and console, too, depending on the stress-testing software's requirements.

4. Install the stress-testing client and console software; refer to the software's documentation for details.

5. Configure each client and the console as recommended by the software's documentation.

In the next few sections, we detail some of the specific scripting challenges we've run into.

Creating Administrative and Other Utility Scripts

Good programming or scripting often focuses on creating reusable code, such as subroutines that can be accessed as or when needed. In the course of stress testing, we have developed a cadre of subroutines that seem to prove useful over and over again, such as the following:

▶ Log in to the SAPGUI and establish a virtual session

▶ Log out of the SAPGUI

▶ Generate a random number

▶ Generate a unique number

- Perform SAPGUI screen-scraping, useful in capturing error and warning messages or basic informational messages like "Credit limit for customer 320030613 changed"

- Perform common comparison routines, useful for incorporating into if-then conditional statements

- Read from an input text file (.txt), Microsoft Excel file (.xls), or other format

- Provide reporting/statistics-capturing capabilities, including writing stress test case information out to a text file

The best tools out there—Mercury's products, making up the HP Performance Center suite—make creating such routines easy if not altogether unnecessary. If you're going with a different tool, note that many times we actually build these subroutines directly into our script instead of calling them. Whether or not we do depends on the likelihood of having to change something, or the need for a specific subroutine, versus our willingness to manage separate subroutines. Regardless, we are sure you will agree that these subroutines save you coding time.

Logging In and Ramping Up

There is more to running a good stress test than simply logging in a few hundred virtual users and letting them run loose. To control the ramp-up of a stress test such that all users actually have the opportunity to log in successfully, the users need to be logged in over a period of time. Why? Because logging in 500 users at once results in many of those login scripts aborting for timeout reasons. HP Performance Center's LoadRunner product takes care of this ramp-up seamlessly. Other tools, such as the SAP Benchmark kits, log in a new benchmark user every second and, in doing so, automatically control login "behind the scenes." Similar programmatic approaches can be developed to stagger SAP logins. The core logic behind this approach is to manipulate the unique number assigned to each virtual user (for example, 0001, 0002, 0003, and so on). Because this unique number is held in a system variable, it is available for use. This kind of a subroutine obviously needs to execute *before* you log in to SAP so it can control when the SAP login process commences. So in keeping with good coding standards, it cannot exist as part of the standard SAP login script or process. Instead, it needs to be executed by the actual functional script, or an "umbrella" script used to execute multiple discrete transactions.

If ramping up users is not built in to your stress-testing software, keep this in mind: When analyzing the data associated with the test run, make sure you toss out all transactions and data associated with ramp-up. Doing so allows you to focus only on the statistics associated with the actual test run. This underscores why it is so critical to track the start and stop times for each individual transaction that is executed—recording start and stop times (again, this is also called "wall clock" time) is performed programmatically in the body of the script's loop, and written to the output file by virtue of the output subroutine called by the script.

Collecting Statistics

Statistics are critical to the stress test; failing to capture the proper source data is therefore akin to throwing away most of the budget money earmarked for stress testing. Best in class tools like LoadRunner and SilkPerformer collect all the input and output data necessary to analyze stress test runs. For those tools that are not capable of this, we normally collect the following data and statistics:

▶ In regard to housekeeping, we capture the virtual client's number or machine name, the test case ID associated with the script (a high-level ID), a "Run Name" associated with the particular script (useful for versioning), and the hostname of the SAP server on which the test user logged in.

▶ It is important to capture general "test run" statistics, such as the current date, the time that the script began, the time that the functional loop began executing, when the functional loop completed (which usually coincides with when the script wrote its reporting/statistics data to an output file), and when the entire script ended.

▶ Capturing business process-specific statistical data, including the name of the transaction screen and how long (response time) it took to display the screen, the screen's business input data (such as a customer number, material number, PO number, and so on), and the screen's business output data (such as the order number created, or an information message noting the fact that a record was updated, or an update failed, and so on).

Other statistical data proves useful, too, though this data may not necessarily be collected via the scripts being executed but instead might be collected through other means. For example, we like to collect test-run data that represents a snapshot in time (such as every 2 or 3 minutes) over the course of a test run. The snapshot data might include the number of concurrent processes executing, the number of users actually logged in and actively using a work process, the disk queue length associated with each of the database partitions, the average CPU utilization of each application, database, and central instance server, and so on. This information is captured in a variety of ways—through another SAPGUI session used for monitoring the stress test run, through Windows Performance Monitor (PerfMon) or other OS-based performance monitoring utilities, and even from the output generated through the testing tool itself.

Sometimes we'll script and run SAP Computing Center Management System (CCMS) transactions along with our test runs so that we can correlate the number of users observed via SAP's ST07 transaction, for example, with what the test tool shows. We are particularly fond of ST07 because it gives us a snapshot of not only how many users are logged in, but how many are actually active simultaneously, how many are actively using a work process at that point in time, how many average user sessions are logged in, and even how many application servers are servicing various functional areas (which verifies that any logon load balancing is working as expected). Transaction AL08 is also useful in that we can see how the users are distributed across different application servers (again, proving whether logon load balancing is doing its job). Automating these kinds of transactions gives us one less thing to worry about when executing the actual stress test runs.

Again, the best stress-testing tools—such as Borland's SilkPerformer and HP's Performance Center suite of products—already have the ability to include this kind of information natively, making our stress-testing project even simpler!

Regardless of how you collect your output and other performance data, it's critical to understand all of the statistics you want to analyze later, as you must actively capture this data during the run. Even the simple task of starting a PerfMon log must be actively performed; we suggest creating a simple checklist of things you want to capture, so that you remember to do so during the actual test runs—without a checklist, we know personally that we would have spent more time *rerunning* test runs to collect forgotten data and less time actually analyzing that data.

Logging Out—Gracefully Ending Your Test Session

When you have completed your test run, or have decided to end or otherwise abort the run, you need to gracefully stop the test. The key here is "gracefully"! It's pretty simple (though time consuming) to kill all of the SAP sessions via SAP CCMS transaction SM04. But from a data-collection perspective, this is not the best answer. Why? Because correctly logging out of the virtual session is critical; an unsuccessful logout can get in the way of collecting statistics associated with the run, and skew the test results, too.

In the best of cases, simply aborting a script only causes you to lose the statistics associated with the last loop in the test run. It doesn't sound like much, but for a test of 1,000 users, losing the results for something between 1 and 1,000 transactions will skew your results and, depending on the number of loops, actually represent a wide margin of error. Some of the 1,000 transactions may just have started, some might be halfway through a complete business process (which then might invalidate the entire business process for the test, given that it never completes successfully), and other transactions may be in the middle of writing output statistics (some of which may be actually written, while others are lost). And worst case, a whole slew of backed-up transaction output that is queued to be written might be lost. This is next to impossible to track, making the whole test run suspect. In fact, none of these cases reflects sound business process or transactional integrity, and therefore should be avoided.

Aborting the activities of a virtual user might be required in some cases, however. For example, if after executing a business process 30 or 40 times, your virtual user 231 gets hung or "stuck" in a transaction (due to poor scripting that did not take an error or other condition into account), you could very well lose all of your statistical data pertinent to that particular user—the orders created, materials moved, and so on. For one or very few users, this is easily dealt with. The output files reflecting activity for virtual user 231 can be purged or simply not considered in the final analysis, for example. But more often than not, you will need an orderly and repeatable method of ending scripts. A few possibilities exist:

▶ Code each script, or set up each package of scripts, to only execute a finite number of times. This represents a method of testing in and of itself, in fact, in that the test becomes more of a race against time than an exercise in throughput.

▶ Code each script to check the status of a systemwide or other variable. If the contents of the variable in a special variable file are "true," end the script. To make the contents of the variable true, and therefore end the test, we suggest copying a new variable file (with the variable already set as true) out to the file share or other location where it currently resides and is accessed by the various scripts (in effect, copying "over" the current variable file).

▶ Similar to the approach described in the preceding bullet, code each script to read the contents of a "status" file; if the contents say "stop," then execute the logoff subroutine to stop the test.

We've used all three approaches with varying degrees of success. The last method can be troublesome, however, if a shared file is used for more than something like 100 users. This is because of the open and read activity that takes place, and resulting "lock" that one user places on the file. Subsequent users can't get to the file, and thus sit around and wait for access. If the wait is too long, these scripts can abort. In our experience, the *best* way around these locking issues is to create a unique "status" file for each virtual user, like status.0231 for virtual user 231. Doing so eliminates file-contention issues, but brings up new issues, including how to manage the process for quickly changing the contents of 1,000 status files. We have used simple batch files to rename the current status file (one that does not contain the word "stop") to another name, and then rename a file containing the word "stop" to status.0231—this works out quite nicely, avoiding every problem that we have ever come across in this regard. Other methods are certainly possible as well.

Additional Scripting Tips and Tricks

Throughout the years, we have come across or developed a few handy scripting tips and tricks that we believe will be beneficial to others. For simple "hardware delta" stress tests (in which we want to compare the throughput of one SAP technology stack to that of another), one of our favorite practices is to avoid running transactions that *create* anything. It's still very important to run transactions that issue *writes* to the database (such as transactions that change sales orders, purchase requisitions, customer credit limits, and so on). But by avoiding inserts, you avoid making the database larger and therefore eliminate much of the need for restoring the database to a known state before each stress test run. This saves a lot of time on a couple of fronts—you don't have to devise a process for warming/populating the database, nor do you have to take up time restoring the database to a known state before each test run—and makes a lot of sense for certain stress-testing scenarios.

We have also learned to use the random number generators that ship with different stress-testing tools. Some of these are quite good, in that they generate a different number or "seed" as expected. Others tend to generate the same sequence of numbers, which is therefore not random, but can be used for predictably unique sequences. We highly recommend developing your own random number generation process, too. Like the serial number example we gave earlier in this chapter, a random number can be easily created by simply concatenating a number of values that change constantly. We often use the virtual client's unique number along with the numbers associated with the current time and date to create a truly random number.

We are also big fans of scripting Basis transactions that can help us automatically gather test statistics. Like transactions ST07 and AL08 discussed previously, transaction ST03 is another excellent tool for gathering post-run response time and throughput metrics associated with a particular test run. In the past, we've coded ST03 in combination with SM51; using SM51, we can select a specific application server (such as the top one in the list). We then follow this up with an ST03 to gather specific dialog steps processed for the run as well as average response time, wait time, load time, roll time, database request time, enqueue time, and so on. After collecting this application server–specific data, we simply run SM51 again and choose the next application server in the list. In all, this is just the kind of data that truly proves an SAP system is ready for prime time, or that one SAP system outperforms another.

In running stress tests, we noticed long ago that it took a whole lot of end users to create the load we needed to generate (as observed in transaction SM50 or in systemwide detail via transaction SM66). As explained earlier, these transactions allow you to display the status of dialog, update, and other work processes, as shown in Figure 33.1. Some of the ways we have artificially and consistently created a greater load on a system during stress testing are

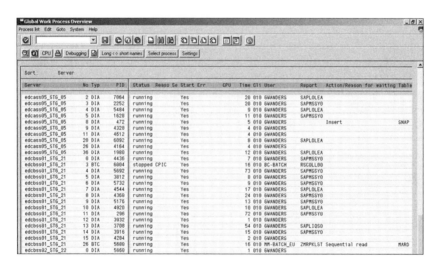

FIGURE 33.1   A powerful cross-application transaction code, SAP CCMS transaction SM66 is perfect for monitoring multisystem SAP landscapes and their active work processes.

▶ Use "noise" scripts. Some of our clients call this *background noise*; regardless, the function is the same—by executing a core set of display-only transactions behind the scenes of your real stress test, you will realize much more activity in the system and create a more-representative stress test. Noise transactions that we have scripted in the past include VA03 (display an order), MM03 (display a material), PA03 (display an employee record), ME23 (display a purchase order), and quite a few other read-only transactions.

▶ Similar to noise scripts, execute a predefined set of long-running queries or reports behind the scenes. A customer's custom "Z" reports can prove beneficial in this regard, and truly help exercise an SAP system.

▶ End a transaction by executing the initial transaction again. For example, if you execute a VA01, you'll go through three or four screens that need to be filled in with input data and processed. At the tail end of the transaction, an order will be created. Run the subroutine to gather your statistics. We then suggest simply running the core VA01 transaction again, only this time refrain from going through the additional screens. Instead, execute a /n and repeat the loop as normal (starting *again* with VA01). The end result is that the load on the system is increased in a regular and repeatable manner, without introducing new or unusual transactions.

▶ Execute a set of scripted Basis (as opposed to functional) transactions to gain a respectable amount of value from early stress testing cycles. This is useful for really basic load tests, especially in the case where no user data is yet available. These kinds of tests best support hardware delta testing, which we spoke of previously. Comparing one system to another can be accomplished by measuring total dialog steps processed for a finite run (of say 30 minutes), or calculating average response time, or simply monitoring the number of times a particular loop of transactions executed. Typical Basis transactions that are available even before any developers customize an SAP system include ST02, ST04, ST06, ST07, OS01, SM50, SM51, SM66, DB02, RZ10, SM37, and a host of others—the idea is to find a set of transactions that not only is relatively easy to script, but also makes reasonably consistent and plentiful database calls or CPU requests, like ST07 depicted in Figure 33.2.

Database Name STG Server EDCDBS23 System MSSQL	SAP Release 640 Time 14:50:33 Date 02/01/2007				
User 4,152 Number of servers 8	all clients Work processes 301				
Application	Number of users			Sess per User	Appl Server
	LoggedOn	Active	In WP		
Basis Components	957	229	20	1.02	8
Financial Accounting	204	15	0	1.00	1
Logistics - General	437	71	0	1.00	2
Materials Management	182	39	0	1.01	3
Personnel Management	2	0	0	1.50	2
Plant Maintenance	413	98	0	1.00	2
Sales and Distribution	205	26	0	1.00	1
Other	1	0	1	1.00	2
Total	2,401	478	21	1.01	8

FIGURE 33.2   SAP CCMS transaction ST07 provides powerful rolled-up user data sorted by functional areas, creating a repeatable load in the process.

For scripting tools that are not SAP-aware, another useful practice is to drive the SAPGUI using keyboard commands as much as possible, instead of performing mouse clicks. That is, if you can navigate via the keyboard to the button you need to click, or the radio button you need to click, you tend to get a more reliable script. And because many of the screens in the SAPGUI support function keys as well as "mousing," it's not too difficult to find keyboard shortcuts. While scripting, right-click the background of the SAPGUI to see the available function key shortcuts for that particular screen.

Finally, yet another handy trick we picked up a few years ago involves using the number of seconds in the current time (0–59) as a way to "randomly" determine which transaction should execute. This is useful in umbrella scripts, which, as we mentioned before, are scripts that essentially execute other scripts based on a set of criteria. We use umbrella scripts and information provided to us by our customers to set up distributions. For example, if our customer tells us that 10% of all scripts should execute FD31, and 30% should execute VA02, we set up if-then logic in our master umbrella script such as "if time = 00 through 05, then execute transaction FD31." This represents 6 of 60 possibilities, and therefore 10%. Similarly, "if time = 06 through 23, then execute transaction VA02." This represents 18 of 60 possibilities, or 30%. As you can see, it's granular enough to handle different percentage loads.

Stress Test Execution During Test Week

With the big week finally upon you, there is much to do, from preparation to final review of both the system to be tested and the supporting test infrastructure, to last-minute assessment of scripts, data, and data analysis processes. You'll want to start early because by the time this is all done, you will probably have time to only run one or two test cases prior to breaking for lunch. We suggest performing a reboot of all servers involved in each test—everything, including the system to be tested and the systems driving the test—prior to officially starting a "run." In this way, all caches are flushed, everything comes up "clean," and a very repeatable test foundation is established. Bring down the test infrastructure first, followed by the test system's web, utility, and bolt-on servers (as applicable), and then the test system's application servers, and finally the database server. Start everything up in the reverse order—database up first, then application servers, then all the other web, utility, and bolt-on servers, then the test infrastructure client drivers, and finally the test consoles.

Next, start the various monitors you will use to collect data on the run. Start two different SAPGUI sessions, kick off PerfMon or start your UNIX performance monitoring utility of choice, and so on. Note the wall clock time on your test run checklist, give the run a name, and then start the actual stress test run by releasing the first script or package. This starts your ramp-up period. Be certain to release each package in the same sequence and using the same time intervals each time you start a run, and note any deviations. We strongly suggest recording the sequence and timing in your checklist, to make sure there is little room for error. Why? Because even a couple of minutes difference in starting hundreds of test users will result in different throughput numbers, and generally skew the test run when compared to other test runs.

Final Preparations Before Test Week Commences

By the time Test Week draws near, all of the gear required to complete the stress test should be in place. That is, the production system or system to be tested must be in place and locked down (in terms of change control) as much as can be expected at this time. All virtual test clients—physical desktops or servers, software, and everything associated with driving virtual clients—must be in place. Any special monitors or consoles to be used for monitoring must also be set up. For example, we require at least two desktops from which to execute SAPGUI sessions, OS-monitoring tools, and so on. Finally, the stress-testing console needs to be cleaned up, customized in terms of packages and scripts, and tested. This will help ensure that Day 1 of Test Week is not wasted performing pre–Test Week tasks.

Leveraging Your Testing Tools

With the first test started, you need to begin monitoring the run immediately. We recommend focusing first on the testing tool's console to ensure that the scripts are indeed running and that virtual clients are indeed being generated and making a connection to your SAP system(s). While monitoring this activity, don't forget to continue the ramp-up process. In our experience, it's common to release between 5 and 10 different packages in the course of 15 to 30 minutes, while simultaneously monitoring the test run. It can take an hour to ramp up a test run of several thousand users!

Monitoring the Stress Test via SAP Transaction Codes

With your SAPGUI and a number of dedicated console sessions per *SAP component*, you will monitor the activity generated by each virtual user. The initial thing to look for is the system activity spikes associated with each virtual client logging in to each system. Again, CCMS transactions ST07 and AL08 are perfect in this regard. When the logon spikes have subsided and the test run has approached the end of the ramp-up period, another set of CCMS transactions becomes valuable:

- ▶ SM66, to monitor how active a particular system is across all application servers and the central instance. SM66 displays all active work processes—database updates, dialog work processes, background (batch job) work processes, and so on.

- ▶ ST06, to monitor disk queues, processor and system utilization, and memory, paging, and similar OS statistics.

- ▶ ST04, to verify that procedure and data cache hit rates are high or otherwise acceptable.

- ▶ ST22, to monitor ABAP dumps.

- ▶ ST11, to review error logs and traces as necessary.

▶ SM21, to review the system log.

▶ ST03, though don't worry about collecting too much data during the actual test run. Instead, we execute one or two ST03 transactions to simply ensure at a high level that actual response times are in the ball park.

Transaction ST03 becomes even more important when it comes time to validate that we actually drove the workload we were expecting to drive. We do this by comparing the number of planned dialog steps to be run with the number that was actually executed. As we see in Figure 33.3, we've run thousands of ML82, IW33, IW23, and other dialog steps— just as we had hoped. Our stress test seems to be working as planned.

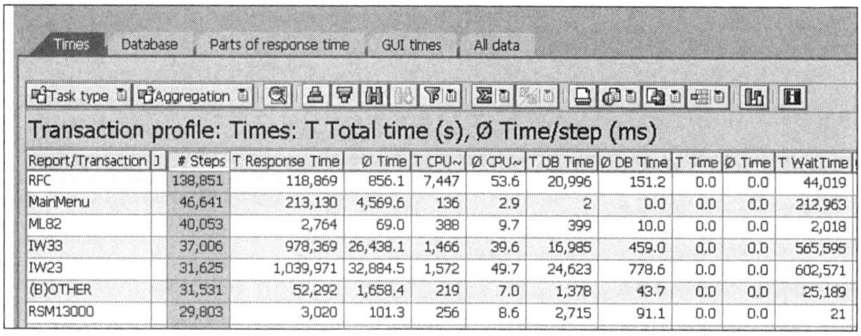

Report/Transaction	J	# Steps	T Response Time	Ø Time	T CPU~	Ø CPU~	T DB Time	Ø DB Time	T Time	Ø Time	T WaitTime
RFC		138,851	118,869	856.1	7,447	53.6	20,996	151.2	0.0	0.0	44,019
MainMenu		46,641	213,130	4,569.6	136	2.9	2	0.0	0.0	0.0	212,963
ML82		40,053	2,764	69.0	388	9.7	399	10.0	0.0	0.0	2,018
IW33		37,006	978,369	26,438.1	1,466	39.6	16,985	459.0	0.0	0.0	565,595
IW23		31,625	1,039,971	32,884.5	1,572	49.7	24,623	778.6	0.0	0.0	602,571
(B)OTHER		31,531	52,292	1,658.4	219	7.0	1,378	43.7	0.0	0.0	25,189
RSM13000		29,803	3,020	101.3	256	8.6	2,715	91.1	0.0	0.0	21

FIGURE 33.3   SAP CCMS transaction ST03 gives us the ability to validate our workload and much more.

While monitoring your stress test via the SAPGUI and CCMS, don't forget to continue to look at the status of the stress test as identified by the tool's monitor. It's not uncommon to "lose" a couple of virtual front ends, for example. However, this needs to be noted so that its impact can be factored in after the stress test run has completed.

Using Test Output for Continuous Improvement

One of the great benefits of a test run's output is that it can be analyzed to support tuning the preproduction system "on the fly." Further, the data can then be used for comparisons, allowing you to measure the real value gained in the tuning and changes made to the system simply by executing another test run. It's a great process, and certainly one of the best ways to tune a system simply because the load placed on the system is so predictable and repeatable.

For this reason, collecting data expressly derived from a stress test run is a must—you cannot afford to "forget" to collect your data, or to lump the test results of many test runs into a master file or another general repository. Do your best to keep both your test runs and your test output data discrete. To this end, we suggest creating a directory structure where each test run is given a directory, and underneath each test run directory are separate folders for input, scripts used, and output data. Copy all of the relevant test-related figures into their appropriate folders. We also create a simple checklist like the one that follows to help us remember what data to collect:

▶ Details related to the complete load-tested solution stack configuration. Of critical importance is to note any changes (compared to the previous run) that were made to the stack, test tool, or approach.

▶ Average ST03 response time statistics for the test run (with all low-level details), especially dialog and update work process response times. Include background response times if applicable.

▶ Dialog steps processed per application server (also available from ST03).

▶ The output files created from each script, which should record input data and output/results for each transaction executed during the test.

▶ Total number of transactions executed (sorted by whatever criteria makes sense in your particular case). This should correlate pretty well to the number of transactions processed.

▶ The number of virtual users that executed on *average* throughout the test, as well as the number of virtual users at the end of the test. Note that there is usually a drop-off of a few users during any test; however, we void a test run if we lose more than a few percentage points.

▶ OS-collected statistics identified previously. And don't forget to copy the PerfMon's or other utility's login to your test run directory structure. In some cases, you might even want to add event or error logs to the output test directory.

▶ Any data collected manually, such as regular "spot checks" recording CPU utilization or average disk queue length and so on.

With all of this collected information, it is then necessary to go through the process of preparing for the next test run. Sometimes this requires restoring the "test" databases for each SAP component. In all cases, we recommend rebooting and restarting each system as previously described to clear all cache and start the next test run with a clean slate—in this way, caches will be predictably populated during the ramp-up period of the next test.

Additional Stress-Testing Goals

When you have made the initial investment in a stress test, and have the infrastructure and scripts in place to accurately simulate how your production environment will behave after go-live, it's very tempting to take this investment one step further and begin doing some additional value-added or just plain out-of-scope stress testing. In our experience, the most common additional test runs performed outside of the core goal-driven testing include

▶ Playing "what if," such as losing an application server to see the impact that its absence has on load balancing

- ▶ Verifying that your failover solution works as advertised, and ensuring that specific failover scenarios operate as expected

- ▶ Ramping up the system to reflect excessive loads; this might include increasing the number of online users, reducing the think time of these online users, increasing the number or intensity of batch processes, and so on

Certainly other scenarios can be tested. We suggest that you discuss these well before Test Week if possible, in case any prior preparation or research would prove beneficial in setting up or executing these test runs.

Playing "What If"

Taking a "what if" approach to additional stress testing can prove phenomenally useful in terms of validating the system's performance. If your company is considering an acquisition, is in the middle of bringing more users into the system, or is simply interested in the impact an MRP run has on the daily production load, these tests are valuable. We believe the key to a good "what if" test is guidance and some level of assistance or preparation from the business units. In other words, you want to understand *exactly what* might be valuable to script, simulate, or test manually. This implies working with the functional or business teams to understand their business processes. You can then add additional "layers" of testing by folding in some of the tests discussed in the next few sections. For example, understanding the impact of an MRP run during a typical day might just be the beginning for you. To really gain valuable insight, you might further want to see the system fail over from one database node to another, or from the primary data center site to the DR site, while in the middle of all of this processing activity. Additional hardware-centric or HA-specific "what if" scenarios are discussed next.

Testing the Failover Process

We have had much experience with the kind of value-added stress testing aimed at testing an organization's HA configuration or failover processes. The possibilities are endless, but the following scenarios are typical:

- ▶ Knock out power to a database cluster node, redundant application server, no-single-point-of-failure disk subsystem, or a dual-redundant network switch, to verify that the system remains up and available, or reacts as expected. It's not uncommon for new failure scenarios to be uncovered in doing so.

- ▶ Simulate a failed disk drive. Speak to your hardware partner for supported ways to perform this test, keeping in mind that unplugging an actively running disk drive, even if it's redundant or protected via RAID, may not be the best or supported method of testing a disk drive failure.

- ▶ Fail your system over to the DR site while you're in the middle of a 1000-user stress test, and see how the system reacts. Run another test to characterize how well the DR site handles the workload. Then fail the whole system back to the primary site to observe how well this piece of the failover process works.

▶ If supported by your technology stack, hot-replace a "failed" component such as a power supply or network card to ensure the process is both flawless and documented clearly.

Finally, test the impact of losing an entire application server, which reflects how well your logon load balancing scheme works, how long users take to reconnect to the remaining application servers, and other performance and availability metrics.

Ramping Up to Excessive Loads

Ramping up your workload to a point beyond what you "expect" to see in production after go-live is a common goal of stress testing once the core goals of go-live viability have been met. Many of our customers look at this in terms of month-, quarter-, and year-end processing. In each case, additional online users and/or batch processes are added to the test's distribution mix.

Measuring specific technology metrics such as disk queue lengths or average CPU utilization can be useful too. For one of our customers, for example, we determined that the average database CPU load would be between 20%–40%. Our goal was then to see how many users the system could host before average CPU utilization across the production landscape exceeded 80%. Other tests were crafted, focused specifically on driving the load on the database server, and then the central instance (which ran on a dedicated server by itself), then specific application servers, and finally a pair of dedicated batch servers.

In another large-scale SAP stress test, we monitored the disk queue lengths observed by different disk subsystem designs. The customer's legacy disk subsystem served as the baseline. A new SAN-based disk subsystem located at a different customer site acted as a target of sorts. Finally, after the customer received its new virtual array, we configured it consistent with different recommendations pulled from SAP Notes and from white papers published by the hardware vendor's SAP Competency Center. All of this resulted in three different configurations that we finally tested. We settled on the design and configuration that resulted in the lowest average disk queue lengths while still meeting the customer's HA and budget requirements.

In yet another case, we executed a set of stress test runs that pushed the customer's preproduction environment almost 180% beyond what would be observed in its typical day-to-day system load. Specifically, its stress test target was to hit 80 concurrent processes. After we achieved this goal, we reduced the think times in the functional scripts and then increased the number of virtual users executing these scripts. By the time we finished, SM66 revealed that nearly *all* (220 of 240) of their dialog work processes were actually being used, and the quantity of work being performed was tremendous by all measurements.

The business value provided in each of these scenarios was the same, in that we proved not only that each customer's SAP technology stack was optimally configured (through iterations of tuning and testing), but also that each system exhibited a certain amount of scalability, or head room. Further, the testing revealed which subsystems or layers of the technology stack enjoyed the head room, and which didn't. By doing so, we also identified future performance bottlenecks that might one day become problematic. Certainly, as

IT budgets became available to perform upgrades over the next few years, each client would be in a position to allocate those dollars to reduce or eliminate future performance bottlenecks.

Extracting the Last Drop of Value Out of Testing

The common goals of stress testing seem to reflect the immediate needs of the production user community—things such as average response times, number of supported users, speed with which batch processing is completed, and so on. However, we applaud those companies that take advantage of stress testing their preproduction environment to verify

▶ That their backup and restore processes work as required

▶ That their DR plans are not a disaster waiting to happen

▶ That their systems management strategy indeed alerts them to performance issues across the technology stack

Certainly, the backup/restore (B/R) process will already have been tested prior to stress testing. What is important here, however, is that the actual B/R solution implemented for production SAP be tested. The significance of this can be easily demonstrated by looking at painful real-world situations, including:

▶ A new tape library was introduced in a customer's production environment. Contrary to best practices, though, no other system in the SAP landscape utilized this specific model of tape library (or any tape library, for that matter). Instead, all other environments relied on a direct-attached older model of tape drive. Had the library been tested during Test Week, it would have been clear that the combination of the backup application, OS drivers, and tape library were not yet ready for "prime time." As it turned out, the customer found this out during an already painful week of go-live.

▶ A customer new to SAP had to deal with learning the intricacies and differences inherent to managing and backing up data residing in a new storage area network (SAN) environment. Maintaining at least one other environment identical to production was not a priority for this customer, either. It learned its lesson the hard way when an issue cropped up during high SAN utilization—the database server simply lost its connection to its data files, corrupting the entire production database as it failed. A firmware upgrade resolved the issue, but a quick 30-minute stress test run would have uncovered this issue weeks before go-live.

▶ A long-time customer decided to implement a clustered database/central instance scheme while going through a database upgrade. The customer clustered its technical sandbox, documented the process for both the database upgrade and the underlying cluster-supported hardware upgrade, and sent two key SAP support members to cluster training. What it failed to ever do, though, was run a backup to completion in its clustered sandbox environment until a week before cutover. At that time, it discovered a bug in the backup software when installed in a cluster. The bug only manifested itself under load, and then only intermittently. A disaster was avoided, but confidence in both the backup solution and the clustering approach to HA was shaken.

You probably noticed at least two embarrassing oversights per issue. First, a stress test would have revealed the flaws that were eventually found either too late or too close to actual go-live. Second, better change control practices would have brought these issues to someone's attention in a more timely manner, too.

As we discussed earlier, testing your DR plan is another important task that needs to be performed prior to go-live and then once a year afterward. Most everyone agrees with this in principle, but when it really comes down to spending the money to test your DR system, too many CIOs and IT directors have *other* plans, and the DR test is "talked through" rather than actually executed. Talking through it is better than nothing, we suppose, but we have a better suggestion—take advantage of stress testing to actually test your DR process *in action* before you go live. Later, when you are in production mode, take advantage of the downtime normally associated with quarter-end or annual change control waves to again test your DR process. This is appealing because it kills two expensive birds with one moderately priced stone. That is, the downtime is already scheduled, so adding another day or two of DR testing only takes advantage of the resources in place, and in our book equates to excellent return on investment.

Other value can be gained from stress testing as well. Any kind of testing that validates that the system will perform as expected, and meet its service-level agreements for availability and performance, represents an excellent testing investment, for example. We like the idea of testing whether alerts are generated when specific performance thresholds are exceeded, how well alerts "roll up" into other testing tools (to support a "single pane of glass" systems management strategy, for instance), and so on.

Other Stress-Testing Lessons Learned in the Real World

In the last few years, we have had the honor to assist countless SAP customers design and execute their SAP stress tests. It's an area of work that we really enjoy, and one that is as valuable to our clients as it is fun for us. The hours are long, but the rewards are great. So, too, have been the lessons we've learned—we hope the following list helps you avoid some of our own mistakes and oversights!

▶ **Make sure you have enough data**—We quickly learned the value of data in a large multicomponent stress test—more data is always better. In this particular case, we had so little transactional and master input data that within a few minutes of a test run, all of it was accessed and just as quickly cached by the disk subsystem. With next to no load on the disk subsystem, the entire test was tremendously skewed; user response times were phenomenal, transactions flew to completion, and the whole effort was essentially a waste of time until we uncovered 100 times more data.

▶ **Don't try to execute a stress test too early in your SAP project implementation—** Good data can be hard to find when you begin testing *too* early. SAP clients change as data is brought in or created, functional areas are updated, and business processes are revamped. This fact manifested itself in scripts that no longer worked a few days before Test Week, due to data combinations being invalid and SAPGUI functional transaction screens actually changing as a result of development.

▶ **Lock down your SAP client as best as possible—**Configurations change, functionality is augmented, and test cycles uncover and remedy issues. Despite all of these changes (which tend to accelerate as go-live draws closer), as much as possible, lock down your client and configuration throughout the script development and test execution phases. And stay flexible, keeping in mind that even in the best of environments, test scripts will need to be changed.

▶ **Not all virtual users are created equally—**Different testing tools exhibit different tendencies and strengths. Some force all users to log in to the system simultaneously, whereas others exhibit a pattern of repetitive activity. This can all be resolved programmatically, but requires time. Thus, do not wait until the last minute to actually test your scripts in a load-testing manner—follow the process we outlined earlier in this chapter, where scripts are tested for functionality, then single-user tested, 10-user tested, and 100-user tested.

▶ **Consider and verify think times—**If a system is designed or sized to host 1,000 concurrent *medium* users (therefore implying a 30-second think time), you need to be sure to include the appropriate think times in your scripting efforts, and then verify that actual "wall clock" time and your programmed think times don't contradict one other. This is especially true as a load is put on your system. Consider the following example: After scripting an SAP ERP VA01 transaction for a customer, we noted in our single-unit testing that the end-to-end process took 3 minutes to complete. With wall clock time of 3 minutes, and direction by the customer to execute 12 sales orders every hour (or one every 5 minutes), we figured we needed to hard-code 2 minutes' worth of think or delay time. When we had 200 hundred of these Sales and Distribution (SD) virtual users executing, however, the average wall clock time jumped to more than 4 minutes. We therefore had to scale back our think times in a big way; otherwise, we would have missed our target of 12 orders per hour per user (by 2 orders per user). At 200 SD users, that would have equated to 400 missing orders, or essentially a very underloaded system!

▶ **Analyze the performance and monitoring data that is derived from a stress test run before you perform another test run—**We've wasted days performing a series of test runs only to discover that more and more of the core transactions were not completing as the user load was increased. Had we looked at the data earlier, it would have been clear that we had a problem (as we had coded an obvious "transaction unsuccessful" message in the error routine used by the scripts; the test's output files were filled with evidence of this irritating little fact).

33

▶ **Be aware of other unintended stress testing outcomes that may prove benefi-cial**—We often prove, for example, that a customized SAP ERP business process (outside of what is in scope for our testing exercise) is poorly coded from a configuration, ABAP, or bolt-on system perspective. In another case, it was uncovered that the customer's reporting system was misconfigured (it defaulted to pulling in all data from all business units by default), bringing the entire system to its knees. Only under load were these problem obvious, though. Both problems were easily rectified (in the latter case, the users were forced to select specific parameters, such as profit center, cost center, and plant). But uncovering these issues was not the explicit goal of load testing in these cases, thus underscoring the unexpected extra value that can come out of a properly executed stress test.

Some of our favorite stress tests have been in support of our own long-time customers performing upgrades and updates to their in-place SAP production systems. These are usually the least time consuming to perform, and often revolve around the introduction of new server or disk subsystem platforms, or a fundamentally new database release. We tend to see a lot of activity in this regard when new or substantially updated processors are released, a new wave in disk subsystem technology drives massive database upgrades, or a new database software release is finally made public.

Summary

Throughout this chapter, we focused on the tasks related to planning for, scripting, executing, and monitoring an SAP stress test. We covered key testing tools, approaches to stress testing, methods of gathering input data, and the work of identifying and gathering post-run statistics. We also presented lessons learned, coding tips and tricks, and more.

Case Study: Developing a Stress Test Plan

With go-live three months away, HiTech, Inc.'s latest SAP NetWeaver implementation is scheduled for stress testing in the next several weeks. You've been assigned to work on the stress test project, and your first task is to co-develop a project plan. Senior management grew tired of spending so much money on this SAP implementation and withdrew much of the funding initially earmarked for stress testing. Further, your direct manager has indicated the need to get as much value out of stress testing as possible. For example, none of the technology teams have had the chance to validate how well the failover solution actually works when under load, nor has the operations team had a chance to see how well its systems management rollup strategy will work.

Questions

1. What kind of preparation and planning tasks need to be developed for the stress test project plan?

2. What kind of tasks related to the actual testing and post-testing need to be included in the stress test project plan?

3. Why is data collection so important to stress testing?

4. Is it possible to execute a low-cost stress test?

5. What other benefits or value should you consider adding to the stress test project plan that will help justify the time and expense associated with stress testing?

33

NOTE

The answers to these questions can be found in Appendix A, "Case Study Answers."

CHAPTER 34

Technical Change Control

At this point in your SAP implementation, your business and solution visions have materialized—the SAP data center and numerous SAP instances are finally running, and the development team is making solid progress. The SAP Technical Support Organization (TSO) should be busy planning for the go-live by now as well. All this activity is at serious risk, though, if you do not give attention to the process of managing technical change—the technology-oriented changes that need to be managed and implemented well before and long after go-live. Note that technical changes are different from the functional and business process changes outlined in Chapter 27, "Functional Configuration Change Control," though many of the processes, purposes, and general tools are similar. Addressing *change management* or *change control*—the terms are interchangeable—is essential to the continued availability and reliability of your SAP systems, just as it is essential to any mission-critical business application in your enterprise.

Change Management Mentality

You cannot expect a productive SAP solution environment to remain static. That is, as functional and business requirements, software upgrades, OS and hardware updates, and other subtle changes are requested or required, the environment will evolve over time. It *must* evolve if only to stay current, supported, and competitive. Although this evolution is good in terms of keeping a customer's employees productive and informed, an enormous opportunity to introduce instability into the production environment exists in the form of changes to the production system. If these changes are not managed well or consistently, the result over time will be much different from the desired outcome—the system will prove to be less than reliable, prone to unscheduled downtime, and more difficult to manage than otherwise required. Worst case, the system might hamper productivity or get in the way of enabling new business innovation.

Fortunately, change management with regard to mission-critical enterprise environments has typically been taken quite seriously. Examples abound of complex enterprisewide business applications being successfully managed from a change control perspective, from mainframe-class and large UNIX implementations to successful client/server-based and more contemporary enterprise environments. All these examples reflect companies that have embraced what can only be described as a no-nonsense "mainframe mentality" to change control—it's taken very seriously, a fact that is revealed by way of high system uptimes, low unplanned outages, and satisfied, productive end users.

Often, when the topic of change management or change control is brought up in the context of an enterprise application such as SAP, managing the functional changes within the application layer itself seems to capture the center of attention (again, refer to Chapter 27). Managing functional changes is important, to be sure, but that very functionality is at risk when technical change is managed poorly. To exacerbate matters, technical changes come from everywhere (see Figure 34.1), from across the technology stack and the organizations tasked with managing these discrete components. And each change ultimately must be reviewed, approved, developed, tested, and eventually "promoted up" the SAP system landscape (in a process called *promote to production*, or *P2P*). With little exaggeration, then, we can say that nearly every member of the SAP TSO will impact, or be impacted by, change control.

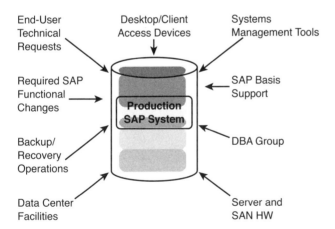

FIGURE 34.1   Changes come from everywhere to affect the SAP technology stack.

Managing and implementing changes is a very precise activity, fraught with systemwide ramifications if addressed less than absolutely correctly day in and day out. And, unfortunately, it is often a labor-intensive task, impacting SAP infrastructure support teams, database administrators, the SAP Basis team, administrators and operators, the SAP help desk/support center, and more, not to mention the training, documentation/knowledge management, and change management teams themselves.

Yes, change management affects much more than just the SAP functional layer. The entire SAP technology stack is impacted. So, too, is the entire SAP system landscape and every phase of implementation. Your management team drives and is affected by changes as well. And finally, change management must focus on human and organizational success factors, because they greatly impact end-user attitudes, behavior, and productivity.

"Change" often goes against the very values held dear by members of an organization. This explains why changes in the daily routine or culture of an organization must be proactively discussed and not ignored. Our natural reaction to change is to deny it at first, and then to simply resist it when we figure out that the change will not "go away." Eventually, a critical juncture emerges—the change is either accepted or rejected, as illustrated by Figure 34.2.

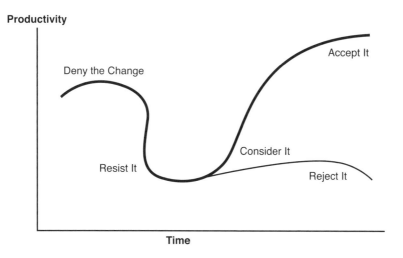

FIGURE 34.2   Our natural reaction to change must be addressed if we hope to actually manage change.

Change is inevitable. Our natural reaction against change must be proactively addressed. It's hard work but the reward for organizations that handle change effectively is compelling. Effectively managing change is all about focusing on SAP's end users and other stakeholders. The idea is to create a more stable, well-performing system, one capable of changing without affecting productivity. Even better, if change can be managed very well, the infrastructure supporting a firm's SAP business processes in effect will become more agile and therefore ready to respond to the changing business needs of the end-user community. Did you get that? *Excellent change control can foster business innovation.*

Thus, the mission of change control often amounts to the following goals:

▶ Providing solutions to users' system problems (ushering in improved business processes), which further tends to improve system utilization or value

▶ Improving system testing

▶ Maintaining documentation

▶ Maintaining training levels

▶ Improving knowledge management

▶ Implementing improved operational processes and procedures

Each of these points is discussed in detail as we step through the remainder of this chapter.

The Real Reason for Managing Change—Stakeholders

Stakeholders in an SAP implementation include anyone with a vested interest in the success of the project. The degree to which stakeholders are impacted by the project vary, and therefore their commitment level varies as well. A common way to break down these commitment levels is by ownership, identity, participation, agreement, and awareness. A change management organization plays a role in managing these stakeholder relations (along with the executive committee, project management office, and other organizations—stakeholders apparently need a lot of attention!). To best address organizational changes such as those driven by an SAP implementation, consider the following guidelines and best practices when it comes to designing or developing a change management organization:

▶ Stay focused on the needs of the stakeholders. This should drive everything from timelines to priorities, the structure of the organization, and how processes are ultimately deployed.

▶ Leverage an experienced change management consultant to review your environment and help design your change management organization.

▶ Get as much feedback as practical from stakeholders, including what they think needs to be done with regard to developing an organization focused on managing change.

▶ Delegate decisions to end users whenever possible. With their decisions driving the project in many ways, buy-in is practically a given, and priorities tend to be naturally maintained.

- ▶ Ensure that the project plan allows enough time to formulate and implement a change management organization.

- ▶ Ensure that the stakeholders understand the impact of your SAP technical designs. To that end, we are reminded of a customer that moved from a single SAP production instance to a federation of systems. The stakeholders needed to understand and accept the impact of this on the business, which was that all reports weren't available from just any system.

- ▶ Rather than trying to control change, take the position that it is more effective in the long run to understand and manage it.

If you follow these guidelines, you will be able to identify easily who the primary people impacted by the project are and develop preliminary stakeholder profiles for the SAP project. And each stakeholder's commitment levels will make themselves known, too. Finally, general change management and communication models may be created with each specific stakeholder and audience in mind.

Change Management Best Practices

In this section, we outline a process commonly used to implement change and identify what we consider to be best-in-class change management practices. Although the labels might differ, organizations focused on managing change with excellence have adopted a process similar to the following:

1. Create a project team dedicated to change.
2. Communicate the vision and goals of this team.
3. Acquire project team resources.
4. Monitor people and organizational issues.
5. Determine change management practices to be leveraged, including tool sets.
6. Reorganize to support these practices.
7. Implement these practices.
8. Monitor completion of the project plan's tasks and milestones.
9. Communicate feedback, revise practices as required, and continue to monitor.

When it comes to managing change, topics like procedures, guidelines, managing to a plan, tool sets, and so on naturally come to mind. Some guidebooks to change suggest an even simpler path to implementing change, focusing on project plan execution, communication plan execution, and stakeholder management. We have assembled a more representative list, though, that reflects both best-in-class and commonly deployed change management practices we've observed in the real world.. These practices are illustrated in Figure 34.3.

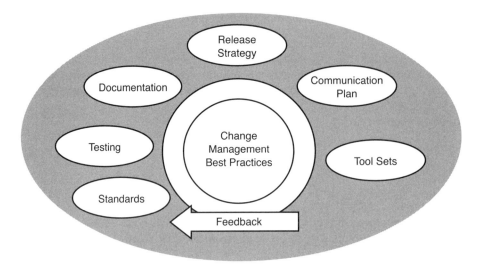

FIGURE 34.3   Change management best practices work together to help ensure that changes are tested and managed both comprehensively and effectively.

The following sections discuss in turn each of these best-in-class (or common, where noted) practices with regard to change management.

Minimizing Change Management with Standards

For most companies, maintaining less of a variety of IT technology—whether this be a certain model of server, or type of disk drive, or version of software package—will cost less in the long run and prove easier to manage than maintaining a mix of products that might better fit each variance and niche requirement within a particular SAP system landscape. For example, at one of our SAP customer sites, the client selected Microsoft Windows Server Enterprise Edition as its standard OS, even though Standard Edition would have been adequate in quite a few instances, and cheaper. Similarly, the customer standardized on a single model of database and application server, even though it provided additional processing headroom in some instances, and therefore cost a bit more up front than other models—in the long run, we all believed that the total cost of ownership would prove to be lower because this client had fewer alternatives to deal with. That is, with less hardware and software variety to run through the change control process every time a new firmware update or service pack became available, stability of the SAP landscape would be better preserved.

This example represents technology areas in which standardization served to minimize the change management activities required to support the SAP landscape. Additional reasons to standardize include the following:

▶ Fewer hardware spares need to be maintained (less costly than maintaining one or more spare hardware components for each component deployed in production).

▶ You can take advantage of bulk buying or quantity discounts (where "20 of these" is less expensive to acquire than "7 of these" and "6 of those" and "2 of that" and "5 of those new ones").

▶ Less training is required for the SAP support staff (no requirement to spend budget money training the operations staff in supporting different variations of the OS, for example, or different disk subsystem platforms, or database releases).

▶ The staff becomes very comfortable supporting fewer hardware platforms and components (no requirement to spend budget money training staff in supporting multiple server models, for example), and support calls are addressed faster.

▶ You will enjoy less unplanned downtime, because components are interchangeable (less risk of having to wait for a hard-to-find or out-of-stock part in the event of a critical server component failure), and less component variety equates to fewer changes that must be initiated, tested, and ultimately promoted to production.

The Core Philosophy Behind Change Control—Testing

Prior to any change being implemented in a system, it must be tested. This is true regardless of the enormity, location, or relevance of the system. In other words, if the system is truly important or otherwise mission-critical to its end users, then it follows that anything that potentially affects the availability of this system must be thoroughly tested first. Sound testing has the following requirements and characteristics:

▶ A highly available and stable test environment is key.

▶ The staff is sufficient to handle a large load of new or changed test projects or "test cases."

▶ To encourage repeatable and rapid testing capabilities, an automated testing tool (or tools) should be leveraged.

▶ Test cases should mirror process design, including exception handling, error corrections, reversals, and so on. By their nature, therefore, well-understood business processes often make the best test cases.

▶ Testing must fully cover and verify all SAP integration points and all possible input data.

▶ Test cases should be able to run "standalone." That is, there should be no dependencies on external data or other test cases, unless testing these dependencies is the goal of the testing.

▶ Testing must help an organization determine the impact that change has on other areas in the SAP implementation or within the company (that is, business process changes).

▶ To be most effective, the individuals tasked with building test cases should be very familiar with the functional or technology area in which they are testing. This includes access to formal training as required.

▶ In a new implementation, the Test/QA phase and related timelines should be broken out from your master project plan, to allow for the granular level of detail required but not typically found or warranted in the master project plan (in other words, a high-level project plan like the master project plan is not appropriate for planning and tracking granular-level test case execution).

▶ The end users should determine what constitutes successful business process output, based on what they also deem as acceptable input.

▶ Functional design teams should be involved early and earnestly, which helps them to understand the high priority of testing and test cases.

▶ Test cases are refined when gaps are discovered.

▶ Changes resulting from testing should be reflected in documentation, from end user–based documentation to test case documentation leveraged by the SAP TSO and more.

If testing reflects the relative importance of a system, it's safe to say that documentation reflects how seriously this is taken—the more critical a system, the better the documentation package should be that supports it. Why? Because documentation directly impacts how effectively the system can be used, managed, and supported. The central role that documentation plays in change management is covered next.

How Documentation Impacts Change Management

Before we begin, it must be understood that the term *documentation* in the context of change management means many things. To end users, the word *documentation* applies primarily to functional test cases we covered in Chapters 26 through 28. Each test case must be documented such that the case is very repeatable, and easily modified as the underlying SAP system evolves with each SAP Support Package and new functional enhancements. The key here is maintaining the data entry points, such as which particular company codes apply to which materials, which storage locations apply to which plants, and so on. All of this is typically documented in a documentation "package."

To the folks tasked with training, *documentation* relates to everything a person new to a job task or position needs to know to become an effective SAP component end user. Thus, documenting the process or workflow associated with each test case is paramount. And these trainers also need to understand how to maintain this documentation, the most effective ways of laying it out and presenting or delivering it (workshops, formal training, Internet-based, and so on), and any delta training required to be delivered between change management waves or release cycles (discussed later).

Documented workflow, process, and system training are all critical because regardless of the goal of a specific set of documentation, it quickly becomes an integral part of supporting a business unit's standard operating procedures.

Up to this point, we have only looked at documentation from an end-user perspective. To the SAP TSO, though, the term *documentation* refers to the various tools and approaches used to manage change. This also includes documenting processes, such as the promote-to-production (P2P) process, or anything regarding timelines (that is, the amount of time a change stays and is tested in the technical sandbox before being promoted to the next system, and then the next, and so on).

Finally, *documentation* to administrative and operations IT professionals means frequently re-documenting the current state of the entire SAP technology stack, and updating how-to documentation as appropriate, such that all changes are easily identified and tracked throughout the life of the SAP component's system landscape.

The Release Strategy Approach to Making Changes

One of the absolute best practices that should be embraced by every SAP shop is the use of *release cycles*—industry leaders running SAP have employed this approach toward managing and implementing technical change for years. As opposed to implementing changes one at a time in an unorganized and less controllable manner, the release strategy seeks to bundle and test changes as part of a release cycle (or simply release) as you see in Figure 34.4. The release is tested as a unit of changes and often implemented on a monthly or quarterly basis. Sometimes referred to as a *change wave* or simply a *wave*, releases facilitate improved planning, scheduling, staffing, and testing, in addition to better controlling costs (that is, costs associated with planned downtime, after-hours hardware/software support, and economies of scale when it comes to unit testing).

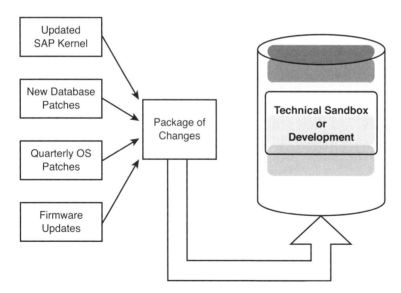

FIGURE 34.4   A good change release strategy bundles multiple discrete changes into a change release, often also referred to as a change wave.

Although a release may consist of many changes at once (all tested in concert with one another), best practices dictate that you layer changes into your SAP environment, keeping most technology stack layers in a consistent state. For example, changing firmware during one release, upgrading SAP functionality in the next, and upgrading the OS during the following wave minimizes later support issues never uncovered during the promote-to-production testing process. The idea, then, is to focus a particular release generally on making large changes in only one layer at a time (when possible, of course), with smaller accompanying changes in other layers as necessary.

A release's contents—the changes to be promoted eventually into production—should be clearly documented on a file share, on a website, or through another means accessible to everyone on the project team, the change management support team, and all stakeholders. A release may consist of the following elements:

▶ A predefined group of business process–oriented changes and enhancements approved by the business

▶ Cross-application components needed to provide integrated solutions in SAP

▶ Support packages, SAP kernel upgrades, and other SAP updates needed to maintain a well-performing SAP system

▶ Incremental SAP Basis upgrades (that is, 4.6C to more contemporary planned release upgrades, for example)

▶ Modifications to SAP extracts and interfaces

▶ Updates or patches to the database and operating system layers of the SAP technology stack

▶ Firmware and other hardware updates required of the SAP technology stack hardware layers

Regardless of the contents of the release, remember that all releases must be promoted up the SAP landscape by leveraging the change management process. Although the rule of thumb tells us there should be no exceptions, emergencies occur. However, as you can clearly see in Figure 34.5, it's much more beneficial to system integrity and reliability that no technical changes ever be put straight into production without some kind of prior testing in another system within that particular component's SAP system landscape.

For SAP implementations with multiple productive instances, a similar though more involved strategy is deployed. A "global" development system is recommended, and through a well-managed client strategy, this single development environment services multiple test/QA, staging, and production environments. As you see in Figure 34.6, such an approach allows for master data to be managed in one system, while also supporting the diverse needs of different geographies, for example.

Exceptions to exclusively using a full-blown formal release strategy exist, however. For example, critical SAP updates needed to address bugs and bombs are often implemented in Emergency Change Release processes. Similarly, critical changes may be put in quickly if data corruption or comparable risks are present.

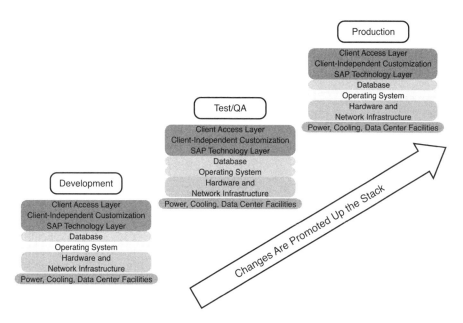

FIGURE 34.5   Promoting changes in any other manner than up the SAP landscape violates basic change management principles.

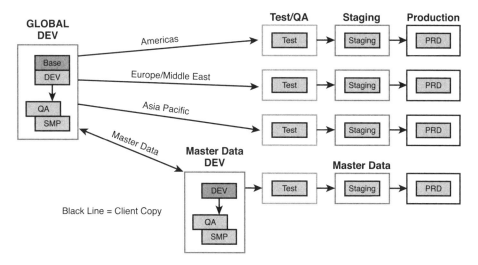

FIGURE 34.6   For SAP implementations that support different geographies, an approach like this Global Path to Production allows a single development instance and its associated master data to support multiple productive instances.

Such changes often include last-minute OS security patches, disk drive and disk controller firmware updates designed to prevent recently discovered data integrity issues, and so on. But these changes still should never be put directly into production; instead, they should be expedited through the change management process.

Finally, before we move on, it should be noted that a sound release strategy does not coincide with quarter-end or year-end processing. For example, if a company embraces a closing schedule based on the calendar year, the end of March, June, September, and December must be off limits to change control waves. Similarly, month-end changes should be avoided as well. Instead, for our calendar-year customers, we endorse the practice of promoting changes into production in mid-February, mid-May, mid-August, and mid-November.

Communication Plan

The difference between implementing changes effectively and implementing them ineffectively can boil down to sound communication. As discussed in Chapter 11, clear communication strategies underneath an overarching communication plan represent another best practice for implementing change. Thus, as the organization tasked with managing change, the change management team must

▶ Understand that communications can always improve, and therefore strive for continuous improvement

▶ Communicate through a standard forum, and in several media if possible, based on the audience

▶ Embrace feedback, so as to improve communication quality and quantity (discussed further in "Feedback—Improving Change Management Incrementally," later in this chapter)

To facilitate the preceding goals while practicing continuous improvement, a communication plan should be put in place. The communication plan seeks to reach all stakeholders, soliciting both input and feedback. It identifies the various stakeholder audiences, embraces different and effective communications media, and includes a mechanism for continuous improvement.

Key challenges to creating and maintaining a good communication plan include differing geographies (with regard to team locations), assumptions, knowledge, expectations, effort, time, and perceptions, barriers between IT departments, barriers between business organizations and IT, and a lack of feedback and two-way communications. To minimize these differences, the following tool sets and approaches are often used:

▶ Monday meetings between the business and the SAP TSO

▶ Regular weekly internal SAP TSO staff meetings

▶ ERP team or other core SAP team meetings

▶ Published meeting minutes

▶ Dialog between management, the business, and the IT groups involved

▶ Project plan schedules with clearly identified tasks, milestones, and responsible parties

▶ Business-unit representation within and between the various IT teams that make up the SAP TSO

▶ Readily accessible change management website

▶ Email between and within the various groups, including the use of standard email distribution lists

▶ Shared knowledge repository as outlined previously in Chapter 6, "Managing Knowledge and the Knowledge Repository"

▶ Various "feedback" approaches (covered later in "Feedback—Improving Change Management Incrementally")

▶ Departmentwide team-building exercises and other nonwork-related activities during which valuable informal communication can take place

The preceding list represents a nice variety of potential communication methods. The next section covers several of the tools and approaches used to manage changes.

Change Control Tool Sets and Approaches

SAP projects are not alone in their need to manage change. Long before SAP projects consumed so many IT and end-user organizations, people somehow managed to implement other enterprisewide projects. Tools and approaches such as the following have long been accepted by IT project management professionals tasked with managing technical changes:

▶ Formal project planning methodologies and training

▶ Management meetings, held to gain high-level management or team leader consensus

▶ Team meetings, held to obtain status updates and ensure that the team is making progress

▶ Communication planning and the tool kits that facilitate this

▶ Change management training—processes, approaches, and practices

▶ Training focused on problem-solving techniques

▶ Training focused on assessment and analysis techniques

▶ Business case management approaches, and training supporting this

▶ Use of subject matter experts, via internal and external consulting resources

▶ Change management software applications

Good technical change control tools reflect the same qualities covered in Chapter 27 with regard to CCM tools. The best of these tools are modular, integrated, intuitive, balanced, and generally accepted.

A good change management tool also hides unnecessary complexity (again, to increase visibility into problem areas) and automates much of the work of managing change. We like HP's Project and Portfolio Management Center product because it reflects the previously listed qualities and is not limited to managing a specific SAP technology stack or product line—various UNIX flavors, Microsoft Windows, mainframe database servers, and more are all supported. And because HP's product supports other enterprise applications, and fits nicely into HP's other software suites, an investment in HP can really pay off across a mixed enterprise landscape.

The capabilities and characteristics outlined in the following list serve as an evaluation guide for comparing the various change management tool sets available today. That is, a change management tool should accomplish the following:

▶ Provide a consistent and repeatable process for managing change across the SAP system landscape

▶ Safeguard the production SAP system from improperly executed or unauthorized changes

▶ Provide audit-trail capabilities of previous changes to the system

▶ Provide the SAP TSO with the information needed to monitor change waves, track priorities and resources, and so on

Such an application minimizes unplanned downtime by reducing risks associated with making changes. And it also reduces the amount of time people need to spend in change control meetings!

When it comes to managing the thousands of table settings and other options within an SAP client, SAP change management will always present a challenge to the organization managing it. By its very nature, the flexibility that end-user organizations love about SAP becomes a driving factor in terms of the amount of time that is devoted to change management. Good change management tools will minimize the time by automating repetitive tasks related to transports, recompiles, system refreshes, migrations, and similar tasks. Thus, any software tool or utility that can ease some of this burden should be welcomed and fully embraced by the SAP TSO.

Feedback—Improving Change Management Incrementally

When it comes to improving any process, it is usually helpful to ask and try to answer the same questions that led to the process being created or updated in the first place. This constitutes a feedback loop when end users and other stakeholders answer the questions for us. With regard to the change management process and organization, then, the following questions are appropriate:

▶ How successful was the change? Were the success criteria drafted at the first change meeting on target or appropriate?

▶ How long after the change did it (or will it) take to stabilize the production system?

▶ Overall, how disruptive was the change to the business? And what can we learn from this, to further minimize the impact of changes in the future?

▶ What individual and organizational benefits of the change have been communicated to our stakeholders?

▶ What have end users sacrificed as a result of the change (such as additional downtime or loss of other functionality)?

▶ What skills and resources were actually required to implement the change? That is, how can we better plan for and execute similar changes in the future?

▶ How well did the change team and project team members understand and execute their roles and responsibilities during the change process? Where can we improve?

We have now concluded our discussion on change management best practices and approaches. In the next section, we take a broader look at exactly how change impacts not only every layer of the SAP technology stack, but every phase of an SAP implementation as well.

Managing the Wide-Ranging Effects of Change Control

As mentioned earlier, changes to SAP can affect everything—the SAP system landscape, phases in the project, the SAP technology stack, and so on. This section details exactly what the effects are and ways to manage them—instead of being managed *by* them.

The SAP System Landscape

One of the most basic tenets of sound change management or change control includes leveraging the SAP system landscape to test changes to the environment. One method often used is a *Technical Sandbox Change Management Checklist*. Such a checklist details exactly how changes are initially introduced into the landscape, and then how they are managed or promoted up the landscape, starting with the technical sandbox.

As you have already read, sound change management practices are essential for maintaining a highly available and well-performing SAP deployment. Such a checklist approach to testing change helps ensure that nothing is missed and that all steps are actually completed successfully. Failing to use a checklist approach risks the success of the project and the integrity of the overall solution, as it impacts the entire end-user community, SAP TSO, and more.

The Phases of SAP Implementation

To understand the role that change management plays in an enterprise SAP solution, it is important to understand the evolution of that solution in terms of phases of systems development—these phases tie nicely into the SAP system landscape previously discussed.

The solution phases described in the following list are based on a typical implementation of an enterprise SAP deployment, the beginning-to-end timeline of which consumes six months at best to perhaps two years or more:

1. **Pilot phase**—This phase allows a prospective SAP customer to examine, test, evaluate, and explore the proposed SAP solution. Here, it is proven that indeed SAP will

solve the business problems at hand. The pilot phase also provides an opportunity to develop training, development, and deployment plans (which serve as a head start and can be updated later), as well as project estimates (in terms of cost and time). This phase can last from 6–8 weeks to perhaps many months. A pilot phase for each SAP component or product is common, as well. A preliminary hardware sizing is beneficial at this point, to ensure that the pilot solution is configured adequately from the beginning, so as to best set the stage for the next phase.

2. **Development phase**—Building upon the technology stack prepared in support of the Pilot phase, this phase consists of customer and/or consulting personnel configuring and customizing the system for use in the target business areas. This phase occupies much of the overall project plan, and typically continues throughout the life of a solution (though perhaps less intensely on initial business areas, to focus on new business areas and SAP components). Initial changes, such as maintenance upgrades and bug fixes, are often performed during this phase as well, hopefully in a technical sandbox or similar system. Thus, within a few months of this phase, you tend to see a fairly stable environment for continued development, and a good foundation for moving into the next phase. During the Development phase, it is also important to begin planning for the expected configuration testing and preproduction deployments to take place next—changes in business assumptions, implementation plans, and a company's particular technology standards roadmap must be reviewed.

3. **Training phase**—Like the Development phase, this phase also begins when the Pilot phase ends. Training of the development team (many of whom are already experienced SAP consultants) and the SAP TSO occurs first. Training of end users and other personnel begins when a preliminary level of configuration and/or customization has been completed. The real work of end-user training commences a few months prior to go-live, however, to help keep their knowledge fresh. After go-live, training continues to some extent for new users of the system. Therefore, like the Development phase, this phase is also ongoing in some capacity throughout the life of the solution.

4. **Test/Quality Assurance phase**—The Test/QA phase begins when the first promotion of code from development to test occurs. This phase is entirely devoted to configuration, integration, and quality assurance testing. Some time a few months before go-live, stress-testing should also take place. Note that the final production hardware sizing also takes place during this phase, typically completed as early as required to address hardware procurement, configuration, and testing lead times. This phase does not end before the Development phase ends. From a change management perspective, the Test/QA phase therefore represents the culmination of individual and packaged change testing—all the individual changes that make up a change release or wave are tested here as a single package, which will ultimately be promoted to production.

5. **Disaster Recovery phase**—Often called the DR phase, this is the phase during which disaster tolerance and contingency plans are identified. For the most mission-critical systems, fully redundant data center facilities are staffed and trained. A cost-effective way we have seen this implemented is by locating an organization's test or

staging system in a different physical location from the production system. Then, assuming the system is sized appropriately and a DR process is in place to allow for failover, the organization is well on its way to working through the remainder of the DR phase, including process testing, documentation, failover and fail-back testing, and so on.

6. **Production (or Production Rollout) phase**—This phase commences the day of go-live as the company and its organizations and business processes become dependent on the data being hosted or managed by SAP. Best practices strongly suggest not going live with multiple SAP components at once, unless they are tied together. In other words, there is usually little business reason (and much more to risk from a holistic perspective) to go live with both SAP BW and SAP SCM on the same day, for example. On the contrary, though, it might make a lot of sense to go live with both SAP ERP and SAP NetWeaver Portal because these products (and the business processes being supported) often work hand-in-glove with one other.

Timelines typically overlap, as you can see in Figure 34.7. Throughout each of these phases, the impact upon the SAP technology stack is significant, too, covered next.

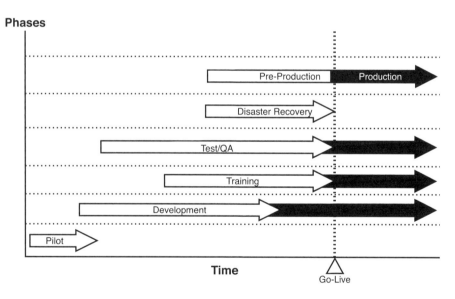

FIGURE 34.7   Note the overlap in phases—SAP implementation timelines rarely support a finish-to-start approach to managing phases.

The SAP Technology Stack

A lot of work goes into configuring and assembling an SAP solution that is supported by its technology stack vendors and effective in servicing its end users. When such a supported configuration is in place, the goal of the SAP TSO should be to minimize technical changes to the stack unless absolutely required. The reasons cited most often for making technology stack changes are

▶ To enhance performance, especially with regard to whatever the current bottleneck tends to be (most often the disk subsystem or a factor related to CPU utilization, such as growth in system usage or volume of transactions)

▶ To ensure stability, such as to address published issues about specific software drivers, database releases, firmware revisions, and so on

▶ To introduce new functionality, such as the need for additional application servers or more horsepower in the existing servers when incremental SAP components, modules, and users are added to the landscape

With these three reasons for making technology stack changes in mind, we'll next touch upon a few scenarios and how each impacts the technology stack, beginning with the SAP computing platform.

Filtering the SAP Computing Platform

Hardware and software vendors typically embrace a rigorous testing process of their own prior to releasing new products. On top of this process, vendors with SAP Competency Centers take the testing to a new SAP-specific level and add what we term an *SAP filter* to the testing process. The filtering process sifts out variables in the SAP technology stack. Thus, instead of trying to support or certify every single hardware platform, controller, software update, firmware release, OS patch, and so on for SAP, the filtering process seeks to test and support a specific combination of the stack's components, and filter out others.

The SAP filter concept is therefore good for the SAP technology vendor, good for SAP AG (which finds itself supporting fewer combinations of technology platform variables), and good for firms running SAP. The only potential drawback is that the final selection of products might be too limited. In reality, though, we have never found this to be the case—vendors are naturally motivated to test/support their latest products or most compelling solution sets. Consider the following list of tested products and releases embraced by one of the authors' favorite SAP Competency Centers, and judge for yourself:

▶ New releases of hardware platforms

▶ Updated firmware releases that address severe stability, performance, or security issues (updating the server's systemboard ROM and the firmware of other hardware components in the configuration is essential for optimal system performance and stability; "flashing the ROM" should be part of your regular server maintenance)

▶ New OS releases specific to previously tested and approved hardware platforms

▶ OS service packs and patches that will not likely be replaced in the next six months, or patches that address critical stability, performance, or security issues

▶ Hardware-specific OS drivers and updates, though typically less often than service packs/patches

▶ New database releases (typically just major releases only, or as specifically requested and funded by database partners or customers)

▶ Database service packs/patches that probably will not be replaced in the next six months, or that address severe stability, performance, or security issues

▶ New major releases of SAP components, historically centered on new SAP Basis releases

▶ Support packages for each major SAP Basis release

Most hardware and software vendors provide a tool or service that proactively notifies its customers of required hardware, firmware, OS driver, and other critical updates. For example, HP has used a Version Control Agent in the past to identify whether the latest supported version of a particular piece of code matches the installed version, or whether the installed version suffers from minor bug or enhancement issues. Check with your vendors to implement a similar kind of capability.

Comprehensive New-Product Testing

To perform comprehensive testing, technology stack partners and vendors should embrace a new-product testing process similar to that described in the following list. These processes are sometimes referred to as *standard test plans* for SAP, and are often employed by large SAP customers as well as technology stack vendors. A valid test plan should be consistent with SAP's general change management recommendations (and its own internal practices), consisting of a process something like the following (for this example, we're focused on a new release of SAP ERP with a new installation of SQL Server 2008):

1. Perform a clean install of the product to be tested, or install a clean technology stack foundation if an upgrade to a particular product is to be tested (the latter is a much more common testing scenario).

2. Perform the SQL Server and SAP installations, noting any issues and resolutions.

3. Log in to SAP via the supported SAPGUI.

4. Perform an SAP data dictionary (DDIC) check.

5. Perform an SAP client copy.

6. Perform an SAP license check.

7. If applicable, import data into or out of the system (more applicable to SAP SRM, SAP SCM, and other components that rely on a core transactional system).

8. Customize existing load scripts (using AutoIt, eCATT, or a more robust tool such as HP LoadRunner or HP QuickTest) or run a "mini" standard SAP benchmark against the system, to simply generate a load. Allow this to run for 12–24 hours (whatever is consistent with your previous testing), serving as a "burn-in" for any other new components in the technology stack. Record the transaction load, average response times observed, and issues.

9. If funded, run a complete SAP Standard Application Benchmark or custom SAP benchmark test, as appropriate.

10. If on the roadmap or otherwise appropriate, use this system to perform delta testing, including database upgrades, hardware upgrades, and so on.

11. Publish the testing results internally or as requested.

Such comprehensive testing by a hardware or software vendor assures the vendor's customer base that the platform in question is truly ready for prime time, and it also allows the partner to say without a doubt that a particular technology stack has been fully tested and is therefore supported.

The preceding example reflects what we call *general new-product testing*, where a change impacts all, or nearly all, layers in the technology stack. If we view the SAP solution as a set of concentric circles, general testing in support of change management is typically performed from the database server out to the other components in the solution, such as the central instance and application servers, and then out to the Internet-enabling computing platform, and finally out to the SAPGUI, WebGUI, or other SAP access software and front-end client hardware used to access SAP systems. As shown in Figure 34.8, then, general testing tends to be the most comprehensive form of testing performed by SAP's partners and largest customers. It represents testing of an end-to-end solution, inside out.

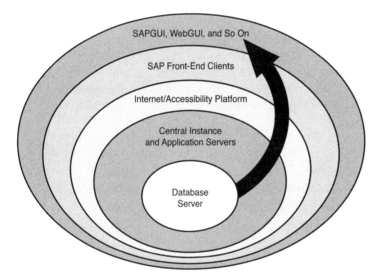

FIGURE 34.8   Comprehensive new-product testing is typically performed against an end-to-end technology stack in an inside-out manner relative to what is tested first.

With managing changes to the SAP technology stack behind us, a discussion of structuring the organization actually tasked with managing change is in order.

Tactical Testing
Other testing tends to be more tactical in nature. This is referred to as tactical, characterization, or delta testing, and addresses a smaller piece of the circle. It also involves less testing in general, often a subset of the standard test plan we looked at earlier. The goal of delta testing is to prove that a new solution component *works* rather than to prove exactly how *well* it works. And in the process, we generally uncover and address installation issues, integration issues, and other issues as they crop up.

After each test is completed, the system log files, event log, upgrade or installation logs, and other pertinent logs are reviewed for errors, and the errors are analyzed. Further testing may then be warranted, sometimes uniquely crafted to isolate or highlight a particular layer or component in the technology stack.

After all testing and error analysis, the new product is either approved or failed (pass or fail, go or no-go). Most testing results are shared with the appropriate internal and external organizations, including product engineering, various software support groups, the OS vendor or organization, the database vendor, SAP AG, and so on through either formal certification processes or informal Competency Center communications.

Organizing and Planning for Technical Change

To stay linked with the entities that drive or create changes, you must integrate a change management organization into your SAP processes and day-to-day life supporting SAP. Doing so also promotes the seriousness of maintaining, testing, documenting, and otherwise managing change throughout the company. To accomplish this, we recommend constructing an SAP support team focused on creating the best end-user experience achievable. Such an organization should have timely or "always on" access to an online change management system; authority on behalf of (and cooperation of) the end-user community; access to the SAP TSO and other resources as required; and more, as discussed in this section.

In our experience, there is no single best answer when it comes to building a change management organization, much less simply naming it. Placing it within the larger structure of the SAP TSO or another group is also a matter of question. As evident from the following list, the teams tasked with managing change can be found across many different organizations, both in and out of traditional technology- and business-focused organizations. Some of the "homes" that SAP change management organizations find themselves a part of include

- Obvious organizations, such as Change Support, Change Management Team, Change Control Group, and so on

- An organization focused on change within a business-management context, including Business Applications Services, Business and Change Integration, Organizational Effectiveness/BPR Management and Business Services, or Business Systems

- Groups tasked with knowledge management, such as SAP Knowledge Management Team or Knowledge Transfer Team

- A group within the general IT organization, such as Information Resource Management Team, Information Technology, or Technology Integration Group

- Part of a larger functional area or business-oriented team, such as Finance and Accounting, Global Supply Chain, SAP Cost Management and Controlling, Operational Accounting, or a Financial Information Support Team

- Part of a training group, including MIS Global Learning Solutions, Training Services, Learning Center, IT Training and Documentation, Change Management and

Training, ERP Training/Information Technology, Training and Process Group, or Technology Education

▶ A group affiliated with customer service or help desk organizations, such as Client Services, Information Support, SAP User Support, or simply SAP Support

▶ A member of the general SAP TSO, with perhaps a title such as Technical Change Management Specialist or something similar

Given this potential variety, however, organizations such as the one illustrated in Figure 34.9 are deployed quite often in our experience.

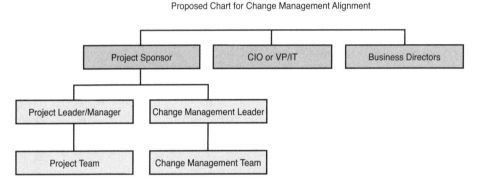

FIGURE 34.9   The change management and project management activities work hand-in-hand in this typical Change Management organization.

In the next few sections we'll take a closer look at the change management review board, the role of the change management manager, and the qualifications of a senior technical change management specialist.

Change Management Review Board

Although the change management team might be focused on managing and implementing changes, a change oversight committee, or *change management review board*, tends to play a key strategic role in larger or more complex SAP implementations, staying connected with the project well after go-live. The review board ultimately serves as the gatekeeper for the release or change wave strategy, refining and enhancing the process as the business or relevant IT organizations require. In this role, the review board actively communicates and coordinates functionally, cross functionally, and across regions or geographies—the review board's scope is as large as the circle of project stakeholders. Traditional review board responsibilities include

▶ Driving standardization of common, global change management processes, and pushing these down into the functional and SAP TSO organizations

▶ Identifying activities and practices that must exist to effectively achieve the benefits expected from each change (or what SAP refers to as an enhancement) to the SAP technology stack

▶ Coordinating and prioritizing changes to achieve improved productivity from the SAP system's end users, including pushing organizations in getting timely decisions made

▶ Measuring improvements in SAP by identifying and publishing Key Performance Indicators (KPIs) provided from each of the business organizations

The review board also often acts as the facilitator for coordinating and communicating resource allocation needs, such as training materials in support of changes, updated work and process flows and similar documentation, access to testing resources, and access to superusers or power users identified as such within their functional areas.

Change Management Manager

The change management manager (a generic title) is a key member of the change management review board, tasked with building and maintaining the change management team and maintaining and refining the change processes adopted by the review board. Because of this, the CM manager must possess not only excellent communication and facilitation skills, but also exceptional business acumen. With these core competencies, the CM manager is equipped to address a number of key responsibilities during the initial stages of the SAP implementation, including

▶ Securing executive sponsorship in support of a formal change management organization

▶ Assessing the critical implementation challenges specific to the project

▶ Developing or refining an existing change management organization

▶ Communicating to all stakeholders the real or perceived impact that changes will have in different organizations, and then working to either expedite resolutions or mitigate risks

---

CAUTION

Don't be tempted to outsource the CM manager position to a third-party contractor or consulting house. Such a role is best served by a loyal employee of the company who is both intimately familiar with the informal and formal power structures within the organization *and* focused on the firm's long-term success.

Ability to align business operations and work processes with new technology is a key to the CM manager job as well, as is an ability to negotiate with the various stakeholder and agents of change in the company. And it must be noted that the biggest opportunity for failure, according to more than a few of our SAP customers, is not gaining the executive sponsorship needed up front. Without this, the CM manager has less perceived authority, and therefore less ability to enforce change control processes vital to the stability of the system.

Senior Technical Change Management Specialist

The senior technical change management specialist position is critical to fill as early in the deployment as possible, as the best candidates will play a significant role in supporting changes even as soon as the data center is completed and the development system is put in place. Don't forget to hire or train a backup technical CM specialist as well. Key skills and experience in the following areas are of the utmost concern:

▶ Change management experience with SAP systems or other large ERP or enterprise solution environments

▶ Organization and change strategy consulting or related hands-on experience

▶ Familiarity with the specific releases and versions of SAP to be deployed

▶ Both outstanding written and oral communication and presentation skills

▶ Ability to work with all levels of the organization, from executives to "single contributor" employees and contractors

▶ Ability to keep a small team focused on working through changes that may prove difficult to implement, including maintaining a high level of resolve on the part of the entire team

Additionally, because the senior CM specialists will probably help the CM manager develop the SAP change management team over time, as well as address day-to-day issues and other tactical issues, the following qualifications are also important:

▶ Change analysis experience in support of implementing and managing SAP enhancements (functional change releases or waves)

▶ Experience with automated testing and building test case models

▶ Ability to lead and educate the business through readiness activities

▶ Ability to draft and maintain clearly written documentation

▶ Experience with establishing training programs

▶ Knowledge of change metrics (how to measure success)

Other typical activities might include participating in the design or redesign of the team, documenting the various business process design sessions or the technology update projects in which the senior CM specialist participates, and so on. Assistance with developing and deploying training curriculum is a common use of this member's time, too, as is helping to continually refine the SAP communication plan. Finally, the senior CM specialist should also be focused on how to plan for, manage, and implement the emergency changes that crop up periodically.

Change Management Lessons Learned

Change management lessons learned abound. We have spoken of various lessons throughout this book that ultimately point back to poor change control practices. If the value of managing changes is still questionable in your mind, consider these real-world examples:

▶ We received a frantic phone call from a customer whose "highly available" SAP/Oracle cluster was down. Apparently, the customer had performed a firmware upgrade on its production disk subsystem *without testing this process in another environment*, and the cluster would not start afterward. We verified that the upgrade process was indeed not performed correctly (actually, it was only half completed), and we worked with our customer to complete the remainder of the process as quickly as possible. Unfortunately, this bad situation was made worse by a harried Basis administrator—we were not called until quite a few totally unrelated changes were made elsewhere in the system, in the name of "cluster troubleshooting." Changes to the cluster itself, and then to the database layer, only served to exacerbate an already tense issue. If the customer had just followed best practices and first performed this change in a sandbox, this "simple" firmware upgrade would have been uneventfully completed well within its maintenance window.

▶ As short-term contractors engaged in testing to support a major change control wave, we were told that everything we needed to acquaint ourselves with the project was communicated via a project plan and other artifacts hosted on an internal company website. Communication outside the project plan was limited—meetings were infrequent, emails were nonexistent, and much of the rest of the staff was located elsewhere. We were expected to understand our role, timelines, and resource and scheduling needs strictly by virtue of this closely guarded project plan. Unfortunately, access to the website was not granted for weeks, and the project manager was not inclined to share the plan via email or otherwise. This forced us, and certainly other third-party contractors, to stumble about in the dark for a while. Our points here are simple—leverage alternative means of communication, and be sensitive to access issues that might impede project progress.

▶ One global SAP implementation project manager was confident that he had put together an adequate change management process, integrating it into how his company planned and deployed IT solutions for business problems across the enterprise. In reality, though, a number of issues spoke to major change management shortcomings. For example, changes made directly to production resources without the benefit of previous testing resulted in many hours of unplanned downtime. Additionally, a lack of a technical sandbox or even a test/QA system had forced all changes to be implemented in the company's development environment. The lesson here: A two-system landscape approach to implementing SAP is not the right answer for most SAP projects; a three-system landscape should be considered as a minimum requirement.

34

▶ One of our customers preferred sticking with its paper-based change control process to alternatively establishing a software-based process replete with full reporting capabilities. Each Friday, a laughable moment in time occurred as the CM manager plopped down her printed stack of completed and outstanding change requests on the conference room table, and began to go through them one by one. Sure, the process worked. But we question how well spent the CM manager's time was as she printed everything, and later keyed into her master plan the updates she scribbled during the weekly meeting on each printed page.

▶ A very large government entity running SAP R/3 was cited by the Inspector General for having "less than adequate" SAP change control procedures in place. The violation? Absolutely all of the SAP support organization—both contractors and employees, developers and Basis personnel alike—had the ability to make changes directly to the production instance. A major no-no! Only very few people (those holding senior technical leadership roles) should have such access at all, and regardless, changes must be made in nonproduction systems and promoted up to the production system.

▶ Many SAP project teams learn too late the value of a sandbox or other technical testing environment that *exactly replicates production*. A technical sandbox allows the SAP project team to experiment with and verify changes prior to promoting the changes into production. In one case, a technical sandbox would have enabled the SAP Basis team members to familiarize themselves with something new to them— using Microsoft Cluster Services to cluster SAP. But to save money, the technical sandbox was not set up in a cluster. Because they had nowhere else to practice and hone their skills, it's no wonder they one day broke their production cluster. They "evicted" the node (kicked it permanently out of the cluster) rather than temporarily failing over the node's resources to the other node, and then they made some scheduled technical configuration changes. Unfortunately, when they tried to reintroduce the first node back into the cluster, they discovered the error of their ways and proceeded to spend the better part of a night reclustering SAP with SQL Server.

▶ With regard to training, one size does not fit all. Some users, such as superusers, need to learn *all* relevant business process options and alternatives, not just the most common options. For these users, "foundation training" or "Intro to SAP" courses are inadequate. As one of our customers found, if you don't train your users, they'll train themselves on the production system. And everyone will suffer the performance penalties as 20 or 30 users simultaneously search every row in a million-row table, pulling up every sales order opened or closed in the last six months, including everything you pulled in from your legacy system being replaced by SAP.

▶ A comprehensive change to master data resulted in lost development time for one of our customers mere weeks before go-live. The exuberant and sleep-deprived developer failed to test her mass update process in a different environment or client, and effectively wiped out half a day's worth of her own and her colleagues' work. She was quite lucky actually; it could have been much worse.

Notice the mention of a *technical sandbox* several times in this list. The sandbox is a "best-kept secret" for many SAP technical support teams. Not only does it enable the SAP TSO to become familiar with SAP operations and day-to-day management without interfering with productive development systems, it plays a key role in the promote-to-production change management process. Let's face it—development is actually a production system in its own right from day one. Just try asking a group of 30 ABAP or J2EE developers if it's okay to reboot the development box so that a potential change can be quickly tested while the expensive developers sit idly waiting for the system to be returned to them, and you'll find the value of a technical sandbox grows exponentially.

Other common real-world issues related to change management include the following:

▸ Conducting onsite training workshops is expensive; computer-based or online training can be effectively hosted internally.

▸ Configuration guidelines and best practices provide a foundation for building and maintaining an SAP solution. The matter of who should be responsible for really doing the work of keeping all this documentation up to date needs to be addressed, however.

▸ The "big picture" needs to be communicated to all stakeholders; they need to understand the amount of change that is typically tested and supported for each change release.

▸ Business productivity must be measured to support the value behind a particular change wave.

▸ The term *superuser* is overused and a bit trite for today's vernacular. What constitutes a real superuser? It used to be synonymous with the person in each functional area who was the go-to person for all the other users. The superuser worked with the help desk to resolve problems, and in doing so made sure that these problems and their resolutions were shared throughout the end-user organization.

▸ The change management process employed by the SAP team probably needs to mimic the companywide approach to managing change, but deviations are common, too (given the unique technologies inherent to SAP solutions).

▸ Feedback must be a natural and easy extension to change control; the more natural this feedback is, the more likely the change control process can be updated in the name of continuous improvement.

With the real-world experiences and lessons learned described in the preceding list, we thought it would make sense to capture a list of worst practices as well, identified next.

Although all the best practices and best-in-class approaches we have discussed about managing change are valuable, change management is also all about avoiding common pitfalls. That is, another goal of change management processes is to avoid repeating history and making common mistakes, or engaging in poor practices that can compromise

the integrity of your SAP deployment or ongoing operations. More than a few SAP implementation teams have learned this the hard way over the years, however. We suggest that
you avoid the change management worst practices outlined in the following list:

▶ **Failing to test in a nonproduction system**—Make firmware, hardware, OS, driver,
or application software changes—including updates or upgrades or applying service
packs or patches—first in the technical sandbox environment; failing to test changes
in the technical sandbox invites unknown performance and availability issues down
the road.

▶ **Ignoring the P2P process**—Failing to adhere to the flow or promotion of changes
or data from the technical sandbox (where infrastructure changes are first tested) to
development (where data originates) to test/QA (if it exists) to training (if it exists) to
the final production solution. Failing to do so compromises the integrity of the
production platform, and therefore negates the value of many of the other SAP landscape environments. Maintaining the history of data objects and configuration
changes as they are moved through the SAP landscape is critical to maintaining a
highly available and reliable solution.

▶ **Initiating configuration changes anywhere other than in development**—SAP
objects should never be modified outside the development system—*do not* perform
these development tasks elsewhere. Making changes directly in production is the
worst-case scenario, of course, because this implies a complete lack of adequate and
appropriate testing. But making changes directly in test/QA, training, and so on is
nearly as bad because the change is not being driven from development, which
makes version control an issue.

▶ **Running additional enterprise applications on the same computing platform
responsible for supporting SAP**—Even if a server has been specifically sized and
configured for multiple applications, we tend to shy away from this practice. Why?
Additional applications complicate the technology stack, make capacity planning
calculations difficult, and make performance guarantees and service-level agreements
much more difficult to uphold. This is why we recommend that other business
applications, including email, database, file/print, audio/streaming video, and even
domain infrastructure, reside on completely separate hardware platforms. Of course,
the growing use of virtualization and the capability of large servers to be partitioned
into smaller servers runs counter to this advice. Unless you're an expert in the performance and change management effects specific applications have on one another,
try to avoid hosting SAP and other systems together.

Summary

In this chapter, we have defined change management, discussed how to implement technical changes consistent with best practices, and looked at how changes impact everything from the project phases, to the SAP system landscape, to the individual technology
stacks residing within each landscape. We then drilled down into organizational complexities, including a common approach to structuring a change management team.

The common theme underlying this chapter should be clear: Your approach to making changes should be conservative and methodical. Changes are an inevitable part of an SAP solution during and after deployment, inviting much-needed new or improved reliability, but also introducing the possibility for disaster into the organization. Our recommendation with regard to change is to play it safe and practice conservative and consistent technical change management as a matter of course. Doing so makes life better for everyone—your end users, the general IT support team, your functional/development teams, your colleagues in the SAP TSO, and so on.

Case Study: The CM Manager

HiTech, Inc. finally needs to create an organization focused on managing technical change. Assist the newly appointed CM manager with answering the following questions.

Questions

1. The manager of technical change is interested in aligning to a technical change process. What do you recommend?

2. How might a technical sandbox environment help improve change management?

3. Should a change ever be put directly into the production environment?

NOTE

The answers to these questions can be found in Appendix A, "Case Study Answers."

CHAPTER 35

SAP Systems and Operations Management

To achieve the ultimate goal of a smooth-running SAP environment, it is important to set the groundwork for the SAP computer operations and systems management teams (or simply "SAP operations"). Normally, this groundwork consists of the SAP Computing Center Management System (CCMS) and Central Monitoring System (CMS, also referred to as "CEN"), manual operations processes, simple paper-based checklists, and a collection of essential utilities and tools ranging from the robust and very detailed SAP Solution Manager to simple command-line utilities. Even if you are implementing the latest SAP NetWeaver technology or are simply managing an older R/3 solution, most of this groundwork, in our experience, varies little.

In the case of SAP shops with expertise in an enterprise systems management application such as HP Business Availability Center (BAC), this groundwork may actually already exist and be quite robust, too. Normally, though, the real work of deploying an end-to-end solution approach for managing your entire SAP system landscape remains to be addressed; this chapter walks you through that process. We begin by making a case for the importance of an SAP operations manual and the role of documentation in general, and then move into piloting and selecting from a variety of enterprise systems management applications, and wrap up with a discussion of various tools and utilities focused at different layers of the technology stack.

> **NOTE**
>
> This chapter stops short of covering operations-related tasks outside the scope of monitoring and fundamentally managing the SAP environment. Much of the operations minutiae related to going live are detailed in Chapter 36, "Preparing for SAP Go-Live."

Although we focus in this chapter on preparing the foundation for going live, it must be noted that all management approaches, methods, tools, and so on are immediately applicable to other systems within your SAP system landscape, regardless of where you find yourself in your implementation or other SAP project plan. For example, your SAP development and test environments are already in use by now. And a technical sandbox, training system, and other components of a system landscape may also be in place. These important systems are absolutely critical to their respective users—expensive SAP developers and essential power users engaged in testing the integration of new SAP-driven business processes. So, although the thrust of this chapter is aimed squarely at crafting an operations and systems management approach, it is not necessarily aimed exclusively at production SAP environments.

What Is the SAP Operations Manual?

The collection of "as is" or "current state" system documentation, day-to-day and other regularly scheduled operations tasks, various installation and operations checklists, how-to process documents, and more constitutes the *SAP operations manual*. A good operations manual therefore supports more than basic computer operations tasks; it facilitates fallback in the case of a change management wave gone awry, and it serves as a blueprint should the need to rebuild all or a piece of the SAP system landscape arise. It serves as an excellent foundation for new-hire training, too. Finally, many of the documentation-specific components of the Disaster Recovery Crash Kit discussed in Chapter 16, "Disaster Recovery Considerations and Solutions," are also fashioned directly from the SAP operations manual, specifically:

▶ Detailed current state information as to how a particular system and its components are architected and configured (for example, server PCI card slot locations, physical disk subsystem disk layouts, OS file system details, and so on)

▶ Step-by-step documentation necessary to install the production system, all access methods, all operations management utilities and applications, and additional documented procedures explaining how to restore the database and other critical data

▶ Operational documentation, such as that which reflects regularly scheduled daily and weekly tasks and more

The SAP operations manual is obviously critical to ensuring a well-running SAP solution, then, as illustrated in Figure 35.1. We next take a closer look at what we consider to be the most important considerations when assembling an operations manual.

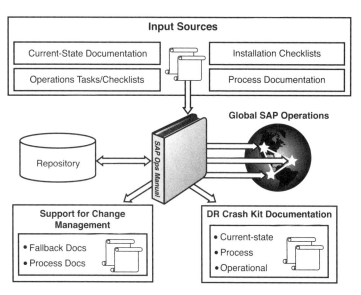

FIGURE 35.1   The SAP operations manual brings critical resources together, and feeds other functions as well.

Documenting Your Current State

Documentation that describes the specific configuration and layout of your unique SAP solution stack is often referred to as *current-state documentation*. Recording the details inherent to your particular hardware configuration, OS installation, database and SAP application configuration, and so on provides critical data necessary to re-create the environment should it be necessary. This level of detail also minimizes complexity and timeframes related to troubleshooting problems down the road—with details close at hand, minutes rather than hours are consumed when it comes time to share configuration data with others helping you to troubleshoot a problem.

In the past, we have spent quite a bit of time documenting complex SAP system landscapes for our own SAP customers. Most of the time, our directive has simply been to get everything "down on paper," using Microsoft Word and Excel. We often then dumped this operational documentation into different presentation media, depending on a client's standards or preferences. Figure 35.2 depicts a common approach we developed for easily collecting and segregating current-state documentation by technology stack layer. We call the resulting customer deliverable the "matrix" because it maps various technology stack components to their properties (or dimensions) in a matrix format. A simple Microsoft Excel workbook divided into technology stack layers by using multiple worksheets and descriptive tabs forms the foundation of this simple but effective approach. Details are either noted within each worksheet, or in a Microsoft Word or other document embedded into the worksheet. In this way, a single workbook becomes a master repository of current-state technology stack configuration data.

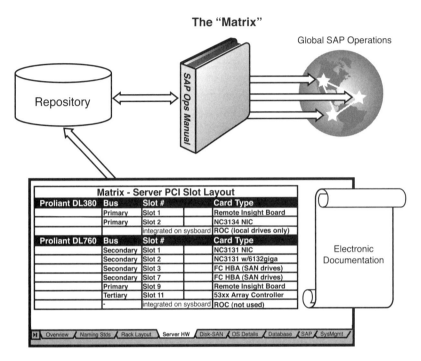

FIGURE 35.2   Our approach to documenting an SAP system landscape often amounts to something that resembles this detailed Microsoft Excel–based matrix.

Documenting Daily Operations and Installation Procedures

With the current state documented, we need to focus our attention on developing daily checklists, installation recipes, and the process for updating our technology stack. Checklists or "run books" are useful in performing routine tasks, such as those related to a set of daily procedures. Installation recipes, on the other hand, are one-time documents that are useful in installing and reinstalling a particular hardware or software component. The idea behind a recipe should be clear—it provides not only a list of "ingredients," but also the precise steps necessary to install a particular solution in a repeatable manner. And because you already have the "ingredients" documented via your own current-state documentation, a recipe can usually be crafted quickly. Update processes, such as those involving updating a hardware platform's firmware or SAP ERP kernel, also benefit from a checklist approach (keeping in mind that future update or upgrade processes from vendors are always subject to change).

Anyone serious about minimizing the time required to install something should invest the time up front to create a comprehensive recipe. Recipes reduce unplanned downtime (if, for example, a problem forces you to re-create a portion of your SAP solution stack). Recipes are also useful tools when it comes time to train your new hires and others involved in installing and supporting a particular layer of the stack. This is why the best of the best—SAP customer sites, hardware vendors, SAP consulting firms, and so on—make use of recipes and checklists, as shown in Figure 35.3. These kinds of documentation artifacts comprising a collection of ingredients and procedures make it possible to deploy proven, repeatable solutions.

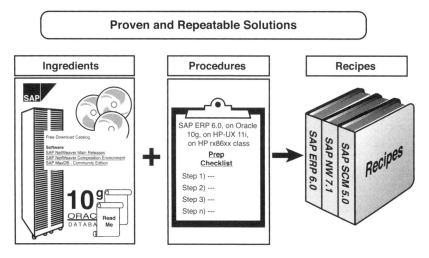

FIGURE 35.3 The right ingredients and proper checklists will create very repeatable solution-guide recipes.

Of course, recipes and checklists may vary in the level of detail that is provided. We have created many high-level SAP installation recipes that are only four to five pages long. These *quick reference checklists*, or "Quick-Checks," help experienced individuals stay on track and perform a procedure quickly. For example, a quick-check for installing Oracle 10g might comprise:

1. Obtain all Oracle media
2. Reserve the technical sandbox
3. Validate Oracle HW and OS prerequisites
4. Perform a backup of the current state
5. Install Oracle per detailed steps outlined at http://xyz.xyz.xyz1
6. Patch Oracle per detailed steps outlined at http://xyz.xyz.xyz2
7. Conduct test cycle 1 for new installations
8. Document all steps and variances
9. Conduct test cycle 2.

As you can see, a Quick-Check is a high-level guide; each step actually comprises many detailed steps. Because all the details are abstracted out of a Quick-Check, it preserves a general process for performing an installation, upgrade, or other change.

At the other extreme, we recommend creating the very detailed checklists necessary to walk through the specific steps for installing and patching Oracle 10g (for example). We recommend including screenshots (in the case of software installations, for example) and even the very basic how-to procedures within the body of the larger document. These detailed checklists are designed for beginners and other novices unfamiliar with a particular process or procedure—anyone who might be called upon to perform an unassisted installation (perhaps in the case of a disaster, or to fall back to a known state, or perhaps in the name of new-hire orientation training). We have been known to help our clients create SAP NetWeaver installation recipes that exceed 200 pages for particular hardware/software combinations, walking the installer through everything from computing platform installation and configuration to SAP NetWeaver step-by-step component installations.

There is one other approach that has proven helpful to us in the past, too. Rather than re-creating the wheel and documenting much that is already documented by SAP, database vendors, and other technology stack technology vendors, we pioneered an approach that we labeled "Delta Guides." A Delta Guide is very much like a Quick-Check, with two exceptions—it's more detailed, and it references other documents published by their respective vendors instead of reproducing that documentation. In this way, a Delta Guide acts as an umbrella over perhaps 10 to 20 other documents, bringing all of these resources and procedures together in one master method or repository. Using this method, not only can system installations be performed quickly, but the work necessary to create and maintain the recipe itself can also be performed quickly because there's no need to recreate the detailed steps outlined by other vendors.

To be feasible, a Delta Guide requires just as much testing and validation as a detailed checklist—we can't assume that a vendor's documentation is 100% accurate, after all! We've all tried to follow installation guides that failed to account of a key step or made important undocumented assumptions. The Delta Guide provides a mechanism for identifying these gaps and assumptions; they are documented to reflect how each gap/assumption is addressed or in some way overcome.

Documenting Other Regularly Scheduled Procedures

Like daily operations procedures, SAP and its technology stack partners also recommend that a set of specific procedures be executed weekly, monthly, quarterly, and even annually. These regularly scheduled operations tasks span the gamut, from facilities to server-, OS-, database-, and SAP-specific tasks; for example:

▶ Archiving tape backups

▶ Verifying SAP failback processes work as expected

▶ Testing disaster recovery (DR) procedures

▶ Performing various security reviews and test cycles

▶ Reviewing and modifying scheduled SAP housecleaning jobs

▶ Executing the promote to production and other processes

▶ Restocking data center consumables

▶ Executing test scripts to compare disk subsystem and SAP application layer performance to historical performance

▶ Benchmarking client-critical network segments

Developing Process or "How To" Documentation

When it comes to operational processes and current state documentation, it's pretty safe to say that these critical components of the SAP operations manual are only made possible by "how to" or *process documentation*. Process documentation amounts to the documentation *behind* your documentation—it describes and details how to perform a particular task, or it references another source (such as an Internet URL or a company-internal file share) where this is further explained. So if, for example, your SAP Daily Operations Checklist calls for an SAP operator to execute transaction ST03N and collect performance statistics related to the number of dialog steps processed each hour over the last four hours, a process document should exist that walks the operator through gaining access to the particular system, executing transaction ST03N, navigating through the various menu and screen selections, and ultimately pulling the requested data out of SAP CCMS.

Considering Documentation Best Practices

In the course of consulting, we have embraced or otherwise come across a number of approaches that we believe represent documentation best practices. The following list details some of these approaches:

▶ **Documentation development**—Although a fair amount of documentation is inevitably developed "on the fly" after go-live, or after changes are made to your system, arguably the *best* way to create documentation is by leveraging your technical sandbox or training system as part of your normal promote-to-production change management strategy. In this way, you can test and record processes and procedures simultaneously, ensuring that accurate procedures are drafted or updated *before* they are required to be executed in the production system.

▶ **Documentation standards**—Creating a consistent and professional SAP operations manual requires a set of documentation guidelines, standards, and procedures. For instance, putting together a document that describes the process for creating documentation, including formats and fonts to use, is a good starting point. Next, a working template to be used for developing new documents is a great time-saver.

▶ **Screenshots**—Precise documentation calls for detail and clarity. Sometimes, the best way to obtain this clarity is to use screenshots, so that complex options and tasks can be clearly displayed to ensure error-free processes.

▶ **Documentation publishing and accessibility**—We have seen all manner of sound publishing practices when it comes to operating procedures, including everything from standard word-processing-based methods (Microsoft Word and lesser packages), to true publishing packages (Quark, PageMaker, Microsoft Office Publisher), to simple HTML-based websites (using Microsoft Word, for example), to

35

feature-rich portals (SAP's, Microsoft's, and Oracle's portal products, to be specific). Simply publishing documentation via the Web, however, seems to be the best way to go all around simply because of the ease of access provided in this way. That is, DR capabilities are strengthened, training capabilities are broadened, and escalation support is enhanced when documentation is available ubiquitously using a standard web browser. And publishing from a web server located at a site other than your SAP data center also enables you to access your documentation in the event of a disaster.

▶ **Documentation maintenance**—Keeping your SAP operations manual up to date requires a time investment. We already mentioned taking advantage of your change management strategy to help keep documentation up to date. Other methods may be preferable, though. One of our customers dedicates 8–16 hours each month to reviewing and updating its current-state documentation and standard operating procedures. Another client makes real-time updates to its hard copies and then "catches up" every few weeks or months as necessary. Although the latter approach is not as consistent as the former, we like the fact that the customer pencils in updates and changes *as they occur*; this helps maintain very accurate documentation. Finally, other clients dump all of their documentation into true document management systems. This approach can enable check-in, check-out, role-based security, access to the documentation repository via a web browser as well as through native Microsoft Word, Excel, and PowerPoint formats, and so on.

With the groundwork of how and what to document behind us, let's now turn our attention to actual processes and products that facilitate SAP systems management.

Systems Management Techniques for SAP

The SAP computer operations team needs to be prepared to manage the various SAP system landscape components being implemented months before go-live occurs. Development systems, training systems, systems that support testing, and so on will all be installed and configured prior to production, and each of these systems will need to be managed to ensure that it is available to its users. This includes *proactively* monitoring hardware and software installed as part of each system, looking for impending failures or circumstances that may cause less than acceptable performance. The systems also must be monitored in a *reactive* manner; reactive management minimizes the amount of time necessary to respond to a failure, therefore reducing unplanned downtime.

This section addresses techniques for SAP systems management. We cover a number of products that support monitoring and measuring the performance of different facets of your entire SAP solution stack, including solutions that take advantage of Java- and HTML-based connectivity. To set the stage, the following capabilities are required of a set of management/monitoring tools:

▶ You must be able to measure and verify end-user response time for each and every end-user transaction. Similarly, you need to be able to do the same for batch jobs and other background processes.

> ► You need to provide a way to tune SAP, the database system, your OS, and your hardware platforms—the entire stack.

> ► You need a method of monitoring your network connectivity, including the ability to identify your specific response-time component attributable to the network.

> ► Your tool sets need to support not only monitoring but also diagnosing your observed performance within and between each layer in your unique SAP technology stack.

In our experience, unfortunately, no single tool can do all of this perfectly in a typical SAP environment. As you will see, though, some of the tools available today come pretty close to providing a truly end-to-end SAP monitoring and management solution. And the "holes" left from these tools can be filled effectively with additional utilities and tools, discussed later.

Leveraging CCMS for Manual Processes and Checklists

SAP's very own Computer Center Management System, or CCMS, forms the foundation for many SAP enterprise management applications and tools in use today. That is, many of the applications in the SAP enterprise management space today leverage the power of CCMS, or more specifically the *data* that CCMS gathers. These enterprise applications simply present this data in unique or more valuable ways than CCMS can, which is much of their value.

Before you can fully understand the real value of an expensive and potentially complex management system, you need to understand not only what kind of data is available via CCMS, but also how to access that data. For this reason, we are a big fan of daily and weekly SAP operations checklists—though manual in nature and therefore more time consuming than automated management approaches, operations checklists force a basic education in SAP CCMS.

Accessing CCMS is simple. For our convenience, SAP created literally hundreds of shortcut Transaction Codes (T-codes) that exist solely to pull performance and availability data out of CCMS. For example, T-codes ST06 and DB02 provide us with OS- and database-specific data, respectively. ST03 and ST04 give us information related to system-level performance. ST07 and AL08 provide us with user-based data, such as the number of users logged in to a particular functional area or executing specific functional transactions. These T-codes are not hugely intuitive, unfortunately. However, several observations are in order:

> ► T-codes that end in "01" (like MM01) are used to create something. Similarly, T-codes that end in "02" are often used to change or update, and those that end in "03" are often used to display.

> ► The first two characters in a T-code typically reflect the functional area or technical area in which a T-code operates. "ST" provides system-related data, "DB" provides database-related data, "RZ" addresses system profile and monitoring data, "OS" reflects OS-related statistics, and so on.

> ► Most T-codes are four characters long, like ST07 or AL08. The majority of other T-codes are five characters.

35

▸ Transactions like SM51 and OS07 can be used to change the application server to which you are connected or logged in to, without logging out and logging back in. In this way, it becomes easier to more quickly collect statistics for multiple application servers within a particular system, for example (if you have to do so manually!).

You can also access CCMS through SAP's basic menu system as well, navigating through scads of different transactions until you find the one that suits your purpose. Of course, this can be time consuming, but in the same manner it can prove quite educational to new CCMS users, too.

Because some of the CCMS T-codes can be quite system-intensive, or can be used to make unwanted changes to the configuration of a system, we suggest a technical sandbox or similar system be made available to the SAP operations and help desk teams when it comes time to learn how to use CCMS.

Automating CCMS Data Collection Processes

Walking through the process of collecting statistics through SAP CCMS can be quite time consuming, especially when multiple SAP system landscapes and large SAP instances are involved. Consider one of our favorite SAP customers, for example. Not only does it maintain a five-system SAP ERP landscape (with eight application servers in both staging and production), but it also operates a four-system environment for both SAP BW and CRM. Collecting and analyzing snapshots and historical statistics across three different production systems, as well as the other supporting systems, could have easily become a full-time job for someone. The right answer for the customer, like most other organizations, ultimately was to evaluate and deploy an SAP enterprise systems management application. Many options exist in this regard—SAP Solution Manager, SAP CCMS and CEN, HP OpenView, BMC Solutions for SAP, and a host of other alternatives—and are discussed later in this chapter.

Evaluating, selecting, licensing, deploying, and then really learning how to use such a potentially complex management application does not happen overnight, however. So in this particular client's case, instead of waiting the 3–6 months to evaluate, install, and configure an enterprise management tool to automatically collect systemwide performance and availability metrics, it asked us to script some of the basic performance monitoring transactions (ST03, ST07, ST04, and more) in the interim.

This scripting is what we are referring to when we talk of "automating" CCMS data collection processes—scripting takes manual processes to the next level, so to speak, and enables these processes to be more rapidly and consistently executed. Scripting allows you to pull displayed values out of the SAPGUI and dump them into an Excel spreadsheet, so that over time you can track things such as average wait times, roll times, DB request times, and so on for dialog response time, background task response time, update response time, and more.

More information about SAPGUI scripting is available on the SAP Service Marketplace and particularly the SDN. Refer to https://www.sdn.sap.com/irj/sdn/sap-gui for more details.

Using CCMS, Transactional Monitors, and CEN

As we have already mentioned, shortcomings in using CCMS to monitor complex SAP system landscapes have helped to greatly drive the development and subsequent popularity of SAP enterprise management tools. SAP enterprise management tools fill in the gaps left wide open by CCMS prior to the newer SAP NetWeaver releases, such as those identified here:

▶ CCMS suffered from an inability to consolidate performance and other data across multiple instances within a single SAP system. For example, a production system with eight application servers, one database server, and a central instance required most CCMS transactions to be executed 10 different times, once per server.

▶ CCMS was less than easy to use when it came to reporting performance, availability, or other metrics across more than one server (a few exceptions existed, but this was generally true). Reports must be generated 10 times, once for each server, and then somehow rationalized afterward.

▶ CCMS by itself could only weakly address any kind of SAP solutionwide data gathering or reporting. Each component had to be addressed separately.

CCMS graphics remain quite limited even today, therefore further impacting CCMS's ability to easily communicate trends and changes in the performance of a system or systems over time. When it comes to T-codes, CCMS is still not very intuitive today, either. T-codes mean little for the most part, and even the short descriptions tied to a particular transaction are not all that helpful most of the time. Learning how to use CCMS, therefore, really requires hands-on hit-or-miss activity (which strengthens our previous argument for providing a technical sandbox to folks tasked with learning and using CCMS).

CCMS is "free"—it is built in to the SAP Basis system, and therefore paid for when you license your particular SAP solution. SAP AG sought to remedy some of the shortcomings of CCMS, though, with Basis release 4.6C when it offered improved monitoring capabilities in the form of *transactional monitors*, a group of transaction-specific dialog monitors accessible via the SAP CCMS Monitors for Optional Components monitor set. It also finally became possible to set up a transactional monitor for each system and even an entire system landscape. This was good for monitoring the performance of a particular set of transactions, like your "top 10" online end-user transactions or background jobs. In doing so, you could easily monitor overall response time, queue time, "load+gen" time, DB request time, front-end response time, and so on across a complex SAP ERP solution, for example.

But this approach was still limited, as it was difficult to address holistic performance of the system outside of the core transactions monitored by a specifically configured transactional monitor. And it was this shortcoming specifically that drove much of the success of third-party SAP enterprise monitoring applications such as BMC Solutions for SAP, HP OpenView, and others in the last 10 years. Never content with standing still, SAP AG continued to improve upon its own native tool sets and offered another management alternative in the form of its Central Monitoring System (CMS, or CEN).

Accessible and configurable via transactions RZ20 and RZ21, the concept of the CEN is to make all alerts of an SAP landscape available in a central CCMS. CEN can run on every SAP NetWeaver Application Server; however, our recommendation is to host CEN on a dedicated SAP NetWeaver Application Server. Alternatively you might want to consider using SAP Solution Manager as the host for CEN. CEN allows you to monitor SAP ABAP, SAP Java, dual-stack, standalone components, and even non-SAP components. Following are some of the CEN monitoring capabilities:

▶ Overall availability of the system, including general status, cluster heartbeat, status of sessions and threads used, and more

▶ Detailed hardware properties, such as disk space, RAM, and CPU utilization, status of system parameters, and so on

▶ Detailed system information, such as the OS or Java version running on each server, its hostname, and similar current-state data

▶ Performance, measured in functional terms (such as the number of documents processed per hour or the average size of these documents)

▶ Performance, measured in technical terms (such as buffer quality and other memory conditions, disk hit ratios, swap/pagefile utilization, and other data typical of CCMS)

▶ Error logs and similar system-generated messages and events

CEN is quite capable today, allowing you to develop custom monitors in addition to leveraging built-in ones. CEN leverages a typical software "agent" approach to monitoring servers; agents are loaded on systems to be managed, thus enabling them to be monitored. The actual agent deployed in each environment differs, depending on the system being managed. The CCMS agent SAPCM3X is used for systems running SAP Basis release 3x, while the CCMS agent SAPCCM4X is for systems running SAP Basis release 4x or higher. The CCMS agent SAPCCMSR is used to monitor components for which no SAP ABAP instance is active, such as the J2EE Engine or TREX.

Using SAP Solution Manager

SAP Solution Manager has been available since Basis release 4.6x. In the short time that SAP Solution Manager has been available, it has improved significantly. Although SAP Solution Manager addresses much more than performance monitoring and systems management, for our purposes in this chapter SAP Solution Manager (operations) provides the following fundamental benefits beyond CCMS, which it leverages heavily:

▶ Can monitor multiple SAP components from a single centralized management console.

▶ Ties directly into support and service functions, both online and through "packaged" best practices documentation. For example, support desk functionality allows your online SAP end users to contact and work with your SAP TSO and SAP's Customer Support Organization in real time.

▶ Extends monitoring beyond mere systems management; it enables real-time business process monitoring, taking transactional monitors to the next level.

▶ Supports Service Level Management (SLM).

One of the latest SAP Solution Manager releases, 7.0, is based on the SAP NetWeaver 7.0 technology. SAP Solution Manager 7.0 is installed as a dual-stack system on either one physical server for minimum system distribution or on several physical servers for maximum system distribution.

We will take a closer look at SAP Solution Manager, and a number of other third-party SAP enterprise systems management applications, in more detail later in this chapter.

Deploying Other Tools and Utilities

Many other tools exist that can aid you in managing your SAP systems. Hardware vendors offer hardware-specific utilities, as do OS vendors, database vendors, and so on. The key here is to find tools that support not only point-in-time snapshots, but also historical analysis. Similarly, there are plenty of infrastructure management applications on the market today that leverage common protocols such as Simple Network Management Protocol (SNMP), Desktop Management Interface (DMI), and Web-Based Enterprise Management (WBEM) to help you manage much of your SAP solution stack—in many cases, in fact, these applications have matured to the point where they even offer "snap-in" modules capable of addressing SAP components, specific databases, and more. But again, unless they are capable of displaying point-in-time as well as historical data, we see little long-term value in them. We will take a look at many of these tools and utilities shortly, after we address a method for evaluating and implementing a systems management application for SAP.

Preparing to Pilot a Systems Management Application

Before an expensive enterprise systems management application or suite of tools is deployed for SAP, it's common to pilot or test drive prospective solutions. After all, there are several different popular applications, many different tools you might wish to incorporate into your broader systems management umbrella, and usually an existing systems management standard with which to contend. To decide which systems management application is best suited, we often follow a basic process like the one outlined here:

1. Develop a specialized subteam

2. Define requirements

3. Explore your environment's unique challenges

4. Review existing in-house systems management solutions

5. Create a short list of prospective solutions

Once the short list is created, each solution candidate may in turn be installed, tested, and evaluated for fit and fitness.

Developing the Systems Management Subteam

To successfully determine the right SAP enterprise management application for your environment, and then successfully pilot, implement, and use it, a strong subteam underneath the SAP TSO is usually developed. In the past, we have seen teams composed of folks from the following groups work well together on a systems management project:

- ▶ Manager of computer operations, who is already responsible for other mission-critical application infrastructure and will eventually be responsible for the team that provides 24×7 SAP infrastructure operations coverage

- ▶ One or two senior technology-focused computer operators who manage the enterprise today, and will eventually be tasked with managing the SAP systems

- ▶ SAP Basis manager or a designated senior technologist

- ▶ A senior technologist from the network infrastructure team

- ▶ A senior technologist from the hardware and OS support groups

- ▶ A technical member of the existing systems management team, if one exists

- ▶ One or two vendor-neutral SAP consultants intimately familiar with the workings of a number of SAP enterprise management packages

This team provides a broad perspective of monitoring and systems management practices over your current environment, and brings needed knowledge and experience in managing SAP solutions, too. We have seen this team given the label of systems management team or enterprise management group (EMG)—for our purposes in this chapter we will refer to this SAP TSO subteam as the EMG.

As it stands, the team may not be comprehensive enough for your particular situation; be prepared to add additional skill sets or additional IT unit representation in the case of complex, global, or otherwise large SAP implementations.

NOTE

If you are extending the monitoring scope from infrastructure- and system-level monitoring to application and/or business process monitoring, it is important to have the relevant business process representative on your EMG team. This individual will understand the requirements related to the business process monitoring part and will help identify the right SAP enterprise management application.

Defining Requirements

With the EMG team created, its first priority is to understand the SAP project's systems management requirements. Sometimes this becomes something of a parallel short- and long-term effort, where a tactical solution and set of processes need to be put in place as soon as possible in support of go-live, although the team also looks at perhaps different approaches or tool sets to address strategic SAP systems management. In the best of worlds, there is enough time to simultaneously define short-term and strategic requirements. Regardless, though, the team needs to develop a first cut of the operational processes that will support the SAP project's service-level agreements (SLAs). This in turn will help narrow down the list of tool sets and applications that may already be (prematurely, of course, at this stage in the project) under consideration, so as to map the capabilities of various applications to the needs of the SAP project's systems management requirements.

In the short term, then, we suggest developing the following:

- ▶ A clear statement of the responsibilities that SAP operations will have in regard to the SAP environment, including where those responsibilities end and are picked up by other groups or teams

- ▶ Clear processes for SAP operations to follow in meeting these responsibilities

- ▶ A similar set of responsibilities for the various groups that may be involved in assisting SAP operations in problem escalation and resolution

- ▶ Clear processes for implementing, documenting, and updating all processes associated with managing the SAP environment

After these requirements are discussed, refined, and documented, we then suggest that the EMG turn its attention to long-term strategic requirements, such as the following:

- ▶ Identifying the owner of the systems management application or tool sets to eventually be installed

- ▶ Rationalizing your SAP systems management approaches with long-term tool sets and approaches that can be utilized across your larger computing infrastructure or enterprise

- ▶ Developing a strategy focused on minimizing monitoring tools by implementing a "broader" systems management application that supports different solutions common to your unique enterprise

- ▶ Deploying niche, specialized, or best-of-breed systems management tools that complement your broader systems management strategy

With requirements nailed down, the EMG can then begin looking seriously at what the company's IT organization is already doing when it comes to systems management, and identifying areas of overlap in terms of common systems management applications that *also* support monitoring and managing SAP environments. But first, we think it's important to understand the real challenges to SAP systems management as we have seen them unfold in the real world.

Exploring Real–World Systems Management Challenges

When it comes to implementing and using an enterprise management application, the actual design of a solution followed by the installation of various software products does not tend to be a problem. Sure, it's a challenge and a ton of work to effectively install, configure, test, and evaluate several systems management toolsets. But the real gotchas in our experience consist of the following:

▶ Fully understanding the regular operational tasks that must be performed day in and day out, or on a regular recurring basis, in an SAP environment.

▶ Identifying the most critical items and conditions to monitor, at the business process, SAP application, database, OS, and hardware levels.

▶ Identifying appropriate thresholds *for each of the critical items being monitored*. If you get too many alerts for a particular condition, for example, your SAP operations staff and the team to which it escalates these issues will become numb to the issue, and a *real* problem may well go unnoticed later (consider the boy who cried wolf).

▶ Identifying appropriate responses to alerts. In other words, which alerts need to be escalated, and at what point, and which alerts can instead be simply noted or archived?

▶ Collecting general references that can illuminate some of the issues likely faced if you choose a particular product or application suite.

▶ Identifying SAP-specific subject matter experts, as the need for product-experienced folks who have implemented your enterprise management solution of choice *in an SAP environment* will avert hundreds of post-implementation support hours in the long run, saving money and increasing your system's availability along the way.

▶ Earmarking a particular person and a backup to maintain your systems management approach. This is key in the long term as well because changes to your SAP environment generally equate to the need to update your systems management console (in terms of adding new systems to be managed, removing old systems, revising thresholds, and so on).

You might have noticed how the solutions for each of the aforementioned gotchas represent systems management best practices. With these gotchas and best practices in mind, let's turn our attention to how your IT organization may currently manage its computing resources. Our hope is that we can leverage some of this in-house expertise and experience to hit the ground running when it comes time to manage SAP.

Reviewing In-House Systems Management Solutions

Looking inward at the suite of management applications, utilities, and tools in place in your organization today makes a lot of sense before further scrutinizing "new" SAP enterprise management applications. For example, if you are running an IBM shop, and have deep experience with Tivoli and other IBM-centric tools, it might save a lot of time and energy to leverage this expertise and implement Tivoli for SAP management as well. The same goes for HP shops, where HP OpenView and Business Availability Center (BAC) might be the best way to go simply by default. Similarly, if you have adopted BMC products across the board, BMC Solutions for SAP might be a natural fit for your organization just because of the pricing and support benefits that can presumably be gained given your existing relationship with BMC.

On the other hand, in our experience even the best general enterprise applications change significantly after SAP is introduced. This can almost eliminate the benefit of implementing a particular enterprise management application simply because your organization already uses it. Why? Because, at minimum, an SAP software agent or similar construct must be added to the technology stack (which itself may very well represent a mixed bag of standards and new technologies). And other agents new to your technical organization may be required as well, bringing with them their own changes and complexities. In short order, the stack with which your IT organization is comfortable monitoring may morph into something very new and different.

A typical example is HP OpenView—thousands of systems management support organizations around the world leverage HP OpenView to manage their network and server infrastructures. But if you want to create an end-to-end SAP management solution, you really need to add OS, database, and SAP agents (HP calls these "SPIs") to various servers within the SAP system landscape. And you might require the deeper capabilities of a snap-in hardware management tool on top of these other changes. Even worse, if you implemented an HP-UX–based solution for network management, for example, but have SAP running on top of a Microsoft Windows or Linux architecture, the actual versions of many of your HP OpenView software components will differ. In the end, the HP OpenView solution originally implemented and understood by your company will hardly resemble the HP OpenView systems management solution implemented for SAP, perhaps negating much of the operational benefit you hoped to gain in the first place.

Regardless, we still like the idea of at least *considering* your current systems management approach when it comes time to investigate the realm of management possibilities. Worst case, you will at least benefit from a pricing perspective. In the next section, we will look at other factors that help you put together a "short list" of enterprise systems management candidates.

Creating a Short List of Prospects

Once you've defined your requirements, identified prospective solutions, and taken a critical look at the systems management applications and related tools you run internally, it's time to develop a "short list" of prospective solutions. It is this list that constitutes the two or three applications you might deploy for evaluation purposes. Where we have been engaged to assist our customers select and pilot an SAP enterprise management application, we tend to narrow down the initial list of prospective management solutions by way of the following categories:

▶ The capability of each potential management solution to address a particular client's requirements. The feature set, capabilities, and underpinning technologies used (especially with regard to clear differentiators) are all important factors. Don't forget to include the current systems management approaches and tool sets, too, unless they are grossly incapable or simply unsupported by the specific SAP solution stack being implemented.

▶ Additional capabilities that, although not deemed critical in the present, may prove valuable in the long run. Examples of these kinds of capabilities might include the ability to schedule and monitor batch jobs running on multiple SAP or other systems (sometimes referred to as a *cross-application batch scheduler*), or the ability to monitor servers running various operating systems, databases, or Internet services.

▶ The underlying method or architecture leveraged by a particular management application to interact with (and therefore monitor) SAP. For example, some applications leverage native SAP ABAP code to manage, monitor, and collect data pertaining to an SAP landscape, but others require deployment of a separate server and associated management database.

▶ Overall cost and licensing structure, which normally includes software, hardware, documentation, and support. Thus, such things as the license cost of a central management console or costs of software agents for each SAP server to be monitored all come into play.

▶ True value provided above and beyond that provided by SAP's CCMS. We usually sum up this by noting what we believe to be a tool's greatest differentiator, like its low cost, vast enterprise systems breadth, superior historical analysis and archiving abilities, robust problem/event correlation, and so on.

▶ The ability to address event management and escalation well, including the ability to route problems to the proper "owner" or on-call entity, and notify responsible parties through multiple channels (via pager, email, cell phone, and so on).

▶ Robust reporting capabilities, including the ability to create standard and ad hoc reports, the ability to define "downtime" and consequently report availability statistics (SLA data), the ability to automatically generate and distribute regular reports (through email or via a website, for instance), and more.

▶ Ease of installation and system maintenance, and access to SAP-specific product support (that is, support tailored to the SAP technology stack being implemented), including the ability to automatically obtain updates or patches and general support through the Internet or other expedient means.

▶ References, or "me too" accounts reflecting other SAP customers running an identical (or nearly so) SAP technology stack, with the identical systems management application being considered. A confident vendor will provide customer names and contact information once they've been told they made the short list.

▶ In-house standards and considerations related to the firm's internal technology strategies or strategic direction (such as a tool's long-term fit in a companywide enterprise systems management project), or access to in-house skill sets.

▶ The ability to implement a particular systems management application within a required timeframe. Some tools take longer to set up and master than others, or are otherwise more complex than others.

Often the "short list" can be further refined simply by virtue of the strengths and weaknesses of your SAP operations, Basis administration, and help desk teams. And your relationship with a particular systems management vendor can also sway your decision one way or the other.

Evaluating Enterprise Systems Management Applications

With the short list of SAP enterprise systems management candidates in front of you, we suggest creating a comparison matrix to facilitate comparing and contrasting the different solutions. We have successfully used a simple Excel spreadsheet approach in the past—the details related to costing can be clearly deciphered in this way, and arbitrary scoring for the categories described in the previous section (plus any others you create) can easily be tallied up to provide a final "score" for each potential solution.

In revisiting the broad category of cost, for example, we like to break down the following line items:

35

- ► **Software**—Includes the cost of items such as the following:

    - ► Basic management console

    - ► Basic agents for each server to be managed

    - ► Uplift for special OS agents required

    - ► Uplift for special database agents required

    - ► Uplift for special SAP component agents required

    - ► Any OS license(s) that may need to be purchased, for a dedicated systems management console or other similar solution-inherent component

- ► **Hardware**—Includes the cost of any required server, desktop, or similar solution-inherent component, such as the cost associated with a central management console or software distribution server

- ► **Documentation**—Includes the cost of printed and electronic versions of all installation and other software- and hardware-based guides or documents

- ► **Support**—Includes the cost of the following:

    - ► Design or architecture support, including any time that needs to be spent reassessing requirements

    - ► Installation support

    - ► Configuration of the product(s), such that a product may actually prove useful in managing your SAP environment; includes figuring out what thresholds to configure, how to monitor specific events, setting up pager/email alerts, and so on

> ▶ Setting up reporting and similar features outside the scope of "configuration," again making a product truly useful and valuable

With regard to support, you need to note whether you can leverage internal resources (company employees or contractors) or require access to external consulting expertise. The trade-off in time versus cost needs to be noted, too, when it comes to engaging consulting resources to install, configure, and support a particular systems management application. All of this usually helps to paint a clearer picture of each systems management option, ultimately illuminating one option as superior over the others.

To help you narrow down your own options, we take a closer look at three common third-party SAP systems management tools in the next sections.

Reviewing BMC Solutions for SAP

BMC offers a wide range of products for SAP, covering everything from discovering the SAP environment to building the related SAP service model and from event management to change management. BMC Application Performance and Availability Management is one of the products found in BMC Software's core systems management application. It provides you with a holistic view of your SAP technology stack, from the SAP application to the database and from the OS to the servers and network.

BMC solutions not only generally integrate into one another, they also integrate with SAP Solution Manager. Though not exhaustive, BMC's strengths include:

> ▶ A large installed base that can be leveraged in terms of deployment experiences as well as consulting and other SAP-related expertise

> ▶ Support for a wide range of SAP applications, from SAP NetWeaver components to SAP ERP, SAP CRM, SAP SCM, and more

> ▶ Software and modules for nearly every supported SAP server and storage system on the market today, including modules for SANs, SAN and network switches, and more

> ▶ Mature support for snap-ins from many SAP hardware vendors today, making it easy to deploy an end-to-end BMC management solution

> ▶ A variety of complemetary products including a cross-application job scheduler (CONTROL-M) and a document/report management tool (CONTROL-D)

With its popularity and proven success in managing SAP environments, BMC is certainly a safe choice to make. At something like twice the list price of some of its less-capable competitors, however, it's not the cheapest offering on the market.

Deploying HP Solutions for Managing SAP

HP's systems management architecture for SAP is arguably the best on the market, marrying a lifecycle-based approach to managing quality, performance, and ongoing operations from one or very few consoles. HP's framework for SAP application management aligns with the ASAP methodology and integrates with SAP Solution Manager. Performance, capacity planning and operations-focused management tools work together to provide real-time operational visibility, enable root cause analysis, and ultimately allow the SAP TSO to solve problems faster.

HP's Business Availability Center (BAC) makes it possible to proactively manage SAP by identifying trends that could negatively affect user response times. It's built-in diagnostic ability can then identify where a problem or potential performance bottleneck lies within and even external to the SAP technology stack.

Performance data is collected by HP's modular Business Technology Optimization (BTO) Smart Plug-Ins (SPIs). SPIs are available for applications such as SAP, various databases such as SQL Server, Oracle, and Informix, OSs such as HP-UX and Microsoft Windows, and other products common to SAP landscapes (such as Documentum, Check Point firewalls, Veritas NetBackup, Software AG's webMethods, and more. SPIs allow you to manage an end-to-end technology stack from a single console; HP's SAP SPI is especially useful in that it brings together CCMS data in a way that makes it easier to analyze performance over time, by user, by transaction, by business process, across an enterprise, and so on. Other advantages of HP OpenView's intelligent agent technology approach include the following:

▶ SAP computer operators and systems administrators are provided with complete and continuously updated graphical maps and views of the SAP solution stack (rather than a less-intuitive list of devices like that displayed by its competitors' products). Further, these maps and views can be tailored for a particular audience, allowing a hardware infrastructure specialist to monitor only specific servers and disk subsystems for which he is responsible, for example, whereas a network specialist's console might be configured to include only network devices and those tools required to manage them.

▶ Specialized maps can be created that are application specific or even business process specific—a line-of-business manager might request a system map that reflects data on new orders taken, for instance.

▶ At installation, the SAP SPI offers instant discovery of the entire SAP system, including dependencies between it and other systems, instances, and processes. Then, with its integration into SAP's CCMS, it can help you manage multiple SAP systems running different release versions while ensuring that end-to-end response-time service levels are met.

HP also provides awesome SAP testing capabilities through its Quality Center suite of products, The PMO and development teams can continue to do their work using SAP Solution Manager, while testing and QA activities leverage HP Quality Center as a central repository for test processes and data. Once SAP go-live has come and gone, the operations team can continue to leverage BAC's integration with HP Quality Center to help track problems and provide the team with good insight into how promoted changes actually operate in production.

Given its breadth of coverage and potential complexity, HP's comprehensive solutions for managing SAP are not installed and configured in a day. A typical HP/SAP systems management implementation from start to finish could easily take several months. But with its robust visibility and the ability to integrate project and portfolio management

35

products with application testing and operations products, going with HP makes sense regardless of your underlying infrastructure or business-enabling technologies.

Considering IBM Availability Center for SAP

IBM Availability Center for SAP provides a centralized way to discover the components and relationships of SAP systems in leveraging other products such as IBM Tivoli Monitoring, IBM Tivoli Composite Application Managers, and IBM Tivoli Application Dependency Discovery Manager.

Similar to BMC and HP OpenView, IBM Availability Center for SAP provides a holistic way to manage an SAP landscape and its underlying resources:

▶ It monitors all SAP components and more in an end-to-end fashion, from SAP transactions to SAP applications, from alerts originating in SAP's CCMS environment to alerts originating in various databases, and from OSs such as AIX and HP-UX to web servers such as Apache and Microsoft IIS.

▶ As with BMC and HP OpenView, in addition to centralized monitoring, management tools are centralized as well.

▶ Performance can be evaluated from an end user's perspective.

▶ SAP environments can be dynamic in regard to adding or repurposing SAP components. IBM's Availability Center for SAP automatically discovers new components and at the same time determines the relationship between these components.

▶ It enables the SAP TSO to identify potential problems before they affect end users and the business.

The IBM Availability Center for SAP is backed by IBM's support organization as well as IBM's Services and Business Partners.

Reviewing Enterprise Management Applications and Lessons Learned

Once you understand the importance of managing your SAP systems, you will want to create a powerful, full-featured enterprise management solution. However, because the time required to really pull this off is generally prohibitive, we have found that the following guidelines help our SAP customers start off on the right foot and keep on track to successfully deploying their enterprise management solution:

▶ Keep it simple; deploy the basic systems management package before attempting to implement additional hardware vendor–specific snap-ins, specialized agents, and so on.

▶ Utilize "out-of-the-box" SAP monitoring capabilities. In other words, refrain from changing the default management parameters associated with deploying the basic package.

▶ Turn off monitoring of parameters that are not of immediate or critical need. Focus on the most critical performance and availability statistics first.

▶ Deploy a "systems management testing" environment for monitoring, and use this environment to initially manage your test and/or technical sandbox systems, so as to evaluate and later refine how your systems management tool performs. Often, this special testing environment is simply an extension to your SAP technical sandbox (in the form of an incremental server and storage, for example).

▶ Adjust SAP and other technology stack performance and HA thresholds based on input from consulting or in-house subject matter experts. At a minimum, in the absence of this expertise, stick with the defaults until you have a better grasp of the tool.

▶ Develop a fall-back plan in parallel to deploying your automated systems management solution, preferably by way of SAP CCMS–trained computer operators and help desk technicians armed with paper "SAP Operations" checklists.

▶ Leverage your "systems management testing" environment to practice continuous review and improvement of your systems management approach both before and after go-live.

Although your SAP enterprise systems management application is being developed and deployed, you would do well to take a look at other management tools and approaches. After all, it's unlikely that a single enterprise tool can address more than 50%–75% of your technology stack, much less *all* of it (HP OpenView is a notable exception, covering perhaps 90% of your stack on its own). In the following section, we detail some of the common tools and utilities that make end-to-end SAP operations and systems management possible by filling in your systems management "holes."

Additional SAP Management Tools and Approaches

Several monitoring and management tools and single-purpose utilities are available to assist you in managing your SAP solutions. Many of these are "free" tools for monitoring hardware components and alerting you of potential issues. HP System Insight Manager (HP SIM), for example, ships with each HP server and "snaps in" to HP OpenView and other enterprise management applications, which can then give you enterprisewide monitoring capabilities from the hardware layer up through the SAP component application layer. Other tools and utilities are built into different components of your technology stack, most notably the operating system layer. Still other utilities and applications can come into play to extend your solution monitoring capabilities, for example, across disparate systems, or up to the client desktop, or down to proprietary storage and tape-backup solutions. In the next few sections, we take a closer look at many of these tools and approaches, and note how truly useful they have proven themselves time and again in our own consulting travels.

Deploying Hardware Management Tools and Utilities

We are big fans of using utilities that typically come bundled with their respective hardware platforms, such as HP's Systems Insight Manager, Dell's OpenManage, and Sun's Sun Management Center. Utilities like these provide a foundation for enterprisewide systems management, often working seamlessly with all-purpose enterprise management applications to provide deeper insight into a technology stack's hardware layer.

Other tools can provide quite a bit of value from an operations perspective, too. For example, after each change control wave at a number of our productive SAP sites, either the SAP operations or Basis team executes a set of scripts that verify the performance of the production disk subsystem. Remember from previous chapters that the disk subsystem tends to be one of the biggest culprits behind SAP performance problems. By executing a set of scripts over a period of 5 to 10 minutes at the tail end of your planned downtime window, you can verify the performance impact that a planned system change may have one last time before turning a system back over to its users. Our two favorite utilities in this regard are Microsoft's SQLIO and the open source Iometer (originally developed by Intel) products. Both are easy to set up and simple to execute.

Other hardware-based tools are also focused on disk subsystems or storage devices. HP OpenView Storage Management appliance and software, for example, allows you to monitor the activity observed throughout an entire storage area network (SAN), from individual disks or groups of disks (called LUNs), to disk controllers, to individual ports on a fiber switch. This granular management capability assists SAP operations teams in quickly identifying the source of SAN-related performance issues that might crop up. It also allows for historical analysis in terms of collecting and analyzing typical throughput numbers observed for specific SAN components under certain conditions (like month-end or seasonal peak processing). Many other disk controller and disk subsystem utilities exist, as well.

Finally, additional hardware management and monitoring tools enable you to monitor specific pieces of your SAP solution stack. Examples include the following:

▶ Tape drive/library management tools and utilities, such as those offered by leading tape backup and restore vendors

▶ Utilities used to manage network infrastructure that interconnects SAP solution components, or software that facilitates managing a server's network cards

▶ Utilities that manage hardware-based IP load-balancing devices, including Java applets and other web-based utilities

▶ Hardware vendor–provided documentation tools

▶ Documentation assistance tools such as SnagIt and PrintKey (for capturing, cropping, and formatting screenshots for documentation)

Of course, other utilities prove themselves useful to a technical support staff day in and day out, such as PKWare's ubiquitous compression tools, SAP's various installation utilities, any number of virus protection programs, and so on. We suggest using the preceding list as a starting point, however, for creating an *operations toolbox* of sorts that matches the monitoring and management requirements of your particular SAP solution stack.

Employing Operating System Management Utilities

At an OS level, we have found without exception that built-in OS utilities such as those associated with Windows and UNIX variants offer immense value to SAP operations teams. Anyone tasked with managing and monitoring an SAP solution needs to add the following utilities to their operations toolbox:

▶ Window's Performance Monitor, or *PerfMon* for short, should be used for any Microsoft-based solution component first to create a baseline and then to monitor system performance proactively on a regular basis. We like to run PerfMon tests after any change management waves (before the system is turned back over to its end users). Similarly, we like to capture PerfMon statistics every 30 or 60 seconds or so, to provide a baseline from which to compare future system performance. Most important in our eyes are disk queue lengths, mix of reads to writes, CPU statistics, RAM utilization, pagefile utilization, and basic network I/O.

▶ A host of UNIX command-line utilities are used regularly in support of day-to-day SAP systems management. One of the most common utilities is vmstat, used to monitor the run queue, swap file page-in count, paging daemon scan rate, CPU status, and more. Another common utility is accessed by executing the single letter *w*, which shows process usage by monitoring load averages and generating an abbreviated Top Sessions report with load averages over 1, 5, and 15 minutes. For a full CPU activity report, top can be executed. And for swap file performance measured as a percentage of swap space utilized, swapinfo is valuable.

Many other utilities and tools are available as well, especially in the world of various UNIX flavors. Refer to your operating system's administration guide for details specific to your OS release.

Drawing Upon Database Management Tools

Naturally, a database vendor's own tools and utilities are most often leveraged for basic database administration outside of SAP's CEN and CCMS T-codes. This includes Microsoft's SQL Server Management Studio and Oracle's Enterprise Manager. However, other tools may also prove useful. Oracle's Statspack utility and UNIX-based bstat and estat command-line utilities are classic examples, as are various SQL trace tools. And iostat, a common UNIX utility, can be employed to display real-time disk subsystem performance, too. Finally, sar, the System Activity Reporter, can be used to report disk I/O and buffer activity.

We also include various data archive utilities and applications under the category of database management tools. Of course, because these tools require a certain amount of database or SAP administration expertise, functional expertise, and the support of an SAP operations team, it's probably not fair to call them strictly operations tools. However, after you nail down an archive solution and approach, the process of extracting business data out of your productive SAP instances and relocating this data to other storage media eventually represents an operational activity.

Extracting More Value from SAP Solution Manager

SAP Solution Manager can fill in quite a few holes that other technology stack tools leave empty. It embraces much more than simply technology management, adding change management and business process management to its core capabilities. SAP Solution Manager brings together SAP's know-how under one management umbrella, and underpins this with service level and help desk capabilities.

For example, its central command station approach to operations management and monitoring can oversee your entire SAP system landscape, even including third-party system interfaces. And because SAP Solution Manager is a self-documenting data repository, it provides great value beyond the operations functions available from its main user interface screen.

The Operations section of SAP Solution Manager includes three broad categories of services, facilitated by detailed process documents as well as traditional SAP consulting engagements:

▶ **Predictive and Proactive Services**—Includes SAP's GoingLive and EarlyWatch services, both of which analyze SAP systems end to end (GoingLive audits your system prior to going live, whereas EarlyWatch seeks to ensure excellent ongoing operations). Note that these services can be performed as a set of self-service procedures, or via more traditional onsite or remote consulting venues.

▶ **Continuous Improvement Services**—Delivered exclusively by onsite SAP consultants, includes analysis or optimization of such things as system administration, storage subsystem performance, SQL statements, and even business process management and more—everything needed to improve the performance and availability of your SAP solution across the board.

▶ **Best Practices**—Reflects best-of-breed documented processes, procedures, and services specific to managing each SAP component.

Beyond these Operations services, though, lie monitoring and support capabilities. Especially valuable are SAP Solution Manager's real-time system monitoring, service-level reporting, and business process monitoring—again, everything needed to ensure a well-performing system. The presence of an online help desk (discussed previously) and the ability to search the SAP Notes database are a huge boon for SAP operations teams. Remember, SAP Notes are provided to SAP's customers to share information regarding corrections and enhancements; SAP Solution Manager's ability to automatically implement SAP Notes rounds out its offerings.

Using the SAP Note Assistant

Outlined briefly in Chapter 27, "Functional Configuration Change Control," another useful tool is the SAP Note Assistant (SAP transaction /nSNOTE). Used to rapidly implement specific SAP Notes (code updates, bug fixes, and so on), the Note Assistant makes it easy to install these corrections to SAP components. Dependencies between SAP Notes, Support Packages, and other system modifications are tracked as each is implemented to ensure that they are implemented in the correct or best order. Together, these powerful capabilities make the Note Assistant invaluable to the SAP TSO, and an important addition to your change management processes.

Prior to the Note Assistant, to implement the corrections and enhancements found in SAP Notes, you had to import them as part of an SAP Support Package (which meant waiting until the support package was released by SAP) or, worse, manually insert the corrections into your own SAP source code. With the Note Assistant, this is performed easily and quickly without the need to touch your own system's source code—a huge improvement in regard to making error-free changes and therefore increasing system availability.

Additional compelling reasons for the Note Assistant are

▶ It provides support for SAP Basis releases from as far back as version 4.5 (implemented as an add-on); as of release 6.10, it is integrated as part of the Basis installation.

▶ Automated implementation of SAP Notes allows you to download the notes appropriate for your particular SAP solution from SAP's Service Marketplace and load them directly into your technical sandbox, development, or development/test systems.

▶ *Dependency resolution* ensures that corrections are implemented in the proper order.

▶ Notes are protected in terms of modifications that your own team may have made to the system, to ensure that your modifications are not overwritten while also guaranteeing that only pristine code is applied to your systems.

▶ The Note Assistant's intuitive user interface and features such as a split-screen editor facilitate fast implementation of SAP Notes, without all of the manual work required in days gone by.

▶ Comprehensive reports regarding the SAP Notes that you have implemented, or the status of SAP Notes in progress, aid in project organization and administration.

▶ SAP Notes can be assigned to particular SAP TSO members for processing; status of their work can easily be checked as well.

With the SAP Note Assistant, handling and implementing SAP Notes makes the process of correcting small bugs in your system easier. This feature, combined with updates and fixes found in regularly released SAP Support Packages, helps guarantee a stable, well-performing SAP environment and represents an excellent alternative when working in SAP environments in which the Service Desk of SAP Solution Manager has not been implemented and configured.

35

Summary

We covered a lot of ground in this chapter, creating a foundation for both SAP systems management and SAP computer operations. We described the SAP operations manual, including both what to include in and how to document the various current-state, regularly scheduled, and how-to documents needed to support an SAP enterprise. We then provided real-world documentation practices, followed by a detailed look at various systems management techniques for SAP. Next, a process for selecting, evaluating, and implementing an SAP systems management application was discussed, backed up with our real-life observations. We also provided our own assessments of three popular SAP management applications on the market today. We wrapped up by identifying common utilities and tools that help fill in the holes left by even the most excellent of enterprise management applications. Our solution stack approach to doing so should prove useful to anyone wanting to identify and add a utility to their SAP shop's operations toolbox.

Case Study: Delivering a Systems Management Best Practices Workshop

You are the member of the SAP support team tasked with positioning HiTech, Inc., to achieve post-go-live operational excellence. Your team lead has asked you to help conduct a workshop covering best practices for managing your unique SAP environments. The target audience is the newly formed enterprise management group (EMG) shared services team, which is essentially a subset of the IT department. The EMG has been instructed to design an SAP management solution leveraging SAP Solution Manager, HiTech's existing HP OpenView monitoring instrumentation, and the IT organization's penchant for manual checklists.

Questions

1. Which additional information do you need to gather prior to the workshop so that you can prepare yourself and the related workshop collateral?

2. How can you bring these initially two separate worlds—SAP and the existing HP OpenView monitoring environment—together?

3. What's your recommendation for how to address the IT organization's use of manual checklists?

4. Could you leverage SAP's native monitoring solutions such as CCMS/CEN and SAP Solution Manager within a larger enterprise systems management framework?

> **NOTE**
>
> The answers to these questions can be found in Appendix A, "Case Study Answers."

CHAPTER 36

Preparing for SAP Go-Live

The big day of go-live is finally close at hand. Go-live is actually nothing more than a point in time; it's just another day, albeit the final milestone in your implementation or upgrade project. But it's the *process* of transitioning from one system to a new one that is the final challenge related to going live on a new system. This process is often referred to as *cutover* and is the focus of this final chapter. Cutover is all about turning on the new SAP system as the user's new system of record, and turning off any existing or legacy systems replaced by SAP.

Critical cutover-related tasks occur well before the big day of go-live, and the planning and preparation associated with these activities occur even further back. Project milestones related to locking down the system from a technical change management perspective, preparing the SAP Technical Support Organization (TSO) for its new support role and responsibilities, and even rolling out the SAPGUI to all future end users are all key to achieving go-live success. And, of course, the huge task of putting to bed all the functional customization of the system, performing final data synchronization between the new SAP system and the systems being replaced, and many other tasks and activities must all be accomplished. It is these high-level technical and business tasks, communications tasks, escalation processes, and other specific activities that make up your *cutover plan*.

The Cutover Plan

Planning, preparing, and executing cutover should all be documented and managed through the use of your project plan. Why so formal an approach? Because there is so much to do, and little room for error. Nearly every member of the SAP support organization is involved, and all of them need to be coordinated in terms of tasks, milestones, and working through critical-path objectives. The job of coordinating all this activity rests with either the SAP project manager or (more often) a designated cutover deployment manager (CDM).

If we take a quick look at the SAP operations team alone, the responsibilities are huge in that even this low-profile team must

- ▶ In keeping with the company's change control processes, work with the technical and functional teams to lock down the production system (described in more detail later in this chapter).

- ▶ Work with the enterprise management group and Basis team to update or reconfigure the enterprise management tools to be used for monitoring production.

- ▶ Obtain any last-minute training regarding ongoing operations.

- ▶ Review and refine all systems-related operations procedures and processes, and ensure that they are clearly defined, understood, and documented. For example, backup/restore, system monitoring, event management, and escalation of issues are all core subtasks that fall under the umbrella of systems-related operations.

- ▶ Ensure that SAP functional operations tasks are addressed. This might include defining your "daily routine" procedures, monitoring and managing batch jobs, addressing on-call support needs, and so on.

- ▶ Assign ownership of all of these processes to individuals within the operations organization, allowing SAP operations to be self-sustaining in the future rather than relying on system administrators to do what actually amount to operational functions.

Event escalation in particular needs to be clearly understood. SAP operations must document which team is contacted (and in what order) for each failure scenario. Typically, an on-call rotation list needs to be disseminated by each SAP support team to the operations team. And within each team, or specific to a particular error or condition, the "event management process" needs to be developed. This includes developing an incident reporting process, a mechanism or tool for tracking and documenting incidents, and a method of reporting. At one of our SAP customer sites, the event management process has been broken down into discrete steps, such as escalating the event to the correct team or person, establishing a conference call with all relevant parties, documenting and tracking an action plan, and building a custom communications process into the company's management and stakeholder teams.

But SAP operations actually has it easy compared to many of the other groups within the SAP TSO! For example, consider the following high-level milestones that must be managed by the client SAP project manager, each milestone consisting of anywhere from a handful of tasks to 10 to 20 discrete supporting activities touching multiple SAP support teams:

- ▶ Establish and staff the SAP help desk and other core support teams and then train and prepare them for their role in supporting go-live, if this has not been done already.

▶ After all post-stress-test tuning changes have been implemented, freeze the production system in terms of technical or solution stack changes.

▶ At a functional level, complete and then freeze all transports, customized settings, and so on related to your SAP component's business processes. Also, establish business cutoff dates and obtain signoff on these dates by each functional group (to prevent anybody from later complaining that the cutoff date was too early and they "didn't know" or had no control).

▶ Load the new system with any required master data (using SAP's Legacy System Migration Workbench or WinShuttle, for example). Creating the data and performing bulk load inserts from a source or legacy system are two ways of handling this.

▶ Transform or change data necessary to populate SAP NetWeaver BW cubes, SAP Supply Chain Management liveCache, and so on.

▶ Freeze all legacy systems some time prior to go-live, so that the final transactional data from these existing systems can be captured and migrated to the new system. This can be done once, prior to retiring the old system, or performed in parallel to keep the old and new systems tightly synchronized for a period of time. Anything from scripting bulk data loads to performing manual data entry may be necessary. And, of course, all of this activity must be carefully communicated to end users, too.

▶ Train all SAP end users and apprise them of the support resources available to them (for example, their superuser colleagues within their own functional organizations, the SAP help desk, key backup or after-hours folks in other SAP support organizations, and so on).

▶ Develop a process for actually measuring the system's availability and performance against its service-level agreements (SLAs). Sometimes called *availability tracking*, this includes defining what does and does not constitute downtime, what constitutes acceptable performance, how to track planned and unplanned downtime, how to measure availability, how to schedule downtime, and finally who will own the tracking process.

▶ Coordinate and validate an *operational review* that determines the readiness of the system. An operational review seeks to confirm technical, functional, operational, and other readiness factors. For example, an operational review of the data conversion process must be performed to ensure not only that the data itself is good, but that the process used to populate the system is auditable. And the readiness of each system process or component must include signoff based on agreed-upon readiness criteria.

▶ Complete tasks related to vendor and partner support and maintenance and management contracts. For example, maintenance contracts, repair processes, access to consulting resources post-go-live, and so on all need to be addressed.

▶ Review the project plan against your implementation methodology of choice to ensure that no stone has been left unturned. SAP Solution Manager maintains roadmaps such as the Enhanced Solution Management Roadmap, which details the

36

technical implementation. In the same manner, the Enhanced Implementation Roadmap for SAP targets project managers and your functional teams.

Of course, none of these activities can occur in a vacuum. Cutover must be underpinned by sound communication and reporting processes, not only for the obvious coordination requirements but also so that no stakeholder is surprised at the last minute by a condition or issue that has existed for some time but has yet to be resolved.

In a nutshell, then, these tasks can be summarized as follows: communicate with your stakeholders, lock down the system, address SLAs, prepare your support personnel, plan for contingencies, work through last-minute issues, train everyone, make sure you didn't miss anything, and do your best to control the chaos bubbling underneath the surface of your project. The details relevant to these tasks are discussed throughout the remainder of the chapter.

Preparing for Technical Go-Live

At least a month before go-live, all of the technical tasks related to updating the system earmarked for production need to be addressed. The most critical of these tasks addresses the issue of change control; any change that must be implemented into production needs to be communicated to the CDM and advanced down the change management path *now*. You want to ensure that each change has ample time to settle in and prove itself within your SAP system landscape. And, just as importantly, you need time should one of the changes lead to an unstable SAP technology stack; backing out a change, or researching new changes and updating the stack, takes time.

As outlined in the Accelerated SAP (ASAP) methodology, you'll also need to focus on last-minute *production support*, which is another way of saying that last-minute issues need to be managed and resolved, and the results of live business processes need to be validated. ASAP never allotted much time for these activities, however; in our experience, nothing less than a calendar month makes sense.

Of course, a great many additional tasks need to be accomplished prior to go-live, too, from fine-tuning your "golden" production business client to completing any final disaster recovery (DR) site updates, to reviewing the system from top to bottom, to finalizing documentation, and so on. The bulk of this chapter is focused on these activities and more.

SAP GoingLive Check and Other Review Processes

A key task associated with locking down the system from a technical perspective involves leveraging SAP's "Predictive and Proactive Services" offerings. The first of these, the *GoingLive* check is usually performed a number of times before go-live. Normally, one is performed prior to your stress test (in support of pretuning and basically ensuring a sound technology stack), and another a few weeks before go-live. It is this final go-live check that ensures you have SAP AG's "blessing" to bring your system live; indeed, it is in SAP AG's best interests as well as your own to smooth the way to post-go-live and the Continuous Business Improvement phase of your SAP implementation.

After go-live, you will still want SAP AG to audit and review your system occasionally. This is performed remotely, onsite, or as a self-service procedure, and is termed an *EarlyWatch service* or *session*. EarlyWatch services have been a mainstay of SAP AG (and select technology partners) for years and help to ensure that your solution continues to run well even in the wake of changes to your business processes or infrastructure.

Today, included with your SAP system maintenance, SAP AG provides two EarlyWatch sessions per year. Most of our customers have these executed via "remote delivery" by an SAP service engineer working over an RFC connection to your system. We recommend that you use the first of these sessions shortly after your first post-go-live change control wave. Use your second EarlyWatch session as you think necessary; in support of performance issues or after major changes to your system are both appropriate uses.

SAPGUI Rollout Mechanism

Prior to go-live, each future end user of the new SAP system needs to enable his or her desktop, laptop, and other access devices to communicate with the SAP system. We use the term SAPGUI generically; as we have discussed previously, there are a number of ways to access an SAP component, including Java- and HTML-based WebGUI interfaces.

The simplest method for small or phased implementations is to make the SAPGUI Front-End CD available via a file share or similar method, and point your users to it. You can leverage logon scripting to automatically install the SAPGUI, too, though we generally prefer to leave this up to the users because the installation takes upwards of 30 minutes depending on your network link and the processor speed of the front-end client.

We have seen more and more SAPGUI deployments enabled through Citrix or replaced (more often simply augmented) by WebGUI deployments and similar means. Where applicable, PDAs, smartphones, and similar hand-held devices need to be enabled for SAP as well.

On the other end of the technology spectrum, it is still not uncommon to see PC support organizations tasked with visiting the desktop of each user and performing the SAPGUI installation based on a standard installation procedure. It is amazing, but certainly not uncommon. If this is your preferred method of rolling out the SAPGUI, we also suggest that SAP default printing and faxing services be set up during this visit as well.

Before we leave the topic of rolling out the SAPGUI, you also want to ensure that your standard desktop or laptop "image" includes the SAPGUI by default. In this way, as your IT organization deploys new or replacement computers throughout the company, your users will not be forced to install the SAPGUI manually. Like imaging your office productivity applications and so on, including the SAPGUI in your master image saves time and reduces complexity and support costs in the end.

Setting Up Batch Housekeeping Jobs

Though you have probably already set up the core housekeeping jobs as part of your unique SAP component post-installation process, a certain number of other "housecleaning" or housekeeping jobs must be scheduled. Review the jobs you currently have scheduled, including the execution status of any job, by running transaction SM37. To add standard housekeeping jobs to new instances, execute transaction SM36 and then click the Standard Jobs button. You can verify that no single job is scheduled to execute twice at the same time from here as well.

Additional jobs beyond the standard ones can now be set up. These can always be executed manually, but we find SM36 helpful when it comes to scheduling housekeeping jobs that should run regularly, or jobs that don't necessarily map well to a traditional calendar. For example, if you need to run a job every Monday unless Monday is a holiday, you can select a more restrictive execution option, such that if the day falls on a nonworking day (according to a factory-based or other calendar), you can configure the system to "Move job to next workday."

Jobs may be specific to an SAP component or more generic. For example, job RSBDCSUB may be executed to process a batch input session. And ZTERRDEL should be set up to run periodically, to clean up application data left undeleted in table TERRD—these are both good examples of cleanup jobs. Other jobs may be used to prepare for executing another particular job, or to report against the status of a specific job, component, condition, and so on. We suggest that you carefully review the Installation Guide, Master Guide, and other core documentation for each SAP component you have installed. Pay particular attention to the SAP Notes referenced by each guide, and review these as well. You will also want to look at SAP Notes that are specific to the Basis release on which your SAP components reside (4.6C or 6.30, for example). And in all cases, refer to SAP Note 16083, "Standard Jobs, Reorganization Jobs," to determine whether any new housekeeping jobs are recommended—as SAP's NetWeaver platform grows to enable greater enterprise connectivity and interoperability, we speculate that more and more standard housekeeping jobs will become the norm.

Final System Updates and Review

A number of weeks prior to the estimated go-live date, the CDM needs to work with the SAP Basis and technical infrastructure teams to carefully review the system that "mirrors" production (for example, the SAP Staging, Preproduction, or Test/QA). When the mirrored technology stack has proven itself to be reliable, only then can the following final technical changes be applied to production:

▶ Promote the final support packages, SPAM, SAINT, and kernel updates, database patches, OS service packs, patches, and hot fixes, and so on into the production environment.

▶ Perform any updates to add-ons, such as the SAP ERP plug-ins. As with everything else, take care to ensure that add-ons are not rushed through the promote-to-production process, as only specific releases of add-ons are supported by specific SAP components.

▶ Perform an additional client copy of your golden client, and keep it available "just in case" and in keeping with best practices regarding data safekeeping.

▶ Make final tweaks to your SAP profiles as needed.

Remember, we recommend obtaining your final SAP GoingLive Check at this time. We also strongly suggest that you quickly follow up these changes with a cold or offline tape backup, and ship the backup offsite for safekeeping. For Windows-based systems, back up the registry of each server in your production environment(s) as well. And keep in mind one of the goals of making these final changes to production—you seek consistency between two or more different systems. That is, by the end of this final change management process, your production environment should be *identical* to your staging, test/QA, technical sandbox, or some other environment within your SAP system landscape. The less identical these environments, the more risk you incur should additional updates or changes be required by the system one day (which is inevitable!), as you will not truly have the benefit inherent to testing changes in an apples-to-apples manner.

Locking Down the System

When your offline backup is safely offsite, take yet another tape (or disk-based) backup and keep it onsite and close by, in case you need it prior to go-live. And lock down the system. In other words, do not make any more technical changes to it. This includes applying last-minute patches and updates, flashing firmware, restringing your SAN fiber cables, swapping out network cables for color-coded ones, and so on. You should even refrain from creating new clients or doing anything else that could potentially impact available disk space. We have seen all of these little things impact the system on the day of go-live. As we were nicely reminded in the Marine Corps Recruit Depot in San Diego after being instructed to halt, "You're done. Lock it up! Lock it up!" In essence, communicate to everyone on the technical team the same thing—no changes allowed, maggots.

Preparing for the First Change Management Package

It might seem strange to be thinking already about making changes to the system, but it's actually very normal; when the system is locked down in preparation for go-live, all potential updates need to be queued for the first change control wave. In our experience, changes still seem to get put in even days before go-live, but this practice is certainly not a *best* practice and should be avoided.

Instead, the SAP support organization needs to begin embracing a mindset that only absolutely critical changes will ever have the opportunity to be implemented rapidly, and then only after having been promoted in an orderly fashion through the SAP system landscape. Some changes will grudgingly be promoted quickly, if they greatly affect profitability or customer satisfaction, for instance. But the bulk of changes will be stored up, to be applied as part of a package or "wave" on some kind of periodic basis after go-live. It is not uncommon for the first change management package to be applied to the system only a few days or weeks after go-live. When things settle down, however, these carefully scheduled mass updates should be applied on a monthly or quarterly basis, and sometimes even less often, depending on the amount of downtime you can afford, if indeed downtime is actually required to implement a particular change.

In the end, you need a very rigorous process for screening any "must have" changes, whether functional or technical. The requests to make changes before go-live are inevitable, and therefore need to be dealt with. If you find yourself with a change request a week before go-live, in our experience a resounding "no" applies most of the time. However, the value of a process for reviewing and validating a critical "Stop the presses!" change—one that could potentially delay go-live—cannot be underestimated.

Final Administrative and Technical Details

Though the system is locked down from a technical perspective, this does not mean that administrative and process details related to *operating* the system cannot be fine-tuned. Nor does it mean that the system is locked down in terms of user-based administration activities, such as creating and modifying roles, or reworking SSO (single sign-on) or central user administration via SAP CUA or SAP NetWeaver Portal. And refining administrative tasks related to daily operations, enterprise management, and so on are all fair game at this point.

Refining Backup and Restore Processes

The enormous amount of data that can be maintained and generated within your production system is remarkable. Most of our customers support single production databases ranging from 500GB to several terabytes, for instance. Factor in multiple SAP components, synchronizing database copies between test, staging, DR, and technical sandbox environments, and the need to at least occasionally back up production file systems other than the core database and logs (such as SAP and database executables, the OS partition, and so on), and the raw amount of production data is staggering.

The need to back up all of this data is critical. Further, the need to actually test whether the tape backup is good is key as well. We applaud those few customer sites that truly embrace regular tape *restore* procedures to ensure true recoverability; their due diligence will pay great dividends one day. In addition to testing the integrity of your backups, though, you must also develop and refine the processes associated with backup and restore, such as

▶ Implementing a grandfather, father, child approach to tape backups, including how often to recycle tapes (for example, every 5 weeks for daily backups, every 5 months for weekly backups, and every 15 months for monthly backups).

▶ Determining the best "window" of time in which to run full, incremental, or other backups.

▶ Determining how often to perform an offline (cold) database backup versus an online (warm) backup. Oftentimes, offline database backups are performed weekly and online backups are performed daily.

▶ Determining how often to dump log files to tape, and whether a disk dump should be used for staging.

▶ Determining how often to ship log files to your DR system, if applicable.

▶ Determining how often to back up other file systems to tape (many of our clients perform this during their weekly offline backups, so as to have a complete "image" of the system no older than a week at any given time).

- ▶ Deciding when a database consistency check might be appropriate, and scheduling it through the SAP or database scheduler.

- ▶ Assembling a schedule for rotating backup tapes offsite, and bringing older ones back "in" to the data center to be reused.

Be sure to document all of the procedures and processes that come out of the tasks noted in the preceding list. Documentation details are covered in depth later in this chapter.

Documenting Output Management Processes

Just as backup and restore processes need to be addressed before go-live, so too do the processes associated with determining which users need which output devices, and then creating and maintaining their relevant printers and fax devices. We suggest creating a step-by-step document, complete with screen shots, when it comes to documenting your how-to output management processes. You also want to document *why* you have chosen a particular approach to printing. For example, if you are setting up all users to print through their own distributed local printers, you want it to be clear to anyone following in your footsteps years later why this approach made sense at the time. The same should be noted for special faxing approaches, SMTP-based communication applications, and so on.

Tweaking Your Systems Management Approaches

Your systems management applications should have been installed for some time now, and the team should be quite familiar with whatever has been implemented. Now is the time, though, to "add" any final servers to your systems management console. The process of adding a server to a management utility is performed in different ways for different applications, but in essence it just means enabling a server to be managed. For instance, it might include

- ▶ Hard-coding or identifying a range of names or IP addresses to discover, thereby adding servers to your system console, so that they can then be monitored and managed.

- ▶ Updating the system console in other ways, such as updating its version control database (used for managing and sharing data relevant to software and hardware updates), updating the database of known bugs and issues, revising performance or other thresholds, defining Key Performance Indicators (KPIs, discussed in detail later in this chapter), and so on.

- ▶ Training or retooling the SAP operations and help desk teams to monitor your production system. This could include any number of systems management tools, such as SAP Solution Manager, HP Business Availability Center, Microsoft Management Console, SAP CCMS/CEN, and so on.

- ▶ Teaching the team how to use an enterprise systems management checklist to verify that the systems are available and performing within tolerances.

The key this late in the deployment is to *not* change any system-level software. Thus, although you may need to enable an underlying service or capability to support systems management (Simple Network Management Protocol [SNMP] and Desktop Management Interface [DMI] are two common management protocols), now is not the time to make these kinds of changes to the technology stack. Similarly, it is also too late to load new, or *update the version* of, systems management agents on your production servers—save these changes for the first change wave.

Managing the SAP Enterprise

A number of miscellaneous tasks need to be performed by the SAP Basis or operations team. For example, it's typical to collect your SAP administrative alerts in a public folder. The contents of this folder should therefore be periodically reviewed and used to populate systems management reports and address other status and service-level reporting.

As another example, you should discuss which tools each operations staff member should have on his or her desktop, and then install and configure those tools. The team then needs to be trained to monitor the production systems when it comes to availability, performance, virus alerts, and more.

Operations will need certain rights (SAPGUI transaction-level security as well as OS-specific) on each SAP server the team has been directed to monitor, too. We suggest creating a global group for operations and providing it with the custom access rights necessary to monitor and manage the system. For specific rights, refer to the tasks outlined in the Daily, Weekly, and other Operations checklists discussed earlier in the book.

Determining Key Performance Indicators

Before you can track and measure your performance or availability, you of course need some kind of metrics. These metrics are often called service levels or Key Performance Indicators (KPIs), and apply to most every team within the SAP support organization. For example, your SAP operations group will be charged with meeting the following KPIs:

- ▶ **Production Job Completion**—The percentage of time that job runs must complete successfully as scheduled. This can range from 99%–99.99%; typical is 99.5% in our experience.

- ▶ **Backup Completion**—The percentage of time that backups must complete successfully. Not surprisingly, the minimum acceptable service level is usually 100%.

- ▶ **Application System Administration**—The length of time between receiving a request (to create a user ID, or reset a password, and so on) and actually completing the request. This might be broken down between "normal" 9–5 business hours and "after hours," and may vary based on the critical nature of the task, too. For example, the target for creating a new user ID might be 90% within 24 hours, whereas a request to change a password might be expected to be done 90% of the time within an hour.

- ▶ **Monitoring Service Levels**—Relates to how long it takes to act after an alert has been received. Some of our customers publish KPIs that promise a 15-minute response or escalation process, for example, after an alert is received by their systems management consoles.

Similarly, the SAP help desk will be expected to quickly respond to help desk calls and resolve them efficiently; just how quickly or efficiently is described by the KPIs assigned to this team:

- **Help Desk Time-to-Answer**—The amount of elapsed time (such as 30 seconds for 99% of all calls) it takes for the help desk customer to reach a human voice.

- **Call-back Response Time**—The time that elapses between entering the trouble ticket and calling back the customer to acknowledge the problem and provide some kind of estimate as to the time it will take to get a technician or analyst onsite.

- **Help Desk Resolution Time**—The time to resolve trouble tickets that do not require service dispatch and can further be easily classified as level 1 (basic issue) or level 2 (moderate) severity. In our experience, 85% of all calls should be completely resolved with 30 minutes or so, and 99% within four hours.

The SAP data center team is tasked with maximizing network and hardware uptimes, and can therefore be tasked with achieving service levels such as the following:

- **System Landscape Availability**—The production system's computing platform might be required to be available during normally scheduled uptime periods 99.9% of the time. Wording an SLA in this way implies that *planned* outage exist outside the 99.9% availability target.

- **Network Availability by User Origination**—Network availability expectations can differ based on whether a user accesses the production system from inside or outside the company-internal network. Such SLAs are usually broken down into external and internal service levels. For example, users accessing the system over the Web might expect these network links to be available 99.99% of the time, whereas internal (and therefore more controllable by the company's IT department) access might be expected in the neighborhood of 99.999% of the time.

- **System Requests**—The time required to evaluate system or service requests and respond to them with schedule and cost estimates. These can be fairly long-term in nature, covering many days perhaps.

- **Service Completion**—The time between the service request response and actually completing the service call.

- **New System Installation**—This is similar to System Requests but is specific to installing a new server rather than responding to a service need on a current system. It's not uncommon to install 95% of all requested new systems within 14 business days, for example (obviously, there's great opportunity for improvement, in part explaining the growing interest in virtualized pools of computing resources).

Of course, hundreds of other service levels need to be defined and recorded for the remaining SAP support organizations—developer teams, database administration, SAP Basis, infrastructure, change control, project steering committee, other programming staff, and so on are all subject to meeting KPIs. Even generic "customer service" and "service evaluation metrics" need to be defined for the entire project.

And although we have focused on measuring KPIs inherent to discrete SAP support teams, it is also common in the first 60 to 90 days after go-live to look at system availability more simply or holistically. For example, one of our favorite customers on the East Coast identified what it called *realistic and conservative* system availability and performance targets. Specifically, after factoring in all layers and components within its technology stack, its goal was to achieve 90% uptime in the first two months, and then improve this to 95% uptime in the third month. After the third month, it would strive for its target three nines of availability. The customer took a similar approach to measuring performance, too; its goal for the first two months was a modest 2- to 3-second average response time across all modules, followed in the third month by an average that did not exceed 2 seconds.

So how do *you* create pertinent KPIs? One sure way is to identify the goals of each SAP team, or to take a closer look at each team's customer. If a team is responsible for performing a certain task, that task is subject to being evaluated in terms of timeliness, quality, and so on. We therefore suggest using this approach as the foundation for creating realistic KPIs by which your solution can be measured. When you understand the tasks, you can determine how easily the data might be collected to prove how well you are performing the tasks. If a task does not lend itself to being easily measured, or requires data that is difficult to obtain, you probably want to pass on using this task as a KPI.

Tracking System Performance

To help ensure that service and performance levels are tracked and met, we suggest *at minimum* dumping your performance and availability data into a database or spreadsheet. Such an approach serves as a data repository and therefore allows for historical reporting. Many of our customers collect this data manually and use it to plot simple graphs that reflect performance statistics and more.

Other customers prefer to collect this data automatically, or have no choice but to automate the process due to their complex SAP system landscapes. We have seen or developed a number of automated approaches that rely on scripted CCMS transactions, similar to the stress-testing scripts discussed earlier in the book.

Collecting and analyzing performance data has long been a strength of enterprise management tools such as those discussed in Chapter 35, "SAP Systems and Operations Management," too. HP's Business Availability Center, Performance Center, and Operations Center suites allow a wealth of SAP technology stack and end-to-end business process performance data to be easily collected and reported against. These tools are supremely effective but not exactly inexpensive. Given the lack of SAP support by many lesser enterprise systems management applications, though, building your own performance management plans may leave you with many gaps with which to contend.

However, a wonderful alternative approach exists—one that can be extended by Borland, HP, IBM, and other SAP-aware tool vendors. Use SAP's very own Solution Manager to validate new SAP implementation KPIs. With its ability to collect and analyze real-time data across your SAP enterprise, SAP Solution Manager can

▶ Help you identify clear and measurable service-level goals

- ▶ Measure and communicate how well you achieve your service goals, based on agreed-upon measurements and KPIs

- ▶ Communicate all of this data through easy-to-understand service-level reports—data is provided for individual servers and for complete solutions

Creating a service-level report is made easy through SAP Solution Manager. Regardless of how you collect and report against your SLAs, though, the key at this stage in your implementation is to ensure that the data being collected is truly useful in proving that SLAs are being met. Thus, *now* is the time to verify that your service-level reporting approaches not only *work*, but work *well*. Once this service baseline is established, fill in the gaps with HP's best-in-class software solutions for SAP.

Managing Company Records

Today more than ever, records retention is an important part of project management. Project employees and contractors need to adhere to company policy addressing how long records need to be maintained. The CDM should work with the SAP project manager to verify that the project's records retention schedule is up to date and that records are kept no longer than required.

We recommend that the CDM appoint a person to analyze project artifacts and other information on a regular basis to determine what needs to be retained and what can be destroyed once its useful life is over. This applies to artifacts stored as a database, an electronic document, an email, and even a physically printed document. When no longer required, be sure to destroy information no longer required for legal or business purposes.

The Changing Role of the SAP TSO

As the SAP system evolves into the butterfly (or "moth," if you're going with the classic gray SAPGUI!) it is destined to become, so too will the SAP support organization tasked with the system's implementation and upkeep. The very nature of the jobs held by many SAP support team members will change in a flash, after go-live comes and goes. And just like that, other positions will completely disappear, to be supplanted by new or morphed roles and responsibilities.

Reaching Maturity: New Responsibilities and Roles

A few weeks before go-live marks a very interesting time in the state of your SAP system landscape. For the first time ever, it will be truly static—if for only a moment or two. During this lock-down, nothing at a technical level will change. Even the functional teams will wrap up their activities, and although their hours will continue to be long and the transports into production will never seem to stop, the nature of the activities taking place at this level will be changing, too.

The big day of go-live marks the beginning of a new phase in the life of your SAP solution that is focused on continuous improvement, a phase that some of our customers call "maturity." We like this term, because it denotes the change in mindset previously

36

discussed. By placing a system into production, you turn the corner from implementation to operations and continuous improvement. This new phase in the SAP component implementation lifecycle is the longest by far, and requires a support organization that plans to stick around for the long haul. But, as we discussed in Chapter 14, the long haul equates to "steady state," and this in turn equates to perhaps a different type of personality requirement than commonly found on the implementation team, one focused on achieving SAP *operational* excellence. Along with this operational mindset must come the desire to manage the system, too, rather than allowing changes to control you.

Shifting Focus to Support/Maintenance

Earlier in the book we discussed the two different personality types, one characterized by a need to climb steep learning curves, and one characterized by the need to achieve steady-state operations. We labeled these, respectively, new project (NP) personality types and support/maintenance (SM) personality types (among other labels). Everyone tends to exhibit a little bit of both personalities, of course, but with the changing nature of your SAP solution, you'll want to seek out or develop people with the latter personality type to be charged with *maintaining* the system.

Besides, with the system beginning its new productive role in servicing your internal and external customers, it's inevitable that some of the project folks assigned to the project will ultimately find less and less of a learning curve to conquer, and will leave. Conversely, the true support/maintenance (SM) personality types on your project will completely enjoy the next few years, as things settle down and they play a role in ensuring that the system delivers the performance and availability that your SAP technology partners promised.

Our point here is twofold. First, as attrition takes its toll on your project team, be sure to find the right people to backfill the various roles left vacant (if indeed the roles need to be backfilled). Second, proactively seek to *relocate* your NP types *before* they leave for greener pastures and steeper learning curves; the current project may be winding down, but it is our experience that other SAP component, technology, or third-party integration projects are often on the horizon. So do your best to retain the people that you and your company have invested so much time in—the payoff can be huge when these same people are leveraged in sister projects.

Beyond Go-Live: The SAP COE

Once go-live is behind the SAP project team and TSO in particular, another team typically is given the systems management and operations reigns. Though it's given various labels, we are fond of the term SAP Center of Excellence (SAP COE). The SAP COE is often just an umbrella organization comprising many of the same teams previously aligned with the SAP implementation. Because it is a higher-level organization than its constituent teams, though, the SAP COE can focus on initiatives that often otherwise fall through the cracks after go-live, such as

▶ Establishing governance processes aimed at providing strategic direction, accountability, and escalation procedures for all teams and potential issues

- ► Maintaining alignment between the business team and SAP technology teams with regard to change management, promote to production processes, business support, IT engagement models, and so on

- ► Documenting and managing changes to "baselines" such as performance metrics, SLAs and to what extent they're being met, and issue resolution identification and management processes

Two of the most important organizations post-go-live are the SAP operations and help desk teams, explored in more detail in the context of cutover next.

Last-Minute SAP Operations and Help Desk Preparation

At this point, the operations team should already have experience supporting SAP. Over the last few months, it has monitored the system from a performance and availability perspective, assisted preproduction users (such as developers and testers) in resolving issues, and so on. The help desk should have been established and staffed by now, and should be currently focused on learning how to report, escalate, and resolve issues. In several cases, however, we have seen SAP customers hold off on putting together the help desk until a few weeks before go-live. It's by no means a best practice, but with everything else going on, it happens. In these cases, it is most often the operations team (or a subset of this team) that is expected to get up to speed quickly. In other cases, we have seen the help desk function outsourced. Regardless, this team needs to be prepared for some pretty unusual things, and armed with troubleshooting tools, escalation processes, and, above all, a customer-service attitude.

In our experience, curious, customer-driven folks comfortable in the role of "jack of all trades" tend to be most successful help desk employees. This is because of the issues with which they will be faced. Our favorite story comes from many years back. A help desk analyst and the Basis team were troubleshooting a recurring performance issue. During the lunch hour every day over the course of a few weeks, the system's response time was rising significantly, consistent with an ever-growing workload. It got to the point where things just didn't add up, however—most of the users would be out of the office enjoying lunch, but the system was nonetheless taking a beating. The enterprising help desk analyst decided to quit focusing on the growing dialog step numbers displayed in CCMS and his performance reports, and instead walked over to the building housing these users. What he found was pretty amazing—lying on top of many users' keyboards were staplers, tape dispensers, and in one case a large claw hammer (how many people have *hammers* in their desk?). As it turned out, one of the users had discovered that his session would not time out if the keyboard's Enter key remained depressed. To this day, we have never quite understood their reluctance to log back in to the system after lunch. The huge transaction load they generated explained everything, though, and this help desk analyst, rather than his more experienced Basis colleagues, solved the problem (and had an interesting story to share for many years).

Final Preparations

Enterprising development, testing, operations, and help desk teams will focus their efforts a few weeks before go-live on ironing out things such as the following:

▶ Job performance expectations. To this end, a "general overview" document of what each post-go-live shift looks like in terms of tasks and responsibilities is useful.

▶ Shift turnover procedures, including when to escalate issues that may have cropped up on a previous shift, ownership of issues, who is responsible for performing various tasks, and so on.

▶ Working with the CDM to gather and publish contact information for the entire SAP project team.

▶ End-of-shift daily, weekly, monthly, or other recurring special procedures (for example, how to execute and manage Friday-night weekly backups that cross over two different shifts, or how to escalate development issues).

▶ How the team will manage changes to documented procedures and test cases; where they will reside, who will update them, and how changes will be validated.

▶ How to provide new SAP team members access to required resources; access to tools, distribution lists, collaboration sites, and so on needs to be granted, and training may need to be made available as well.

The team may also be tasked with managing both the old and new systems, too, if the decision was made to run parallel systems (a decision that in some respects mitigates the risk of go-live but complicates the business while creating a lot of additional work for many). Preparation must therefore take into account the time that will be required to monitor and manage both production systems during this time period, especially with regard to staffing. Finally, central to many of these monitoring tasks is the importance of maintaining "as-is" and process documentation, discussed next.

Updating Installation Documentation

As the technical "current state" of your SAP environment changes and subsequently affects operations and performance, these changes need to be tracked. We have found recording the following data quite useful not only in getting new SAP implementations started off on the right foot, but also in tracking changes throughout the implementation:

▶ All hardware-centric data, such as server and disk subsystem models, serial numbers, drive layouts, PCI slot details, and so on

▶ Logical diagram of your unique SAP environment, illustrating the various system landscapes, server topology, functionality hosted by each system, level of business criticality, and so on

▶ Logical diagram illustrating the network topology that interconnects the servers, and provides access to front-end clients, back-end resources, the Internet or company intranet, and any other important details

▶ Physical diagram (sometimes called a "floor map" or data center layout) showing where all of the SAP hardware resides in the data center

▶ Physical diagram that details the contents of each rack

With the current "rolling" state of the system documented at a point in time, the operations and help desk teams can then turn their attention to process documentation.

Updating Process Documentation: Run Books

Unlike point-in-time documentation, procedural or process documentation seeks to walk its reader through how to perform a task or activity. Thus, we often call these "how-to" documents, and collectively refer to many such documents as "run books." A how-to document should be able to be referenced for any installation or operational aspect of the system. Fortunately, many how-to documents exist in the form of SAP whitepapers, SAP Notes, Installation and Master Guides, partner-provided documents, and so on. In the past, though, we have had to create specific process documents for the following:

▶ How to perform server hardware and OS-related tasks, such as "How to Upgrade Server Firmware," "Installing a Server Through Scripting," "How to Set Up an OS Software Stack for SAP," and "Installing MSCS for SAP-on-SQL Server."

▶ How to manage SAN hardware how-to docs, such as "How to Create SAN Disk Volumes," How to Manage SAN Performance," and "How to Map SAN Volumes to Logical Drives."

▶ How to perform database software-related how-to docs, including "How to Install Microsoft SQL Server 2005 and Service Packs for SAP."

▶ How to implement specific SAP components or install options, such as "How to Install Central User Administration" or "How to Download SAP NetWeaver BW Web Queries to Microsoft Excel."

▶ How to perform specific post-installation procedures, such as setting up a printer or the Transport Management System, installing and uninstalling the SAPGUI, configuring operation modes, executing a client copy, applying support packages, using SMLG to set up logon groups, and so on—many of these processes are documented by SAP AG, but our versions include screen shots and other details to leave little to chance.

▶ How to install and manage bolt-ons, such as "How to Install SAP GRC," "How to Install FACSys," and so on.

▶ How to use various utilities and application suites to monitor performance, operations, and availability.

▶ How to perform various tape backup and restore processes, perform database backups, and more.

▶ How to address problem analysis and resolution processes, such as "How to Ide[ntify] and Analyze Connectivity Issues," "How to Identify and Analyze SAP Techno[logy] Stack Performance Issues," and "How to Identify and Analyze SAP Printing

36

Updating your process documentation is critical because these processes can be complex and therefore subject to error, and because these processes are typically not static; they change depending on the modifications made to the technology stack. Thus, we recommend that you never postpone updating your documentation. In our experience, when documentation is postponed, it rarely ever gets done—other projects and "emergencies" invariably continue to crop up, pushing the documentation out further and further along your timeline. Thus, by the time you find a spare moment, you might very well have forgotten the processes to be documented.

Addressing Future Service and Support

One day, your system will fail. It is inevitable; even five nines of availability still equates to a small amount of unplanned downtime. And even if your unplanned downtime numbers are small, you will still require *planned* downtime to implement changes to your business processes, technology infrastructure, or any number of elements or components inherent to your technology stack. It is for these reasons that, well before you need it, you need to arrange for mission-critical support services for your SAP environment. As you will see in the next few pages, this support umbrella hails both from deep within your SAP support organization and from traditional external sources.

At a minimum, you need to collect contact and escalation information for each technical element or component in your stack—from top to bottom. We recommend obtaining not only the usual "1-800" vendor support information, but the deep technical links as well, such as contacts at each partner's SAP Competency Center or SAP second- and third-level engineering groups. Add to this *local* vendor contact information, such as pre-sales and post-sales team members, field service, account management, and any special consulting organizations with SAP experience that are within a few hours of your data center. Finally, augment this external technical contact data with your internal organizational charts and on-call lists, and your team will be well prepared when unexpected issues crop up in your system.

As we alluded to before, this information is typically maintained by the SAP operations or help desk organization. A great way to maintain all of this service and support contact information is through an easily accessible "Quick Reference Support Matrix" document or web page kept on your company intranet (along with the rest of your as-is, process, and other documentation). Many of our customers keep their lists of on-call company-internal resources separate from external contact information due to privacy issues—it's common to include home and personal cell numbers in your rotating on-call lists,

nile Support Agreements

is to draft a support agreement between it and SAP AG, its hard-partners, and any other SAP technology vendors. Normally, service vels; more comprehensive service levels, or faster service response er monthly or annual support fees. A support agreement also arious companies represented in the agreement will collaborate with other partners to provide technical and business process support to their mutual customers. Things like processes for problem escalation, expectations during problem resolution, and so on need to be documented and understood between all parties.

Beyond standard service and support agreements, many customers also choose to execute "consulting on demand" or other reactive services agreements. Most of the time, these are SAP-specific in nature, focused on Basis support, functional support, or integration troubleshooting services. We have seen these executed for particular system components, though, such as access to deep SAN expertise or e-commerce skills. The key here is that the customer has the paperwork done to quickly access a specific resource, so that in the event of a critical issue, no time is wasted putting a service agreement in place.

Leveraging Joint Escalation Centers

Most everyone is familiar with working through basic technology issues with vendors and partners—typically, a partner's first-level support center is contacted, and a trouble ticket or "case" is created to help document the information and process used to solve the problem. For a single-vendor solution whose support center is well versed in a solution, a resolution to an issue can be obtained pretty fast. Unfortunately, it's impossible to implement a monolithic technology stack for SAP; various hardware platforms, disk and database subsystems, operating systems, and of course SAP components equate to multiple partners, each with a first-level support center. Thus, it might seem that the most typical support model employed by a customer would require no less than three or four trouble tickets, one with each partner. All of these partners would be provided the same redundant data (the nature of the issue, how it manifests itself, details relevant to the issue in terms of technology or business process, and so on), subject to the individual interpretation and biases of each partner. In doing so, coordination between the different partners and SAP AG would be cumbersome at best, and finger-pointing would be an inevitable byproduct of such an inadequate support model.

What SAP customers really need is a support model that melds a hardware partner's expertise in IT management and infrastructure with application and business process expertise inherent to SAP AG. This is where *Joint Escalation Centers (JECs)*, *Global Solutions Centers*, or *Joint Solution Services* come into play. For our purposes here, we will refer to these simply as the JEC. Regardless of the name, technology partners that are serious about supporting their SAP customers will participate in, or create, an organization or service offering that

- ▶ Takes ownership of escalated first-level issues

- ▶ Addresses the needs of both technology and business process issues

- ▶ Is capable of reproducing integration and interoperability issues in a lab environment

- ▶ Can access, stage, and test the specific technology stack gear deployed in one of their customer's SAP environments

- ▶ Has deep ties into both SAP and their own back-end product engineering organizations

36

▶ Performs their work in a manner that promotes communication between the customer and the JEC, as illustrated in Figure 36.1, and ultimately facilitates rapid problem resolution

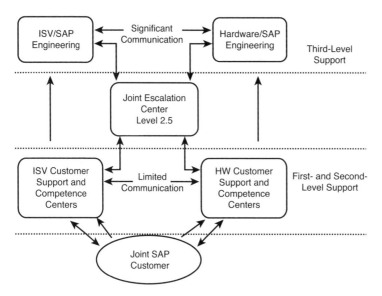

FIGURE 36.1   A Joint Escalation Center represents a key support component, facilitating communication and problem resolution between SAP AG, itself, and the customer.

All of this troubleshooting and testing is performed through a joint-staffing model, in which the engineers and consultants hail from both SAP and its technology partners (HP, IBM, Dell, Fujitsu, and so on). SAP's PartnerPort in Walldorf, Germany, meets these criteria, and houses many a "global" SAP competence or support center. Other implementations of the JEC model exist as well. For example, most of the major independent software vendors (ISVs), such as Microsoft, Borland, Oracle, HP, Sun, and IBM, maintain support organizations that are tied to various partner organizations and SAP AG resources. And some of the hardware partners have assembled JEC resources or service offerings in various key geographies as well.

With these kinds of capabilities, a day in the life of a JEC revolves around diagnosing and resolving interoperability issues, addressing performance issues, modeling business process failures, advising and directing the solution-sizing efforts of their respective SAP Competence Centers, and more. The JEC is uniquely positioned to not only work with back-end engineering resources to help them understand how issues manifest themselves, but also to implement the fixes in a lab environment to *prove* it. And the JEC further proves its work in testing regularly published ISV-provided or hardware-specific fixes, patches, updates, service packs, and so on. As a customer of SAP, you want to be sure to understand and take advantage of the PartnerPort and other JEC-like organizations tasked with supporting SAP solutions.

Thus, if we review the goals of the previously discussed support agreements, clearly the JEC represents where the rubber meets the road. It is the JEC that addresses filling in the support holes left by multiple first-level support organizations or competence centers staffed in a one-sided manner. Even a modest investment of two or three engineers can pay off in a big way in terms of improved customer satisfaction and therefore longer customer relationships. As most of us are aware, it takes a lot more effort to win a new customer than it does to maintain an existing one; the JEC serves this purpose, and creates a best-in-class support environment that will attract *new* customers as well.

The First Week of Go-Live

When the system is finally turned on for use by its end users, you have achieved go-live. This is very different from technical go-live, when the system was locked down and no changes were allowed from a technical perspective. Go-live is actually synonymous with "functional" go-live. However, unlike its technical counterpart, it is unlikely that the system will indeed be locked down for long after the big day of go-live comes and goes. Big changes will of course require downtime, and will therefore be relegated to regularly scheduled change waves. But smaller changes and tweaks to the system will continue to be made and promoted to production as usual, leveraging the Transport Management System (TMS).

Turning the system "on" is by no means the end of the road, though—we've covered a few of the activities that must occur post-go-live throughout this book. In the concluding sections of this chapter, we take a closer look at this critical week, including how to

▶ Monitor the system during the first critical week of go-live

▶ Obtain feedback on the SAP production solution, to promote the idea of continuous business process and technical improvement

▶ Evaluate how well the various SAP support teams performed during the implementation

▶ Celebrate!

The goal of go-live is a "nonevent." That is, well-planned and executed SAP implementations merely make a new productive system available to end users, who in turn are well prepared to begin using it. The transition from the old way of doing things to the new solution should therefore be seamless. We have been fortunate to play a part in countless SAP go-live weeks, and we want to share how the various teams accomplished this greatest of goals—an uneventful go-live—next.

Monitoring During Go-Live Week

The foundation of a smooth go-live rests on monitoring critical performance, availability, and other system characteristics, and rapidly communicating this information throughout the team. To this end, we have seen all of the following approaches prove useful:

▶ During the first week of go-live, twice-daily status meetings between the technical, functional, operations, and help desk teams keep everyone on the same page.

▶ Developing an anticipated list of most frequently asked questions (MFAQs), updating it daily through help desk feedback, and publishing it to the end-user community in an easily accessible format (for example, a website) is important. Covering basic topics that explain such things as how to access the system, log in, reset passwords, and so on saves everyone time.

▶ Ramping up the help desk to handle more calls, as discussed previously, is also essential. Further, communicating the top-ten questions and resolutions throughout the team (to update the MFAQs) and escalating critical issues are important as well. Both of these will serve to reduce help desk call volume.

▶ Monitoring SAP CCMS throughout the day (every hour or two the first few days, stretching out to snapshots a few times a shift by the end of the week) is the most important thing the SAP Basis and infrastructure team can do. The idea is to proactively identify impending performance issues. We suggest regularly running through SM66, ST06, ST04, DB02, ST03, AL08, ST07, and ST02 at minimum this week. Add ST11 (to display error logs) as necessary, and use a daily operations checklist to monitor additional parameters and conditions, too, until you've automated these kinds of activities.

▶ The database administrators need to monitor how well the RDBMS and disk subsystem are performing, from a hardware, operating system, database, and SAP CCMS perspective.

▶ The DR team must examine how well the DR solution appears to work. That is, it needs to verify that log shipping works as expected, or that the cluster is operational—whatever DR solution was implemented. There should be no surprises, because all of this should have been performed previously, but it's still essential to perform the due diligence during go-live week.

▶ The network infrastructure and data center team needs to monitor the performance of all internal and external links binding the SAP system landscape together, and to other systems.

▶ The data center or operations team also needs to monitor events generated by the system and captured by the systems management applications and tools. In addition, special attention must be paid to basic infrastructure power and cooling during this first week, to catch any trends in utilization of these key assets before they become a problem (this first week will find *all* of your SAP hardware and supporting infrastructure up and running, which may not have been typical in the past).

▶ The functional or programming teams need to remain available to discuss business process issues with the help desk (and end users, perhaps). This also includes monitoring the number of ABAP dumps created (ST22), to determine where rapid fixes can be implemented.

▶ Reviewing the technology stack, to verify that no changes have been made unbeknownst to the team, is still a good idea at the end of day one and again at the end of the week. In other words, it's important to verify that no changes are being made behind the scenes, circumventing change control.

While the core technical and functional constituents of the SAP support organization are busy collecting, monitoring, and analyzing the performance of the system, the project management team needs to address related tasks, as communicated next.

Planning for Feedback and Continuous Improvement

Though we use the term lightly, a number of knowledge "databases" exist at this point. For example, the knowledge repository should contain all project definition and success criteria, TCO analyses, sizing data, staffing plans, testing scripts and results, project deliverables, and so on. Partners will also maintain system-level or other data relevant to your project. Additionally, the master project plan and all of its iterations (as it was revised over the course of the project) will reflect changing needs and the impact of scope creep. Enterprise systems management tools and utilities will contain a wealth of data by the end of the first week after go-live, and this data will continue to grow in terms of both volume and its ability to chart historical trends. The change control system will house similar data, though from a functional perspective as well as a technical one. Finally, the cases created using the help desk's tracking tool will serve as a database of issues, resolutions, and trends. All of these "databases" can be leveraged to provide project feedback to the team, and help to focus the efforts of the entire SAP support organization in the weeks to come.

Much of this documented feedback will highlight what the team did right, and what could be improved upon. It will underscore what cannot be changed, what should change, what worked, and what did not. And performance data collected during the first week of go-live will serve as a baseline for the system, a starting point against which updates to the system will be measured. As time passes and the SAP project's players change, this initial collection of information will help level-set newcomers, too.

But perhaps more importantly, this information will serve as the foundation for continuous improvement in the system. Like a baseline in a stress test, all of the data that describes the system's current state will be used to measure the impact of future state changes. Thus, everything from the technical infrastructure to the actual business processes that execute through the system will play a role in continually improving the system across the board.

Additional data should be proactively collected through surveys. Think about it—by the time the first week of go-live has come and gone, most of the production system's users will be using the system enough to begin causing inevitable issues that were not caught during functional, integration, or stress testing. You'll see performance issues, issues with users locking tables needed by other users (and thus "locking one another"), issues with data, and so on. Many of these issues will be relatively minor, and will continue to crop up for several more weeks. However, many of these issues will be minor enough to not warrant a help desk call, and therefore you'll have nothing formal to track. This is where surveys comes into play. Conducting a brief survey every week will give users a chance to report on these minor issues—issues that may become more critical if left untended. We like to use the ZipSurvey utility to collect this additional information, though your organization may already be using one of the many other utilities available.

Simply *having* all of this information is only the beginning, though. To put continuous improvement into action, the team needs to embrace action as well, as follows:

▶ The SAP and client project managers along with the cutover deployment manager need to perform a final review of the SAP master implementation plan to ensure that all milestones have indeed been completed, and to communicate project management lessons learned to the steering committee and senior project staff.

▶ A final high-level "Project Lessons Learned" document, consisting of individual feedback documents created by each SAP team, needs to be assembled and distributed in *electronic* format by project team leaders; each team leader should focus on communicating lessons learned related to his or her area of responsibility. Because this approach ties all organizations together, take care to request only a page or two of lessons learned from each group or team leader—this will allow you to create a document of manageable size and phenomenal value, especially useful if you are preparing to launch similar projects or add new SAP components to your enterprise environment. Be sure to include things that went well, things that could use improvement, things that didn't work too well, and things to be completely avoided.

▶ The core SAP customer-facing and technical support teams need to review the top 10 or 20 most common help desk calls every week, to update or fine-tune MFAQs, automate more assistance, and ultimately reduce call volumes by working through these issues.

▶ The team responsible for systems management needs to review its tool sets regularly. It's often possible to automate responses to certain business and technical events, or automatically escalate issues to the appropriate teams. In the same way, you will find issues that pop up as events that really don't qualify and can be summarily noted or even ignored; the better you fine-tune your enterprise management application, the fewer near-worthless events you will be forced to manage.

▶ The SAP Basis and infrastructure team needs to push many of the standard performance monitoring responsibilities over to the systems management team, by helping it to identify typical performance thresholds and to characterize trends. It also needs to push standard systems administration to the operations team, and user ID maintenance/SSO responsibilities to the help desk. In doing so, the Basis team not only develops "backups," but also frees itself to work more closely with the functional, development, and change management teams going forward.

▶ The functional and programming teams need to focus on developing, testing, and implementing business-driven, user-motivated changes. A testing process that encompasses built-in functional and stress-test milestones will help promote continuous improvement in the code that they author. Regularly reviewing system dumps, revising workflows as directed, and in general embracing change management will consume the rest of their time, while promoting continuous improvement as well.

And though not precisely a continuous-improvement *process* per se, a high-level appraisal of the team's performance needs to be communicated verbally via the final team meeting of go-live week. We have seen these meetings used to underscore the important roles held by key team players, and to communicate how well the team worked together to achieve the project's objectives. Normally, one-and-a-half to two hours is about right, though the best of these are wrapped around something like a long catered lunch of prime rib and lobster. Don't misunderstand the importance of this verbal appraisal (or "go-live lunch," if applicable), though; the feedback from the project leadership team to the team itself can be huge in terms of improved morale and ultimately future performance.

Completing a Post-Implementation Evaluation

Although continuous improvement plays a role in ensuring that the system continues to better meet the needs of its end users, a one-time *post-implementation evaluation* is commonly used to obtain formal, concise feedback shortly after go-live. It is normally the product of the client SAP project manager, though many organizations and individuals play a role in shaping it. After this evaluation form has been crafted, it is shared with the following organizations:

▶ The manager of each key business unit or other customer organization. If different from the manager, the lead person within each business unit responsible for working with the SAP support teams also needs to complete the evaluation.

▶ Each manager or team leader tasked with any level of responsibility for the project. For small to medium-sized implementations, we have seen *every* member of the IT group that supported an SAP deployment be given this form; because feedback is the goal, that's not a bad idea.

▶ Key implementation and technology partners, especially core project managers and senior technologists.

After the results are collected and tabulated, they should be used to provide feedback to the entire team. And we have found these useful when it comes time to write employee reviews or to justify that a consultant's contract be extended, too.

Bestowing Proper Congratulations

Earlier in the book, we recommended a number of compensation alternatives in addition to pay increases, promotions, cash and other bonuses, training opportunities, and so on. Proper congratulations for go-live should certainly include one or more of these, too, depending on an individual's role and success in the project. Team recognition is important as well. But we still maintain that the most important thing, the thing that will help you to retain your top talent and key steady-state personnel, is judicious and honest use of congratulations and praise—both individually and from a team perspective.

Especially during the week of go-live, or shortly thereafter, the project management team, and company management team in general, has a unique opportunity to make a lasting

36

impact on its key employees and long-term contractors. We use the term "key" loosely, too, as we believe that an SAP implementation or upgrade is only successful when a team of people proves that it works together exceedingly well. Thus, we look at praise and general congratulations in terms of layers—we like to see a performance bonus doled out to the *entire team*, no exceptions.

On top of this, though, we feel that there is great value in activities such as the go-live lunch discussed earlier, or getting together for a formal banquet or other event after hours to dole out more targeted awards and sincere words of thanks. It is at these celebrations that public praise carry the most weight. These are especially heady events when the budget can absorb the cost of hosting both its SAP project team members and their spouses or significant others.

As we said before, on top of the meal we like the idea of handing out awards. Some of these should be light and humorous, to keep the event a bit more celebratory. Others should be targeted at the top performers, though, typically the various project managers, team leaders, business leads, senior solution architects, and other senior technical staff. Cash bonuses are always nice, but gift cards and the like are appreciated as well.

Though not nearly as frequent as they should be, we have also seen gifts handed out to family members; gift cards to nice restaurants, enclosed within handwritten cards personally thanking them for allowing the project to "steal away" their spouse during the project, are excellent. Remember the family, we say, and you'll build long-standing bridges to your valuable employees and other team members.

Summary

Here we are at the end of our journey, and you've read about what it takes to plan for, execute, and take live an SAP system. In some cases, you may have used this book as a roadmap for implementing or upgrading SAP or perhaps integrating a new SAP component into your existing enterprise. Regardless of the scope, congratulations are in order! We genuinely hope that we were able to help you avoid some of the landmines we've personally stumbled over in past years, and that you've enjoyed the journey along the way.

In this final chapter, we walked through the process known as cutover. You learned that cutover is much more than go-live, or the instant in time when your new SAP solution is finally turned over to its anxious end users; instead, it refers to the entire transitional process, from planning for the big day to administration and operations, to running parallel systems, to synchronizing or executing last-minute data loads, and much more. We also addressed the final administrative and operational details necessary to prepare you for the big day, and discussed how the SAP support organization will need to change. We wrapped up the book with a quick discussion of service and support agreements followed by a detailed description of how to monitor the new system, address continuous improvement, and reward your SAP support organization during the first critical weeks after go-live. Again, congratulations!

Case Study: The Cutover Plan

As you are nearing go-live, you've been asked by HiTech, Inc. to answer some questions coming out of the executive committee pertaining to cutover and what the project team and SAP TSO in particular need to focus on.

Questions

1. What are several of the key tasks found in the SAP cutover plan?
2. How will the SAP support organization change after go-live comes and goes?
3. Outside of collecting data through the help desk and call ticket systems, what's another important way to collect information relative to potential post-go-live issues?
4. What two roles tend to be tasked with managing the cutover process?
5. When it comes to employee retention and recognition, what is the most important thing to remember?

> **NOTE**
>
> The answers to these questions can be found in Appendix A, "Case Study Answers."

36

PART V

Appendixes

Case Study Answers

Chapter 1

1. The key difference between best practices and common practices is cost. Few companies spend the money required to adopt and maintain best practices, whether business related, technology related, or otherwise, simply because best practices are comparatively expensive. Often, an approach that approximates "good enough" provides a better balance of cost and capabilities to an organization. When these "good enough" practices become commonplace, they become de facto common practices.

2. Innovation relative to adopting SAP comes in two flavors: business innovation related to adopting SAP in the first place, and technical implementation innovation. The latter form of innovation might reflect a firm's ability to implement a new SAP business application less expensively than competitors, or set up its ongoing IT operations and systems management more cost-effectively, or by introducing a nimbler SAP computing platform and IT processes.

3. There are several "most important things" relative to SAP. The classic priority revolves around change and how to manage its introduction and then encourage its adoption. At a higher level, though, SAP requires attention to people (end users as well as IT professionals), processes (business, technology, and project management), technology (relative to its adoption and how it drives business innovation), and finally money (budgetary realities, ROI targets, and TCO targets). These are the primary priorities of an SAP implementation.

4. SAP often changes its naming conventions to reflect improved capabilities or simply for marketing reasons. The mySAP.com label has been replaced by SAP Business Suite (which comprises SAP's business applications) or SAP NetWeaver (if we're talking about enabling technologies or products, such as SAP's NetWeaver Portal or Business Intelligence offerings). Similarly, SAP's Web Application Server, or WebAS, has given way to SAP NetWeaver Application Server.

5. The term "SAP" is often used (misused!) to refer to any of SAP's business or technology applications or products (rightly called *components* but nonetheless also called applications). To refer to SAP's business applications, insert the word *SAP* in front of the component (for example, SAP ERP, SAP ERP HCM, or SAP SCM). For SAP's NetWeaver components—products used to enable access or provide a specialized service for SAP's Business Suite components—insert the words *SAP NetWeaver* in front of the components (for example, SAP NetWeaver Portal).

Chapter 2

1. There are probably several reasons why HiTech is implementing SAP, including the need for improved integration between different systems of record, the need for improved operational reporting, and the need for improved strategic reporting.

2. The project sponsor is responsible for developing project buy-in at the highest levels of the organization. It's probably the CIO's most important role at this point.

3. Although the CIO is a reasonable choice for sponsoring the project, the role would be better filled by the company's CFO—the executive responsible for financial performance and the one who will benefit most broadly from the firm's adoption of SAP. If HiTech's president were available, this would be an excellent option as well (though often the president has too many other responsibilities to do an outstanding job as project sponsor).

4. Once the SAP data center is ready, it's typical to have the SAP development system installed, along with a technical sandbox for the SAP TSO. For large implementations, a business sandbox is necessary as well, for initial prototyping and piloting.

5. There are several reasons why HiTech's implementation might fail. The issues associated with buy-in need to be addressed immediately. Further, the company's functional areas have developed silos of information, each having its own systems and IT personnel, which will make it difficult to develop functional and computing platform buy-in. Further, system issues related to inconsistent information, poor planning visibility, numerous bug fixes, and other, unknown issues will also make it difficult to work through master data and initial functional specifications.

Chapter 3

1. The four strategic dimensions spoken of by long-time SAP implementers include the firm's business strategy, its operational strategy, its organizational change strategy, and its technology strategy.

2. Instead of viewing technology strategy from a technology stack perspective, it might be helpful to view it in terms of front plane, cross plane, and back plane perspectives.

3. The four-bucket business driver taxonomy includes "must haves," "should haves," "nice to haves," and "blue sky stuff."

4. The three organizational change models that have been shown to be effective with regard to SAP implementations include Lewin's unfreeze/refreeze model, Burke and Litwin's Change Model, and Orlikowski and Hofman's Improvisational Change Model, the latter of which was developed for large-scale IT projects such as SAP ERP.

5. Guiding principles often include what not to do, what to avoid, or what to circumvent, alongside an organization's operational principles, standards, and preferences.

Chapter 4

1. Business, application, and technology specialists useful in creating an ERP solution vision may come from many places, including SAP AG itself, your systems integrator (SI), your preferred enterprise hardware, software, and services partners, and of course from your own technology teams.

2. We described four primary technology perspectives. The first, conservative, is the least risky of all approaches and reflects a conservative technology perspective that prizes system availability above all else. A mainstream perspective is less risky but still seeks a lot of company when it comes to technology decisions (mainstream companies want to be able to point to many other companies who have adopted the same technology). Close followers, the third technology perspective, invest in proven technology but take risks in areas where they might gain a competitive advantage. Finally, firms who embrace a leading-edge technology perspective seek to get a jump on the competition at the risk of adopting less than proven or mature technologies.

3. Yes, there's a fifth technology perspective as well—handing the system over to an outsourcer or hosting partner.

4. System landscape dimensions or characteristics include simplification, performance, high availability, disaster recovery, scalability, the need to support training requirements, security, system accessibility, manageability, cost, and more.

5. An ERP solution vision builds upon the firm's business vision, transitioning focus from business-inspired wishful thinking and business requirements to how this vision may be realized by way of SAP's components and technologies. An ERP solution vision takes the organization's business vision and gives it legs. It turns a set of requirements into an SAP-specific application blueprint reflecting SAP technology–specific and business application–specific attributes capable of meeting both an organization's business needs and its financial goals.

Chapter 5

1. HiTech incurs the lowest relative risk if it decides to leverage its in-house talent and expertise represented by its baseline skills and competencies and implement an identical technology stack for the new SAP SCM system. Risk increases as HiTech deviates from its core competencies—perhaps not a whole lot in some cases, but the idea behind a delta analysis is to identify the impact that each change has on the project's cost. Thus, as HiTech considers alternatives perceived to be lower cost, such as a Windows Server 2003 platform or implementing IBM DB2 on HP's ProLiant line of servers, it needs to factor back in the risk associated with changing its standards and everything that such changes demand.

2. No; don't read too much into the raw delta analysis numbers in and of themselves. Whether a number is a 20 or a 40 means little. What matters is the difference between the numbers, the deltas. The difference between a 20 and a 40 is quite significant, so the 40 is likely a better solution, but probably not "twice as good."

3. Regarding HiTech's database standard of Oracle9i, as long as Oracle9i is still supported by the new server/OS computing platform and is currently not affected by the requirements of the release of SAP SCM to be implemented, its risk factor is 0. Of course, you'll still want to factor in the impact of not being on a current Oracle release (and the fact that an Oracle upgrade would be imminent).

4. Beyond initial acquisition costs, ensure that HiTech is assessing each technology stack's ongoing support and maintenance costs. Pay particular attention, for example, to server, OS, database, and disk subsystem costs over time, followed by ongoing people and process considerations.

5. A risk factor of 4 represents a very low-risk way to go, in light of the fact that a maximum of 10 for each of the five key solution stack layers equates to a possible 50. Moving to a different vendor's server and disk subsystem platforms, and introducing Windows with the same Oracle9i release, would give us a much riskier 21 (5 + 10 + 6 + 0 + 0) compared to staying with a current updated platform. An even riskier decision would be to bring in the new servers, disk subsystem, and OS, and top it off by supplanting Oracle with SQL Server. Such a solution stack might represent a 29 (5 + 10 + 6 + 8 + 0)—a very significant risk indeed when compared to a 4.

Chapter 6

1. It is important for an organization to capture and preserve its collective knowledge for several reasons. Knowledge capture leads to knowledge retention and the ability to transfer and share that knowledge across the organization (rather than see it leave). KM can then be used to manage organizational change, quickly train new employees, support RFIs and other similar processes, support technical system operational excellence (therefore reducing unplanned downtime), and ultimately avoid repeating the same mistakes.

2. The following knowledge is typically maintained in an SAP project's knowledge repository: planning and project-related knowledge, staffing knowledge, knowledge related to the project's business vision, requirements, and functionality, knowledge related to the project's solution vision and SAP applications or business scenarios, SAP system landscape knowledge, and finally all the knowledge detailing each SAP system's installation and configuration.

3. The concept of metadata as it relates to a knowledge repository speaks to the fact that the repository houses data about the SAP project (rather than the raw transactional and master data that will eventually be created and utilized by the business in the course of using SAP in production).

4. Capture "must haves," "nice to haves," priorities, dependencies, and so on to help people looking back on the project understand why a certain business decision or particular piece of functionality was implemented while other decisions or functionality were put on hold.

5. Though HiTech has deployed various pockets of knowledge repositories, the SAP Content Server makes the most sense going forward; it's the most robust knowledge management tool used by the project, and would serve very ably as a project-wide knowledge repository.

Chapter 7

1. Your primary consideration should be what the language requirements are of all project stakeholders. Secondary considerations include approaches to support any local language requirements.

2. Establishing a project charter is included in the initiating process group. The project charter formally authorizes the project, describes business drivers behind the project, and includes a high-level scope statement.

3. The three close-related tasks that need to be addressed prior to concluding a project or project phase are conducting the administrative project close, obtaining formal client signoff, and performing the contract close process.

4. The project charter, preliminary scope statement, and preliminary project budget are developed within the initiating process group.

Chapter 8

1. An IT-centric PMO organization is probably in place at the firm. Emphasizing business requirements over IT requirements may be one solution to improving performance in the structure.

2. Migrating from an IT-centric PMO to a PMO reporting at the executive level may be a viable solution to better balance business and IT concerns.

3. The four steps of creating a PMO include articulating the type of PMO you intend to build, selling the PMO concept within your organization (followed by obtaining approval and funding), staffing the PMO to support the firm's functional and organizational requirements, and periodically examining the role and effectiveness of the PMO.

4. SAP Solution Manager is not something that you set up in a couple of days on your PC. It was possible to do this in earlier versions of some of the tools contained in Solution Manager (ASAP or ValueSAP). Solution Manager requires its own infrastructure, server(s), operations and functional management personnel, and a trained user community. Although you need to implement Solution Manager to obtain SAP support, you might be too far down your project path to open up a project to implement the functionality you intend to use.

Chapter 9

1. There are two primary reasons a "technical" project will require SAP functional resources. First, in many cases core functionality is significantly changed in newer SAP versions, requiring the guidance of functional consultants to (at a minimum) update your Business Blueprint document and related customization, update training materials, and support revalidating system functionality. Additionally, experience tells us the more that you have customized your existing system, the greater the chance is that the "technical" upgrade will overwrite some of your customizations, reverting back to standard SAP functionality.

2. Master data loads are not typically part of a technical upgrade unless the upgrade has made a change to the required master data set. This is yet another reason to include functional consultants in your technical upgrade project. Best practice is to uncover a data gap of this nature during system validation versus being hit with a major surprise after going live. (Don't laugh—this exact problem has happened!) Lesson learned: Do not skip any upgrade steps unless advised to do so by your functional and technical leads.

3. There is no single correct or even best answer to this question. It is customary to conduct two or three rounds of testing in a typical project, but the exact number of tests required is a function of the overall complexity of your environment. As an example, it is essential for a retail company to perform as many tests as necessary to confirm that the configured SAP system combined with master data loads will be able to process customer orders, perform billing and shipping, and generate invoices on the first day following system cutover. In our experience, many firms do not devote the appropriate amount of time to conducting business acceptance testing, which can lead to post-go-live surprises.

Chapter 10

1. It is important to identify those people on your staff who have prior SAP CRM or SAP Basis (technical) experience and ask them to participate on this team. Also identify domain experts within your company who have institutional knowledge of how your processes are structured today, supporting terms of business support teams like sales and the customer contact center, and IT support teams responsible for systems, storage, and so on.

2. Because you are more interested in gathering data, you would issue a Request for Information (RFI) to gather information on the potential vendors who have domain expertise implementing SAP CRM systems. This serves the dual purpose of sharing information about the potential project, thus helping create a short list of prospective partners.

3. Selection criteria should not focus solely on price. It should give equal weight to the experience and caliber of the consulting partner's team, its success in the marketplace, and its financial strength. You can check customer references provided by the partner; however, these references often are vetted in advance by the partner to

ensure that they'll give a positive reference. You're better off having some of your technical staff present in the consulting partner's oral presentations to pepper its staff with questions regarding not only the presentations but also the items on their resumes. This will enable you to see how well they are able to think on their feet and determine how deep their experience is.

4. Conduct a project kickoff meeting in which scope, schedule, key milestones, critical success criteria, and ground rules are set. During this meeting, define project roles and introduce key team members to each other.

Chapter 11

1. Given the importance of communication, your primary consideration should revolve around the language requirements of all project stakeholders. Secondary considerations include approaches to support any local language requirements.

2. Tools facilitating a good communication plan include the phone, email, wikis, blogs, webcasts, podcasts, and any number of collaboration tools.

3. Program managers are often found inside your organization leading other significant projects or business functions or departments. Alternatively, hire an outsider with a strong industry background and experience with SAP implementations.

Chapter 12

1. OldBoy's IT organization needs to fundamentally change lest the whole group be outsourced or folded into HiTech's existing IT organization. Thus, revolutionary or transformational leadership is called for; a leader practicing evolutionary or incremental change probably will never overcome OldBoy's biases and entrenched approach toward maintaining the status quo.

2. Transformational leadership as described by Burns (1978) and Bass (1990) is most appropriate. The new leader will need to "transcend their own self-interests for the good of the group, organization, or society; to consider their longer-term needs to develop themselves, rather than their needs of the moment; and to become more aware of what is really important" (Bass, 1990). To pull off the planned changes, leaders described as those who have the admiration, loyalty, respect, and trust of their followers are necessary. This describes the kind of leader known as transformational.

3. Outside of traditional authoritarian leadership style based on position and formal authority, OldBoy's current leaders probably exercise a lot of transactional leadership to get things done in the organization today. "Do this for me, and I'll do this for you" is probably commonly heard from OldBoy's managers today.

4. Servant leadership has been shown to be effective in organizations in which formal authority is lacking; this may not be the case at OldBoy, given that the new program manager will presumably enjoy a position of authority granted by the HiTech executive leadership team. Regardless, pure servant leadership has little hope of being

successful at OldBoy (given the need for transformation). However, such leadership atop a foundation of authoritarian leadership has been proven successful in a host of diverse organizations and might represent a sought-after attribute in the best candidates. A leader's penchant for "breaking bread" with his or her followers could prove useful at OldBoy, so as to build and strengthen the personal relationships the new leader needs to make hard decisions while still maintaining the support of the team.

5. Although the best initial candidate for OldBoy is a transformational leader, once the project is underway and transformation has served its purpose, the organization will need to focus on streamlining operations. In this case, a transactional or contingent leadership style has been shown to be most effective. Management by exception will help such leaders focus their energy where it yields the greatest return; the transactional leadership style is adept in maximizing an organization's potential for greater efficiency.

Chapter 13

1. Desirable SAP business team members include not only the most talented members of the organization, but also the members known for having vision. Experience, communications skills, and trainability are key qualities.

2. SAP business team members may be found at the executive and managerial levels as well as in front-line positions as subject matter experts.

3. Hiring backfill positions to support legacy processes or hiring consultants to train existing personnel can both be valid training approaches, and may even be combined into a hybrid approach.

4. To encourage effective working relationships, form an SAP integration team or hold projectwide integration meetings so that the various business areas are naturally inclined and encouraged to plan and work together.

5. Key lessons learned include the following: create a top-down model, set clear role definitions, and keep members engaged through regular communication. Additionally, recognize SAP business team limitations, identify knowledge deficiencies, balance current workload with the SAP project's demands, facilitate excellent business-developer relationships, balance experience against inexperience, focus on quality rather than quantity, and cut your losses before it's too late.

Chapter 14

1. SAP environments are complex by nature, so you want to make sure that the new team member has enough time to understand your SAP technology stack, SAP components, the system's bolt-ons and other integration points, and so forth. The more time your new team member can spend with the to-be-replaced SAP Basis specialist, the better. There is much to transition, from daily change management and operations to existing projects, planned activities, go-live schedules, and so on.

2. In this chapter we highlighted several staffing approaches, from résumé to interview to staff testing, and from try-before-you-buy to our best practices approach rapid deployment. We recommend the rapid deployment approach because it combines the best of the other staffing methodologies and demands the most rigor.

3. Qualified internal candidates might be found within HiTech's existing SAP Basis or infrastructure support organizations. HiTech might also be employing qualified technologists in other enterprise support teams.

4. Depending on whether your to-be-replaced SAP Basis specialist is leaving in two weeks or in two months, you might want to consider the try-before-you-buy approach. A systems integration partner like our fictive GOSAP Consulting could certainly help you in this situation. Not only could it most likely provide an experienced SAP consultant within days, but GOSAP could also introduce HiTech to SAP implementation best practices, software tools, and experienced SAP consultants comfortable with helping you address installation and patching needs, daily SAP operations, deep infrastructure support requirements, and more.

Chapter 15

1. A natural approach to assessing the technologies and solutions that make up an SAP system is to look at the system from a technology stack perspective. Direct subject matter experts in the HA assessment team to focus, for example, on the data center/facilities, the disk subsystem platform, the network infrastructure, the server hardware platform, each server's OS configuration, the SAP ERP database's configuration, and finally the SAP application layer itself.

2. The data center provides the foundation for an SAP business system in terms of underlying power, cooling, and rack mounting needs. Without a sound foundation, all other technology stack solutions and approaches may prove ineffective when needed most.

3. Outside of the core SAP ERP system, be sure to also assess all critical bolt-ons or integration points necessary for business processes to run to conclusion. This often includes tax calculation programs, faxing and email solutions, enterprise print solutions, and other SAP systems that, combined, serve the business's needs.

4. Reliability is measured by MTBF and speaks to how well a component withstands or avoids failure, whereas fault tolerance reflects a duplication of these components or resources. Although both are important, most attention is given to increasing fault tolerance because computing platforms today generally are highly reliable. Fault tolerance is often increased by installing and configuring redundant power supplies, disk drives, network cards, and other resources. Beyond such basic fault tolerance, server clustering and SAP central instance replication also increase an SAP system's fault tolerance.

5. Calculate the difference in the number of hours a system can deliver (for example, 2 nines) versus what you need it to deliver (for example, 4 nines) by multiplying .99 times 8,760, multiplying .9999 times 8,760, and subtracting the difference. In this

case, this equates to 8,672.4 minus 8,759.124, or 86.724 hours worth of extra likely downtime the system we succumb to as configured on an annualized basis—more than three extra *days* of unplanned downtime!

Chapter 16

1. HiTech must develop, document, and regularly execute a tape recovery testing process that encompasses pulling tapes from offsite storage, restoring a copy of the production database with the tape, and verifying that the database starts up and SAP can be accessed.

2. A DR documentation maintenance process must be established; every month or quarter, the DR Crash Kit's documentation must be reviewed and updated. This will represent a fairly significant investment in time and money but should be treated as part of the cost of maintaining this insurance policy.

3. Clusters that span the primary data center and DR site (essentially a "stretch cluster") serve both HA and DR purposes. Dual data center strategies commonly employ such stretch clusters, using their DR site to double as the host for nonproduction systems.

4. A compressed promote-to-production process does not allow changes that have an effect over time—such as the introduction of software updates that exhibit a memory leak—to exhibit the problem. This can result in changes being prematurely permitted to be installed, leading to unplanned downtime and perhaps some additional planned downtime necessary to ultimately correct the issue.

Chapter 17

1. The most critical system availability problem involves poor processes in the midst of key personnel unavailability. For example, if your primary SAN SME disappears on vacation for three weeks and you suffer a SAN technical failure, your knowledge management process should get you through. If the KM process is broken, however, you're in trouble.

2. Several organizational methods can increase organizational availability and therefore the availability of the systems the organization supports, including staff alignment, broad/effective communication, and intentional career development. Along similar lines, organizations should also develop intrateam backups and pursue team-to-team clustering.

3. When it comes to planning for high system availability, the intersection of the following processes with people SPOFs mandate special attention:

   ▶ Knowledge management

   ▶ Change and release management

   ▶ Systems management

▶ Capacity planning/resizing

▶ Load testing

▶ HA failover and failback

▶ Backup and recovery

▶ Server and SAN build/deployment

4. The four roles found in the DRO include the SAP recovery manager, communication liaison, technical recovery team, and review/certification manager.

Chapter 18

1. As the lead solution architect for this resizing effort, you should probably engage IBM again given that it is the incumbent. However, it's not uncommon to engage competing vendors, particularly when price is a factor or the incumbent is not inclined to support a desired platform. In this case, Dell, Fujitsu, HP, Sun, and Unisys should be contacted.

2. To ensure an apples-apples comparison, create a project in the SAP QuickSizer and share the results. By ensuring that all SAP hardware partners use the SAP QuickSizer data (particularly the number of SAPS your system needs to support), you level the sizing playing field.

3. Concurrent users typically reflect 20% to 50% of the number of named users (concurrent users are the number of logged-on users who are active in the system and thus working simultaneously).

4. In the case of new systems, or to obtain a rough estimate of a new hardware configuration, a user-based sizing is not only simple to conduct but appropriate. With regard to the subsidiary's particular situation, a user-based sizing would be useful for budgetary sizing. However, throughput-based sizing would be more precise.

Chapter 19

1. An SAP sizing exercise is an iterative process; indeed, as a long-time SAP customer (from previous acquisitions), HiTech has been through sizings and resizings. SAP's hardware and software technology partners will be anxious to work with HiTech for many reasons, including the opportunity to sell new products and services to HiTech. However, HiTech needs to be prepared to identify data such as those associated with online user characteristics (heavy, medium, and low), batch load assumptions, peak monthly and seasonal workloads, and so on. HiTech also needs to be ready to conduct sizing workshops and conference calls as it balances what the business needs with what the business and IT organizations can afford to spend, all within the context of IT's core competencies, technology standards, and skills.

2. Technologists typically are biased toward technology they are comfortable with or knowledgeable of. In the case of SAP infrastructure, this generally refers to hardware platforms, operating systems, and database versions.

3. Probably the two most prevalent and polarized biases are those regarding UNIX versus Windows operating systems, and Oracle versus SQL Server databases. Given this, an IT organization faces special challenges to implement an IT solution counter to what it knows and is comfortable with. Many IT organizations have pulled this off in the past, sure, but it requires active management and transformational leadership—the kind of leadership that can bring about a change in mind and attitude as it seeks to achieve something new.

4. Super-sizing, or the process of including incremental horsepower in an SAP sizing, is called for when avoiding the risks of undersizing is worth the investment in additional CPU, memory, and network bandwidth, additional servers and disk space, HA solutions that probably exceed the business's requirements, and so on.

Chapter 20

1. As we highlighted in this chapter, it is critical to pursue the proper training at the proper time. Not only does training require a fair amount of your time, but it's also pretty expensive. Granted, you will receive "world class" training experience independent of where you attend it and who delivers it. SAP provides its *SAP NetWeaver – Web AS Implementation and Operation* course, which will teach you the fundamentals of the SAP NetWeaver platform and how to operate it.

2. The fact that you have been working already in the SAP NetWeaver environment is excellent. It will give you a jump-start when you attend your first SAP training courses, and will help you to ask the right questions (in light of your previous exposure to the SAP application). From a timing perspective, it's recommended to attend training just before you need it, preferably several weeks in advance. In this way, you will know you have time to digest what you learn. Be prepared to get a lot of information. SAP tends to provide you with at least one big notebook full of PowerPoint slides and other documentation.

3. The SAP system landscape includes three systems that specifically target training. The technical sandbox targets the SAP support team (technical teams), the business sandbox is intended to train configuration specialists and developers, and the training system is geared toward training the system's end-user community.

4. SAP certification is generally very desirable. Do everything to convince your manager that you need to attend the certification course or track that reflects your area of responsibility. This will set you apart from others, give you the confidence you are looking for, and help you to receive more of the subject matter expert respect you need when implementing SAP.

Chapter 21

1. Data center services and resources common to all SAP applications include power, cooling, network, disk subsystem, racking, and cabling.

2. With regard to racking clustered servers, each node should be housed in a different rack (preferably in a different area of the data center from the other nodes). This helps avoid situations in which a single event (such as a failed section of floor tiles) might bring down all nodes in a cluster and therefore bring down the application itself.

3. Server consolidation and elimination (essentially the same thing) represent the primary focal areas for green data center initiatives.

4. Storage area networks (SANs) and similar high-performance disk subsystems not only house an organization's data (and therefore its lifeblood) but also provide a foundation for excellent performance, resilience against failures, and ultimately overall system reliability. With more than 80% of all performance issues historically related to disk issues, designing and deploying a robust disk solution is paramount.

Chapter 22

1. The best time to capture lessons learned is at the close of significant project activities or milestones. Similarly, before any key resources walk out the door (from developers to functional specialists, to Basis technicians, help desk support personnel, and so on), be sure to capture and incorporate their knowledge into the project's knowledge repository or other KM resource.

2. We are primarily concerned with capturing lessons learned to avoid repeating the same mistake and to provide consistency in project activity execution. This will reduce costs significantly over a project's lifecycle. Best practice is to include formal lessons learned communication activities in your project plan.

3. Favorable project activities include determining that actual effort is less than planned effort. Unfavorable project activity might reflect that actual effort is greater than planned effort. Significant variances of both type need to be incorporated in future project activities.

4. In terms of greatest impact, establishing a highly detailed or granular cutover process and related cutover preparation activities benefits most from lessons learned; by its nature, cutover needs to be tightly scheduled and controlled. Any area of your project that does not contain slack time may also be fine-tuned by incorporating lessons learned.

5. Changes to the resource mix will affect your project's average blended resource rate. Increasing the number of onshore resources and decreasing the number of near-shore and offshore resources will have an unfavorable budget effect, for example. Conversely, increasing the number of a project's offshore resources and decreasing

the number of onshore resources will result in a favorable budget variance (keep in mind that changes in the mix itself might also dictate changes in required support staff).

Chapter 23

1. The SAP NetWeaver 7.0 Master Guide is an ideal starting point for your SAP infrastructure planning activities.

2. The SAP Note for the installation of your OS/database combination of SAP NetWeaver 7.0 would be a great place to start.

3. There is no longer a general guideline for Windows pagefile sizing (outside of reading the specific SAP component's installation guide).

4. You could install the JRE on a remote host, download the SAPinst, and run it from there.

Chapter 24

1. The NetWeaver 7.0 Master Guide lists the software units required for a given IT scenario, as well as the installation order and system landscapes. In this case, a Java system with usage types EP and EPC is required.

2. No, you will not require the SAPGUI. This IT scenario requires a Java-based system (AS Java), which is managed from a web browser. Incidentally, no other clients except a web browser are required for this scenario.

3. The installation guide for the platform and database—in this case, the NetWeaver 7.0 SR3 Java on Linux: Oracle Installation Guide—provides the list of post-installation steps. Some of the post-installation steps will be specific to your database and OS configuration. Updating Oracle statistics is a good example of this type of post-installation activity.

Chapter 25

1. The ERP 6.0 Master Guide lists the software units required for a given business scenario, as well as the installation order and system landscapes.

2. No, do not wait to apply Oracle patches; they should be applied during the Oracle database installation. You do not want to continue the SAP installation until all relevant Oracle patches have been installed.

3. Use transaction SPAM, the Support Package Manager, to install ABAP support packages.

4. You can download support packages from the SAP Service Marketplace.

5. You always want to make sure you have updated the SAP kernel and applied the latest required support packages *before* releasing the system.

Chapter 26

1. The transaction code to start configuration is SPRO from the SAP Easy Access menu.

2. The first set of configuration tasks is to set up the organizational structure of the company implementing the SAP ECC 6.0 solution using the information provided in the BBP document.

3. Programmers are looking to receive concise and clear functional specifications from the functional developers to understand what needs to be developed.

4. The programmers will develop the technical specification based on the inputs provided in the functional specification.

5. The transaction code to execute the ABAP Development Workbench is SE80 from the SAP Easy Access menu.

6. The transaction code to view all the configuration tasks created via transports is SE10 from the SAP Easy Access menu.

Chapter 27

1. The change control board (CCB) comprises a CCB chair, a change control manager (or project change manager), and one or more originators, evaluators, modifiers, and verifiers (all of whom reflect seasoned developers or configurators attached to various business processes and SAP functionality).

2. Arguably, the SAP change control manager's primary responsibility is effective and broad communication. With so many organizations and the project's fundamental functionality at stake, functional changes must be managed and coordinated well—impossible with less than stellar attention to communication.

3. WinShuttle features a batch input mode (making it much faster than test tools using the slower GUI scripting mode) and more granular security than tools like SE16 (enabling a user to only view data related to a particular company code or plant, for example). It also provides separation-of-duties capabilities (to separate people who create scripts from people who can only execute scripts).

4. Several types of tools are useful to functional change management organizations, including change control management (CCM) tools, e-signature tools, SAP enhancement tools, document management tools, and various go-live tools.

Chapter 28

1. For older versions of SAP products and components, SAP offered CATT (Computer Aided Test Tool). More recently, eCATT has been included with all components based on SAP Web Application Server 6.20 or greater.

2. Several third-party tools are available that support business process testing. Look to a suite of functional/quality testing tools from HP, and other tools from Borland,

Compuware, IBM, and others. Pay particular attention to tools that are certified for eCATT.

3. The LSMW is used to migrate master and other legacy data to SAP by way of recorded transactions. Without good and abundant data, comprehensive functional testing is impossible.

4. By focusing on the entire testing process for SAP while automating and enforcing quality standards, HP Quality Center eliminates much of the risk inherent to the testing process, and thus reduces the time and cost required to implement SAP.

5. Automated testing tools are preferable to manual testing for many reasons, including the fact that manual testing is time-consuming, prone to errors, tedious, expensive, and involves users that must be coordinated, housed, given breaks, provided system access, and so on.

Chapter 29

1. Development changes can be made faster and easier through an SOA architecture because the architecture itself is broken up into layers of processes and services that are designed to be interoperable and used across different business processes and different business contexts. These services can be thought of as building blocks, each of which represents business functionality that can be assembled and reassembled in multiple ways. The building block approach is inherently agile because it is designed for change. In the same way, this approach also reduces costs because services can be reused, thereby eliminating redundant functionality that otherwise would need to be reconstructed each time.

2. NetWeaver uses the System Landscape Directory (SLD) as a central information database from which the relevant products and systems of the system landscape can be queried for development and configuration purposes.

3. The Business Process Engine is predicated on unbounded processes, while the Workflow Engine refers to embedded processes.

4. The process of systems integration—where people, business applications, processes, and data are combined to create a seamless and useful business system—is changed only in the context of the tools and approaches at our disposal as SAP developers.

Chapter 30

1. The team of five people can be easily categorized into project workers (or new project personality types) and steady-state workers (or support/maintenance personality types); in this case, there are two project workers and three steady-state workers.

2. Three leadership behaviors that greatly affect employee retention include intellectual stimulation, inspirational motivation, and individualized consideration.

3. There are many keys deemed essential to employee retention. We've focused on six of them: understanding what motivates the team, addressing salary requirements, practicing regular and meaningful communication, delivering well-deserved praise, providing performance-oriented and other incentive bonuses, and offering training and career path opportunities.

4. The two project workers might be motivated by additional training and the promise of new and different projects on the horizon. Think about where their experience and technical prowess might be better used as HiTech continues to implement new SAP components and other enterprise systems. Be sure to intellectually stimulate and inspirationally motivate these workers, pushing them to innovate as the opportunities arise. And reward useful innovation in a tangible manner—public recognition and cash are ideal.

5. The three steady-state workers might feel best rewarded by the opportunity to "finish what they started" and help take over steady-state operations and maintenance after go-live. The use of bonuses and especially long-term equity incentives might be especially useful in encouraging these team members to carefully document the system's current state and operational processes.

Chapter 31

1. Front-end printing is warranted when the primary criteria is ease of administration rather than strict security, centralization, mission-critical printing (such as checks), or high-speed printing options.

2. Central User Administration could be implemented to avoid maintaining users in the individual systems.

3. To best address a rapidly growing database, implement an archiving strategy. A company might also investigate the functional areas responsible for the bulk of data growth and seek to change how the business is configured.

4. Available options include performing an SAP system copy to another system or using a data migration tool to extract HR production data to a client on another system.

Chapter 32

1. This is actually a bit of a trick question—we would recommend testing the disk performance both before and after joining the cluster. But we also test from the bottom of the technology stack up, so we would recommend testing the disks before verifying the cluster operations.

2. It should not be necessary to establish a baseline for CPU performance. The CPU tools are used to compare the performance between servers—there is not a lot of value in establishing a baseline except to use for comparison. For example, future firmware updates to a server's systemboard warrants CPU performance testing if only to quantify to what degree performance has been affected.

3. A lower benchmark test number is desired for tests that try to crunch their way through a set workload; in this case, the workload itself is constant while time is variable. The faster the workload is processed in terms of time, the faster the CPU. On the other hand, a higher number is desired for CPU tests seeking to showcase a CPU's throughput or how much work was processed in a given amount of time. In this case, time is the constant while the workload itself is variable. For example, a test might seek to process as many calculations as possible in 10 seconds.

4. We absolutely recommend that you execute a standard suite of test runs after every change to the disk subsystem. You should then compare them to your baseline numbers to verify that performance has not been impacted (or to quantify impact).

Chapter 33

1. Tasks related to preparing and planning for stress testing include pretuning the SAP technology stack, selecting a stress-testing tool, determining the technical skill sets and other resources (including time commitments) required to support stress testing, setting up and configuring the stress test infrastructure, analyzing business processes and mapping them to SAP components/functional areas, working with the business groups associated with these SAP components and functional areas, scripting the business processes, uncovering the data necessary to execute the scripted business processes, and developing a process for "warming up" the database.

2. Testing and post-testing stress test tasks include determining how to execute and monitor each test run, collecting performance and other output data, confirming that the stress test runs are valid, analyzing the data to determine how well the system performed under load, and conducting iterative testing and tuning cycles to increase system performance.

3. Data collection—or more precisely, uncovering enough data—is critical to stress testing. Business scripts that only exercise the same data over and over again are worthless because the data is quickly cached by the hardware, database, and application cache. When data is cached, subsequent executions of the same transaction fail to put any load on the system; the data is immediately accessible out of memory rather than load-generating disk I/O, and therefore the stress test fails to represent reality.

4. Low-cost stress tests are possible by using virtualized test tool suites, including tests that leverage freeware.

5. Stress testing can provide value beyond performance validation and testing/tuning in the form of validating that the system's HA clustering or DR solution works well under load, that backup/recovery processes work well under load, and even that the firm's systems management strategy provides alerts when performance thresholds are exceeded and generally works as expected.

Chapter 34

1. A basic technical change management process might include addressing the following: technical standards, testing processes, documentation/knowledge management, release strategies, communications plan, and tool sets related to holistically managing technical change.

2. A good technical sandbox, especially one that is identical to production, allows for experimenting with and verifying the breadth of changes that will eventually be promoted to production *well before* these changes are introduced to production. This also gives the SAP Basis and other teams the chance to familiarize themselves with new technologies, versions, and releases, thus helping ensure the promote-to-production process goes smoothly.

3. Inevitably, a change will need to be implemented directly into production lest a major security or severe potential availability issue be ignored in the short term. The risks related to a decision to circumvent the promote-to-production process must be weighed carefully against the expected benefits—typically for emergencies only. If at all possible, try to test a proposed change in at least one other system first.

Chapter 35

1. It is important for you to understand the customer's SAP environment. You must understand what kind of SAP applications and components the customer is running (SAP ECC 6.0, SAP EP, TREX, ITS, and so on). Also, you want to understand whether these SAP instances are pure ABAP, Java, and/or dual-stack environments because this will help you determine a possible SAP management solution. In addition, find out whether the customer has already implemented SAP Solution Manager and, if so, which release the customer is running and which type of SAP Solution Manager scenarios have been implemented (Solution Monitoring, Service Desk, Change Management, and so on).

2. HP offers so-called SMART Plug-Ins (SPIs) for various applications, including SAP. The relevant SMART Plug-In for SAP is the SAP SPI. It allows you to connect to the SAP instance and to deploy various monitors. One of the monitors is the CCMS monitor. It gathers CCMS-related alerts and forwards them to HP OpenView Operations (Management Console).

3. Manual checklists provide an excellent foundation for ensuring that recurring operations are take care of. Use manual checklists to train new hires as well. Once the team is adept at managing SAP, seek to automate the steps in the checklists.

4. Absolutely. As a matter of fact, it is the right approach to leverage CCMS and CEN and eventually even SAP Solution Manager. A possible solution for your customer could be to set up and configure a central CCMS environment (CEN) hosted by SAP Solution Manager. CEN receives every SAP-related alert from the SAP satellite systems through SAP CCMS agents. The SAP SPI will gather and filter alerts available on CEN and forward them to the customer's existing HP OpenView environment.

Chapter 36

1. Critical cutover-related tasks include project milestones related to locking down the system, preparing the SAP support organization for its new role and responsibilities, rolling out the SAPGUI, synchronizing data, and performing a host of project managements tasks related to communications, escalation processes, and similar activities.

2. Go-live changes the SAP support organization from a focus on retaining project workers to a focus on retaining overall talent, many of whom are probably better characterized as support/maintenance (SM) personality types. As positions vacate, it's important to backfill those positions with the right person—post-go-live probably means more steady eddies.

3. Conduct surveys using a tool such as ZipSurvey to collect perceptions and other information from your SAP user community.

4. The job of coordinating cutover rests with either the SAP project manager or a designated cutover deployment manager (CDM).

5. The most important thing is honest and timely congratulations and praise (though cash will top the list of any surveys you administer!).

SAP Acronyms

3G	third generation
4GL	4th-generation language
ABAP/4	Advanced Business Application Programming/4
ABC	activity-based costing
ACC	Adaptive Computing Controller (SAP)
AD	Active Directory (Microsoft)
ADAM	Active Directory Application Mode (Microsoft)
ADK	archive development kit
AFS	Apparel and Footwear Solution (SAP)
AGATE	Application-Gate (SAP ITS component, application server side)
AIM	AOL Instant Messaging
AIX	Advanced Interactive eXecutive (IBM)
ALE	Application Link Enabling (SAP)
ALV	ABAP List Viewer (SAP)
AM	Asset Management (SAP ERP module)
AP	accounts payable
API	application programming interface
APMP	Adaptive Partition Multiprocessing
APO	Advanced Planner and Optimizer (component of SAP SCM)
APS	Advanced Planning and Scheduling

AQ	Advanced Queuing (Oracle)
AR	accounts receivable
ASAP	Accelerated SAP (SAP methodology)
ASCS	ABAP Central Services (SAP)
ASP	application service provider
ASUG	America's SAP Users' Group
ATEC	Authorized Technical Education Center (Microsoft)
ATP	Acceptance Test Plan
	Available to Promise (SAP)
ATR	availability through redundancy
B2B	business to business
B2C	business to consumer
BAC	Business Availability Center (HP)
BAdI	Business Add In
BAM	business architecture methodology
BAPI	Business Application Programming Interface (SAP)
BBD	business blueprint document
BBP	business blueprint phase
BC	Basis (SAP module)
	Business Connector (SAP product)
BCS	business critical services
	business continuity services
BDC	batch data communication
BEx	Business Explorer (SAP)
BI	Business Intelligence (now refers to SAP BusinessObjects, formerly a NetWeaver component)
BIA	Business Intelligence Accelerator (SAP; now called SAP BW Accelerator)

BIC	best in class
BOBJ	SAP Business Objects
BOD	business object document
BOM	bill of materials
BOR	business object repository (SAP)
BOSS	Business Object System Server (IBM)
BPCS	Business Planning and Control System (SSA product)
BPI	business process integration
BPEL	Business Process Execution Language (for Web Services)
BPM	business process management
BPML	Business Process Modeling Language
BPO	business process outsourcing
BPR	business process re-engineering
BPX	Business Process Expert (SAP online community)
BSP	Business Server Page (SAP)
BTO	build to order
BU	business unit
BW	Business Warehouse (SAP NetWeaver BW, formerly NetWeaver BI)
CA	Computer Associates
	Continuous Access (HP)
	Cross Application (SAP products atop modules)
CAB	customer advisory board
CAF	Composite Application Framework (SAP)
CAGR	Compound Annual Growth Rate
CAL	Client Access Licensing (Microsoft and others)
CATS	Cross Application Time Sheets (SAP)
CATT	Computer Aided Test Tool (SAP)

CBI	computer-based instruction
CBT	computer-based training
CC	Competence Center (SAP)
CCB	change control board
CCM	change control management
	change control manager
CCMS	Computing Center Management System (SAP)
ccNUMA	Cache Coherent Non Uniform Memory Access
CDSA	Common Data Security Architecture
CE	Composition Environment (SAP NetWeaver)
	Concurrent Employment (SAP ERP HCM)
	Concurrent Engineering
CEA	chief enterprise architect
CEN	CENtral monitoring system (SAP)
CEO	Chief Executive Officer
CFO	Chief Financial Officer
CI	central instance (SAP)
CIC	Customer Interaction Center
CIO	Chief Information Officer
CIS	Customer Interaction Software
CISC	Complex Instruction Set Computing
CKO	Chief Knowledge Officer
CLO	Chief Learning Officer
CMM	Capability Maturity Model (ITIL)
CMO	Chief Marketing Officer
CMS	Change Management System

CND	could not duplicate (failure verification)
CO	Controlling (SAP ERP module)
COBOL	Common Business Oriented Language
CoE	Center of Excellence (or Expertise)
COGS	cost of goods sold
COHO	Corporate Office/Home Office
COM	Common Object Model
	Component Object Model
COO	Chief Operating Officer
CORBA	Common Object Request Broker Architecture
COTS	Commercial Off-The-Shelf
CP	capacity planning
CPI	cost performance index
CPIC	Common Programming Interface Communication (SAP)
CPFR	collaborative planning, forecasting, and replenishment
CPM	critical path method
CR	contingent reward
CRC	Content Repository Content (SAP)
CRM	Customer Relationship Management (generic, and SAP component)
CSF	critical success factor
CSM	candidate status matrix
CSO	Chief Strategy Officer
CSP	capability support pack
CSS	cascading style sheets
CT	Chief Technologist
CTO	Change and Transport Organizers (SAP)
	Chief Technical (or Technology) Officer

	configure to order
CTP	capable to promise
CTQ	critical to quality
CTR	click through rate
CTS	Change and Transport System (SAP)
CUA	Central User Administration (SAP)
D&B	Dun & Bradstreet
DB	database
DBA	database administrator
DBMS	database management system
DDE	dynamic data exchange
DDIC	Data DICtionary (SAP)
DDoS	distributed denial of service
DEV	Development (SAP system landscape)
DfR	Design for Run (EDS/HP)
DHCP	Dynamic Host Configuration Protocol
DI	Development Infrastructure (SAP)
DIA	DIAlog work process (SAP)
DISA	Data Interchange Standards Association
	distributed Internet server array
DLL	dynamic link library
DLT	Digital Linear Tape
DMS	document management system
DNS	domain name server
DP	data processing
	Demand Planning (SAP SCM module)
DQL	Data Query Language

DR	disaster recovery (or recoverability)
DRCK	disaster recovery crash kit
DRM	Data Replication Manager (Compaq/Digital DR product)
DRO	Disaster Recovery Organization
DRP	distribution requirements planning
	disaster recovery planning
DRS	Distributed Resource Scheduler (VMware)
DSO	Data Store Object
DTR	Design Time Repository
DTS	distributed transaction system
DW	data warehousing
DWDM	Development Workbench Demos (SAP)
DynPro	Dynamic Program (SAP)
EA	enterprise architecture
	enterprise applications
EAF	Enterprise Architecture Framework (SAP)
EAI	enterprise application integration
EAM	Enterprise Asset Management (SAP)
EBITDA	earnings before net interest, taxes, depreciation, and amortization
EBP	Enterprise Buyer Professional (SAP SRM component)
EBS	Enterprise Backup Solution (HP)
ebXML	Electronic Business XML
EC	European Commission
	Enterprise Controlling (SAP ERP module)
eCATT	Extended Computer Aided Test Tool (SAP)
ECC	ERP Central Component (SAP component)
	Error Correction Code (or Error Code Correcting)

ECM	Enterprise Compensation Management (SAP)
	enterprise continuity management
EDI	electronic data interchange
EDS	Electronic Data Systems (an HP Company)
EFT	electronic funds transfer
EHS	Environmental Health & Safety (SAP)
EIP	Enterprise Information Portal
EIS	Executive Information System (SAP)
EISA	Extended Industry Standard Architecture
EJB	Enterprise JavaBeans
EM	enterprise management
EMA	enterprise management architecture
EP	Enterprise Portal (SAP; replaced by NetWeaver Portal)
EPC	Enterprise Portal Core (SAP)
EPIC	Explicitly Parallel Instruction Computing
EPS	earnings per share
ERD	Emergency Repair Disk (Microsoft)
ERM	enterprise resource management
ERP	Enterprise Resource Planning (generic, and SAP component)
ESA	Enterprise Service Automation
ESB	enterprise service bus
ESM	enterprise systems management
ESMTP	Extended Simple Mail Transfer Protocol
ESOA	Enterprise Service Oriented Architecture (SAP)
ESS	Employee Self-Service (generic, and SAP)
ETA	estimated time of arrival
ETC	estimate to complete

ETL	extraction, transfer, loading
EU	European Union
EVA	economic value added
	Enterprise Virtual Array (HP storage)
EVM	Enterprise Volume Manager (Digital/HP)
FAQ	frequently asked questions
FASB	Financial Accounting Standards Board
FDDI	fiber distributed data interface
FFMS	factory floor management systems
FI	Financial Accounting (or Financials; SAP ERP module)
FLOPS	floating point operations per second
FM	Funds Management (SAP)
FRICE	forms, reports, interfaces, conversions, enhancements
FRU	field replaceable unit
FTE	full-time equivalent
FTP	File Transfer Protocol
FUD	fear, uncertainty, and doubt
FY	fiscal year
GAAP	Generally Accepted Accounting Principles
GAL	Global Address List (Microsoft)
GbE	gigabit ethernet
GBU	global business unit
GDS	Global Data Synchronization (SAP)
GIF	Graphics Interchange Format
GL	general ledger
GM	gross margin
GNOME	GNU Network Object Model Environment

GNU	GNU's Not Unix
GOSIP	Government Open Systems Interconnect Procurement (U.S. Government)
GPS	global positioning system
GRC	Governance, Risk, and Compliance (SAP component)
GSA	General Services Administration (U.S. Government)
GSM	Global System for Mobile communications
GUI	Graphical User Interface (generic, and SAP)
GVC	global value chain
HA	high availability
	High Availability (VMware product)
HACMP	High Availability Cluster Multiprocessing (IBM)
HBA	host bus adapter
HCM	Human Capital Management (SAP equivalent of HR)
HP	Hewlett-Packard Company
HPC	high-performance computing
HR	Human Resources (SAP ERP module)
HRM	human resource management
HSM	hierarchical storage management (or manager)
HTML	Hypertext Markup Language
HTTP	Hypertext Transfer Protocol
IA	Intel Architecture
IAC	Internet Application Component (SAP)
IBM	International Business Machines
IC	individual consideration
	Interaction Center (SAP)
ICAP	Interactive Communicating Applications Protocol
ICE	Internet Content Exchange

ICM	Internet Communication Manager (SAP)
ICOE	Industry Center of Expertise
ICP	Internet Content Provider
ICX	Inter-Cartridge Exchange
IDES	International Demonstration and Education System (SAP)
IDL	Interface Definition Language
iDOC	Intermediate Document (SAP)
IE	Internet Explorer (Microsoft)
IETF	Internet Engineering Task Force
IIA	idealized influence [attributed]
IIB	idealized influence [behavior]
IIS	Internet Information Server (Microsoft)
IM	instant messaging
	inspirational motivation
	Inventory Management (part of SAP Materials Management)
	Investment Management (SAP ERP module)
IMAC	installs, moves, adds, and changes
IMG	Implementation Guide (SAP)
IOBJ	InfoObject (SAP)
IP	intellectual property
	Internet Protocol
IPC	Internet Pricing Configurator (SAP)
IPO	initial public offering
IRJ	iView Runtime for Java (SAP technology)
IRR	internal rate of return
IS	Industry Solutions (SAP)
	information systems

	intellectual stimulation
ISA	Industry Standard Architecture (PC bus)
ISAPI	Internet Server Application Programming Interface (Microsoft)
ISO	International Standards Organization
ISV	independent software vendor
IT	information technology
ITAR	International Traffic in Arms Regulations
ITI	Information Technology Industry Council
ITIL	Information Technology Infrastructure Library
ITO	information technology outsourcing
ITS	Internet Transaction Server (SAP product)
ITSM	Information Technology Service Management
iVIEW	Information View (SAP)
IX	Internet Exchange
J2EE	Java 2 Enterprise Edition
J2SDK	Java 2 Software Development Kit
JAD	joint application development
JARM	Java Application Response Measurement
JAS	Java Application Server
JCA	Java Component Architecture
JCo	Java Connector
JDBC	Java Database Connectivity
JDK	Java Development Kit
JEC	joint escalation center
JIT	just in time
JMAPI	Java Management API
JMS	Java Message Service

JMX	Java Management Extension
JRE	Java Runtime Environment
JSP	Java Server Page
JSPM	Java Support Package Manager
JV	joint venture
	journal voucher
KM	knowledge management
KMT	knowledge management tool
KPI	key performance indicator
KVM	keyboard, video, mouse
KW	Knowledge Warehouse (SAP component)
LA	letter agreement
LAN	local area network
LDAP	Lightweight Directory Access Protocol
LDB	logical database
LE	Logistics Execution (SAP ERP module)
LLP	limited liability partnership
LMS	learning management system
LO	Logistics (SAP ERP module)
LOA	letter of agreement
LOB	line of business
LOE	letter of engagement
LPar	Logical Partition
LSB	Linux Standard Base
LSI	Large Scale Integration
LSMW	Legacy System Migration Workbench (SAP)
LSO	Learning Solution (SAP)

B

LT	leadership team
LUN	logical unit number
LUW	logical unit of work
M&A	mergers & acquisitions
MAC	Media Access Control
MAPI	Messaging API (Microsoft)
MAU	Media Access Unit
MBO	management by objectives
MBWA	management by walking around
MCA	Micro Channel Architecture (IBM)
MCP	Microsoft Certified Professional
MCSD	Microsoft Certified Solutions Developer
MCSE	Microsoft Certified Systems Engineer
MDBMS	Multidimensional Database Management System
MDCD	Mobile Data Collection Device
MDM	Master Data Management (SAP component)
MES	manufacturing execution systems
MI	Mobile Infrastructure (SAP)
MIB	Management Information Base (SNMP)
MII	Manufacturing Integration and Intelligence (SAP)
MIME	Multipurpose Internet Mail Extensions
MIPS	millions of instructions per second
MIS	management information system
MLQ	Multifactor Leadership Questionnaire
MM	Materials Management (SAP ERP module)
MMC	Microsoft Management Console
MMX	MultiMedia eXtensions

MOF	Microsoft Operations Framework
MOM	message-oriented middleware
	Microsoft Operations Manager
MOU	memorandum of understanding
MPC	Manage Projects and Consulting (SAP ERP module)
MPCS	manufacturing planning and control systems
MPLS	Multi-Protocol Label Switching
MPP	massively parallel processing
MPU	Microprocessing Unit
MQM	manufacturing quality management
MRO	maintenance, repair, and operations
MRP	manufacturing resource planning
MSCS	Microsoft Cluster Service (or Server)
MSMQ	Microsoft Message Queue
MSN	Microsoft Network
MSS	Manager Self-Service (generic, and SAP)
	manufacturing support services
MSSQL	Microsoft SQL
MTBF	mean time between failure
NAS	network attached storage
NCA	Network Computing Architecture (Oracle)
NDA	non-disclosure agreement
NetBEUI	NetBIOS Extended User Interface
NFS	network file system
NIC	network interface card
NLB	Network Load Balancing (Microsoft)
NNTP	Network News Transport Protocol

NOC	network operations center
NOS	network operating system
NSK	NonStop Kernel (Tandem/HP Operating System)
NSP	network service provider
NT	New Technology (Microsoft)
NTAS	New Technology Advanced Server (Microsoft)
NTCDC	NT Crash Dump Collector
NTFS	NT File System (Microsoft)
NUMA	Non Uniform Memory Access
NW	NetWeaver (SAP)
NWDI	NetWeaver Development Infrastructure (SAP)
NWDS	NetWeaver Developer Studio (SAP)
OAG	Open Applications Group
OAGIS	Open Applications Group Integration Specification
OCX	Object Linking and Embedding Custom Control
OD	organizational development (or design)
ODBC	Open Database Connectivity
ODG	Oracle Data Guard
ODS	operational data store
ODSI	Open Directory Service Interfaces (Microsoft)
OEM	original equipment manufacturer
OFS	Oracle Failsafe
OID	Oracle Internet Directory
OLAP	online analytical processing
OLE	Object Linking and Embedding (Microsoft)
OLTP	online transaction processing
OM	Organizational Management (SAP ERP HCM)

OODBMS	Object-Oriented Database Management System
ORB	object request broker
OS	operating system
OSF	Open Software Foundation (of The Open Group)
OSI	Open Systems Interconnect
OSS	Online Service System (SAP)
	operations support systems
	open source software
P2P	peer to peer
	promote to production
PA	Payroll (SAP ERP module)
	Personnel Administration (SAP ERP HCM)
	Precision Architecture (HP)
PAE	Physical Address Extensions (Microsoft)
PAM	Product Availability Matrix (SAP)
PAR	Portal ARchive file
PAT	profit after taxes
PBT	profit before taxes
PC	personal computer
PCD	Portal Content Directory (SAP)
PCI	Peripheral Component Interconnect
PCM	project change manager
PCR	Personnel Change Request (SAP ESS/MSS)
PD	Personnel Development (SAP ERP HCM)
PDA	personal digital assistant
PDC	Primary Domain Controller (Microsoft)
PDF	Portable Document Format (Adobe)

PDK	Portal Development Kit (SAP)
PDU	power distribution unit
PERL	Practical Extraction and Reporting Language
PGP	pretty good privacy
PI	Process Integration (SAP component; formerly SAP XI)
	Plug-In (generic, and SAP)
PIT	process improvement team
PLM	Product Lifecycle Management (SAP component)
PM	Plant Maintenance (SAP ERP module)
PM1	Project Manager 1
PM2	Project Manager 2
PMBOK	Project Management Body Of Knowledge (PMI)
PMI	Project Management Institute
PMO	program management office
	project management office
PMP	Project Management Professional (PMI)
PMU	Project Management University
PNG	Portable Network Graphics (file format specification)
PO	purchase order
POE	point of entry
POJO	plain old Java objects
PoR	plan of record
PP	Production Planning (SAP ERP module)
PPDS	Production Planning and Detailed Scheduling (SAP SCM module)
PPI	Processor Performance Index
PP-PI	Production Planning—Process Industries (SAP SCM module)
PPTP	Point-to-Point Tunneling Protocol

PRD	production (SAP system landscape)
PS	Project System (SAP ERP module)
	professional services
PSA	persistent staging area
PY	Payroll (SAP)
Q&A	questions and answers
QAS	quality assurance system (SAP system landscape)
QC	Quality Center (Mercury/HP)
QM	Quality Management (SAP ERP module)
QoE	quality of experience
QTP	Quick Test Pro (Mercury/HP)
R/2	Release 2 (SAP mainframe OLTP Product)
R/3	Release 3 (SAP Client/Server OLTP Product)
R&D	research & development
R&E	research & engineering
RAC	Real Application Clusters (Oracle)
RAD	rapid application development
RAID	redundant arrays of independent (or inexpensive) disks
RAM	random access memory
RCA	root cause analysis
RDBMS	relational database management system
RDP	rapid deployment program
RDSSP	rapid deployment SAP staffing process
RFC	Remote Function Call (SAP)
	request for comment
RFI	request for information
RFP	request for proposal

RICEFS	reports, interfaces, conversions, enhancements, forms, and SAPscripts
RISC	reduced instruction set computing
ROA	return on assets
ROI	return on investment
ROIC	return on invested capital
RPC	remote procedure call
RPO	recovery point objective
	recruitment process outsourcing
RRI	Report-Report-Interface (SAP BIA)
RTO	recovery time objective
SaaS	software as a service
SADT	structured analysis and design technique
SAN	storage area network
SAP	Systeme, Anwendungen und Produkte in der Datenverarbeitung
	Systems, Applications, and Products in Data Processing (original American translation)
	Systems, Applications, and Products (a later, simplified translation)
	Shut up and Pay
	Select another Package
	Say another Prayer
	Suffering and Pain
	Salary Advancement Program
	Scare a Programmer
	Slow and Pointless
SAPGUI	SAP Graphical User Interface
SARBOX	Sarbanes-Oxley
SBX	Sandbox (SAP system landscape)

SC	supply chain
SCE	supply chain execution
SCM	Supply Chain Management (generic, and SAP component)
SCOPE	Supply Chain Optimization Planning and Execution (SAP)
SCP	supply chain planning
SD	Sales and Distribution (SAP ERP module)
SDK	service delivery kit
	service developers' kit
	software development kit
SDLC	systems development life cycle
SDM	Software Deployment Manager (SAP)
SDN	SAP Developer Network
SEM	Strategic Enterprise Management (SAP)
SET	secure electronic transactions
	sizing evaluation team
SFA	sales force automation
SFC	shop floor control
SFI	shop floor integration
SG&A	selling, general & administrative
SGA	System Global Area (Oracle)
SI	systems integration (or integrator)
SID	system identifier (SAP or Microsoft)
SIG	special interest group
SIM	Systems Insight Manager (HP)
SIPP	SAP implementation (or infrastructure) project plan
SKU	stock keeping unit
SLA	service-level agreement

B

SLD	System Landscape Directory (SAP)
SM	Service Management (SAP)
	Solution Manager (SAP)
SMB	small and medium business
SMD	Solution Manager Diagnostics (SAP)
SME	subject matter expert
	Small/Medium Enterprise (SAP)
SMP	symmetric multiprocessing
SMS	Systems Management Server (Microsoft)
SMTP	Simple Mail Transport Protocol
SNA	Systems Network Architecture (IBM)
SNIA	Storage Network Industry Association
SNMP	Simple Network Management Protocol
SNP	Supply Network Planning (SAP SCM module)
SOA	service-oriented architecture
SOAP	Simple Object Access Protocol
SolMan	Solution Manager (SAP)
SOW	statement of work
SPI	schedule performance index
	Smart Plug-In (HP)
SPO	SPOol work process (SAP)
SPOF	single point of failure
SQA	software quality assurance
SQL	structured query language
SQL2K	SQL Server 2000 (Microsoft)
SQL2K5	SQL Server 2005 (Microsoft)

SRM	Site Recovery Manager (VMware)
	Supplier Relationship Management (SAP component)
SSCR	SAP Software Change Registration
SSH	secure shell
SSI	server side include
SSL	Secure Sockets Layer
SWOT	strengths, weaknesses, opportunities, threats
SysMgt	systems management
T&M	time and materials
TCO	total cost of ownership
TCP	Transmission Control Protocol
TDMS	Test Data Migration Server (SAP)
TemSe	TEMporary SEquential object storage
TFT	thin-film transistor
TFTP	Trivial File Transfer Protocol
TIFF	Tagged Image File Format
TME	Tivoli Management Environment
TMF	Tivoli Management Framework
TMN	Telecommunications Management Network
TMS	Transport Management System (SAP)
	Tape Management System (IBM)
TNG	The Next Generation (CA-Unicenter)
TOC	table of contents
TOG	The Open Group
TOGAF	The Open Group Architecture Framework
TP	transaction processing
TPC	Transaction processing Performance Council

TPM	third-party maintainer
	transaction processing monitor
TPS	transactions per second
TQM	total quality management
TREX	Text Retrieval and EXtraction (SAP)
TRS	text retrieval system
Ts & Cs	terms and conditions
TSO	technical support organization
UDB	Universal Database (IBM)
UDDI	Universal Description and Discovery Interface
UDI	Universal Data Integration
UDP	User Datagram Protocol
UM	unified messaging
UME	User Management Engine (SAP)
UML	Unified Modeling Language
UPS	uninterruptible power supply
URC	Utility Reference Customer (SAP)
URL	Uniform Resource Locator (Web address)
USB	Universal Serial Bus
V	Update work process (SAP)
V2	Update2 work process (SAP)
VAR	value-added reseller
VAS	vision and architecture services
VBA	Visual Basic for Applications (Microsoft)
VC	venture capital (or capitalist)
VCB	VMware Consolidated Backup
VI	virtual interface

VLAN	virtual local area network
VLDB	very large database
VLP	visionary leadership and planning
VM	virtual machine
VNC	virtual network computing
VPar	virtual partition
VPN	virtual private network
VTA	virtual tape library
VTDPY	virtual terminal display
VUIT	visual user interface tool
W2K	Windows 2000 (Microsoft)
W3C	World Wide Web Consortium
WAD	web application designer
WAIS	wide area information server
WAN	wide area network
WAP	Wireless Application Protocol
WAS	Web Application Server (SAP; informal)
WBEM	Web Based Enterprise Management
WBS	work breakdown structure
WebAS	Web Application Server (SAP; succeeded by SAP NetWeaver Application Server)
WEM	Web Experience Management
WF	Workflow (generic, and SAP)
WGATE	Web-Gate (SAP component of ITS, web server side)
WIP	work in process (or progress)
WMI	Windows Management Instrumentation (Microsoft)
WOM	Web Object Management (IBM)

WOSA	Windows Open Services Architecture (Microsoft)
WP	Workplace (SAP component, replaced by Enterprise Portal)
WRB	web request broker
WS2003	Windows Server 2003 (Microsoft)
WWW	World Wide Web (Internet)
WYSIWYG	what you see is what you get
xApps	composite applications (SAP)
XI	Exchange Infrastructure (replaced by SAP PI)
XML	eXtensible Markup Language
XRP	extended resource planning
Y2K	Year 2000

Index

NUMBERS

A

C

How can we make this index more useful? Email us at indexes@samspublishing.com

D

J - K

How can we make this index more useful? Email us at indexes@samspublishing.com

How can we make this index more useful? Email us at indexes@samspublishing.com

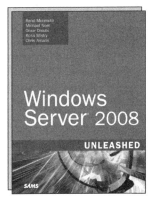

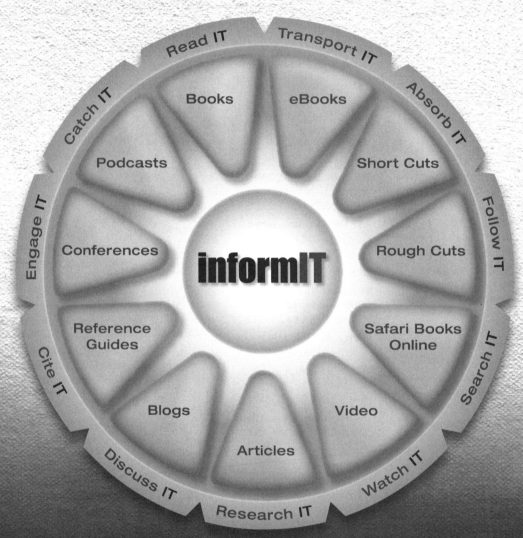

George W. Anderson
Charles D. Nilson
Tim Rhodes

SAP Implementation
UNLEASHED

A Business and Technical Roadmap to Deploying SAP

SAMS

FREE Online Edition

Your purchase of **SAP Implementation Unleashed** includes access to a free online edition for 45 days through the Safari Books Online subscription service. Nearly every Sams book is available online through Safari Books Online, along with more than 5,000 other technical books and videos from publishers such as Addison-Wesley Professional, Cisco Press, Exam Cram, IBM Press, O'Reilly, Prentice Hall, and Que.

SAFARI BOOKS ONLINE allows you to search for a specific answer, cut and paste code, download chapters, and stay current with emerging technologies.

Activate your FREE Online Edition at
www.informit.com/safarifree

> **STEP 1:** Enter the coupon code: CKXSFWH.

> **STEP 2:** New Safari users, complete the brief registration form.
> Safari subscribers, just log in.

If you have difficulty registering on Safari or accessing the online edition, please e-mail customer-service@safaribooksonline.com

Addison
Wesley

Adobe Press

ALPHA

Cisco Press

Press
FINANCIAL TIMES

IBM
Press

lynda.com

Microsoft
Press

New
Riders

O'REILLY

Peachpit
Press

PRENTICE
HALL

Que

Redbooks

SAMS

SAS
Publishing

Sun
microsystems

WILEY